D1226611

ALICE NEEL

ALSO BY PHOEBE HOBAN

BASQUIAT: A QUICK KILLING IN ART

PHOEBE HOBAN

ALICE
NEEL

THE ART
of
NOT SITTING PRETTY

ST. MARTIN'S PRESS ☙ NEW YORK

ALICE NEEL. Copyright © 2010 by Phoebe Hoban. All rights reserved. Printed in the United States of America. For information, address St. Martin's Press, 175 Fifth Avenue, New York, N.Y. 10010.

All works by Alice Neel © The Estate of Alice Neel. The Estate of Alice Neel includes works in the collections of Hartley Neel, Richard Neel, their respective families, and Neel Arts, Inc.

Jacket photograph of Alice Neel by Sam Brody reproduced courtesy of Sondra Brody

Other Painting and Photograph Permissions:

Paintings:
31. Reprinted courtesy of Galerie St. Etienne, New York

Family Photographs:
Frontispiece image: Photograph by Sam Brody, reprinted courtesy of Sondra Brody
6., 9., and 10. Reprinted courtesy of Pablo Lancella
16. Reprinted courtesy of Cristina Lancella
17. Reprinted courtesy of Ralph Marrero
24. Reprinted courtesy of Getty Images
32. Photograph by Sam Brody, reprinted courtesy of Sondra Brody
Except as noted above, all photographs are reprinted courtesy of the Estate of Alice Neel.

www.stmartins.com

Book design by Jonathan Bennett

Library of Congress Cataloging-in-Publication Data

Hoban, Phoebe.
   Alice Neel : the art of not sitting pretty / Phoebe Hoban.—1st ed.
      p. cm.
   ISBN 978-0-312-60748-7
   1. Neel, Alice, 1900–1984.   2. Women artists—United States—Biography.   I. Title.
   ND1329.N36H63 2010
   759.13—dc22
   [B]
                                                                    2010035781

First Edition: December 2010

10 9 8 7 6 5 4 3 2 1

FOR MY FATHER, RUSSELL HOBAN

Contents

ALICE NEEL

CHAPTER ONE

Studio Still Life

Her paintbrushes and glasses still rest by the easel in the apartment on 300 West 107th Street, where Alice Neel spent the last twenty-two years of her life. The living room overlooking Broadway, which also served as her studio, is filled with furniture circa 1950. In the next room, lying on top of a dresser, is a faded snapshot of José Santiago Negron—the father of her oldest son, Richard—a handsome Puerto Rican musician who later became a priest. The surfaces are strewn with artifacts: two animal skulls, an odd menorah with five, instead of the standard seven candleholders, and three sitting ducks—wooden decoys which Neel humorously referred to as herself, Sam Brody, the filmmaker and photographer who was her longtime companion and fathered her second son, Hartley, and John Rothschild, her erstwhile lover and close friend. There are paintings everywhere—on the walls, stacked in the hall. Everything has been left just as it was when Neel lived and worked here, covering hundreds of canvases with ruthlessly honest portraits of the people who intrigued her, from neighborhood children to Andy Warhol.

Like the Pollock-Krasner House in the Springs, where Pollock's half-filled gallons of paint and cans of brushes remain in suspended animation, Neel's place has been frozen in time since her death in 1984. But unlike Pollock's studio, which has been carefully preserved as a temple to its former resident genius, no effort has been made to sanctify the Neel home; like the artist who lived there, it remains strikingly uncontrived. All that's missing is the powerful presence of Neel herself.

The quintessential Bohemian, Neel spent more than half a century, from her early days as a WPA artist living in the heart of the Village, through her Whitney retrospective in 1974, until her death ten years later, painting, often in near obscurity, an extraordinarily diverse population—from young black sisters in Harlem to the elderly Jewish twin artists Raphael and Moses Soyer to the American Communist Party chairman Gus Hall to Linus Pauling—creating an indelible portrait of twentieth-century America.

An avowed sensualist, Neel painted unflinchingly naked (often literally) pictures of her lovers and the contemporary movers and shakers of the time, including many fellow members of the left-wing, activist art world. "I'm cursed to be in this Mother Hubbard body," she once said. "I'm a real sexy person." At the same time, she was a resourceful single parent, raising two sons, first in Spanish Harlem, then on the Upper West Side near Columbia University. Neel was highly attuned to complex issues of motherhood, and her raw, intimate nudes of pregnant women, from friends and neighbors to her own daughter-in-law, are among her signature works.

In every aspect of her life, Neel dictated her own terms—whether it was defiantly painting figurative pieces at the height of Abstract Expressionism, convincing her subjects to disrobe (which many of them did, including, surprisingly, Andy Warhol), or finessing scholarships for her sons at the Rudolf Steiner School. No wonder she became the de facto artist of the feminist movement. (When *Time* magazine put Kate Millet on its cover in 1970, she was asked to paint the portrait.) Very much in touch with her time, Neel was also always ahead of it. Although she herself would probably have rejected such labels, she was America's first feminist, multicultural artist, a populist painter for the ages.

Neel managed to transcend her often tragic circumstances, surviving the death from diphtheria of her infant daughter Santillana, her first child by the Cuban painter Carlos Enríquez, with whom she lived in Havana for a year before returning to the United States, where Carlos later joined her; the breakup of her marriage; a nervous breakdown and several suicide attempts when she was thirty, for which she was institutionalized for over a year; and the terrible separation from her second child, Isabetta, whom Carlos took back to Havana, where she was brought up by the Enríquez family. Neel also lost much of her work when Kenneth Doolittle, her lover from her Village days, burned and slashed some three hundred of her pieces.

Although Neel suffered enormously, she never became a victim. Unlike Frida Kahlo, whose work brilliantly fetishized her personal pain, Neel transformed her deepest wounds into her most humanistic work. And unlike Mary Cassatt, who beautifully chronicled family life in the nineteenth century but never married or had children, Neel painted from firsthand experience of the vicissitudes—and rewards—of marriage and motherhood. She accurately called herself a "collector of souls," and spoke of her oeuvre, in hommage to Balzac, as "the Human Comedy." "I paint my time using the people as evidence," she once said.

The story of Alice Neel is the story of a fiercely unconventional woman and artist who, without ever being a careerist, managed to carve out a significant niche in art history through sheer tenacity, a keen intellect, and a tireless drive to paint the truth. Her prolific output captures a universe of powerful personalities—and documents an age. Neel painted through the Depression, McCarthyism, the revolution of the sixties, and the feverish eighties. She was in her late sixties before she began to receive serious critical acclaim. Today she is widely considered a major twentieth-century artist.

Neel's life is not just the saga of a great American painter; it is a great American saga. Born into a proper Victorian family at the turn of the century, Neel came of age during suffrage, struggled through the Depression, and lived through the women's liberation movement and the sexual revolution, reaching her prime in a time when she was finally permitted to do—and even celebrated for doing—just what she had strived to do all along: forge the life of an independent woman who was first and foremost an artist. Neel's personal and artistic growth was often at odds with the century that shaped both her and her work. But when the antiestablishment sixties arrived, Neel, then herself in her sixties, arrived, too. The lifelong iconoclast and rebel against institutional values was finally at one with her era.

Neel knew many of the important political and art thinkers of her day, as evidenced by her portraits of people as wide-ranging as Meyer Schapiro, Linus Pauling, Kenneth Fearing, the Beat legend Joe Gould, apocryphal author of an "Oral History of the World" (whom she famously painted with three penises), Frank O'Hara, Robert Smithson, and Andy Warhol.

She was also enough of a cultural character to have appeared as a cameo in two movies and in several books. Neel is the basis for a feisty WPA artist played by Elsa Lancaster in the 1948 film *The Big Clock*, from Fearing's 1946 novel by the same name; Susan Sarandon played Neel in *Joe Gould's Secret* (2000), in which her infamous portrait of Gould appears; and the novelist Millen Brand portrayed Neel in two of his best-sellers, *The Outward Room*, 1937, and *Some Love, Some Hunger*, 1955.

From the start her work was both personal and political: Neel participated in the first Washington Square Outdoor Art Exhibit (one piece, *Degenerate Madonna*, drew protests from the Catholic Church and had to be withdrawn). She was a member of the Artists' Union, and in 1936, she created an audacious work called *Nazis Murder Jews* of a Communist torchlight parade. Neel was a long-term member of the Communist Party USA (with an FBI file to prove it) and painted many Party leaders. In 1953, Neel commented on Cold War policy in her powerful painting *Eisenhower, McCarthy, Dulles,* portraying a terrible trio hovering over the western half of the globe. She was also highly aware of issues of race, and painted members of the civil rights movement as well as other influential black figures.

But Neel was no naïve folk artist. A witty, well-educated, and worldly woman, she studied at the country's first all-woman art school—the Philadelphia School of Design for Women (now Moore College of Art & Design)—receiving awards for two consecutive years in her portrait class. Robert Henri, a founder of the Ashcan School (and one of Edward Hopper's mentors) had taught at the Philadelphia School in the late 1800s and was still considered its foremost artist. His book, *The Art Spirit,* inspired a whole generation of artists. Neel's work followed in the realist tradition of Henri and Thomas Eakins in its effort to portray the essential truth of its subject and to explore social diversity. But Neel pushed this envelope to its utmost edge, into a realm uniquely her own.

Neel's portraits are incisive psychological studies of her models. Indeed, posing for Neel was an experience in itself. In a reverse form of "talking cure," Neel entertained her subjects—and disarmed them—with a nonstop stream of racy stories, politics, and philosophical musings. Curator John Perreault had a vivid recollection of modeling for Neel. "I'm posing stark naked; Nancy, her daughter-in-law, is coming in and out of the room; Alice is chatting away about the Depression and this boyfriend, and that boyfriend. She looked like a grandmother—a *Saturday Evening Post* grandmother. She had that beauty that an older woman can have. She had great eyes; she had the devil in her eyes. She had a foul mouth, and she was a vicious gossip. So there I was, lying naked in front of a vicious gossip."

Another model, artist Benny Andrews, described Neel's clever ploy for capturing her prey in its most vulnerable state. "It was interesting because she would just come up with these stories. In fact, that was one of the things that was so effective about her, because then you were listening, and you were interested in what she was telling you, so you got involved in that. I always said she was looking at you like an X-ray, and you were sitting up there laughing at her jokes while she was seeing right through you, and you didn't even realize it."

One of the last paintings Neel made was one of her rare self-portraits. At eighty, Neel cast as relentless an eye on herself as on the hundreds of subjects of her long career. Perched on a chair, the artist known for her scathing nude portraits is stripped down to her quintessence. Naked but for her glasses, a paintbrush, and a rag, she bravely renders herself with neither clothing nor props, her aging body equipped just with the tools of her craft—her vision and her deftly wielded implements—as if to make the definitive statement of self-expression: "I paint, therefore I am." The flesh may sag, may, as Neel put it, be "dropping off the bone," but the artist and her ability to paint remain forcefully intact. It is a radical departure from the standard artist's self-portrait, and in its stark veracity beautifully illustrates Neel's original and enduring American vision.

"The road that I pursued, and the road that I think keeps you an artist, is that no matter what happens to you, you still keep on painting," she once said.

CHAPTER TWO

Childhood's Canvas

Alice Neel always knew she wanted to be an artist. Her "Rosebud" moment was her earliest memory as an infant: the color red. "Whenever I
think of writing a biography, I think of . . . the color red in our living room.
My mother said I could not have remembered it because I was only about
six months old."

Highly conscious of herself as the protagonist in her own drama, Neel
sometimes framed her self-reflections: "If I wrote a biography . . ." (meaning, of course, autobiography). Instead, she painted one: Neel's canvas was
a membrane through which the artist experienced the world. Her entire
oeuvre is a powerful "Remembrance of Things Present."

As art, her hundreds of paintings emphatically stand on their own. As
biography, they are inextricable from the vivid verbal narrative which Neel,
who achieved fame and an audience later in life, polished and stylized over
the years: a dazzling and seductive cycle of anecdotes and reflections that
brilliantly limn her character, much as her indigo blue outline defines
many of her subjects. No wonder she had a difficult time parting from her
work, hoarding it tenaciously. (Even when she actually sold something, she
sometimes made a copy.)

"I tried to capture life as it went by—art records so much, the feeling,
the beliefs, the changes," she wrote. "One of the reasons I painted was to
catch light as it goes by, right hot off the griddle. Now that doesn't mean
that the work has to tell *about* your life, I mean it can be abstract or anything, but the vitality is taken out of *real living*."

Alice Neel's lust for "real living" was in direct response to her stultify-
ing background. Even today, her hometown, Colwyn, Pennsylvania, just
outside of Philadelphia, exudes a sleepy provinciality; there are trolley
tracks bifurcating the main street, and the trolley still runs. You can take

the same route Colwyn's most famous citizen would have taken as it rumbles through the drab little town.

And Neel, from the time she was a young girl, would have made an indelible impression. As Marilou Usher, a Colwyn denizen, recalls, "My mother, Isabel Huston Spahr, saw Alice on the trolley, on the way to a Sunday school picnic when Alice was about fourteen. She was in awe of her. She remembered her as very Bohemian. She was different than everyone else." That would ultimately set Neel apart, not only from her hometown but from her family, who were nothing if not outwardly respectably conventional. "If I could have met myself in that little town, that would have been a wonderful thing for me," she said. Instead, she had to invent herself.

Neel's life and career were a violent rebellion against the values of her tiny hometown, with its numbing normalcy and rigid constraints. Although she returned frequently to her home—seeking comfort from her mother between recurrent crises—she was hell-bent on escaping its deadly confines. Neel would lead a life that was wild even by Bohemian standards, and create a deeply original body of artwork. It would be shaped by three potent forces: her relentless and transcendent desire to paint, her ongoing struggle with the sometimes mundane, sometimes tragic hardships of poverty, and her adamant refusal to conform. Neel was uncompromising in her absolute drive. In the end, it is that which enabled her to survive—and to leave an enduring mark.

*   *   *

Alice Neel was born on January 28, 1900, in nearby Merion Square, now known as Gladwyne (a town she would return to after a nervous breakdown in 1930). "If I ever write a biography, I'm going to call it 'I am the century.' I'm four weeks younger than the century," she liked to say. When she was about three months old, the family moved to Colwyn—a working-class town of narrow streets and small wood and brick row houses—which boasted one of the country's first black baseball teams, the Hilldale Club. At the time, Colwyn, which is located southwest of Philadelphia and is part of Darby Borough in eastern Delaware County, had a population of about twelve hundred.

Neel's family history is as sketchy as the backgrounds of her mature paintings: If the family ever kept records, they have long since been lost. Neel was the fourth of five children born to economically lower-middle-class parents with somewhat distinguished genealogies. Her father, George Washington Neel, who was a clerk for the Superintendent Car Service of

the Pennsylvania Railroad, came from a long line of opera singers in Philadelphia, ending with his parents, who died when he was between the ages
of twelve and fifteen. (As an infant, he had even appeared onstage in an
opera.) His father was a Civil War veteran.

Her mother, Alice Concross Hartley, was, according to family lore, a
descendant of a signer of the Declaration of Independence, Richard Stockton. Stockton and his wife, the poet Annis Boudinot Stockton, had six
children, four daughters and two sons: Julia Stockton (married to Benjamin Rush, also a signer of the Declaration), Mary, Susan, Richard, Lucius,
and Abigail.

The most definitive link that can be established between Alice's mother,
whose maiden name was Hartley, and Richard Stockton, is not directly
through Richard, but through his brother, John Stockton. John was the
great-great-great-grandfather of a woman named Rhoda Stockton, whose
great-great-great-uncle was Richard the signer. Rhoda married a man
named Johh Huff, and the couple had nine children, including a daughter,
Mary, who married William Hartley, whose lineage is unknown. Hartley
fought in the Civil War. There seems to be no further or more immediate
connection.

Although she was proud of it, Neel herself was confused as to her mother's precise place in the Stockton family tree. She told Richard Polsky, who
interviewed her in 1981, that "Rhoda Stockton was a sister of Richard Stockton, who signed the Declaration," that John Huff owned a shoe factory in
Philadelphia, and that Mary was never seen in anything but a "black satin
gown," à la John Singer Sargent. She recalled, in a written reminiscence,
that her grandmother "was the daughter of a woman who was a sister of a
hero of the American Revolution and a wife of my grandfather who was a
courier in the calvary in the Civil War. She lived until I was eight or nine,
and was slight and dark with a small waist. She was always well-dressed
and rather elegant. I still have a piece of purple satin ribbon from her funeral, which I was considered too young to attend."

Apparently, there was also a wealthy side of the family that included
Alice's great-uncle on her mother's side, Linley Walsh, a liquid-soap manu-
facturer, and his wife, Julia. As a Quaker, according to Alice, Walsh refused
to advertise and ultimately lost everything, including his country house in
Cape May. Neel's mother grew up knowing some of the old, rich families of
Philadelphia, which perhaps accounts for the fact that Neel always depicted
her as "cultured."

The only thing George Washington Neel inherited from his parents was a lifelong bias against Bohemians. According to Alice, he was vehemently "anti-Bohemian," a sentiment Alice Neel's own children would also later come to express. Although her father's family had been well-off when he was a child (Alice had a picture of him with his own pony), his mother died when he was young, and at nine he went to live with an aunt. At twelve, he moved to a boardinghouse and took a job hanging beef at a butcher shop. At seventeen, he began working at the Pennsylvania Railroad, eventually becoming head clerk of the accounting department.

By Alice's account, he was a "little gray man," quiet, passive, and totally dominated by her mother. She depicted him in two paintings, nineteen years apart: *The Family*, 1927, in which he is a tiny coal-bearing cipher, and the poignant, austere *Dead Father*, 1946. His most striking feature was his large nose, which caused his wife to joke that he was an "Irish Jew."

Alice Concross Hartley was an ur-Victorian. In that sense, she took after her mother, who was, according to George Neel, "the most disciplined Victorian I ever heard of." Thirty years Alice's junior, George (also known as "Georgie") was a highly eccentric college professor, prone to colorful turns of phrase. George's comments are among the only remarks on record (except for those of Alice Neel herself) regarding Neel's childhood home and family antecedents.

"Now my Grandmother Neel [Alice Neel's mother] was a disciplined Victorian, I mean to the nth degree, but her mother was even more so," recalled George in a 1987 interview. "Her mother, my great-grandmother, was a perfectionist of discipline, and everything had to be exactly as she ordered it." Her father (Neel's great-grandfather), on the other hand, was a "big, blond, American of English descent." A heating expert, he had installed the first central-heating units in Pittsburgh, and he frequently traveled.

Alice Concross Hartley had four sisters, Maimie, Lillian, Julie, and Jenny (a younger sister, Florence, had died of diphtheria), and a brother. While Mrs. Hartley may have been totally puritanical, her husband apparently had a drinking problem, and Alice Sr. would let him in when he found his way home in the wee hours.

"My great-grandfather was a heavy beer drinker and when he came home at night he was loaded. My great-grandmother wouldn't let him in. She was a Puritan of the severest code and nature," said George. The girls, Lily, Maimie, Alice, Julie, and Jenny, slept in a large walnut bed, all five of them, crosswise in the bed. But my grandmother snuck downstairs and slept on the settee, so that she could let her father in when he came home drunk, and she said, 'Well you know George, I loved him, but he did stink of beer and I didn't like that.'" When she ran her own household, Grandmother Neel prohibited any liquor in the house, but according to George, "Albert and my father, Peter, and Alice always snuck it in."

Life chez Neel was a matriarchy. "My mother was the real head-of-the-house type," Alice told Frederick Ted Castle in 1983. "My father didn't even care to be boss. He was a nice philosophic person. I was more interested in my mother because she was bright, she knew more and she was quicker on the draw."

"My grandfather was a gentle and quiet man who was ruled by my grandmother. My grandmother was the boss," agreed George Neel, who described her as a complicated and conflicted person. According to him, "My grandmother was a charming conversationalist. She never spoke but in a conversational tone, she never told a complete story, and she was always the most cheerful person I have ever known. My grandmother was exceedingly determined, exceedingly organized, exceedingly regimented, but she was also kindly and gentle really, or at least she had learned to become so. She was mean, but on the surface she was a lady."

George (whom Alice would paint in 1982 [*Georgie and Annemarie*] as an effeminate man with well-manicured hands, seated side by side with his much older German wife) described Alice (at least as an adult) as just the opposite. "Alice did everything imaginable to be anything but a lady. Her habits were always essentially disgusting. Her fingernails were dirty. Alice didn't like to bathe; Alice had a habit of eating her bread sideways. She could never do anything like any normal person would do. Alice spilled everything. Every time anything got exciting, Alice screamed and squealed." Alice, said her nephew, "decided already as a very small child, 'This house is unbearable. Therefore I must make a world of my own beyond it.'"

By the time Alice was in high school, the family had moved twice. Their third house, at 408 Colywn Avenue, was by far the nicest. Part of a pair, it was really half a house, cream-colored, with forest green trim. It was up on a hill that dropped precipitously down to the stone-paved street. To its right was the bridge that led to the railroad; there was also a flight of wooden stairs leading down to the train. There were two forest green wicker rocking chairs on the front porch. All three houses still stand. Today the house at 408 Colwyn Avenue no longer has a cream-and-green exterior. But inside the rooms remain essentially the same—small and low-ceilinged, with dark bedrooms up the narrow stairs.

Alice had the back bedroom; there was also a small sitting room at the top of the stairs with an oval table that in later years had a lamp with a shade that Alice had painted with images of corn husks, and a round ceramic dish that she had painted with a fish. A bookcase held a history of the United States bought for Alice's brother Peter, who became a college professor.

Downstairs in the parlor, furnished with an oak settee, an easy chair, and an oak rocker, there was more Neel artwork: A still life of zinnias by Alice hung above Grandfather Neel's beloved radio, and a watercolor of downtown Havana painted by Carlos Enríquez was displayed between the two chairs. The dining room had a massive Tiffany dome above the round oak table. There were also a heavy oak sideboard, two built-in china cupboards, and another rocking chair next to Grandmother Neel's Victorian spool-turned sewing stand with its marble top.

As Neel recalled it, "In the dining room was a plate rack and beautiful wallpaper, of an elegant kind, heavy with a rich dark red patterned border, and on the rack really beautiful plates which had belonged to my grandmother [Mary]. . . . There were china closets in this dining room with the plates all arranged very artistically and a bay window. It was really very nice. But for me too small, and besides I didn't like the fact that the house was one of a pair. I wanted it to be standing all alone with the lawn all around it, not a so-called yard such as we had."

In a striking cross section of this childhood home, a dun hued watercolor painted in 1927, Alice used the house to provide an almost Freudian analysis of the family dynamic: There is her father, hauling coal up from the cellar; her mother, wild-eyed and nearly hysterical, scrubbing the dining room floor; Alice pensively cradling her first baby, Santillana; and her brother Peter, impervious to the melodramas being played out beneath him, on the top floor, studying French for his classes at Temple University.

George Neel painted a telling picture of Grandmother and Grandfather Neel at home after their children were grown. As a young boy, he would play pinochle every evening with his grandparents, with Grandmother Neel priding herself on her ability to read the cards upside down. She would boast that "your grandfather can count pretty well, but he can't count half as fast as I do."

Alice's father, meanwhile, would amuse himself by making little drawings of neighbors and dogs. "Alice got her drawing interest from her father— not from her mother," George Neel said. "My father, Albert, and Alice looked very similar."

Grandmother Neel had a commanding personality. Equally impressive was her misogynistic attitude. "My grandmother was a male chauvinist. She hated all women. Women were for her absolutely unimportant. The only thing that mattered with any woman was she had to be rich, or she was nothing. She couldn't even be politically important. Either she was rich and fashionable or she was nobody. Then she said to Alice when Alice told her she was going to paint, 'Why do you want to be a painter? Don't you know you are only a girl?'"

Or as Neel herself recalled it, "I don't know what you expect to do in the world, Alice. You're only a girl." Neel would later say the comment made her "ambitious."

Neel's mother's patronizing remark was as much a reflection on her intense frustration at the severe limitations of her own era as it was a perspective on her daughter's future. Alice Concross Hartley was a competent, intelligent woman miserably inhibited by staid Victorian constraints. As Neel later said, "Everything in her life was induced by being so frustrated." Her mother's enforced inertia—with its tacit entrapment and despair—was both a cautionary example and a challenge to Neel, who had, fortunately, been born on the cusp of a time when women began to gain some vestige of freedom. In reacting to her restrictive background, Neel would exploit that newfound freedom to its maximum extent.

Neel's mother also said, "None of us will ever be remembered." Alice's father, however, seemed to sense Alice's singularity. "Well, I am not so sure about Alice," she remembered him saying.

From an early age, Alice Neel's quirks were apparent. She was a child consumed by anxieties and indecision. Clearly stifled by the prim Victorian household, where by the time she was three or four years old, "there was already a wall between me and the reserve of my mother," she was showing signs of neurasthenia (duly noted by the family doctor). "I was hypersensitive as a child," Neel told Eleanor Munro, who interviewed her for a WNET television program on women artists that became the 1979 book *Originals*. "If a fly lit on me, I'd have a convulsion. . . . There was a stuffed cat I lived in terror of. For all I know my human images originate in terror. It may be I need to exorcise something."

Even Sunday school frightened her. "The tale of Christ nailed to the cross would send me into violent weeping and I'd have to be taken home. Also I remember a film they showed at the church of the horrors of delirium tremens that quite unnerved me and prevented my sleeping for many nights." She was also plagued with ambivalence, "going into a fever" over even the most minor decisions, like whether or not to have hot chocolate or coffee. Her mother later said she was "jumpy as a cricket on a hot stove."

Neel's uncertainty undermined her sense of self. "Other people loomed too large. Everybody could knock me off base so that it was hard for me to be myself. I'd make such an effort to be what they wanted, a pretty little girl, that I wouldn't be myself at all. As for that, I doubt if I was really myself until my mother died when I was fifty-four."

Although physically Neel was indeed conventionally pretty, with round cheeks, blue eyes, and red-gold hair, "I was an unknown quantity. That's what my mother used to say," Neel told Joan Kufrin, author of *Uncommon Women*.

But despite her psychological and emotional insecurity, Neel maintained one strong conviction: "Even as a child, I was sure there were three things I could be: a writer, a painter or a sculptor." She was even more emphatic in her oral history with art historian Patricia Hills: "I always wanted to be an artist. I don't know where it came from. When I was eight years old the most important thing for me was the painting book and the watercolors. When I was very small, about 5 or 6, my most important Christmas present would be a coloring book."

Later, Neel would say that she had been bitten by the "the bug, the virus, Art." It would be her often tortuous lifeline. It was her refuge—her way of coping with her constant dis-ease. "When I first began to paint that was my only real life, really. That was the only place I acted natural. That was where I was completely myself. Because in life itself I was not ever completely myself. I've had a lot of lonely wretched times, but then I would paint in them."

Alice loved drawing violets and rose of Sharon, which grew around the two-story house in abundance. There were also three rows of pear trees—the vestige of a former orchard. In the backyard, there were maple trees and a garden tended by her father: nicotiana, lilies that Alice's mother hated—she called them "swamp things"—and an impressive bevy of blue hydrangea bushes lining the house. (Alice would later paint them in *Still Life, Rose of Sharon*, 1973.)

Neel used to go to Tribbet's farm, "the only real farm left in this little suburb," to pick the "first May lilies . . . then the violets, beautiful rich purple . . . I would take them home for the house, and for my mother who always loved them. Then star of Bethlehem all over the ground . . . then later buttercups, a whole field of them beautiful and yellow in the sunshine. . . ."

But even Tribbet's farm had its dark places; the buttercups grew near "Ann's Rock, a dangerous place, so that even as you enjoyed and picked them you were a little afraid. Ann's Rock was an enormous rock covered with Isinglass a great distance from the ground below, from which an Indian girl named Ann had jumped, so it was said, because her white lover deserted her. Now a strange shabby dark man sometimes lurked there, and there were nameless things about him, things that made him dangerous to children, that everyone talked of so that as soon as you saw him, you had to run away. . . ."

"I was just a child then, but I remember all the flowers, what they looked like: elephant ears, and four o'clocks and scarlet sage," she said. "When I was in high school, I loved botany class. We had a bean that sprouted, and I made beautiful paintings of the bean and the sprouting. They looked like Ellsworth Kelly drawings. . . ."

One Christmas, when Neel was eight, she got a paint book with apples and flowers. "I was a romantic and that was the most exciting thing for me. Not like the one they gave me when I was ten, with the Katzenjammer Kids. I hated that. I read how Picasso loved [that comic], but I hated that hideous dog and those frightful kids," she told Karl Fortess when he interviewed her in 1975.

Neel hated the book because, like the stuffed cat and the story of the Crucifixion, it scared her. From the time she was an infant, she was also deathly afraid of the dark. "At night I'd turn on my side in bed and look out the door at the gaslight in the hall. With one eye I could see the light, and with the other I couldn't, and I thought the eye that couldn't see was blind. . . . The minute the light went out, I thought I was blind, so I was terrorized at night. W. H. Auden says that people with night fears never will become nice people. I had these fears, but I wouldn't tell anyone. . . . I internalized everything. Mother and my older sister were different. They were elegant ladies. They didn't make any noise, but their emotions went outward. Mine all went inward."

Neel, however, described herself as "extremely attached" to her mother. "She had a strong, independent character, stronger than I, but she was terribly nervous. She could have done anything, run a big business establishment. She was very well-read and very intelligent, and she had a terrific capacity, but she couldn't compromise." According to Neel, this is why she was able to "run the roost."

But beneath the maternal hierarchy ran a troubling undercurrent. According to George, "My grandmother, who was so charming and who was so really matriarchial and Victorian, really suffered from a level of hysteria and possibly schizophrenia, but had learned how to balance this world so well."

As Neel put it, "She was so superior, so sensitive, she couldn't bear anything. . . . I had to keep her happy all the time." Indeed, in one of her last interviews, Neel told writer Judith Higgins that her therapist hypothesized that she had become a portraitist as a result of intently studying her mother's face, which, she said, "had dominion over me," for signs of her conflicting and unpredictable feelings.

According to Neel, her mother, who was often moody, "needed sunshine because it was very easy for her to fall into dissatisfied morbidity, never very deep or lasting, but still the sunshine helped her to feel that life after all wasn't so bad, although everyday there was evidence that it really wasn't what one expected and hoped for."

Half a century later, Neel conjured up a remarkable childhood memory of that sense of apprehension and discontent:

> . . . Do you remember your mother and your father, how they struggled, the little people, and that house they thought was so nice, and it was nice, on a street that had once been a pear orchard. . . . Then all the present melted away, and I could smell one of those thunderstorms that come up around five o'clock, just when supper is being prepared, and first the sun disappears, then there is a feeling of threat and a light breeze, fitful and chaotic springs up from nowhere, the leaves on the pear trees rustle. Next it grows darker with heavy grey clouds in the sky and a yellowish light, the wind lashes the pear trees and the little sickle pears, green and reddish on one side, begin to fall. Then rain in great drops. Inside the house my mother gets more and more nervous, the peals of thunder terrify her and make her rush around. You mustn't stay on the porch for the lightning is attracted to wet wood. The street is full of falling pears and the rain fills the gutters with water. After the storm a lot of little urchins in bare feet and scant clothing rush out to pick up the pears. It is frightful not to be able to do this also. You can feel the good wet mud and grass on your feet, what fun, but you aren't allowed to do it, and you see your mother is so frantic that you give it up out of sympathy for her. Instead you get out the tablecloth and begin to set the table to show her that everything is normal.

Neel did not derive much comfort from her siblings, who were not close to each other in age or temperament. Alice's sister, Lily, ten years older, was her diametric opposite. "Small and dark," Lily was as straightlaced as her mother, and an accomplished seamstress. "My sister made the most magnificent clothes so I tried to sew but I never could. So it was something I always hated," Alice recalled. According to Neel's daughter-in-law Nancy Neel, "When Alice was born, Lily was like a little mother, and she made beautiful clothes for her. Alice was like a little doll, and she dressed her and she took care of her." But Lily married and left home young. Her husband, Chadwick Scott, was one of the architects of the Holland Tunnel. He later became gravely ill and had to be carried to work. They had a son named Jimmy.

As time went on, the two sisters grew significantly apart, although Alice told Richard Polsky that she loved her sister. "Later on she became a bone in my throat because she only loved me as long as I was an accessory of hers. . . . When I began to have my own life, which she felt was a little scandalous, then it was another story." Indeed, Lily later turned on Alice. As Neel told Jonathan Brand, "She was wonderful to me when I was little. It was just when my life got so wild that she became a menace."

The family's firstborn son, Hartley, had died of diphtheria before Alice was born. Her brother Albert, who was twelve years older, was a true eccentric, a mama's boy who didn't marry until he was thirty-nine, and obsessively raised dogs, flowers, and pigeons. Neel did one watercolor, *Obie's Corner*, 1926, done in a similar style to that of *The Family*, of a neighborhood bar that Albert used to take her to, where, Alice recalled, she would dance a jig on the counter.

Alice's brother Peter, who was five years younger, had fathered George out of wedlock, then married the child's mother, Dorothy, and moved back home for a year, leaving the infant with his wife's family in Pennsylvania. Neel's son Hartley says Peter was also "peculiar, really bizarre—very loud and self-centered, the spoiled child of the family." He played the saxophone, and drank and gambled to excess.

Still, Peter ultimately became the dean of Monmouth College, in New Jersey. Eventually his vices caught up with him; a serious smoker, he burned to death in bed. Observed George of the Neel children, "None of them had any grace or gratitude toward their parents. And the parents served the children as though they were organized slaves to them. They didn't want children. Therefore they felt that they had to take care of these chicks especially well." Although Hartley says Alice was fond of both her brothers, she never spoke about them to interviewers; it was almost as if they didn't exist.

Alice's memories of elementary school were the archetypical experiences of the perennial outsider. Unlike her classmates, she was prone to existential thoughts. "She'd tell the other kids, 'you know your mind is really a strange thing, you are always thinking,' and someone would say, 'What am I thinking about now?' and she would say, 'You are thinking about what you are thinking about,' and the other children would beat her up," her son Richard recalls. Once, when a teacher insisted she do something she didn't want to do, she planted herself on the ground and declared, "I am the Rock of Gibraltar."

At fourteen, Alice attended Darby High School, where she excelled in math. She did not take art classes, although she drew, not very confidently, confining her sketches of people to the very edges of the page. She also copied covers of *The Saturday Evening Post*—"you know, the gorgeous girl with her hand out and a drop of rain falling," she told curator Henry Geldzahler.

Art provided Alice's only outlet from her repressive childhood. It wasn't just her household that was stifling, but the "benighted" town of Colwyn itself. "Although in the spring it was beautiful," Neel told Patricia Hills, "there was no artist to paint it. And once a man exposed himself at a window, but there was no writer to write it. . . . There was no culture there. I hated that little town. I just despised it. . . . And in the summer I used to sit on the porch and try to keep my blood from circulating. . . . Because boredom is what killed me. There was nothing to stimulate my mind except my mother."

When she was a teenager, Neel's mother took Alice to the theater, concerts, and ballets in Philadelphia. Neel recalled seeing *Faust* at fourteen, and she particularly admired Sarah Bernhardt and Elonora Duse as actresses. She also saw performances by the ballerina Pavlova and the Polish pianist Paderewski. Neel told Hills her mother took her out "so I wouldn't get pregnant," indicating a certain popularity with the opposite sex. "She took me to *Faust* to show me what happened to girls that strayed from the straight and narrow," Alice recalled. But it is likely that Mrs. Neel, whom Alice described as "intelligent and well-read," enjoyed culture herself.

Still, by the time she was in her early teens, "I felt like their parent," Alice said of her mother and father. "They seemed very innocent and naïve." When her brother Peter, who raised rabbits, mentioned that one of them was about to have babies, "a dim silence fell over the whole house. You didn't mention things like that," she recalled.

Meanwhile, Alice tried to be responsible, taking a business course in typing and stenography during her last two years of high school, despite the school superintendent saying she was too bright to waste her time on such things. "This was the stupidest thing I ever did in my life. But nevertheless, I did it. They came to see the family, they told them I was so great in mathematics I should never do that, but one thing the family never interfered with. . . . I could do as I pleased, so I took this course," she told Karl Fortess.

Between feeling a duty to her financially strapped family, who were saving money to send her younger brother, Peter, to college, and the constant distraction provided by the boys in her class, her junior year was, it seems, particularly stressful: "I had a small nervous breakdown when I was seventeen, only a small one, but I remember not being able to hold my head up for a couple of months. It came from repression, from growing up in a very puritanical atmosphere," she told Eleanor Munro. She also mentioned it to Patricia Hills. (While it is unlikely that it was diagnosed as such, or even noticed by anyone in her family, her lethargic condition was the precursor of a full-fledged breakdown a decade or so later.)

In a scrap of journal-like writing, Neel described her state of mind at the time, which appeared to have been a result of teenaged sexual frustration and holding down a part-time job:

> Well you see I should have been exercising when I was a weak white adolescent. I never had the money to go with the others so I just sat on the porch and got sexual. Then I learned to click clack typewriter letters beautifully to get money. I click clacked them and hated it. I was so tired always. I didn't know what to do with the money anyway. I bought heavy supplies that made me sick. I used to itch and feel awful in stuffy restaurants and my eyes were blurry and I felt so sexual. . . .

This was the same year that she went to New York for the first time. "I did love New York at first. I went to the Metropolitan. Such was my hunger for art that I remember three or four rooms, not only every picture in them, but how they were hung as well."

When she graduated on June 28, 1918, in a ceremony that the 1919 Darby High School yearbook indicated was unruly, she passed the civil service exam and got a job with the Army Air Corps in Philadelphia, making twenty-two dollars a week working as a file clerk and girl Friday for Lt. Theodore Sizer (who later became an art historian), and "meeting lots of Air Force officers." She worked at various civil service jobs for three years, eventually making thirty-five dollars a week and taking art classes at night at the School of Industrial Art and a smaller school in downtown Philadelphia.

Even then, she had her own idiosyncratic way of doing things. When an old-fashioned art teacher criticized her naturalistic method of painting hair, suggesting she simply color it in, she told him, "Well, that isn't the way the hair goes. I don't want to put in a tone." When he told her, "Before you conquer art, you'll have to conquer yourself," Alice retorted, "That's not for you to say because you are only my beginning teacher."

By the time Alice began classes at the Philadelphia School of Design for Women, in 1921, she had proven that she had the two qualities she deemed essential for the life of an artist: "You know what it takes to be an artist? Hypersensitivity and the will of the devil. To never give up."

As she further explained: "Hypersensitivity, because in order to be an artist you have to react intensely. And then you must have the will. I had a very strong, adamant self. That is proved by the art I have produced. Now I don't know how you arrive at that. But in my case I believe it came about because other people had such a strong effect on me."

Neel used portraiture as a framing device; a way to *contain* both life and people—and the intensity of their impact on her. Her trademark draughtsmanlike outline—in itself a frame—is a painterly metaphor for Neel's artistic survival instinct. Portraiture provided the perfect aesthetic distance. On canvas, Neel could create "a world, and I could do as I liked in it."

CHAPTER THREE

Designing Women

In the autumn of 1921, Alice Neel was the model of the young working woman. She had just returned from Pittsburgh, where she visited her sister Lily, and got a job at a bank. Although she was still living at home, she was earning thirty-five dollars a week at her civil service job. And she had just answered an ad for a job opening at Swarthmore, which paid thirty dollars a week. But walking home from the job interview, Alice had an epiphany. This was not the life she wanted: It was clearly time for her to push her interest in art to the next level. "Art was in the back of my mind always," she said.

As she later elaborated, "For me art was a necessity, apart from being a profession. There was something obsessive about art for me. And I think that's one of the main—the best—reasons that people go into art and stick to it, because it's essential to them feeling that they're living, no matter how uncomfortable it makes them."

On November 1, 1921, Neel was admitted to the Phildelphia School of Design for Women. She specifically chose the school over the more famous Pennsylvania Academy of the Fine Arts for four reasons: First, it was a women's school, and she wouldn't be pursued by men. "I was very beautiful then and all the boys chased me. . . . I chose a women's school so there wouldn't be anyone there to distract me," she told Munro. Second, it differed significantly from the Pennsylvania Academy of the Fine Arts, Mary Cassatt's alma mater. "I didn't want to be taught Impressionism," Neel declared. "I didn't see life as Picnic on the Grass. I wasn't happy like Renoir." Neel emphatically despised those "yellow lights and blue shadows." And third, "I didn't want to be taught a formal form. At least where I went it wasn't too well-organized, but you had freedom. You could do as you wanted, which was really the most important thing in my life." Perhaps even more important was the fact that although it had classes in com-

mercial illustration, the Phildelphia School of Design also had a school of
fine arts.

The school's registration pages indicate Neel was admitted to the school
of fine arts on November 1, 1921, and switched to illustration about a year
later. But Neel always said that she initially enrolled in the illustration
course "because I still had the idea of making money," and that after a just
short time she shifted to the school of fine arts. (Since Neel graduated with
a fine arts degree, it would appear her version is correct.) Neel only informed her parents that she was studying fine arts after the fact.

"The truth is I deceived them," Neel told Cindy Nemser. "They didn't
interfere with it because they knew how much I wanted it, but at first I told
them I was going to be an illustrator. Of course I soon realized that that
was not for me, and I was trying to do things that were completely impractical—just to be a good painter was impractical—it required complete
concentration. It also required that whatever money you had had to be put
into art materials. I had my own secret life at art school."

Neel paid the one-hundred-dollar tuition for her first year at the school
out of her own savings. Thanks to her obvious talent, she was soon given
the Delaware County Scholarship for the remaining three years of her
studies.

The history of the Philadelphia School of Design for Women itself
mirrors the changing attitudes toward women's education and their role in
society from the mid-nineteenth century through the early twentieth century, a pivotal generational shift from the Victorian era to the industrial
age, when the first seeds of women's rights began to blossom and women
emerged as a viable workforce. If Neel's mother, who was betrothed by the
time she was eighteen, had been brought up to believe that the only thing a
woman could do was marry well and run a household, Neel herself emerged
at a time when women were combatting the rigid hierarchies of their pre-
decessors, going out into the workforce, and finally winning the right to
vote. (In 1920, the year women won suffrage, Neel herself was twenty.)

As the school's 1922 pamphlet, "An Experiment in Training in the Useful and the Beautiful," begins:

> Anyone familiar with the education of girls and women today can
> hardly realize what kind of instruction was given them only as
> short a time ago as eighty years. Girls with conscientious mothers
> were taught to be expert housekeepers in expectation of marriage.
> People with some means, whose children it was thought would

not ordinarily be thrown on their own resources, gave their daughters what was called a fashionable education. This generally included fair penmanship, a limited knowledge of their mother tongue, a very little arithmetic, a few words or phrases of French . . . and some drawing or painting . . . If any such samples of such work now exist, they will be found stored in attics with their faces to the wall. The accomplishments also include the learning by rote of a few melodies or dances for the piano. If a girl of some education happened to be thrown on her own resources and did not care to marry or had not the opportunity, she had nothing upon which she could fall back for support. . . . Such a dependent became a hanger on, a barnacle.

Founded in 1848 by Mrs. Sarah Peter, the wife of the British consul William Peter, the Philadelphia School was one of the first trade schools in the United States for women, and the first of a handful of women's design schools that emerged in the mid-nineteenth century. Initially established in a single room in the Peters' residence at 320 South Third Street, it started out with one drawing teacher and ultimately expanded to include teachers of ironwork, paper hangings, calico prints, and woven textiles, as well as wood engraving and lithography.

The idea was that women could be taught marketable skills in the commercial arts, turning the crafts they had hitherto learned at home into wage-earning skills. The school fulfilled a twofold need: to give women a trade and to provide trained designers for the local industries, including textiles and household goods.

Eventually, the endeavor outgrew the Peters' residence, and the Franklin Institute agreed to fund its move to a larger building at 72 Walnut Street. By 1851, the school was doing so well that its students were earning an income from their work, of which they kept three-quarters; the fourth quarter went to the school for expenses. In 1853, when Mrs. Peter moved back to Cincinnatti, the Franklin Institute took the school over. At that time, the school had just three departments and less than sixty pupils: Drawing; an Industrial Department, which applied drawing, shading, and coloring to the art of designing paper hangings, textiles, et cetera; and the Department of Wood Engravings and Lithography.

In 1880, the school moved into an imposing block-long mansion with a large garden, formerly owned by the actor Edwin Forrest, on the corner of

Broad and Master streets, where Alice Neel first entered its doors. (The Forrest mansion is now a designated historical landmark and houses the Freedom Theatre. The school moved in 1959 to its present location at 1916 Race Street.)

"The school had great towering rooms and this marvelous collection of statues. It was completely conventional. But they had the most magnificent collection of classic statues I ever saw in my life. To me it was just heaven to be there," Neel told Fortess, "They had a magnificent Michaelangelo's Moses and they had the Elgin friezes. They had marvelous things." As for the mansion itself, "It was magnificent. Architecturally it fit perfectly with the buildings around it."

The collection of plaster casts that made such an impression on Neel was used to teach the students drawing, before they progressed on to a life class. According to Moore's 1921–1922 catalog (which includes among its illustrations Neel's oil portrait of a young woman), The Fine Arts Course began with first-year classes in cast drawing, pencil-drawing composition, oil painting, perspective, the theory of color, the history of art, and painting; second-year students studied portrait and antique painting with Paula Balano and Henry Snell; and third- and fourth-year students studied life class and portrait, modeling, painting, pictorial design, and costume-model sketch class.

"It is so arranged," the catalog explained, "that the student, through steady progression from simple to complex, may develop the power to represent objects faithfully and learn their forms and aspects, while at the same time, by constantly interchangeable use, she acquires equal facility in the handling of pencil, charcoal and brush."

Typically for the time, drawing was a foundation of the school's academic training; it was a skill that Neel would put to expert use throughout her career, even when draughtsmanship was at its most unfashionable. Neel used drawing as both a compositional tool, to map the elements on the canvas, and as an integral part of her painting technique. "For me, drawing is the great discipline of art," she would later say. "Usually I place everything when I start by drawing on the canvas in thin blue or black paint directly from the model."

The Philadelphia School stuck to a fairly traditional curriculum, and by the time Neel arrived there, had acquired the nickname "the Philadelphia School for Designing Women," because many of its students were unmarried.

Still, in choosing the Philadelphia School over the Philadelphia Academy of the Fine Arts, Neel was, in part, choosing the aesthetic precedent of Robert Henri over that of Mary Cassatt. (Cassatt was America's leading Impressionist, and, as a successful nineteenth-century female artist, one of Neel's immediate antecedents. But her beautifully rendered portraits of mothers and children—subjects Neel herself would later radically transform—ultimately stuck to the conservative.)

Although he taught at the Philadelphia School of Design for only three years (1892–1895), several decades before Alice attended the school, Robert Henri, who along with John Sloan founded the Ashcan School, was the most famous artist associated with it, and his book, *The Art Spirit,* published in 1923 (when Alice was in her second year), informed an entire generation of artists. Neel took its tenets—that realism represented one of the highest orders of art, and that its goal was to embody the absolute truth rather than the beauty of an individual—deeply to heart. Indeed, she took his book with her to Cuba and gave it, as a token of friendship, to the novelist Alejo Carpentier. "Paint what you feel. Paint what you see. Paint what is real to you," Henri exhorted.

As one of the founders of the Charcoal Club, which included William Glackens, George Luks, Everett Shinn, and John French Sloan (also known as the Philadelphia Four), Henri espoused the realistic portrayal of city life, including its ghettos and street scenes—hence the name "Ashcan School" (and one of its successors, Social Realism)—and the philosophies of Emerson, Whitman, Zola, and Thoreau. In 1907 the group, which by now included other artists, became the "The Eight," several of whom were key to the seminal 1913 New York Armory Show, which officially ushered in the American age of modern art.

Henri, who studied with Thomas Eakins, started out as a landscape painter, but his reputation rests on his uniquely expressive style of portraiture. He believed in capturing his subjects spontaneously, in a single sitting, and he taught his students "to work with great speed . . . get the greatest possibility of expression into the larger masses first. Then the features in their greatest simplicity . . . Do it all in one sitting if you can. In one minute if you can. There is no virtue in delaying."

As he wrote about his portraits of children, "I am not interested in making copies of pretty children. What I am after is the freshness and wonder of their spirit, the beauty that so often lies back of an awkward or even homely exterior until it is searched out." Among his students were Edward Hopper, Rockwell Kent, George Bellows, and Stuart Davis. Neel's later career would powerfully reflect Henri's influence, from his subject matter to his ideology.

Harriet Sartain was the dean of the school during Neel's time there. She was a member of an eminent Philadelphia family dedicated to the arts; the granddaughter of engraver John Sartain and the niece of Emily Sartain, a well-known painter who ran the school from 1886 to 1919. It was Emily who instituted a life class for the study of the full-length nude figure—the class which Alice singled out as her favorite—quite aware that twenty-five years earlier Eakins had been fired from the Pennsylvania Academy of the Fine Arts for allowing women to paint male nudes—"even though the male model had a jockstrap on," Neel said. (Actually, it was a loincloth, which Eakins had removed from a male model in the presence of female students.)

Alice didn't have much respect for Harriet (whom she wrongly called "Emily" in her interview with Hills), describing her dismissively as "a very conventional lady." A landscape painter who had been the first instructor at the Graphic Sketch Club, Harriet was a firm believer in art as "beauty in the largest sense," and a thorough knowledge of art history. "Tradition is our springboard," she would say.

This stodgy attitude was reflected in her classroom. Neel recalled one assignment given by Harriet: a brick wall, which Neel represented as "romantic," with ivy and deliberately chipped bricks. Harriet singled out a painting done by a classmate, Vera Weber, "the daughter of the Weber paint people, who did one with a rule," as the best. "But this Aunt [Emily] came from Paris and they were all up on the wall, and she pointed to mine and she said obviously that is the best. But still the woman [Harriet] never took back the fact that the other one was the best."

By her own account, this sort of thing seemed to be a repeated experience for Neel. While her talent was instantly recognized—and she received several awards during her time there, including one for best painting in life class—she clearly didn't conform to the school's academic conventions, or, for that matter, to its sensibility in general. Not only were girls required to wear hats and gloves as they came and went from the school; they were certainly expected to respect, rather than challenge authority as Neel did on more than one occasion.

Neel's favorite teacher was Paula Balano, who taught anatomy. "There was one very good teacher, a woman, Paula Balano, who used to design stained glass windows for a living. And she was great because she taught you to draw, and she taught you anatomy at the same time, so it wasn't just the cold medical stuff of anatomy. She would teach you, for instance, that the bone in the nose ends here. The mouth has a circular thing like a rubber band, so when you get old it is pursed in. She was great. She once said to me, 'The things that are hard for other people are easy for you, but the easy things, you can't do,'" Neel told Karl Fortess. (She was still moved to tears by the memory fifty years later.) It was an oddly prescient comment, given Neel's later life experiences.

Neel had nothing but "contempt," however, for Henry Snell, a convivial type known by the students as "Uncle Harry," who dressed up as Santa Claus for Christmas. "Once I took him a landscape that was all horizontal on purpose, and he said 'now this needs a few verticals,' so he put in charcoal trees. Of course that destroyed it for me and as soon as he got out of the room, I took the verticals out because I didn't want verticals. That's what it was all about you know. But he was a nice old man," she told Fortess. "Then we did landscapes. Henry Snell criticized that. He was a very inferior teacher. Still it was good to have someone to stimulate you to do that branch of things. . . ."

Alice, who had a hard time doing the lettering required for the course, also disliked her illustration teacher, George Harding, who had been a pupil of both Howard Pyle and George Bellows. But she valued one comment he made to another student: "Now, if you could add your clever drawing to this girl's feeling—you'd be really good." Neel explained, "*I* was the feeling . . . but that didn't entitle me to anything, you know."

Neel also took a life course, where the students drew from live nude models. "Of course that to me was heaven, just heaven. And one of the first things I did was a male nude." (Until the end of the nineteenth century, women in public art academies were not permitted to study live nude models of either gender. Neel's generation of female art students was the first to be permitted to study live male nudes, an academic experience that would later prove pivotal to her work. Neel would become known for her many nudes, including several notorious portraits of naked men.)

"We had another teacher, R. Sloan Bredin," Neel recalled. "He was so excited about art he used to perspire just talking about it, even though it was winter. And then he said, 'What is that little thing on his face?' and I said, 'Well that's his moustache,' and he thought it was absurd that I'd put the moustache. But after all I was naïve—the moustache was there so it was there. Why he thought it [the picture] was great was the composition, the legs, the muscles, all of that. . . . I was good at drawing and won all the prizes. But what I also had was a fantastic memory. I trained it. I made myself paint from memory something I saw every day."

Still, Neel said, she was "too rough for the Philadelphia School of Design. . . . I didn't want to pour tea. . . . Once I painted a sailor type with a lighted cigarette . . . this shocked them." Neel prided herself on the realistic depiction of the sailor's lit cigarette, and said that the reason she didn't receive the prestigious Elkins award with a European scholarship (given to her friend Rhoda Medary when she graduated in 1923), was that "they liked pictures of girls in fluffy dresses better. . . ."

To escape the staid confines of the Philadelphia School, Neel and her closest friends at the school, Medary and Ethel Ashton (of whom she later made a striking painting, *Ethel Ashton*, 1930) would take classes together at the Graphic Sketch Club, which met on Sunday afternoons and used real people, including "old, poor and city people, an Asian and a young black child," as models. The Sketch Club was free and attracted not only art students but also painters of different styles. The three young women would also take their easels to the Reading Railroad yards and the market on Ninth Street—certainly not the usual subject matter of the Philadelphia School of Design students.

Neel's social conscience, which would play such a big role in her later work, was already making itself felt. She was keenly aware of class differences. "There were all these rich girls who went there [the Philadelphia School of Design] as a finishing school. At the start I went out to lunch with them, but I realized that wasn't what I was there for, so I gave up everything and became a grind . . . For three years I worked so hard I nearly destroyed my own talent. I worked so hard because I had a conscience about going to art school. Not for my own family, but for all the poor in the world. Because when I'd go into the school, the scrubwomen would be coming back from scrubbing office floors all night. It killed me that these old gray-headed women had to scrub floors, and I was going in there to draw Greek statues."

Every day, Neel would travel to school on the 8:03 train from Colwyn, get off at Pennsylvania station, and take a bus to Broad and Master streets. She'd return home by the same route at around 6:00 P.M. Even when she was not in classes, Neel was constantly drawing: "I'd go wait at Penn Station, and I'd even sketch people sitting in there."

Alice also occasionally painted at the center-city studio that Rhoda Medary and Ethel Ashton had rented at 622 South Washington Park Square.

The neighborhood was filled with painters, and the three-room space overlooked the park. Her friends kept an easel there for her, and the studio would
later provide a temporary refuge during a major crisis. But for now, Alice
used it rarely; it was far from the school, and the one time she cut classes to
get there, she was punished. Instead, she dutifully returned home each day
after classes.

By the end of her third year, Neel appeared to be on the verge of another
potential nervous collapse—not just from overwork in her classes but, as
she herself put it, "from going to the theater with boys every night." She
told Fortess she had dated a young architect and seen most of Shakespeare.
"I didn't like him physically. Still, I saw all the great plays really and he
was very aesthetic, very artistic. But he didn't really know about painting
so much."

Neel later described her response more viscerally:

> Well, then there was Jim. He made me sick. . . . He used to shiver
> with emotion. He used to wriggle damp wriggles of emotion. He
> was good though—he was clever and English. He used to give me
> dollars for art's sake. He knew a lot about art. I'd fold them up
> and put them in my shoe. The little square would press my heel, it
> made me feel powerful. Nobody could make me stop the school as
> long as I had dollars.

Despite her ambivalence about Jim, Alice had no qualms about taking
his money. In order to get a much-needed break in the country, Neel enrolled in the Chester Springs summer school, run by the Pennsylvania
Academy of the Fine Arts, which had a six-week course in outdoor portrait-
painting classes, drawing, and painting. She paid her tuition with thirty
dollars she had gotten from Jim.

In accepting money from someone with romantic intentions toward her
that she did not reciprocate, Neel established a behavioral precedent. She
would later engage in a major long-term relationship that followed much
the same pattern.

Jim, like most of her previous "dates," presented Neel with a classic dilemma: "If I liked a boy physically I didn't like him mentally, and if I liked
him mentally I couldn't stand him physically. That was partly my mother's
fault. Those Hartley girls were hell on wheels. They were too domineering
in some terrible way." But all that was about to change.

Although Alice completed only half the course, her three-week stay would radically transform her life—and her work. It was at Chester Springs that Neel met Carlos Enríquez, with whom she fell passionately in love and whom she would marry the following year.

CHAPTER FOUR

En Plein Air

It was an idyllic setting for a summer romance: a series of quaint build-ings and barns that constituted the open-air studios of the Chester Springs Country School. Established in 1916 by the Pennsylvania Academy of the Fine Arts on the site of a Civil War orphanage, the school was located in a picturesque corner of Pennsylvania, near Phoenixville, now known as Yel-low Springs, thanks to the convergence of three natural mineral springs, including a yellow spring rich in iron. The property was a medicinal spa in the eighteenth and nineteenth centuries, attracting such celebrities as the opera singer Jenny Lind (one building is named after her).

Situated on one hundred rolling acres, the Chester Springs summer school compound had a number of buildings, including a former stable, "the small barn studio," with its huge skylight, a nineteenth-century hotel turned dormitory, a swimming pool, and tennis and croquet courts. But the primary attraction was the great outdoors. Taking a page from the Im-pressionist tradition of *en plein air* landscape painting, "The chief object of the academy in establishing a school in the country is to afford fine-art instruction in the open air, with all the beautiful surrounds of nature her-self, in order to supplement instruction within the walls of classrooms. . . ."

For Neel, who had just spent three years toiling at the Philadelphia School, located in the heart of a bustling urban neighborhood, Chester Springs must have literally provided a breath of fresh air. The old build-ings had porches that overlooked lush green hills and meadows. There was a charming courtyard, where students gathered to paint (although classes were held all over the campus). There were winding tree-lined lanes, a ga-zebo, and even some "Oriental Bog Gardens," landscaped in the 1920s. "The rare charm of the old revolutionary place and its delectable country-side have made possible the only summer school of art in the United States of this sort," according to a 1925 newspaper clipping.

There are no records documenting the initial meeting between Alice Neel and Carlos Enríquez de Gómez, who arrived at Chester Springs after attending Curtis Business School in Philadelphia. Carlos, like Alice, was intent on becoming a serious artist, and came across as an exotic Bohemian. But, in fact, he was from one of the wealthiest families in Havana, where his father, a major sugarcane-plantation owner, later became the physician to Cuba's president Gerardo Machado. His parents were completely against his artistic vocation and, after he had proven to be a recalcitrant student at several high schools in Havana, including an Episcopalian and a Catholic school, sent him to business school in the United States, hoping to reform him.

Even years later, Alice enthusiastically described him as "gorgeous," and Carlos was, in fact, tall, dark, and handsome. In high school, he had been nicknamed "the Mosquito," as much for his high-strung energy as his high-pitched voice. He was thin and wiry, with wavy hair and a trim mustache. In old black-and-white photographs, his physical intensity and dashing nonchalance are striking. A picture of him and Alice as sweethearts at Chester Springs, sitting on their favorite bench under a tree, shows him sporting a dapper bow tie. Carlos was an infusion of vivid color into the muted palette of Alice's life. "That was the first time I really fell in love," Neel told Munro.

On the surface, at least, it appeared to be a classic case of opposites attracting; the sensual foreigner, with his expressive eyebrows and voluptuous lips, and Alice, a prim young blonde whose conventional "dairy maid" looks belied her true nature. But in many ways, he and Alice were kindred spirits. Both had grown up in a provincial area outside a major city—Carlos was born in Zulueta, a rural village, and didn't move to Havana until he was a teenager. Both loved to read. As a boy, Carlos was particularly enamoured of the works of Alexandre Dumas and Sir Walter Scott. Both drew from a very young age. Carlos illustrated the covers for his school magazine.

In addition, both were deeply antiestablishment. "Carlos rebelled all his life. He didn't accept his family's values or take advantage of their wealth," according to his biographer, Juan Sánchez. (Indeed, in later years, Carlos would cause his family much consternation because of his constant opposition against the government. Machado himself once told his father, "Well, doctor, your son is an insolent bastard, and if he doesn't leave Cuba on his own, and quickly, I'm going to throw him out!")

Unlike Alice, however, who took a business course to help support her family, although she was "a whiz at mathematics," Carlos was "very bad at mathematics," which is why, he told her, his parents had made him go to Curtis Business School. "But he really loved art and was always painting. As soon as he finished his business course, he took this art course," Neel told Cindy Nemser. According to the school's records, Carlos attended Chester Springs from May 15 through July 24, 1924. Neel was there just three weeks, from July 1 through July 24.

Although Alice was about six months older than Carlos, he appeared to be far more sophisticated. At the time, she was, in her own words, "the most repressed creature that ever lived." At nearly twenty-five, she had scarcely ever spent a single night away from her parents. And while her hair was fashionably cut in the 1920s bob of the "new woman," she certainly wasn't a flapper. (She even complained about the Charleston: "the forced gaiety and jumping up and down of dancing.") It's easy to see how Carlos could have swept Alice completely off her feet.

But if it was nearly instantaneous, the first phase of their romance was also short-lived. Like Alice, Carlos didn't get along well with authority figures. Although Alice said that he was expelled from the school for "doing nothing much more than taking walks" with her in the evening, he was at loggerheads with the head of the school, Professor D. Roy Miller. "After failing in various prep schools, in 1924 I entered the Pennsylvania Academy of [the] Fine Arts. But I wasn't lucky. Professor Miller decided to kick me out," Enríquez said.

According to Sánchez, Miller, who was also a teacher, did everything in his power to make Carlos, who had a defiantly different painting style, fail. As Carlos wrote in a letter, "When the student doesn't paint like the teacher, he has to fight hard to make himself recognized." In the unedited transcript of Neel's interview with Eleanor Munro, she says that he fought with the head of the school, who threw him out.

Still, according to Gerald and Margaret L. Belcher, who interviewed a Chester alumna for their book *Collecting Souls, Gathering Dust*, Carlos and Alice had already attracted notice by their brazen behavior: They cut classes, strolled hand and hand through the woods, arranged private evening rendezvous, and, taking advantage of a costume trunk that was also used for sketch classes, even showed up at the school's masquerade party in drag—Neel dressed as a man, and Enríquez as a glamorous flapper.

Not that the colony was so staid: According to Sandy Momyer, the archivist for Chester Springs, the covered walkway that connected the men's and women's dormitories proved quite convenient for late-night assignations. And many of the city girls were thrilled to have a chance to cut loose, wearing shorts and smoking cigarettes outdoors, much to the dismay of the local farmers.

Although school authorities were apparently concerned that if things continued, Alice might get pregnant, according to Neel herself, the relationship had not actually been consummated. In her later account to Munro of why she delayed going to Havana with Carlos once they were married the following summer, Neel said that she and Carlos never slept together before they went to Havana in 1926. "Now by then I'd had too much experience of a kind, but never the real thing," she said in the published interview. What she actually said was, "I had millions of clitoral orgasms, but I never had the real thing. I was always having sex but also conservative. Anyway, I was terrified of the whole thing." In any case, the pair were in their mid-twenties, old enough to do as they pleased, despite the fact that they were both still supported, in part, by their parents.

Before things could progress any further, Carlos was recalled to Havana by his father, who had been notified of his expulsion by the school. Despite his seeming independence, the "rebellious" young artist left immediately. It would be almost another year before he and Alice were reunited. But Carlos continued his courtship from Cuba. A surviving letter to Alice, embellished with charming sketches, captures the lyrical, poetic spirit with which he pursued her—and his teasing, idealized image of her:

LA HABANA, 1924
Sweetheart, rest in a green lawn looking to you and the sky while your fingers tramp around the ringlets of my hair. How wonderful would it be for us to see the rest of the world in each other's eyes and wait for the moon to come out . . . Talking to the mountains, far away, a tale of witches.

Watch the stupendous silhouette of the trees against the clouds and imagine a grotesque face. How wonderful it would be if you were a lost princess in the woods and of course as the legend always says, I riding a horse will find you crying. "Weep no more, my fair lady," I'll say, for I have a kingdom in my heart for you.

Dear we rode together . . .

How wonderful would it be to watch the day come that your kisses all mine will be, and your hands as lotus flowers in mine will be, in winter to warm them and, together we will read at

*twilight, when the sun is sinking in the sea, then you will tell
me I love you with the same tenderness and same fire as today.
Will you dear?*

*Oh yes, for the sea have to be empty and the sky without
stars before you stop loving me . . .*

*. . . Every night I send a kiss to the window he will find you
he will find the three tiny windows in your room. For I've told
them of the little bench under that tree where at sunset we used
to sit and watch the elves . . .*

*Please window, take her a kiss from these lips which only
can say "I love you Alice."*

It is signed, *Yours forever Carlos,* with the date October 15.

*   *   *

At the top of the letter is a drawing captioned "Alice, my beloved sweet-heart, Oh, life like that" of a sultry Alice in a "fancy dress" and "fancy skirt," running her fingers through Carlos's hair. She has a patch of "frekles" [*sic*] on one wrist. Carlos, wearing a bow tie, a striped jacket, and polka-dotted socks, head on her lap, is smoking a cigarette. An arrow points to his "tiny moustache." Farther down are the trees, with their "grotesque silhouette," and two tiny dark embracing figures, labeled simply "Us."

CHAPTER FIVE

Limbo

Although there is no question that Alice was totally besotted with Carlos, she continued to see Jim. She later recalled her brief summer romance in somewhat more cynical terms:

> Well then one summer Jim gave me $30 and I went to summer art school. It was wonderful. Well there I met a sleek skinny black hairdo Spanish boy and of course loved him. He was the type that lived by his wits—not [that] that's a mistake. He lived off his family—but I didn't care about money then; I was so romantic. Well we loved each other.
>
> Then the teacher put him out so I went too—I got $8 back of the $30 Jim gave me. He borrowed $5 because he was so broke but he never paid it back—he forgot. Well then his family—they were wealthy. O [sic] they ordered him back to Cuba so he went. He wrote me a letter every day. I was crazy about him. He'd send cables on Sunday. He sent me a bottle of perfume once but it got broken in the mails and my mother—well you may imagine she paid $2.50 duty on an empty bottle. He wrote once that he didn't like to think of me going to theaters etc. With other people or staying home alone. He'd send me $50 to go with mother. It was such a relief I cried because I didn't have fifty cents to buy writing paper with—well he never sent it.

Given the long-distance distraction provided by Carlos (and the immediate attention from Jim), it's not surprising that Neel completed her fourth year of school on automatic pilot. Already alienated from many of the other students, she kept even more to herself. "After I met Carlos, I went back to school, and although I worked hard, it wasn't like the other years, it wasn't as good," she said. Although she still advanced, "the year was sort of ruined by the fact that I wanted to be in Havana even then and marry."

She began to spend more time at the Washington Square studio, painting characters from the park that she, Rhoda, and Ethel had asked to model (including the man with the lit cigarette). She was no longer seeing various young men, as she had the year before, waiting instead for Carlos's whimsical letters.

She became much more vocal about her increasingly "anti-bourgeois" attitude, and her only time socializing at school was not with her classmates, but with the janitor and his wife, Hugh and Mary Coyle, nicknamed by the students "Mom and Pop." A photograph of Neel in the school's 1925/1926 yearbook shows her, seated, back to the camera, in an advanced portrait class. The picture of a young woman propped up on her easel is very different from the rough, bare-chested sailor she painted at the studio, a raw precursor of her Spanish Harlem work. She also portrayed herself naked on a vase as Lady Godiva.

In Havana, meanwhile, Carlos coped with the separation in his own way. He turned his professional painting debut at the 1925 Salón des Bellas Artes into a Valentine with his portrait of a girl "en plein air"—"his fiancé," Alice Neel. He also reunited with his childhood friend Marcelo Pogolotti, who showed a painting of a laundress. (Among the other painters in the show were Eduardo Abela, Víctor Manuel García, and Amelia Peláez, who, along with Enríquez and Pogolotti, would soon form the core of the Cuban Vanguardia movement.)

Pogolotti mentioned the painting of Alice in his autobiography, *Of Clay and Voices*: "Carlos exhibited a portrait of a young blonde in the open air, seated upon the grass, who it turned out would later become his wife, Alice Neel, a painter of talent, whose rather brief stay in Havana left good and lasting memories."

The meeting rekindled the friendship between Carlos and Marcelo, which would continue throughout their lives. (Pogolotti would also remain close to Neel, years after she left Havana.) "For me, there was not any other moment happier than that. As I would have expected, he hasn't abandoned his painting vocation. He has a job [the Independent Coal Company] with a steady salary that gives him the freedom to do what he wants," Pogolotti wrote of Carlos.

Like Alice, Carlos was still living with his family—in a huge house in Reina. Enríquez and Pogolotti would meet up each day for lunch or dinner at the Nuevo Mundo restaurant on fashionable Obispo Street, and soon developed a painting routine. "Our points of view mostly coincided with respect to the Cuban artistic climate, and we regretted its underdeveloped nature and aridity. There was a need to educate a public indifferent to arts and letters. . . . On the other hand, Cuba offered rich, virgin material for the artist who was able to discover and interpret it. The work we had before us was tremendous, but we made a pact not to abandon painting under any circumstance," Pogolotti wrote.

The two would spend each weekend painting a different part of the city, or hiking to the fields, hunting for landscapes. "After some intense work, we would return to nightfall, dine with good appetite and examine our respective paintings, making friendly critiques that gave us footing for long conversations and considerations about art and literature in general, since Carlos had always been very inclined to reading. His father, a renowned physician . . . liked to tell paradoxical stories about medicine and comment on the most recent theories. But as a cultured man, he was one of the rare people in Cuba already subscribed to *Revista de Occidente*, a publication that we read with gusto. It was then that Ortega y Gasset's "The Dehumanization of Art" reached our hands . . ." which, with its insistence on the irrelevance of humanism and the idea of an "objective purity of observed reality," in service of the new art, had "a huge influence on Carlos." He would translate the essay for Neel, who some fifty years later still referred to it in interviews.

Carlos and Alice both sought refuge that year in painting, often with their friends, although Carlos, it seems, enjoyed this period more than Alice. In addition to having lost interest in her academic training, she was having a tense time at home, where her mother had still not forgiven her behavior at Chester. Neither Carlos nor Alice had given up the belief that their summer romance was more than a three-week fling, and that they could eventually reunite.

But that didn't prevent Alice from continuing to encourage Jim's attentions. "Then I did a dirty trick," she wrote. "I let Jim dangle for a year so he'd give me money. Sometimes I would mean it when I told him I didn't know what to do, but all the time I loved the other one. Well then one day I got a cable—he was coming. I had a green silk handbag Jim bought for me with me when I met him."

"Could you come as far as Colwyn to see me?" Alice had plaintively written to Carlos in response to his October 15, 1924, letter. Although she never sent her plea, Carlos arrived in Colwyn in late May 1925, nearly a year after they had first met. Alice's erstwhile suitor was welcomed by Alice's parents, who were particularly impressed with his perfect manners and his family wealth.

According to George Neel, Alice's mother "absolutely adored" Carlos. "She said he was the only man she ever met that had manners." A few years later, she would observe that "he had marvelous manners and no money." But Alice remembered her mother remarking, "He is very interesting, but I don't think he is dependable."

In the days after Carlos returned, Alice virtually disappeared from the Washington Square studio, which had served its purpose as a retreat from both school and home. Now she spent all her time with Carlos. Rhoda and Ethel had not even met her fiancé when she suddenly announced that the two were married. The marriage certificate, dated June 1, 1925, states that Carlos Enríquez de Gómez and Alice H. Neel were wed by Elisha Safford, a Minister of the Gospel, in Darby, Pennsylvania (in accordance with the license issued by the Clerk of the Orphans' Court in Delaware County, Pennsylvania).

The ceremony took place at the Darby Presbyterian Church, a big stone house of worship built in 1854, in "the manse," with Alice's parents as witnesses. "Well I couldn't help it—I married him. He made a big fuss and tried to get out of it, when I told him to give the minister $20—but he didn't have the nerve to refuse," Alice wrote.

Just a few days later, Alice, with Carlos and her family in attendance, graduated from the Philadelphia School of Design for Women. The commencement took place on Wednesday, June 3, 1925, at 3:00 P.M.; a reception in the school's courtyard followed. Entertainment included music and an exhibition of the students' work. When the awards were announced, Alice Hartley Neel, as she was referred to in the commencement program, did not receive, as many had assumed she would, the Elkins European Fellowship, which went instead to a classmate, Peggy Goodell. Still, Neel's talent was, for the third consecutive year, recognized: She won the John Sartain award for general achievement and ability, giving a year's study in the school, and the Kern Dodge Prize—twenty-five dollars for progress in painting from life.

Neel would never take advantage of the extra year of study. A new chapter, one that would make an indelible imprint on her life and her work, was about to begin.

But not before Neel succumbed to a paroxysm of indecision and self-doubt that brought her life to a standstill for nearly eight months. Once again, Neel confounded stereotypes. Her sister, Lily, had come from New

Jersey to help Alice pack. But instead of leaving on a blissful honeymoon, Neel suddenly stopped cold in her tracks and refused to leave the country with Carlos, despite the fact that she clearly loved him. Her parents, particularly her mother, were dumbfounded. Their twenty-five-year-old daughter (by 1925 standards already a spinster) had found a cultured, well-to-do husband, one who doted on her, and she was acting like a stubborn ten-year-old child.

While Carlos waited for her to come to her senses, patiently spending several more weeks at the Neels, Alice fled the house every day, seeking refuge in the studio she shared with Ethel and Rhoda, often arriving before they did each morning. She would go with Rhoda to buy lunch provisions at the market, then paint the rest of the day. She didn't discuss her dilemma with her friends, nor did she tell them under what conditions Carlos finally gave up and left Colwyn.

Neel had been brought face-to-face with the "awful dichotomy" she would later express with such force when she became a mother. Right now, it was only a fear, not a fact, but Neel's ambivalence about subsuming herself into marriage and, inevitably, motherhood (and doing so in a totally foreign environment, Carlos's home, Havana) when her foremost desire was to paint, was an almost unthinkable leap.

"He sent me money to come to Havana. He thought I was a normal American girl. I had every appearance of being utterly normal and beautiful. But I couldn't go. I couldn't go. It was the worst agony, because I really wanted to go," she would later say, in an effort to explain her behavior.

It was not until Carlos returned that Neel's terrible quandary was resolved—at least on the surface. Just a month after her twenty-sixth birthday, Enríquez materialized in Colwyn. "So he came back in February and got me, and I finally went down, and got pregnant right away. I'd eaten my heart out all those months, and then afterward I had no rest," Neel said. Her stay in Havana would prove to be pivotal to Neel and her art. But the "dichotomy" had not been vanquished.

CHAPTER SIX

Tropical Soul

Up until this point, Neel's farthest excursion from home had been to the Jersey shore, where her parents rented a summer cottage. Her honeymoon with Carlos started on a train from Philadelphia to Key West, where they caught the overnight boat to Havana. The train, which took about twenty-four hours (Neel recalled having a private compartment), connected them to one of the many steamships that plied the bay between Florida and Cuba. The Peninsular and Occidental Steamship Company ran several vessels (*The Governor Cobb, The Florida,* and *Cuba*) between Key West and Havana. Period brochures show swank staterooms, promenades, and even a "writing room," a hint of the glamorous city ahead. But it was wasted on Neel, who immediately got seasick. "I bravely got on the boat at Key West," she told an interviewer, "and in two minutes I was lying down and couldn't get up. I vomited solidly all the way from Key West to Cuba."

Neel's tropical odyssey began even before they set off for Havana. En route to Key West, the couple took a detour to Palm Beach, where the pair met up with Carlos's friend Pogolotti, who would also become a lifelong friend of Neel. The three of them, sketchbooks in hand, instantly attracted the press, as they would throughout Neel's time in Cuba. According to an unidentified newspaper account, which unwittingly took Carlos and Pogolotti at their word:

> Helping to spread the fame of Palm Beach, a trio of artists, Miss Alice Neel of Philadelphia, Don Carlos Enríquez and Marcelo Pogolotti of Havana, Cuba, are daily sketching many of the show places of the famous winter resort.
>
> Señor Enríquez is a staff artist for a Havana magazine while Señor Pogolitti is sketching scenes to be incorporated in a book showing various scenes around the world in a tour he is making.

The trio are clever draftsmen, transferring their thoughts to the sketch pad with fountain pens. Each stroke of the pen must be correct because there is no chance for erasures.

Friday the trio was photographed for a motion picture news reel. Their presence on the Lake Trail drew much attention and a great deal of curiosity.

From Key West, it is just a six-hour journey by boat to Havana. The ships arrived at the boat terminal facing the graceful Plaza de San Francisco, with its Fuente de los Leones (a replica of a famous fountain in Spain, decorated with four lions) and the lovely Basilica Menor de San Francisco de Asis. Despite the short distance from the United States, Neel's new city might as well have been another universe.

It's difficult to imagine the intensity of Neel's first impression of Havana. Nothing could have prepared her for the sheer exoticness of the tropical port, from its flora and fauna to the rich resonance of its language. The city had a lush, lyrical quality, in keeping with its lilting, omnipresent music. "Spain touched everywhere by the tropics, the tropics—without a tradition—built into a semblance of the baroque," wrote Joseph Hergesheimer in his 1927 edition of *San Cristóbal de la Habana,* pronouncing the city "Rococo."

Havana was drenched in light and color. As an old tourist guidebook put it, "You see tortuous cobbled streets, balconied buildings with elaborate iron grilles and stupendous carved mahogany doors, sidewalks shaded from the sun in pillared arcade effect. You notice the cool, plant-filled patios, the lush tropical foliage in little parks scattered everywhere through the city, the vivid, unmixed glorious colors. It's the color that gives Havana its perpetually fiesta-like appearance. There is color in everything: it gleams in the buildings and the rooftops, glows in the flowers and foliage, is gay in the tiled walls, and bright in the complexions and clothes of the women." And then there were the "crystal light" and "printed shadows" heightened by the proximity of the sea.

Neel must have been equally overwhelmed by the extravagant luxury of the Enríquez household. Having grown up in cramped, dark, low-ceilinged rooms in a working-class town, Neel suddenly found herself not only in a glamorous cosmopolitan city but living in a marble-floored mansion with gracious rooms, wide hallways, and huge arched windows. (Alice referred to it as a "palace.") There was even a charming balcony off the bedroom that she shared with Carlos, overlooking a small garden, where peacocks

strutted. Within walking distance of the house was the magical Malecón—
the curving seaside balustrade that was a favorite promenade for upper-
class Cubans. At six each day, "the Hour of the Promenade," Neel, Carlos,
and her in-laws would tool along the Malecón in the Enríquez's chauffeured
Rolls-Royce.

It would be Neel's first—and last—encounter with such material wealth.
Years later, she still marveled at the Enríquez's lifestyle. "Carlos's father
was the most famous doctor in Havana, Doctor Carlos Enríquez de Gomez.
You can't imagine how they lived," Neel recounted to Hills in her oral biography. "The family had seven servants. One was a cook who just cooked
all day. She did nothing but cook—Josephina. I remember going out in the
kitchen and eating fried banana before dinner. At lunch they had their big
meal. We'd start with soup, fish, well you never saw anything like it. It was
just fantastic, on the grand scale you know. His mother as a girl was dressed
by slaves. And they lived in this white palace in El Vedado, with peacocks
walking in the garden. I had a room like Romeo and Juliet's with marble
floors and a balcony. My God, it was fantastic."

Alice and Carlos lived with his parents for about eight months. As an
American, Alice was certainly not expected to conform to the strict turn-
of-the century etiquette that until recently had been required of Cuban
upper-class women, who were not allowed to roam the city freely, but were
either driven to the shops and restaurants or confined to their homes or to
private clubs like the Biltmore Club and the Vedado Tennis Club (leading
Alejo Carpentier to say that until 1925, Havana was "a city without women").
Indeed, as Hergesheimer wrote of his first impression of Havana in the
early 1920s, "What struck me at once was the fact that there were, practi-
cally, no women along the streets. It was a tide of men. . . . Havana was a
city of balconies, barred windows, of houses, impenetrable, blank to the
streets, but open on the garden rooms of patios."

By the time Neel arrived, that was dramatically changing. According to
the historian Louis Pérez, Neel's generation of women in Cuba led parallel
lives to American women during the Roaring Twenties. "These were not
women who stayed behind curtains," he says. "There was a real sense of
pushing boundaries and breaking taboos."

Cuban women smoked in public, drove cars, and had shrinking hem-
lines. They found ready-made role models in American film stars: Mary
Pickford as the optimistic ingenue; Clara Bow as the flirtatious flapper.
Even American-style short hair became à la mode: There were bobbed-
hair contests, and in 1925 a fashion writer declared "bobbed hair has tri-

umphed in Cuba." The newly liberated hairstyle symbolized a newly liberated lifestyle. Neel didn't necessarily see it that way. "It was backward and the women were very conservative. Not that they were stupid. It was just the rules. They even thought it was dreadful if a woman was in the streets too much. 'Siempre en la calle' was considered a very derogatory remark about a woman," she told Cindy Nemser.

Neel's behavior must have been a constant affront to her affluent, old-fashioned in-laws. Alice consorted with the servants; she would spend time in the kitchen with Josephina, practicing her Spanish. "I wasn't made to sit in the patio and do embroidery," she said. In the evenings, she would go out to join Carlos and not return until the wee hours. "I used to go meet Carlos at a restaurant called El Nuevo Mondo, and we used to stay there so late that the garbage man would be coming."

And there was a much more profound tension: In April, just two months after her move to Havana, Neel discovered she was pregnant with her first child. "I should have had some birth control thing, because I was then simply an ambitious artist. . . . But anyway, when I got pregnant in Cuba, that was it. Of course, Carlos' father was 100 per cent against abortion."

The looming fear that had initially prevented Neel from traveling with Carlos to Cuba was now a physical reality. And by July 1926, when Alice was about six months pregnant, she would convince Carlos to move out of El Vedado to an apartment on the waterfront, near the Produce Exchange. (Although the Enríquez family would have far preferred their new granddaughter to be brought up in their beautiful, well-staffed home, Alice refused to return there.)

But in the meantime, Neel was intent on not letting her pregnancy prevent her from painting. She and Carlos liked nothing better than to take a bus from El Vedado to the poor sections of town, Alice colorfully dressed in the native garb. Equipped with their paintboxes, "like van Gogh," they would stroll the streets and paint the street people. "All we did was paint day and night," she said. Although she complained about the heat, and commented that Cuba was "too happy, with all that bright sun," Alice was struck by the "tropical light," which she tried to capture in her paintings.

The scenes in these outlying neighborhoods were in vivid contrast to the elegant streets of El Vedado. As Neel described it, "There the Afro-Cubans would be dancing: they'd dance like mad and run into the bushes—you know for what. They'd use this strange language, part African and part Spanish, and what dancers! Wild, you know. Nicolas Guillén, a Latin-American writer, claims 'that the spirit of Cuba is mulatto.'" (A spirit

Enríquez was later to famously capture in his own paintings, including one of his best-known works, *El Rapto de las Mulatas*, 1938. Carlos's work would also be noted for its use of tropical light.)

Neel was particularly taken with the bearing of these Cuban women. "They have more self than American women. They are highly sophisticated. The American woman was weak compared with the womanliness of the Cuban woman." And with the extreme rift between the rich and the poor. "There were people who were hugely wealthy and the bitterly poor were much poorer than I had ever seen," she told Barbara Diamonstein. "The rich used to cut all the trees small so you could see their great houses. And the poor were just wretched, they were on the streets."

Several works from this time survive; a painting of two beggars (whom Alice and Carlos paid to pose) and another of a mother and child. Neel was already documenting "the people as evidence of her time." There is also a dreamy portrait of Carlos, in the tobacco-tinted palette she then favored; this painting was exhibited in her first group show in 1927. Although almost academic in style, Neel's work at the time had a fluid brushstroke. She depicted Carlos as the epitome of the Latin lover. This was the man who opened up an entirely new world to her, and the painting reflects all the passion of Neel's initial infatuation.

But for Neel, the real revelation was the community of artists of which she and Carlos quickly became a part. This was a heady time not just for Neel but for Cuban culture itself. "We completely lived the vie Bohemienne," she told Nemser. "It was more civilized there than here. The writers and poets and artists all got together, so there was more of an overall culture than there was here." Besides their close friend Pogolotti, Neel's circle included poet Nicolas Guillén, Alejo Carpentier, Cuba's leading novelist, painter Víctor Manuel García, Domingo Ravenet, Martí Casanovas, Jorge Mañach, Juan Marinello, José Manuel, Valdés Rodríguez, and Juan José Sicre, among others.

Havana circa the mid-20s was a place of major political and cultural flux. Neel's stay, though brief, coincided with the birth of the Cuban modern art movement, of which she became an integral part. Havana would have a lasting influence on both her life and her art. "My life in Cuba had much more to do with my later psychology," she told Hills. "It conditioned me a lot." She would also later say that being married to Carlos gave her a "Latin mentality." She was referring as much to the politics as to the culture.

When Neel arrived in Havana in February 1926, it was more than a quarter of a century since the 1895–98 War of Independence. In January 1899, four centuries of Spanish domination had finally ended, but the U.S. military occupation had just begun. It would be another three and half years, until May 1902, before José Martí's dream of a "Cuba Libre" was realized, and Cuba became, in name at least, no longer a colony, but a republic. Still, the United States' political and economic control remained omnipresent. U.S. domination would not end until the revolution in 1959.

The 1920s, according to Pérez, was "the coming of age of the first generation of the Republic born in free Cuba. It was a period of remarkable political, cultural, and artistic effervescence, what you could call the first Cuban generation."

Cuba's love-hate relationship with the United States was fomenting. The country was still in the midst of a major U.S.–fueled sugar boom—the "Second Dance of the Millions." However, by 1926, when the price of sugar went down by nearly half, Cuba's economy was already beginning a downward spiral, which culminated with the Depression in 1929.

In May 1925, General Gerardo Machado was elected Cuba's fifth president. Although he ran as a member of the Liberal Party, by the time of his overthrow during the 1933 coup, he was perceived as a brutal tyrant responsible for the death of thousands of political insurgents, and was ultimately toppled by U.S. diplomatic intervention.

In 1926, however, his minister of public works, Carlos Miguel de Céspedes, was overseeing many of the great architectural projects of the period, from the continuation of the newly expanded Malecón to the new capitol building to the paving of the Central Highway. In the previous decade, Havana was already a favorite resort of the rich—particularly rich North Americans. The many country clubs of El Vedado—the Havana Biltmore Yacht and Country Club, the Cuban Athletic Club, and the Jockey Club— were social epicenters where wealthy American families could hobnob and entertain their guests. (The DuPonts even established their own club, the DuPont Country Club, on the vast expanse of beach they had acquired.)

By the 1920s, Havana had become known as "the Monte Carlo of the Western Hemisphere." The city was a hot spot of fancy clubs and literally thousands of bars, from La Florida to the Plaza Bar and the Paris Bar. "Havana is becoming a second home for that section of the smart set which formerly spent its winters on the Riviera," exclaimed Basil Wood's seductively titled book, *When It's Cocktail Time in Cuba*. "It is hot, it is wet, it is, in its easy tropical way, Wide Open," wrote Bruce Bliven in a February 1928 article for *The New Republic* entitled "Cuba and the Winter."

Pérez describes it vividly: "There was live music, people in white dining coats, the racetrack [at Oriental Park], the bath clubs, an amazing casino. Havana in the 20's was quite an astonishing place." "The moment to go to Havana was youth, the moment for masked balls and infidelity and champagne," advised Joseph Hergesheimer. (When Prohibition was at its peak in America, the rum was flowing freely in Havana, a major incentive to wealthy tourists.)

Although Havana maintained its multicultural, melting-pot identity—rich with Spanish and African influences—the North American hegemony was pervasive. Perhaps nothing symbolized that as much as the influx of American cars in the early twenties, with Fords becoming ubiquitous. "Foot It and Go" ran the Ford Motor Company's advertising campaign, giving rise to the Cuban term *fotingo*. Even the taxis were Fords, with people colloquially "catching a Ford" rather than catching a cab.

Beneath Havana's shimmering surface, though, other, revolutionary forces were at work. During the 1920s, as the upper classes and "entrepreneurial" bourgeoisie thrived, the political dissidents and labor movement leaders were rapidly organizing, striving to assert Cuba's national identity, largely in reaction to the oppressive U.S. influence. In 1923, the Junta for National Renovation was founded by Havana professor Fernando Ortiz, which demanded labor, education, health, and legal reforms. The poet and activist Rubén Martínez Villena formed a political action group, the Cuban Action Phalanx, which then became part of a larger group of intellectuals, the Grupo Minorista.

Nineteen twenty-five alone saw the formation of the Third National Labor Congress, which merged the Cuban trade unions into one entity, the Confederación Nacional Obrera de Cuba (CNOC), and the Cuban Communist Party. In May 1927 (the same month as the pivotal Exposición de Arte Nuevo) the Grupo Minorista published its manifesto, stating, among its primary precepts, the desire for:

> The revision of false and tired values; the introduction and popularization in Cuba of the latest artistic and scientific doctrines, theories and practices; the economic independence of Cuba and against Yankee imperialism; against political dictatorship in the world, America and Cuba; against the excesses of Cuba's pseudo-democracy, the falsity of Cuba's suffrage and for the effective participation of the people in government . . .

Politically and culturally, a wave of nationalism was rising, and the Vanguardia art movement (like the Grupo Minorista) epitomized its ideology. Their goal was to create art emblematic of an authentic Cuba. (Four of the Vanguardia painters were active members of the Grupo Minorista.)

> We fully condemn and negate the art of the nineteenth century, the service instrument of capitalist bourgeoisie. The central issue of modern art is to return to emotions: situate oneself with pure intentions before the spectacle of the world and of life, and describe, with a simple and clear language, the emotion of everyday life.

Art historian Juan Martínez identifies 1924 to 1927 as the "embryonic" period of modern Cuban painting. It was at this time that the cadre of a dozen or so painters who would become known as the Vanguardia movement—including Enríquez, Pogolotti, Jorge Arche, Amelia Peláez, Victor Manuel, Antonio Gattorno, Eduardo Abela, Domingo Ravenet, and Wilfredo Lam—began to first show their work. Most of these painters had originally been trained in the Cuban academic style—many at San Alejandro Academy of Fine Arts. Now they were taking motifs they had encountered in Europe—particularly Paris—Fauvism, Cubism, Surrealism, and applying them to "lo Cubano"—Cuban tradition and folklore. (Although they were also inspired by the nationalism of the Mexican mural movement, they wanted to create an original Cuban style, incorporating current painting techniques.)

The new European-influenced work began to emerge in a handful of solo shows by painters including Victor Manuel García and Antonio Gattorno. Neel even had her own solo show in the fall of 1926, possibly at a small gallery or an alternative bookshop; the location is not recorded, nor did Neel remember it in later years. According to the Belchers, it contained about a dozen paintings—of women, mothers and children, and beggars.

In October, Neel's family came to visit. Their timing couldn't have been worse: They arrived the day before the great hurricane of 1926. Pogolotti dramatically described the "apocalyptic" damage in its wake:

> The storm had been wild. Dozens of masts and some chimneys stood out from the waters of the port. A steamship was missing half of its upper decks . . . clearly revealing a cross-section of the

rooms and cabins. . . . Seventeen cadavers, some in postures of
rigid action, lay in a small boat near the end of the avenue. . . .
The bronze eagle from the monument honoring the victims of
"The Maine" came flying out to the edge of the gardens of the
Hotel Nacional. The trunk of a palm tree had passed through a
beam as if it were a giant knife. The examples of incredible devas-
tation are too copious and well-known to list. The hurricane of
'26 has passed into history as one of the more devastating that
Havana has ever suffered.

Pogolotti also recounts Neel's parents' astonishment: "After hearing for
awhile with shock and suprise, cement decorations falling to the ground and
branches breaking, they asked, 'Does it always rain like this here?'"

Alice later recalled the stressful visit in an interview: "You can't mix
people. My parents came down to visit me and my Cuban husband. It was
crazy to try and mix them. They were very rich Cubans and they lived on
another scale. My parents couldn't speak Spanish. The biggest cyclone they
ever had in Havana happened when my parents visited down there. It was
just frightful."

On December 26, 1926, Neel gave birth to a daughter, whom she and
Carlos named Santillana del Mar, after a small town in Spain. Neel never
forgot the intense pain of her labor. "So I had this baby. They're more animal than we are, in Havana, and for them to have a child is the most normal
thing in the world. For me, it was a major event. They don't give anesthesia there. Now I couldn't stand Anglo-Saxons. I couldn't stand their soda-
cracker lives and their inhibitions. I loved Latins. But I wasn't a Latin, and
for me to have a baby without anesthesia was frightful. In the end, it had
been eight hours of agony."

By now the little family was living in a small house on 3 Revolucíon in
La Vibora (the Viper), "two steps from the bus stop," as Pogolotti put it, on
Havana's edge, with "walls a yard thick." It was a more conventional neigh-
borhood than the one by the wharves, but it was also removed from "la vie
Bohemienne."

But the Neel-Enríquez household created its own artistic diversions. As
Pogolotti writes in his autobiography, *Clay and Voices*:

Every Saturday we would meet there to paint someone ready to
pose as a model, whether it be a friend or someone interesting or
strange we had found somewhere, or we met in some agreed upon

place to paint an attractive landscape that was unfamiliar to us. At night we dined in some restaurant which attracted us by its particular food, its location or its novelty. . . . On Sundays, we did what we could to finish paintings from the previous day. Sometimes, at dusk when there was insufficient light to paint, we rented one of the old cars sitting patiently by the bus stop and we took a tour of the surrounding countryside. Alice had a tendency to use neutral, rich colors with good tonal quality, but these painting motifs did not suffice for the Cuban interpretation. Her artistic sensibility was nevertheless exceptional and her taste and comments never lacked in interest.

Despite her intelligence, Pogolotti was amused by Neel's "Anglo-Saxon" gullibility; he and Carlos had convinced her, for instance, that there were gardens near Naples where macaroni grew on trees. Alice also had them in stitches with her odd habit of turning her back on her canvas and looking at it upside down through her legs to get a different perspective.

According to Pogolotti, "Carlos was fond of bringing home the most exotic people he could find," citing as an example a tall, skinny American they saw painting the Morro and persuaded to come to lunch. He ended up helping paint the inside of the house in his underwear. There was also the Japanese painter who came to dinner, consumed several glasses of wine, and when the Jamaican cook laughed at his animated rendition of Japanese songs, threw plates at her.

*   *   *

Just a few months after Santillana's birth, in March–April, 1927, Neel-Enríquez made their formal debut as a significant art couple. Together, they showed their work at the XII Salón de Bellas Artes, sponsored by the Asociacíon de Pintores y Escultores. (Shades of Stieglitz and O'Keeffe?) According to the pamphlet for the show, each had seven paintings: Carlos's work included several landscapes and portraits, including one of his infant daughter, Santillana; Neel showed all portraits, including the sepia-toned 1926 painting of Carlos nursing a glass of wine. They were a sensation.

In a glowing review of the show in the *Paquena Gaceta*, Martí Casanovas singled out their work: "There is an evident parallelism of tendency and an almost simultaneous advance in the work of this extraordinary couple. . . . Alice Neel and Carlos Enríquez set the tone of the Salon, and we could almost say the Salon has been made for them." Calling their work a "revelation," Casanovas went on to say that their work redeemed the show from being "sterile and utterly useless."

Images of their work were reproduced in two issues of the bimonthly publication *Revista de Avance*. Both the April 15 and April 30 issues of *Revista de Avance* included a page of reproductions: Neel's portrait of Enríquez and Enríquez's painting *Intima*, which seems to be of Neel, and his *El Callejón de Luhan*. The April 15 issue gushed on its "Almanaque" page about "the extraordinary marriage" of Neel and Enríquez, "that joins in delights of conjugal life, its adventures and ambitions."

The April 30th edition added two charcoal drawings: *Apuntes* (a mother and child and a man), by Neel and *Casas de Burguess* (a street of houses) by Enríquez, and included a caption on the work of "Neel-Enríquez" that praised its "wide and juicy brushstroke," its "spontaneity and great richness of temperament" and its "audacious and free vision . . . this is the marvelous and heroic art of Neel-Enríquez."

The Vanguardia movement made its official debut in May 1927 with the first Exposición de Arte Nuevo. It was sponsored by the avante-garde magazine *Revista de Avance*, of which Enríquez was a founding member. (The publication ran for only three years, from 1927 to 1930, and proclaimed as its mission the desire for "movement, change, advance, even in the magazine's name. And we want absolute independence—even from time!")

The Arte Nuevo show was nothing less than a declaration of the new art movement. Although *Revista de Avance* called the work "militant," "new," and "avant-garde," Martínez points out that much of it represented "mild versions of European modern styles." The show included paintings by Eduardo Abela, Rafael Blanco, Gabriel Castaño, Víctor Manuel García, José Hurtado de Mendoza, Luis López Mendez, Ramón Loy, Marcel Pogolotti, Lorenzo Romero Arciaga, Alberto Sabas, José Segura, Carlos Enríquez, and Alice Neel, whose work once again attracted special mention.

Neel showed portraits, including *Sombero Negro*, *Naturaleza Muerta*, and *Madre e Hijo* (her 1926 painting of a mother and child). Enríquez exhibited both portraits and landscapes, including *Phoebes*, *Desnudo Rojo*, and *Palmas Gemelas*. Their work garnered positive reviews. Carlos's work was the focus of a column by Martí Casanovas, who also wrote the preface to the show's catalogue. (There was also a photograph of the couple, both wearing jaunty hats, apparently taken onboard the *Miami*.) Two of Enríquez's nudes of Alice were removed for being "too exaggerated." These were later reproduced in the May 15 issue of *Revista de Avance*.

But if May 1927 marked the advent of the Vanguardia movement (and Neel's arrival as a successful professional artist), it also marked the abrupt end of Neel's Havana sojourn. In later interviews, Neel never really discussed her reasons for leaving Carlos and Cuba, but clearly she and her in-laws were at loggerheads. In addition, it must have been becoming increasingly obvious to her that Carlos was not capable of supporting a wife and child on his own—he had long since stopped working at the coal company, which had closed down, and he was getting an allowance from his father. It is also unlikely that Neel could have continued to paint seriously with a tiny daughter in tow—nor would she have been likely to turn Santillana's upbringing over to the nanny the Enríquez family might have employed.

The "dichotomy" had caught up to her, and before the end of the month, while her paintings were still on view at the watershed art show, Neel and Santillana returned to Colwyn. She arrived back at her childhood home more in defeat than victory. But she hadn't permanently separated from Carlos; he would join her there in October.

As for Carlos, wrote Pogolotti, "Since Carlos' wife left for the United States with the Little Santillana, she of the pretty round face with two round black disks, I invited him to accompany me on some explorations."

CHAPTER SEVEN

(You Can Go) Home Again

Although she returned to her childhood home in the spring, when everything was in full bloom, Neel must have found her surroundings even more depressing and dreary after the bright "tropical light" and bustling street life of Havana. She had escaped her rigid American life only briefly; now she was once again trapped in the small house with her family—although this time with a child of her own, which totally changed the picture.

The Neel household during the six months before Carlos arrived to reunite with his wife and daughter consisted of Alice, her mother, her father, and her older brother, Albert, and her younger brother, Peter, who was attending Temple University, but was home for the summer. At thirty-nine, Albert was finally about to get married and leave home, but in the meantime he and his many dogs were all over the house. Alice and five-month-old Santillana took up residence in Alice's old bedroom. Although she begged her mother for the front room, which had more light, that was her mother's bedroom and out of the question.

Neel had no income at this point, and couldn't afford oil paints and canvas, so she turned to watercolors, producing pieces that capture her clearly despairing state. *The Grandchild*, 1927, depicts her father in his smoking jacket, with Santillana on his lap. The child's round black eyes punctuate this painting with its only spark of life; Neel's father, holding the baby, is an almost amorphous dull brown shadow. Neel described his attitude, quoting Thoreau, as one of "quiet desperation."

The watercolor *The Family* (previously mentioned in chapter 1) renders with enormous economy and power the Neel family compound, a psychological prison. The picture looks like the cross section of a dollhouse. But its inhabitants appear more like inmates than family members. Climbing up the stairs from the cinder-colored basement is her stooped father, coal bucket in hand. On the middle floor, the heart of both the house and the painting, Alice, face downcast, sits passively in a rocking chair, cradling Santillana, while her mother, crouched on all fours beneath the round oak table, madly scrubs the floor, an hysterical look on her Munch-like face. The top floor is dominated by Peter, bespectacled and reading a book—the only person in the household free to pursue his own interests. The watercolor displays as transparently as a Rorschach test Neel's tormented feelings at being sucked back into the family's dysfunctional psychodynamics.

Neel described this key work to Hills some sixty years later with dry humor: "My brother is upstairs studying French. He was going to Temple University. I had just come home with this baby and I'm sitting holding the baby. My mother is frantically cleaning the floor, and down in the cellar my little, gray father is carrying up coal for the stove in the kitchen. My mother couldn't stand the confusion. She has a wild look; no doubt she saw the future. I was too goofy to see it."

Chances are Neel didn't feel "goofy" at the time, but in a state of complete paralysis. Although she went with her parents to the Jersey shore, as always, for the summer months, she made no effort to go into Philadelphia, or to reconnect with her friends Rhoda and Ethel. She hibernated at home, waiting for Carlos to snap her back to life.

She didn't have to wait very long. Carlos resurfaced in Colwyn that fall, and he, Alice, and Santillana moved to New York City, to an apartment on West Eighty-first Street, a large furnished room, where Neel said she painted a "great number of watercolors," mostly "street scenes of New York . . . the people and the life around me. That's my thing really!" she told Nemser.

Still, Neel's watercolors of this time express what seems to have been her own "quiet desperation." A second painting called *The Family*, but this time Neel's family of choice, not her family of origin, shows the artist naked from the waist up, leaning wearily on the bed where Carlos and Santillana are reclining. Carlos's expression is one of sadness; Santillana, once again, is characterized solely by her black raisin eyes. (The painting seems influenced by Edvard Munch, and is reminiscent of his work *The Vampire*.)

Neel's 1927 pinched watercolor portrait of Carlos is in stark contrast to the sensual oil painting of him she had made just the year before in Havana. This time, Carlos sits alone at a table, his plate, cup, and glass empty, his face a study of pensive unhappiness. And finally *Mother and Child*, 1927, another watercolor echoing subject matter she had first painted in Cuba, shows Neel herself, head capped, nunlike, face pious and, again, downcast, a pale toddler on her lap with a white halo of a hat; this 1920s Madonna and Child are sitting on a park bench, framed by barren trees. The artist's palette is brown (as it was in Cuba), the watercolor equivalent of daguerreotypes, as if she had yet to discover color. (The piece is a precursor of Neel's sad 1930 painting *Mother and Child*, set in a cemetery.)

Neel's desperation was in great part economic, and she would take two jobs during the next few years—one briefly at Fanya Foss's Art Deco store on Madison Avenue, and the other at the National City Bank. (Contrary to previous accounts, Foss did not own a bookstore in Greenwich Village, according to her children, Michael and Toni Lawrence.)

Carlos's decision to live in the United States with Alice and their child had literally cost him. His parents sent him a pittance, and the couple would soon find themselves living at subsistence level, or, as Alice put it, "We began to starve to death. We had both left out the fact that you had to eat and live somewhere and he got very little from his family. We thought we'd make out as artists, which was just absurd; even now it may take some time; then it took even more."

But meanwhile, they were living New York City, the very epicenter of modernity. New York in the 1920s, as historian Ann Douglas puts it, was "a modern scene in action crying for comment, tantalizingly ready to express and be expressed. It was a photo shoot inviting models and masqueraders, a play in the vast business of being cast, a movie set calling those ready, like [F. Scott Fitzgerald] to live inside their 'own movie of New York.'" As Fitzgerald wrote of New York in 1920, ". . . I remember riding in a taxi one afternoon between very tall buildings under a mauve and rosy sky; I began to bawl because I had everything I wanted and knew I would never be so happy again."

Douglas records the astonishing fact that New York City's population doubled in size between 1910 and 1930, and lists among its new inhabitants the Bohemian A-list: Scott and Zelda Fitzgerald, Sinclair Lewis, Hart Crane, Katherine Anne Porter, Thomas Wolfe, Edna St. Vincent Millay, Marianne Moore, Dorothy Parker, Edmund Wilson, John Dos Passos, George S. Kaufman, Paul Robeson, Langston Hughes, Duke Ellington—the list goes on and on, telegraphing the fact that New York was on the brink of becoming a cultural capital of the world. There was literature, film, theater, dance, and music—this was the birth of the Jazz Age and everything it entailed. "New York in the 1920s," Douglas writes, "was a magnet attracting and concentrating the talents of a nation."

The New Yorker magazine was founded by Harold Ross in 1925, the same year that *The Great Gatsby* was published. The Harlem Renaissance (1919–1929) was well under way, giving rise to an extraordinary array of black culture—from the poetry of Hughes and the writing of Zora Neale Hurston to the jazz of Satchmo and the photography of James VanDerZee.

Everything about the city seemed to be about newness and speed. New York's spiky skyline was in its infancy: The skyscrapers that appeared to pierce the clouds above the city were just being conceived—the Chrysler Building began construction in 1928; the Empire State Building was completed in 1931. That newfangled invention, the automobile, was running rampant in a city that still didn't have quite the necessary infrastructure to support it.

In May 1927, Charles Lindbergh completed the world's first transatlantic plane flight, in the *Spirit of St. Louis*, just around the time Neel found her way back to Colwyn. Radio and film were entering popular culture for the first time: The first feature-length "talkie," *The Jazz Singer,* was made in 1927. Sacco and Vanzetti, whose trial for bank robbery and murder had been a cause célèbre for six years, were finally electrocuted in August 1927. (Mike Gold, who would become a mentor to Neel, was one of those who marched to protest their sentence.) That same summer, the Babe hit sixty home runs, setting a record not broken until 1961. Isadora Duncan, whose autobiography had just been published, died in September 1927, strangled by her own sinuous scarf.

As for American art in 1927, although New York had yet to arrive as the new art capital of the world, the major players were already finding their way to the mecca. De Kooning had just recently moved to Manhattan from Hoboken; he was working at Eastman Brothers and living in a boarding house on Forty-ninth Street and Sixth Avenue; Arshile Gorky settled in the Village by the following year. One of Edward Hopper's first solo shows opened at the Rehn Gallery on February 15, 1927; among the works were his famous *Eleven AM*, *Automat*, and *The City*. It would be three more years before Jackson Pollock would arrive at the Art Students League to study with Thomas Hart Benton; Mark Rothko had studied there briefly in 1924 and 1925, taking a still-life class with Max Weber.

The mid-20s in American art was a time of transition. The 1913 Armory Show had engendered a new era of art, introducing Americans to the possibilities of European modernism, including Impressionism, Post-Impressionism, Symbolism, Fauvism, and Cubism. The 1,250 works ranged from Duchamp's seminal *Nude Descending a Staircase* to Matisse's *The*

Blue Nude to Picasso's *Head of a Woman*. But it also included works by
Stuart Davis, George Bellows, Edward Hopper, John Sloan, Childe Has-
sam, and Mary Cassatt. It was introduced by its organizers, the Association of American Painters and Sculptors, with the statement:

> The members of this association have shown you that American
> artists—young American artists, that is—do not dread, and have
> no need to dread, the ideas or the culture of Europe. They believe
> that in the domain of art only the best should rule. This exhibition
> will be epoch making in the history of American art. Tonight will
> be the red-letter night in the history of not only American but of
> all modern art. . . . [We] felt it was time the American people had
> an opportunity to see and judge for themselves concerning the
> work of the Europeans who are creating a new art.

Of course, the show had its detractors. Fairfield Porter, not only a painter
but a critic, said, "The Armory Show was a complete disaster for American
art because it made people think you'd got to do things in a certain style.
American art was provincial before and it became more provincial as a result of the Armory Show." Still, the stage was being set for a new generation of artists to challenge the academic past.

But in 1927, de Kooning, Rothko, and Pollock had yet to evolve the
unique, mature styles that would revolutionize not only American art but
the history of modern art itself: The three famous Abstract Expressionist
artists were still painting fairly traditional figurative work, and American
Scene painting was about to become popular. Indeed, Rothko's subject
matter at the time was often urban street scenes or fellow subway passen-
gers. This was the heyday of the Ashcan school (Robert Henri's *The Art
Spirit* had just been published four years earlier), which made the common
man its subject and eventually gave rise to a spin-off genre, Social Realism, which in the 1930s had politically radical and even heroic connotations but by the 1950s would be completely marginalized.

Neel would have her first success in the United States as a Social Realist
painter, particularly during the WPA period. But in 1927, working in
watercolors, she had yet to develop her signature aesthetic, although her
work of this period is striking—and strikingly different than that of her
American contemporaries; her own idiosyncratic blend of Expressionism,
Symbolism, and Surrealism often sharpened with satire.

*   *   *

At this point, Alice and Carlos were still constantly painting. "When we were together, all we did was paint," Neel told Munro. "In Havana that's all we did and in New York that's all we did. In 1927, 28 and 29." Enríquez's work at the time reflected his location: He sketched skyscrapers and jazz clubs. Meanwhile, both Neel and Enríquez also attempted to find employment. Enríquez continued to contribute work to *Revista de Avance*, and according to Alice eventually ended up doing some simple and "stupid" drawings for American newspapers.

In late 1927, Neel answered a newspaper advertisement for work in a small Madison Avenue shop. The store was owned by Fanya Foss, a screenwriter whose second husband, Gordon Kingman, became a supervisor of the folklore division of the Federal Writers' Project. (In 1938, the division published *The Italians of New York*, a book about Italian neighborhoods and landmarks. Although Neel didn't meet him until a decade later, one of the photographers who worked on the book was her future partner, Sam Brody.)

According to her son, Michael Lawrence, Fanya Foss stocked her antique shop with objets d'art picked up around the world by her first husband, the writer Edward Dahlberg. Her daughter, Toni, also remembers her selling scarves "painted by Isadora Duncan's husband." Six years Neel's junior, Foss had been born in Odessa, Russia, and moved to New York at the age of three. (She and her mother arrived in the United States with diamonds sewn into the lining of their coats.)

As some of Neel's later portraits attest, Foss was lovely in a slightly exotic way, olive-skinned and dark-haired, physically Neel's diametric opposite. Although she was already on her second marriage when Neel met her, she had as yet had no children. She was a well-read intellectual who at one point worked as a librarian at Columbia University, then during the WPA on the Federal Writers' Project, and moved to Los Angeles, where she married her third husband, the actor Marc Lawrence, in 1942. She became a well-known screenwriter under contract to RKO. Her credits include *Affectionately Yours*, *Girls Under 21*, and *The Richest Man in Town*, in addition to television scripts for shows such as *Have Gun—Will Travel*. She had also lived in Paris, where she met Ford Madox Ford, who asked her to represent his magazine, the *Transatlantic Review*.

Foss had interviewed a number of applicants before Alice came in, and Michael Lawrence says that his mother instantly discovered a kindred spirit in Neel. Or, as he later wrote in a letter to *Art in America*, they "shared an early feminist independence and a thirst for sexual life."

Foss had married Dahlberg when she was only seventeen, against her father's wishes. She lived on Cornelia Street, just across from where Alice later lived with the sailor Kenneth Doolittle. According to her daughter, Toni Lawrence, she loved talent and surrounded herself with artists. She appreciated Alice's work, and was one of the first people to actually buy paintings from Alice. She acquired some half a dozen pictures, including portraits of herself, several of her son Michael, and a few still lifes and street scenes.

"I bought Alice's early periods," she recalled. "I feel close to them because of memory. Also because it's charged with her past, her poverty, her early struggle, her telling environment and reflected her art on an emotional level which gave them depth, strength, insight, and meaning."

She did not buy the painting *The Intellectual*, 1929, in which she is depicted as an intellectual dilettante, languishing in an armchair, her dress unbuttoned to reveal her breasts, while off to the left an earnest, book-wielding woman engages her in conversation, and Alice, armed with six limbs, minds her impish-looking daughter. "She was a friend of mine, Fania [*sic*] Foss, the pretentious lady with the breasts hanging out, which is artistic liberty on my part. She did Grade B movies," Alice later said.

In Foss, Neel found an equal, someone with passions and beliefs as powerful as her own, even, as Foss's son puts it, "when they went against the grain of reason and practicalities." "She and Alice were a good match; they could both be very blunt and had good strong egos," Lawrence observes, as is apparent from this portion of a brief reminiscence Foss wrote about Neel for a posthumous show in Los Angeles in 1985.

> I met Alice Neel during the Depression of the Thirties. [In fact, she met her in 1927.] I had an Art Deco shop on Madison Avenue and was in need of a sales lady. Fifty hungry women applied. Alice was the last one to be interviewed. I liked her bright personality, smile, and the watercolors she showed me. I hired her. A few days later she brought her cousin Carlos, a Cuban, around. Dark-skinned Carlos against her fair complexion was surely a most unlikely relative. Alice was to change her story later: Cousin Carlos turned out to be her husband, and to add to this new revelation, she also confessed to being pregnant. Many times I remember feeding all of them in the back of my store at lunch. This was no time for Art Deco. The shop failed. Alice had her baby. Carlos took the baby to Cuba to his family and went to Paris, leaving Alice to live on her wits. The photograph of Alice and myself was

taken on the steps of the apartment house I lived in on Cornelia
Street in Greenwich Village. Alice lived across the street. I was to
witness many of her early struggles, her loves, longings, jealou-
sies and fights. Kenneth Doolittle, burning her paintings in a
crazy frenzy, Sam Brody and his insane temperament. John Rothschild, who remained her constant supporter and lover throughout her life.

Foss not only witnessed some of Neel's difficult episodes, including the
incident in which Doolittle destroyed much of her work (according to Foss's
son, she discovered him in the midst of this act and prevented him from
destroying more), she wrote about Alice's private exploits in an unpublished
novel optioned for film by Garson Kanin, which many years later led to a
"vituperative" argument and falling-out between the two old friends.

No doubt she also witnessed the increasing stress between Alice and
Carlos, who by now had moved to a cheaper apartment on Sedgwick Avenue in the Bronx, just off the highway and the Harlem River. (Alice did a
watercolor of her neighborhood at the time, *Harlem River,* 1927.)

While the tension that had existed between the couple in Havana arose
from Neel's discomfort with Carlos's family and their haute-bourgeois values, in New York the tension resulted from a combination of poverty, com-
petitiveness, and the realities of being a nuclear family when Alice did not
necessarily always want to perform the traditional role of wife and mother.

As her nephew, George Neel, put it, "My grandmother said, 'You know,
he [Carlos] was a gentleman, but he had to wash his own underwear.' And
Alice would not do any of those so-called menial tasks of wife and mother.
And they were both young romantic artists who were going to be really
artists . . . and they both were painting and Alice was determined to do
more than her husband."

Certainly Alice, even with an infant and a job, continued to enjoy painting and spending time with her friends in the Village. It was around this
time that she first met Nadya Olyanova, who had gone to the Art Students
League with Marcelo Pogolotti. Olyanova later became a celebrated graphologist. She was a brilliant and somewhat decadent character, whom
Neel depicted in a number of paintings, including the sinister 1929 *La Fleur
du Mal.* Olyanova was also the model for *Degenerate Madonna.* For her
part, Olyanova, with whom Neel would become close over the next few years,
used to call Alice "Malice Neel." (It was through Nadya and her husband,
Egil, that Neel would meet Doolittle.)

Whatever the marital issues may have been between Alice and Carlos at the time, nothing prepared them for the tragedy that occurred that winter, when Santillana, who up until then had been a "very beautiful, healthy, child," got diphtheria, then prevalent, although, as Neel bitterly told Hills, only a year later the vaccine became available. Alice must have been terrified when Santillana became ill, with symptoms that could have included nausea, chills, high fever, and neck swelling. In the 1920s, there were between 100,000 and 200,000 cases of the often-fatal upper-respiratory disease a year in the United States, many of them children.

Neel tried everything in her power to take care of her sick daughter. According to the Belchers' book, she tried to break Santillana's fever by "burning a spiritus lamp." But Neel clearly remained full of guilt and remorse. Marcelo Pogolotti told his daughter, Graziella, that Santillana had also been malnourished.

In the autobiographical piece Neel wrote called "Money," which begins somewhat satirically and ends up tragically, she hauntingly lamented the circumstances that may have led to Santillana's death:

> Do you know how much an oil stove costs? About $5. . . . But you see if I'd had the money—the green lovely dollars the shining quarters to buy a coat with maybe I wouldn't have caught layrngitis so badly if we hadn't had to live in one little room the baby maybe wouldn't have caught it like she did and then if I could have paid a doctor I wouldn't have been so slow to call one and then it was so cold oh so cold if only I had had an oil stove to keep the room warm at night. Oh my god a black oil stove haunts me. I told him we needed it but he's so used to trying to get out of spending any money for necessities that it's a habit. And then I got tired and frightened and weakminded. Well she died mostly from the goddamned discomfort. Well how do you expect one to feel about money. Well after that his family sent him some but I didn't like to eat because I knew the baby dying had earned those meals for us.

Evidence seems to point to the fact that Neel took the baby, then ten months old, home to Colwyn, enlisting the aid of her mother. "She must have died there," said George Neel. "How else explain the stains on the settee?"

Alice told her daughter-in-law, Ginny Neel, of her horror and disbelief at

seeing Santillana's tiny corpse. "It was so horrible because she looked totally fine, she looked perfect in every way, but she was dead." As Neel wrote
in "Money," the same minister who married her and Carlos performed the
funeral rites for their first child.

Santillana del Mar died just shy of her first birthday and was buried in
the family plot in the Arlington Cemetery in Drexel Hill, Pennsylvania, on
December 9. There are no tombstones marking any of the Neel family
graves, which are located in the Sunnyside Section of Arlington, perhaps
because they couldn't afford them.

"In the beginning, I didn't want children. I just got them. But then
when she died, it was frightful," Neel told Hills.

The coming year would produce several memorable watercolors as Neel
attempted to process her intense grief. *After the Death of the Child,*
1927–1928, expresses with almost unbearable poignancy the loneliness and
silence of the solitary parent passing a lively playground. The central figure is attenuated, Munch-style—the human as exclamation point—its face
reduced to a stylized *Scream*-like skull. The painting is anchored by a
coffin-shaped building and a sharp black tree.

The disturbing *Requiem,* 1928, shows several embryonic sea creatures
hovering near a prone corpselike figure that is hugging an invisible bundle
to its breast, while a black grim reaper clings to its back as intimately as a
lover or a shadow. It's unclear whether the figures are on the shore or sub-
merged underwater. Two tiny boats are stalled on the static waves. The entire painting is done in dull mud tones and is singularly lifeless.

And finally, the clay-colored *Futility of Effort,* based on an early sketch
Neel made when Santillana died. Painted a full two years later (1930), the
picture expresses the primal feeling of failure that overwhelms any parent
whose child, defying the natural order of things, dies first, rendering for
naught all the care and nurturing it has been given. Neel here conflates her
subconscious guilt with a newspaper account of a child strangling to death
between two bedposts—in Neel's rendition, it looks like the child has died
in its own crib. There is the vaguest outline of an adult, heedless, outside
the door, and the window is a black hole in space, as much a reminder of the
vaginal opening through which a child enters the world as the void following death.

Neel herself later proudly called the painting "revolutionary." Although
art historians have commented that it evokes Ensor, Neel told an interviewer that at this point she had never seen the work of Ensor, and that
the painting was "right out of my experience." She had, however, seen

the work of Matisse, and its tone and composition are reminiscent of Matisse's *The Piano Lesson,* 1916, which also relies on gray and emphasizes a child's head, a figure to the right, and a triangular form to the left. As Neel pointed out to Nemser, "Even Picasso only used gray and white when he did the *Guernica.* Color is just too cheerful and happy for this sort of situation."

Neel also talked about the painting in her interview with Eleanor Munro. "I had had that child in Havana, and she died in New York just before she was a year old, of diphtheria. There's a picture I made, three years after, that's a distillation of that and so much else: *The Futility of Effort.* Into it went the amount of effort you put into having a child. Pregnancy. All the rest. Then the tragedy of losing it. Everything. Everything."

CHAPTER EIGHT

Futility of Effort

It is not surprising that Neel got pregnant with her second child almost immediately—by late February 1928, just three months after Santillana's incomprehensible death. "After Santillana's death I was just frantic. . . . All I could do was get pregnant again," she told Hills, calling her situation at the time "a trap." But it is likely that getting pregnant was the instinctive reflex of a bereft mother attempting to fill the gap left by the loss of her first child, and giving herself—and Carlos—a second chance.

Despite their poverty, Neel and Enríquez managed to take pleasure in some cozy evenings in the early days of her pregnancy. But even these moments of warmth were seasoned with despair.

> The two little lamps in the room make circles of light surrounded by darkness. Carlos smokes a white cigarette which I love to see in his dark hand against his dark face . . . it is a pleasure to walk out on our little porch and breathe the fresh night air. I remember dinner smells, different air, tropical nights—love in the beginning, me dizzy with many thoughts become vague and formless. How can I tell if I feel happy or sad. It seems to be neither. Perhaps it is youth that is leaving me—sweet sharp youth—
>
> Life has given me her bitterest cup to drink so why should I fear the shades or the suggestions of sorrow. The long desolate twilight when I am often here alone the house pale lights and foggy shadows the bridge a thing of classic beauty against the dramatic sunsets—all the spirits of all the artists coming up before me . . . and then I hear the door downstairs open and Carlos comes in. He is always smiling—he has a good kind nature and usually his arms are full of bundles. Then he kisses me and we make little false enthusiasms over a fresh mackerel that we will eat almost

toasted in oil and white potatoes and with their skins on which
with a little butter and salt will make a delightful supper. The
bread is also hot and crisp and as we eat the fragrant smell of coffee lends to it all such an atmosphere of well-being and at least
momentary pleasure that I forget for a moment the burning and
deferred ambitions of my dark-eyed companion—forget how he
loves to have supper with gay company—and wine—and voluble
Spanish conversation. Forget that he has to make imbecilic newspaper portraits forget we are poverty stricken—that my clothes
are shabby and ugly—that over a year ago I had a sweet baby,
that my soul is heavy for remorse for many things—

After Foss's shop closed, Neel got a full-time job at a bank. "When I was
pregnant with the second child we didn't have any money in New York
and he [Carlos] was a rich boy, he didn't know how to do anything and his
family sent him money, but not enough. So I got a job in the National
City Bank. I was always very smart, you know, and I could always type and
add and do everything, so I got a job there. I found it was so much easier
than painting. . . . I had to leave when I got too obviously pregnant, but I
was amazed at how easy it was, the work there."

Neel recorded her dispiriting experience at the bank's employment offices when she first went to apply for a job. After removing her hat for a
mug shot for her identification card, she nervously filled out the application before being interviewed and completing a typing test. She was
asked for a urine sample, and to strip for a physical examination by "an
insufferably bored doctor, middle-aged," and a "homely nurse. . . . All
this you do, trembling because . . . of course having lied like a trooper to
get this far on your journey." Then there was another long wait before she
was told to return another day. She spent the time making mental notes,
which she later typed up:

You enter a splendid building, marble and imposing, and take the
local elevator to the fifth floor. Your first thought is how sad
that so many people are unemployed, for the room is full of people.
Young girls, frivolously dressed, but with very serious expres-
sions, young men of every type, reminding one of the many
nations represented here, and older men with iron grey hair,
whom you already expect to fail to get anything, knowing the
prejudice for anything past its prime. Also there are a few little

boys, prematurely old in long trousers, but with very childish faces, some with lemon colored hair.

The account indicates Neel's natural acuity as an observer, a skill that was always in play, even when she wasn't standing in front of a canvas. She didn't let her working hours entirely stop her from painting, however, and this only added to the tension with Carlos, most of whose art at this point was for pay.

"A terrible rivalry sprang up between Carlos and me. He had to make money any way he could, stupid jobs like drawings for newspapers, on a very low level, although some of the drawings were elegant—upper-class girls riding horses for Saks Department Store, which had opened on Fifth Avenue in 1924." (Horses would figure prominently in Carlos's later work in Cuba.) "His family sent us money, but not enough, and he did terrible drawings for the newspapers, you know—commercial art." Although Alice didn't mention it, Enríquez also sent illustrations of New York scenes, including dancers in Harlem nightclubs, to *Revista de Avance* back in Havana, where they were published.

Despite Carlos's efforts, "we really almost starved to death," Neel said. It was a struggle to even afford such staples as milk: "The milkman just came and you who do not know bitter poverty can little realize the powerful feeling I have, when like today, I am capable of paying the milk bill. . . ."

The constant strain of poverty did nothing to blunt Neel's naturally competitive edge. She described being "consumed by an actual fire of jealousy. . . . In the case of Carlos there are more complications, for when his work is awfully clever, I feel selfish and wrong to insist on painting and so hold him back—but think of a long bleak life of stupidity and yet I am so nervous perhaps I never will do anything."

After a visit from her friend Fanya and her husband, Gordon, Neel succumbed again to her fears of the "awful dichotomy."

I lay in bed just screaming inside—sick and destroyed—the room squeezing in close to me in a black circle, then widening—all my dreams and desires clear canvas and new wooden stretchers all the pictures in my brain that I've been saving—and the work to do in this house—the terrible foolishness and failure of our lives—the fact that in a week or two I'll be in the hospital, white and business-like, but I hate hospitals.

Neel's account of her visit to the hospital just before her second child was born is full of the poignant but brutal imagery that soon found its way into her painting *Well Baby Clinic*. She described the "coarse" women she saw there, with their "heavy faces and blunt fingers."

> . . . I feel sorry for them all—can realize their hard burdens, but I hate their stupid faces and I hate like hell to be their thin white robed companion. When I look at their poor bodies I begin to imagine where and how and under what romantic dream they all indulged in that so enjoyable privilege—the act of life. . . .
>
> . . . And sometimes their life is too hard and their children die or are killed in the crowded streets and grief completes what labor has so well begun and their heavy bodies and blank grief stricken faces grow to look at the streaming luxury of the rich— without even desire or envy so heavy has been their loss. For now all the wealth and comfort of the universe could not restore the children they have lost—perhaps for want of an oil stove on a damp and foggy day—or a doctor in time.

*   *   *

Neel gave birth to Isabella Lillian Enríquez on November 24, 1928. She and Carlos called their daughter "Isabetta." (According to Isabetta's husband, Pablo Lancella, they got the name from a voluble Italian family in the hospital, who kept shouting it out.) Her birth certificate, issued on December 3, states that Isabetta was born at Fifth Avenue Hospital at 105th Street and Fifth Avenue to Alice Hartley Neel, age 27 (housewife) and Carlos Enríquez, age 28 (artist).

Just several weeks later, Neel documented her memory of childbirth with the remarkable painting *Well Baby Clinic*. The work is a return to the use of oil paints, and quintessential Neel: skeptical, psychological, and powerfully cynical. Neel was already embarking on a lifelong career as the anti-Cassatt. She recognized as much in herself. "*Well Baby Clinic* makes my attitude toward childbirth very dubious. I wondered how that woman could be so happy, with that little bit of hamburger she's fixing the diaper for." As she said, "When people would mewl over little kids, I just wanted to paint them."

The painting depicts a maternity ward with rows of beds filled with writhing, faceless infants. One mother, teeth bared, is about to breast-feed her child. A nurse cradles a baby, while the woman with the "hamburger" prepares a diaper. To her right is a gentler image, "that nice-looking one"— Neel herself, with Isabetta. A doctor proffers pills. Neel referred to the contrast between the clinic's neat white walls and pure nurses' outfits and the "sloppy humanity there, all ragged at the edges. . . . The walls look so hard and neat and the people so mangy and wretched."

It is certainly one of the least sentimental depictions of new motherhood ever created. The painting is also very much in keeping with the painfully personal pieces Neel was painting during this period, when much of her work was unabashedly autobiographical.

Neel suffered from phlebitis immediately after Isabetta's birth, causing her to be confined to bed for a few weeks, and to walk with a cane for several months. Alice spent some of her confinement writing a strange short story, "The Dark Picture of the Kallikaks," which describes the primitive coupling in a swamp of a young woman, Nona Kallikak, "the last scion of her disreputable family," and Unik Edwards, a young man from the upper class. (Nona is also the name of one of Nadya Olyanova's friends, whom Neel painted in a 1933 double nude portrait of the two, which she called *The Two Little Tarts*, but this character does not appear to be based on her.)

Although Hills remarks that the story reflects the 1920s preoccupation with eugenics and the differences between genders and classes, its raw sexual energy is its most striking feature. The story contains a passage which has a satiric pornographic tone that would later surface in Neel's intimate watercolors of herself and John Rothschild. Certainly the "most repressed creature that ever lived" now had an overt and worldly view of sex.

> Nona bent more and more backwards and then leaning against the bank gradually lay down, her black eyes more sad and strange than before. Unik Edwards didn't care. He unbuttoned her loose blouse. He kissed her white stomach, her round white breasts one in each hand he pushed them together. They looked like white birds then and he kissed their pink beaks. The flat thick slit of Nona's mouth was working in and out rhythmically with primitive emotion. And now the sharp clean shaven lips of Unik fell into the soft red jelly of Nona's lips. She felt his watch tickling on her bare white belly, the buttons of his vest hard places in his soft wool suit. She felt his motions were too jerky and she did her best to mold him with the slow passionate movement of the purple mud.

It's unclear if Neel eventually went back to her job at the bank. But apparently Carlos spent much of his time taking care of Isabetta, as Neel returned to the Village with her paint box, seeking out her friends Nadya Olyanova and Fanya Foss. Not much work survives from this period, and in later interviews, Neel tended to leave 1929 out altogether. But she expressed her desolate state of mind, despite her new child, in several poems written at the time.

> *My house is beside a river of lead*
> *I build a snow woman*
> *My brown fingers dream of blood red*
> *Warm earth in Cuba*
>
> *I burn my snow woman's*
> *Black coal eyes and still I am*
> *Not warm*
>
> *Water has mixed with the marrow of my bones*
> *My spine a ramified icicle . . .*

The poem's ending sums up Neel's sorrow:

> *the grey of this sad house*
> *beside the river of lead*
>
> *my tropical soul*
> *frozen in ice*
> *molded with pain*

The next two years would prove to be more than the couple's seriously strained union could bear. The continuing poverty, the bickering that resulted from the fact that while Neel was still painting for her own pleasure, Carlos was forced to do advertisements, and the fact that Neel, who at least for part of that time had a day job, was often not at home, all took an eventual toll.

According to George Neel, the two artists, whose marriage was becoming increasingly "rocky," used suggestive drawings to taunt each other. "Well, his entertainment was drawing tunnels and her entertainment to taunt him was drawing bridges. And he must have drawn a picture of Alice lying on the bed with the train going into the tunnel." The subtext, according to George, was that "she was essentially promiscuous and she didn't cook and take care of things." (George Neel was not talking about Alice's actual sexual proclivities, as much as her general attitude.)

Although, like any young mother, Alice proudly posed for photographs with Isabetta as an infant, she wasn't particularly enamored of caring for an energetic toddler—at least not as revealed by her own hand in the ironic but honest *The Intellectual*, painted around this time. While Foss, pretentious or not, is portrayed as a lady of leisure, Alice, excluded from the intellectual comraderie, a blank look on her face, can do nothing but cope with her child.

The portrait is as much about Neel's overt envy of Foss's mental and physical freedom as it is a comment on Foss's "pretentiousness." Here, Neel depicted her relentless dichotomy: Clearly she would have preferred discussing literature to baby-sitting Isabetta. Even the fact that Neel found the time and energy to do this watercolor and the scene it depicts—Neel visiting her friends in the Village—indicates her inclinations.

In another poem written at the time, Neel decried the different lots of men and women. While the men can "put all their troubles in beautiful verses," the women "poor fools, they grumbled and complained and watched their breasts grow flatter and more wrinkled . . . and no one loves their grumbling, sad, sour dry with red and shiny knuckles."

The stock market crashed on October 29, 1929, setting off the Great Depression in the United States. Alice and Carlos had experienced their own personal poverty for several years; now the whole country was plunged into a devastating economic crisis of historic proportions. It's hard to estimate the immediate impact on the young couple, although the money coming in from Carlos's parents, with the Cuban sugar industry also in a tailspin, completely dried up. (According to her nephew, George, Neel was forced to ask her sister Lily for help.) But the sights Neel saw at the time created indelible images that would permanently affect her art.

"People starved," she told Lucille Rhodes, who interviewed her for a documentary. "Men sold apples on the street. You know, 'Buddy can you spare a dime'? It was a starving world. On West Fourth Street, there used to be a figure sleeping in every doorway, and in the park, bums used to sleep and they'd wrap their legs with newspaper at night, and then in the morning they'd burn them. Nobody had enough to eat. It was frightful."

Still, Carlos drew a Christmas card that year that the two sent to friends, including Fanya Foss and Gordon Kingman: It shows himself, Alice, and a perky Isabetta, with a traditional Christmas tree and Christmas turkey. It would be their last major holiday together as a family.

CHAPTER NINE

The Bell Jar

Oh I was full of theories
Of grand experiments
To live a normal woman's life
To have children—to be the painting and the painter . . .

I've lost my child my love my life and all the god damn
business
That makes life worth living.

—ALICE NEEL

On May 1, 1930, Neel's life took another traumatic turn. The plan, or so Alice thought, was for Carlos to take Isabetta to Havana to visit his parents, who had never met their granddaughter. Neel was to join them there, and then they would all travel to Paris.

It seems, though, that Carlos may have had something else in mind. He telegraphed his friend Pogolotti, announcing his arrival in Havana. Wrote Pogolotti, "He abandoned New York and his wife, taking with him the second child so his sisters could take care of her."

According to Neel, Carlos's Havana visit was originally to have been for only about a month. But events soon unraveled in a radically different way. When his parents, whose income was still suffering as a result of the Depression and its impact on the sugar market, said they didn't have the money to fund the trip to Paris, he went by himself with money he got from his friends, leaving Isabetta with his family in Cuba. His friends had been criticizing him for some time about his bourgeois lifestyle in America, and urging him to follow his vocation as an artist in Paris. Now he was gone, along with Isabetta.

Alice learned these brutal facts through a letter (from Paris) she re-

ceived from Carlos early that summer. Although Carlos had initially said
he would send for her in a couple of months, when he had made enough
money, "I realized that was just the end of everything. I was left with the
apartment, the furniture, a whole life, and it was finished. Because he was
very weak, and I was abandoned," she later said. Neel had lost not only her
husband but, for the second time in two and a half years, a daughter. She
would only see Isabetta, who was brought up by Carlos's sisters, Julia and
Sylvie, several more times during her lifetime.

Neel's emotional agony is clear in a dream she recorded at the time:

> Carlos went away. The nights were horrible at first. . . . I dreamed
> Isabetta died and we buried her right beside Santillana. Well
> then I was crying alone in a room and someone came and said
> they were moving the cemetery and that when they dug up those
> two baby coffins they could see them moving inside. . . .
>
> Isabetta was alright—just like now. . . . I was afraid to look—
> her head was alright, only now she had long black hair—but her
> hands and arms were like mummies all cracked and dried. I had
> to save her from breaking them off. She was tall—as old as she
> must be by now—and the hands you could see them getting bet-
> ter, coming back to life. If only dreams were life—they are in a
> way only shorter.

There are conflicting and unreliable accounts of both Neel and Enríquez as parents. According to Juan Martínez, neither parent was particularly suited to that responsibility. Although in later years, the Cuban
branch of the family painted Alice as a questionable mother, at least to Isabetta, Martínez doubts that Enríquez proved to be much of a father. "I am
not so sure knowing what we know of him later that he would want children, because he was the worst father there was. I don't see why, with all
the ideas he had in his head of going to New York, going to Europe, living
this kind of life, why would he want children? And when they did have
children, they didn't seem to have been the best of parents, either one of
them. What I'm saying is that toward the children they were both wacko.
You cannot say that one was worse than the other. I mean the whole incident of taking her back to Havana and leaving her there with his sisters. If
you ask me, probably both in the back of their mind that's what they
wanted—just let's find a place where this child can be brought up. We've
already had one die on us."

The Cuban branch later clung to a story, quite possibly apocryphal, that Enríquez had at one point discovered Isabetta in her bassinet on the fire escape as it was beginning to snow, while Alice, oblivious, was painting. According to Marisa Diaz, Isabetta's childhood friend, who says she heard this anecdote from Isabetta herself, "She didn't take care of Isabetta. She needed to be fed and she [Alice] would go out of the apartment and leave her alone. One day she left her on the fire stairs and forgot her completely. She was only a few months old and Carlos found her almost frozen to death and decided to take her to Havana. And then he left her there and went to Paris to paint. That story she told me from her family."

But Martínez heard that Isabetta had been left out on the ledge by both parents while they were throwing a party. "I came by this story that they threw a party and she was crying and they put her out on a ledge so she wouldn't bother them, and it was snowing. So it seems to me that they, both of them, were unfit parents." (Neel's two sons, Richard and Hartley, whom she brought up more or less single-handedly, strongly question both versions of the fire-escape story.)

From the Cubans' point of view, though, Neel had never been a conventional mother. She had let neither her pregnancy nor having an infant interfere with her artistic agenda in Havana, and she had made sure that Santillana was not brought up in the Enríquez household. And then she had taken the child back to the United States, where Santillana had died. She had made a permanent impression on her Cuban in-laws, and it's possible the discomfort over her unorthodox behavior had still not faded.

In the first weeks after Carlos left, Neel, who seemed to be in complete denial, initially reveled in her freedom to paint whenever she pleased. That her life with Carlos and Isabetta was ostensibly over was too terrible for her to comprehend. "You see, I had always had this awful dichotomy. I loved Isabetta, of course I did. But I wanted to paint," she bluntly told Hills.

Now that her family was gone, Neel's immediate response was to feverishly subsume herself in her art. "At first all I did was paint, day and night." Her parents came to visit her that spring, and they took a day trip to Coney Island, where Neel immediately painted an uncomfortable-looking young couple from memory (*Coney Island Boat*, 1930). She then visited her parents in Colwyn, later doing a picture of a couple she saw on the train; in this one, the woman is pregnant, but while she looks "miserable," her male partner looks happy.

She was no more able to explain to her parents what had happened with Carlos than she could to herself. At first, she beseeched her mother to let Isabetta live with her and her father in Colwyn. "You see, I asked my mother if I could keep the little girl there with me, because they would have brought her up, and that would have meant my giving up painting because I would have cared for her. But my mother wouldn't do that. She said, 'No, I've raised my own family.' She wasn't like these good mothers. If she had taken Isabetta for a couple of years, everything would have been simpler," she told Hills.

Yet another account exists of how Isabetta ended up staying in Cuba. According to Diaz, "I know at that beginning they [Carlos's family] asked her [Alice] to take Isabetta back when Carlos went to Europe, and she said no, she preferred Isabetta to be where she was, because she would be better taken care of. Alice was sick at the time—maybe that could be a reason—and she didn't have money." Neel herself told more than one interviewer that "the Cuban inlaws would have brought Isabetta to stay with me" but that after her mother said no, "I was much too proud to ever ask her again."

She explained it to Patti Goldstein slightly differently. "His family would have brought her back to me—but guess what? I was already divided between art and the little girl, although losing that little girl is partly what gave me the breakdown. After all, I'd lost the other baby when she died, and now this one was only a year and a half old. But when I asked my mother if the baby and I could come live with her, she said 'No, I've had one family and that's enough.' I couldn't stand the humiliation of asking her again and I couldn't show any emotion."

One way to have kept Isabetta with her might have been to have gone to Cuba herself to get her, but as Neel unsentimentally told Jonathan Brand, boiling it down to her Bohemian attitude toward money, ". . . it would be too bourgeois . . . other women get supported. If I had been a practical, hard-hearted woman, I could have gone down to Cuba and taken Isabetta, and I would have gotten supported."

Whatever the actual truth of the matter—that Carlos's family was insistent on keeping the child or that Neel's ambivalence prevented her from taking any conclusive steps to recover her daughter—it became a fait accompli. Isabetta remained in Havana. "Isabetta was bitter. She had every right to be. Her father was no help. She wasn't close to her father either. He abandoned her. He brought her to Havana, took her away from her mother, and then he went to Paris," says Isabetta's husband, Pablo Lancella.

With Carlos gone, Neel was not in any shape to care for a child. She was barely able to care for herself. She couldn't afford car fare or lunch, and in her hyperactive, adrenalized state, she ate little or nothing. Within a short time, she lost nearly twenty-five pounds.

In order to make some money, Neel sublet the apartment she had shared with Carlos and Isabetta on Sedgwick Avenue. She probably also wanted to escape the insistent memories of her missing family (including Santillana). Once again, she retreated to Colwyn, living with her parents at home. But every day she tried to escape the reality of her situation by going to Rhoda and Ethel's studio on Washington Square in Philadelphia to paint. Her life revolved around the images on her canvas. She couldn't let herself see beyond her easel. "I had a terrible life. But in a very short space of time, I turned out any number of great paintings," she said.

These included several striking portraits of her studio mates: Ethel Ashton, conceived boldly as an "uncompromising" nude, who nonetheless looks ashamed of her own thick body, which crowds the frame, and a slim Rhoda, also nude, except for a necklace and a wide-brimmed blue hat. (Interestingly, Neel's recent spate of introspective paintings ceased.) Neel was in a sort of "manic" state that was starting to wind down. "Your senses are never more acute than before you have a nervous breakdown. You're hyped up. In three months of June, July and August, before the middle of August, I painted some of my best paintings."

The frenzy of escapist activity took its toll. On August 15, Neel collapsed after experiencing an eight-hour chill and intestinal cramps. As she herself put it simply, "One of the reasons I had the breakdown, I never showed any grief." Now she was completely overcome. "I just opened up and everything let go. Then I had Freud's classic hysteria. I died every day."

Neel remained bedridden at home for nearly eight weeks, under the care of her mother and a local doctor. She recalled this time of "dying spells" as torture, "dreading this falling apart, which happened every single day." She described it vividly to Hills: "It's a complete breakdown of the nervous system. And you get weaker and weaker. . . . I lost weight. I would lie there perspiring . . . you are absolutely convinced you're dying. But I never made a sound. You see, one of the reasons I had this frightful breakdown—I never gave normal vent to my emotions."

Neel's repressed grief at the recent traumas she had experienced, from Santillana's death to losing Carlos and Isabetta, played a primary role in her psychological breakdown. But on another level, Neel's condition may also have been brought on by her own guilt at her unconscious relief at being liberated from the family responsibilities that curtailed her artistic desires; in a sense, by leaving with Isabetta, Carlos had removed the source of Neel's dichotomy. According to Freud, the "pathogenic mechanism of hysteria" includes "the emergence of a wishful impulse which was in sharp contrast to the subject's other wishes and which proved incompatible with the ethical and aesthetic standards of his personality."

Neel later told Munro, "If only I'd had five hundred dollars, I wouldn't have had the nervous breakdown. I had gone every day and worked in my studio . . . If I'd had a few hundred dollars, I could have had a show, but as it was three months after he [Carlos] went away, I had my first nervous chill." Once again, poverty played a major role. Tellingly, she seems to be saying that if she had succeeded with her painting at the time, she could have sustained the significant emotional loss she had suffered; that it was not being able to make her art career work, rather than that she had lost her husband and child, that led to the breakdown.

She was more explicit in another interview: "Instead of being able to do anything about my art, I had a nervous breakdown instead. But if I'd have had some money, I wouldn't have had it, I don't think. I was evenly divided between my family life and my art life. I was delighted to be able to paint again."

In October, Neel's parents, unable to cope with her continuing deterioration, took her to Philadelphia's Orthopedic Hospital. But the care Neel received there only exacerbated her fragile state: The doctors kept her from painting, instead forcing her to sew, something she hated as a result of her childhood rivalry with her sister, Lily. Neel was unable to paint the "great masterpieces" she saw all around her. She was confined to a ward, where the conditions were "frightful . . . there was a little girl chained to the bed and an old woman dying."

Sessions with a psychiatrist didn't help. While telling him she wanted "nothing but the peace of the grave," Neel, ever the observer, focused on his hands, noting how impotent they looked. By Christmas, Neel had reached her lowest point. The contrast of the "normal" holiday with its cheerful carols only heightened her sense of complete despair.

As A. Alvarez writes in *The Savage God*,

> A suicidal depression is a kind of spiritual winter, frozen, sterile, unmoving. The richer, softer and more delectable nature becomes, the deeper that internal winter seems, and the wider and more intolerable the abyss which separates the inner world from the outer. Thus suicide becomes a natural reaction to an unnatural condition. Perhaps this is why, for the depressed, Christmas is so hard to bear. In theory it is an oasis of warmth and light in an unforgiving season, like a lighted window in a storm. For those

who have to stay outside, it accentuates, like spring, the disjunc-
tion between public warmth and festivity and cold, private despair.

When Carlos, whom Lily had summoned from Paris, sending him money
for his fare, appeared at her bedside in January, like some kind of overdue
miracle, Neel was unable to feel any sense of rescue or relief. "Carlos wanted
to return to Paris; he wanted to take me; he wanted everything. But it was
too late. I was too far gone. . . . Three months before, it would have saved
me—going to Paris. But then it was just too late. The disease was on its
way, whatever the disease was."

Carlos visited Neel several times, and he accompanied her to Colwyn
when the hospital released her in January. But Neel was in no condition to
be released. Even the taxi ride home threw her into a nervous fit, and later
that night she attempted suicide by sticking her head in the gas oven. It
was a threat she had heard her mother use against her father often enough.
(Neel remarked that when they discovered her in the morning, her brother
originally thought it was her mother.) Fanya Foss later recalled, "During
one of my periodic visits to New York, Alice and I sat in her kitchen when
she told me after Carlos left she went to live with her family. One morning
they found her after an attempted suicide by gas. And her father's singular
comment on the suicide was how high the gas bill will be. And how we both
laughed at what her father said."

Neel's situation as this point was one of total desperation. No sooner was
she back at Orthopedic Hospital than she smashed a glass and tried to
swallow the shards. This time, they strapped her to the bed. The next day,
her mother, who had never been to visit her in the hospital in all the previous
months, came to transfer her to the suicidal ward at Philadelphia General
Hospital. (According to George Neel, it was his mother and a friend of hers
who made this trip because, "my grandmother refused to go.") Meanwhile,
Carlos's efforts to soothe Neel were fruitless, and he returned to Paris, where,
she later said, "he had a girlfriend. He was a frivolous character."

Neel's verbal description of the next several months in the suicidal ward
is horrifying; equally disturbing is the desolate pencil drawing she made
of it, *Suicidal Ward*, 1931. First she was given a spinal epidural—"to see
if I had a veneral disease." For the next few months, Neel, like the other
patients in the ward, got up at five in the morning to eat breakfast with
rubber utensils. She was surrounded by others in all states of mental and
physical distress, from a woman next to her who died on Easter morning

(the orderlies decided not to change her nightshirt when they realized she would be dead in a few hours) to a woman who refused to eat and had to be intubated, to one who threw flowerpots.

Neel spent all day longing for the night and "oblivion," in a room with a barred window, under the surveillance of the night attendant, when "between the cries and groans there are intervals of silence . . . how horribly lonely my soul is on this last horrible adventure. I who always needed companionship so. . . ." She soon became incontinent. And she contemplated suicide daily, first by jumping down the laundry chute and later by strangling herself with a stocking. "I couldn't pull long enough or hard enough. You cannot commit suicide unless you—in a moment of frenzy—you do something irrevocable."

It seems almost certain that Neel would not have survived her stay. But a sensitive social worker discovered her and, according to Neel, impressed by her good looks, despite how thin she was, asked her how she had gotten there. Neel's instant response: "Well I'm a famous artist, but they don't believe it." Apparently she had tried to tell them about her show in Havana. The social worker gave her a drawing pad. Neel refused to draw the psychiatrist called in to see her first artistic effort in months. "You're the enemy," she told him. But it was the initial step toward her being sent to a private sanitarium. Neel's lifeline—her art, which she had not been allowed to practice ever since her hospitalization—had literally saved her. "It was the drawing that helped me decide to get well," she told Munro.

By late May 1931, a little over a year after Carlos's abandonment, Neel was sent to an asylum run by Dr. Seymour DeWitt Ludlum, head of the Neuropsychopathic Department at Philadelphia General Hospital. It was at the Gladwyne Colony in Merion Square, Pennsylvania, the very town where she had been born, that she began her slow and painful recovery.

CHAPTER TEN

Resurrection

"I was a neurotic. Art was my salvation."

—ALICE NEEL

The link between artistic genius and insanity is so often invoked that it has become cliché. But scientific evidence indicates that it is not coincidental that creative luminaries ranging from Byron to van Gogh to Virginia Woolf all suffered from suicidal depressions; according to data, the rate of manic depression and major depression in artists is from ten to thirty times more than that of the general population.

Some artists, like van Gogh, famously represent the extreme of this spectrum, epitomizing the myth of madness and creativity. Others, like the late sculptor Louise Bourgeois, who battled daily panic attacks her entire life, courageously cope; indeed, their art is often their best coping mechanism. Bourgeois has stated that her art is a "form of therapy" that prevents her from doing actual violence to others or herself.

And then there are those whose inner terrors tragically converge with external events to create insurmountable pain. In the wake of multiple traumas—the fire that destroyed his studio and work, the colostomy for colon cancer, the car accident that broke his neck and temporarily paralyzed his arm, and finally the breakup of his marriage when his wife, Mougouch, left him with their two children, Arshile Gorky hanged himself at age forty-four, after scrawling the note "Goodbye my Loveds." "In a state of negative paralysis, and with his family gone, he felt his world fall apart. Yet although present misfortunes precipitated his suicide, depression surely was the principal cause," wrote his biographer Hayden Herrera.

By the age of thirty-one, Neel had already suffered several profound misfortunes, and she was to experience more in the next several years. But despite her statement that she was "suicidal her whole life," her frequent description of herself as a "hypersensitive" child, and her tendency toward overwhelming "nervousness," Neel never totally succumbed to her despair; she proved herself to be a survivor. Painting was her survival method. "I'm very high-strung and nervous," she told one interviewer. "In a way, I overreact to everything. Painting portraits is a way of coming to grips with this."

Even during her breakdown in 1930, the diagnosis was "no psychosis," Neel told Hills. "So I was never out of my mind." Like many intellectuals of her generation, Neel was familiar with and fascinated by Freud's early theories (hence her self-diagnosis—that she had suffered from "Freud's classic hysteria"), but it wasn't until 1958 that she began psychotherapy. She later credited her therapist, Dr. Anthony Sterrett, with giving her the confidence to break out of obscurity.

Although severe trauma triggered her breakdown and her two subsequent suicide attempts in 1930, Neel never again tried to kill herself. Like Bourgeois, she skillfully used her art to maintain her equilibrium. "If I don't paint for certain lengths of time, I get into frightfully morbid moods, but the minute I begin to work, I'm cured. Sometimes though, after I've finished a painting, I feel like an untenanted house, utterly alone." (As beautifully expressed in her painting *Loneliness*, 1970, a picture of an empty chair by an empty window, which Neel once said was the closest thing to a a self-portrait.) "But guess what? If I like the picture it's all okay because I have this terrific feeling of elation. I did what I wanted to do."

Or, as she said to Joan Kufrin, author of *Uncommon Women*, "I'm a trained neurotic. I had a frightful breakdown, and you don't go through that without learning a lot of self-control. Even if you get into a sanitarium, the person that gets you out is yourself. You get yourself in, and you get yourself out. Now if you have such terrible things happen that you really go under, it may be hard for you to cure yourself. But nobody else can. You have to come around to the opinion that you don't want to be like that and fight it. It took a whole year out of my life."

*   *   *

Nestled on several verdant hillsides in Lower Merion Township, just outside Philadelphia, the Gladwyne Colony was Neel's personal Magic Mountain, a private sanitarium with a unique cast of characters. Although she stayed there only about five months (as opposed to Hans Castorp's seven years), it was here that Neel gradually struggled back to health.

The colony was the brainchild of Dr. Seymour DeWitt Ludlum, an innovative psychiatrist who had first come across the quaint remnants of

Rose Glen, a 1835 cotton-mill town (on Mill Creek), just outside Merion Square, in 1910, while riding on horseback from his home in Merion to Mill Creek Valley. He bought the property—fourteen buildings on thirty-five acres—two years later from the mill owner, William Chadwick, and established the Gladwyne Colony, which operated for the next 54 years.

Born in 1876, Dr. Ludlum was in the forefront of those who believed that psychiatric disorders often had physiological sources or components—the basic mind/body connection. He studied at Rutgers University and at Johns Hopkins, graduating in 1902. Over the course of his career, he published more than fifty-five papers, primarily dealing with physiological changes in patients with mental disease, the best known of which is "Physiologic Pathology in the Schizoid and Affective Psychoses," published in 1955. At the time he founded the Gladwyne Colony, he was chief of staff of the Neuropsychopathic Department of Philadelphia General Hospital. He also maintained an office in Philadelphia, where he saw outpatients. For a while, some of his mentally disturbed patients lived with him in Merion, and it was in an effort to expand their housing that he first thought of starting his own sanitarium.

At its peak, the Gladwyne Colony housed as many as one hundred patients, ranging from the violently insane—who were incarcerated in locked rooms and strapped to their beds—to those well enough to walk the grounds. (Some were simply old people whose wealthy relatives didn't want to care for them; one woman was there merely because she was disfigured.) There were about thirty-five staff members, from dining room waiters to nurses to groundskeepers. The colony employed a variety of therapeutic methods, including electroshock therapy, then in its infancy; physical therapy, which was also relatively new at the time; vocational therapy, such as crafts; and psychotherapy. Patients were prompted to engage in activities they enjoyed.

"When able, patients were encouraged to work on the grounds, plant gardens, care for the many animals at the Colony, and participate in therapeutic crafts," according to the Lower Merion Historical Society's *The First 300: The Amazing and Rich History of Lower Merion.* "If you were to drive through the village, you could scarcely tell the patients from the employees. They practice tree surgery and flower cultivation, they are given chores to do and are entrusted with responsibilities. You see them taking walks and on hikes, or feeding the ducks and geese paddling in the shallow, placid creek. In addition to outdoor games and recreation they work at weaving, painting and other arts and crafts and when the weather isn't kind they indulge in indoor games or watch television," reads a description in the *Mainline Chronicle*, March 28, 1957.

Still, it was not unusual to see patients sitting on the lawn in straitjackets. "There were people in straitjackets and people playing tennis," says Sandy Ronan, Dr. Ludlum's granddaughter, who lived just up the hill from the Colony, in a house called Birdside. Built by Dr. Ludlum and her father, Seymour DeWitt Jr., Ludlum's only child, it was whimsically embellished with scavenged bric-a-brac. (In the 1950s, with the advent of psychopharmaceuticals, says Ronan, who lived there until 1957, the tenure of the colony completely changed.)

Physically, Gladwyne Colony was quite beautiful, a sort of Sleepy Hollow hamlet, with stone buildings of various sizes and well-kept grounds, including gardens and a tennis court. The buildings were located on both sides of Mill Creek, along the juncture of Rose Glen and Mill Creek roads, all within walking distance of each other. On the east side of the creek, there was the two-story Inn, a former post office and general store, which housed the offices; the second floor was used for patient intake and evaluation. Near that was Chadwick, the former mill house, which had the dining room where patients not restricted to their rooms had their meals. Dr. Ludlum had converted a blacksmith's shop into a modern-day laboratory, replete with specimens and instruments, including a fluoroscope. Across Mill Creek were the Towers and the Mill, the dormitories where the patients lived.

It is likely that after being evaluated, Neel was lodged in the Towers, the impressive former miller's mansion, which, in addition to the imposing stone tower from which its name derived, included a lounge with furniture upholstered in floral prints, a pool table (in its own pool room), magazines and books, and a phonograph. Neel describes it as "a gorgeous, beautiful house." It is probably here that the parties Neel refers to in her oral biography took place. (It was also here on the first floor that the electroshock room was located.)

Neel also used to visit Dr. Ludlum's home, Fernside, a stunning stone house that is still standing, impeccably renovated and occupied by Dennis Milstein and Richard Lebert. On the same side of the road are the ruins of a solitary dovecote, and across the creek, up the hill, the stone foundations of the Towers, with its arched doorways.

Neel's memories of the Gladwyne Colony were highly positive, although they include some offbeat details. She referred to Dr. Ludlum as "a wonderful experimental psychologist . . . a wonderful person. . . . It was a lovely place and there I got as well as I could." Her stay there, for which her family paid forty dollars a week—a steep fee for the time—would later figure in the description of the experience of the psychiatric patient in her friend Millen Brand's best-seller *The Outward Room*, published in 1937. (Recalled Millen Brand's son, Jonathan, "Alice painted him [Millen] in 1937, when he became a literary sensation by writing about Alice emerging from the psychiatric hospital. The novel was *The Outward Room*.")

According to Neel, she was initially put into the "suicidal ward" at the colony. Ronan believes this would either have been the Mill or the building next to it, the Guard House, which housed the most violent patients, who were shackled in chains or locked in cell-like rooms. But Helen Dixon, the daughter of Ellen Porter, a nurse who worked there during Neel's time, (from 1928 until 1958) says that there really was no suicidal ward, and it is possible that Neel was put on the second floor of the Inn, where patients usually stayed at least a week in order to be evaluated by Dr. Ludlum. According to Dixon, Neel would have had one ankle shackled to the bed until she was evaluated.

Neel's first memory of the place, which she repeated to several interviewers, was of hearing someone playing the song "Just a gigolo . . . everywhere I go . . ." on a phonograph. Neel said that she was put in a room with a woman who wrapped her corset in bunting, like a baby, and sang it to sleep. This woman also took exception to Neel's drawings, tearing one up because it was the "work of the Devil."

According to Neel, when Dr. Ludlum evaluated her, he told her, "You wouldn't have to be here if you would swear not to commit suicide," and she was transferred to "this big house where they had mental patients, not suicidals." Neel slept in a room with one of the nurses, although Dixon states that this was unusual. She also remarks that Dr. Ludlum would have been unlikely to have been convinced that Neel was not suicidal until he had observed her for at least a month. (He didn't make daily rounds.)

A tall, distinguished-looking man, Dr. Ludlum was fifty-five years old during Neel's stay at Gladwyne. Although Dixon describes him as stern and formal, always dressed in a suit and bow tie, his colleagues from the Philadelphia Neurological Society recalled him as "a connoisseur of good food, fine wine and a genial host and a delightful companion," who liked to yacht in his spare time. He married his second wife, Mabel Stewart, in 1920. According to Dixon, she was a highly sophisticated woman, "always dressed to the nines," who spent most of her time in Philadelphia. He was also, says Dixon, "a maverick, always experimenting."

Neel's quirky anecdotes include dancing at a party with a "genius" who had "over-studied," a former court stenographer who kicked people (and whom Neel, of course, depicted in a drawing), and a tennis player who clobbered a therapist with his racket. She also recalled sitting "out on a terrace with wisteria, the most beautiful place," possibly at Dr. Ludlum's home, Fernside, where, she said, "Dr. Ludlum used to hug me, and he'd say, 'Why don't you look in the mirror and get well.' I was very pretty, with golden hair, and he said, 'You're so foolish, you can't imagine.'"

From her first days there, she was already making art. Neel's self-prescribed therapy were hour-long warm baths. (In Brand's book, the character also takes baths: "Body that had lain in the warm baths, the running water holding her in hours of blanched calm.")

"I worked at getting well. It was a deliberate process. Even intellectual. For instance, I read a very ordinary American novel published in installments in a magazine. Waiting for each issue, looking it up, reading the sections in order, made me exercise my brain."

She tried to follow the advice of a "deaf woman doctor" who advised her to give up "the habit of worrying." "I began to try to explain it to myself. That I never had been able to ask for room for my nervousness. I'd never been able just to say, 'Look I'm frightfully nervous,'" she told Munro. Or, as she explained to Hills, "I learned to realize it was my own fault. I pushed my brain back; then, after it got back there, I was much worse off. Then I trained myself to come back. I am now more normal than normal."

Eventually, she became continent again, and she regained her memory of Spanish, which she had lost during the breakdown. She began to feel well enough to leave the sanitarium, although Dr. Ludlum had made her an unusual offer. "Dr. Ludlum had a wonderful house," she recalled. "And he said, 'I'll make it into a wonderful studio for you, and you could live here.' You know, like van Gogh." (The third floor of the house was a garrettlike room with large windows, and it's possible that Neel occasionally painted there. And Dr. Ludlum, as mentioned above, had previously allowed patients to live with him.)

Although by today's standards, such unorthodox behavior as a psychiatrist hugging his patient, especially outside the clinical setting, and suggesting that she essentially live in his home would be considered so inappropriate as to bar him from practice, this was the 1930s, and the current (overused) term "sexual harassment" had not yet been coined, nor were the rules regarding doctor/patient relationships so rigidly observed.

According to Dixon, "I never saw him hugging patients in my presence.

I do know he hugged my mother now and again. I know he was flirtatious with her. She was a tall, blond, good-looking lady, but it was never a problem. She worked there for thirty years. He was a very caring person in whom people had a lot of confidence."

Dixon recalls being taken to his laboratory when Dr. Ludlum performed a fluoroscopy on her mother, who was found to have a malignant stomach tumor. (Years later, she learned that Dr. Ludlum, who paid for the operation to remove the tumor, told her mother that the hospital had told him she was four months pregnant at the time.) Still, it would have been unusual to begin with for a patient to be in the doctor's private home, says Dixon. "That means he must have taken her on a walk from the Towers down a long driveway, across the bridge, and into his home. If she had agreed to live there, she would have been alone a lot of the time, since he was often in Philadelphia," she adds.

Dr. Ludlum had a spotless record and was considered eminent in his field. Indeed, when he died, he received numerous tributes from his colleagues. There is nothing to suggest that anything untoward occurred between patient and doctor.

But according to Neel's account, she asked to be released from the asylum shortly after he suggested she stay on a more permanent basis. Perhaps Dr. Ludlum's close personal interest in her was becoming oppressive.

Dixon says that on at least one occasion she had seen Dr. Ludlum put his arm around her mother, and that a beautiful young supervisor named Marion, who came to work at the Gladwyne Colony and who befriended her, ultimately left because she was made uncomfortable by his familiar behavior. It is possible that Neel felt the same way.

Writes Brand of Dr. Revlin, the psychoanalyst in *The Outward Room*:

> Ever since he had known her, he had taken more than a routine interest. "Case," that was it at first. Then professional pride, generosity? She had to admit there was generosity. A long and difficult analysis. Yet the feeling she had towards him was not in this. Doubt. How did she feel? Lately, at each talk with him—She knew he was kind, open with her, but he kept her at times from fully understanding certain things about herself, that was it— she felt that she had never found out completely all that he knew, that he was leading her up to something. . . .
>
> "Is there any other reason why you'd be happier outside?"
> "No." "You're sure? Be honest." She hesitated. "Yes," she said.

"To have escaped me, could that be it?" She felt her face flushing. "Yes."

". . . I think you know we're reaching a kind of—that we are coming towards something. Perhaps what you are going to tell me is the same as what I am going to tell you."

In this excerpt, it is Dr. Revlin's probing questions the patient wishes to escape (leading up to his indicating that she has an Oedipal complex regarding her father, who is significantly "weaker" than her mother, who "orders him around") rather than any romantic advances, but it captures an unease that Neel herself may have experienced.

Neel attributed her wish to leave to not wanting to be part of a special group. "I have always had a perfect horror of being in a little group apart from the main group, in fact I never went to Woodstock or any of these artists' colonies because I thought there was a certain sappiness." She told her family she was "well enough to come home." Dr. Ludlum agreed. In September 1931, Neel left the Gladwyne Colony. In later years, she never referred to Dr. Ludlum with anything but respect and admiration.

CHAPTER ELEVEN

Next Stop, Greenwich Village

The three strands that weave the core of Neel's sensibility as a painter were now in place: Cuba had permanently activated her radicalism; her devastating experiences in the mental hospitals and at Gladwyne Colony had given her a profound, firsthand knowledge of psychological vulnerability and breakdown; and the Depression had reinforced her innate sense of social conscience. Her inclusion in the WPA easel program, which she joined in 1935 (she had joined the Public Works Art Project, or PWAP, in 1933), would forge these separate threads into Neel's signature style.

And, if Neel weren't already to the manner born, her several years in the Village completed her transformation from a still somewhat provincial artist into a full-fledged member of Bohemia. It was also at this time that she was introduced to Marxism, and in 1935 she joined the Communist Party, becoming a long-term member. Finally, this key period also marked Neel's first serious art foray in New York. In 1932–1933, she participated in half a dozen shows, including her memorable debut in the first Washington Square Outdoor Art Exhibit.

*   *   *

When Neel left the Gladwyne Colony in September 1931, she returned, as always, to Colwyn—childless, penniless, and with no immediate plans. Her only certainty was her consuming need to paint. The Washington Square studio she had shared with Ethel Ashton and Rhoda Medary, which had provided an erstwhile refuge in past years, was no longer available. Rhoda had recently married and moved, and Ethel had rented a new studio.

A poem at the time reflects her sense of ennui and despair, what she called her "great renunciation." "Now I know I'll never be strong enough mentally or physically to put the things I see and feel in any concrete form. They'll just be grey and yellow shadows in my skull," she wrote. During this fallow period, Neel actually forced herself to sew a complicated linen outfit, complete with gores and scallops, which she "wore for years." It is almost as if she made the suit as a form of penance, a sort of haircloth shirt.

Neel remained at loose ends until she got a call in the early winter from Nadya Olyanova, her fascinating old cohort from the Village. Nadya was now living with her husband, a Norwegian named Egil Hoye, in a house they had rented in Stockton, New Jersey. She invited Alice to join them. Neel stayed with the couple on and off for several months that winter.

Nadya was a graphologist who would later attain international renown. According to her great-nephew, Victorio, a flamenco dancer, who had a brief incestuous affair with her when he was twenty-one and she was a recent widow in her early sixties, "She was kind of like a spider with a fly in her web. She was a wild woman. There was something about her that was dark and tenebrous. Her sexuality was kind of decadent." Of her relationship with Neel, he recalled, "Nadya said that all Alice did was paint penises. She called her 'Malice Neel.'"

Many years later, Olyanova analyzed Neel's handwriting and included the analysis in her second book, *Handwriting Tells* (1969). The left-handed artist had penmanship that veered to the right, indicating, Olyanova said, "her preoccupation with people."

> Described in *Arts* magazine as probably of the greatest portrait-
> ists of our day, Alice Neel has all the signs in her handwriting to
> bear this out. She has the compulsive drive of the creative artist,
> as shown in her long t bars, some of them with hooks on the end,
> and a vivid imagination, disclosed in the t bars consistently above
> the stem, which derives from her childhood world of fantasy . . .
> her insights are keener than average, and she paints the souls of
> humans. . . . Her curiosity is insatiable.

Born in Kiev in 1900, Olyanova, according to Neel, was originally named Edna Meisner, although Victorio says her name was Ethel Neidish. She studied with Alfred Adler in the early 1930s and by the mid-30s had a weekly radio show on WOR. Her intense dark looks are aptly captured in the painting and watercolors Neel did of her at the time, including the disturbing *Degenerate Madonna*, 1930. As Neel herself put it, "She represented Decadence to me." She would realize this dark vision in several other pieces, including *Nadya and the Wolf*, painted in 1931, *Nadya and Nona*, and *Nadya Nude*, both painted in 1933.

Still, the house in Stockton was a hub of social activity, with a regular flow of Nadya and Egil's friends, some of them New York artists. For the first time in over a year, Neel began to feel like her old self, to "return to real life." Neel's travails had provided her with ample material—not just for painting but for transforming some of her worst experiences into compelling anecdotes for an admiring audience, many of whom were men. (This would become a lifelong skill.) Among the visitors was a sailor named Kenneth Doolittle, with red hair and a sly "Mephistophelian" aspect, at least as depicted in a watercolor Neel made at the time. He looks even more devilish in a 1931 oil portrait; seated, with a walking stick, he is dressed in a suit and tie, fedora hat, brown overcoat, his narrow, masklike white face sporting a bristling red mustache, his eyes piercing.

"He was very clever," she told Hills. "He played a banjo and sang interesting workers' songs, such as 'Old Rock Candy Mountain.' He had been a Wobbly and traveled across the country." Or, as Neel described him to Munro, "an addict, but an interesting fellow." Neel's mother did not approve of her association with Doolittle, and chastised her: "Why don't you go stay with your sister in Teaneck, instead of out there with that dirty old sailor?"

But Neel's relationship with Doolittle continued to develop during "the dead of winter," and by early 1932 they moved together back to New York City, to the heart of the West Village, a flat in a carriage house at 33½ Cornelia Street, where Neel would live with him until December 1934. The four-story rear building overlooked a small yard. The entrance was a small door in a brick wall, marked "33," right next to an old-fashioned blacksmith's shop.

"I lived with a sailor, a rather interesting chap who played the guitar and sang and was rather nice except that he liked dope. He had a coffee can full of opium. I didn't dare smoke opium since I had just had this nervous breakdown, but they smoked opium at my apartment. This chap and Kenneth Fearing became so elegant and refined under the influence of opium," Neel told Nemser.

Neel's depiction of Doolittle, both verbally and on canvas, is an arch and dismissive, if seductive, caricature. But according to those who knew him later, the real-life man was more appealing, both physically and intellectually. And politically, he and Neel were completely aligned. They were both committed Communists, and they both regularly picketed in demonstrations. (It was through Doolittle that Neel first met many Party members.) During the McCarthy years, they both drew the attention of the FBI, although Doolittle was actually blacklisted as a result of his union activities and CPUSA membership.

Pictures of Kenneth Doolittle in his early twenties in Hollywood, where he tried for a short time to become an actor, show a handsome young man with rakish blond sideburns and an almost James Deanish look. (He even had a bit part in a Lon Chaney film.) Always a dandified dresser, with an elegant gait, he was clearly what his friend Stanley Maron describes as "the kind of guy that women would go for." He sported a rose tattoo on his left shoulder.

When he moved with Neel to Cornelia Street, Doolittle was twenty-nine and Neel, just out of the sanitarium, was thirty-two. Perhaps at the time, Doolittle was the brash, volatile fellow frequently described by Neel, a sensualist who lived the Bohemian life, indulged in drugs with his literary cronies, and became wildly jealous when Neel received male attention. But by the time he married and became a father, a little less than decade later, he had, according to his family, completely reformed and become a dedicated parent and loyal labor organizer.

Kenneth Waldron Doolittle was born in Schenectady, New York, in 1903. When he was four or five, his father, Van Ness Doolittle, who taught elementary school and at one point was a letter carrier, died of consumption, and his mother, Anna Waldron, placed him in a local home for children, the Troy Male Catholic Orphanage. Van Ness, also an orphan, was descended from English religious dissidents who had settled in America in the 1600s.

Anna had a hard time making ends meet, and worked picking hops in the fields, which was not considered a particularly respectable job for women at that time. During the summers, young Kenneth would join his mother on his uncle Clarence's farm, where, like the other family members, he would be put to work.

When he was about ten or eleven, Anna remarried. Her new husband was an African-American man named William Bryant, whom she had met during a summer job as a waitress at a Lake Lucerne resort, where he was a chef. Bryant worked as a Pullman porter on the railroad, and he also played piano. As soon as they were married, he insisted that they bring Kenneth home.

Recalls Doolittle's son, Tom, "They picked him up at orphanage and went straight to the train station and then they all took a steamboat, the Hudson dayliner, from Albany to New York City." At first they lived in Harlem. But the racism the misegenated family encountered soon forced them to move to an all-black community in Jersey City.

Doolittle had a sister from his mother's first marriage, Norma, who lived with their aunt, Cora. Doolittle lived with his mother, Bryant, and their two sons, his half brothers, Jack and Bill. He was quite close to William Bryant, whom he called "Pop," but the interracial family had to keep moving, and Doolittle only completed school through sixth grade.

Doolittle's early years sound like something out of Joseph Conrad. When he was fourteen, his mother died in the great Spanish flu epidemic. At sixteen, he went to sea, after an unpleasant incident on his uncle Clarence's farm. Doolittle was introduced to Marxism during his very first shipboard experience. As his son Tom recounts the story, the shipmate had brought him onboard to meet the captain. "Before he could say a word, he was punched to the deck by the captain, who said he wanted 'to show you who is master of this vessel,' emphatically making it clear that 'the law is my fist.' A fellow sailor offered him a lovingly wrapped book, suggesting he consider it his bible. The book was Karl Marx's *Das Kapital*."

Doolittle, an autodidact and voracious reader, became an engaged social activist for the rest of his life. Indeed, he and his wife, Mary, whom he met while unionizing an upstate New York shoe factory, Endicott and Johnson, later helped organize the 1199 Hospital Workers Union, in which he served as a delegate.

True to his strong antifascist convictions, Doolittle volunteered to fight in the Spanish Civil War, where he served in the famous Abraham Lincoln Brigade, and was one of the last men to return to America. (Neel, in one of her few flattering remarks about him, conceded his heroism.)

Doolittle spent ten days behind fascist lines. After being wounded by shrapnel in the Gandra retreat, he finally managed to make it across the Ebro River at night, by floating on a raft that he had fashioned out of reeds. He was pulled from the river on September 9, 1938, and was placed in a hospital in Barcelona, where his wounds became infected. He then had an allergic reaction to the horse serum given to him in a tetanus shot. He remained in the hospital from September 1938 through January 1939. According to his military papers, he was released with full disability:

> Sir Antonio Cordon Garcia, Vice Secretary of the Land Army of the Department of National Defense and through delegated authority, Sir Jose Ernesto Vidal, major-in-chief of the Technical Secretariat of the Vice Secretariat, I certify that Doolittle, Kenneth, who has belonged to the company of the battalion of the 15th brigade in the rank of soldier, having combated under the Govern-

ment of the Republic has been certified as totally disabled by the inspector of health of this Land Army due to wounds received in combat with the enemy on the 8th day of September of the year 1938. On being given passport to his country on this date, the government of the Republic makes known its gratitude to the aforementioned soldier for the work he has done in favor of the liberties of the Spanish people. Being also ascribed the benefits of a pension designated for the disabled of the second war of the Spanish independence and this is Barcelona 29 of November, of 1938.

Over the years, Doolittle kept in touch with fellow veterans, and his daughters recall him singing the song "Vive la Quinze Brigade," with its jaunty chorus, "Rumbala, rumbala, rumbala!" Says his oldest daughter, Karla Buch, "He had a great bass voice and he could really sing that nicely." Doolittle treasured his trove of military memorabilia, and kept his archive of medals, papers, and correspondence, which is still intact, in a trusty metal box.

By all accounts, Doolittle was a charismatic character: erudite, a bit macho, full of moxie, and fond of sayings. He told Stanley Maron that Neel had had "a heart as big as an apartment, which she wore on her sleeve." But he also said that she was "prey to the monkeys," meaning that she was promiscuous. His wife, Mary, bore a noticeable physical resemblance to Neel, with long, light hair and a full-bodied figure. According to Karla, "They were a similar type. He liked a full-chested woman, curvy. He used to talk about Alice Neel, what beautiful hair she had. He said he loved strawberry-blond hair, and that was the one feature I knew that she had. He also talked about her features—that they were retroussé. He always liked that kind of a look on a woman."

He and Mary had three children, Karla (named after Karl Marx), Tom (after Thomas Paine), and Sarah (after Sarah Roosevelt). He later told his children that he didn't marry Neel because he didn't think he could depend on her, that he feared she was unstable and would not be a reliable person to have children with. "He wanted to have a family, family was a big thing for him," said his daughter Sarah Eisenberg. "He didn't trust her stability and loyalty. He felt that it was not a safe thing to have kids with her." (Ironically, Mary, who suffered severe postpartum depression after the birth of her third child, Sarah, was institutionalized for a year, and remained a depressive the rest of her life.) But Doolittle's evolution into a staunch family man was several years after the Cornelia Street days, where,

from 1932 to 1934, he and Neel lived what he later called the "original
Bohemian" life.

*   *   *

It seems inevitable that Neel's life would include a sojourn in the Village,
which could have been tailor-made for her antiauthoritarian sensibility.
Even its streets refused to conform to Manhattan's standard numbered
grid. The Village wasn't always home to artists. Originally called Green
Village because of its forests and meadows, it occupied a portion of lower
Manhattan, just south of what became Fourteenth Street in 1811—when
Manhattan first imposed its grid system—and north of Houston Street,
and spanning from Third Avenue on the East Side to as far west as the
Hudson River. A smallpox epidemic had caused a major migration from
the southern tip of Manhattan into the "Village," by now called Greenwich
after an estate built by an "early privateer." Then, as now, its central landmark was Washington Square Park, with its famous arch, which started
out as a potter's field and was used for hangings as late as 1822.

By the mid-1850s, the north end of the park had gone upscale, lined with
beautiful town houses, most of which still stand. (These provided a picturesque setting for the 1880 novella *Washington Square*, by Henry James,
who was born nearby.) South of the square were the more downscale
Irish, Italian, and black neighborhoods—and most of the famous cafés,
taverns, and speakeasys.

Although it had already firmly established itself as a cultural epicenter
by 1912, Greenwich Village was unofficially anointed New York's (and possibly America's) capital of Bohemia on January 23, 1917, when Gertrude
Drick, a young painting student of John Sloan, arranged a hodgepodge
insurrection that included Sloan himself, Marcel Duchamp, and the actors
Forrest Mann, Betty Turner, and Charles Ellis.

Armed with a picnic, Chinese lanterns, cap guns, and balloons, they
climbed to the top of Washington Square arch and declared the secession
of Greenwich Village from the rest of New York City, as "a free and independent republic." They even signed a parchment formalized by a "Great
Seal of the Village." The declaration, read by Gertrude, was an early piece
of performance art: She repeated the word "whereas" ad nauseum. Sloan
memorialized the event in his etching *Arch Conspirators*.

The Village stood for virtually everything that was antiestablishment—
from its politics to its sexual mores to its various and fecund forms of art.
But even by 1917, it was also a self-conscious tourist destination, and at
times a caricature of itself. Still, when Edna St. Vincent Millay (who would

soon become as famous for her sexual exploits and drug habits as her poetry), moved to Waverly Place in 1918, she quickly met Theodore Dreiser,
Malcolm Cowley, and Hart Crane, and, of course, John Sloan.

By the time Neel arrived, fourteen years later, the Village's Bohemian
golden age had peaked. Its famous early days, when Mabel Dodge first
hosted her celebrated salon at 23 Fifth Avenue, Max Eastman founded *The
Masses*, and the Provincetown Players was first established by Jig Cook
and Eugene O'Neill, were long since over. But the Village remained the hub
of New York's cultural community. Everyone lived there, from Raphael and
Moses Soyer, with whom Neel became friendly, to Sinclair Lewis, Ford
Madox Ford, and Moss Hart. (In his book, *Exile's Return*, published in
1934, Malcolm Cowley stated his mandate for those who found their way to
the Village: "Each man, each woman's purpose in life is to express himself,
to realize his full individuality through creative work. . . .")

As Ross Wetzsteon puts it in his preface to *Republic of Dreams: Greenwich Village: The American Bohemia, 1910–1960*, "Many major movements in American intellectual history began or were nurtured in the
Village—socialism, feminism, pacifism, gay liberation, Marxism, Freudian-
ism, avant-garde fiction and poetry and theater, cubism, abstract expressionism, the anti-war movement and the counterculture of the sixties. And nearly
every major American writer and artist lived in the Village at one time or
another."

Wetzsteon's list includes nearly two pages of novelists, poets, intellec-
tuals, and artists—from Louisa May Alcott to Jack London to Thomas
Pynchon to Norman Mailer to Edgar Allan Poe, Walt Whitman, Conrad
Aiken, Wallace Stevens, and Allen Ginsberg. And although the Abstract
Expressionists are the Village's storied painters, Albert Pinkham Ryder,
Winslow Homer, and Diego Rivera also lived there. Add to that list
Alice Neel.

Prohibition ended shortly after Neel arrived in the Village, and the neighborhood was full of Bohemian cafés and bars that were finally allowed to
sell alcohol legally after a hiatus of four dry years. From Neel's apartment
on Cornelia Street, between West Fourth and Bleecker, it was an easy walk
to the Jefferson, a twenty-four-hour diner at the junction of Sixth Avenue,
Greenwich Avenue, and Eighth Street, or to the sidewalk café at the Brevoort
Hotel on Fifth Avenue and Eighth Street, a popular meeting place for Village radicals.

There was the Belmar, the Jericho Tavern, the Village Square Bar &
Grill, Goody's, and the Rochambeau. There was also Alice McCollister's,

an old-fashioned Village restaurant on Eighth Street, and Stewart's Cafeteria at Sheridan Square, which, according to the legendary Joe Gould, whom Neel painted in 1933, was "the most popular late-at-night Bohemian hangout in the Village." (Although according to Gould, the "Bohemian" talk by the mid-thirties had changed from sex and art to Lenin and Trotsky.) There was Aunt Clemmy's, on Ninth Street near University Place, and the Minetta Tavern. Of course, Neel probably didn't frequent these places to eat: Like many of the other impoverished Village artists, she depended on a program of "one free meal a day" organized by "some screwball." Gould refers to having just such a meal at the Fair on 103 West Third Street.

Although Doolittle was not himself an artist per se (he did amateur street photography and he also helped Neel stretch canvases), he knew everyone in the neighborhood—which was virtually crawling with painters, poets, and eccentric characters, including Gould, of whom Neel made one of her most famous portraits, branding for all time the tiny self-described author of the "Oral History of the World" as a man with multiple organs. As Gould himself wrote in his unpublished essay, "My Life," "In February, Alice Neel did a portrait of me and a nude, which was grotesque, to say the least. It was not really a nude because I insisted on a cigarette holder, but she endowed me with three penises." (She also did an elegant pencil drawing of him, fully clothed in an uncharacteristic suit and tie, and another small clothed painting of him.)

Gould later called the nude painting "an underground masterpiece," predicting that someday it would hang in the Whitney (where, in fact, it hung during her 2000 retrospective) or the Metropolitan. *Joe Gould* has also, literally, been well hung at the Tate, where it remains on loan. In it, Gould, with a devilish sparkle in his eyes, sits on a stool, his three! prominent penises like so many Russian onion-shaped domes, his name and the date of the painting enblazoned between his legs. On either side of the übernude oral historian, his body, from the waist down, is repeated as a framing motif. He's clearly uncircumcised in both of these half-nudes. (Neel said this was an advertisement against circumcision.) In one hand, he is clutching the cigarette holder (also, of course, phallic). Neel sometimes humorously referred to the painting as "Variations on an Old Theme on the Source of Russian Architecture," since she said his testicles looked like "St. Basil's upside down." As Malcolm Cowley later said on seeing the painting, "The trouble with you, Alice, is that you're not romantic."

Essentially homeless, Gould depended on his friends and the kindness of strangers, constantly begging alms for the "Joe Gould Fund" to support himself and his supposed historical opus. Neel helped him by altering some of his hand-me-down clothes and feeding him "spinach and vinegar." Gould's usual diet was a Depression special—"tomato soup"—made by pouring catsup into hot water, a habit that did not endear him to the local eateries that regularly gave him handouts.

As Neel wrote about Gould:

> "Ship ahoy Joe Gould." So would Joe Gould announce himself in the Village of 1932. Many would not open the door not wanting to be annoyed by this lost representative of a lost cause. His cause was man, or rather a man, a single individual human being, against all the things he considered stifled the feelings and expression of man. An American Don Quixote too far from the Middle Ages to have Don Quixote's grandeur. His own mental processes were tainted by the same frivolity he despised so much. On the stairs sometimes as he was leaving, he would declaim "workers of the world ignite arson and fire buggery you have nothing to lose but your Janes." He looked like Uncle Sam, and in 1933 I painted him, mainly because I had seen a painting of E. E. Cummings of Joe where he looked like Leon Trotsky. It is true there was something of Trotsky in the sharp little face and pointed beard, but also something fundamentally Yankee.

Neel quoted Gould as being fond of saying, "In the summer I'm a nudist and in the winter I'm a Buddhist, and I have delusions of grandeur. I think I'm Joe Gould."

Neel's last memory of Gould was at the Minetta Tavern. "'Why Joe,' I said, 'you remain so stable in the midst of such great change.' My companion smiled and said 'Well Joe, you see when she looks at you she thinks of a stable.' Joe put his head on one side, birdlike, blinked and said, 'Well, that's probably because she's to the manure born.'"

Gould's story would later be memorialized by Joseph Mitchell in two famous *New Yorker* pieces, "Professor Sea Gull" and "Joe Gould's Secret." Although Gould was notorious in the Village as the author of his perpetually in progress "Oral History of the World," Mitchell ultimately came to the conclusion that the book was apocryphal. All Gould ever wrote was a small number of essays about his own life, from his father's death to his own time at Harvard. A few of these pieces were in fact published in literary magazines of the time, in *Broom, Pagany*, Ezra Pound's *The Exiles*, and *The Dial*, but Gould's major activity was constantly and compulsively revising them, leaving numerous iterations scattered at the homes of his friends. (He left about half a dozen such pieces with his friend Millen Brand before the two became estranged.) Neel's portrait is thus a canny, though unconscious, metaphor for Gould's obsessively repetitive endeavors.

Wrote Mitchell of the portrait, which he saw many years later, "Anatomically, the painting was fanciful and grotesque, but not particularly shocking; except for the plethora of sexual organs, it was a strict and sober study of an undernourished middle-aged man. It was the expression on Gould's face that was shocking. . . ." Mitchell went on to describe Gould's "seagull" dance, which he would occasionally do at parties. "Quiet," he would cry out. "I'm doing a dance. It's a sacred dance. It's an Indian dance. It's the full-moon dance of the Chippewas." His eyes would glitter, his lower jaw would hang loose like a dog's in midsummer and he would pant like a dog, and on his face would come a leering, gleeful, mawkishly abandoned expression, half satanic and half silly. Miss Neel had caught this expression.

As Neel told Mitchell at the time, "I call it 'Joe Gould,' but I probably should call it 'A Portrait of an Exhibitionist.' I don't mean to say that Joe was an exhibitionist. I'm sure he wasn't, technically. Still, to be perfectly honest, years ago, watching him at parties, I used to have a feeling that there was an old exhibitionist shut up inside him and trying to get out, like a spider shut up in a bottle. Deep down inside him. A frightful old exhibitionist—the kind you see on the subway. And he didn't necessarily know it. That's why I painted him that way."

Neel later criticized Mitchell and his musings on Gould. She said he was a "cute, folksy writer" and that his account of Gould "had an O. Henry ending, it was so vulgar." She continued to believe in the existence of at least part of the "Oral History," pointing out to several interviewers that "Harvard just bought eleven chapters. It was not as big, neither was it one chapter. . . ."

Neel was in her element in the Village, with its society of peers, forging friendships with the writer Millen Brand and his wife, Pauline, who lived around the corner from her; the poet Kenneth Fearing; the flamboyantly homosexual critic Christopher Lazar; the writer Max White; and Sam Putnam, who wrote for the *Daily Worker* and was famous for translating *Don Quixote*. Putnam stayed in a spare bedroom at Cornelia Street for a while, and, according to Neel, was usually drunk, a "dipsomaniac." She thought of him as a "broken ruin."

Neel later referred to this crowd as "the Beat of those days," adding that her subjects of choice were the "neurotic, the mad and the miserable." As she wrote at one point, "Those were the days not far from the twenties when there was a tendency among Village intellectuals to laugh at oneself. Dalí was painting Freudian dreams and hungry folk would often not mention any real problems but would seem to be entirely concerned with the newest trends and the latest thought."

She was also friendly with the Soyer brothers, although not overly so. She may have been a bit rough for them, given their conventional and tight-knit domestic lives, and for her part, "I never palled around with them. They were never on the WPA, because they are Jewish and their people took care of them." (Neel was mistaken: in fact the Soyer brothers were on the WPA program.) Not only that, she felt they had an entirely different psychology. "I grew up in America, so I never would call myself an artist, but they grew up in Russia . . . so they were always proclaiming that they were artists." Neel knew Fanya Foss from the old days. And then there was Harold Rosenberg, who was a regular visitor to Neel's studio in the Village. (In fact, she claimed that she lent him two paintings so he could get onto the WPA.)

Neel would paint all of them, incorporating German Expressionism and Symbolist influences to create her own spin on the emerging genre of Social Realism. Her *Christopher Lazar*, 1932, shows the "queen of homosexuals" in several different guises, and reveals his penchant for "rough trade." Then there is her harrowing portrait of Putnam, done in 1933, complete with the dramatic jagged scar that bisected his forehead, and later her extraordinary portrait of Kenneth Fearing (1935).

And they, in turn, depicted her: Millen Brand in several novels (notably *The Outward Room*, 1937, and *Some Love, Some Hunger*, 1955, in which Neel is the graphic designer Rose Hallis); Kenneth Fearing in his 1946 noir classic, *The Big Clock*, which later became a movie starring Ray Milland (with Elsa Lancaster as the Neel character, a larger-than-life WPA painter); and Fanya Foss in her huge never-published roman à clef.

Brand and his wife often dropped in on Neel and Doolittle. In his 1934 journal, Brand noted, "Pauline and I were walking through the Village and rang Alice Neel's bell. The door clicked open when we reached the house, and Kenneth (Doolittle) met us and took us in. . . . 'How's Alice,' I said to Ken. 'All right,' he said. 'She's upstairs doing some typing, you know, for money.' [Brand crossed out his next sentence: "Anything to make a few dollars."] As Alice was busy, Ken didn't take us up."

Indeed, the house Neel lived in became the main setting of *The Outward Room*. The other people who lived there were a German artist named Dagmar Hammond and her daughter, Cooky, who sometimes slept in Neel's bed and was terrified of Joe Gould. "Joe Gould no come," she would say each morning, according to the October 2, 1934, entry in Brand's 1934 journal. (Dagmar and Cooky later acted in the stage adaptation of *The Outward Room*.)

Fanya Foss's depiction of Neel during these days was taken straight from life, and its transparency caused a rift in the friendship when Neel later discovered it. Foss's Alice is an artist named Kate, just out of the sanitarium and living in the Village with a sailor named Steve. She has an ex-husband back in Cuba called Ernesto, who has taken their daughter, Juanita, to Havana. Not much is left to the imagination, from Kate's fading beauty to her wry and scatological remarks. Foss described Kate as "plump, with thick legs and fat ankles that ended in her shoes like a pig's hoof. . . . She had come up fresh and blooming after a year in a sanatarium, and was it because she could make herself forget?"

She's introduced in the book at the Washington Square outdoor exhibit, anxiously overseeing her portraits. Foss lost no time establishing the Alice/Kate persona: "I must paint his picture some day, with his hands like wilted asparagus," Kate says to Rachel (the Foss alter ego). "That's just what he's afraid of. You do justice to your friends," Rachel replies. "What's the matter with my portraits," laughed Kate, "they look like the sitters don't they?" "Too much so, God help them. One doesn't like the unadulterated truth."

As for the Steve/Kenneth character, although pictures at the time show Doolittle as a trim figure with a mustache, Foss's Kate says of him, "Sometimes I have the illusion that his face is a rat's face. Those small sharp eyes and that long thin nose of his, always ferreting out news. . . . Still it's lucky I met him. Helped my cure. You know, I don't like to sleep alone."

Neel herself described him vividly in a poem:

> *In the beginning, when I loved him I used to notice*
> *The blood red pink rose on his shoulder*

Blue leaves and prickley [sic] *thorns*
The blue star on one arm
The horse-fly. . . .
I used to think his pointed face with tan trimmings
Looked carved in stone, chaste, wistful as his then sensitive
nostrils expanded out the cigarette smoke.
He looked oriental and Irish
Refined and plebian
Intellectual and bovine
The "Man with the hoe" of Millet
A thin-faced witty Irishman in a bowler hat
On Patty's day—a green shamrock in his buttonhole . . .

     *   *   *

The Washington Square outdoor market was a watershed event for Neel, transforming her life both artistically and personally. It was there that she met two key figures, the painter Joe Solman (an organizer of The Ten) and John Rothschild, who would become her lifelong companion and one of her strongest supporters.

The fair took place from May 28 to June 5, 1932, and was organized along the perimeter of the park. As *The New York Times* described it: "New York has just had its first open-air art show, staged in Washington Square by the artists of Greenwich Village. New to us, these outdoor exhibits are familiar sights in several European cities, and in Philadelphia. . . . Hard times have hit the artists of the Village; the outdoor sale was held to help them market their wares and perhaps to gain recognition for their talents."

A photograph of Neel at the time shows her in a peasant-style blouse, standing proudly in front of her paintings, which are hung on the park's wrought-iron fence. Among the works she showed were several disturbing depictions of motherhood: *Well Baby Clinic* and *Degenerate Madonna*, which the Catholic Church forced her to remove.

(She may have also shown *Symbols [Doll and Apple]*, 1932. This unusual canvas, done in a style reminiscent of Dalí and Kahlo, shows a naked female doll with an apple in its crotch, an apple in one hand, a large blood-red glove on the other, and a crucifix and palm fronds in the background. Some critics have seen it as Alice's version of a sacrificial Eve, a painful shrine to broken maternity or, as she herself put it, "All of this is humanity, really." Neel later called the painting "sexy.")

Joseph Solman was showing his works nearby. Solman, nine years Neel's junior, would found the group The Ten in December 1935, along

with Mark Rothko, Adolph Gottlieb, and six other now lesser-known artists, (despite their name, there were actually only nine of them). The Ten
was formed to oppose the hegemony within the art establishment (including the Whitney Museum) of American regional painting and such American scene painters as Grant Wood. They had their own brash, diverse style,
which included elements of Expressionism, Cubism, and early Abstract
Expressionism. "We didn't have much use for social art or regional art,"
said Solman. He also became the editor in chief of *Art Front* magazine, for
which Neel did some illustrations. Solman would become a champion of
Neel's work.

Recalled Solman of the first time he met Neel, "We each had space around
the park on the iron fences to hang our pictures, and I had five of my early
gouaches. She [Neel] was only a couple of steps from me. . . . So I saw this
stuff and I said, 'Gee, I kind of like those things you tackle, New York
scenes like I like to tackle, under the el and all that sort of stuff,' so we got
to talking and we got friendly. I remember being very impressed with a
picture of a young child, a daughter, I think, that died early in life. . . .
One was a very original picture of the Sixth Avenue el or one of those els. I
was impressed with the boldness with which she did them."

As for the impression made by Neel herself, "She was a little like a dairy
maid, a little plump, pink-cheeked, and so on, and very daring in her speech.
I don't mean that she used cusswords, but the way she described people
was incisive, sharp, and original—like her paintings, like her portraits.
She didn't damn with faint praise. She damned with exclamation marks.
I thought she was very funny. She looked to me like a dairy maid."

But she didn't act like one. "I remember she was friendly with a good-
looking sexy blonde and took her down to the village on Eighth Street and
introduced her to people. Whether that woman was a semiprostitute or
something, I'm not saying she pimped for her. But I had the impression.
She introduced me to her, but I didn't know her name or who she was. But
she was very aggressive."

Recalled Herman Rose, who also met Neel around this time: "She liked
guys. And she went for me. I think she had a crush on me. I wouldn't say
she was pretty; she was beautiful. And she was very—I don't know how to
say it. She threw herself around openly. . . . She was a free spirit even compared to today. There were not many women like her. . . . Well, she was
like an Isadora Duncan in our period. The thing I do remember about her
was her painting. It was very bold and very beautiful and just like her character, really."

One day, as Neel peddled her artistic wares by the park, a well-dressed man approached her and enthusiastically praised her work, particularly *Well Baby Clinic*. It was John Rothschild, who, despite his last name, was not related to the wealthy Rothschilds. He ran a progressive travel agency called the Open Road. Rothschild had studied at Harvard, and his outward demeanor could not have been more different from that of Neel's lover, Doolittle. He was bald, smoked a pipe, and had distinctly upper-class manners. (Foss creates a satirical portrait of him with her fictional character Dr. Lehvy, who has an exaggerated Harvard accent and purchases the Neel character's portrait of Kenneth/Steve.) Rothschild would play a major personal role in Neel's future life. But for the moment he presented himself primarily as an ardent supporter of her work and followed up this first meeting by inviting her and Doolittle up to his apartment for drinks.

This was a pivotal period for Neel. Her career moved forward in incremental steps. She participated in the second Washington Square Outdoor Art Exhibit in mid-November and presumably attended the November 20 tea and discussion at the Jumble Shop on Waverly Place, to which she and the other artists were invited by Juliana Force, the director of the Whitney Museum.

In January 1933, Solman helped get her into a small show at a bookstore in the Village, the International Book and Art Shop on Eighth Street, run by Joseph Kling. Three of Neel's works, along with some by Solman and Max Sivak, were exhibited for a month in the back room of the store. And she received her first American review, in the *Philadelphia Inquirer*, on March 10, 1933, when J. B. Neumann included some of her work at the Mellon Galleries in Philadelphia in the show, "Living Art: American, French, German, Italian, Mexican, and Russian Artists." "Among the Americans," wrote the *Inquirer* critic, "there is a one-time Philadelphian, Alice Neel, whose 'Red Houses' and 'Snow' reveal the possession of interpretive gifts out of the ordinary. There is nothing 'pretty' about these pictures, but they have substance and honesty."

She was also mentioned in Philadelphia's *Public Ledger* on March 19. "Of the American canvases one prefers 'Inciting the Mob,' by Elsie Driggs, with its Daumier feeling and its more modern color sense. . . . 'Snow' by Alice Neel (one-time Philadelphian) for its bleak, glaring economy. . . ." That same month, she showed work in an exhibit organized by the Artists' Aid Committee. She had a second show organized by them that October.

On December 26, 1933, Neel enrolled in the Public Works of Art (PWAP) Project, the precursor to the WPA. "I started doing revolutionary paintings when I lived on Cornelia Street," she said. Although Neel meant the term in a political sense, her subject matter and its treatment could also be highly provocative: whether it was the Gould multiple-penis painting, which could not be shown in public for decades, or her *Desperate Madonna*, which the Catholic Church found so offensive. Neel's work would be strongly shaped by the Roosevelt years, the Depression, and its antidote, the WPA.

CHAPTER TWELVE

The Easel Project

*"I came to Greenwich Village New York in 1932, and people were
starving. Then Roosevelt was elected. He said, 'one third of a nation is
ill-housed, ill-clothed and ill-fed,'"*

—NEEL INTERVIEW WITH JUDITH ZILZCER, OCTOBER 27, 1981

The Depression was at its peak in the winter of 1932, just before Franklin
Delano Roosevelt entered the White House. Neel had been in the Village
almost a year. The unemployment record was estimated as close to 25
percent—some fifteen million people. It was common to see entire families evicted from their homes. Bernarda Bryson, Ben Shahn's widow and
the former president of the Artists' Union, interviewed at one hundred,
vividly recalled seeing a family who had just been evicted standing with
their three children in front of their house in Columbus, Ohio. "People
couldn't pay their rent and the landlord threw them out. You'd see the
movers moving their furniture out of their house. There were things you
saw in those days that stayed with you forever."

The economic crisis hit cities particularly hard, and urban landscapes
became harsh studies in human suffering. In New York City, as in most of
the cities and towns across America, there were breadlines, unemployment
lines, and an eruption of "Hoovervilles"—cardboard and tin shanty-
towns—that sprouted up in parks and mushroomed under bridges.

When Neel attended a meeting at the Russell Sage Foundation (which later
resulted in her painting *Investigation of Poverty at the Russell Sage Foundation*, 1933), she heard pitiful stories, including that of a woman who lived
with her seven children under an overturned automobile. As artist Will Barnet recollects, "When I first came to New York, breadlines were blocks long.
Everybody lost everything. So you were faced already with a social situation,
and if you couldn't respond to that, you had to be a jackass of some kind."

By early 1933, ten thousand artists were out of work. Special relief agencies had been set up for artists as early as late 1932, when Audrey McMahon and Frances Pollak ran the Emergency Relief Bureau (ERB). (McMahon, the subject of an unkind 1940 portrait by Neel, who called her "arsenic and old face", later became the regional director of the New York department of the WPA.) But it was the establishment of the Public Works of Art Project in late 1933 that had an immediate impact on New York artists.

The PWAP, as it was known, was run by Whitney Museum director Juliana Force. Although it only lasted seven months, from December of 1933 to June of 1934, it gave employment to some 3,749 artists, including Neel, who enrolled in the program the day after Christmas, 1933. (Neel was so happy to have been signed up, she came home and painted *Snow on Cornelia Street*.) It produced some 15,633 works of art. In its intention and operation, the PWAP was the precursor to one of the greatest creations of FDR's New Deal, the Works Progress Administration's Federal Art Project (FAP), which began in August of 1935 and ended in 1943. According to her employment records, Neel was on the project from September 1930 through August 1942, making her one of the first artists on the WPA, and one of the very last to get off it.

Neel's years in the Village were thus literally framed by the far-reaching political and social consequences of Roosevelt's revolutionary New Deal. Although she often compared her humanism to that of Balzac, to a great extent, Neel was in spirit, sense, and sensibility what one might call a "Roosevelt" painter. Her worldview was shaped by that era and she practiced nearly from the inception of her New York art career the genre that came to be known—and was ultimately marginalized—as Social Realism, a politically conscious movement characterized by its unsparing representation of social injustice and its hero worship of the poor and working class. Major artists of the movement at the time included Ben Shahn, Moses Soyer, Jack Levine, Reginald Marsh, Philip Evergood, William Gropper, and Isabel Bishop.

Unlike many of its proponents, however, Neel went on to evolve her own transcendent style. Still, there are certain constants in her work that date back to the WPA period: She never veered from the brutally penetrating gaze she had developed during these Depression years, and her subjects were a deliberately diverse and democratic mix, including many fellow travelers in the labor and civil rights movements. The era's influence on Neel's work extends past content to form: Neel took a page from WPA photographers like Walker Evans and Dorothea Lange and focused on searingly honest portraits of common people.

Volumes have been written on the organization, execution, and impact of the Works Progress Administration, which had four cultural departments: Art, Music, Theatre, and Writers'. The Art Project alone had eight divisions: murals, easel painting, photography, sculpture, graphics, posters, motion pictures, and the Index of American Design. A phenomenal amount of art was produced by some five thousand artists. According to Hills, the WPA/FAP artists produced some 2,500 murals, over 17,000 sculptures, 108,000 paintings, 200,000 prints and 2 million silk-screen posters. In New York City, artists painted 200 murals in public buildings, and produced more than 12,000 paintings, 2,000 sculptures, and some 75,000 graphics works.

Like its famous murals, the WPA had an epic sweep. It is almost impossible to overestimate the wide-ranging effect of this unprecedented national patronage system on the lives and works of the artists involved—and on the cities in which they lived. Memorable murals materialized (many still extant) on public buildings across the country, from post offices to schools to hospitals. For the first time on a national scale, and during a period of devastating hardship, American artists were government-funded, with little or no restriction, in terms of content, imposed on the art they produced. (There was, however, a prohibition against nudes.)

Neel nonetheless ran afoul of authorities on several occasions—including breaking the rule against nudes. According to Neel, an "even better" version of her three-level painting, *Synthesis in New York*, 1933, had actually been destroyed by the WPA's office because it included a nude figure, and was thus considered too "indecent" for public display.

The benefits of the program weren't just financial. For the first time, art, rather than being considered an intellectual luxury, was being classified as wage-earning work. Artists of the time felt an uplifting sense of unity: Artists of the world unite! They were imbued by a sometimes naïve idealism about the possibility of social change.

As Raphael Soyer recalled in a catalog for the 1983 exhibit "Social Concern and Urban Realism: American Painting of the 1930s," curated by Patricia Hills, "Those were economically difficult times, but spiritually exhilarating. We looked forward to a bright future. We had hopes that when Fascism and Nazism would be overcome, we would have a good world."

In organizing so many individual artists, from realists to modernists, under one umbrella, the WPA also served as a network that introduced artists and their work to each other, creating a burgeoning community that outlived the program itself. The WPA, in effect, sowed the seeds of the New York art world.

Says Barnet, who worked as a printmaker on the project, doing work for Orozco, the Soyers, and Gropper, among others, "The WPA was perhaps the institution, if you want to call it that, that made America the center of the art world. Because the artists for the first time were able to paint pictures and be paid for them. Now, there had never been a period like that in the history of America. That meant that they could develop as artists, and not necessarily social artists, either, because the murals and the different things that were done had other aspects to them that were beyond just social statements. They were aesthetic statements. The modernist movement was flourishing, too. So the WPA was perhaps the key to the history of American art, in terms of giving it a tremendous push into being the universal center of the art world for many, many years to come."

Neel was on the easel project. This included artists of every ilk, from American Scene and regional painters to the early Jackson Pollock, Mark Rothko, Ad Reinhardt, and Milton Avery, to those Social Realists more frequently associated with the WPA, such as Philip Evergood, Joseph Solman, Herman Rose, Robert Gwathmey, and Jack Levine.

As Neel recalled in 1981 in an interview with historian Judith Zilczer, "I was on the New Deal Art Projects for ten years, from 1933 to 1943. It was in the spring of 1933 when I was first employed by the Public Works of Art Project, and the following spring I was transferred to the WPA. I worked as an easel painter, and I don't know how I would have eaten without this support. . . . The WPA was marvelous. It was a great creative venture."

In a statement made for a catalog of a 1977 show of WPA art at Parsons School of Design, Neel went into more detail. After receiving a letter from the Whitney Museum:

> I was interviewed by a young man who asked me, "How would you like to paint for $30 a week? This was fabulous as most of the artists had nothing in those days and in fact there were free lunches for artists in the Village. Also, $30 in those days was $120 or more now. This was the PWAP, which preceded the WPA and paid a little more. Also one was chosen for the quality of one's work, and not for necessity. However, about four or five months later it was turned into the WPA, which paid $26.88 a week. . . . For this sum I turned in a painting 23 by 30 inches every six weeks. The country was in a severe depression and there was no

welfare or social security so people just starved and were evicted from their homes. All the artists were on the Project. If there had been no such cultural projects there might well have been a revolution.

As Barnet puts it simply, "It was a Godsend because things were so bad, so terrible."

By September 1935, according to her WPA employment records, Neel was making $103.40 per month. Artists on the easel project delivered their finished works to the supervisor at 110 King Street in Manhattan. Neel's work on the artists' projects included *Investigation of Poverty at the Russell Sage Foundation*, a stark, somber painting in which a jury of grim-faced men and two concerned stenographers listen to the weeping plea of a witness, and the somewhat similarly composed *Magistrate's Court*, painted in 1936.

Streetscapes included the other rendition of *Synthesis of New York—The Great Depression*, 1933, which she never turned in. The painting, which is similar to another painting of that period, *Ninth Avenue El*, 1935, evokes a desolate urban landscape bisected by an elevated train track; the few people have skull-like heads. Oddly, winged clothing mannequins circle the sun like crazed angels. Like her earlier image of her family, it is a multileveled cross section.

Although she wasn't turning in the nudes she painted at the time (such as the suggestive *Nadya and Nona* and *Nadya Nude*, both done in 1933), Neel still managed to provoke the authorities, when in 1939 she turned in a painting, *Fish Market, Upper Park Avenue*, which her supervisor, John Lonergan, decided showed too much blood. "Not everyone likes blood as much as you do," he remarked. Neel dutifully removed the excess blood, but some years later, when Neel discovered some of her WPA work being sold for canvas, she bought back the painting (a scene reenacted by Elsa Lancaster in the movie of Fearing's *The Big Clock*) and restored the blood.

Godsend or not, the WPA was also a bureaucracy, and the artists often found themselves at odds with its red tape, fueling a level of activism perhaps not seen again until the sixties. The period gave birth to a number of influential artists' organizations and publications. The first was the John Reed Club, an artists' offshoot of the American Communist Party; formed in 1929 and named after John Reed, a founder of the American Communist Party and the author of *Ten Days That Shook the World*. John Reed

Clubs soon proliferated in other cities. Neel attended the John Reed Club at least once. In September 1933, a band of artists formed the Emergency Work Bureau Artists' Group to represent themselves in WPA matters ranging from conditions at work sites to artists being unfairly taken off the WPA payroll. By May 1934, this group had become the Artists' Union.

Neel, who was a member of the Union, benefited from just such an intervention when Joseph Solman complained on her behalf. Some of Neel's pictures weren't being allocated (turned in and designated for public buildings) because, according to Solman, "her pictures were a little difficult. She turned a person inside out. If she did a portrait of you, you wouldn't recognize yourself, what she would do with you. She would almost disembowel you, so I was afraid to pose for her. I never did pose for her."

Recalled Solman, who was the chairman of the grievance committee of the Artists' Union, "If we had a grievance, we would tell our grievance to the head of the project on Fifty-seventh Street, where they had a WPA office. So one time, because she didn't allocate many pictures, they were going to demote her to teaching. I liked her work, so I went down and met with the people who were hiring, firing, and changing your allocation, and I met with the woman who was the boss of the New York project, Audrey McMahon, and I made a speech for Alice's work. They put a couple of her paintings up, and they said, 'We can't allocate her work.' 'Allocate her work? She's too original!' I said. And I made a whole speech for her, about how much I liked her work and how original she was, and so they left her on [the easel project]. I saved her from being pushed over to the teaching division. Of course she knew it, how good she was, how original she was. She was too original to be allocated. In other words, I saved her from that fate. I am very proud of it. She was very appreciative of the fact that I did it."

The Artists' Union and later the American Artists' Congress also organized picket lines and strikes. Audrey McMahon recalled one revealing anecdote. "Some picket lines had their amusing sides. One of these took place in front of the colonel's office at Columbus Avenue, while I was in conference with him. The colonel was furious, denouncing 'those Reds,' and boiled down to the street with me, to give them a piece of his mind. There we encountered not one, but two picket lines, and they were not at all in harmony with each other. . . . The Artists' Union pickets (the colonel's 'Reds') carried signs reading 'McMahon employs armed guards,' which I was dismissing with a laugh, when the colonel assured me it was true. He had placed a guard complete with revolver outside of my office, and I had known nothing about it! Signs carried by the other picketers said 'Send McMahon back to Moscow—McMahon is a Red.' The colonel was delighted."

Solman recollected an incident that may have been the famous 219 sitdown strike at the WPA headquarters, in response to people being taken off the payroll. "About 200 or more artists were picketing the offices used by the project administration on the corner of 57th street and Lexington Avenue. The occasion was a new round of firings. The police wagons appeared and this time they decided on a wholesale arrest, no one excluded. When we arrived at the 17th precinct, James Lechay led the long line of prisoners. 'Your name,' bellowed an officer, pad and pencil in hand. Picasso came the firm response; that was a sufficient cue. Cezanne, Da Vinci and Peter Breughel followed. When my companion Martin Craig gave the name of his idol James Joyce the policeman muttered, 'How did an Irishman like you get mixed up with this mob.' "

Even the names of Michaelangelo and van Gogh did not bring a spark of recognition. "We could not call home, but the police were willing to phone messages for us," he recalled. "Thus, when my wife, who along with Craig's wife was expecting us for dinner, answered the phone, she heard this pronouncement; 'James Joyce and George Seurat have been arrested and are at the 17th precinct.' " Neel was an active participant in such protests. She recalled marching in Artists' Union demonstrations, including a strike against May's department store.

The artists didn't just march when they wanted to discuss, question, or protest; they published. The magazine *Art Front* was a joint publication of the Artists' Union and the Artists' Committee of Action. Started up in 1934, it soon became a must-read for its stringent political and critical essays, written by some of the most famous writers and artists of the time, including Harold Rosenberg, Meyer Schapiro, Louis Lozowick, Philip Evergood, Jacob Kainen, Joseph Solman, and Moses Soyer. Solman became its editor, and once again his friendship with Neel paid off. "I got one of Alice Neel's pictures in one of the issues of *Art Front*. That little girl that I described. I always remember that picture."

In 1935, another important artists' organization was initiated, the American Artists' Congress, conceived as an outgrowth of the John Reed Club, which had just folded. A "call" to the new congress was published in the "Revolutionary Art" issue of *New Masses* (October 1, 1935) and signed by over three hundred artists. The call resulted in the First American Artists' Congress, a historic public conference held from February 14 to 16, 1936,

at Town Hall in New York City. Its major themes were antiwar and antifas-
cism. It was attended by thousands, who heard luminaries like Lewis
Mumford, Stuart Davis, Meyer Schapiro, José Clemente Orozco, and David
Alfaro Siqueiros speak.

Recalls Barnet, "It was crowded with about five hundred artists. And
the artists were from every kind of movement—academic, realist, modernist, surrealist, you name it. Every visual culture was there. And this meeting was hilarious, because Orozco was the speaker and he didn't speak very
well. His English was broken and not very clear. But when he finished
speaking, there was such applause, for so long. I've never been to a meeting
where the audience was so taken. It was just overwhelming. It was just a
feeling of unity among artists as to what was going on in the world. That
moment was sort of like a golden age of unity between artists and the politics of the time." (Barnet also recalls Siqueiros dropping a revolver on the
floor, to stunned silence.)

The papers from the conference, which included such sessions as "The
Artist in Society," "Problems of the American Artist," and "Economic
Problems of the Artist," were later published and soon sold out. Such issues were also hotly debated by Social Realists and modernists alike at the
Artists' Union, which often held its exhibitions at the legendary ACA Gallery, founded by Herman Baron in 1932, which continues to show politically concerned art to this day. The arguments would continue long afterward
at Stewart's Cafeteria, at nearby Sheridan Square.

The conflict between figurative and abstract art would eventually evolve
into a full-fledged aesthetic battle, but for the moment, Social Realism was
the dominant movement. Social Realism was influenced in part by the
Mexican muralists Diego Rivera, José Clement Orozco, and David Alfaro
Siqueiros, all of whom visited New York during this period. Indeed, Bernarda Bryson (who later became the president of the Artists' Union) met
her future husband, Ben Shahn (then married to another woman), in 1932,
when he was working as an assistant for Rivera on the infamous mural entitled *Man at the Crossroads Looking with Uncertainty but with Hope
and High Vision to the Choosing of a Course Leading to a New and Better
Future*, for Rockefeller Center, which included an oversize image of the
head of Lenin. (Rivera later became a Trotskyite.)

When Rockefeller asked Rivera to eliminate the head, the artist refused, and the mural was later removed—but not without considerable
protest, including a demonstration. The furor resulted in the creation of
the Artists' Committee for Action. Wrote Rivera in his 1932 essay, "The

Revolutionary Spirit in Modern Art," "The social struggle is the richest, the most intense and the most plastic subject which an artist can choose." And, although he also reviled "easel painting" as a luxury beyond the proletariat, he could have been speaking for Neel and her stated goal of capturing the Zeitgeist when he wrote, "The artist is a direct product of life. He is an apparatus born to be the receptor, the condenser, the transmitter and the reflector of the aspirations, the desires and hopes of his ages."

Although Social Realism is the school of art most associated with the WPA years, as were the Mexican muralists, the modernists, most of whom were budding Abstract Expressionists, were also honing their skills at this time. Jackson Pollock studied with Siqueiros in the 1930s, and Willem de Kooning worked for the mural division of the WPA, headed by Burgoyne Diller—which included a "decorative mural" (read: abstract) for a low-income-housing project in Williamsburg, where Stuart Davis was also commissioned. Stuart Davis's abstract mural for radio station WNYC, now owned by the Metropolitan Museum of Art, and Gorky's stunning *Modern Aviation* panels for the Administration Building at Newark Airport, most of which were unfortunately destroyed in the 1940s, were considered some of the best murals to come out of the WPA. In 1937, twenty-eight abstract artists formed the American Abstract Artists group. The hegemony of Social Realism over abstract art would be dramatically reversed several decades later, with the advent of the 1950s and the triumph of Abstract Expressionism.

*   *   *

Meanwhile, a specter was haunting the intelligentsia and the art world—the specter of Communism. A convergence of historic events, from the failure of capitalism and the rise of organized labor, to the success of the WPA, America's grandest-scale socialist experiment ever—combined with a heightened awareness of activities in the Soviet Union, contributed to making Marxism the prevalent political movement in the circles frequented by Neel. Its impact on the art world would be immediate and lasting.

In his 2002 book, *Artists of the Left*, Andrew Hemingway states that, starting with the Great Depression, the Party was "the most powerful ideological and organizational force on the left for more than two decades, and a major influence in American culture." Hemingway traces the CPUSA (Communist Party USA) from the publication of the *New Masses* in 1926—an effort to reincarnate the radical publication *The Masses*, which had folded in 1917—to the 1950s and the onset of McCarthyism.

The Communist Party "were the only ones who made sense of the Depression," said Annette Rubinstein, a well-known teacher and Marxist critic who ran a literary salon in the 1940s and 50s. The Party was also instrumental in organizing the American Artists' Congress in 1936.

Marxist ideas, promulgated by prominent thinkers from Walter Benjamin to Meyer Schapiro, permeated the cultural and critical milieu. Benjamin's seminal essay, "The Work of Art in the Age of Mechanical Reproduction" which was published in 1935, argued for a theory of art that, instead of using modern modes of art production—particularly film and photography—to "process data in the Fascist sense," would be "useful for the formulation of revolutionary demands in the politics of art." At the first American Artists' Congress in 1936, Meyer Schapiro read his paper, "The Social Bases of Art," which proclaimed that the artist must renounce individualism and align himself with the proletariat.

The Congress itself had come about in response to the onset of the Communist-initiated Popular Front period. The Party's new policy, instituted in 1935, terminated the John Reed Clubs and urged Leftist organizations to unilaterally join forces against Fascism, forming a "Popular Front."

Writes Serge Guilbaut in *How New York Stole the Idea of Modern Art:* "The Popular Front was a haven in which progressive intellectuals [including of course, artists] could work in a communal spirit and even achieve a certain prestige (the ranks of the CPUSA swelled from 12,000 in 1929 to 100,000 in 1939)."

Guilbaut quotes Daniel Aaron's *Writers on the Left,* who describes the Popular Front's broadbased appeal:

> Now you could be for every kind of social reform, for the Soviet Union, for the Communist Party, for proletarian Literature—for everything and anything that was at one time radical, rebellious, subversive, revolutionary and downright quixotic—and in doing so you were on the side of all the political angels of the day . . . on the side of all oppressed colonial peoples in the world. In short, this is the only period in all the world's history when you could be at one and the same time an *ardent revolutionary* and an *arch-conservative* backed by the governments of the United States *and* the Soviet Union.

"It was very heady, the period," says Charles Keller. "It was very exciting because a lot was going on. The Depression was still on. Roosevelt was the president and he instituted some pretty radical laws, which the Communists were instrumental in pushing for: Unemployment insurance, Social Security, and all of these various assistance programs, including the WPA art program, were causes that the Communist Party was very involved in, with demonstrations and with educating the public."

Joseph Solman recalled an extraordinary May Day parade to Union Square. "My God, those days! They had a May Day march down Fifth Avenue. The cooks who belonged to the restaurant union, they had these cook hats. You'd see about a hundred of them with those hats on leading the parade of the restaurant workers. It was fantastic to see. I wish I had painted it."

In *Art and Politics in the 1930s: Modernism, Marxism,* and *Americanism,* Susan Noyes Platt argues that the art of the period, particularly Social Realism, should be viewed not as a self-contained art-historical genre, but as virtually inseparable from the period's politics. After Hitler's rise to power in 1933, "the Communists broadened their goals to invite all artists to join in a Popular Front against war and Fascism," she writes, continuing:

> I believe that Communism was of central importance in the decade, and that politics and activism were its determining characteristic. More than that, I feel that characterizing the Thirties in terms of individual artists and styles, the traditional methodology of art history, eliminates the ideological forces and political arguments that shaped the art. This fact is most obvious in the case of Social Realism. Speaking of a Social Realist "style" separates the production of the art work from its complicated position within the Popular Front, the Communist Party and The New Deal.

Social Realism mirrored the New Deal itself. The artwork funded by the Works Progress Administration under the Roosevelt administration was intended to be "public work," work the public could relate to and that would be placed in public venues such as post offices, schools, and hospitals; hence the many street, factory, and strike scenes. It was an art form that reflected the economic conditions that created it. Its unique government patronage was the direct result of the Depression, and on the WPA program, the artists themselves became members of the very working class they were heroically depicting.

As Solman wrote, "The WPA artist . . . felt an inevitable alliance with the new surge of trade unionism for unskilled workers (CIO) sweeping the country . . . the heated discussions taking place everywhere concerning the New Deal, the welfare state, socialism, and communism in the Soviet Union . . . the artist became a self-esteemed citizen of his country, feeling his product was a viable commodity and beneficial to it."

As party and class lines blurred between the despised bourgeoisie, brought to its knees by the Depression, and the newly idealized proletariat, the Communist Party did its best to exploit this gaping chink in capitalist armor. A major ploy was to infiltrate and influence the trade organizations and unions that multiplied like rabbits. The artists' unions proved particularly fertile ground.

"Participation of the Communist Party in artists' organizations of the Depression, sometimes even from their beginning, need not be denied . . ." Lincoln Rothschild wrote in an essay in the anthology, *New Deal Art Projects*. Rothschild outlined some of the Party's activities, which included creating "fractions" within the organizations themselves.

Bryson, then head of the Artists' Union, recalled that it was basically taken over by Communists. "We had a meeting every Tuesday night. The meetings were very exciting, but you had to watch your step. Particularly as being the head of union, I had to watch and to be aware of what was going on. Once I saw that the Union was being kind of taken over by the Communist Party, which it really was, that was very painful. Because I was so idealistic at the point at which I joined the Artists' Union." Yet Bryson herself remained a Communist, attracted by "the potentialities of political theory and actuality."

Said Bryson of the Roosevelt years, "I think the word 'idealism' would fit in there pretty nicely, because I did consider the New Deal as the absolute apex of political potentiality in this country, and I thought that so long as we stood for what we believed in, we were doing the right thing." And what most people at the time believed in was a united front to fight Fascism.

Said Charles Keller, "The issues were very clear. One of the big lessons that the people on the WPA learned was cooperation. They worked collectively and they didn't compete with each other. They all moved forward as a body. The American Artists' Congress was an example of pulling together artists of various stripes. They never discussed style in the American Artists' Congress. They never discussed schools. They just said, 'We're here to be united, to be free, to be artists, by making sure that fascism doesn't take over.'"

But what seemed so appealing in theory proved far more problematic in practice, as is so often the case with political movements. While the intelligentsia initially embraced the ideology offered by the Communist Party in the guise of the Popular Front, its various members and factions reacted to the onslaught of actual historical events—from the Moscow Trials of the mid-thirties (often referred to as the "Show" Trials), during which many of Stalin's opponents were executed, to the 1939 invasion of Finland—in myriad and convoluted ways, with a major and insurmountable rift forming between the Trotskyites and Stalinites. What it boiled down to was how many atrocities could ultimately be sanctioned in the name of the movement.

"If the Communist system, as exemplified by the U.S.S.R., provided the most definitive economic alternative to the collapse of capitalism in 1929, it nonetheless was as unstable a model as capitalism itself," writes Pamela Allara, considerably understating the matter. She continues:

> After Hitler's rise to power in 1933, it appeared to be the political alternative to fascism, but its authority was undermined as early as 1934 by Stalin's purges of dissidents; by the end of the decade, the Nazi-Soviet Pact in August 1939, and the Russian invasion of Finland in November 1939 destroyed for many fellow travelers their faith in the Soviet system. Given the course of international politics, it is hardly surprising that the Communist Party USA was fraught with internal dissension, and that Marxist literary and artistic theorists in the United States could not provide a translation of changing Soviet policies appropriate to the vernacular of the American Milieu.

Many would-be "fellow travelers" found that they could not support a political system that perpetrated the same heinous crimes as fascism, whether that system took the Stalinist or the Trotskyite line. And the defeat of the Spanish Republic did nothing to strengthen the core belief in Communism.

The changing political climate had an immediate impact on art, as the tide gradually began turning against proletarian art, synonymous with Social Realism, which was now increasingly seen as "propaganda." *Partisan Review*, for instance, began arguing once again in favor of the individual over the masses, setting the stage, at least ideologically, for the advent of Abstract Expressionism. Explains Guilbaut: "The estrangement of the intellectual was the justification for his withdrawal from real politics, but it was also an explanation for his ability to rise above the mundane and reunite art and politics into a vision of a revolutionary culture. The alienated man became the radical man."

For Neel, the personal and the political had always intersected. During the 1930s, she was surrounded by Communists, from her Wobbly boyfriend, Doolittle, to her friend Sam Putnam. Her mentor and close friend, Mike Gold was one of the country's foremost supporters of Socialism. He was the editor of *The Liberator*, for which he also wrote a column, and was one of the founders of *The New Masses* (where he served as editor-in-chief). An impassioned promoter of proletarianism, Gold earned a reputation as the "Dean of U.S. Proletarian literature," after the 1930 publication of *Jews Without Money*, his fictionalized account of growing up on the Lower East Side.

Although she said she went to the John Reed Club only once, Neel joined the Party in 1935 and continued to espouse Party politics the rest of her life, even financing her own show in the Soviet Union in 1981. True to form, she greatly admired Fidel Castro, writing a letter to him in the 1960s, and doing both an etching and a drawing (now owned by Jenny Holzer) of Che Guevara. To this day, a poster of Lenin remains on the kitchen wall of the apartment her family still maintains at 107th Street.

Says her friend, the writer Phillip Bonosky, "Everybody was a Communist then. The art movements were very sharply influenced by Marxism, and it was right down her alley. The Marxists were the only ones who recognized her. She was not only an artist, but a woman, not only a woman but a lost woman; she was an unmarried woman and she had everything against her. But she found a home there. She found people who respected her."

Marxism provided not only what seemed to be a viable ideology, but, observed Hemingway, "One of the key things is the way that the Communist cultural movement, with its various organizations, functioned partly as a social nexus for these people."

For Neel, that meant not only being a member of the Artists' Union in the 1930s but, later, taking classes with V. J. Jerome and Howard Selsam at the Jefferson School of Social Science in the 1940s and 1950s. She also accompanied *Masses & Mainstream* editor Charles Humboldt to Annette Rubinstein's literary salon—the Writers and Critics Group, where she met such contemporary luminaries as Howard Fast.

Jerome, like Bonosky, would become a lifelong friend. As Neel told Hills, "V. J. Jerome was a very good friend of mine. I took many courses at the Jefferson School with Jerome and Howard Selsam. He loved me, V. J. Jerome, he'd come up to Harlem to see me. He especially loved my mother, who looked rather upperclass English, you know." Neel even made a special visit to see him after he was released from Lewisburg Federal Penitentiary, where he had been incarcerated for violating the Smith Act.

According to Hemingway, Neel "is representative of that type of woman, artist, and intellectual who gravitated to the Communist Party because— whatever its limitations—it offered the most sustained critique available of class, racial and sexual inequality."

Given Neel's intellectual leanings and political beliefs, it would have been an anomaly had she not joined the Party. What set her somewhat apart from other fellow travelers is that, although she said she quit twice, she remained a more or less lifelong member of the Party, even if she didn't adhere to—or admire—its bureaucracy. (Rubinstein, for instance, left the Party in the early 1950s, in solidarity with Congressman Vito Marcantonio, for whom she worked as an aide, and his support of the American Labor Party.)

Neel continued to do work for *Masses & Mainstream*, to illustrate Bonosky's books, and to paint Party leaders well past the 1950s. (Some of these portraits were featured in her 1951 show at New Playwrights Theater, organized by Mike Gold, who also wrote the introductory essay.)

"She remained absolutely kind of stalwart in her public support of Communism in the USSR," says Hemingway. "I think the commitment was very, very deeply felt. As an artist she was thoroughly committed already to a particular notion of personal freedom, and her attraction to communism was partly that she thought that that model of personal freedom would be realized for everyone through it. However misguided and blinkered that might seem to us now, for many people at the time, it was very much a reality. I think that there are certain ways in which probably her involvement with the Party encouraged Neel's focus on the portrait, which is where her real gift was. I don't care for those so-called social pictures, the pictures of demonstrations. I think they are very weak. In a sense I think the Communist movement helped to license and give weight to the value she put on the genre [of portraiture.]"

Her work directly reflected her beliefs, from her 1930s portraits of Sam Putnam, Max White, and Pat Whalen to her protest paintings *Nazis Murder Jews*, and *Uneeda Biscuit Strike* to her later "proletarian" portraits of the 1940s and 1950s and well beyond: the union leader Bill McKie, 1953; the journalist Art Shields, 1950; the American Communist party chairman Gus Hall, painted in 1980; her friend and mentor, Mike Gold, 1952; and another Party leader, Mother Bloor (Ella Reeve) depicted, saintlike, in her casket (*The Death of Mother Bloor*, circa 1951).

What Allara refers to as Neel's "proletarian portrait gallery" reveals its Marxist influence in two ways. Neel's portraits of Party leaders, like much

Social Realist art, are visually similar to Soviet propaganda posters of the 1920s and 1930s, particularly those featuring heroic figures, whether laborers or leaders. (Ironically, when Neel finally had a show in the Soviet Union in 1981, Gus Hall objected to having his portrait shown because he felt it personally lionized him.)

And her use of portraiture to iconize ordinary individuals—her Spanish Harlem neighbors, for instance—is very much in the spirit of Marxist thinking. Wrote Gold in his essay "Towards Proletarian Art," "The masses are still primitive and clean and artists must turn to them for strength again." As Gerald Meyer observed in his article, "Alice Neel: The Painter and Her Politics," "Neel represented an exemplar par excellence of the Party's hopes for a socially conscious contemporary artist. Her paintings were accessible art, which depicted ordinary people of all races and ethnic backgrounds in ways that captured and dignified their actual state of being."

Her Communist Party involvement would earn her a thick FBI file, opened in 1951 and not closed until nearly a decade later, and two memorable visits from FBI agents. As Neel herself explained it, "I joined the Party several times. But you know what? I'm not a bureaucrat, by nature. I hate bureaucrats. You know what I am, I'm an *anarchic humanist*."

Charles Keller, who was the art editor of *New Masses* from 1945 to 1948, believed Neel's work itself expressed her commitment to Marxist ideology more than being a good CPUSA member would have. "She never showed any particular discipline or devotion to the [Party] work, but she showed her views through her work, which I think was more important in many respects then the Jimmy Higgins's work distributing leaflets and organizing meetings. Both had to be done."

CHAPTER THIRTEEN

A Man's a Man for All That

"You know I picked husbands not like regular women do, but like men pick wives, because they are beautiful or amusing or charming or something. Never because they can pay the rent."

—ALICE NEEL TO ELEANOR MUNRO

If Neel had a tragic flaw, it was her judgment when it came to men. Or perhaps it comes with the artistic territory: arguably Lee Krasner, Elaine de Kooning, and even Frida Kahlo, who gave as good as she got, suffered well-known tragedies and humiliations at the hands of their mates. The major difference is that they were married to geniuses. Although several of Neel's lovers were her intellectual equals, and Enríquez went on to become a major twentieth-century Cuban painter, it is Neel who left the enduring mark.

Neel had just met a man, Rothschild, who would become her staunch champion for the rest of her life. But she was not free of her present entanglement with Doolittle. And, by her own account, she had never fully gotten over Carlos Enríquez. "When I lived with him [Doolittle] I still loved Carlos," she told Patti Goldstein in 1979. "Doolittle would say, 'Well, we three are all very happy living together.'" Or, as she told Barbaralee Diamonstein, "I really didn't care too much about either of them [Doolittle or Rothschild]. I was still more or less in love with the Cuban."

In early 1934, Neel got her chance to reunite with her husband (she and Carlos would never officially divorce) and the father of her first two children. Several major events in Enríquez's life had converged, and, according to Neel, a real rapprochement was in the offing. (Carlos even sent his sisters as would-be emissaries.) But Neel seemed to suffer a repeat of the emotional paralysis she had displayed when she first married Carlos, and was initially unable to leave Colwyn and travel with him to Havana. Once

again, she froze. At a key moment in her life, Neel was completely passive
and unable to take any conclusive action. She offered no real explanation—to
Carlos, her interviewers, and perhaps even to herself.

"Now that year, in 1934, Carlos wanted to come back," Neel told Hills.
"His mother had died [on August 30, 1933]. He had just returned from
Paris [it was actually Spain] and he wanted to come back. But here I was. I
was living with Kenneth Doolittle, pursued by John Rothschild, and I was
too stupid to see that I could have had Carlos back. I really would have
liked to have Carlos back, but I couldn't."

Fanya Foss offered a hint of what she observed of Neel's attitude in her
novel. In an early chapter, Ernesto (Carlos) writes to Kate (Neel) that he is
living in a garage behind his father's house, which he has converted into a
painting studio, and that the baby is well. "Kate's face lost her freshness
and roundess when she spoke of Ernesto," wrote Foss. "The hell with them.
I've learned to do as they do, use everything in your work and forget
ethics. . . . No maudlin sentimentality for me. If he can forget, so can I,
I'm not going to spend my life moping and pining."

Neel took the path of least resistance and stayed with Doolittle. Her life
in the Village went on, although she was taken off the PWAP payroll in
April because she failed to deliver an appropriate painting, even after several attempts. She had been given the assignment to paint a picture of "one
of the phases of New York City life." At first, she didn't turn in anything at
all, then she brought in a painting that appeared to have been painted
"the night before, on brand new canvas . . . that did not represent more
than one day's work."

Perhaps Neel's fantasies about the possibility of rejoining Carlos were
distracting her, or maybe the attentions of John Rothschild were encroaching on her relationship with Doolittle. The picture Foss painted in her
novel of life in the cold-water flat at Cornelia Street is a sordid one, with
Neel and Doolittle constantly bickering over everything from money (they
were living on home relief and later on Neel's PWAP and WPA payments)
to food to Neel's acquaintanceship with other men. She managed to temporarily escape these mounting conflicts that summer when she rented a
small cottage in Belmar, New Jersey, with her parents.

Neel had, by default, rejected Carlos's overtures. But if Carlos did not
reenter her life, her daughter Isabetta did, at least for a few months. Neel
managed to have a brief reunion with Isabetta, a beautiful child now nearly
six years old, when Isabetta visited Belmar from Havana. It was the first
time she had seen her young daughter since she was an infant.

Neel seized the rare moment to paint her infamous nude portrait of Isabetta, a painting that she would later feel compelled to re-create. Up until
this point, Neel, who would become famous for her nudes, particularly pregnant mothers, had limited them to images of her friends and lovers—Nadya,
Nona, and Rhoda; Kenneth Doolittle and soon John Rothschild. This was
the first—but hardly the last—time she would strip a family member bare.

It is a truly remarkable artistic gesture, as if she were laying claim to the
very essence of the girl, who at this time was her only child; inculcating her
bond to Isabetta by rendering her in paint. (A self-referential and ephem-
eral bond compared to that formed between hands-on parents and their
progeny—the reflex of an artist, rather than that of a mother.)

And what must it have been like for Isabetta, who had had no contact
with her mother in four years, a long time in such a young life, to have
stood there, naked and vulnerable, as Neel focused her full attention on
her daughter in order to paint her. Perhaps that explains the strong—if not
defiant—look on her face. (One wonders if her father had ever had her pose
nude; his tame Isabetta portrait of the same year shows her in a sleeveless
dress, looking older than her years.)

It was clearly an important picture for Neel, since she made sure it was
photographed (there's even a picture of her and Doolittle standing with it,
Neel's arm casually draped over the top of the frame), not knowing it
would later be destroyed. And after its destruction, she repainted an almost exact replica of the original, if anything strengthening her daughter's
thrusting pose. (Neel also made one other image of Isabetta at the time,
capturing her in a more traditional and innocent attitude—hair in childish
pigtails, fully dressed, although, oddly, with the crotch of her underwear
exposed.)

The notorious painting has an uneasy, haunted resonance. Neel later
remarked to Hills in a rather offhand manner that at first galleries refused
to show it because it was "indecent;" and later they knowingly referred to
it as "Lolita." Even today, naked images of children (particularly created
by their own parents—think of Sally Mann) remain controversial. And the
photographs of nude little girls taken by Charles Dodgson, or the famously
suggestive paintings of Balthus, still evoke a certain queasiness.

These were the only paintings she had done of her daughter since she had
painted her from memory in 1930, shortly after Carlos took her to Havana.
Neel would never again paint Isabetta, whom she would only see two more
times during either of their lifetimes, and it is perhaps fitting that the nude
portrait she made of her daughter stands out as one of the most striking

images of her career. As Neel told Munro, "My second child . . . came back to see me when she was six. I made a magnificent painting of her—that I sold just before I got famous for a song to a chap that lived in Sweden. . . ."

That "chap," Jonathan Brand (who actually lived in Denmark), also owns the 1930 portrait of Isabetta, a rigid doll-like figure clutching a stuffed dog, the canvas a grid of ancient slash marks (courtesy of Kenneth Doolittle). As Neel told Brand in a 1981 interview, "That's emotion in its purest form." Of the nude painting, she said, "I love the 'Isabetta,' do you know why? Her elegance."

*   *   *

It's unclear whether Doolittle visited Belmar at all that summer, but Neel's relationship with him had been unraveling for months, and it didn't improve when she returned to Cornelia Street in September. Understandably, Doolittle couldn't tolerate Rothschild's attentive presence. As Neel described Doolittle to Barbaralee Diamonstein, "He was very jealous and possessive by nature. He was also an early drug addict. . . ." Or, as she told Henry R. Hope, "Doolittle was a real male chauvinist. He thought he owned me."

Neel did take some responsibility for being a coquette. "You know what the problem was? I was too good-looking. Too many men pursued me. I had this red-gold hair, I was clever, I liked people, and I liked being the life of the party. . . . So I had a completely double life. I was myself, but for social reasons I was that other person. In one way it was very useful to me. It made all the boys crazy about me."

For all Neel's strident independence, she seemed to have a high tolerance level when it came to her treatment from men. According to Solman, there were frequent tumultuous fights at Cornelia Street. And, at least as fictionalized in Foss's novel, the quarrels could be physically violent, with Doolittle striking Neel, and at one point smashing a fishbowl. (Allara describes the relationship as "decadent." She also describes Neel's rarely shown 1933 pencil drawing of a tormented and hunched-over Doolittle collapsing "under the influence of drug withdrawal" as "an early representation of drug addiction.") Neel told Jonathan Brand that in addition to cocaine, Doolittle had also used heroin, when he was working in Chicago, probably sometime in the 1920s.

Whatever the rising level of tension in the Neel/Doolittle domicile, or its causes, things reached a shocking conclusion that December. In later years, Neel gave only glancing accounts of her relationship with Doolittle, from its onset to its climax. But she repeated the story of its traumatic ending (with minor variations) in every interview, referring to it with unalloyed horror as a personal "holocaust." (Indeed, in one interview she segued right out of the loss of her work to the loss of Isabetta, referring to them both with the phrase "I've had such awful things happen," a telling association.)

As she described it to Munro, "Now in the meantime this guy that was pursuing me, John Rothschild, he got more arrogant in his pursuit. I had slept with him a few times already and he began to really pursue, and the sailor found out about it and destroyed all my work—got high on cocaine or something. Although they used to smoke cocaine in the apartment, Kenneth Fearing and Kenneth Doolittle . . . It was a holocaust. He burned all my clothes, all my paintings. Sixty of them, and three hundred drawings and watercolors. He burned up a fortune. I never recovered from that."

She embellished the story even further when she told Cindy Nemser that after she met a "well-to-do liberal, a Harvard man named John," Doolittle got jealous and "cut up all my work and my clothing. . . . He used a curved Turkish knife. I just got out of the house in time or I would have been murdered. It was frightful."

She gave a slightly different account to Hills: "In the winter of 1934, Kenneth Doolittle cut up and burned about sixty paintings and two hundred drawings and watercolors in our apartment at 33 Cornelia Street. Also, he burned my clothing. He had no right to do that. I don't think he would have done it if he hadn't been a dope addict. He had a coffee can full of opium that looked like tar off the street. . . . I had to run out of the apartment or I would have had my throat cut. This was a traumatic experience as he had destroyed a lot of my best work, things I had done before I ever knew he existed. It took me years to get over it. . . . They were also personal history."

Strangely, one of the few watercolors to survive the mass destruction was a portrait of Doolittle himself.

Doolittle told his friend Stanley Maron that he cut up all her paintings after she jilted him. "What am I supposed to do?" he told Maron he'd asked Neel. To which she'd supposedly replied, "Go to Spain and fight the fascists." Maron also says Doolittle "talked about using heroin—talked about injecting it."

A very different image of Doolittle emerges from the accounts of his children, and from Maron, who met him in the 1960s and considered him a mentor. Perhaps his experiences in the Abraham Lincoln Brigade had permanently changed him. Or he had rehabilitated his lifestyle in order to function as a married man and father.

According to Doolittle's children, he acknowledged to them that he had destroyed Neel's work, and expressed regret. As his younger daughter Sarah Eisenberg recalls, "He said 'I ripped up a bunch of her paintings. I was just so hurt.' He was devastated. He felt betrayed." Many years later, Doolittle even personally apologized to Neel.

His son, Tom, has a totally different take on the episode, which he says was, in fact, neither frenzied nor "drug-fueled." "My uncle Bill told me that this was not an act of rage. It was a very conscious thing. He felt extremely betrayed. He knew what was going on with Alice, and had already arranged for him and Bill to live in a new apartment. Two things happened to my father with women: He had been abandoned by his mother, and then he found this love, Alice. I don't remember him talking about any other women besides his mother and Alice."

Doolittle's children, moreover, adamantly refuse to believe that he ever threatened Neel with a knife. "It just does not seem possible in my father's makeup to injure a person. That's just so out of character," says Sarah. "It's just not the way he operated; objects might be injured, but not people. Not an animal, not a cat or dog." And he was, according to Sarah and Karla, "the opposite of a male chauvinist. His whole life, he fought against all forms of chauvinism and oppression."

They also reject the idea of Doolittle as a heavy drug user, or someone who ever injected heroin. "He said that he experimented when he was a sailor, here and there," says Sarah. "He was the kind of man who was very straitlaced at the time he was raising children, to the point where my aunt and mother said we were the only family in the neighborhood who didn't have a liquor cabinet." Adds Tom, "I always saw him as a sober person. He told me he used heroin once, when he was at port in Hamburg in the early 1920s, and that if he had stayed there, he would have had a problem. To my knowledge, he never did it again."

The destruction of so many years of work was a central tragedy of Neel's life. While she remained reticent about the death of Santillana and the loss of Isabetta, she never hesitated to launch into the Doolittle story, frequently reliving it for interviewers and lecture audiences. Perhaps it was simply easier to talk about than the profound earlier tragedies, which, after all, involved human life.

Fanya Foss expressed the profundity of this loss in her novel:

It was ironical that she who had hoarded the moments of her experiences should find not one remnant left. She who had hated to
lose even the smallest thing, had now nothing left to remind her
of what had once been alive and scintillating with light. Her dead
baby . . . No longer would she see in the drawing those dark liquid eyes of her child, who had eyes like her father. No longer
would she have the small picture of Ernesto . . . on the walls had
hung her memories, her life, which she had gloated over like a
miser over his few sad pennies. Her work had been a resurrection
of the past.

Neel fled Cornelia Street, never to return. "When I left Cornelia Street,
I left a life," she said. She wasn't on her own, however. She moved first into
a hotel room with John Rothschild and later to an apartment on East Sixtieth street that he had set up for her.

John would play a central role in the rest of her life, but her relationship
with him would not become a lasting romance.

Moving On

I cry and my tears are for no one
In a tropical city
speaking another language
To a little girl who is my daughter . . .

Do you see that man with a cap over his eyes
Walking under the light
He used to be my lover . . .

Those paintings torn and ripped
Those drawings burned
They are the work of Fifteen years.

—ALICE NEEL

In the wake of the "holocaust" created by Kenneth Doolittle, Neel turned to John Rothschild, who instantly came to her rescue. Once again, there is a far more complicated back story than what Neel later told interviewers. In fact, according to the Neel family, during this time she had gotten pregnant by Doolittle. She even alluded to it in a poem: "He used to love me and then a big white stomach came between us. He began to see me as a stomach."

Neel didn't want to bear Doolittle's child, although it seems unlikely she discussed it with him. Using money provided by John, she got an abortion. Says Richard, "Alice told me that the abortionist was a woman, and that when she asked her what the child's sex had been she wouldn't tell her."

Now that she was homeless, Rothschild first put Neel up in a hotel on West Forty-second Street, and then at Hotel Fourteen on East Sixtieth Street, which she described as "that swank hotel." "I lived there for several months. You see, he was the money man," Neel told Munro. She also called him her "super-aesthete."

Her infidelity with Rothschild may have triggered Doolittle's fury, but that in no way affected Neel's continuing attachment to a man who functioned, as one friend later put it, as her "Benefactor." A good part of Rothschild's appeal was his unflagging support of Neel's work and his access to the nicer things in life, either through his own money or that of his network of wealthy friends.

Nobody could have been more of a contrast to Kenneth Doolittle than Rothschild. If Doolittle was a street-savvy autodidact who had been brought up in an orphanage, Rothschild was a Harvard graduate from a distinguished Jewish family, with the breeding to prove it. He was extremely fastidious in his attire, manners, and personal hygiene. (Neel's first portrait of him, done in 1933, shows a refined-looking man in a suit and tie, eyes closed and chin resting delicately on his hand.) "A Harvard man par excellence," as Neel described him. "Upper class, Jewish."

His grandfather had emigrated from Germany in 1848 and established a dry-goods store in Flat Rock, New York. His father, Alonzo, was Abraham Lincoln's biographer, the author of *Lincoln, Master of Men*, published in 1906, and a posthumous book, *Honest Abe*. Along with his brother, Meyer, John's uncle, who became a trustee, he was an early member of the Society for Ethical Culture, joining in 1879, just three years after its founding. ("The society was a refuge for German Jews who were seeking to assimilate," explains Marc Bernstein, the society's archivist. The core of its belief system was ethics, rather than theology, and it functioned for some as Judaism without the Jewishness.) The two brothers also founded the American Gem and Pearl Company.

Alonzo also established a gazette called *Jewelers' Weekly*, and quickly made enough money from it to move his family to Cambridge, Massachusetts. There he enrolled at Harvard in the Lowell adult-education program, while his wife attended Radcliffe. After graduating, he became a Lincoln scholar. In 1915, when he was fifty-four, Alonzo drowned in a tragic swimming accident in Beaumont's Pond, in East Foxboro, leaving his widow with little or no money. Still, the fact that he was a Harvard alumnus made it easier for John when he applied there, entering the class of 1917 and graduating in 1921.

Although he had no wealth of his own, John had an innate knack for connecting with the wealthy. At Harvard, he had become friendly with George D. Pratt, Jr., nicknamed "Gid," who was two years his junior. When he graduated, Gid's mother, Mrs. George D. Pratt, of the Glen Cove Pratts, invited John out to their Long Island mansion and asked him to mentor Gid, giving him the financial means to do so. Thus the seeds of John's left-wing travel agency, the Open Road, were sowed.

John and Gid went to Europe and recruited about half a dozen student leaders from different countries and brought them to the United States, where they introduced them to student organizations at American colleges. By 1925, John Rothschild had created a nonprofit organization called the Open Road, which arranged traveling seminars and exchange programs. Through the Open Road, he organized one of the first student groups to go to Germany and the Soviet Union.

In the meantime, John married Alice Edgerton, whom he met on a commune called April Farms, in Massachusetts. A Quaker, she was disowned for marrying John, a non-Quaker, in 1924. In 1925, she gave birth to a son, Joel. In 1926, the family traveled to Paris with one of the early Open Road tours. By 1927, John had divorced Alice, who was teaching at the Hessian Hills School in Croton, New York, where Joel and his mother lived in the house of Max Eastman (founder of *The Masses*).

According to Joel, his parents marriage split up over John's relationship with a painter named Erica Feist, whom he met on one of his Open Road trips to Germany. Erica became John's second wife, and they had a son named Amos, Joel's half brother. While John kept an apartment in New York, Erica, Joel, and Amos lived in Pennsylvania. Erica Feist was the sister-in-law of Charles Garland, the founder of April Farms, and she also worked as a teacher at an experimental commune/school called the Living House.

It was indirectly through Erica, who had introduced her to John, that Neel came into contact with Muriel Gardiner, the famous author and psychoanalyst, who was active in the anti-Nazi movement and is said to have been the model for Lillian Hellman's character Julia in her book *Pentimento*. Gardiner would later become Neel's patron, giving her an annual stipend.

John was still married to Erica when he met Alice in 1932. At first, it seems, the relationship was one of refined escort/patron and needy Bohemian. Alice acknowledged she slept with John early on, but she was never really romantically interested in him, although his friendship and companionship were of major importance to her. The dynamic of her relationship with John was a replay of her youthful involvement with Jim, the architect she had brazenly "dangled" for money, during the period when she first met Carlos. John, however, seems to have had, at least initially, hope of something more.

Neel lived at the hotel on East Sixtieth Street for several months in early 1935, eventually leaving there to stay with various friends in the Village. Her extraordinary pencil and crayon drawing *Joie de Vivre* depicts Alice and John the week after she left Cornelia Street, while they were staying at the Forty-second Street hotel. A satire of their sexual high jinks, John, naked except for one sock and one shoe, is dancing with three sows, one of whom, clearly meant to be Alice, is being penetrated by the other shoe. Beneath the frolicking man and his porcine playmates, two dancing wine bottles kiss. The parodic and pseudopornographic style of this piece and the two companion watercolors made in the next few months are unlike anything else Neel would ever do, combining shocking candor with biting satire.

Although he continued to spend time with Neel, John still had a family in Pennsylvania. But by the summer of 1935, he had officially left his wife and children, possibly with the intention of eventually marrying Neel. The two spent that summer in Spring Lake, on the New Jersey shore, in a little house that she later purchased, with assistance from her parents and John. The red-shingle, one-story cottage was near the railroad station, with its rhythmic sound of steam engines. It had a small yard with beautiful trees, including weeping willows and a maple. A small screened porch led to a living room with a fireplace, and a kitchen with a dining nook and an old coal stove. (In later years, it was a wonderful summer haven for her two young sons.) Although she eventually got a larger place in Spring Lake, Neel would return to this seaside retreat for the rest of her life.

It was an interesting interlude, and one that produced some singular work. It also seemed to crystallize Neel's relationship with John, shown in a 1935 portrait in a white suit and hat against the sea. The picture looks harmless enough, but to Neel it epitomized John's insipid core. "I painted him in a hat, that's when I decided to get rid of him. . . . I thought anybody that could take that much joy out of the hat and suit, there was something wrong with him. . . . He was utterly empty. He really had the makings of a voyeur in that way." Not surprisingly, Neel's pragmatic side won out. "But I didn't really get rid of him because he kept pursuing me and I had such a hard life that it was very nice to go to Longchamps or the Harvard club for dinner."

Even though some of her watercolors of their sexual life are compellingly erotic, Neel was not drawn to John in the way that she had been to Carlos or Kenneth, or that she would be to her next lover, José. Neel's choice in men was like a dark thread that ran through the fabric of her life.

While many artists opt for an anchor in a mate, Neel sought something else—drama or passion, or both. But she found John neither dangerous nor exciting.

Her watercolor *Alienation* shows John standing, naked except for his red slippers, hugging his arms to his chest, by the bed, where Neel reclines, possibly postcoitus. They are neither together nor apart. They are not touching each other, and John's crossed legs and arms create a posture of either defense or defeat. Neel later said of her piece, "It had nothing to do with sex. It was alienation. He had just left his wife and a couple of children."

Equally "alienated" is the unique bathroom scene, painted a little later, at an apartment where John was living with V. Henry Rothschild on Gramercy Park. In it, both Alice and John are urinating, Neel on the toilet, Rothschild into the sink. While Allara describes the scene as presex, with the couple relieving themselves so they won't be interrupted later, it could just as well be postsex, despite his erect penis. Neel, legs splayed, is either putting up or taking down her hair, while Rothschild, positioned over the sink, holds an object which could be a condom or a shell in the palm of one hand. The black-and-white-tiled floor, black base of the sink, and black bathtub mat provide a sharp counterpoint to the two pallid figures, both of whom, despite their intimate activities, look utterly forlorn.

In September 1935, Neel got onto the WPA's easel project, making $103.40 a month, according to her records, although she said it was $26.88 a week. Neel knew that at this point John assumed she would live with him. Indeed, Erica had even offered to fix up an apartment for her. But Neel got fed up with all the "chit and chat" about it. Now that she could afford it, she went out and found an apartment of her own, on West Seventeenth Street, for twenty-five dollars a month. As if to further prove her independence from John, Neel actually spent the weekend with Kenneth Doolittle, going on a "trek" with him and "hitchhiking up through Pennsylvania to visit some of his relatives, who were farmers in New England. . . . It was a *strange* trip. It was the end of the whole business."

As to why she would spend time with Doolittle after he had destroyed her work, Neel told Hills, "I couldn't change that easily." She was hardly oblivious to the impact of her behavior on John. "God that was a weird trip, and John while I was doing that, he was driving over to where I had an apartment on West Seventeenth Street every night to see if I had come back yet. John took an awful lot. But I realized later that that's what he liked, really."

The apartment on West Seventeenth Street was unheated, but once that amenity was supplied, Neel thoroughly enjoyed the place, which also served as her studio. John would often join her for dinner, and, according to Neel, particularly "loved to take care of the laundry." When Neel wouldn't let him live there with her, John moved just a few blocks away, to a beautiful apartment which he dutifully decorated. At first, Neel said she would move in with him, but when it became clear that she had no intention of doing so, he then moved into an "elegant apartment on Gramercy Park," belonging to a friend, V. Henry Rothschild (no relation), a lawyer.

Neel may have been tortured by the dichotomy of losing her independence to a domestic life. But she had no trouble painting the woes of the working class during the day and then going over to V. Henry Rothschild's apartment for dinner served by a private chef. "He had a Filipino cook, so I had my upper-class evening," Neel opined to Hills.

The Social Realist pieces she did during this period include *Longshoreman Returning Home from Work*; *West 17th Street*, with its funeral going on within an apartment that is "For Rent," while outside a vagrant is rummaging through a garbage can; the bleak-looking *Ninth Avenue El*; and *Magistrate's Court*, where Neel went with other members of the Artists' Union who had been picketing.

"I enjoyed the luxuries of the rich, but sympathized with the poor," Neel remarked. "I always loved the most wretched and the working class, but then I also loved the most effete and most elegant."

Rothschild also routinely took Neel out for upscale dinners. "One of the fascinations of him in the thirties was that everybody was starving and he used to take me to Longchamps and the Harvard Club, and they had very good meals, you know. . . . He was a great companion," she said, adding, "I once said to him: 'The only compatible life we have together is across the dinner table.'" Rothschild and Neel remained regular dinner companions for decades, through several other relationships on both sides. "He pursued me all his life. It was very strange. He liked aspiration more than realization," Neel said.

While Neel clearly enjoyed the material luxuries he offered, the primary thing that Rothschild gave her was support—both financial and emotional—for her work. "He was absolutely convinced of her stature as an artist, to begin with," says his son Joel. "He was fascinated by her work. This was a continuous leitmotif."

During these early days on the WPA, she also painted a series of impressive "proletarian" portraits. *Max White*, 1935, gives a glimpse of

Neel's future technique: Seated, he confronts the viewer with his straight-forward gaze, his large hands prominently spread on his knees. Two other paintings from that year are also vintage Neel: the remarkable *Kenneth Fearing*, which with its symbolist iconography—a bleeding skeleton in place of a heart, a tiny infant by his elbow (his wife had borne him a son the night before), characters from his poems in the foreground, and the el as background—is oddly reminiscent of Frida Kahlo's work. When Fearing saw the painting, he told Neel to "take that Fauntleroy out of my heart."

"The reason I put it there, Neel later explained, was that even though he wrote ironic poetry, I thought his heart bled for the grief of the world."

And then there is the heroic *Pat Whalen*, the waterfront organizer, painted with his huge clenched fists planted firmly on the June 16 issue of the *Daily Worker*. The Whalen portrait forcefully meshes Neel's political views with her unique skills as a portrait painter, foreshadowing much of her later work.

"When I painted Patty Whalen, I had just recently painted 'Joie de Vivre,' that one with the man with his penis waving. You know, I adjusted myself to different aspects of life. I loved to hit the depths and then at night to eat in the Harvard Club," Neel told Hills.

CHAPTER FIFTEEN

José and Spanish Harlem

Rothschild's relationship with Neel began as a classic case of unrequited love. As it evolved into a long-term but nonexclusive attachment, John at times acted masochistic, and Alice supplied the sadistic edge. In later years, John's son Joel often observed Neel verbally lashing out at John, perhaps because that was the only way she could tolerate his continuing generosity. (By this time, of course, John had had several other lovers, as had Neel.)

"I spent evening after evening in the presence of both of them, watching the way in which Alice almost defined herself by putting John down," Joel says. "Alice had a dependence on John, and I think the dependence she had really bothered her, and she resented it. But even when she was saying something very unsparing, it was said with humor, as a joke. She would criticize his style of life. He was absolutely too bourgeois. She would comment on his always wearing a tie. She would make fun of him for the Harvard Club and the good meals, as though that somehow made her feel less indebted to him." (And she wasn't called "Malice Neel" for nothing.)

Apart from the personal attentions he paid her and material comforts he afforded her, Rothschild also loyally promoted Neel's work, trying to arrange portrait commissions. As his son puts it, "It was as though John had adopted her as a client of his fund-raising and connection-making abilities." Despite John's best efforts, these commissions would frequently backfire because Alice sabotaged them, whether in person or in paint. Either she didn't want to part with the portrait or the subject found it too unflattering.

They would remain fixtures in each other's lives, but Alice and John's Belmar summer fling, with its bittersweet "alienation," was the closest they would get to a romantic relationship. Indeed, Neel was actually out on the town with John, in late 1935, when she first encountered her next great love interest, José Santiago Negron. In José she found an irresistible combination of the working class and the elegant, the sexual and the spiritual. She lost no time finding her way back to the nightclub where they had seen him perform.

Slim-hipped as a matador, and turned out in a fancy ruffled shirt or bolero jacket, José played the guitar and sang quaint Spanish folk songs at a place called La Casita. He was ten years Neel's junior, and worlds apart from the relatively staid John, with his bald pate and habitual pipe. The seductively handsome musician was the stereotype of an inappropriate choice for a mate. But Neel couldn't restrain herself. Physically at least, the slender, dark, exotic José reminded Neel of Carlos, her first great love. "You know what he was? He was a substitute for my Cuban husband although he was completely different," she told Cindy Nemser. And years later, she still took credit for making the first move.

"I went to the nightclub with John, and I had on a silver lamé dress that was beautiful," she told Hills and other interviewers. "And José was charmed with all this wealth and elegance." The dress, of course, had been bought for Neel by John. "Toward José I made my one aggressive action. I went down there one night, to that nightclub, and I knew José was going to want to come home with me, and he did."

Her first rendezvous with José did not, however, prevent Neel from spending that same winter weekend with John. "Maybe it was Vermont, because I remember a roof with snow." But the romance with José had begun in earnest, and Neel was soon spending the wee hours at La Casita, mesmerized by José and the other acts at the club.

"I wish I had a record of his playing. I was in the nightclub every night where he played. It was a wonderful nightclub, La Casita in the Village, founded by a man who was a pianist in Spain who left because of Franco." Neel recalled that after José finished his act, a singer named La Argentinita and her dancing troop, "who took most of their dances from houses of prostitution in Latin America," took over. "I'd come home just when the lights were going on about five o'clock in the morning. I remember my mother noticing some wrinkles around the edge of my eyes saying to me you are too young to have those. That's because I stayed up all night, every night."

Still, Neel claimed to be attracted to more than just José's physical charms. "José had a spiritual streak. I think you can see it from the way he holds the guitar," Neel told Hills. Her 1935 portrait of him, his guitar cradled on his lap, has a noticeably pensive air. (Although he would marry four times—two more times after his relationship with Alice, whom he never married—José, who was born Catholic, ended up becoming an Episcopal priest. His nephew, Ralph Marrero, says he was always deeply religious. But if he was "spiritual," it was certainly not in the conventional sense.

José Santiago Negron was born to Rosa and Eliada Negron in Corozal, Puerto Rico, in 1910, the second of nine children (three of whom died before the age of sixteen). Eliada owned a small farm and provided livestock to the local butchers. In 1928, Antonia, José's oldest sister, moved to New York, and soon afterward sent for José, who finished high school in the United States and briefly attended New York University. His sister Jenny Santiago decribed José as "very debonair, very intelligent. He was the most intelligent of all of us. He went to college, which the others did not."

Despite his college education, José worked as a soda jerk in an ice-cream parlor during the day and sang in bars and nightclubs in the evenings, according to Sheila de Tuya, his daughter by his first wife, a Jewish woman named Molly Smith, whom he married when she was in her late teens. (De Tuya, who was born in 1935, first learned that José was her father when she was sixteen.)

When Molly was pregnant with Sheila, she discovered that José was "running around" with other women, which probably included Alice, who met him around that time. Molly was so angry that she threw his guitar out of their tenement window. "As far as I know, Alice was the next in line," says Sheila. (José would also abandon Alice once she had an infant.)

Not long after Alice met José, he moved into her apartment at 347½ West Seventeenth Street. In just a few months, José had achieved what John hadn't in a several-year courtship. "I guess he captured Alice's heart with his Bohemian singing and whatnot," says Ralph Marrero. Alice continued working for the WPA, now receiving a bit less—$95.44 a month. She also began to receive some minor acclaim.

In early 1936, her 1930 painting *Futility of Effort*, of the child strangled between the bars of its crib, now retitled *Poverty*, was published in the Art Union's magazine, *Art Front*. "During the Depression I called it 'Poverty,'" Neel explained to an interviewer. "Because then it was considered self-indulgent to talk about the futility of effort. But poverty was something that everyone understood." Whatever she called it, Neel remained enormously proud of the work. As she told Nemser, "I think it was a very revolutionary painting in this country. I don't think that anyone was doing anything like that. It was an experience felt and painted."

In September 1936, Neel's painting *Nazis Murder Jews*, a potent depiction of a Communist-organized torchlight protest in which Neel and some of her WPA colleagues marched, was exhibited at the ACA Gallery, in a show of five winners in a competition sponsored by the American Artists' Congress. While it garnered attention, Neel's painting received a mixed review in the *New York World-Telegram*.

Wrote Emily Grenauer, "[It] would be an excellent picture from the point of view of color, design and emotional significance, if the big bold black and white sign carried by one of the marchers at the head of the parade didn't throw the rest of the composition completely out of gear by serving to tear a visual hole in the canvas."

But the very point that Grenauer objects to is what gives the painting its power, and Neel is unique among her fellow artists at this time in bringing specific attention to the Nazi persecution of the Jews. Around the same time, Neel painted *Uneeda Biscuit Strike*. Both paintings are Neel at the peak of her Social Realist period. (Her identification with the genre, at first a boon, would later become a professional bane to her career.)

*   *   *

> *For how I have loved you with all my heart*
> *that you were better than you seemed to be*
> *Loved your faults, your eyes, your hands your mouth*
> *Your spirit which at times was beautiful*
> *But now I see you in a baser light*
> *A rat who scuttles off the ship that's going down*
> *You've lived with me a year and several months*
> *On Tuesday morning my poor premature baby was born and died*
> *On Thursday you rush madly to your wife*
> *Entreated her to live with you. You couldn't bear failure you*
> *suspected me of weakness*
> *And then this shriveled petty mind*
> *Denied this baby life to a stupid little night club scene . . .*

This first stanza of an undated poem by Neel records a painful narrative: that she gave birth to a premature child, and that José threatened to leave her and return to his wife, saying, according to the next stanza, "I don't live with a pregnant woman."

In January or February of 1937, Neel, whose last child, Isabetta, had been born eight years earlier, became pregnant. But in July 1937, when she was six months into her term, her water broke and she was hospitalized. She told Richard that she had given birth to a little girl, who had been strangled by her umbilical cord. Two letters at the time, one from her mother on July 12 and one from Nadya Olyanova four days later, seem to indicate that José might not have been particularly attentive at the time.

Her mother wrote: "You poor child, suffering so, and no one with you. . . . I am so very sorry for you, but for myself delighted. You don't realize all you would have had to face. You say your breasts are so sore? Be awfully careful of them, seems odd they should hurt so, as it was 5½ months still when you were here last Monday. . . . When do you leave the hospital? Stay as long as you are able . . . take care of yourself and don't think of traveling until you are perfectly well."

Nadya begged her to visit, so she could take care of her, suggesting she get some word through John, and that she take care of herself and "don't get wreckless." Soon afterward, she and José moved to 129 MacDougal Street.

Although she was still receiving money from the WPA and José made some money playing at clubs, the couple, like everyone else at the time, was constantly hard up. A letter written to Millen Brand from MacDougal Street offered him and his wife, Pauline, a landscape for fifty dollars. "I'm horribly broke and besides I'd much rather old friends like you had it and I probably should give it to you, but I gotta eat," she wrote. Shortly afterward, she wrote to say she was in the country, but that a friend, Ann Patterson, would be staying at her place on MacDougal Street and would give him the picture and that "The financially arrangement is perfectly o.k." Finally, she wrote to thank him for his money order. "I hope you continue to like the picture—that's the acid test you know—time—the only judge in fact."

By the end of 1938, Neel was pregnant again. Although John offered her money for an abortion, Neel used the money to buy a phonograph instead. As Richard (who would be born nine months later) recounts, "It was an Ansley radio-record player, and the first thing that she heard on that Ansley was the overture to *La Traviata*. Whenever she heard that piece, this story would come up."

Perhaps anticipating the birth of her child, or because, as she had lamented, the Village had become too honky-tonk, Neel abandoned downtown and Bohemia to take up residence in Spanish Harlem, where she would remain for twenty-four years. (Her painting *Flight into Egypt* shows the two of them, Neel with a swollen belly and José carrying his guitar, walking north through Central Park.) She and José moved to an apartment, 8 East 107th Street, just around the corner from his family.

Recalls Marrero, "Alice lived on the ground floor of a building between Madison and Fifth avenues." It stood by itself, with empty lots on either side. "She was very kind. She advised my mother, Antonia, and my grandfather how to get assistance, because this was Depression time, and my grandfather got a job with the WPA." Alice was also quite close to Rosa, José's mother. "She and Alice would have long conversations in Spanish. Alice spoke perfect Spanish." (Although Alice told Patricia Hills that at first "José's family lived with us and it was a disaster," only José's brother, Carlos, and his wife, Margie, lived with her briefly.)

Nineteen thirty-eight was, in many ways, a banner year for Neel. She became the only woman member of the short-lived New York Group, founded by Jacob Kainen, which also included Jules Halfant, Herb Kruckman, Louis Nisonoff, Herman Rose, Max Schnitzler, and Joseph Vogel. "Now when I was on the WPA, I was in a group, seven men and me. So you see, I was already a very good artist," she said. But that didn't mean that Neel was accepted as an equal. "They were so embarrassed because I was a woman, but I didn't feel any different from them." As Solman put it, "Some were social expressionists, some were romantic expressionists, and then there was Alice."

That spring, Neel had her very first solo show in Manhattan, at Contemporary Arts, on 38 West Fifty-seventh Street, from May 2 to May 21. The gallery produced a brochure for the exhibit, which included sixteen paintings; among them were street scenes, landscapes, and portraits. The May 14 issue of *ARTnews* reviewed Neel's New York debut:

At Contemporary Arts a Pennsylvania artist, Alice Neel, is holding her first one man show in New York. Beneath the appearances of people, houses and landscapes, this artist searches for both general forms and particular personalities. The "classic front" of a building and the portraits of Mr. Green [sic] and the children Luisito and Amos are characters made real and familiar to the observer. Much of Alice Neel's work is based on flat decorative patterns which are invariably subordinated to the mood of the subject. When the artist departs radically from reality she falls short of her poetic aims. "Landscape," an attempt to create a fanciful vision of a tiny hut on an island atop a hill, is an example of her less felicitous style.

The bespectacled Mr. Greene, a family friend who lived in the Village and was something of an intellectual, is depicted as a dapper bon vivant in a gray suit, cigarette dangling between two fingers, legs jauntily crossed. Luisito was José's younger brother, painted when he was eight. Dressed in a stiff white shirt and black shorts, the dark-haired child sits solemnly in a chair, his large brown eyes and full red lips expressive and sad.

A precursor of her striking 1946 painting of Richard, also at eight (possibly done in the same chair), *Luisito* is one of Neel's earliest portraits of children—apart from her startling image of Isabetta—and follows firmly in the tradition of Robert Henri. "I am not interested in making copies of pretty children. What I am after is the freshness and wonder of their spirit," Henri had once written to his mother. Henri's focus on children, particularly ethnic children (he was one of the first American artists to paint black children in a realistic manner), had an obvious and direct influence on Neel ever since, as mentioned earlier, she had first read his *The Art Spirit* while in art school).

The New York Times also reviewed the show. The critic Henry Devere may have been the first to remark in print on Neel's painterly sense of sarcasm:

> Alice Neel in her debut at Contemporary Arts tempers her firm constructions with a somewhat sardonic humor in which a couple of remarkable cats play a part. Her "Classic Fronts" (red brick facades) and a still-life with torso and sprays of foliage are outstanding in the show. It is an excellent first.

Although there is little or no documentation of the portraits of Luisito (which belongs to José's family), Mr. Greene (who was a friend of Alice), or Amos (who was John Rothschild's son by his first marriage), apart from their mention in *ARTnews*, these paintings mark, in fact, the advent of Neel's long and extraordinarily fruitful Spanish Harlem period. For the next two dozen years, many of Neel's subjects would be those who lived immediately around her, from family members to neighbors to people she saw in the street. As Neel explained to Nemser about her move to Spanish Harlem, "You know what I thought I would find there? More truth. There was more truth in Spanish Harlem."

Neel had a great affinity for both the people and the place. Her Spanish Harlem paintings are uniformly strong, although often brooding. Her recording of her multicultural milieu brings to the fore her social conscience, her empathy for the underdog, and her love of Latin culture, starting from her earliest days with Carlos in Cuba. Her deep attachment to the community is evidenced by an undated poem she wrote:

> *I love you Harlem*
> *Your life your frequent*
> *Women, your relief lines*
> *Outside the bank, full*
> *Of women who no dress*
> *In Saks 5th Ave would*
> *Fit, teeth missing, weary,*
> *Out of shape, little black*
> *Arms around their necks*
> *Cling to their skirts*
> *All the wear and worry*
> *Of struggle on their faces*
> *What a treasure of goodness*
> *And life shambles*
> *Thru the streets*
> *Abandoned, despised,*
> *Charged the most, given*
> *The worst*
> *I love you for electing*
> *Marcaronio, and him for being what he is*
> *And for the rich deep vein*
> *Of human feeling buried*
> *Under your fire engines,*
> *Your poverty and your loves*

Whether they are of neighborhood children—Georgie Arce, a pair of anonymous black sisters—or her own extended family; José's sister Margarita with her three young children, and José's brother Carlos in the unforgettable *T. B. Harlem*—Neel's images from her twenty-four years in the neighborhood rank among her best work.

Within the next three years, Neel would be included in some four group shows (including three in 1938) at the Contemporary Arts gallery, which was founded by Emily Francis in 1931 to sponsor "mature American artists."

Just several days after Alice's solo show at Contemporary Arts came down, she was included in a show of work by the New York Group at the ACA Gallery which; since its founding, had promoted social art. "Drawings and paintings can fight too," its founder, Herman Baron, once said. As the New York Group's statement in the catalog put it:

> The New York Group is interested in those aspects of art which reflect the deepest feelings of the people: their poverty, their surroundings, their desire for peace, their fight for life. However, we believe that this laudable attitude can best be transformed into living art by utilizing the living tradition of painting. There must be no talking down to the people: we number ourselves among them. Pictures must appeal as aesthetic images which are social judgements at the same time.

The show ran from May 23 through June 4. Neel had two paintings in the exhibition: *Poverty* and *Well Baby Clinic,* which, although they reflected social concerns, were primarily about Neel's personal life. They were also both about childbirth, an interesting choice, considering she was the only woman in the group. Works by other painters fell solidly within the Social Realist genre, such as Jules Halfant's *The Eviction,* Max Schnitzler's *WPA Lunch Hour,* and Herb Kruckman's *Railroad Workers.* (The positive review, entitled "Exhibitions of the Week: First Showing of a New and Democratic Art Group," mentioned all the artists but Neel and Louis Nisonoff.)

Although they weren't included in any of these shows, Neel also did some wonderfully intimate portraits of José just after she first met him, celebrating his sultry beauty. An early 1935 watercolor of Alice and José as an exotic Adam and Eve shows a Botticelliesque Alice in the background, José, painted with a Gauguin-like naïveté, front and center, his right hand drawing the eye to his crotch. A rosy pastel, *José Asleep,* 1938, shows only the musician's head and arms, which Neel compared to "tropical plants."

There is also a striking painting (1938) of a somnolent José in striped pajamas, propped up in a chair, his wavy hair tousled, his head leaning heavily on his hand. (José often slept during the day, since he worked late into the night.) A charming watercolor from the same year shows the two lovers in bed, Alice's red hair fanned out on the pillow, a dreamy look on her face, and José on his side, in a white T-shirt that highlights his dark skin. These are still the halcyon days of their relationship, which will end in the winter of 1939, shortly after Neel gives birth to her first son, Richard.

"I was out in nightclubs every night. I did the tango, the rhumba, all those dances. Richard is the product of nightclubs," she later joked.

CHAPTER SIXTEEN

More Truth

The New York Group had its second and final show at ACA, from February 5 to 18, 1939, before permanently disbanding. Neel exhibited three paintings: *Rosa*, a picture of José's mother, *Movie Lobby*, and *59 E. 106th Street*. The show was not reviewed.

Wrote Kenneth Fearing in an introduction: "With its second showing the New York Group gives lively emphasis to its original program. 'There must be no talking down to the people,' they said a year ago and didn't. . . . These pictures . . . are as savage, as primitive as man is in today's civilization; as civilized, as sensitive, as the individual against the contemporary background of sheer chaos." A symposium, held during the exhibit, including a panel discussion by Philip Evergood, John Graham, and Jacob Kainen, raised the notion that the "real revolutionary art" was abstraction.

The Social Realist movement was beginning to wane, although it wouldn't disappear into near oblivion until the 1940s. Global events played a direct role in its demise. Wrote Philip Rahv in the *Partisan Review* in 1938, in response to the Moscow trials, "The failure of Capitalism had long been assumed, but the failure of Communism was a chilling shock and left the intellectual stripped of hope and belief in progress, with only himself and his own talents to rely upon."

The Nazi-Soviet Non-Aggression Pact of 1939 and the invasion of Finland had brought about the destruction of America's Popular Front, causing the disintegration of the American Artists Congress, shortly after Stuart Davis, Lewis Mumford, and Meyer Schapiro resigned. Along the way, the beliefs of many Communist sympathizers were destroyed.

Originally founded to oppose war and Fascism, the Congress was branded a Stalinist pawn when it resolved to support the Pact, endorsed the invasion of Finland, and revised its policy of boycotting Fascist and Nazi exhibitions. According to the declaration of a "Trotskyite" dissident group founded by Meyer Schapiro, "The Congress no longer deserves the support of free artists." By mid-June, 1940, Schapiro's group had formed the Federation of Modern Painters and Sculptors, a supposedly apolitical group to promote "the welfare of free progressive art in America."

Social Realism was now being dismissed, as "poor art, for poor people," as Arshile Gorky (who was on the WPA along with Pollock, De Kooning, Rothko, and Guston, among others) scathingly put it. Balcomb Greene sharply criticized Social Realism, as "the soap box speaking instead of the man."

It was this soap box, some felt, that had been put to use in art that supported the causes of the American Artists Congress, which had ultimately been taken over by the Stalinists. The members of the Federation of Modern Painters and Sculptors, in particular, hoped to find a "non-illustrative" way to express their response to world events.

The fall of Paris in June 1940, when the Nazis invaded France and marched down the Champs Élysées, stunned the world and signaled the beginning of a seismic shift of global power from Europe. In parallel with the changing map of political power, there was a concurrent shift of intellectual and cultural influence. Paris, the City of Light, the beacon of modern art, had been unseated. The stage was set for America, and particularly New York, to become the capital of the modern art world.

Harold Rosenberg memorialized the historic moment in his essay, "The Fall of Paris," in the *Partisan Review* in 1940:

> Paris represented the international of culture. . . . What was done
> in Paris demonstrated clearly and for all time that such a thing as
> international culture could exist. Moreover, that this culture had
> a definite style: the Modern. . . . But the Modern in literature,
> painting, architecture, drama, design, remains, in defiance of
> government bureaus or patriotic street cleaners, as solid evidence
> that a creative communion sweeping across all boundaries is not
> out of the reach of our time. . . . No one can predict the center of
> this new phase. For it is not by its own genius alone that a capital
> of culture arises.

The early roots of Abstract Expressionism, already nascent in the modernist work of Stuart Davis, Arshile Gorky, and Willem de Kooning, were just beginning to take hold. Although she was included in several group shows at Contemporary Arts between 1939 and 1942, Neel would not have a solo show for another five years, and would not show at ACA again until 1950. This was the start of the obscurity that would engulf her for more than a decade.

In July 1939, Neel's WPA payments were adjusted to ninety dollars a month, and in August, she was terminated from the WPA, a situation which turned out to be temporary but was repeated several times before the WPA itself was terminated by Congress in 1943.

That summer, for the first time in more than a decade, Neel once again found herself functioning as both an artist and a mother: Just two months before she was due to give birth to her third child, Isabetta arrived for a visit to Spring Lake, where Neel was staying along with her parents, José, and possibly his daughter, Sheila. Neel hadn't seen Isabetta in five years. By now she was a strikingly lovely young girl, with long dark hair. Not much is known about the circumstances of the visit. The only thing that is certain is that Isabetta told her family in Havana that she would never go back there again.

Marisa Diaz, a childhood friend of Isabetta's, who grew up with her in Havana, says that Isabetta never discussed it with her. But, says Diaz, "With her mother that was something there that happened that Isabetta didn't want to go back." Diaz says that the "assumption is that there was someone who may have molested Isabetta. One of [Neel's] boyfriends, because she hung around with very low-class people, and Isabetta was such a beautiful little girl. But whatever it was, it was something so serious, Isabetta didn't want to back again. She wanted to see her aunt [Lily] on her mother's side. She liked her very much. But she didn't want to go to her mother's house. . . . The aunts [Carlos's sisters Julia and Sylvia, who were bringing Isabetta up] told me this. Something very, very, very strange happened there. A little girl came back from one of her vacations saying, 'I don't want to go there again. Don't ask any questions.' She didn't want to talk about what happened there, but something that made her feel very ashamed."

According to a family friend, America Villiers, Isabetta called the police and asked them to contact her Cuban aunts, who were staying at a hotel in New Jersey, and they came and got her.

Nancy Neel, Alice's daughter-in-law, and her assistant from the late 1960s through the mid-1980s, recalls hearing about Isabetta's visits, both the one when she was six and the second and last visit just before Richard was born. "The only thing Alice ever said, and I'm not sure which time it was, is that Isabetta was walking on the beach with Alice. And somebody said,

'Oh, what a cute little girl.' And she picked up a jellyfish and threw it at him. And Alice said she thought it was a very strange thing to do, but she attributed it to the fact that she didn't speak English, so she misunderstood and thought of it as an advance. But again if it was 1939, she would have been eleven, and probably she was just beginning to develop. And you also have to think that when she was up that summer of 1939, Richard was born in September, but Alice would have been very pregnant. She might [have felt very jealous]. Alice said that she [Isabetta] used to put a pillow on her stomach."

"She came to see me when she was ten," Alice told Munro. "But when she was ten, I was pregnant with Richard by the Puerto Rican . . . but my sister in Teaneck turned them against me . . . I did see her once after at a hotel." Certainly seeing Alice pregnant must have evoked conflicting feelings in Isabetta, who had grown up without a mother in her life, and that may have been enough to make her decide never to visit again.

(A photograph at the time seems to indicate that José and his daughter, Sheila, were also at Spring Lake during Isabetta's visit. The fact that Alice was not only pregnant, but that her partner had a little girl who wasn't Alice's daughter, may well have also confused and disturbed Isabetta.)

It is impossible to tell what might actually have occurred, because no real facts are known about the incident, if there even was one. By today's standards, given the widespread occurrence—and reporting—of pedophilia, the assumption of potential molestation is not a surprising interpretation of what may or may not have happened in Spring Lake. And the cultural gap between what was perceived as proper and appropriate here and what was acceptable in Cuba in the 1930s has to be taken into account.

The Cuban relatives' hostile attitude toward Alice, fueled in part by her own sister, Lily, who disapproved of Alice's lifestyle and who was close to Isabetta (who spent her third year of high school with Lily in Teaneck), must also be factored in. Possibly they conflated Isabetta's decision never to return to Spring Lake with her posing naked during her earlier visit. Although they never directly witnessed Neel's relationship with Isabetta, the Cuban part of the family clung to the most extreme possible interpretation of any episode that was reported back to them. Whatever the truth of the matter, Isabetta did not see her mother again—and then only briefly—until she was an adult.

On September 14, 1939, Neel gave birth to her first son. She and José called the baby boy Neel Santiago, although his name became, on and off, in elementary school, the awkward Neel Neel. (In seventh grade, when he joined the Boys Choir of the Heavenly Rest, he became Richard Neel, at least in the choir. And, finally, when he went to boarding school, he became, once and for all, Richard Neel.)

"I was in the hospital when England declared war on Germany," Neel told Hills. She shared her hospital room with Goldie Goldwasser, and duly documented the vestiges of Goldwasser's difficult labor. *Childbirth* or *Maternity* depicts a contorted, bruised woman, her huge nipples echoing her blackened eyes.

Although she was terminated from the WPA in August, Neel was reassigned in October. She was able to support herself, José (who still made a bit in nightclubs), and their new son, Neel, especially since she recalled her rent at the time as being only twenty-five dollars a month. Ralph Marrero remembers visiting as a child, and seeing the newborn Richard lying in his crib. When he asked how babies came into the world, "José looked at me impatiently and said in Spanish that they come out of the cunt." Alice apologized for his crude behavior.

Marrero recalls Alice as "very handsome, like one of those characters from an Ingmar Bergman movie. I remember how Alice was with José. She was very kind to him and he was a little rough with her and very lazy and slept all hours of the day," says Marrero. "Alice really captured José's laziness in that picture of him sleeping. They weren't a good couple because of his laziness. Alice wanted to get up and do things."

Whatever José's domestic foibles, the three never had a chance to settle into a regular family routine. In December, just two and a half months after his son was born, José left Neel. It was the second time he had left the mother of an infant he had sired; Molly lost José to Alice when her daughter, Sheila, was born.

In later years, Neel never expressed either surprise or even much regret at José's behavior. "Well, you know how Spanish men are? He was always 'enamorado'—always chasing the girls. This didn't bother me so much because I wanted freedom to paint, but when I had a baby with him, my son Richard, it seemed worse."

But when Rosa, who was close to Alice, asked José why he had left her, he had a different explanation. "I was tired of getting horns," he said, possibly referring to Alice's ongoing relationship with John Rothschild. Says Jenny Santiago, "She wasn't heartbroken, no not for my brother, I don't think so. They had all finished, and then she got somebody else [Sam Brody.]" Marrero agrees. "I don't think Alice was interested in staying in touch with José. Alice was more interested in her art and José was more interested in himself."

Once again, when she was faced with a traumatic event, Neel was curiously passive. "Of course José should never have done what he did. It was wrong . . . He never should have left like that. I could have tried to stop him," she told Jonathan Brand. "But the whole thing sickened me. I thought it was so frivolous. We had lived together for five years . . . why pick this time when this little kid is maybe four or five months old and just leave like that? I thought it was frightful."

In later years Neel was much more nonchalant in recounting her reaction to José's departure. "I kept on living in Spanish Harlem and I kept on painting . . . I used to work at night when the baby was sleeping. I was more an artist than anything," Neel told Nemser. "If you decide you are going to have children and give up painting during the time you have them, you give it up forever. Or if you don't, you just become a delittante [sic]. It must be a continuous thing."

And she described José's abandonment almost casually: "A couple of months after Richard was born, José ran off with a saleswoman at Lord and Taylor's. She was very young and glamourous."

The saleswoman was Ruth Lovett, who was probably no more than sixteen or seventeen when she was swept off her feet by José. "My mother was sixteen years old, absolutely gorgeous. She was a model," says Paul Negron, the youngest of Ruth and José's three sons. "We called her the 'China doll.' She was just beautiful, real tall." Pictures of Ruth show a slender, beautiful young brunette—physically Alice's complete opposite. Ruth's childhood was difficult. Family lore has it that she and her brother, Warren, were left in an orphanage by their mother, who, after telling them she would return, disappeared forever.

For a time, José and Ruth lived right around the corner from Alice and Richard, at 1263 Fifth Avenue. Although she and Ruth kept their distance, Alice remained quite close to José's family, particularly his mother, Rosa, and his brother Carlos and sister-in-law Margie, all of whom she captured in memorable portraits. *The Spanish Family*, 1943, is a picture of Margie with her three children, and Neel's haunting *T. B. Harlem*, 1940, shows Carlos after his lung was removed.

Says Jenny Santiago, "We all used to see each other because Alice always came to visit Mamma. She was Bohemian, *'elle est a Bohemia,'* but my mother accepted all her ways because she loved her. Alice used to make

1.

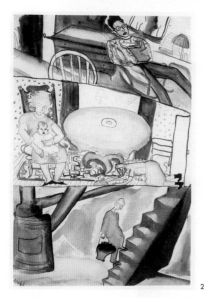

2.

3.

1. *Carlos Enríquez*, 1926, oil on canvas, 30 ½ x 24 inches:
Alice's romantic rendition of Carlos, portrayed as the
passionate Latin lover in Havana, during the early days
of their marriage.

2. *The Family*, 1927, watercolor on paper, 14 ½ x 9 ¾
inches: In the dollhouse: an almost Freudian analysis of
Neel's family dynamic in her childhood home of Colwyn,
Pennsylvania.

3. *Carlos*, 1927, watercolor on paper, 12 x 7 inches: This
pinched watercolor portrait of Carlos is in stark contrast
to Neel's sensual oil painting a year earlier.

4.

5.

4. *Futility of Effort*, 1930, oil on canvas,
26 x 24 inches: One of the saddest paintings
in Neel's oeuvre, it expresses her despair at
the death of her infant daughter Santillana;
echoing modernist motifs, including those in
Matisse's *The Piano Lesson*.

5. *Well Baby Clinic*, 1928, oil on canvas,
39 x 29 inches: Done not long after Isabetta's
birth, this is certainly one of the least
sentimental depictions of new motherhood
ever created, and very much in keeping with
the painfully personal pieces Neel was painting
during this period.

6. *The Intellectual*, 1929, watercolor on paper,
10 ½ x 15 inches: Neel's biting evocation of
her friend Fanya Foss, who is free to pursue
her intellectual interests, while Neel has
sprouted extra limbs to deal with her child,
Isabetta.

7. *Bathroom Scene*, 1935, watercolor on
paper, 10 x 8 ¼ inches: In this unique take
on intimacy—or the lack of it—Neel depicts
two lovers—herself and John Rothschild—
relieving themselves after sex.

8. *Kenneth Doolittle*, 1931, pencil and
watercolor on paper, 13 ¾ x 10 inches:
Although Neel never spoke about him
without referring to his destruction of her
work, Doolittle possessed both rakish charm
and a committed social conscience.

6.

7.

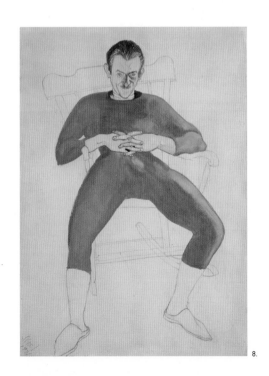

8.

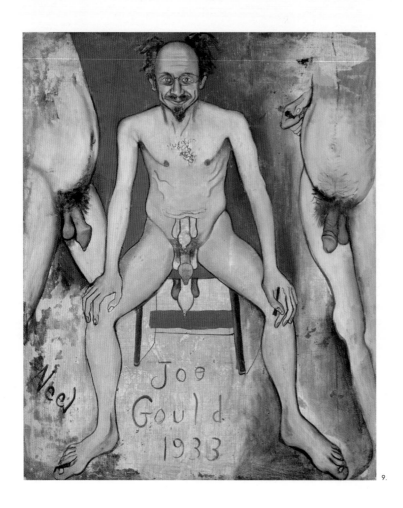

9.

10.

11.

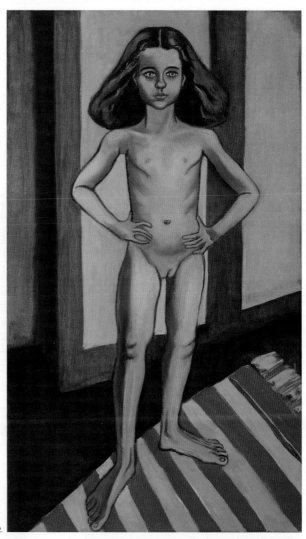

12.

13.

9. *Joe Gould*, 1933, oil on canvas, 43 x 31 inches: Neel's iconic work of this Village legend fully captures his manic megalomania and his quirky exhibitionism.

10. *Kenneth Fearing*, 1935, oil on canvas, 30 ½ x 26 inches: The poet Kenneth Fearing "bleeding for humanity," as Neel put it. Neel has channeled Frida Kahlo to give her friend, who wrote *The Big Clock*, which features a flamboyant artiste based on Neel, the look of a Mexican reliquary.

11. *Pat Whalen*, 1935, oil on canvas, 27 x 23 inches: Neel's heroic portrait of waterfront organizer Pat Whalen forcefully meshes her political views with her unique skills as a portrait painter.

12. *Isabetta*, 1934, oil on canvas 43 x 25 ¼ inches: Neel's shocking response to seeing her estranged daughter for the first time since she was taken by Carlos to Havana at one-and-a-half years old. When an earlier version was destroyed, Neel repainted it.

13. *José*, crayon on paper, 1935, 12 x 9 inches: According to Neel, "José had a spiritual streak. I think you can see it from the way he holds the guitar."

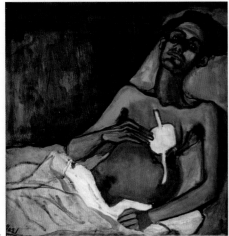

14. *TB Harlem*, 1940, oil on canvas, 30 x 30 inches: This haunting image of José Santiago Negron's brother Carlos, who had his rib removed as treatment for tuberculosis, is a powerful example of Neel's Spanish Harlem period.

15. *The Spanish Family*, 1943, oil on canvas, 34 x 28 inches: This painting of Margie, who was married to José's brother Carlos, and her three children, evokes the sensibility of Spanish Harlem.

16. *Two Girls, Spanish Harlem*, 1959, oil on canvas, 30 x 25 inches: Neel was influenced by Robert Henri and the Ash Can school in her effort to portray the essential truth of her subject and to explore diversity.

17. *Fire Escape*, 1946, oil on canvas, 36 x 24 inches: Neel told Henry Geldzahler that her image of stark buildings outside her window proved that realism could be as good as abstraction.

18.

19.

18. *Sam/Minotaur*, 1940, oil on canvas, 30 ½ x 24
inches: A devilish, horned Brody with a bristling
black heart anchors the canvas; over his right
shoulder is the frightened, screaming Richard.

19. *Alice and Richard*, 1943, gouache on paper,
22 x 15 inches: This heart-rending portrait of mother
and son, both hollow-eyed and traumatized, is
painted in harsh, atypical hues. Neel documented
the truth of her situation, even if she was unable, or
unwilling, to change it.

20. *Richard*, 1946, oil on canvas, 26 x 14 inches. Neel
raised two sons in Spanish Harlem: Richard, her son
by José, and Hartley, her son by Sam Brody. Here he
is depicted in an almost Early American style.

20.

21.

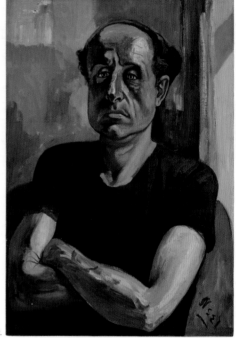

22.

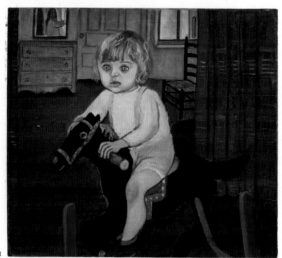

23

21. *John in Striped Shirt*, 1958, oil on canvas, 28 x 22 inches: The most reliable of Neel's amours, John, though steadfast, never quite captured her fancy; instead he provided her with companionship and "upscale dinners at the Harvard Club."

22. *Sam*, 1958, oil on canvas, 32 x 22 inches: Brody was Neel's longest term live-in partner, and the one with whom she shared the strongest intellectual bond. While his volatile temper made living with him fraught with psychological and physical drama, Neel was deeply attached to him on every level.

23. *Hartley on the Rocking Horse*, 1943, oil on canvas, 30 x 34 inches: Neel raised two sons in Spanish Harlem: Richard, her son by José, and Hartley, her son by Sam Brody. Here Hartley is depicted in an almost early American style. Neel can be glimpsed in the mirror.

you love her. And my mother was always crazy about Richard and was very close to him. My mother always used to give Alice money. Alice was always broke. Well, she lived on welfare, but she had a maid, Francisca." When he was a toddler, Richard used to play with Ralph and his other cousins in Central Park.

José had little or nothing to do with Richard. Says Marrero, "I don't think he was curious about seeing his firstborn son. I don't think he was much into Richard. As a matter of fact, even the children he had with Ruth he was never close to. He might have seen Richard once in a while."

Recalls Richard, "I remember meeting him one time with Alice, and he bought me a milkshake, and I was so nervous being around him that I pulled my glass away and some of it spilled on the counter."

But if José was a totally absentee father, Neel had another, more serious concern. Although apparently his vision was fine when he was born, when he was a little over a year old Richard's eyesight had deteriorated to the point where he could barely see.

According to José's medical records, at one point he had had syphilis, says his son, Joseph Negron. Extremely widespread before the advent of modern antibiotics, syphilis infected a great number of famous historical figures, including Napoleon, Charles Baudelaire, Beau Brummel, John Keats, Paul Gauguin, Leo Tolstoy, Franz Schubert, Henri Toulouse Lautrec, and writer Isak Dineson—the list goes on and on. (In fact, Marcello Pogolotti, Carlos and Alice's friend from Havana, eventually became blind from syphilis.)

It is well known that syphilis can be transmitted in utero from a mother to an unborn child. If left untreated, it can damage the heart, aorta, brain, eyes, and bones. Among its more serious consequences are blindness and insanity. It can also be fatal. In the pregnant mother, it can cause miscarriages and stillbirths. Neel apparently gave premature birth to a stillborn child when she was six months pregnant, in July 1937. Although it is unclear what caused the premature birth, Alice told Richard that the baby was stillborn because it had been strangled by its umbilical cord.

Neel told several friends, including Nadya Olyanova, that José had syphilis. Further, she admitted to more than one confidante that José had syphilis during the time that she was intimate with him. And Richard himself acknowledges that Alice told him José had syphilis. In Neel's circle it was assumed, at the time, that Richard's blindness had been caused by syphilis.

Today, syphilis is commonly treated with penicillin, but in the 1930s, during the period Neel was with José, penicillin, which had been accidentally discovered in 1928, by Alexander Fleming, had not yet been isolated and used as an antibiotic. Although it was available to soldiers during World War II, it wasn't until the late 1940s that penicillin was mass-produced and became commercially available and widely used.

During the war years, syphilis was extremely prevalent. At the time, the Wasserman test, first developed in 1906, was a common method of seriological diagnosis. This test, which produced many false positives, as well as false negatives, was first superceded in the 1930s by the Hinton test. Since then, far more accurate diagnostic tests have been developed.

Richard's eyes were apparently fine at birth. But about a year later, they swelled up, and it was found that his vision was about 90 percent impaired. Neel consulted a general practitioner, Dr. Erwin Schiff, who conducted a Wasserman test, which proved negative. But Richard's eyes continued to get worse over the next few months.

For most of her life, Neel attributed the fact that her son by José was legally blind to a vitamin A deficiency, rather than the possibility that he had contracted a disease in utero. In fact, she was adamant in blaming Richard's damaged eyesight on Sam Brody and the extreme health-food diet he imposed—and that she apparently went along with.

Although vitamin A deficiencies are rarely seen in the United States, and Richard also had an apparent heart murmur when he was twelve or thirteen (another possible symptom of congenital syphilis), Richard's memory of his diagnosis and treatment make the likelihood of a vitamin A deficiency appear to be more feasible than would conventionally be the case. (In the early 1940s, syphilis would have been considered the much more likely possibility, which is why the doctor ordered the Wasserman test.)

According to Richard, it was Sam who eventually found an ophthalmologist, Dr. Max Goldschmidt, who had emigrated to this country from Germany between the two World Wars, and had practiced at the University of Leipzig for eighteen years prior to the advent of Hitler. (Goldschmidt would have been likely to have seen cases of vitamin A deficiency in Germany after the first World War.)

Although his medical records are not extant, and he was far too young to remember the details, Richard says that, according to Alice, Dr. Goldschmidt immediately diagnosed him with a vitamin A deficiency. The doctor also told Alice that it was the first time he had seen such a case in America. He hospitalized the child, then about sixteen months old, and gave him vitamin A injections. Over the next few months, Richard's eyes improved, and when he was next examined, he moved toward a light source, and Dr. Goldschmidt told Alice that he could see again, although his vision was still impaired.

Richard then returned to the care of Dr. Schiff, who prescribed that he remain on a vitamin-A rich diet and take Videlta drops (a form of cod liver oil) as per the following note:

> *Erwin Schiff, M.D.*
> *784 Park Avenue*
> *New York City*
>
> *July 9, 1941*
>
> *The child Neil [sic] Santiago has been suffering, since I saw him first on January 1, 1941, from keratomalacia due to a vitamin A deficiency. This condition has improved greatly. There is no gonococci infection present, and the Wasserman reaction was negative.*
>
> *I suggest that he continue his present diet. An indication of this follows:*
>
> *Breakfast: eight ounce of milk, one boiled egg, bread and butter, orange juice*
> *Forenoon: fresh fruit*
> *Lunch: vegetables, potatoes, grated liver with butter*
> *Mid-afternoon: fresh fruit*
> *Supper: vegetables, six ounces of milk, orange juice*
> *Five drops of Videlta daily*

Dr. Goldschmidt was Richard's ophthalmologist until he was in his teens. When Richard was about twelve, he recalls the doctor telling him, "Do you know what would have happened if I hadn't diagnosed you correctly?" "I would be blind," Richard responded. "No," Dr. Goldschmidt replied, "You would be dead."

According to Dr. Gerald W. Zaidman, an expert in pediatric corneal disease, an infant or young child with a vitamin A deficiency severe enough to cause blindness would probably have malnutrition, as well as other symptoms, including the failure to thrive. In North America, blindness caused by keratomalacia from vitamin A deficiency is extremely rare.

Dr. Frederick Wang, a clinical professor of ophthalmology at Einstein College of Medicine, also points out that keratomalacia is rarely seen in this country. Moreover, he adds, "if one gives vitamin A (through diet or systemically) the reversal of the condition is dramatic. But any scarring of the cornea that occurred may persist."

Blindness caused by congenital syphilis is attributed to insterstitial keratitis and secondary scarring of the cornea, and it can occur in children up through their teenage years, although not commonly in children as young as one or two. And children with congenital syphilis can also get other eye infections, individually or in combination, including chorioretinitis and uveitis, both of which can also cause blindness.

Everything about Richard's blindness, including the era in which it occurred, would have led most practitioners to assume he had congential syphilis. But there seem to have been extenuating circumstances that make the vitamin A deficiency diagnosis credible.

Alice told members of her family that Sam had put salt in Richard's bottle at least once, and that Richard, who was terrified of Sam, routinely vomited at the sight of him. Years later, a family member found a news clip in Alice's wallet regarding instances of salted baby's bottles. When she was asked about it, Alice replied that Sam had done that to Richard. "She sat down heavily, and put her head in her hands, and said 'I did the best I could.' It was sort of a moment of darkness."

Both Dr. Wang and Dr. Zaidman concur that, if indeed, Richard were on an extremely restrictive diet, it would be possible for him to be deficient in vitamin A, although, "it would have to be a very strange diet in this country," says Dr. Wang. "However, if a vitamin A deficiency were the wrong diagnosis, the injections wouldn't have helped at all, so that makes the vitamin A deficiency seem more likely.

"And," says Dr. Wang, "if he were only getting empty calories, Richard could have been vitamin A deficient, without appearing to be malnourished." It seems possible that perhaps both Alice and Sam neglected the infant, and only realized the dire consequences when it was too late.

Dr. Gerald Zaidman points out that having first tested Richard for congenital syphilis as a cause of his eye problems, it is unlikely that a reputable ophthalmologist, who saw a patient not just once as an infant, but anywhere from several to a dozen more times over more than a decade, would have repeatedly misdiagnosed him, even if he had gotten the diagnosis wrong the first time.

Although the vitamin A treatment improved Richard's vision (which would not have been the case had he had congenital syphilis), it did not totally restore it. Dr. Zaidman suggests another possibility: that Richard sustained retinal damage that the vitamin A could not completely reverse, and that in addition to that, if his visual deprivation continued for months during a key developmental time, he could also have suffered from amblyophia. That is, even if his eye had healed through the vitamin A therapy, it might not have properly developed in order to operate normally. In such cases, doctors often prescribe a patch, and indeed, Richard said he was eventually given a patch when he was about five.

For the purposes of this biography, the actual cause of Richard's blindness is not significant. This medical issue is relevant for just two primary reasons: the question of how Alice may have dealt with it and how this might lead to a deeper understanding of her psychology and character.

From at least her twenties on, Neel had learned to survive terrible traumas: the death of Santillana, the permanent estrangement of Isabetta, her own suicide attempts and institutionalization, the Depression, and the destruction of much of her work by Doolittle. Somehow, through death, attempted death, and major loss, she had persevered.

It is impossible to know if Neel knew that José was syphilitic when she first had intercourse with him, or if she was aware that syphilis could cause a premature birth during pregnancy. Even if she had known that she may have been a carrier, penicillin was not available at the time, although there were other treatments. Neel told a confidante that Richard's eyes had been prophylactically washed out at birth. It is highly doubtful that Neel realized that she could give birth to a child with congenital syphilis and went ahead with her pregnancy anyway.

Neel was an intelligent, educated woman, but in the 1930s, sexual health was not publically discussed the way it is today, and she may have been unaware that syphilis can be passed in utero. One assumes this is not a risk she would have willingly taken, and that she would have performed whatever precautions she could in order to prevent potential contagion.

What perhaps is more to the point is how she dealt with Richard's near blindness. She chose to demonize Sam for blinding her child, though, in fact, it was he who eventually located Dr. Goldschmidt. And surely Alice herself had some control over Richard's diet. If he were vitamin A deficient, she would be as much to blame as Sam for going along with whatever restrictions he imposed.

Was this her way of exonerating José and herself, Richard's parents, from any other medical possibility? Or was it her method of punishing Sam, who systematically tortured Richard throughout his childhood? Whatever the real cause of Richard's legal blindness, how did Alice live with the knowledge that, wittingly or unwittingly, whether it was through José or through Sam, she had, even if indirectly, caused such terrible damage to her beloved son? Her dubious choice in partners had, in the end, exacted an awful toll, not just on her, but on her children.

Says one person close to Alice, "What is it that makes an artist an artist? The final thing is the art. But the fact is that a lot of really creative people lived tortured existences, not in the classic sense of the starving artist and all that, but maybe in order to be creative you have to be out there in some imaginary world. You have to be out there not seeing what you see, and not seeing what's in front of you."

Alice often told Hartley how tormented she was by Richard's condition. "She told me any number of times how she suffered every day with Richard's eyes. And that's exactly the way she said it. And in some of the paintings she did show Richard's eyes as abnormal. She had to be living with it. She saw it in his face."

Neel tried to compensate in various ways. When he was in first grade, Richard was sent to a sight-conservation class at P.S. 6, a well-known public school. He also went to the Lighthouse for extracurricular activities, where, among other things, he got free music lessons. Later on, when he was in college, Alice would type his school papers for him, although she also did that for Hartley.

Says Hartley, "Whatever happened, Alice was absolutely tortured by it. She used to say 'I don't go a day without thinking about all these things.' She had to forgive herself. Maybe she didn't accept the major responsibility, but maybe she did. I do think Alice felt terribly guilty about it. I think she suffered about it. I think she tried to make it good."

However else Alice managed to live with such disturbing thoughts, she also relied on the survival strategy she knew best: She channeled her emotions into her art.

Isak Dinesen, whose father had had syphilis, contracted syphilis from her husband, Bror Blixen, and was plagued by it the rest of her life. The disease had infected her spine, and she suffered a range of terrible symptoms that produced crippling pain, from stomach cramps to joint aches.

Blixen's full-blown case was for a time infectious, and she was forced to forfeit sex. She seems to have convinced herself that it was a Faustian bargain—that her storytelling talent was given in exchange for her continuing abstinence from carnal pleasure. "I promised the Devil my soul, and in return, he promised me that everything I was going to experience hereafter would be turned into tales," Judith Thurman quotes Dinesen as saying in her biography of the author.

Neel herself never gave up sex. But there is no question that she made tremendous sacrifices—deliberate or not—for her work. And these sacrifices affected not only Neel but those closest to her.

For his part, the disease does not seem to have had any lasting deleterious effect on José. In the early 1940s, he went into the army. A conscientious objector, he was a member of the Medical Corps, stationed in Okinawa, Japan.

By that time, he and Ruth had two sons, John and Joey, born in 1942 and 1943, respectively. Ruth had inherited property and a small fortune from her aunt, and when José returned from overseas, the family moved to Palm Beach, Florida. José opened a short-lived ice-cream parlor, Snow White's, then worked as a postal carrier. Eventually, he got a degree from the University of Miami and began teaching English and Spanish at a tony private school, Grameckies, and even wrote a how-to book on teaching languages.

But, say his sons, Paul, Joseph, and John, all of whom are practicing Christians, José never got over his womanizing ways. "He had a roaming eye," says his son Paul. "My mother was a very introverted, quiet woman and just wanted to fall in love and have a family. My mother never ever got over José. It was a disaster; she had a semi–nervous breakdown over it."

"He chased everything in a skirt, that's just the way he was," says his son Joseph. He also liked to gamble at the dog track. "He was a terrible, useless father, but he did teach us to play baseball."

Richard visited Palm Beach once as an adolescent, accompanied by his friend from the Steiner school, Dave Freeman. Recalls Richard, "When I was around twelve, I stayed with José and Ruth (and his half-brothers) for about ten days. I was introduced to Coca Cola, which we didn't drink at our house, and I learned how to sell cigarettes at his store." Freeman remembers José as "easy-going, Latin, sort of a dreamer."

As a college student, Richard visited José in Florida, and also later stayed with him several times in San Miguel, Mexico. By then, José had divorced Ruth and had moved to Mexico with his third wife, Helen Mabbott (whom he met while he was still with Ruth and Helen was married to someone else). He became an Episcopal priest. He officiated in a church in Haines City, Florida, and also served as the rector of the Church of the Holy Family in Monterey, Mexico.

Neel didn't see José again until many years later, when she painted him in New York City in 1966. In 1969, she, along with Richard and Nancy, visited him in Mexico. The last time she saw him was in the summer of 1975, when he baptized Victoria in a glorified birdbath (embellished by Alice) out at Spring Lake.

Several decades later, he developed Parkinson's disease. He lived for a time with his son Joseph and his family in Hobe Sound, Florida, then moved to his brother Louis's in Miami, and finally entered a nursing home, Salerno May Manor.

He died there on February 15, 1992, at the age of eighty-one. His obituary stated that he was survived by his sons, John, Paul, and Joseph Negron, Richard Neal (*sic*) and Sheila Detoya (*sic*), thirteen grandchildren, and three great-grandchildren.

In later years, Neel was often quite dismissive when she spoke about José. "You see what I liked were these glittering, unstable, undependable, irresponsible personalities . . . José, God I spent more time being bored by him because, after all, his intellect, it wasn't so much. But if he'd play the guitar and sing he was wonderful."

CHAPTER SEVENTEEN

Enter Sam

Neel's personal life, like her art, owed a debt to the WPA. Neel met Sam Brody at a WPA meeting in January 1940, scarcely a month after José had left. (Brody was later kicked of the WPA for refusing to sign "some obscene loyalty oath.") Neel was introduced to the tall, striking man by a friend, a sculptor named Blanche Angel. (Neel had done a pastel of her pregnant in 1937.) "She said he was a great photographer and he could make some great pictures of your baby," Neel told one interviewer. Brody would father her next child and be her partner for nearly the next two decades.

There was, Neel recalled, an immediate attraction. "He was such a show off, such an intellectual. He came home with me that night. And of course he fell in love with me immediately. He was very gallant when he fell in love. He brought me flowers, and he came every day. He told me he had divorced his wife because she had had an affair with a traveling salesman. Of course this was a pure lie. He was completely married with two children."

Sam would later say that he had first really fallen for Alice when he saw her at home serving food to guests with typical nonchalance. Says his widow, Sondra Brody, whom he married in 1959, "Alice always had a kind of low-grade buzz around her as this non-Jewish WASP woman artist who hung out in Spanish Harlem, so it attracted attention. She was very social about people coming to her house. She was serving ice cream. She was very generous about food. If you came to her house, she would cook up something and people would partake. When Sam was there, she dropped some ice cream on the floor and she reached down and picked it up and stuck it on her plate. And I guess that appealed to him."

It was a messy, if rather domestic, beginning to what evolved into a complicated relationship, as full of emotional—and sometimes physical—violence as of passion, psychological connection, and intellectual support.

Despite—or perhaps because of—the intensity and volatility of their part-
nership, Brody would become Neel's longest live-in lover.

Brody's courtship only intensified after a chance encounter with José.
"[Sam] came a couple for times for dinner. . . . José came and gave me
some money and played the guitar. This made Sam furious. He said, 'Oh,
you are being serenaded again,'" recalled Neel. "And of course he went
after me much harder." Just a few weeks after meeting Neel, Brody moved
into the apartment at 8 East 107th Street.

Things were made even more messy by the fact that Brody was indeed
married—to a Russian woman named Claire Murray Blitz, with whom he
had two children, Julian and Mady. They had married young, when she
was eighteen and he was twenty, and lived for a while in Europe before returning to the United States. (Julian was supposedly conceived on the boat
back from Paris.)

Like many of Neel's previous partners, Sam brazenly overlapped women.
Indeed, he ultimately had five children by three different women, all of
whom he married at one point or another. Even though Sam spent his days
with Alice, he managed to visit his family every afternoon. (It was a pattern he would later repeat some years later when he met Sondra. "Sam was
good at overlaps," she says.) Neither Alice nor Claire was aware of each
other's existence, at least not at first.

Samuel Brody was, in many ways, Neel's ideal match, in terms of intellect and interests. His sophisticated discourse was a welcome relief from
what Neel called the "poor intellectual fare" of Spanish Harlem. But he
had a deeply destructive side that would take a terrible toll on both Neel
and her sons.

Brody was born in London, in a house at 89 Church Street, on January
1, 1907. His parents were Abraham and Sophie Brody (shortened from the
original Brodetsky). His father, who had emigrated from Russia, was a
"journeyman" tailor. "He was an extraordinary person, a brilliant person,
a socialist himself who was a tailor all his life and whose parents were in po-
groms in Russia. He led the family out of Russia to England and to Paris,
where he also sold furniture, and then finally to the promised land here,"
says his son David. Sam's mother, who came from a family of peasants, was
illiterate. Sam Brody was about five when the family moved to Paris and
about sixteen when they moved to the United States, first to Richmond,
Virginia, where they had relatives, and later to the Bronx.

Although his father always worked, the family was quite poor. According to David, in both London and Paris they lived in the "slums." Brody had an older sister, Ethel, who died young of rheumatic fever, and a younger brother, Louis. Sam took after his father, both in looks and in explosive temper. "His father would hit him with a baguette of French bread, but he was small and it could hurt. He had bad memories of his father's temper," says David. His father's personality was also very much, says his son, a product of childhood poverty and "deprivation and struggles since the day of his birth. He was poor all his life."

If Brody took a single lesson from his childhood, it was the importance of social activism. In a 1977 interview, Sam Brody said, "My old man was a journeyman tailor whose life was consumed and ground to dust in London, Paris and New York sweatshops. Yet he still found time to initiate me into the eye-opening truths of Marxism and the unorthodox notion that living and acting for social change was more important than making a lot of money at the expense of one's fellow man." Brody's idealism was bred in the bone. "He held true to his beliefs to the very end," says his son.

Brody was a brilliant autodidact. He had gone briefly to the Sorbonne, but never completed his studies. "My formal education consists of less than a year in New York's high school for precocious boys—Townsend Harris at CCNY. Picked up the little I've learned from roaming the book-stalls along the Seine in Paris, the used bookstalls on 125th Street, and the incredible library of the YMHA at 92nd Street and Lexington Avenue in New York," he told Tony Safford in an interview published in *Jump Cut* in 1977. According to his *New York Times* obituary, he also attended schools for still photography and film. He worked for a while at the Communist Party's national book-distributing center on 125th Street, "doing a little editing, Jack of all trades."

Brody saw his first film as a child in Paris. "The earliest film I can re-member and I was only then believe it or not about five years old because we left London when I was about six, we didn't call them movies. We didn't call them cinema. We called them 'living pictures.'" But it wasn't until see-ing *The End of St. Petersburg* in a Broadway theater that he was irrevoca-bly hooked. "That had terrific effect on me. It was the first Soviet film I had seen. To me it was a revelation. I didn't know that films could have so much power, such an effect on an audience and I decided, 'My God if I could just partcipate in any way in the making of films, in creating this sort of thing.' That's how it started, you see."

Brody saved up and about a year later bought a camera at Willoughby's.

By 1926, he was shooting still photos and films at labor strikes, including one in Passaic, New Jersey, and another in 1929 in Gaszonia, North Carolina, and volunteering for various organizations.

He went to France briefly, and heard Eisenstein lecture at the Sorbonne on February 17, 1930, which he later wrote about for *Close Up* (April 1930): "It is nine o'clock in the evening. In a small lecture hall at the Sorbonne University in Paris, nearly two thousand people are crowded together to witness a private showing of *The General Line*, and hear S. M. Eisenstein lecture on the 'Principles of the New Russian Film.' But before it could be shown, the screening was shut down by French police, causing a demonstration, which did nothing to dampen the enthusiasm for Eisenstein's lecture."

In 1931, he was volunteering for several organizations, including the Independent Labor Defense, which helped "protect workers' rights in cases of eviction and layoff and so on," and "several people suggested we do some still photography." Brody along with a friend and colleague, Lester Balog, acquired still cameras and began taking photographs of labor issues, which they then printed and sold to "left wing and union publications, especially the Daily Worker," Brody told an interviewer in 1987.

Recalled Brody: "Little by little, that developed into a project for forming an organization which would make both films and stills and we said what should we call it, and that was the birth of the Film and Photo League. . . . We had a program which covered every contingency, whether it was anti-fascism or anti-unemployment, the Film and Photo League had a crew out there, and we shot film which was shown as widely as we could get it distributed, those days mostly in the halls of labor unions."

Whether that was the birth of the Film and Photo League, or, as he had stated a decade earlier, the League grew out of "the cultural activities of the American section of the Workers International Relief (WIR), an international organization dedicated to supporting striking workers materially and culturally," is unclear. " 'The camera as a weapon in the class struggle!' was our slogan," he recalled.

On March 6, 1930, a huge Communist demonstration of the unemployed marched into Union Square. Way ahead of the curve, Brody recognized the innate power of live news clips. In May, he wrote in the *Daily Worker*:

> I want once more to emphasize the news film is the important thing. That the capitalist class knows that there are certain things it cannot afford to have shown. It is afraid of some pictures. . . .

Films are being used against the workers like police clubs, only more subtly, like the reactionary press. If the capitalist class fears pictures and prevents us from seeing records of events like the March 6 unemployment demonstration and the Sacco-Vanzetti trial, we will equip our own camera men and make our own films.

To accomplish this goal, the League established the Harry Alan Potamkin Film School: to train "working class filmmakers." Brody himself taught at the school, along with Joseph Freeman, Leo T. Hurwitz, Lewis Jacobs, and David Platt.

In 1931 and then again in 1932, Brody worked on filming the Hunger Marches to Washington, as well the Bonus March. "I was a member of a group of four cameramen sent by the New York section of the Workers Film and Foto [*sic*] League to cover the activities of Column 8 of the National Hunger March on its way to Washington from New York City. Soon there will be shown to the workers of New York the evidence gathered by the keen eyes of our cameras. This evidence is totally unlike anything shown in newsreels taken by capitalist concerns," he told Tony Safford. "Our cameramen were class-conscious workers who understood the historical significance of this epic march for bread and the right to live." These were 35-mm silent films, relatively crude and propagandistic.

Explained Brody: "The Workers Film and Photo League carried on the struggle on two fronts: (1) by making films aimed to bring the proletarian message of class struggle to the working class audience; and (2) to expose and combat the Hollywood lies that fill the American screens. During the early Fascist films we would boycott and picket. We occasionally went so far as to plant stink bombs in the theater. And today Hollywood films still replace what ought to be, and has the potential to be, a highly progressive art. . . . The most escapist art, is by that very fact, sterile at best and reactionary at worst. This art abdicates the artist's responsibility to society and social progress. Daumier, Goya, Eisenstein, Balzac, Robeson, Hogarth, YES: De Kooning, Hollywood, Emshwiller, Anger, Kandinsky, Kine, NO!" No wonder Brody was such a staunch supporter of Neel's work.

Compared to the "pap" churned out by Hollywood, for Brody and the other young progressive would-be filmmakers in the Workers Film and Photo League, "the Soviet films and the writings of their makers were a welcome revelation guiding us through the heretofore unknown territory to where we could learn the basic grammar of the medium, both in the making and the writing about films."

Brody later wrote film criticism, including a column for the *Daily Worker*, "Flashes and Close Ups," and contributed to the journal *Experimental Cinema*. He also wrote a column for *Film Front*—"From Up in the Gallery," under the pen name "Lens"—that eviscerated Hollywood films and the critics who praised them. And he occasionally contributed film commentary to *New Masses*.

To him, the "revolutionary content" of the Russian films was inextricable from their innovative technique and aesthetic. Indeed, he felt that seeing these films "helped push the intellectuals and the artists of the 1930s towards a more Marxist and revolutionary outlook on life in general. How can you separate the Russian Revolution from OCTOBER?"

It's easy to see how Neel would find such steadfast devotion to the proletarian cause irresistible—that, combined with the fact that Brody was tall, dark, and attractive, with thick black hair, a high forehead, intense eyes, an impressive nose, an appealingly full lower lip, and beautiful hands. (Neel caught his brooding intensity—and his expressive hands—in a 1940 portrait.) He spoke with a slight accent, which only seemed to accentuate his extensive vocabulary. "He was very clever and very intelligent," she told Hills. "And the ladies loved him. He was good-looking, he was smart, he was terrific. And 100 percent an artist."

There was something else in Sam that Neel must have recognized instantly: an infallible radar for sensing someone's vulnerabilities. But while Neel confined her most stringent analysis of people, which sometimes bordered on crucifixion, to the canvas, Brody resorted to a full-frontal verbal assault. Few people could tolerate it. "He was so smart, when he'd pick on people, he'd know exactly the bad spot in them," Neel told Hills. "There was something uncanny in his capacity to tear people down."

As a result, there were few serene moments in the Neel-Brody household, where verbal sparring was a thriving blood sport. "Sam in a tirade was completely eloquent. He knew all the hostile words in the English language," says Phillip Bonosky, a Marxist author and longtime family friend. "He was verbally ruthless." But, adds his wife, Faith, "Alice was no pussycat, either."

As Hartley observed, "Out of the chaos of the emotional situation, Alice somehow teased out some higher reality for herself. I don't know how to say it exactly, but she got energy from the emotional stress and intellectual jousting that went on in these interactions."

The two were fiercely loyal to each other's work. "Alice was sure he was one of the best photographers in New York," says Bonosky, and Sam was

"Alice's most loyal admirer; he loved her art." Yet they could eviscerate each other over almost anything.

"They would have screaming matches with each other," recalls Sam's daughter Mady, whom Alice painted four times—as a child of about three, as a twelve-year-old, and as a teenager. "When they argued they got very loud, and sometimes Sam would storm out and Alice would bring out some chocolate ice cream and we'd all sit around and relax while he was gone, and sometimes she'd be the one to go out."

Most often, it was the children who fled, the two boys "cowering at the bottom of the stairs," as Hartley put it, until things calmed down.

Sam was also known for going after other people, sometimes physically. On more than one occasion, he violently chased would-be collectors of Alice's work out of the house. Joe Lasker, a fellow artist and friend from the forties and fifties (Neel did his portrait in 1968), was present when Sam threatened to kill a friend, Steve Rappo, with a butcher knife. "I said, 'How can you live with this guy?'" he recalls. "And Alice said, 'Ah well, that's who he is.'"

And at one point, he supposedly punched John Rothschild. Says Sondra, "Sam knocked him [John] out. It's a famous story. I think he whacked [old] Rothschild once. Because he was jealous, because he knew that Rothschild had been in Alice's background. See Alice came with a lot of clutter. Sam came with clutter, too. But by the time Sam met Alice, you could say that Alice had more clutter in her life than Sam was prepared for. She had Doolittle and she'd had Enríquez. She'd had the previous two kids, and then there was Richard. I mean, Alice came along with clutter. Now Sam was drawn to the clutter and the romance of Bohemianism. But he also liked boundaries. He liked both. We all like our appetites satisfied, but we like to go home for dinner, you know."

Brody's temper and jealousy expressed itself in other ways than brandishing blades and punching out John Rothschild. He took a violent dislike to Richard, and "as time went on he abused Richard," Neel told Hills. In Andrew Neel's 2007 documentary, *Alice Neel*, Richard spoke for the first time publically about being the victim of Sam's physical (not sexual) abuse, which had started when he was an infant and continued until he left home for boarding school at fourteen.

"He used to kick me under the table all the time. He kicked me under the table, and one time I screwed up enough courage to say 'Stop kicking me under the table.' Well, she had to go out that evening and he beat me up. He really did. I mean, that was probably one of the worst incidents. . . . It was intermittent, but it was physical violence and it was directed at Alice and it was certainly directed at me."

But Richard didn't need to put this abuse on the record; Neel herself had already done so from the very beginning in a number of drawings and paintings done in 1940, her first year with Brody. In *Sam and Richard*, 1940, a drawing that has since been lost, a vicious-looking Sam is tightly clutching Richard. And in the disturbing painting *Minotaur*, 1940, a crazed-looking, horned Brody with a bristling black heart and a clenched fist anchors the canvas. Over his right shoulder, effectively blocked from rescue by Sam's body, a terrified Richard screams and cries. When Brody later discovered this painting, he tried to destroy it, but Neel patched it back together.

Still, in January 1941, about a year after meeting him, Alice was pregnant with Brody's child. In February, she was terminated from the WPA, only to be reassigned in March. On September 3, Neel gave birth to Hartley Stockton Neel. Shortly afterward, the family moved to 10 East 107th Street in Spanish Harlem.

By October, an arrangement was made through the Federal Works Agency enabling Neel to place Richard (then called Neel) at the Winifred Wheeler Day Nursery in exchange for teaching, for which she also received fifteen dollars a week. She taught there for two years. In the meantime, Brody's legal wife, Claire, discovering Brody with a baby carriage, became aware of Alice's (and Hartley's) existence.

Says Sondra, "Sam was always chasing women. He was unfaithful to her pretty systematically, like a lot of left-wing men; it was a badge of honor. That was one of the subtexts of radical life. And sex is always fun, too; it's what you do. And Sam did it well. He was a sexy man. Claire found out Sam had had a child by Alice by following him one day and seeing him pick up the baby. It was very painful for Claire to have discovered that not only was her husband having an affair but he had a child by another woman." Claire and Sam later divorced, although they would remain in touch and at one point even consider a reconciliation.

The birth of Hartley did nothing to ameliorate Sam's feelings toward Richard. "Sam's attitude toward Hartley was entirely different from his attitude toward Richard. . . . And this created a very difficult situation," said Neel in an uncharacteristic understatement. "At times he went away, often for the better part of a year. I was glad he went."

Neel took advantage of his absence to paint her reaction to the situation. In *Subconscious*, done in 1942, during the winter nights when her two young sons were asleep, Neel didn't mince paint in depicting the horror of her homelife. As she explained the painting to Hills: "I am holding Richard, whose head is about to roll off . . . Right in front is Sam with that chin, reduced to an idiot. At the right is John as a statue, discreetly turning his head away. There are a couple of little blood marks on the sheet. On the edges of the canvas are the gods of sickness. The color lavender means insanity."

Neel's oeuvre contains a significant number of paintings of children with their parents, from *Linda Nochlin and Daisy*, to *The Spanish Family* to the many images of her sons and her daughters-in-law, Nancy and Ginny, with Neel's six grandchildren. And most of them emphasize the realistic anxiety and stress inherent in the responsibility of parenthood.

Her brutal depictions of Sam with Richard, and the heartrending 1943 portrait of herself with Richard, both hollow-eyed and traumatized, which is painted in shocking, atypical violent purple and blue hues, occupy a class of their own. Like a visual journal, they are Neel's way of acknowledging and documenting the truth of her situation, even if she was unable, or unwilling, to change it. (Even when she painted Sam holding Hartley, in a portrait done around 1945, the fear factor is evident.)

If Neel was so miserable, but even more to the point, if she saw Sam physically hurting her son Richard, why didn't she either leave or make Sam leave? "Part of me is very inert," Neel told Brand. "I had the two children. I had the house. I had a basis of living. I wasn't going to leave that or give it up, or change it, do you understand? So I stayed there. Sam would go away for a month and it'd be so dull and frightful that I'd be glad to see him. Then he'd stay for a month and he'd be so impossible I'd be glad to see him go. Well, of course, he'd use these fights as a way of getting away."

José's sister Jenny recalls her mother's anger at Alice for staying with Brody. "My mother heard about it because Alice was dumb enough to tell my mother that he almost broke Richard's arm and my mother said, 'Why don't you tell his father about it?' But she never did. She never told José about it, but she told my mother, and my mother was very angry at Alice. How she can allow Sam to maltreat her son. Those things happen with stepfathers. They don't love the child. He couldn't love Richard. Like I told you, he was always jealous of José." Alice told several people, including Richard himself, and later Phil Bonosky, that Sam had broken Richard's collarbone.

Says Richard, "I was too young to know whether he broke my collarbone or not, but Alice always said that he did. She always said that he beat me up around the head and shoulders while I was in my crib. It would be story time, and then, you know, instead of hearing about Little Bear or something, you would hear about how your collarbone was broken, or how whenever he came into the room you threw up. That's what I would do when he came into the room. That's the kind of stories that I would hear.

"He would terrorize me. You know, when I was learning how to read he said, 'If you learn how to read I'll kill you.' I mean, this guy was beyond comprehension. He was like the Devil. He was like Mephistopheles out of Faust. Alice told me that Sam said that if she pushed me off a cliff, he would buy her a piano.

"It was the threat of physical injury that terrorized me. I mean he could say, 'filthy Puerto Rican,' and make fun of Spanish people and stuff like that. It's you're small and he's big, and you're helpless. When you're a child, you're helpless. When I was a kid, she told me, 'There's the Society for the Protection of Children,' and I said, 'I want to go there.' She said it not once, but dozens of times. She had the police up once," Richard recalls.

"It was just a very lousy situation, Hartley may not have lived in terror, and he didn't, but he had to live with a very ambivalent type of person, who was a monster and yet it was his father. He had his problem and I had mine."

Hartley frequently came to Richard's rescue. Richard was also looked after by Bonosky, who took an intense interest in the boy and spent many hours with him. "He [Sam] discriminated against Richard in many ways," Hartley says in the film. "You know Richard and I stuck together very much. But at times it was a situation that was just awful, is all I can say."

In the documentary, Richard states it bluntly: "The fact is that she tolerated this person she knew was abusing me for years and years. I mean, I didn't hold that against her, but the facts are the facts. I mean, the world isn't just you. The world is you and your relationship with the other people, and you have to deal with your situation and other people have to deal with theirs."

Even with her high level of tolerance, it is difficult to understand how Neel remained in such a destructive situation. But despite her determinedly unconventional lifestyle, Neel in some ways conformed to the stereotypical model of a woman confronted with domestic violence.

Observes Fiona True, codirector of the Center for Children and Relational Trauma at the Ackerman Institute for the Family, "Alice was unable

to act protectively towards Richard, yet demonstrated ambivalence by telling him of the existence of the child protective agency, speaking to people
about the injuries he sustained, and even at one point calling the police.
One could speculate that she, as someone who was apparently extremely
self-involved, elevated her own need to work, the financial security she
needed to do that, and her psychological need of the intense, volatile relationship with Sam, over the needs of her child."

In so many aspects of her life, True adds, "Neel defied the stereotypical
norms for women, but in this aspect she mirrored her contemporaries,
whose dependency on men compromised their ability to protect either
their children or themselves. Her own history of powerlessness, reflected
in the traumatic loss of her daughters, may have made her feel even more
vulnerable, and convinced her, on a primal level, of her impotence in trying to bring about a different outcome with Richard."

As adults, both Hartley and Richard have had nothing but praise for
their mother, whom they adore and revere. "If she had been satisfied with
the paradigm of what women were supposed to be in her era," says Hartley, "she would have accomplished nothing, okay, nothing. She might have
been the greatest housewife and mother and all that. This was the other
side of the coin."

Richard even goes so far as to say that despite the suffering he experienced as a child, having Alice as a mother was a worthwhile tradeoff. "She
was a good mother. She was a very good friend to me. And the fact that she
might not have been able to give me the protection that I might have gotten
somewhere else, that's a fact. But suppose I got the protection, but I didn't
get something else. It's just one of those things that we have to deal with.
Every single one of us has to deal with what we're dealt, and the people we
are exposed to. And it was a gift to have her as a mother, certainly. There is
no question about it."

In November 1942, Neel moved to a new apartment on the third floor
at 21 East 108th Street, where she raised both her sons, remaining there
until the early 1960s. (Although her employment records indicate that
her last payment from the WPA was in August 1942, Neel claimed to be
among the last eleven artists to come off the WPA, which was officially
terminated by Congress in the summer of 1943.)

Her final WPA assignment was to scrape armbands worn by guards in
case of a German raid. "They made people on the Art Project, regardless
of how good they were, correct little mistakes on the armbands. I never

corrected one, because I thought I was too good for that. I had joined [the WPA] to paint masterpieces, not to scrape armbands." Instead, she spent all day chatting with fellow artists, turning in an already-corrected bundle at the end of the day. Neel immediately went onto public assistance, which she would continue to receive through the mid-1950s. It was the end of an era.

CHAPTER EIGHTEEN

Painting in Oblivion

A 1944 photograph of Neel by Brody shows her cross-legged in front of an avalanche of her work, bracketed by Sam's stern portrait and the dour depiction of Audrey McMahon. Her own face looks serious and somewhat worn. This striking image was printed on the invitation to her show at the Pinacotheca gallery (March 6 to March 22), Neel's first solo exhibition since May 1938.

Among the twenty-four pictures on display were *Symbols*, *Portrait of Sam*, *Dead Child*, *Nadya and the Wolf*, *Mady*, *Puerto Rican Girl*, *Green Apples*, and *The Walk*, which was singled out in a decidedly mixed review in *ARTnews*:

> Neel's paintings at Pinacotheca have a kind of deliberate hideousness which make them hard to take even from persons who admire her creative independence. . . . Nor does the intentional gaucherie of her figures lend them added expression. However, this is plainly serious, thoughtful work and in the one instance of "The Walk," it comes off extremely well.

Howard Devere, in *The New York Times*, was kinder:

> Alice Neel, at the Pinacotheca, is represented by realistic, romantic, and expressionistic paintings that reveal a healthy, half-humorous attitude towards life. Occasionally, in more tersely symbolic work, a reticient Pathos makes itself felt . . . Mischievous humor sometimes becomes sardonic, as in a café portrayal. A Prokofieff [sic] flavor may be detected here and there.

But, as Neel observed, "That was the last year she [the gallery director, Rose Fried] showed anything with a figure in it. She became a very pure abstractionist after that and she didn't even want to show me anymore."

By now, the tide had almost completely turned against Social Realism, the genre through which Neel achieved success in the 1930s. Originally a boon to her career, her association with what was now seen as an archaic art movement had become a bane.

It was a pivotal moment in the art world, but Neel didn't veer from her own sensibility. She would never be someone who catered to trends. "I never followed any school. I never imitated any artist. I never did any of that," she said. She had long ago determined her own path, and she stuck to it, regardless of the negative professional consequences.

That same spring, Neel bought back some of her WPA canvases, sold at 4 cents a pound to a Long Island junk dealer, who peddled them to Henry C. Roberts, the owner of a secondhand store in the Village, where they were quickly snapped up by art lovers and the artists themselves. An item about this appeared in *Life* magazine (April 17, 1944, illustrated by Neel's *New York Factory Buildings*) and later inspired a scene in Kenneth Fearing's 1946 *The Big Clock* (in which Neel is depicted as an over-the-top Bohemian artist, replete with a vermin-infested loft and four love children fathered by different partners). "Selling the WPA paintings as scrap canvas for 4 cents a pound was disgraceful. . . . They just sold them as spoiled canvas to wrap pipes with," Neel later told Hills.

The fire sale of WPA art was a perfect metaphor for the backlash against Social Realism, which had not survived the series of world-changing historical events between 1939 and 1941. The art movement epitomized an ideology that had been debunked.

*   *   *

Just as external, global forces drove the American art forms of the 1920s through the very early 1940s, internal, personal dramas would drive the dominant art forms of the mid-1940s and the 1950s: Surrealism, Cubism, and Abstract Expressionism. There was an increasing interest in expressing individual rather than collective concerns.

"In response to World War II and the intellectual climate generated by it, the future Abstract Expressionists came to believe that they faced a crisis in subject matter. Prevailing ideologies—socialist, nationalist, and Utopian—and the styles identified with them—Social Realism, Regionalism, and geometric abstraction—lost credibility in their eyes. Unwilling to continue in known directions or to accept any other dogma, the Abstract

Expressionists turned to their own private visions in an anxious search for
new values," wrote Irving Sandler in his introduction to *The Triumph of
American Painting*.

During the period when artists' political and social beliefs were being
strenuously put to the test, from the Depression through World War II, the
artists themselves were also being exposed to important new aesthetic influences. These ranged from seminal shows at the Museum of Modern Art,
founded in 1929 by Alfred Barr, and Peggy Guggenheim's gallery, the Art
of This Century, to seminal writings by Meyer Schapiro, Harold Rosenberg, Clement Greenberg, and Sam Kootz. And then there was the enormous impact of the wave of European émigré artists, including such leading
proponents of Cubism, Dadaism, and Surrealism as Max Ernst, André
Breton, Marcel Duchamp, and Salvador Dalí, all of whom fled to New York
in the late 1930s and early 1940s.

In the fall of 1936, the American Abstract Artists group was formed; by
spring, 1937, they had inaugurated an annual show and were distributing
pamphlets which proclaimed: "Abstract art is the most legitimate and authentic expression of contemporary international culture." The purpose of
the group was "to unite American abstract artists; to bring before the public their individual works; and to foster public appreciation. . . ."

The Museum of Modern Art mounted an important early show called
the "Twentieth Century Painting of the School of Paris," followed by
"Cubism and Abstract Art" in 1936. In 1937, "Fantastic Art, Dada, Surrealism" introduced Americans to the Surrealists: The nearly seven hundred works included Man Ray's *The Lips*, Max Ernst's *The Hat Makes the
Man*, and Meret Oppenheim's *Fur-Covered Cup, Plate and Spoon*.

Neel was familiar with the Surrealist movement; among her papers is a
1933 announcement for an early Salvador Dalí exhibit at the Julien Levy
Gallery. In all likelihood, she heard about—even if she didn't see—the
short-lived Bonwit Teller windows designed by Dalí in 1939. She may also
have read *View*, a New York–based Surrealist journal founded in 1940.

A major Picasso exhibit (Picasso: Forty Years of His Art) opened at the
Museum of Modern Art in 1939. That same year, the Museum of Non-
Objective Painting (which later became the Solomon R. Guggenheim Mu-
seum) opened; its collection included an important group of Kandinskys.

In 1939, *Partisan Review*, which only a year earlier published essays by
Trotsky promoting "revolutionary" art ("the function of art in our epoch is
defined by its relation to the revolution"), published Clement Greenberg's
"Avant-Garde and Kitsch," which decried the mass art, or "kitsch"—what

we now call popular culture—as a product of the industrial revolution and totalitarian regimes, suggesting that only under socialism could the taste of the masses be raised to high (read: modern) art. Stated Greenberg:

> Capitalism in decline finds that whatever of quality it is still capable of producing becomes almost invariably a threat to its own existence. Advances in culture, no less than advances in science and industry, corrode the very society under whose aegis they are made possible. Here, as in every other question today, it becomes necessary to quote Marx word for word. Today we no longer look toward socialism for a new culture—as inevitably as one will appear, once we do have socialism. Today we look to socialism simply for the preservation of whatever living culture we have right now.

The avant-garde had, wrote Greenberg, repudiated revolutionary as well as bourgeois politics:

> Hence it developed that the true and most important function of the avant-garde was not to "experiment," but to find a path along which it would be possible to keep culture moving in the midst of ideological confusion and violence. . . . "Art for art's sake" and "pure poetry" appear, and subject matter or content becomes something to be avoided like a plague.
>
>   It has been in search of the absolute that the avant-garde has arrived at "abstract" or "nonobjective" art—and poetry too. . . . Content is to be dissolved so completely into form that the work of art or literature cannot be reduced in whole or in part to anything not itself.

The article, in effect, gave artists the freedom to divorce their art from politics. Their enemy was not totalitarian regimes, per se, but the mass culture they inevitably engendered. As Greenberg later wrote, "Some day it will have to be told how anti-Stalinism, which started out more or less as Trotskyism, turned into art for art's sake, and thereby cleared the way, heroically, for what was to come." Greenberg himself, of course (who became the art critic of *Partisan Review* in 1940 and of *The Nation* in 1942), had a major hand in "what was to come" as one of the primary promoters of Abstract Expressionism.

In 1942, Peggy Guggenheim, who was married to Max Ernst, opened her gallery, the Art of This Century; its design itself, by architect Frederick Kiesler, was a Surrealist statement. The curvilinear walls were canvas, the paintings unframed and suspended by cables or cleverly mounted on hinged wooden cantilevers (which resembled sawed-off baseball bats). Guggenheim was instrumental in both introducing American artists to European modernist traditions and, even more importantly, in showing the artists who would become the Abstract Expressionist stars.

She was among the first to appreciate the early work of Jackson Pollock and Robert Motherwell, including them in an exhibition of collage in April, 1943, as well as the "Spring Salon for Young Artists" in May, giving both artists their first one-man shows. Guggenheim was also key to establishing the careers of Mark Rothko, Hans Hofmann, and Clyfford Still. Pollock's one-man show took place in November 1943; by 1949, *Life* magazine had somewhat sardonically anointed him America's Greatest Living Artist.

Remarkably, she also mounted two shows devoted exclusively to women. "Exhibition by 31 Women," which included works by Djuna Barnes, Frida Kahlo, Gypsy Rose Lee, Louise Nevelson (who had had her first solo show at the Karl Nierendorf Gallery in 1941), Meret Oppenheim, Hedda Sterne, Dorothea Tanning (who would later marry Max Ernst), and her own daughter, Pegeen Vail, among others, opened at the Art of This Century gallery in 1943. And, in 1945, the exhibit "The Women" included work by Nell Blaine, Louise Bourgeois, Lee Krasner, Perle Fine, and another dozen or so female artists, whose names have been lost to history. Neel was not among them.

Neel had, however, thanks to her WPA connection, made it into a show organized by Sam Kootz at Macy's in 1942, which included 179 works by 72 artists, among them Gorky, Davis, Rothko, and Gottlieb, all of whom had also been on the WPA, "and nearly every other modernist painter in New York."

Just the year before, Kootz (who published his books, *Modern American Painters* in 1930, and *New Frontiers in American Painting* in 1943, and opened his own gallery in 1945), had sent a wake-up call to the somnolent New York art world, with a provocative letter to *The New York Times* challenging American artists to experiment:

> The pitiful fact is, however, that we offer little better than a geographical title to the position of world's headquarters for art. . . .
> I probably have haunted the galleries during the last decade as

much as have the critics, because of my anxiety to see new talent, intelligent inventions. My report is sad. I have not discovered one bright white hope. I have not seen one painter veer from his established course. I have not seen one attempt to experiment, to realize a new method of painting. . . . True, some years ago, we had a rash of class-struggle painting, but the boys didn't have their ideas straight, and they killed what they had by shamelessly putting those ideas in the same old frames—they made no effort to invent new techniques to express their thoughts. . . . Anyhow, now is the time to experiment. . . . And all you have to do, boys and girls, is get a new approach, do some delving for a change— God knows you've had time to rest.

Kootz hit a nerve, causing an outcry among artists. The *Times* art critic, Edward Alden Jewell, described the letter as a "truly shattering bombshell" and urged artists to organize and "prove it to Mr. Kootz that the picture he drew of American art today is far too black." Sparked by Jewell's suggestion, the so-called "Bombshell Group" organized a show at the Riverside Museum in the spring of 1942.

One of the last organized stands of the Social Realist movement was the forming of Artists for Victory, Inc., in 1942, which held several major juried shows at the Metropolitan Museum, including a show of 1,418 American artists in January 1943. In what amounted to a counter-exhibit, members of the Federation of American Modern Painters and Sculptors organized a show at Riverside Museum from January 17 to February 27, 1943. Its catalogue implicitly criticized the work of the "Artists for Victory." Wrote Barnett Newman:

We have come together as American modern artists because we feel the need to present to the public a body of art that will adequately reflect the new America that is taking place today and the kind of America that will, it is hoped, become the cultural center of the world. This exhibition is the first step to free the artist from the stifling control of an outmoded politics.

Not that everybody agreed on exactly what the new art should be. Jewell negatively criticized the Federation of Modern Painters and Sculptors third annual show just several months later, in June 1943, singling out for special approbation two paintings, by Adolph Gottlieb and Mark Rothko.

"You will have to make of Marcus Rothko's 'Syrian Bull' what you can. Nor is this department prepared to shed the slightest enlightenment when it comes to Adolph Gottlieb's "'Rape of Persephone.'""

The two artists responded by writing forcefully to *The Times* what amounted to a manifesto of their beliefs. "We do not intend to defend our pictures. They make their own defense. We consider them clear statements. Your failure to dismiss or disparage them is prima facie evidence that they carry some communicative power. . . . We feel that our pictures demonstrate our aesthetic beliefs, some of which we, therefore, list:

1. To us art is an adventure into an unkown world, which can be explored only by those willing to take the risks.
2. This world of the imagination is fancy-free and violently opposed to common sense.
3. It is our function as artists to make the spectator see the world our way, not his way."

They went on to further enumerate the value of "simple expression of complex thought, large shape, the picture plane and flat forms." And to "assert that the subject is crucial and only that subject matter is valid which is tragic and timeless. That is why we profess spiritual kinship with primitive and archaic art."

Like many of the other modernists (including Pollock, who at the time was in Jungian analysis), they were consciously influenced by the prevalent theories of Freud and Jung. The nebula of a powerful new American art was emerging.

As Arshile Gorky put it, "The stuff of thought is the seed of the artist. Dreams form the bristles of the artist's brush. And as the eye functions as the brain's sentry, I communicate my most private perceptions through art, my view of the world."

Alice Neel was acutely aware of the changing forces in art. As an avid reader, she kept abreast with publications, from the *Daily Worker* to *The New York Times*. She was even personally acquainted with some of the modern art world's movers and shakers, including Harold Rosenberg, from her old Village days, and John Graham, author of the influential *The System and Dialectics of Art*, who used to visit her with his wife in the forties.

Still, up in Spanish Harlem, Neel continued to operate in her own orbit. She stubbornly stuck to her personal aesthetic—an idiosyncratic blend of Social Realism and Expressionism—just as she stuck to her Communist ideology. Neel's adherence to figurative art—despite her consciousness of the current art movements—would doom her to several decades of obscurity.

"I just went my own way," she later said. "[Hans] Hofmann . . . had taken America by storm with his 'push and pull' and, you know, he had huge classes in which they all pushed and pulled together."

As she told Barbaralee Diamonstein, "All during the forties and fifties, New York was nothing but Abstract Expressionism and nobody painted people or anything like that. . . . They wouldn't even let people-painters get a foot in the door. But during that time I couldn't give up what I was interested in for what was the fashion, so I kept right on painting. . . ."

Neel could have adapted to the new style; indeed, she tipped her hat to modernism repeatedly as early as the 1930s—by including first Surrealist and then, in the mid-1940s, Abstract Expressionist gestures and marks in her work, usually relegating them to the background, where she no doubt thought they belonged. Her paintings at the time provide further proof that Neel's insistence on realism was an informed choice, not a necessity.

Neel successfully flirted with Surrealist motifs in three highly disturbing pieces of the time: her 1940 portrait of Sam with Richard, *Minotaur* (which was also the title of a French Surrealist magazine); her drawing *Sam and Richard*; and her 1942 painting *Subconscious*, none of which resemble her contemporaneous work. And then there are the curious anamorphic images that swirl in the background of her 1945 painting *How Like the Winter,* in which Sam is reading the latest news about World War II.

Neel also knowingly used Abstract Expressionist tropes in a number of canvases. In her innovative essay, "Some Notes on Women and Abstraction and a Curious Case History: Alice Neel as a Great Abstract Painter," Mira Schor emphatically states that "Neel is as great a painter of abstract expressionist marks as de Kooning or Chaim Soutine."

While that greatly overstates the case, Schor makes some valuable points in her description of how Neel used the space around the subjects in her portraits—the peripheries of the painting as well as the backgrounds—to:

> reach into the vocabulary of abstract expressionism, placing thick, violently embodied strokes of paint to the side of and to some extent independent of the figure and the conventions of portrait painting. If the style and quality of these marks is similar to marks by expressionist artists such as de Kooning or Soutine . . . Neel activates the relationship between figure and

ground in a manner consistent with the goals of artists such as Barnett Newman and critics such as Greenberg, who emphasized the essential flatness of panel painting. Neel, however, does so within a representational frame that includes the rendering or referencing of a three-dimensional space.

Citing Neel's 1952 portrait of the art historian Dore Ashton, a noted Abstract Expressionist critic, Schor continues:

> Bold intensely brushed areas of orange, red, and purple crowd the uncharacteristically flatly rendered portrait, so that the figure has the sculptural boldness of a Picasso from the same period. But these abstract areas of color may be exactly as narrative and literal as the background images in the Kenneth Fearing portrait. . . .

About Neel's portrait of Robert Smithson, Schor writes:

> Many a painter could make an entire career from the richness of abstract painting she deploys in the small area of his cheek alone.

Neel herself later commented on her nod to abstraction in her strikingly composed 1946 painting *Fire Escape*, which, with its strong linear strokes, is reminiscent of Franz Kline, yet powerfully expresses the penned-in lives of herself and her Spanish Harlem neighbors. (*Falling Tree*, 1958, done during the period when Neel was attending the Abstract Artists Club, is another strong example of her fluency with the form.)

Says Schor, "The way I would describe it from the point of view of a painter, there's a sculptural quality to the paint mark as a thing of itself, not just to represent something, an application of paint in the weight of paint, the color of the paint, the rapidity or confidence of the brushstroke. Her painting is not intuitive. She's not an outsider. She is a master at the craft of painting, which allows her tremendous freedom. What you always feel in her work mid to later career, is that she could paint anything—and she knew it."

*   *   *

To her professional detriment, humanism—and all it stood for, not just artistically but politically—remained more important to Neel than careerism. (Neel would not begin to consciously strategize her career until nearly a decade later.) As previously mentioned, she was a member of United

American Artists, a 1939 offshoot of the Artists' Union, which in 1942 became the Artists League of America, essentially a labor union for artists. She continued her active commitment to Marxism, in her life and in her work, whether she was doing illustrations for *Masses & Mainstream* (including *The Trial of the Twelve* and *Judge Harold R. Medina*) and books by her friend the Marxist writer Phillip Bonosky, or painting CPUSA and labor leaders.

"Abstract Expressionism was becoming very attractive then," Neel later said. "I'm not against abstraction. Do you know what I'm against? Saying that man himself had no importance. . . . I am a humanist and that's what I see and that's what I paint." She would not have another solo show until 1950.

Neel summed up her professional fate in the documentary made by Nancy Baer. In the 1940s and 1950s, "I'd go to galleries that would say, 'Oh well, you're just an old-fashioned artist.' Well, many things: I was a woman. I never traveled with the pack. I did as I pleased. And I always dealt with humanity, more or less. And, of course, all during this period of Abstract Expressionism, no one did that. That was considered old hat, you know."

CHAPTER NINETEEN

Domestic Dramas

Despite the domestic Sturm and Drang, which came and went with Brody's peregrinations, Neel's next five years, from 1945 to 1950, were relatively staid, though sadly punctuated by her father's death in May 1946, at age eighty-two. Neel took the occasion to paint a remarkable portrait—her first of him—the day after his funeral in Colwyn. "He was a good and kind man and his head still looked noble. I didn't set out to memorize him, because I was too affected. But the image printed itself." In its elegant simplicity, the flattened corpse, starkly embellished with pale lilies and two pink roses, *Dead Father* evokes Mexican funerary images.

Neel's fine portrait of Richard, done the same year, seated with one arm hooked around a chair, shares with her earlier (1943) painting of her younger son, *Hartley on the Rocking Horse,* a distinctly Early American look. (Neel, wielding a brush, can be partially seen, reflected in a mirror in the background.) Both boys were enrolled first in the Winifred Wheeler nursery school and then in the Rudolf Steiner School, where Neel managed to get them full scholarships. She chipped in by doing a portrait for the school's annual fund-raiser. The school's pedagogical mission followed the theories of Steiner, who promoted the Waldorf model of education, a holistic approach integrating physical, intellectual, and emotional development by combining fine arts, movement, and practical arts with the study of humanities, science, math, and technology. As such, it was very much in keeping with Neel's humanistic beliefs.

Her work at the time ranged from several relatively sympathetic portraits—*Dick Bagley's Girlfriend,* 1946, and *Josephine Garwood,* 1946—to stylized streetscapes like *Fire Escape* (she told Henry Geldzahler the composition of that painting proved that "realism can be as good as abstraction"), and *Central Park in the Afternoon,* 1946, both of which show her continued playing with modernist motifs, including Surrealism and

Cubism. (There are two paintings entitled *Fire Escape*. Neel may have been referring to the carefully composed second one, 1948, a study in shades of brown.)

Then there was her poignant picture of her newly widowed mother (1946), done the summer after her father died, out at Spring Lake. "I realized later that the willow tree [barely seen in the background], which I had included in the painting, was also in the early American mourning pictures. My mother's life was just a shambles after my father was dead."

Her moody, minimalist 1947 seascapes, *Cutglass Sea* (almost identical in composition to *Sunset*, 1963) and *The Sea*, were also done at Spring Lake (more Arthur Dove than Neel). Her first portrait of Meyer Schapiro (she would do a second a quarter of a century later) is almost cartoonish, brightly hued and noticeably flat; the famous art critic and historian is posed oddly, clutching his left hand as if reluctantly taking an oath.

Neel spent her days painting in the big front room overlooking the street. "The paintings were always there, the smell of oil paint. That is something which was there from the dawn of consciousness," says Richard. Recalls Hartley, "We were on the third floor, but the apartment had a very good view of the street. There was a little grocery store on the corner. It was very much a family neighborhood in those days. The smells of wonderful food would sort of float through the windows—chicken, rice and beans—and there were always noises in the street. We had a big sound system there that was fantastic. It was really a warm environment. Alice used to play the piano, too. Of course, we took lessons. My brother played the violin for a while. I played the trumpet. And we all had to play the recorder at the Rudolf Steiner School."

The apartment on East 108th Street was a classic six-and-a-half-room railroad flat with many windows. The front room led into Alice's bedroom, which, in turn, led into the boys' bedroom, a playroom, the hall, a small room off the hall, which later became Richard's room when he was at Columbia, a bathroom, and then the kitchen, with an old-fashioned dumbwaiter that amused the boys. "The apartment was fairly big," says Hartley. "It was very nice, with wood floors. It was kept for the most part very well. Alice had it painted. Alice was not a slob."

It was not, however, very private. "In order to access the front room, Alice's room, you had to go through our room," says Hartley. The small private room off the hall was the only one with a door. Alice often had people over in the evening, which meant there could be a procession of visitors through the boys' room.

"Our room was the transition between two rooms," Hartley explained in his son's documentary about Alice. "So people would come in and at a certain place have to pass through our room to get to the main room, living room, or studio. So even if they came at ten o clock at night, and we would be in bed, they would go through the room. . . . There were people who read to us; there were people who told us stories. As a child, you know, you appreciate it as your world. Meanwhile she had her world in the other room right next door. . . . We met so many blasted lives."

According to Hartley, "Alice had a lot of interesting friends, and people would come to see her art. Usually there were sort of high-powered intellectual conversations going on with a lot of classical music. Among Neel's friends at the time were Phillip Bonosky, Michael Gold, Frank Gentili, Mr. Greene, the Wheelwrights, Max and Polly Freeman, and Gordon Kaplan, who taught at Columbia. Mr. Greene, of whom Neel did the lively portrait, would often read to the boys, as did Bonosky, who also made up wonderful stories about a character named Joe Weasel.

And then there were the intermittent boarders, all of whom had stories of their own. For a while, a woman named Jean Steel and her daughter, Suzie, lived with the Neels. And there was their maid, Manzi, who lived in the apartment for about a year with her daughter, Julie. And the Dutchman with a drinking problem, named Aef Grattama, who built Alice's kitchen shelves, and whose battered lover, Peggy, Neel painted with a blackened eye (*Peggy*, 1949).

Because Neel was living on welfare, which she considered "sort of an extension of the WPA," according to Hartley, a government investigator periodically appeared—"a case worker making [his] rounds. Usually there was some warning, a letter or something," he says. "We had to hide the TV and later the phone. We hid the phone under the pillow. We had the TV in a big cabinet and could close it so you couldn't see the TV. We still have that television. It was a Craftsman. It had a beautiful chassis made out of stainless steel."

According to Hartley, the family managed to maintain a "nice lifestyle" despite the occasional visits of the investigator. "I never feared the investigators. We weren't that happy when they came, but I only remember them coming a couple times, and it didn't really enter into our picture very much. The only reason it was sensitive is that there is something embarrassing about being on welfare, you know. It's a certain stigma associated to that."

"We knew pretty early, or at least I knew, that we were on welfare, and of course I was terribly ashamed of that," realls Richard, "You would just compare the way we lived with our classmates and it was a cut below," he says, adding that they didn't have a real refrigerator until he was in the seventh grade (they used an old-fashioned icebox) or a telephone until he was in college, in the 1960s.

Every once in a while, Neel would get caught affording her children some forbidden luxury. Says Hartley, "She was taking us to ballet, performances, and concerts and so forth, and you weren't supposed to do that. I guess she was seen with Richard at some concert with decent clothes on and she got reported for it." (As Dorothy Pearlstein pointedly observed, Neel's Marxist learnings made her an expert at manipulating the system.)

"Alice was a resourceful mother," says Richard. "But," he adds, "she was totally irresponsible. Just the fact that she would leave us alone in the apartment when we were just kids. But you know, that's the way she was. One time we destroyed the record collection and threw it out of the window." At the time, the boys were, respectively, five and three years old. Leaving her children unsupervised was, according to Richard, not an everyday event. But it occurred more than once.

"I am sure after that happened, she didn't do it as often," he says, "but she did leave us alone, and if it were today, you'd read about it in the paper, but in those days it was different. She couldn't hire a babysitter. She didn't have that kind of money."

Despite living close to the bone, Neel provided her children with as many comforts as possible. Hartley recalls a Lionel train set, a rocking horse, the annual Christmas tree, and carrots for the Easter bunny. "We had Siamese cats. We had an assortment of things—guinea pigs, white mice, hamsters. We had two alligators. We had little ducklings. Alice was trying to provide us with the whole range. We had a couple of dogs." (That included a formidable boxer named King.)

As a mother, Neel was a study in contradictions. On the one hand, she brilliantly finessed and finagled on her sons' behalf, wrangling excellent educations for both boys, with full scholarships to the Rudolf Steiner School; High Mowing, a progressive boarding school in New Hampshire; and finally Columbia University. In addition to ballet lessons for Hartley, whom Neel hoped might become a dancer, and music lessons for Richard, whom she wanted to become a pianist, Neel also arranged for Richard to go to a special school for the blind and to get "talking books."

"We didn't feel deprived," says Hartley. "You know, I have to tell you we were lucky. We were going to a 'fancy' school, at a fancy address. I have to say we knew that others had more, but it wasn't something that we were particularly jealous of. I mean, we were overprivileged in a way, altogether. We had a country house in New Jersey (Spring Lake) that Alice wasn't supposed to have, either."

On the other hand, her Bohemian lifestyle meant that her sons were exposed to a range of complicated people, including not only her lovers (for most of their childhood, this meant primarily Sam and John) but also her lovers' lovers. Sam seemed to have a rotating bevy of romantic interests, including one young woman who stayed in the apartment and whom Alice took care of after she tried to kill herself. (For a while, Alice not only accommodated her, but also her furniture, which filled the place.) Alice recounted one tale of both José and Sam sleeping with the same woman, Winifred Mesmer, "a promiscuous girl who had posed for me nude" within short order of each other. (Neel's 1940 portrait shows her as a solid, big-breasted blonde.)

Some of Sam's other lovers at the time included Janice Loeb, the sister-in-law of photographer Helen Levitt, who advised Neel to get rid of Sam. As Neel told Brand, "Hartley [then about four] said to me, 'Janice laughs when Sam carries her upstairs.' I once found her little white gloves under my bed. You know what it reminded me of? The White Rabbit in *Alice in Wonderland*."

Around the same time, there was also Vicki, whom Sam had met in California. Neel ran into her one night when she was supposed to meet Sam at the YMHA. Neel, who was wearing "a little hat and veil," recalled, "I was better-looking than Vicki." Said Sam, on witnessing the unexpected encounter between his two lovers, "I hate and despise both of you." The women retreated to the ladies' room, where Neel "gave her an earful."

And while he was with Neel, Brody actually even got married for a second time, in 1950, to a woman named Marilyn, with whom he had a son, Christopher. "Why did you marry her?" Neel asked him when she eventually found out. "She made me," was his reply.

Even her youngest son chided Neel about Sam. "Hartley as a boy said to me, 'Why don't you weigh his virtues and his flaws?'" As for Alice herself, "I had a taste for collectors' items. Strange people. People who were essentially irresponsible, undependable. Don't publish me as a female Don Juan. I was not promiscuous. I was much too Puritanical. . . . The last extra-marital affair, [he] was only 37 . . ." This was in 1959 or 1960, with a Russian named Vladimir who worked at TASS. Neel slept with him as late as 1969.

Meanwhile, Alice continued to sleep with John, whom she perceived as "an old habit" but who nonetheless continued to provide dinner escapes to Longchamps and assiduously tried to arrange portrait commissions. "The great thing about John was that he was tolerant. He didn't care what happened. He didn't care who I had, or anything else, he still wanted to take me out. He still had some interest in my fate," Neel said. "John never gave me up, never, even though he married a couple of times. He married a woman 25 years younger in the early 1940's," Neel told Hills. "Sam used to make big fusses and scream and yell when I went out with John. But since he did as he pleased, I did as I pleased," she said.

John adroitly managed to sidestep Sam while continuing to serve as both Neel's lover and benefactor. Says his son, Joel, "John would not go visit her if Sam was there. He was appalled about what Sam was doing to the boys and he was appalled at what Sam was doing to Alice, but it was pure self-defense. John had no intention of putting himself in the path of that madman."

Despite the difficulty of dealing with Sam, as well as Neel's own problems with potential models (at one point, King, the boxer, tried to bite a particularly wealthy prospect, who swiftly punched the dog), John did his best to hustle work for Neel. "He was absolutely convinced of her stature as an artist," says Joel. "He was fascinated by her work. He was continuously concerned with promoting her recognition, and getting her the compensation to support her art. She became a cause, so every week or so, he would round up a possible sitter, someone who would purchase a painting. This story of his continuous efforts to find patrons, and the difficulty that he had doing this is an entire story in itself. It's a saga."

During this time, Phillip Bonosky was also a major presence, acting, according to his own description, not only as Alice's close companion but as a kind of surrogate father to the boys.

Certainly such domestic dramas, combined with financial pressures, and, of course, the volatile relationship with Sam himself, had a strong effect on Neel's sons. "As a child, you want stability, security; that's human nature," Hartley, who was seven in 1948, later said. As an adult, Hartley completely disowned Sam and asked Richard to do the same. "I never forgave my father, and if you know anything about psychiatry, that's not good."

Richard, two years older, was even more blunt. "I don't like Bohemian culture, frankly. I think that a lot of innocent people are hurt by it. I consider that I was hurt by it. And the people that engage in it really don't care about or don't feel responsible for those around them and [who] depend on

them. If people are in that position you don't put them at risk by your behavior. . . . Absolutely I do feel I was put to risk."

Neel's sons were not her only children affected by her unconventional
lifestyle. Back in Havana, her estranged daughter, Isabetta, having just
been jilted by the young man she was supposed to marry, settled for her
second suitor, Pablo Lancella. A wedding announcement was sent to Alice's mother in June 1948. Shortly afterward Isabetta and Pablo came to
the United States on their honeymoon. They planned to visit Lily, and a
meeting was even arranged with Alice, apparently at her request, in a
New York hotel. Although it's unclear exactly what happened, the first
encounter between mother and daughter in nearly a decade did not go
particularly well.

According to Isabetta's cousin, Marisa Diaz, Isabetta, who was pregnant
with her first child at the time, was too nervous to even go through with it,
and told her husband to tell Alice she couldn't meet her. But according to
her friend Eileen Goudie, "She mentioned that during her honeymoon
they were at this hotel in New York. She told me that was devastating for
her, that encounter with her mother. . . . I don't know what happened; it
was awful."

Nancy Neel says that from Alice's description of the meeting, it seemed
that Isabetta was ashamed of her. "The way she looked, the way she lived.
That she really didn't give respect to her in any way. It was sort of embarrassment to her as an adult."

Pablo Lancella actually saw Alice when she arrived at the hotel, but he
says he never asked Isabetta what happened next. "As I walked across the
lobby she [Alice] came across. I was amazed. She was the spitting image of
Isabetta. It was absolutely incredible. I sat in the lobby and waited. I didn't
think it was my business. I knew that Isabetta was very hurt about it."

Alice had also apparently invited Isabetta and Pablo up to the apartment, either before or after the hotel appointment. Recalls Richard, "Alice
said, 'Isabetta is coming up with her new husband to visit us at 21 East
108th Street. You are going to meet your sister.' And we were all ready for
them to come, and they didn't come."

And there is also another story, told by Georgie Neel, that is far more
painful. (Although it is unlikely that he fabricated it, there is no other record of this story, nor are Isabetta's husband and her friends familiar with
it.) Georgie told Gerald and Margaret Belcher that he drove Neel's mother
out to Teaneck for dinner at Lily's with Isabetta and her new husband, and
that Alice made an abortive attempt to connect with Isabetta.

As Georgie recounted it, "Isabetta and her husband were honeymooning in New York from Havana. And we were invited to Lily's for dinner. We arrived about four thirty in the afternoon. Isabetta was there. Her husband was there. I was surprised when I met my cousin. She was small, a little larger than my grandmother, not a lot taller than my aunt Lily, who was a small woman. We were assembled at the dining table.

"And we had just begun to eat a fruit cup when Alice entered . . . and Lily screamed, 'Oh my god!' And Alice entered the room. 'Oh, hello. Isn't this wonderful. Well here I am.' And she sat down. And the conversation was then strained. Alice was friendly, but rather boisterous . . . I don't know how she got there. All that I know is that she mentioned getting a cab. There was no place set for her . . . But somehow she found out that they had been invited to Lily's for that dinner and she got there. I think later Alice mentioned to me that Isabetta's husband had notified her. But Isabetta refused to speak to her mother, and would only address Chadwick Scott (Lily's husband).

"After dinner we moved into the living room and we sat for a few moments . . . Alice went to the toilet and . . . I looked at Isabetta and I said, 'Couldn't you be a little bit nice or polite to your mother? I think it's been many years since she's seen you.' And she looked at me and she said, 'My mother is a whore and I will never talk to her!' Alice then returned, and I looked at my grandmother and she looked at me, and she said, 'Georgie, we're going home now.'

"We never mentioned it again in our lives, ever. I only remember Alice telling the husband that since they were touring New York they could meet for cocktails at such and such a hotel on some occasion, and I do believe that he met with her. But Isabetta refused to speak in any way to her mother. And when we got in the car my grandmother said, 'I never want to see them again.' And I don't believe my grandmother ever went to see my Aunt Lily ever again, to the best of my knowledge. And that's the last time Alice ever saw her daughter."

CHAPTER TWENTY

Monsters and Victims

Phillip Bonosky's relationship with Alice, Sam, Richard, and Hartley was extended and complex. Although they flirted with the notion, there was never a sexual relationship between Neel and Bonosky. But he was more than just a friend. For a good part of the late forties to mid fifties, he, Neel, and Brody formed an often painful triangle, and he was intimately entangled with her sons, with whom he spent significant periods of time. The relationship healed wounds on all sides, even if it opened others. Bonosky was estranged from his own five-year-old son, Danny, by his first wife, Jean. The Neels came into his life when he was at a low point, desperately missing not only Danny but any semblance of family.

Bonosky was born in Duquesne, Pennsylvania, a steel-mill town, in 1916. His father, who had emigrated from Lithuania, his brothers, and even his sister were all involved in the steel industry. "Our whole life was involved in steel," he recalled. His family was poor—one year his father made fifty dollars to support eight children, and Bonosky developed his adamant anti-capitalist attitude early.

He was also a brilliant student, an editor at his high school newspaper. "There was absolutely nothing for me. So I had to leave. I left home. Good-bye." After briefly riding the rails, he arrived in Washington, where he settled, getting a job with the WPA "measuring clothes" to come up with a national average. Bonosky's politics were further forged by his exposure to things ranging from corrupt southern senators to stockpiling food during the Depression—"people pouring out milk because they wouldn't sell milk before cost, and all the rest of the horrible things that happened. People were evicted by the hundreds of thousands from their homes. So how could you love a system like that?"

Bonosky first met Neel at the offices of *Masses & Mainstream*, where he was an editor (as was Mike Gold). Neel asked him to sit for a portrait,

and in early March 1948, he came up to her apartment every afternoon for
a week, posing between one and four. They quickly became fast friends.
Bonosky, a keen and garrulous observer, would keep a journal for the next
thirty-some years, creating, in effect, his own voyeuristic portrait of Neel
and her family. (There are close to three hundred pages devoted just to his
interactions with them.) His impressions are vivid and unsparing, and
open an often disturbing window onto the quotidian of the Neel-Brody existence during this time.

In his first journal entry about her, just a few days after starting to pose,
he summed up Neel and her past and present life. During their painting
sessions, Neel lost no time telling him about her childhood, the devastating loss of Carlos and Isabetta, and her unconventional relationships with
José and Sam. After dispensing with her recent history, he recorded the
profound impression Neel and her paintings had initially made on him,
providing a firsthand picture of Alice at age forty-eight:

> MARCH 6, 1948
> . . . Alice is a plump, red-haired one-time beauty, with blue eyes
> and the clear porcelain complexion that often comes with those
> features. With her long hair down she reminds you of those
> grave High School girls in middy blouses and long skirts you
> see in old photos during their graduation ceremonies. She
> chatters in an almost hysterical way when she only half-knows
> you. My first impression of her was that she was crazy; later, I
> began to glimpse what was wrong. She'd never been able to
> make a living and is now on relief. The house is up in Harlem,
> in the Puerto Rican section; it's a tenement but she has a lot of
> rooms and pays only $36 a month. . . .

Her work made an even stronger impression than her looks and demeanor:

> She showed me her canvasses. She has car loads of them. While
> I sat on the chair she brought out, with naive, child-like enthusi-
> asm, with laughter and chortles and assurances that I'll think
> she's depraved, canvases such as I have never seen before: mon-
> sters, monsters, monsters. All psychopaths to one degree or an-
> other, their neuroses charging through their eyes and coming out
> of their ears; in one case she even laid bare the brain of her "hus-

*band", the one that pinches her eldest son. She shows him in
many poses, all hideous, all demanding straight-jackets.*

*She showed me the pig woman and asked me what I thought
of her own father whom she displayed lying dead in his coffin,
and Sam Putnam with a deep crack in his forehead and fingering
a whiskey glass, and Joe Gould, the Village character, who
wanted to be painted nude, or rather his testicles to be: and there
they are about a dozen views of them, red and purple, while the
hideous grinning ugly human stood proudly above them.*

*Her portraits of children are the only ones—or of a Negro
woman or Puerto Rican—you could call "sympathetic." She has
a few landscapes and houses, which I liked. But all in all my
flesh shrank and my skin crawled as canvas after canvas was
pulled out for me. I told her if she painted me anything like them
I would murder her. She laughs uproariously and protests that
never, never, never would she do such a thing!*

In this same entry, prior to having ever met him, Bonosky described Sam:

*A Jew . . . who is obviously a pathological case of some sort. I
met both the boys. The eldest one is almost totally blind as a
result of a dietary deficiency when he was just a year or so old.
The youngest boy's father who seems to flit about the country,
pounces down on them from time to time and while he's there, he
tortures and abuses the eldest child and showers psychopathic
affection on the younger one, his own. Alice herself is torn by
her feelings for and against him and doesn't know what to do.*

Far from being repelled by the complicated family dynamics, Bonosky
was clearly smitten with Alice and her brood from the start. He would remain an integral part of Neel and her family's life for the next few decades,
although his first two years were the most intense. A writer by profession,
he employed novelistic detail to document the domestic dramas.

MARCH 9, 1948
*I cannot get the picture of the Neels out of my mind. I see her,
red-haired, buxom, smiling, apologetic—and her canvases of
maniacs. I see her slim elder boy with his delicate face and
great big dark eyes that can't see. I see his arms reaching up to*

*catch the ball and always the ball slipping through, no matter
how big it is. His younger brother, with his big blue, alert eyes,
his impudent little gestures . . .*

*The older boy leans over a book until his face is almost
touching the page and so reads. And yet he moves swiftly and
gracefully, and all the time you can feel the boy, as if caged,
holding up his blind eyes to you and sensing you as if from
somewhere behind them.*

According to Bonosky, although he was two years younger, Hartley was
already acting as the protector to both his mother and brother, even offering to help out financially.

*One day, too, when she started to send him out for bread, she
found there was no money, and, big-eyed, he said, 'I'll give you
all my money from now on,' and bringing her every penny he
picked up or was given.*

Bonosky was particularly fond of Richard, and it soon became his mission to save him from Sam. From the moment Phil first encountered Sam
in Alice's kitchen, he focused mercilessly on Sam's treatment of Richard,
as noted in the following entry:

MARCH 15, 1948
*I was due for a sitting, and I had promised the kids there I'd
have my birthday party with them. So, loaded with candy and
a big cake, I arrived, and Alice greeted me with her characteristic effusion, telling me en passant that "Sam" had arrived. . . .*

*Then the kids came, the "tough," touchingly impudent
Hartley; the boy who tears my heart when I look at him, the
slender, sensitive boy, with the great dark, unseeing eyes, and
they were full of excitement. . . . Hartley snuggled up to me
and I read him a Hans Christian Anderson [sic] fairytale
while Neil listened. Alice busied herself washing dishes,
happy, happy in her eyes . . . and then came a knocking on the
door, and in came Sam.*

*He recognized me from the painting. I had already seen him
in many a pathological interpretation on Alice's canvases. We
talked in the kitchen. There occurred a little episode that*

*shocked me. Alice had been telling me that Sam hated Neil
and at night used to creep into his room and tell him, "I'm
going to kill you!" Pinched him, insulted him. Neil, full of
excitement, came up to him, asking for attention, saying, "A
girl fell down in school and fractured her skull!" Sam looked
at him and said painfully, "That's not funny, Neil [sic]." Without a word, the boy broke from him and ran into the next room.*

This first experience of Sam's treatment of Richard would soon pale in comparison with later incidents. Before long, Phil was picking Richard up at school and taking him on various outings, including down to his own studio apartment on the Bowery. They were soon nearly inseparable.

APRIL 12, 1948
*. . . I felt strange walking down the street, holding this par-
tially blind little boy's hand, answering his questions ("How
much money do you earn?")
. . . Looking at this gentle, slim little boy, with his brown face
and dark eyes, never quite seeing you, the one eye askew—I felt
myself shaken. But he was obviously in love with me; or rather,
yearning much for affection and for a father, he unloaded all of
it on me. I'm probably the only person who has ever accepted
him as an individual. . . . Then, at home, Alice, who was
painting the portrait of a Puerto Rican woman—a beautiful
woman, too—covered me with gratitude. She revealed to me
that Neil [sic] had turned down an invitation by Sam to go to
the circus so that he could spend the afternoon with me. "Suppose," Alice quoted herself as saying to him, "he doesn't come?"
"He'll come," Neil had replied. "He told me." Suppose I hadn't.*

The attachment between the two continued to evolve, with Richard even voicing envy when Bonosky introduced him to a female friend. "'Are you go-ing to marry that girl that was with you then?' he asked anxiously. 'No,' I said, 'Do you want me to?' 'No,' he replied, smiling happily." Bonosky seemed to be aware that his attentions to Richard were creating a mutual dependency.

APRIL 19, 1948
*He was waiting for me outside the blind school, looking pa-
thetic all by himself, with that lost listening expression on his*

*face. I knew he wouldn't be able to see me until I was almost on
top of him. But he broke into a smile when he did, and there was
a surge of relief over him as we walked—he skipping happily—to the Elevated. . . . In the restaurant he went over his list
of friends and shyly included me. I had been a little late
meeting him and had almost become panicked at the thought of
causing the crushing disappointment and disillusionment that
would have come over him; at the same time, what will this turn
into?*

By May, Bonosky was fantasizing about living with Alice and serving as
a father to her sons. It was a fantasy he would continue to seriously toy with,
even after he married his second wife, Faith, in 1955.

MAY II, 1948
*At Alice's I find no pretensions, but simplicity; I relax there,
have the kids clamber over me, watch her smiling with that
touching happiness that says, look, my children are happy!
And she? She's so free of greediness; of selfishness. She says
of life: you've never given anything and I expect nothing;
and this cries out to me—this same absolute lack of
illusion. . . .*

*She's been beaten hard, very very hard; and she's learned all
the sly, wonderful, ways of outwitting the worst in life, of sneak-
ing through, and cunningly slipping away just when it seems
you're pinned down for the slaughter. So she's a thief; I love
that! I love the guerrilla way she goes through the stores and,
poor as she is, takes what she wants, slips it under her dress,
merrily. With a flash of her eyes, too! One for our side!* [Neel,
according to her family, had a charming lifelong habit of
shoplifting.]

*Yes I feel at home there, and I wish I could throw all the silly
difficulties out of the way and do what I want. Go there, live
there, be their father, be her lover.*

Given Phil's obvious infatuation with Neel and her sons, and what
was becoming an overt triangulation between Neel, Sam, and Phil, there
were frequent tensions. Phil was hypersensitive to the least infraction on
Sam's part. On his side, Sam bristled at the mere presence of Bonosky,

whom he had christened "Cardinal Bunzoveky." They were worse than oil and water:

JUNE 5, 1948

He [Richard] sat at the table, his hand guarding his face; his face looked like the mask of terror, the dark eyes looking larger than ever. When S. is in the room his body becomes taut. S. was planning to go to Chinatown for a meal, and A. said that she and Neil [sic] would stay behind. "Why?" asked I. "I haven't been invited," she answered. "What do I have to do?" S. cried. "Get down on my knees? If you think I'm going to beg you . . ."

No, she said, she'd stay with Neil. "There's no reason why Neil can't come," I said. "Do you want to come, Neil?" His face lit up shockingly. It was evident that he had been listening to our conversation that would have left him out, his heart sick. Sam would ordinarily not have taken him; but now he had no choice.

So we left her behind. She would drink wine, perhaps, because it consoled her. Neil, alive now, took my hand, and Hartley took my other. They (even Sam's kid) preferred me to Sam. On the way down, Sam was solicitous about Neil, who, unaccustomed to this solicitation, made Sam repeat each inquiry twice before he understood it wasn't an insult.

Hartley, who is a most engaging little showoff, sported in the restaurant, amusing everybody. He insisted on sitting by me and laying his head on my lap. He seemed so much like Danny [Bonosky's estranged son].

. . . We brought home a paper container of lobster for A., who seemed surprised. When she put them to bed, Neil said to her, "Why don't you marry Phil so he can be our daddy?" "Oh," said Hartley, "I'm going to tell Sam!" But this he would never do. "When Sam comes into the room," he tells me, disgust on his little boy's face, "he always starts yelling . . ."

Sam makes Neil's life a torture. For some reason he has an intense, neurotic, hatred of him, insults him, hits him, threatens to kill him. When Sam walks suddenly into the room, Neil jumps.

I toy with the idea. Why not? I like Alice a great deal, I fit into the house, the kids love me. Why not? I admire her painting; she's an honest, hurt, generous woman, with too much misery. No wonder she paints those monsters!

Despite, or perhaps in part because of, Sam's behavior, Bonosky's feelings for Alice and her children continued to grow.

JUNE 22, 1948

*Saturday I brought Neil [sic] here and he promptly began to
clean up the place. Later, he asked me if I would be his
father, and I said yes, his secret father. He hugged me and
put his face against mine and peered into my eyes with his
great almost-blind ones. Everything surged up in him; his
face was radiant. Later I told him: "You don't have to
worry when Sam abuses you. Remember me. Do you understand?" He wants to live with me now and plans for the
winter.*

    *We spent the afternoon with Alice. Neil climbed over me,
pure love in his eyes. He had told Alice all the plans he had
made, and this begins to worry me. Alice had given her
consent. She thinks it's wonderful for him that we have established this relationship. Sam, meanwhile, had taken Hartley to
the zoo—always alone, and Neil is the stepson, receiving all
the abuse. He needs me, and so I respond to him.*

    *I go out and play a solitary game of ball with Neil, whose
face flushes and whose passion in playing—for he has to
overcome so many obstacles—is deeply moving. When we return,
Sam and Hartley are there. In a moment of privacy Hartley looks
at me and signals me. Then he climbs on my lap—leaving, in a
sense, his father. . . .*

    *Alice brings out her canvases. Some old ones this time, and I sit
and marvel at them. I feel absolutely no compunction about
saying I love her work. I think she has a distinct style, a great deal
of suffering, sometimes torture, in her work; but even in her worst
monsters you see not only what they've done, what they are—but
that they are also victims.*

"Monsters" and "victims" is an interesting choice of words. Bonosky
was now functioning as Richard's "secret father," and perhaps performing
other "secret"—and not-so-secret—roles. This included courting and comforting Alice, assuaging her every time Sam stormed out, without taking
into account that his own behavior—both overt and covert—might be pro-
voking some of Sam's outbursts. But while they continued to get closer (in

some ways, he was serving as her secret lover) Bonosky and Neel stopped short of an actual physical relationship:

JUNE 29, 1948

The kids rolled over me and climbed on me and made me tell
them stories. Quite by accident I invented a character who
became fabulous and before I was home again I had constructed
a dozen and more stories about him: Joe Weasel. The kids love
him. Neil [sic] monopolized me, clinging to me, wanting to feel
my presence, so much so that Hartley was jealous and I tried to
make up to him somewhat. Neil calls me his father now.

Last night I went up to the Neels', where Sam was and spent
a grim evening with them. Their hostility broke out openly and
they fought before me, while little Hartley jumped out of bed to
try to stop their fighting. Sam tortures Neil; in the bathroom he
called him a "filthy Puerto Rican" and spit in his face. He tells
Alice that they could have a good life together if she'd get rid
of Neil. While Sam is there Neil almost looks pale to me.
Hartley tells me: "Sam spoils all the fun. When you come we
can't play with you." He tells Alice, rushing out of the room
briefly, "I got to go back and protect Neil."

Finally, Sam leaves. He has another apartment and is
supporting some other woman. Who nobody knows. He leaves
his coat hanging on a chair and comes rushing in, his face
pale, Alice tells me, crying, "My wallet's in my coat!" He gives
Alice $20, altho she's penniless. He makes $88 a week.
. . . Then I rise to leave. At the door, we linger. I feel I
should kiss her, but don't.

Six months later, the pattern seemed to have been set: Phil as the willing witness to, and even participant in, what he perceived as Alice's domestic hell. And so it went through 1949, with Bonosky occasionally threatening to abandon ship as the situation became intolerable to him, only to be irresistibly sucked back into it.

DECEMBER 15, 1948

Meanwhile, Alice goes on with her golgotha. When I'm
up there and talking to the two of them, they declare a kind
of truce, and we have a good evening. But the next day I

*learn that S. had kicked Neil [sic]. He keeps the other
woman, too.*

*We were sitting there, and Alice had taken out many
pictures I'd never seen, and Sam said suddenly, "Here, I'll buy
them all!"—bourgeois—initiation—and then threw Alice
$30, carrying through the act. But the $30 is what he gives her
each week, and he was buying her life with it.*

*"I don't care!" she cried, her face lit up almost savagely, "I
want him to go, I want him to leave! I want him to get mad!"*

Although Neel's convoluted relationship with Sam was the closest she
came to a "marriage" after Carlos, and although she was thoroughly engaged with him on every level, money seems, once again, to have been part
of her motivation to maintain the relationship.

Bonosky would continue to record his relentless observations of the complex dynamic between Neel and Brody through the 1960s, after Sam had officially moved out. Even a decade later, their "guerrilla warfare" remained
the same; "S. and A. pass through like leopards on the prowl from time to
time: the tenseness of hunter and hunted and sometimes they swap roles."

JANUARY 12, 1949
*Spent yesterday at A's. We talk and talk—always about herself
(and her ego is formidable), about S., about her wrecked,
tangled life of which, it's obvious to me, she's proud (if un-
happy); it's the ruined tragic life of the artist, a drama show,
and she plays it to the hilt—all the while that it's true. We could
have an affair, that's obvious; but I shy away from triangles
(even though it's not such of a twosome right now). N. is passionately attached to me, and while I'm there, I protect him from
S., who, for my benefit, makes a hideous show of affection for
him. (When he embraces N., A. tells me, sometimes he squeezes
his bones till they crack!)*

*She has a gesture—a stylized gesture of tragedy and grief—
whenever we touch on some aspect of her battered life. She casts
down her eyes, pulls in her head a little, and stares at the floor
[with] slightly arched eyebrows. But she told me I always dispel
her gloom, and she thanks me for being the only healthy person
she knows.*

Sunday I arrived in the afternoon, and found only Sam there.

We sat and faked talked about literature in the kitchen. There he was, his ant-eater's nose, his air of a tank-town Hamlet about to stalk off the stage with his cloak thrown about him in a grand gesture (he parodies himself like that), his slightly dazzling eyes (and here the dazzling refers to the eyes and not to their effect), the taut, animal tenseness. . . .

There was a tiny knock on the door, and I went to open it. There N. stood, like a little boy who had run away from home and it got dark—wistful, tired, frightened; but he was glad to see me, and glad he wouldn't be alone with the ogre. S. made a loathsome show of affection for him, while N. stood like a bow-string quivering in his arms. . . .

Finally, Alice and Hartley arrived; they'd been skating. A. was, as usual full of impressions (she couldn't walk to the corner without a vivid impression to bring back) about the skating rink. The question of supper came up, and this unexpectedly aroused the slumbering panther (a tattered, noisy-fierce panther), who wasn't going to get any food. Finally, he was prevailed on to go out and brought back lentils from which he made delicious lentil soup.

The kids were put to bed—N. quietly into the little room always fearful of pinches and pokes from S.—and we retired to the front room, the room full of beauty—and talked. Talk went on desultorily from one thing to another, until it reached one of A's relatives, an engineer who is dying but who works three times a week by being bodily carried to the office. A. was telling about it, and grew somewhat sentimental and forgiving, and then S. exploded. He hated those "Jew-baiting, reactionary bastards!" Didn't they conspire to take A's first child away from her? . . . Etc. Etc. A. vainly trying to reply.

And so, like a madman, off to bed. In the kitchen, she sits wondering (this is now almost professional)—wondering what she'd done to set him off, being sick about, wondering, wondering. "What keeps you to him?" I ask. "Is it the $30 a week he gives you?" But she doesn't really know.

Monday she woke with a beating headache and had deep pains along her back all day—from the argument, she said.

JANUARY 16, 1949

Spend more and more time uptown. We sit in that beautiful front room surrounded by canvases, and we talk. I've already come to anticipate all her attitudes, which have become classifiable. Everytime I arrive, she's in profound despair, sometimes she's physically suffering, from S's abuse. When she relates the details, I only shrug now. Since the obvious answer—get rid of him—is the impossible one, what's there to say?

All the men she's had! The sailor who cut up her canvases, José, Neel's father, whose head she has served up on a platter in one of her canvases—whom S. is madly jealous of, calls a pimp, and whom Alice calls "a lightweight"—the first one, the Cuban, then S. She showed me pictures of her daughter—a beautiful girl; yet when she was with her sister in Jersey a few years ago, Alice made no attempt to see her [or none that she told Bonosky about, since her meeting with Isabetta probably occurred not long after the summer of 1948].

Yesterday I asked her what it was in herself that contributed to all the debacles. She thought a moment, and answered that probably it was because no man can endure for long a woman who is superior to him in any way and attempts to reduce her in one way or another. "And then," she said, "I got bored with them." "Why did you go after them—the monsters?" She tightened her fists and gritted her teeth. "I had to reach my sexual aim!" she cried.

We had a bottle of wine, and finally S. came in, looking proper and even quiet. Suddenly she was seized with glee, and began to bring out hats and pose with them, decorating Sam with them as he sat in the opposite chair trying to talk to me. Her face was pink, her cheeks were plump—she gave a hoochie-koochie twist, and laughed. "Oh, let me be!" she cried.

She told me that Neil [sic] had told her that he loved me, that I was just as nice always. We had a long day together yesterday. Movie for hours, and then we ate a Chinese lunch, and I took him home. He was happy.

But nothing was quite that simple in the Neel household. One of Sam's amours (Marilyn) had threatened to commit suicide over him, and was now, incredibly, staying with Alice, Sam, and the kids until she recovered.

Bonosky and Brody almost came to blows after Bonosky asked the woman to leave. (As previously mentioned, the following year, while he was still living with Alice, Sam would marry Marilyn, with whom he had a son, Christopher.)

FEBRUARY 23, 1949

. . . S. came out of the room. I decided to go home. As I was leaving, it started: "I'm sick of people," he cried, "Sick of them. And you—you ordering her out of the house as if you owned it!" "What are you talking about?" I cried. "Don't tell me!" he screamed. His face began to assume the classic mask of the insane, distorted eyebrows, glittering eyes staring out of his face—I wanted to smash it! Then he launched into one of his diatribes, with which I've already become more than familiar— only this time it was directed against me—and screamed and screamed at me. . . . Alice began to shriek. "Get out of here!" screamed the maniac. "And don't come back!"

Alice started me toward the door. "Please go," she cried. "Please go." Suddenly out of the bedroom, little Hartley, naked as the day he was born, came running and began pushing me out of the house. As Sam passed through the room, he shouted at me, "Pus bones!"

Alice begged me to leave and accompanied me downstairs. I told her, "You're a fool, Alice!"

I left the place, so disgusted I didn't even want to think about it. It was just too damned much now!

I was tired when I got home and went to sleep without my usual wine. Basically, my feeling was one of relief that all this was over. I had witnessed too much that was hideous, had listened to too much that was just revolting, to want anymore of it.

Next morning there was a telegram. From Alice. She asked me to meet her and the kids at school. It was raining outside. I rode up and met her.

"He wants to apologize to you. He's so conscience stricken, he said that he'll even go down on his knees. . . ."

"Good God, Alice," I said. "You ought to get rid of him. You know that, don't you? You know I'm not going to let myself get pulled into his vortex. The guy bores and disgusts me and I

don't want to have anything to do with him. I'm not coming up
for awhile. I'm sick of it. As long as you tolerate him. It would
be better to starve on what you get for relief than take what he
gives. . . ."

S. had managed to gather around him certain women and
children on whom he vents his psychoses; somehow he has
found a necessity in them to be flogged—perhaps—and so has
them bound. But it's more sinister than that. He's clever to the
point of machievellianism—and completely transparent—but
he gets his victims. His son wants to kill him; A. thinks she
might; N. wants to kill him; dozens of others I've met abhor
and hate him. And yet he operates. The reasons for him are for
a psychiatrist to probe into. Myself, I think he's beyond hope.

By the spring of 1949, things had escalated even further. Richard, then
all of ten years old, had begun standing up to Sam, and even threatened to
go to the police.

APRIL 18, 1949
When I took N. home last night, he begged me to wait outside
and if S. was home he'd put a note in the mailbox and then
come with me back home. I tried to dissuade him, tried to
convince him A. would be home. He left me and minutes later
I saw his head pass the open window and then S's, in an
attitude of unmistakable abuse. I shivered standing there, and
my heart felt sick to think the little boy suffering under that
bastard's abuse. I'd seen him in action before and I knew what
it was like. I'd also seen N. sitting at a table, his hand up to
his cheek, shielding himself from the very view of the man!

I've decided to tell A. that I can't endure to be part of this
anymore. If she keeps on with S. and all his torture of N., and then
as long as I can't do anything about it, at least I can get out of it.

This whole episode became a mad nightmare. Last week when
I was up there, I was told they were going to drop S. A shiver went
down my back, for I would not see that psychopath in action.

MAY 21, 1949
N. told me that he took S. into the bathroom the other day
and told him everything he had against [him]. Told him that he

knew that S. had broken his collarbone when he was a child,
and that if he continued to abuse him, he would go to the police.
A. tells me S. came out later, white, and said, "I'm leaving.
It's no longer safe for me here. If I stayed here, all I'd do is
think of ways of murdering him."

Still, at the time, Bonosky could no more extricate himself from Alice
than she could extricate herself from Sam.

MAY 25, 1949
With A. the problem is maze upon maze. She's such a porten-
tous personality. She already had a couple histories, of which
only one of them would be enough to stagger the average guy.
Once, she fascinated me like something I don't know; but bit
by bit this began to fade. The insane complications of her life
just weighed me down.

Again, she wants me to pull her out of her trap by her hair;
but who in the world am I? "Why don't you concentrate on
me?" she asked the other night. "I'm worth saving." "We have
only enough for ourselves," I answered. "We need what strength
we've got for our own life." I'd fit into her life like just another
detail of her crazy quilt.

But oh, how I'd go for her if other things were equal! I'd never
met such a fascinating, and what's more, still beautiful woman.

It's odd, our relationship; it exists I think, through the
children: and through S. We talk about one or the other. I forget
sometimes what my role's supposed to be with her: I forget
simply because my mind forces me to forget. . . .

In May, Neel's illustration of Bonosky's story "The Wishing Well" was
published in *Masses & Mainstream,* as was her illustration for his story
"Walk to the Moon," published in the *Daily News.* Around this time, she
also did several satirical illustrations for *Masses & Mainstream* of Judge
Medina and a virulently anti-Communist witness, Angela Calomaris, whom
Neel called the "stool pidgeon," both done during the 1949 trial of Communists (the "Trial of the Twelve") under the Smith Act.

America was on the cusp of the McCarthy era. Although Neel was now
more self-conscious about her Communist ties, she went to the occasional
"party club meeting" and she kept up with the *Daily Worker* and *Masses &*

Mainstream, as indicated by this letter she sent to Phillip Bonosky in the summer of 1949:

> *Would you mail me your* Sunday Worker *this week. I'd love to have it every day but I'm afraid I'd draw attention to myself having it delivered here as I'm sure no one else in S.L. [Spring Lake] takes it—maybe they wouldn't even know what it was. Is it delivered wrapped up. Anyway, if it isn't too much trouble send me this Sunday's and all the others you have when you get this letter—I don't mean old ones but Monday in case you've finished with it. Also I'd love to have the last Masses and M. I'll send you the money for it.*

From another letter:

> *Mother reads the* Philadelphia Enquirer *and yesterday the governor of Pennsylvania came out advocating hanging communists to telegraph poles—the governor no less, not a hoodlum. He told this to the legions.*

*   *   *

Meanwhile, Sam's inappropriate displays of temper and psychological cruelty continued, even outside the household. Hartley recalls the terrible visit of his father to camp Glenbrook up in New Hampshire that resulted in the camp's director forcing Sam to leave. Neel, who, among other things, turned to Bonosky as a confidant, wrote him a letter in July 1949, about the incident.

> JULY 9, 1949
> *Sam made a dreadful abortive journey up there and they wouldn't permit him to remain or to take Hartley out for the afternoon—so he raged at Mr. Harrer (the head of the camp) and called him a nazi and a jew-hater—well you may imagine the scene. Of course I think Mr. Harrer might have relaxed the rule considering how far Sam came and that he didn't know about it—still he didn't so he just had to come back frustrated.*

And Joel Rothschild, who never saw Sam be physically violent with Richard, was horrified by one scene he witnessed: "The worst I saw was to have him walk across a book that Richard was trying to read. He was down on the floor [with his face close to the pages], trying to read a book, and the image of Sam tramping on that book was not something you forget."

But, adds Rothschild, "Alice fought for her kids and that meant fought for Richard. She defended him as best she could and she worked very hard to give them the protection that she could."

Rothschild, who recalls Neel's place as "a large but crowded East Harlem apartment, dilapidated but lively and filled with paintings," had a bad early experience with Brody: "He was a very nasty person. Alice had all sorts of people who boarded with her temporarily because she needed the money, and I had a very brief affair with one of her roomers. We were sitting in the kitchen and just at dusk, Sam came in and jumped on the table between us and unscrewed the lightbulb. No explanation."

Rothschild also remembers Sam buying and cooking hotdogs for himself and Hartley, but excluding Richard from the meal, including the large bowl of ice cream served as dessert. "What I saw was horrendous. That was the level of meaness."

The months passed, and Bonosky still couldn't break away from the Neel family, even when he saw Alice in the worst-possible light, as much predator as prey, pinning down her quarry in paint. And even after Richard told him he was carrying a knife in self-defense.

> NOVEMBER 4, 1949
> *Only then did I realize the profound corruption of this woman whose round smiling face hides so much that is deadly. Now I understood the depths of what it is that keeps him to her, and her to him. She had only lately "survived" his affair with the girl who had rented the room, and this had come on the heels of the other affair (the girl who is supposed to be pregnant); the girl whom she welcomed into her home, tortured in her role of the spit-on and abused and yet relishing it.*
>
> *For how does she get "above" it? She lies in wait and paints them; here is where she really lives and doesn't care what happens on the "outside". She endures S. because she has made a dozen canvases of him, accurate down to the last ruined atom.*

And yet Neel, who never stopped painting, was also capable of doing a very empathetic picture of Brody's daughter, *Mady*, 1949, notable for its Modigliani eyes, bold lines, and solid reddish background.

NOVEMBER 26, 1949

*N. comes to see me Friday and when I ask him whether S. is s
till mistreating him, he says yes; and then he shows me a knife
in his hand and adds: "I always carry this with me." I look
at his half-blind face, watch him as he sits eating, sunk in
whatever dream of his; I see him from a distance trying to
recognize my face in the crowd, and he holds that lost look until
I come upon him, and then it dissolves into a look of pleasure
and assurance.*

NOVEMBER 27, 1949

*Spent the whole day with the kids. They come knocking on my
door at 11:30, and I'm still in bed. They're jubilant, for in the
night it's snowed. H. takes his shoes off and crawls into bed
with me, for I'm afraid to get up till the room warms; then N.
joins him and the three of us glow like puppies together under
the covers and I tell them two stories:* Ichabod Crane *and a
tale from the* Wind in the Willows. *Finally I get out of bed and
make breakfast for all three of us. (Because of N's intense
jealousy, F. had left yesterday; also, she said, to save me money.)
We played games on a pinball machine I have, and then
went outside to have a snowball fight. . . . We returned and I
made sandwiches for them. Then we played more, and they
got a little hard to handle. N., who lives so tensely on the
edge that anything makes him lose his balance, shrieks at the
top of his voice when he wins; and finally, in some melee, he
jams the door with a pole and I get sore. We part with a cloud
over us.*

DECEMBER 2, 1949 FRIDAY

*I went to see N. perform as the "'arrator" of a puppet show at his
school. There A. was at her booth selling chances for an oil
painting. We went out for coffee and talk, and she told me that
[Charles] Egan was up to see her work, but didn't seem to be too
impressed and she doubts that she'll get a show from him. As
usual she invites dissection of herself, and I try my hand
half-heartedly.*

*There she is, matronly, wrapped in a gray coat and wearing a
dirty dress. She's doing this in order to help partly pay for the*

kids' tuition. . . . The show begins. It's the story of Hansel and
Gretel and I hear N's clear soprano voice, speaking the part of
Hansel behind the scenes. It goes on, and when it's over, N. comes
out proudly and kids say: "You were good, N." and he glows
happily.

Then I think of him sitting in the kitchen with his hand
protecting his face from the sight of S. as he tries to eat soup.
He doesn't know if S. will suddenly rise and grab the plate and
throw the soup on the floor or over him. He doesn't know
whether S. will reach under the table and pinch him, or kick
him, or call him "dirty Puerto Rican," or promise that when
he's sleeping he'll come in and kill him. Or worse, take him in
his arms and pretending to embrace him crack his bones.

Although Sam's treatment of Richard was a constant source of pain and guilt for Alice, she found ways to rationalize it. "You know Sam was always crazy about these children," she told Jonathan Brand. "He's mad about them. His whole life centers on his children. Yes, of course *his* children, you know the other children, he could kill all of them. He saw some Puerto Rican child on the street and he could be nice to him, it's just that when there's some other child in the house, his tribalism comes out, you know. Ancient Hebraic tribalism."

Bonosky recounts Neel saying to him and his wife, Faith, in the late 1950's. ". . . Do you think it's right—I'd come home and find Neel's [Richard's] head bloody, and Sam would say he fell against the radio; he liked music so much, he'd lean against it." When Faith asked Alice, "But why did you stay with him, then?" Alice replied, "Well you know, there is something wrong with me, too."

According to Bonosky, she would try to "unravel her relationship" with Sam, asking herself, "Was I wrong? Should I have kept him? Should I have let him keep beating Neel [Richard]?"

But, as she would say to Bonosky in 1959, after Sam had moved out, "Sam is good at bottom. Can you imagine my life—I had to choose between my child and my love. . . . And yet I miss him. He made life interesting."

She must have also found ways to rationalize Sam's abuse of her. Sam liked to spit at people when he was angry, and he would also hit and shake Alice, although not routinely. Says Richard now, "He was abusive to Alice in a fashion most women wouldn't tolerate." Richard recalls Sam actually spraying DDT in Alice's face at one point. "He got angry at her, so he got out the DDT. She was coughing for a few days after that."

Sondra, who would have a son, David, with Sam in 1958, and marry him in 1959, acknowledges that he was extremely volatile. But, except for his knocking down Rothschild and "whacking a few guys" and, at one point, Sondra herself (he hit her across the face with some gloves) does not believe he was physically violent toward Richard.

Sondra says, "[He was] not a hitter, because his father hit him. He had bad memories of his father's temper. Sam was not a hitter. No. He might have shaken Richard; he might have been angry at something Richard said. He might have been jealous of Richard. Sam fought with people. He upset people around him. He also charmed them. And you could either walk away, fight back, or ignore him. He brought a certain Sturm and Drang with him. But Alice brought stuff with her, too, and it was comforting to blame things on Sam. Alice was seeing a married man and got pregnant by him and had a child by him. Does she bear any of the moral responsibility for this?"

Sondra concedes that Sam's behavior could be ugly. "Sam did one thing that was obnoxious. He spit at you. If he got really angry. He was an angry man and he did angry things. But it's just useful to always remember that that is not the complete picture."

Says David, "Alice claimed my father abused Richard, that he was responsible for him going nearly blind. At one point a story circulated on regular basis: she said my father starved him. My memory of him was that he had really bad moments with me, and other moments were extraordinary and wonderful. He taught me more things than could put in an encyclopedia. And so he could be the minotaur, and he could also be a teacher. But his volatility would short-circuit things in his life, and it would short-circuit things like friendships. I heard some of the sensational stories after she was dead," he says, referring to the story about Richard's blindess being caused by Sam's restricting his food.

Like his mother, Sondra, David does not think his father would have been physically violent. "When she [Alice] was alive I saw Richard and my father together, and interacting quite normally for many, many years, and seeming to get along." David, Sam, and Sondra also spent time with Alice, Richard, and Nancy out in Spring Lake. Still, "I was in the room during some of the moments of conflict with my father, when Alice would say some pretty horrifying things about the way he raised Richard."

David recounts an anecdote his father told him about trying to feed

Hartley cereal: "And he opened up the box and a big rat jumped out and it certainly contaminated the rest of the food, so he couldn't feed Hartley breakfast that morning and they had no food. They had no money and he described the rage that he flew into—he took a broomstick and chased the rat around until he cornered the rat and beat him to a bloody pulp—and that's the response of someone whose fury comes out of not being able to feed their child. So then to tell me that he would deprive Richard . . . Well, I guess Alice's argument was that because Richard wasn't his natural child that he put Richard in a separate category. My mother will have her own story of Sam Brody and I think in the end it will be a positive one, because as difficult a man as he was, and as black as a sort of core of fury that he had in him, he was still essentially a very compassionate person, and he simply wouldn't have done something, not consciously, to deprive Richard. I just don't believe that."

David said that in his experience, Alice was quite capable of standing up for herself. "To some extent I think Sam met his match with Alice, but Alice didn't so much as always stand up to him as avoid him at moments. I mean, I think that were times in her life when she fled from Sam Brody."

As Alice herself later described her relationship with Sam, "You know what Sam and I were? 'Homicidal meets suicidal.' That's all it was. Just as simple as that."

Some sixty years later, Hartley paints a more nuanced picture of his child-hood home, while acknowledging its destructive elements. "I would say that that's not totally inaccurate," he says of Phil's overall depiction. "It wasn't awful all the time; that's a tremendous simplification. When Phil was there it was often awful for whatever that business was between Sam and Phil and Alice. Phil was a little bit holier than thou in his attitude and judgmental, which I thought was very interesting. But there were many good times be-tween those two, Alice and Sam—many times for hours just sitting in the front room listening to music that they appreciated, even reading things back and forth to each other. They were good times. Now bad times were random and things would set people off, but there was a lot of consensus there—consensus about politics, consensus about aesthetics and art and music."

As for Sam, "Sam hated people that he didn't know in the house. Other situations that would stress him or aggravate him were when people came over—Phil, Joel [Rothschild]. And so they saw things that weren't going on all the time. Phil being there could be an irritant to somebody if they thought they were the master of the house. It's a pain in the ass to come in and find somebody hanging around all the time. Now I think it was useful to

Alice to have Phil, and she liked Phil certainly, and he was a very entertaining guy. You know he could tell a good story, he was an interesting guy; he was a leftie; he was in touch with the *Untermensch*. We were happy to see Phil, because he concentrated on us."

They especially enjoyed outings with Phil. "Amusement parks, baseball games, this and that and so forth. He had a little apartment in the Bowery. It was a one-room apartment that was heated with a kerosene stove. I'll never forget that smell. And we used to go down there and we'd spend the night. We slept on the floor. And in the morning Phil would make, like, bacon and eggs and he had a little hot plate. This was primitive."

"You know, Phil was good," recalls Richard. "I mean, I would go to a film with him, and he would tell me what happened during the film and stuff, and we saw a lot of films together."

But when Sam went on a tirade, nobody was safe, says Hartley. "I'll tell you what it is. If two dogs attack each other, you step back because they might bite each other going after the other dog. . . . It's just the sort of instant chaos of the situation, because whether it was Phil or Alice or Alice and Sam and Phil all in one little orchestra, it was not nice to be there, and whether you were a son or a relative or a friend, you got the hell out of there; you know nobody wanted to be there for that."

Except perhaps for Alice, who seemed to thrive on drama and discordance. "I mean if things were going too smoothly, she'd throw a monkey wrench into it," says Richard. "And it wasn't just with Sam. It was at family dinners or something like that. She would get bored, and then all of the sudden people would be raising their voices and shouting and screaming. You know what she was? She was outrageous. Alice was outrageous." (Even with the staid John, who didn't rise to the bait, Alice's usual modus operandi had always been to goad him.)

Olivia, Neel's oldest granddaughter, also remembers how much Alice liked to provoke people. "Alice was of the belief that you should find out what people don't like and *give plenty of it*. As Thanksgiving we would have almost scripted fights," she recalls.

"Alice really liked the Sturm and Drang of it," Hartley says, simply. "She enjoyed the give-and-take of a relationship that was not on the sort of 'bourgeois,' middle-class, stupid level, okay, where everybody plays a little role and so forth. Alice was a complicated person. Alice didn't see things the way other people see them. And probably part of her greatness as an artist is that she had an imagination about what something was, and it might not be what she thought it was. I always said Alice didn't know the difference between a Fifth Avenue bus and a fire truck."

Hartley is less forgiving of Alice's tolerance of Sam's cruelty to Richard. "Alice could cover her tracks when she was responsible for something, too. And whatever happened to Richard, she bears a minimum of 50 percent responsibility—more, because it's her kid. It's her relationship with somebody else; she knows what's happening. And like Phil says in the movie, she forgave Sam everything because he loved her work. But you know there's no forgiving everything if it's your kid. So Alice is at least 50 percent responsible, probably more, in the context of this. Richard wasn't the sole suffering one. We both suffered. Richard was subjected to the physical part of it, even though I got hit a couple times myself, but it wasn't in the same way that Richard got hit. We were in it together. When you are hiding at the bottom of the stairs because of fear . . .

"It could be bad when Phil wasn't there. But if Phil was there, it was most likely to be bad. So we didn't want Phil to come when Sam was there, that was an automatic unallowed state, like in physics. . . . it would rapidly deteriorate and the minute either one of them would show up when the other one was there, trouble, trouble, it's going to be trouble and you could say, 'Hey, I'm getting out of here right now.'

"But whatever led to that, I think Alice was very much a part of it. Obviously if Sam and Phil were alone, they might not have gotten along, either, but Alice stoked it. Because she was in the middle of it, and it was all about her to a certain extent. The three did not work out. That's like two dogs, and you bring another dog in that doesn't get along with one of the other dogs and before you know it they are all killing each other.

"Alice may have been unconscious, in terms of blinded by her own role in this, or affection for somebody. . . . She didn't forgive Sam everything, but she realized her culpability in it. It complicated everything, so she had to forgive herself. You know what I mean; that made it much more. If it was just one bête noire, we could all hate him. But she knew that she was responsible. Maybe she didn't accept the major responsibility, but maybe she did."

In a stunning metaphor, Hartley compares his mother's behavior with her casual attitude toward driving, a skill she never mastered: "She got in the car, you know, not knowing what the implications were, necessarily, not knowing that she was driving around a ton and a half of steel down the

road, that if it hit something, it would knock it to bits, and to a certain extent that was the way she sort of lived. . . . She didn't care about cars and
fences and crap like that. . . . And for that you have to laud her. . . . What
was important to her was this core. She had this tremendous obsession
with art, with painting."

In the Middle of the Road

At the age of fifty, when many of her contemporaries were already grand-mothers, Neel had two young children, nine and eleven, to raise. Still attractive, although increasingly plump and blowsy—her hair was piled loosely on her head and she often wore a housecoat—she also had her hands full juggling Sam and John. Although she painted daily, between her self-imposed exile to Spanish Harlem and her unwavering devotion to realist work during the age of Abstract Expressionism, it is not surprising that her career stalled in the forties and fifties, despite a few shows here and there.

She was getting some work from *Masses & Mainstream*, including the illustrations for Bonosky's stories. In April, a drawing called *Relief Cut* was published. But it wasn't until the end of the year that Alice resurfaced in a gallery, with her first solo show in six years.

The day after Christmas, 1950, Alice's one-man exhibit opened at the ACA Gallery. The show, which ran through January 13, 1951, had been arranged thanks in part to Neel's old friend from the New York Group, Herman Rose, who had brought her to the attention of ACA's assistant director, Abram Lerner.

(In a 1986 letter to the Belchers, Lerner recalled Neel as looking, "lovely and delicate." He also noted her "tremendous ego, marked sweetness," and contrasting "unpleasantness and a touch of paranoia." Lerner saw Alice, in other words, in all the idiosyncratic and contradictory glory that so capti-vated Phillip Bonosky.)

Recalls Herman Rose's wife, Elia, "Herman Baron and Ellen ran the gallery and [Herman] told them about Alice, and they didn't like her work especially. I think [Herman] and Abram Lerner and Joe [Solman] were involved in getting her a show there."

Alice, as always, was an acquired taste. And it says something about the loyalty of her WPA friends that between them, Rose, Solman, and Mike Gold were involved in not only helping get her the show but also in writing the brochure, and even reviewing it.

Solman wrote an exacting introduction:

> Alice Neel is primarily a painter of people. Waifs and poets, friends and Puerto Rican neighbors come in to sit for her—and she probes one without sermon or sentimentality. At times, an element of foreboding, akin to that in the work of Munch, creeps into her work; and there are portraits that are almost vivisections. But always her communication is so irresistibly direct that a great intensity infuses her work.

Seventeen paintings were included; among them were *The Spanish Family*, the lovely rendering of José's sister-in-law-Margarita with her three young children against a delicate filigree of wrought iron; *Fire Escape*; *Sam*; *The Sea*; *Edward Pinckney Greene*; and *Dead Father*. The paintings were sold at prices ranging from $150 to $500.

For someone who had been off the radar for so long, Neel managed to garner some impressive reviews, including one from *The New York Times*:

> Emotional values predominate in Alice Neel's paintings of people at the ACA Gallery. Her approach is frankly Expressionistic; she uses a great deal of black, accentuates the profile lines, and catches figures in strongly individual poses. And its dramatic intensity succeeds because of unmistakable artistic sincerity.

Alice's friend Mike Gold, who wrote regularly for the *Daily Worker* (his column was called "Change the World"), took the occasion to praise Neel's Social Realist style:

> Alice Neel, whose paintings will be shown at the ACA Gallery 63 E. 57th St. beginning today, is perhaps the first painter to pioneer in portraying the spirit of the Puerto Ricans living in New York. . . . The friends of Alice Neel, including Fred Ellis and other painters, feel that her "one-man" show at ACA will reveal to the world of painting a new star of social realism. Included among her portraits are one of Mercedes Arroya [*sic*], a trade union leader of the Puerto Rican people, and well known for her heroism.

More to the point, Gold gave Neel an opportunity to espouse her highly unfashionable beliefs:

> "I am against abstract and non-objective art," said Alice Neel to this reporter, "because such art shows a hatred of human beings. It is an attempt to eliminate people from art, and as such is bound to fail. Rembrandt and Titian gave us a whole universe in their portraits, but this modern art is good only for wallpaper or textiles. . . . But for me, people come first. . . . I think I have tried to assert the dignity and eternal importance of the human being in my portraits."

The *Arts Digest* review was also positive:

> . . . Alice Neel has vigor, a warm earthliness and a careful sense of color which avoids the blatant but does not lack force even when it remains quiet. . . . Described as "a painter of people," she is at her best with rich, and one would suppose, perfectly recognizable liknesses of her Puerto Rican friends and neighbors. Another of the highlights is a curiously unsentimental portrait of her dead father, lying as peacefully as anybody could wish in his casket, clutching a couple of dead roses.

Perhaps indicative of Neel's low profile at the time, the reviewer called Neel a "veteran" New Yorker, while at the same time erroneously describing this as her first one-man show.

ARTnews, which Alice claimed not to read, had a more mixed response. Wrote Stanton Catlin:

> Alice Neel's informal portraits and domestic still lifes are somber projects of city tenement life. Her pictures are unevenly excecuted but the people and objects which she represents from this grey and bare environment have a quiet strength and dignity.

Still, Baron, who was not a real fan of Neel's, did not choose to champion her work, which, under any circumstances, but especially during the early 1950s, was a hard sell. The gallery also showed Abstract Expressionists, whose triumphant transformation of the art world was in the offing. (In 1949, when *Life* magazine profiled Jackson Pollock, the article was ironically subtitled "Is he the greatest living painter in the United States?" signaling the fact that the Ab-Ex stars were, for better or worse, about to become household names.) It is not surprising that in late 1949, when Charles Egan, whose gallery would be pivotal to many of the Ab-Ex artists, came up to Alice's apartment to look at work, he expressed no interest; what's more surprising is that he made the trek up there at all.

And then, of course, there was the political content (and obvious affiliation) of much of Neel's work. McCarthyism (the term was coined in 1950) was rampant. Although she didn't know it at the time, by March 1951, Neel was already under FBI surveillance, which could have begun as early as 1948. But she was never subpoenaed to testify at the Committee for Un-American Activities, as were a number of her friends, including Millen Brand. (As a "reliable source" advised the Bureau in 1951: "The subject appears to suffer from mental psychosis and in the informant's opinion she is in need of psychiatry and was in need of treatment for many years prior to 1951.")

Neel had just one other show in 1951, this one arranged by Gold at the New Playwrights Theatre, which continued to mount its overtly leftist plays during the fifties, duly attracting the attention of the FBI. (There was a two-page write-up on March 10, 1951, of the organization and its leftist activities and productions, such as Herb Tank's *Longitude 49* and Howard Fast's *The Hammer*, in Neel's file.)

Neel's show was held in the basement of a church at 347 East Seventy-second Street from April 23 to May 23. It included two dozen works. Among them were some of Neel's most blatantly Social Realist paintings. The striking *T. B. Harlem*, Neel's picture of José's brother, whose treatment included having a rib removed, was on the cover of the brochure; other pieces were *The Spanish Family*, *Magistrate's Court*, *Investigation of Poverty at the Russell Sage Foundation*, *Mike Gold*, and *Uneeda Biscuit Strike*.

The opening of the show featured a panel discussion on "Realism vs. Abstraction." One of the panelists was to have been Gold himself, although, in fact, he didn't make it. Gold dubbed Neel the "Pioneer of Social Realism" in his introduction to the brochure, a political statement that read as much as a diatribe against abstraction as a paean to Social Realism:

> Alice Neel has never allowed them to dehumanize her. This is heroic in American painting, where for the past fifteen years Humanity has been rejected, its place given to mechanical perversions, patent-leather nightmares and other sick symbols of a dying social order.

Alice has for years lived with her children in a Harlem tenement. Her studio is the kitchen and her models the neighbors and these streets. She comes from an old Philadelphia family dating back to the Revolution. But her paintings reveal that here is her true family. In solitude and poverty, Alice has developed like a blade of grass between two city stones. She has become a superb craftsman, and the first clear and beautiful voice of Spanish Harlem. She reveals not only its desperate poverty, but its rich and generous soul.

Some of the melancholy of the region hangs over her work. This is as inevitable as the sadness in the work of Gorky or Chekhov. But there is also their truth and their unquenchable faith. Alice Neel is a pioneer of social realism in American painting. For this reason, the New Playwrights theater, dedicated to the same cause, presents her paintings to its audience, who will know how to understand, appreciate and encourage one of their own.

Although Neel's New Playwrights' Theatre show escaped the notice of the critics, it didn't escape the FBI, which in May 4 and May 14, 1951, entries quoted Gold's *Daily Worker* article and his introduction in its entirety in its extensive file on Neel. (The FBI may have also been the only agency to notice that Neel had a piece, *Let Them Live*, in a small show at the Hotel Brevoort in June.)

While Gold's words must have been gratifying to Neel, this was just the sort of thing that branded her permanently as a Social Realist (and confirmed for the FBI her Communist ties) right at the time that the Abstract Expressionists were boldy putting themselves on the map. Despite his good intentions, Gold might as well have labeled her as terminally passé. She would have only one more show for the rest of the decade.

Neel's New Playwrights' Theatre show overlapped by several days a seminal moment in Abstract Expressionist history: The Ninth Street Show, which ran from May 21 to June 10, and included sixty-one artists. Nothing could have more clearly illustrated the yawning gap between Neel and the current art world.

A virtual Who's Who of the emerging Abstract Expressionist and New York School movements, the show included everyone from Willem de Kooning, Jackson Pollock, Robert Motherwell, Fairfield Porter, Ad Reinhardt, and Franz Kline (who designed the poster) to Joan Mitchell, Helen Frankenthaler, and Lee Krasner. The opening itself was a mythic event: For many, it was a first glimpse of the new painting style, if not its creators.

(Several months earlier, *Life* magazine had published Nina Leen's iconic photograph *The Irascibles*, picturing fifteen of the avatars of Abstract Expressionism, who had banded together to protest the "American Painting Today—1950" show at the Metropolitan Museum of Art. The virtually all-male group—Hedda Sterne was the only female—dressed atypically in suits, included de Kooning, Gottlieb, Reinhardt, Pollock, Still, Motherwell, and Rothko.)

It would be another several decades before Neel became anything like a part of the contemporary art scene. In the mid-fifties, she began attending meetings at the legendary Artists' Club, on Eighth Street, "to be with other artists." (It was at the Club that Alice met Robert Frank and Alfred Leslie, who would put her in the classic 1959 Beat movie *Pull My Daisy*.)

Her isolation was more or less complete, both figuratively and literally. Neel took her own road: Not only did she continue to paint figurative work at the peak of Abstract Expressionism, but she lived more than a hundred blocks from the epicenter of the modern art world, with its downtown studios and galleries. (Not many midtown galleries or museums in the then tiny art world were located much above Fifty-seventh Street.) And while for decades artists had famously summered or taken up residence in the Hamptons, particularly the Springs, Neel spent weekends and summers in Spring Lake, the furthest cry from any semblance of an art scene.

Harold Rosenberg's historical essay defining the new art movement, "American Action Painters," appeared in *ARTNews*. In it, he declared:

> The big moment came when it was decided to paint. . . . Just to PAINT. The gesture on the canvas was a gesture of liberation, from value—political, esthetic, moral . . . At a certain moment in time, the canvas began to appear to one American painter after another as an arena in which to act—rather than a space in which to reproduce, re-design, or "express" an object . . . What was to go on the canvas was not a picture but an event. The painter no longer approached his easel with an image in his mind; he went up to it with material in his hand to do something to that other piece of material in front of him. The image would be the result of this encounter. . . . Call this painting "abstract" or "Expressionist" what counts is its special motive for extinguishing the object . . .

This was ostensibly the diametrical opposite of what Neel—who was not only a realist, determined to record the object, but first and foremost a portrait painter—had in mind when she approached a canvas. For her, the easel would always be a window onto the psyche of her subject, if not herself.

She continued to include the occasional subtle gesture, as it were, to Action Painting, particularly in her treatment of backgrounds, where she also displayed her awareness of Surrealism and Symbolism: *Harlem Nocturne*, 1952, *Sunset, Riverside Drive*, 1957, which bears a striking resemblance to *Cutglass Sea*, done a decade before. To Neel, that's where such embellishments belonged. She reserved the foreground for her real interest: the realistic subject.

Wrote Bonosky on April 27, 1955, "A has felt martryized not only for her political opinions—for being a woman, and an artist to boot, and a mother, but also because she refused to go along with the current, the fashionable current, 'the abstract linoleum design' school. She stuck to reality—her kind perhaps, but it was real, and it's remained a recognizable comment on life, real life."

Says Bonosky, "She was very bitter about being marginalized like that, being wiped off the map, simply because she insisted on being a realist."

Neel was not the only realist artist who felt marginalized by the ascension of Abstract Expressionism. As artist Jack Levine, who was friendly with the Soyers, through whom he met Neel, put it, "We were mugged! It's a bitter pill that I swallowed a long time ago. We didn't realize the extent of it. It took a lot of money and it took a lot of press to put Abstract Expressionism to where it got. It was like a seizure of power. It cost me something, and I'm still busy catching up." Says Joe Lasker succinctly, "Abstract Expressionism was the new broom—it swept everything else away."

More important, ultimately, to her career than her two shows, was an interesting experiment Bonosky had suggested. Neel had always done spontaneous "show and tells" for her friends, relatives, and supporters.

As Joel Rothschild recalled, "I probably visited Alice a dozen times when she put on her show, which means that she got out painting after painting after painting after painting, commenting on them and so forth. And the paintings were magnificent, but her presentation of them, and the scene that she created, was magnificent. Somebody said that she had a completely clean unconscious. By which they meant that everything came out, you know, and she was at her best. Let's put it this way: You sit down to dinner with her and you would get some of this bubbling, but she was by far at her best when she was showing you her paintings. This was not just an exciting artistic experience but it was a type of theater which was unparalleled. When she was finished with one, she would then go and get another, and there was the anticipation. What will she bring out? What will it be? And it was such a rich collection that if you saw thirty of them, it would take the whole evening. And you had hardly scratched the surface."

It was Bonosky who realized that Neel's colorful remarks regarding her paintings would make a galvanizing lecture. On March 27, 1953, Neel delivered her debut lecture at the Jefferson School, screening two hundred slides. She was introduced by Mike Gold, with Joseph Solman providing critical commentary. The lecture was, of course, reported in her FBI file, which also included a clip of a *Daily Worker* mention:

> On the last of the Friday evenings, March 27, an enthralled audi-
> ence saw 200 colored slides of paintings by Alice Neel, following
> her entire development, discussing with the artist the problems
> of realistic and working class painting, frequently breaking into
> applause at particularly striking scenes.

Such lectures, which included a slide show with extemporaneous remarks, would become a classic Neel performance. Not surprisingly, she excelled at the form, charming and entertaining audiences with her startling portraits and their equally shocking backstories. Throughout the seventies and even eighties, Neel traveled to colleges, museums, and other venues around the country, promoting her work. Philip Pearlstein remembers her giving a lecture to a rapt audience at the Educational Alliance. Benny Andrews remembers Neel shocking the students at the very proper Chapin private school with her liberal use of four-letter words and "talking about sex and everything, and this was Chapin, so my God, it's like the nineteenth century."

                    *   *   *

Meanwhile, Neel's domestic situation was shifting. That same March her brother Albert died (which the family learned by telegram just in time to attend the funeral). Her mother, who was ailing, had been living with Albert and his wife, Nelly. Now she came to live with Neel in Spanish Harlem, as captured in her memorable 1953 portrait *Last Sickness*. The deeply personal image of Neel's mother, wearing a plaid bathrobe, her hair thin and straggling and her face frozen in a fearful, pained expression, is a visual essay on mortality. "I'm tired of death," Neel told Bonosky. "When I looked at Mama there—a shrunken little old thing, that had no connection with the alert tart woman she was, that cured me of any last love of death."

On May 25, 1953, the FBI wrote up the "Communist-controlled" organizations at 35 East Twelfth Street, which included the *Daily Worker*. Attached as an exhibit was a program for play that included an advertisement for "Alice Neel, Class in Painting and Drawing, Studio 939, 8th Avenue. For information call circle 6 5138 Wed evenings 8–11 pm."

Although she didn't speak about it much, Neel occasionally taught classes to bring in extra income. As Alice later told Joan Kufrin, ". . . I used to give classes sometimes. There are a lot of women that study art, at menopause age. I had them come to the house. . . . It's a mean thing to say, really. I shouldn't say it, because it's perfectly all right to study art at any age, but they're in the late forties, fifties. And they're nice. But even though fifty people study art, you maybe only get one artist out of it."

On June 18, the FBI missed an opportunity to spy on Alice at Union Square, where she, like hundreds of others, congregated to protest the trial of the Rosenbergs. "Look what happened to the poor Rosenbergs, for being imagined to have atomic secrets. I went down to Union Square to hear them speak in 53, the night before they executed the Rosenbergs. And do you know what happened, the neighbors were already taking the furniture out. Wasn't that frightful. They stole the gate they had at the top of the stairs to keep the children from falling, they took the piano. Oh that was a horrible business, you know."

Alice kept the FBI, which believed she was officially married to Sam Brody, baffled by lying about her age by fourteen years. Despite numerous efforts, they were never able to officially verify her birthplace and date, even after they determined, through her son's birth certificate, that she had been born in 1900. But they nonetheless continued to gather information on her. Their notes sometimes read like a routine from the Keystone Kops:

A reliable informant advised that the subject was sympathetic to the Communists and associated with a number of Communists. She is reported to have painted portraits of several individuals who were Communists. Another reliable informant advised that in 1951, the subject became engaged in a political discussion at an art gallery, at which time she expressed pro-Soviet views. Reliable informants advised that subject and husband are CP members as of 1948.

Reads a November 30, 1953, entry, which also states that Neel was born on August 7, 1914.

In the fall of 1953, Richard Neel entered High Mowing, a boarding school in Wilton, New Hampshire, on a full scholarship. Hartley would join him there two years later. Alice wrote Bonosky a long, sad letter about Richard's leaving home:

AUGUST 19, 1953
Don't you suppose I've anguished over the business of Neel going away and also changing his name but my main reasons are he wants to. Just why he changed his ideas about going away I don't know but about 5 of his classmates are going and there is always the fact that his life is scarcely "carefree" although I've done my best to make it so, because of the horror injected into life by Sam. And he of course is always the main target.

Also when we got up there she made the money angle so attractive—$200 for everything and it doesn't have to be paid all at once. It must cost that much just to feed him. I know I'm taking a chance to let him go like that but I think he has some depth of feeling and right now with mother sick most of the time things get so complicated and also as I said before that raging wolf "Sam." All summer I've tried hard to get rid of him but the more I'd like him to go (for good this time) the more passionately he wants to stay.

By now I feel more than schizophrenic, that's only two divisions, isn't it. I feel multiphrenic and since I'm essentially "simple-hearted" or at least, I like to be, I get so tangled in my own thought I stop thinking just in self-protection.

I hate liked the devil to see Neel go and I know I'll miss him like mad but he's so set on it and you know I prefer to give people what they want.

Why couldn't you come down for a couple of days by bus. It's $3.00 round trip, the children would "love" to see you and me also and we really need it. From Mon to Fri there's never anyone here so the field could be yours.

Neel leaves on the 13th of Septmber—the day before his birthday and I dread it.

We'll be in before that as I want to get his eyes examined.

P.S. There is another factor in this Neel business. When Hartley and Neel alias Richard, disagree or scrap, then Sam attacks Neel violently and now that Neel is so big it is both better and worse, better because he can protect himself, worse because the proportions become more dangerous. Don't think I'm protecting Sam, quite the reverse, because after all Neel isn't 14 yet— but the whole situation becomes so ugly.

In an undated letter, Neel also wrote:

Phil, dear . . . it's true I feel weighed down by experience and somehow not much smarter about "now." Will I be able to bear them away? At first one resists children, tries to keep on with one's life, etc, however as time goes on more and more one becomes that normal thing—"a parent" and relates with it. Then suddenly you can see that you aren't going to work with this [word unclear] forever and you aren't even sure of a pension and life yawns in front of you, that same big black terrifying hole you've always been afraid of. Still I'm not sure I feel like that, by now I know so much if only I can work and life really doesn't look like a big black hole but something that sits poised on the edge of a marvelous era—and people are wonderful—capable of almost anything really. If only the apartment isn't ice cold and my arthritis so painful that I won't be able to function. . . .

I'm working like mad painting Richard Neel and Hartley Neel. I've done one painting of Neel—strong I think—I'm never sure. Well you'll see it. I've been very bad to Sam so I expect him to leave right after the children. Also I think the sadism of such a gesture will appeal to him—I'll be better off if he does. I always appear to the world in a conditional state because of his violent behavior. . . .

Neel's mother lived with her for nearly a year, until her death, at age eighty-six, from complications from a broken hip, on March 1, 1954. Neel had always fought depression, but her mother's death triggered a downward spiral during the next few years. Friends were concerned as Neel gained weight, sometimes drank excessively, and generally let herself go.

As Bonosky wrote in a June 14, 1955 entry, "I arrived at A's at 3. A opened the door. She was dressed in some kind of flimsy gown—perhaps nightgown—which showed her body. She has a careless way with her 'charms' as though she wanted to deal with you without reference to her femininity. (Though she brings that into play, too, when it suits her.) She lets go; She'd drink herself silly each night if she had company to do it with."

By March 1954, the FBI, using information gleaned from a letter sent to them by a source in Miami, had pegged Neel as a "muddled, romantic, Bohemian type Communist idealist who will carry out loyally the Communist sympathizer type of assignment, including illegal work if ordered to do so. . . . Alice Neel talks the straight Party line passionately even in the presence of total strangers. She complained . . . that the Communist Party gives her nothing more important to do than pass out leaflets and to paint signs." Still, they continued to surveil her for several more years, even reopening her file as late as 1961.

In the summer of 1954, Neel had her last show until 1960, once again at the ACA Gallery, thanks to the efforts of her friend Joseph Solman. "Two One-Man Exhibitions: Capt. Hugh N. Mulzac, Alice Neel" ran from August 30 to September 11 and included eighteen paintings, among them *My Sons*, *Bill McKie*, *Alice Childress*, and *T. B. Harlem*.

The show received a mention in *ARTnews*: "Alice Neel, veteran of previous New York shows, continues to view the human face—even that of the child—without tenderness or compassion. Gaunt and austere, her portraits of Negroes, hospital nurses and young boys are strongly delineated and blocked in with bold color." The paintings sold from $150–$700.

There was also a dismissive review in *Arts Digest*: "The artist seems to stress in a rather insistent, exclamatory fashion how interesting she finds each sitter, but she failed to make them interesting to us either as people or as paintings." This was the final discouraging word on the artist before a resounding six-year silence.

In mid-April 1955, according to Bonosky's journal, Sam temporarily moved out and rented a room, blaming Alice for "conspiring with the FBI to evict him from the house."

That same spring, Neel made a fictional appearance as an artist named Rose Hallis in Millen Brand's latest novel, *Some Love, Some Hunger*, which was published to acclaim. Wrote Brand:

The best artist available for color was Rose Hallis, a free-lance designer. . . . Rose had that flair for life in the mingling of colors:

she would be the one for this assignment. With or without paint, she had life.

She was at the stair railing, leaning over, as he walked up. She was wearing a dark, loose dress, and her long hair was wound and knotted. "Hello," she called down. "Oh, it's you, Liam, it's Ed." Her older boy, Liam, (she pronounced his named Leem) strained over the railing to see. He had poor eyesight . . . She glanced after him. He's listening to a Borodin quartet, isn't that awful? At his age. Only twelve. To crouch at a loudspeaker and listen to music. Finley hates it. Finley was her other boy . . . "Come in, you look so well dressed . . . Clothes can make you mature, can't they. I mean if you can afford them, you must be a few years older at least." She smiled, a smile naïve and tired, and glowing. "Now if I dressed well, I'd look younger."

"You are young, Rose."

Her smile burned. "You're kind. Don't be kind. I have arthritis and my hair is turning gray. Look." She held out a strand of her hair . . .

"I've done a new painting," Rose said. He brought his attention back to her. Across the room, on a piano, a piece of music moved in a summer draft . . . "Would you like to see it?"

A certain eagerness in her—he would have to see it. She led him to her large work-room in the front, a room of high molding and figured plaster ceiling, smelling of turps, her easel stood empty, like a window.

From an end of the room, the Borodin quartet was crashing faintly. Liam had his head down against it, his eyes shuttered.

"This I have to listen to while I paint."

"Does it bother you?" he said.

"It depends. If I want it quiet, I make him pose for me. I've painted him twice as much as Finley."

She was lifting a rectangle that lay flat against the wall, turning it out and resting it on the base of the easel. On the canvas a man sat holding a child in his lap. The man's face was distraught, the child's face, relaxed. "It's this generation you know—adults seeking refuge in the repose of their children. Not repose really. It's a kind of natural poise children have. A kind of tact . . ."

Yes, her strength was color. Although walls and corners of the rooms gave her pictures depth, her figures or objects were out-

lined in purple gray or gray without any intention of shadow. Her
dimensions were color.

As he kept looking at the hunched, taut man holding the child
against him, he said, "There's even love in the child's face."

"Yes, how they fool us!" she said. She glanced at Liam. "They
hate us, really, you know."

"Hate?"

"We all put them aside. They get in our way. They know they
get in our way and they want to and they hate us. . . . Don't un-
derestimate children's hate. It's just lucky they can't do much.
When I was a child, I used to dream for hours at a time how to
kill my mother. Oh, not just Mama, everybody . . .

". . . And you should see Liam and Finley. Liam looks so sweet
there, listening to music," she folded her hands with an angelic
expression. "But when Finley comes . . . or when I want him to
be still. No." She passed her hand tiredly over her face. "Don't
talk to me about children."

In his novel, Brand also used a story about "Foxy and Catty" that Richard had supposedly made up when he was a child, and paid him a dollar for
it. But after discussing it with Bonosky (who actually wrote the story with
Richard, according to his journal), Richard asked for more. When the
book was finally published, Brand sent him ten dollars.

As Bonosky noted in his journal on May 15, 1955:

*She had his book chastely inscribed to her and the two boys. Her
eyes were rounded.*

"Why, Phillip, he got it all from here—all of it!"

"Really?"

*I remember how incensed she was once because he pulled out
his notebook and took down some remarks of hers right in front
of her eyes.*

*"So many writers have used me in their books," she said, with
a trace of complacency.*

"Don't you mind?" I said.

*"Mind? Why should I? I think that would be petty. Besides,
what can you do? In any case, nobody has really caught me. . . ."*

*Which is true. She has so much colorful surface that there's
no incentive to go beneath.*

"I think you could do me best."

"You wouldn't like it if I did. . . ."

"You'd paint me black?"

I shrug. "I wouldn't picture you the way you would want me to. . . ."

"Anyhow," she said, "he doesn't catch it. He has N. and H. there, and listens to N. singing, and you know he doesn't even say that his voice was beautiful. . . ."

"Has he got my story in?"

She nodded. When I borrowed the book later from her I found that B. had indeed included the story I pretended N. had written. I must say I had a kind of admiration for the economical way in which he put all things to his purpose.

*   *   *

Throughout most of the fifties, Alice continued to receive vigilant attention from the FBI, which got information from various sources, including someone whom the FBI believed was either her sister or sister-in-law. The Bureau ultimately confronted her directly on October 11 and 17, 1955.

Hartley recalls the incident: "We were there. We let them in. We were playing in the playroom. They came in their trench coats, these two Irish boys. Boy, Alice took care of them. She said, 'The only thing I don't have in my collection are FBI agents. Would you please step in the other room? I can paint you. . . .' They just got red in the face and left." Although it was later said she asked them to pose nude, Hartley says that never happened.

According to the October 31, 1955, entry in her file, the first visit, at 11:05 A.M., was terminated after five minutes because visitors arrived. "The subject at the time of the initial contact was cordial and a future contact was set up for an unspecified date."

The second interview lasted about half an hour, from 6:35 P.M. to 7:10 P.M. "At the outset of the interview the subject was cordial. However, when the purpose of the interview became apparent to the subject, she refused to furnish any information concerning her activities, associations, or affiliations. The interview was pressed at this point, but the subject remained adamant in her refusal to furnish any information to this Bureau. Attempts were made to engage the subject in conversation on any point with negative results and accordingly the interview was terminated."

But although she successfully shook them off, Neel was quite upset by the intrusion. As Bonosky noted in his journal, October 20, 1955, "Up to A's yesterday. She told me she'd another visit (FBI) and once again matched

wits with the 'vistors.' They were Irish. She tried a little Geneva spirit on
them, and they assured her that the 'hunt' would go on. She made them
leave. But was so shaken all night she couldn't sleep."

At this point, it seems, the FBI gave up, at least temporarily. "A review
of instant file fails to reflect any recent subversive activity on the part of
the subject. Her name has been deleted from the Security Index. In view of
this, no further investigation is being conducted to ascertain the correct date
and place of the subject's birth and this matter is being placed in a closed
status pending receipt of additional information which would warrant its reopening." However, three years later, the FBI resumed their investigation,
and in 1959 Neel's status was "subject retained on Communist Index."

In a late entry, another informant advised, "From my experience with
Alice Neel, I can swear that she is an avowed, uninhibited, outright Communist and sympathizer toward all Communistic aims and gains in every
thought she has and word she speaks. She is angry and furious against our
keeping Red China out of the U.N. . . . She attends all lectures she can,
given by Communist or Socialist followers in N.Y.C. She is devoted to and
admiring of Paul Robeson, his son also, and approves of their being Communists. She blames the United States for all the Robesons have suffered at
our hands because of our hatred and intolerance of non-white citizens. . . ."
Neel's case was finally closed in 1961.

(In 2005, the artist Jenny Holzer turned some of the partially blacked-
out pages of Neel's FBI file into emblematic prints.)

*   *   *

The mid to late fifties were a difficult time for Neel. Although she was painting, she wasn't showing. Still, this is when she did some of her best pictures
of the "Spanish Harlem Period." These include her grinning portrait of
Georgie Arce (1955); a painting of another neighborhood boy, *Call Me
Joe*, 1955, the memorable portrait of sisters, *Two Girls, Spanish Harlem*,
1959; the odd *Religious Girl*, 1959; and the painting she later called *The
20th Century*, the succinct, bleak, brown *Rag in Window*, 1959.

Physically, Neel continued to let herself go. In April 11 and 15, 1957,
journal entries, Bonosky remarked:

> *Last Saturday I remembered she'd sat around in her favorite
> costume, a dirty green slip and a dirtier dressing gown . . . . When
> I dropped in Saturday night to see A, I found her in that old
> olive-colored coat, pinned over with safety pins and underneath
> she had nothing on but an old slip. This costume of hers drives*

her sons frantic. Her hair was unmade, she looked tired and she
was a bit sick.

In May 1957, Neel received some shocking news: a "curt note" from her
sister, Lily, stated, "Elizabeta wants me to tell you that Carlos died in his
sleep last night." Enríquez, who had been impoverished, alcoholic, and ill
for some time, died on the eve of the opening of a solo show. He was found
in a chaise lounge at his simple but charming studio, Hurón Azul, on the
outskirts of Havana, which during the forties had become famous for the
intellectual salon he hosted every Sunday.

According to Bonosky's journal, May 29, 1957, Neel showed little or no
emotion on learning about the death of the man who was her first great
love, the father of her two daughters, and legally still her husband.

> *"Did the death of your husband," I asked, "affect you much?"*
> *She laughed. "No, not much." Then she added: "But at the same*
> *time it did, you know." She'd been thinking about Carlos. "You*
> *know," she said, "how unfair the relationship between men and*
> *women was in Cuba. There's no Cuban who hasn't had a woman*
> *by 15, let's say; and anyone who can't get one is put down as a*
> *fool, or there's something wrong with him. They early get used to*
> *separating sex from love; and when they come to you—to me,"*
> *she said, "they already have a tremendous advantage over you.*
> *That was an unsatisfactory part of our relationship. He was so*
> *sophisticated already sexually, but for me, of course, who had*
> *had no experience, it was altogether different. . . . When I was*
> *down there, his sisters would say to me, 'Do you know Carlos is*
> *out with a girl tonight!' And I'd say, 'With a girl!' And they'd*
> *say, 'Who would you rather have him out with—a boy?' They*
> *were bound in by custom, but they had their own way of manipu-*
> *lating the situation; they were very clever and malicious. . . . I*
> *can't tell you how I felt to get back to New York!"*

In the same entry, Bonosky succinctly and cynically summed up Neel's
credo:

> *She's worked out her own code of behavior, whose cornerstones*
> *are two: 1) her freedom to paint; 2) the well-being of her two*
> *boys. For 1, she will surrender everything else, and what other*

*people place high—the sanctity of one's flesh in bed—she subor-
dinates to this superior law of her life. And the second also
comes lower—but higher than anything else but the first.*

*What other people strive for and cannot live without—good
furniture, good clothes, a conventional acceptance by society,
etc., etc.—she gives up without any sense of loss whatsoever.*

*What misleads most people who see her life is suggested in
that. Naively, a person who suffers if her wardrobe isn't replen-
ished every season thinks A. suffers too; but she doesn't. Or the
woman who believes herself shamed to Hell eternal if she has
carnal relations with a man not her husband believes this preys on
A's mind; but it doesn't.*

*Of course she pays. She pays all right, but in that desperate
exchange that one makes with fate, she's not altogether a loser.*

But Neel's apparent indifference to Carlos masked deeper emotions. A
few weeks later, Bonosky witnessed Neel's reaction when a guest at her
house began singing Spanish songs. As he put it in his journal:

> *Alice's face changed suddenly and strangely. As she listened to
> those Spanish tunes and words, she looked like a woman in exile
> hearing the accents of her native land. . . . At one point she
> cried, "Oh, this Spanish atmosphere!" She shuddered and
> hugged herself. Her husband had died only recently, the Cuban,
> and his death released a flood of memories. She thought then of
> Neel's father, the Puerto Rican, and later we were to listen again
> to his voice on a couple of cheap, home-made records . . . and as
> we listened, I watched Alice's face fill with the kind of memory
> that comes back to your face when your face remembers the whole
> body. . . . When Alice sang a song, her voice came thin and girl-
> ish, so innocent and sweet and her face reflected the same purity.*

Later, Alice showed Bonosky and his wife, Faith, an early portrait of
Carlos. "It was the romantic picture of a Spanish grandee, sitting at a café
table with a glass of amber wine before him," Bonosky wrote

That was then: In the long interim since Alice had last seen him, Carlos
had become the very embodiment of the mythic *romancero guajiro* that he
would make famous through his painting and writing.

Romancero Guajiro

In the twenty-seven years since Carlos had left Neel, Enríquez had established himself as one of Cuba's leading artists, a figure of legendary status. Enríquez was famous not only as a foremost member of the Vanguardia movement, but also renowned as the author of three novels, *Tilín García* (1939), published during his lifetime, and *La Vuelta dey Chenco*, and *La Feria de Guaicanama*, published posthumously in 1960. His books focus on the same subject matter as his art: the indigenous Cuban spirit, which he celebrated in his "Peasant Ballads." Says Graziella Pogolotti, a leading cultural critic (and Marcelo's daughter), "He is one of the most important artists in Cuba in the twentieth century."

After returning to Cuba briefly, in May 1930, Carlos had his first show in Havana since 1927, which opened at Las Asociación de Reporteros de la Habana in June. It was immediately closed down because of its sexual content. The show reopened at a new venue, the law offices of Emilio Roig de Leuchsenring.

In August, Carlos left Cuba to spend several years abroad, in Paris, Italy, and Spain, joining friends who were already in Europe, including Marcelo Pogolotti. Recalls Graziella Pogolotti, "My mother always said that when we all used to live in Paris, and I was a newborn little baby, sometimes they didn't have money to buy a bottle of milk. And Carlos wouldn't say a word, but he would disappear, he would vanish. He didn't have a penny either, but he would go and play billiards with some friends, and with that he would get the necessary amount to leave a bottle of milk in front of the door. And my mother never forgot that."

He became acquainted with the work of the Surrealists in France, and participated in several shows in Spain, in both Oviedo and Madrid. He also illustrated the French and Spanish editions of *The Terror in Cuba*, a pamphlet published by the Young Cuban Revolutionaries against Machado.

Enríquez returned to Havana in January 1934. Soon afterward, he had a show of work he had done in Europe at the Lyceum. It too was closed down on opening night, again because of its explicit sexual content. Once more the show was moved to the law offices of Emilio Roig de Leuchsenring. Carlos's often-scandalous career had begun in earnest.

In his work, Enríquez exalted the Cuban national identity, its essential *cubania*—particularly its peasant roots. Both his paintings and his writings revolve around *romancero guajiro*—rustic or peasant romances.

As Enríquez himself explained it, "I am presently working on what could be called 'peasant ballads,' that is to say the painting of the Cuban peasant in his environment, surrounded by something mysterious and fantastic that fills his solitude with curious legends, which emerge out of his direct contact with the earth." The art historian Juan Martínez, author of *Cuban Art and National Identity* and *Carlos Enríquez: The Painter of Cuban Ballads*, calls this genre "Creole Ballads." (Martínez points out that Enríquez's trope of the *romancero guajiro* emulates, to a certain extent, García Lorca's poetry cycle *Romancero Gitano*, or *Gypsy Ballads*, published in 1928.)

The protagonist of *Tilín García* is a *guajiro*; he also appears as an iconic image in much of Enríquez's painting. A pistol and blade-wielding hero on horseback, Enríquez's *guajiro* conquers the landscape—and its women—with equal machismo. This swashbuckling folk idol, prone to physical violence, is also a kind of Cuban Robin Hood. Whether he is destroying flowers or ravaging women, the *guajiro* has social justice and the good of the Cuban people at heart.

Enríquez's painting *El Rey de los Campos de Cuba*, (*The King of the Cuban Countryside*, 1934) epitomizes his depiction of the *guajiro*. A long-haired, musatchioed figure with a broad-brimmed sombrero, he sits astride a rearing horse, his hand on the trusty blade being pulled from its sheath. Painted in an early version of Enríquez's celebrated style, the figure shares both Cubist and Surrealist influences. But they are merged into a genre that is pure Enríquez, particularly the "transparency" technique used in painting the *guajiro*'s banditlike—but diaphanous—mask. To the left of the noble *guajiro* are two vague figures who may be guards or police. In the background is the fertile Cuban countryside, shown as two large breast-like hills studded with tiny palm trees. *El Rey de los Campos de Cuba* was awarded a prize in February 1935, at the Primera Exposición Nacional de Pintura y Escultura.

Later that same year, in the December issue of the magazine *Grafos*,

Enríquez defined for the first time the genre he was developing in an article entitled, "The Criollismo and Its Basic Plastic Interpretation." In 1936, he coined the term *romancero guajiro* to describe his work.

Tilín, the quintessential *guajiro*, is a character Enríquez clearly identified with. At one point, Tilín fires his gun at a bunch of harmless orchids attached to a tree, their parasitic and feminine delicacy trigger a primal response:

> Without knowing it, he was one of those primitive men, of elemental emotions. In him, the women admired his violent decisiveness in lovemaking, his lack of femininity, and the impetuous savagery with which his desires were translated into actions. He was earthy. He emanated from the furrow of the earth, like an animal he could perceive the occult and the supernatural which originate from the earth. . . . He came to feel oppressed by the delicacy of the landscape, and, like an automaton, urinated on the wildflowers which colored the fields yellow, white purple and yellow.

Enríquez, like Neel, rebelled against his upbringing through both his lifestyle and his art. They both relished the scandal caused by work considered either too political or too erotic. If Enríquez's family's money came in part from sugarcane, sugarcane (and by extension the economy of the United States) was the sworn enemy of the *guajiro,* as illustrated by this passage from *Tilín García*:

> And this was when the *guajiro* saw himself displaced, frightened off, deprived and chased away from the small land-owners themselves, they became slaves of the sugar-cane growers, of other small pieces of land only ashes remained and they were entrapped by the new landowner's stores, having to work for their food . . . their coffee plantations, worth fortunes, were burned to plant sugar cane. . . . The seeds of the land were abandoned, to plant sugar cane.

Says Pogolotti, "Enríquez and my father and the other painters of that movement believed in the total rejection of all that would seem or look bourgeois. Adds Martínez, "Enríquez was out to scandalize the Cuban bourgeoisie. Maybe because he had been born into it. He also had a big ego and that certainly helped make him notorious in the way that he wanted to be notorious."

Enríquez considered raw sexuality to be an essential element of lo Cubano. Overt, sometimes shockingly graphic images permeate both his painting and writing.

> When Tilín met her, she was a complete and lustful mulata whose armpits were the thermometers of the lust which agitated her body; her pointed and erect tits had a perpetual shaking movement, allowing an occasional view of her nipples, dark and shiny like wet chocolate . . . they were like bullets of desire looking through the window of life . . . That was when her sensuality became art, the motion of her body left voids in the air it displaced; the rhythm of her walk became dense like the jungle, and only one small movement which shook her tits, her flanks and her eyelids, spoke of the brutal passions which stirred within her complete womanhood.

(It is interesting that Neel's 1928 short story, "The Dark Picture of the Kallikas," has a similar visceral sensuality.)

In *El Rapto de las Mulatas*, 1938, perhaps his most famous work, two *guajiros* in cowboy hats, mounted on horses, rape two apparently willing mulatto women. The painting is a swirling, sensual tangle of rearing horses and violated, enraptured women. Enríquez used the transparency technique that became his trademark to great effect in his nudes. Images are slightly blurred, as if seen through a scrim or a Vaseline-coated lens. A picture like *El Trópico*, 1947, a lush male fantasy of a sinuous black nude with pointed nipples, posed against tropical plants, has a nearly pornographic feel.

"The technique is soft and somewhat transparent. The tropical light erases the distances, sometimes turns solid objects into liquid, fuses the colors and transforms the quality of the materials," Enríquez wrote in 1944, describing his work to Alfred H. Barr, the director of the Museum of Modern Art, where the artist participated in several shows.

Although their styles couldn't be more different, Enríquez and Neel explicitly overlapped in subject matter at times. *Primavera Bacteriológica*, painted in 1932, depicts a headless woman on a toilet, giving herself a douche. It is oddly similar to Neel's self-depiction in the 1935 erotic bathroom watercolor she did of herself and John Rothschild.

Their 1934 portraits of the young Isabetta are a study in contrasts (Enríquez's sentimentalized version looks almost like a Keane). But there is an image in *Campesinos Felices* (*Happy Peasants*, 1938), Enríquez's satirical painting of starving peasants—a small fierce figure of a nude girl, whose posture, legs firmly parted and arms akimbo—mimics Isabetta's in Neel's 1934 nude of her, although Enríquez had never seen it. His *Virgin del Cobre*, 1933, is similar, in both palette and style, to some of Neel's early, somewhat Surrealist work, particularly *Requiem*, 1928, done just after Santillana's death and two years before Carlos's departure. They also both did double female nude portraits—although Neel's *Nadya and Nona*, 1933, was not explicitly lesbian, as were several Enríquez did in the 1940s.

Throughout the mid to late 1930s Enríquez continued to explore his Creole ballad themes. In early 1936, he participated in the Exposición de Pintura Moderna III Circulo de Amigos de la Cultura Francesca, along with Amelia Peláez and Domingo Ravenet. In August of that same year, he showed work in a painting exhibit at the Lyceum with Peláez, Ravenet, and Víctor Manuel Gracía. In 1937, he was part of the Exposición de Arte Moderno in the spring. He also painted a mural at the José Migues Gómez high school in Havana.

In 1938, Enríquez's work was shown in Mexico City, at the Galería de Exposiciones del Palacio de Bellas Artes, during the Exposición de Arte Cubano Actual. *El Rapto de las Mulatas* won a prize that June at the second Esposición Nacional de Pintura y Escultura in Havana.

Nineteen thirty-nine was an important year for Enríquez. He moved to the outskirts of rural Havana, to El Hurón Azul, a rustic house and studio he had built with money he had inherited after his father's death. He published *Tilín Garcia*, his first novel, and he had his first show in the United States, a group exhibit at the Riverside Museum in New York. He also "married" Eva Fréjaville, a noted writer and beauty—and the wife of his former best friend, the novelist Alejo Carpentier. Carpentier never forgave him for seducing Fréjaville away.

As Graziella Pogolotti succinctly tells the story, "Carlos and Alejo, who was a very close friend of Enríquez, and Eva used to go out together. The three of them were in Carlos's car, and at a certain point, Carlos said to Alejo, 'Get out, because Eva is going to stay with me.'" But, as her father recalled in *Of Clay and Voices*, "The three of them were traveling in the middle of the Malecón in broad daylight, when Carlos suddenly stopped the car and asked Eva if she preferred to continue with Carpentier, or if she would go with him. When she answered with the latter option, Carlos asked Carpentier to get out of the car. When Carpentier, thinking it was a joke, went to the Blue Ferret, the painter theatrically brandished a pistol."

Enríquez painted a gauzy nude fresco of Fréjaville in the main room of El Hurón Azul. She was also the subject of a disarming nude portrait painted on the studio's bathroom door and now displayed at Havana's Museo Nacional de Bellas Artes.

The sparkling rum bottles that line the path to El Hurón Azul, buried neck down, were put there by Enríquez and his cousin, to help him find the way home at night when he was drunk—which happened more often than not. (Carlos also used to use the bottles in his studio. Smeared with paint, they were quite beautiful, and coveted by visitors, including his daughter, Isabetta.)

Despite its Cuban-style terra-cotta roof, the odd little cottage, which is hidden behind a bright blue fence, looks nothing like the neighboring houses. Some say it was modeled after a Pennsylvania railroad station, a vestigial reference to his studies in Philadelphia in the mid 1920s, and, perhaps, his pivotal relationship with Neel.

El Hurón Azul—the Blue Ferret—takes its name from the ferrets that populated the area. The artist killed one of the animals, skinned it, painted its skin blue, and nailed this totem to his door. The studio soon earned an almost-mythic reputation—not just for its picturesque ambience and famous owner but also because of the salons Enríquez hosted every Sunday.

Throughout the mid-1940s, El Hurón Azul was a celebrated cultural hotbed for the Cuban intelligentsia. "Everybody who was anybody that was part of the culture in Havana came out to El Hurón Azul for those Sunday gatherings," says Martínez.

"It was the splendid era of El Hurón Azul," Pogolotti recalls. "I have a vivid memory of visiting El Hurón Azul with my father as a child. Carlos would welcome as many as forty or fifty friends on Sunday. The consumption of rum and beer was quite high, and people would be holding forth both in- and outdoors. There would be artists and writers from Havana and artists from other countries. Things would begin in the morning and continue all day, until very late at night. They would be discussing everything having to do with literature and art. Nobody wanted to be the first to leave."

From 1940 to 1943, Enríquez participated in a number of high-profile art shows in Havana. He completed his second and third novels, *La Vuelta del Chencho* and *La Feria de Guaicanama*. In 1943, Enríquez's work was exhibited for the first time at the Museum of Modern Art, from March 31 to May 9, in a show entitled, "The Latin American Collection of the Museum of Modern Art." (It is unclear if Neel was aware of or saw this show.) He also had a one-man show at the Lyceum in Havana, from June 17 to 28.

Enríquez and Fréjaville spent the end of 1943 into early 1944 in Mexico, where he met the famous Mexican muralists Diego Rivera and José Clemente Orozco. Rivera showed his work at the Palacio de Bellas Artes. Enríquez also spent some time studying fresco painting with Orozco.

Nineteen forty-four was another banner year. Besides two solo shows, one in Mexico City and the other in Manzanillo, Oriente Province, Cuba, Enríquez gave a conference, "El Surrealismo," which was coordinated with Marcelo Pogolotti's art show "Nuestro Tiempo." Both took place at the Frente Nacional Antifascista.

Enríquez participated in a second show at the Museum of Modern Art that spring. From March 16 to April 30, his work was included in the first show of its kind in the United States, "Modern Cuban Painters." But sadly, his "marriage" to Fréjaville ended when she left him for another woman. "For Carlos Enríquez, this was the most humiliating thing that could ever happen to him," says Pogolotti. He would later do several paintings of lesbian lovers.

In 1945, Enríquez went to Haiti to study history and folklore, including voodoo. He showed his work in a group exhibit at Port-au-Prince, "Les Peintres Modernes Cubains," which ran from January 18 to February 4, followed by a one-man show from April 23 to May 6 at the 12th Exposition du Centre d'Art. During this time he met the woman who would become his third (and last) "wife," Germaine Lahens.

Returning to Cuba with Lahens, Enríquez continued to be productive. In 1946, he was given an award for his painting *La Arlequina*. He also had work shown internationally—in exhibits in Mexico, Argentina, and Washington, D.C. In 1947, Enríquez had another solo show, this time at the University of Havana, La Sociedad Universitaria de Bellas Artes. He collaborated on several works, designing the set and costumes for a one-act ballet, with music by Hilario González and choreography by Alberto Alonso. And he illustrated a collection of poems, *El Son Entero*, by his friend Nicolás Guillén. In 1949, Enríquez participated in several important shows, one of modern Cuban artists at the Palacio Muncipal, in Havana, and another at the Lyceum.

In the early 1950s, Germaine left him. It was the beginning of a steady decline for the artist. At first, his career didn't suffer. That year he was in three group shows in Havana. The following year, he, along with other

Cuban artists, including Amelia Peláez and Wilfredo Lam, were commissioned by Esso Standard Oil to paint a mural on O Street in the Vedado, his old Havana neighborhood.

But Enríquez's habitual drinking had begun to take a serious toll on his health. He frequently fell, first injuring his foot, then his head. In 1953, he was hospitalized for foot surgery. After that, he used a cane. His painting, *Dos Ríos*, 1939, honoring José Martí, was awarded "best painting to capture not only the chronological circumstances by the spirit of the hero" by the Comisión Nacional del Centenairo de Martí.

The following year, Enríquez had another solo show, December 10–30, at the Galería Nuestro Tiempo. In 1955, when Havana's new national museum at the Palacio de Bellas Artes was completed, several of his paintings were placed on permanent view.

The year before his death, Enríquez's work was shown in numerous exhibits, including one at the Lyceum, one at the University of Havana, another at the Lyceum, and the 8th Salon National de Pintura y Escultura at the Palacio de Bellas Artes.

Says Pogolotti, "The last years of Carlos Enríquez were actually very sad. He was bankrupt and ruined, and little by little he was left alone. Some of his friends were not true friends. He suffered a lot. He was an alcoholic. He would fall down. He would be left unconscious for hours and hours. At that point, he frequently suffered from very serious headaches, and he was hospitalized. They discovered that the headaches were caused by fractures, which left to heal by themselves would press on nerves in the brain, so they operated on him a number of times to break his bones again and reconstruct them. It was horrible. He spent months in the hospital. I think part of his memories while at the hospital are in his last novel, about a dead man who comes out of the hospital and receives a fortune. And he starts to distribute the money among his neighbors and friends. These were his final years." One of the portraits he made at this time was of Maria, the young daughter of the last woman who took care of him when he was ill.

Enríquez died at El Hurón Azul on May 2, 1957. Perhaps fittingly, it was the day that his sixth solo show in Havana was scheduled to open. The house had no phone, and the curator was furious at Enríquez's unexplained absence. Only later did he learn that a neighbor's daughter had found the artist, three months shy of fifty-seven, dead in his chaise lounge by the fireplace. At his side was his dog, Caliban.

The show opened a few weeks later, now called "Exposicíon Póstuma de Cuadros de Carlos Enríquez," at the Galería de Arte de Editorial LEX.

Enríquez would go on to have numerous posthumous shows, including an exhibit representing Cuba in the nineteenth Olympics in Mexico City.

El Hurón Azul became a museum. It was taken over by the local municipality, Arroyo Naranjo, in 1981, then closed for six years, during which time it was lovingly restored and its collection of original art carefully curated.

It's a quirky cottage, complete with a fireplace (unheard of for a tropical climate) surrounded by the lovely nude fresco *Las Bañistas* and a "haunted staircase," which Enríquez believed a ghost used to climb.

To the right of the fireplace is a bookcase filled with books signed by some of El Hurón Azul's famous visitors: among them Pogolotti, Félix Pita Rodríguez, and Nicolás Guillén. The wall facing the mural contains a number of paintings by Enríquez, including a fierce bust of José Martí and an exotic pink-hued portrait of Germaine. The tiny living room leads in the back to a small tile-floored kitchen with a stained-glass window, which opens onto a backyard, and in the front to a bedroom, where a vitrine holds his letter to MoMA director Alfred Barr.

But it is upstairs that one feels the true spirit of Enríquez. The stairs themselves hold ghostly painted footprints; today they are protected by Plexiglas. The garretlike studio above looks onto the richly tinted countryside, where cows graze, much as they did in Carlos's day; a neighbor, perhaps a modern-day successor to Enríquez's mythic *guarijo*, works his land with an ox-drawn plow.

*   *   *

Once again, Neel's household was morphing. Richard graduated from High Mowing in the spring of 1957 and moved back home to attend Columbia University on a full scholarship. And Sam, who had been carrying on a serious relationship with a woman named Sondra since 1956, had pretty much moved out by 1958, although he still spent a fair amount of time at Alice's.

Sondra, who at the time was married to someone else, was charmed by Sam from the instant she saw him. "I met him in front of a health food store, doing push-ups," she recalls. By the fall of 1956 they were regularly spending time in a rented room together. (Neel apparently had no knowledge that Sondra existed, and Sondra was unaware that Sam, who was adept at juggling two households, was keeping up domestic business-as-usual at Neel's.)

By the summer of 1957, according to Sondra, he was living with her, although Alice was still somewhat in the dark about the relationship. By the following summer, however, she could no longer deny it.

As Phillip Bonosky wrote in his journal on June 10, 1958:

She complains and grieves over S. now as if she'd only met him
yesterday and been betrayed by him for the first time today. He'll
leave me for good, she cries, leave me for this 23-year-old girl!
Then she tells us that a woman with a young baby has always
been irresistible to S.

Sondra and Sam's son, David, would be born on June 18, 1958.

Still, although they no longer really lived together, Sam remained a
major presence in Neel's life until the end, outliving Alice by three years.
And the drama had not subsided. Richard recalls a 1958 episode that took
place right after the publication of a small book, *The Tune of the Calliope*,
which included some illustrations by Neel.

Saul Lishinsky, an artist who had organized, contributed to, and written
its introduction, was at the Neels with his wife, Estelle. Alice, Sam, Richard, and the Lishinkys were having a pleasant enough visit when Richard,
then a student at Columbia, made a remark that echoed Alice's own comment about why she had attended the Philadelphia School of Design for
Women—that he liked the fact that Columbia "was all men, because I wasn't
distracted by women in the classroom."

Sam was instantly infuriated. He shouted, "You filthy male chauvinist!" says Richard, who then pulled out a switchblade he had been given
by Sam's brother, Lou. "Sam got some scissors, and we sort of parried
around the room. Estelle had never seen anything like this, and she blew
up like a blowfish. Well, Sam left, and nothing happened, but it was a
close call," he says. "And that was the thing that got Alice to get him out
of there."

Neel's 1958 *Self-Portrait*, one of only several she would ever create, bears
testimony to her psychological state at the time. In spare ink on paper, she
depicts herself as a hollow-eyed skull, one eye dripping black tears, many
teeth missing.

That same year, Neel began analysis. Her therapist was a former podiatrist, Dr. Anthony Sterrett, who practiced on East Seventy-third Street.
Neel had met him through John Rothschild. John's son, Joel, who consulted him for a foot infection, remembers Sterrett as a youngish man in
his mid-thirties, Neel would only go to him for about two years. But she
credited him with giving her the confidence to promote her own work.

Neel explained to Hills that she had first consulted Sterrett at the suggestion of doctors at Columbia-Presbyterian, where she had gone for "nervous disturbances," later determined to be cardiac arrest. (She would get a pacemaker in 1980.)

"I was analyzed in 1958, not by a psychiatrist, but by a psychologist. . . . If it hadn't been for the psychologist my work would never have gotten before the world. I must give him credit. If I hadn't gone to him, I never would be known at all today. He would say: 'Well why don't you send to these shows? Is it because you're not as good as they are?' I'd say, 'Oh no, I'm much better.' But he'd say: 'Why don't you send?' I had a block, I still have it, against publicity . . . against the outside world. There's something of the pack rat about me. I reached the conclusion that if I painted a good picture, it was enough to paint a good picture, because I couldn't fight the world. I was never a go-getter."

Still, in March 1958, she complained to Bonosky, "Why can't I get a gallery? Here I am, a genius—and I need to show my canvases. I'm innundated with them."

According to Neel, it was Sterrett who got her to screw up the courage to call Frank O'Hara, whom she wanted to paint: the resulting images (1960) were breakthrough paintings for Neel. In the first, she depicts O'Hara as a beautiful young man: "a romantic, falconlike profile with a bunch of lilacs." In the second, he is ravaged. "His teeth looked like tombstones; the lilacs had withered. When he saw the picture he said, 'My God, those freckles.' But the Fauves went that far." This portrait, which Neel said expressed his "troubled life," was reproduced in *ARTnews* in 1960, a first for Neel. (O'Hara, a hero of the New York School of poets and painters, would be tragically run over on a beach on Fire Island just six years later.)

Whether it was Sterrett's influence ("He was practical with me and that was the right thing," she said) or simply the fact that with her children grown she had more time to devote to her art, Neel's career would begin to turn around in the 1960s.

And there was another major factor. Although there is some doubt as to the actual date Sam really left for good (he certainly spent less time there after David was born in September 1958), Neel told Jonathan Brand that Sam officially moved out on January 1, 1959, even though according to Bonosky he apparently cooked a turkey dinner on New Year's Day.

They would stay in fairly close touch for the rest of her lifetime (and she also saw Sam's children, Mady, Julian, and David), but Alice and Sam never lived together again. (Sam would die in 1987, three years after Alice, from a terrible fall down the stairs at his Connecticut home.)

CHAPTER TWENTY-THREE

Pull My Daisy
(from Flower to Power)

"Poverty isn't enough for me anymore. I can get things now out of other classes. . . ."

—ALICE NEEL TO PHILLIP BONOSKY, 1960

Neel entered her next decade, which would chart the beginning of her extraordinary comeback, as somewhat of a cult figure, thanks to playing the mother of the "bishop" (art dealer Richard Bellamy) in the 1959 Beat film *Pull My Daisy*. Directed by Robert Frank and Alfred Leslie, the underground classic stars an A-list of downtown Beat characters: Allen Ginsberg, Gregory Corso, Larry Rivers, Peter Orlovsky, David Amram, Sally Gross (Bellamy's wife), Robert and Mary Frank's son, Pablo, and Alice Neel. Wearing a funnel-shaped hat, she briefly plays "A Mighty Fortress Is Our God" on the organ. The movie was produced by Walter Gutman, the financier, art critic, collector, and avant-garde filmmaker (*Circus Girls*, *Clothed in Music: A Dance of the Body*, and *The Grape Dealer's Daughter*). Neel painted him in 1965.

With its free-form, improvised cinematic style, its jazzy, faux stream-of-consciousness narration by Jack Kerouac (reciting the third act of his play, *The Beat Generation* over silent footage), and music by David Amram, the quirky film captures the iconoclastic spirit of Beat poetry and Abstract Expressionism. Not much actually happens: a group of poets and painters assail the unlikely bishop with questions about Buddhism and ironic riffs on what is holy: "Are glasses holy, is baseball holy, holy, holy. . . ." The zany scatting eventually ends up as a musical jam session.

"I never understood this goofy little masterpiece as it was being filmed," wrote Rivers in his memoir. "But it was pleasurable playing a stoned train conductor carrying a kerosene lamp in the company of such Beat luminaries."

As Bonosky remarks in his journal, on April 12, 1960, after seeing the movie:

> *A. in it looked more part of it than even the professional "beat." There's one scene where she's standing on a warehouse platform while the "bishop" is haranguing the people, and she actually shivers with cold. This isn't in the script, I'm sure; the day was cold. How curious, however, to see her on the screen, looking, she told me then, exactly the way she usually feels— depressed.*

For most of the twenty-eight-minute film, Neel simply sits on the couch. Says Leslie, "I first met Alice in 1945 at some party and she asked me to come pose for her. She said I looked like a faun, because I have pointy ears. I loved Alice and thought she was a wise and funny and very courageous person. And when I thought of someone for this part who was matronly but also had an edge, the first person I thought of was Alice."

Recalls Amram, "Alfred was brilliant at directing people who weren't actors. It was a few weeks of constant chaos, with all this screaming and craziness going on. It was like being a hostage negotiator or a master psychiatrist to take this crazy group of people and actually make a lovely and delightful film. With *Pull My Daisy*, we captured a moment in time." As for Neel herself, "We all admired her so much. In the art world at the time, she wasn't nearly as appreciated [as she should have been]. I think she is appreciated now more than ever."

According to Neel, the filmmakers, whom she had met at the Artists' Club, picked her for the part because "I looked like a conventional American type. I had a hat then, and orange gloves and an orange scarf. I went and there was Allen Ginsberg. So I said, 'Oh are you taking the part of Allen Ginsberg?' And he said, 'No, I *am* Allen Ginsberg.' Gregory Corso was there, looking just like a gargoyle that had jumped off a building in France." Neel got twenty-five dollars a day for appearing in the film, but the notoriety it gave her at the time was incalculable.

Neel also contributed to Leslie's "one-shot review," *The Hasty Papers*, published in late 1960, which included squibs by cultural icons ranging from Jean-Paul Sartre to John Ashbery, William Carlos Williams, Terry Southern, and Jean Genet. Neel's statement, in which she first framed herself as a latter-day Balzac, appeared under a reproduction of her infamous Joe Gould portrait:

. . . I decided to paint a human comedy—such as Balzac had done in literature. In the 30's I painted the beat of those days— Joe Gould, Sam Putnam, Ken Fearing, etc. I have painted El Barrio in Puerto Rican Harlem. I painted the neurotic, the mad and the miserable. Also, I painted the others, including some squares. . . . Like Chichikov, I am a collector of souls. Now some of my subjects are beginning to die and they have an historic nostalgia, everyone seems better and more important when they are dead. If I could make the world happy, the wretched faces in the subway, sad and full of troubles, worry me. I also hate the conformity of today—everything put into its box.

When I go to a show today of modern work, I feel that my world has been swept away. And yet I do not think it can be so that the human creature will be forever verboten. Thou shalt make no graven images.

Neel would continue to go to the Club through the mid-1960s. Her participation in the contemporary scene, however glancing, marked the beginning of a turning point in her career. Although she had a small solo show at her friend Geza de Vegh's Old Mill Gallery in New Jersey in September 1960, and in August 1961 her 1935 Kenneth Fearing portrait appeared on the cover of *Mainstream*, the sixties were a time of deliberate change for Neel. She began to seek new venues, new subjects, and even a new palette, as exemplified by her 1960 dual portraits of Frank O'Hara, which shockingly recorded the noted poet and art critic, who was also a curator at the Museum of Modern Art, as both an angel and a demon—perhaps illustrating Neel's attitude toward his dual role as artist (poet) and art-world power (critic and curator).

In the first, light-tinged portrait, O'Hara, haloed with lilacs, boasts the regal profile of a Roman coin. In the second, sepia-toned portrait (like dried leaves), the lilacs are a rusty blur, and O'Hara's face is caught in a frightening, wrinkled, wild-eyed grimace.

The second painting was reproduced in the December 1960 issue of *ARTnews* to accompany a review of a four-man show at the ACA Gallery (Alice Neel, Jonah Kinigstein, Anthony Toney, and Giacomo Porzano), which ran in December. It was a one-two punch for Neel. Critic Lawrence Campbell singled out her work:

Miss Neel made the strongest impression. She has been painting for years but for some unknown reason is rarely seen in exhibi-

tions. The best of her paintings here were portraits which combined a speaking likeness, with an intense, cool, lowering
Expressionism. She uses a black, sinuous line to grab the edges of
her figures, but it is not the line which makes them striking, it is
a haunting power. Her paintings cast a spell.

The half-dozen works on display included both renditions of O'Hara,
two of Miles Kreuger, *The Baron's Aunt*, and *Lovers*. The show was also
reviewed by *The New York Times*. Wrote Stuart Preston, "Alice Neel shows
some portraits that grip their sitters in a relentless grasp."

Just as importantly, Campbell wrote an encouraging note in the vistors'
book at the gallery, "Bravo, Alice Neel!" Neel contacted him and he became a long-time supporter.

Neel also made other important new connections, including the art
critic Hubert Crehan, who gave her a ride home after a party, and stayed to
marvel at her vast hoard of paintings, including *Miles Kreuger*, which he
admired as "great art." "I converted him from being a follower of Clyfford
Still to being a follower of me," Neel said. Crehan, whose portrait she painted
in 1961, would be instrumental in the next phase of her career. In early
1962, he organized a solo show at Reed College, in Portland, Oregon. He
also wrote a major profile of Neel for *ARTnews* (October 1962), the first to
establish her status as an important contemporary artist.

The fashion in the art world, dominated for nearly two decades by Abstract Expressionism, was beginning to change. Nineteen-sixty marked the
cusp of the Pop era, and a return to some semblance of realism. Figurative
painting was back. Neel's portraits may have been a long way from Warhol's iconic soup cans and Lichtenstein's everyday detritus, which famously
made their appearance in "the Store" on East Second Street in early 1961,
but they no longer looked like a throwback to the Depression and Roosevelt years. This was especially true since Neel's style in the sixties was
looser, lighter, in every way more masterly than her work of the previous
three decades.

The black outline, noted by several reviewers in the fifties, softened into
a fluid signature blue. The canvases themselves got larger, brighter, more
vivid. The figures in them were not working-class heroes and neighborhood characters anymore, but, as often as not, art-world celebrities. Neel
brought all her significant wit and wisdom to bear in depicting—sometimes
to the point of broad caricature—these other survivors of the "rat race."

Her perspective is now that of an insider rather than an outsider. Her

1962 portraits of a young Robert Smithson (Neel called him "wolf boy")
and of art dealer and "snake" Ellie Poindexter, a study in lemon yellow
(which, like the Resnick/Passlof portrait, was done from memory), are as
canny as they are intense. (When Smithson, who himself was then working
on blood-covered papier-mâché Christs, objected to Neel's attention to his
bloody acne scars, Neel retorted, "Why Robert, you wouldn't let me have
even a little blood and look how much blood these Christs have.")

The sly humor in Neel's humanism asserted itself, reaching its apotheosis by the early 1970s; consider her portrait of curator John Perreault as
a sultry odalisque, or her clever homage to Andy Warhol's shoes in an
otherwise remarkably poignant painting.

Now in her early sixties, Neel was no longer the Bohemian femme fatale,
but she was still a feisty radical artist, and the countercultural renaissance
of the sixties provided her with the perfect backdrop for her own long-held
predilections. The era was a celebration of the personal freedom Neel had
fought for for years. As the decade unfolded, with its political and sexual
revolution, from its bawdy experimentation to its idealistic activism, Neel,
always ahead of the curve, was finally in synch with the Zeitgeist. The ob-
durate nonconformist was at last coming into her own.

Her career emphatically reflected the seismic shift in cultural sensibility: Between 1927 and 1964, Neel had only about half a dozen solo shows.
During the last twenty years of her life, from 1964 to 1984, she had over
sixty.

*   *   *

Although Neel called 1963 her breakthrough year, her career really began
to coalesce in 1962. This was also the year that she made her final residential move, from Spanish Harlem, her domicile of over two decades, to the
large apartment at 300 W. 107th Street and Broadway, with a big bay window in the front room that served as her studio, which her family keeps to
this day.

In January 1962, fifteen of Neel's paintings were exhibited in the solo
show organized by Crehan at Reed College. Several months later, Thomas
Hess and her old friend from the Village days, Harold Rosenberg, made
their way up to Spanish Harlem to consider Neel's work for the Longview
Foundation Purchase Award, given by Dillard University in honor of un-
derrecognized artists. (Neel, who certainly qualified, received the award
that September.)

In late May, Neel had three paintings at the Kornblee Gallery's response
to the Museum of Modern Art's show "Recent Painting USA: The Figure,"

which had somehow omitted a number of significant figurative painters. Neel
was in excellent company: the show, which ran through June 15, included
Milton Avery, Philip Pearlstein, Fairfield Porter, and George Segal. Her dev-
ilishly antic *Milton Resnick and Pat Passlof*, executed from memory, continued her chronicle of the contemporary art world. "Milton Resnick in his
best clothes, going to Lee Krasner's show at the Pace Gallery," Neel remarked. "When I painted them, you know what Harold Rosenberg said?
That I should have that in a tent and charge a dollar admission."

The show, along with several others, engendered an article in *ARTnews'*
summer edition. Entitled "U.S. Figure Painting: Continuity and Cliché,"
which posed the question, "Is there a new kind of American figure painting?" Neel's work was analyzed, along with that of Fairfield Porter, Alex
Katz, and Elaine de Kooning. Wrote Valerie Peterson:

> Alice Neel's portrait of Edward Avedisian opens up like an expen-
> sive box of chocolates; overindulgent, excessively Oscar Wilde,
> eccentric and opulent . . . seeing her subjects exposed is like
> dreaming yourself nude on Main Street at high noon, Easter Sun-
> day, and only her consistent good humor and knowledge that she
> is equally vulnerable makes her penetration possible to take.
> Miss Neel's double memory portrait of Patricia Passlof and Mil-
> ton Resnick is a tour-de-force of innocent incision, direct like a
> child's family portrait; it is a narrative of private emotions that is
> good natured yet really belongs in the closet with the skeletons.

That same month, Neel had several paintings at a "Portraits" show at
the Zabriskie Gallery (June 4–30), which placed her in context with several dozen celebrated artists, including a few from the New York School:
Nell Blaine, Larry Rivers, Elaine de Kooning, Leland Bell, Marisol, Alex
Katz, Mimi Gross, Red Grooms, and Robert De Niro.

At her invitation, Neel even briefly worked in Elaine de Kooning's studio on Broadway and Eighth Street. She painted *Eddie Fisher* and *Dr.
Lester Johnson* there. "She stole my technique," Neel told Jonathan Brand.
"But maybe it was worth it. . . . Bill de Kooning, you know, came to her
studio and thought this was just great."

(While like Neel, she is preoccupied with hands, Elaine de Kooning,
who began doing portraits early in her career, created a signature style by
combining figurative painting with Abstract Expressionism. Most famously, she did a commissioned portrait of President John F. Kennedy,

1963. Her 1962 portrait of Frank O'Hara is in stark contrast to Neel's
literate psychological studies: De Kooning's busy Abstract Expressionist
background nearly engulfs her subject.)

Irving Sandler recalls that around this time Neel asked him to pose for
her, but he refused because she was "like a voodoo person who would stick
pins in me." (Nonetheless, he later suggested she speak at the National
Endowment of the Arts, where, he says, "she held them in the palm of her
hand.")

In September, Neel made the move to her new apartment, with its pan-
oramic view of Broadway, where she would live and paint for the rest of her
life. It was not far from Columbia, where both her sons were now attending
school—Richard at Columbia Law School and Hartley at Columbia College. Later that month, she appeared in a two-man show at the Camino Gallery, as part of a "gala co-operative opening of eight galleries just off Tenth
Street, between Third and Fourth avenues."

The year culminated in triumphant *ARTnews* piece by Hubert Crehan.
Although she would be the subject of hundreds of major articles over the
next two decades, it was Crehan who first effectively transported Neel into
the milieu of the modern art world. His feature article, "Introducing the
Portraits of Alice Neel," illustrated by eight powerful paintings, appeared
in the October issue of the magazine. Wrote Crehan:

> Anyone who would make a dogmatic claim that modern portrait
> painting is dead is in danger of having to seal his lips on this sub-
> ject after seeing the paintings of Alice Neel.
>
> There are revelations to be made in painting people today, and
> she makes them. There are risks to be taken in doing portraits,
> and she takes them.
>
> Alice Neel with a pure ingenousness has created an asylum of
> saints and sinners, a rogue's gallery that makes a place for the
> Beatific and the Beat. Her world is the demi-monde: Village Bo-
> hemia, Spanish Harlem (where she has lived for twenty years),
> the world of artists and poets, the world of homeless radicals, dis-
> placed and deranged persons, like a Scandinavian baron and a
> dark-skinned motherless child. . . .
>
> She paints portraits that come alive and that have style and
> meaning. She is a master of a technique which can reach a high and
> convincing level of expressiveness. She is a painter whose work
> has individual character. There is a place for this work. It is an

achievement of portraiture in our time and I have no doubt that it
will come to be recognized for its rightful value . . .

After striving in New York for nearly four decades, Neel had profession-
ally arrived. It was not the first time she had received some level of recognition; Neel had achieved that in the 1930s. But this time, her success would
be sustained.

*   *   *

Neel signed with the Graham Gallery, which would represent her for almost the next two decades, in October of 1963. Although the ACA Gallery
had shown Neel on and off in the 1930s, 1940s, and 1950s, she had never
been selected to join their roster of artists. Now, finally, for the first time in
her career, Neel had formal gallery representation; an artistic home. It was
significant validation that her work was, at long last, being taken seriously.

The Graham Gallery, founded in 1857, was originally an antiques business, specializing in decorative arts and objets d'art. In the 1930s, James
R. Graham, a member of the fourth generation of the family, began to show
art of the American West, including the paintings of Frederic Remington
and Thomas Moran. By the 1940s, its representation of paintings had expanded, with a focus on "late 19th century and early 20th century American art, American modernism and realist artists in the tradition of The
Eight."

By 1963, when Neel joined the gallery, it was being run by James and
Robert C. Graham, Sr., along with Joan Washburn. Robert ("Robin")
C. Graham, Jr., also worked in the business. As the 150th anniversary
book on the gallery puts it: "James Graham & Sons first showed the work of
Alice Neel in 1963. That year represented a professional breakthrough for
the artist, who had enjoyed little success before 1960. After the first important article on her work appeared in *ARTnews*, her recognition as an artist
steadily increased. She had not had a one-person show in New York since
1954, and before that only three, in 1938, 1944 and 1951."

According to this same gallery history, in 1964, Robert Graham's daughter, Kathryn, sat for Neel, wearing a red dress. Apparently, she was not
"particularly pleased with the portrait, a common reaction by the subjects
of this artist whose strong opinions and uncompromising vision did
not generally lend themselves to complimentary portrayals. In 1968 Robert C. Graham Sr. sat for his portrait and the results were much more
flattering."

The Graham Gallery, where Neel remained through 1980, would have a

total of eight Neel shows: 1963, 1966, 1968, 1970, 1973, 1976, 1978 (a retrospective), and 1980, her final year there. Neel received steadily good
press, which exponentially increased in praise and quantity as the years
went on. By the time she left the gallery to join Robert Miller, only several
years before her death, Neel was famous.

In September 1963, Neel saw her old friend Millen Brand for the first
time in nearly a decade. The friendship had unraveled over a big fight with
Sam, who had called Millen a "monster." Brand recounted the visit in his
journal:

> *This afternoon I went up to see Alice Neel at her new apartment
> at 300 W. 107th Street. . . . She took a handsome large apart-
> ment here for $200 a month. It was partly for the boys. . . .
> "Both my boys are squares, but nice you know. But I thought
> they'd be, Richard a singer or something, and Hartley," I forget
> what she said, writer or painter or something. But Hartley is
> going to be a doctor.*
>
> *We talked in a torrent, all the years between Sam, Kenneth
> Fearing, Max White, Sam Putnam, Rachel Fearing, Bruce, and
> on and on. I guess it's ten years since I last saw her, because of
> the trouble with Sam. She says Sam is back living with his wife
> (she took the baby and left him) and he lets Alice alone now.
> The boys have practically disowned him. . . .*
>
> *Alice has had some good notices and now has a top gallery
> and is going to have a big show in October. Her prices are going
> up. She wanted eight hundred for her portrait of Carol [Brand's
> daughter]. Then she said out of friendship, I could have it for
> five hundred. . . .*
>
> *But Alice hasn't changed, looks the same, the same sweetness
> and acuteness. And blames Sam for giving her a guilt complex.
> "Neil's eyes and of course I stayed with Sam. There I was in Span-
> ish Harlem and nobody knew what I was doing and Sam under-
> stood. He was so intelligent. And had such good feet and mine
> were so bad. Those good feet," and she laughed.*

Neel's very first Graham show, from October 1 to 26, was an unqualified
hit. It garnered the lead review, a rave, in the October 1963 issue of *ART-
news*. Wrote Kim Levin:

Alice Neel is having a long overdue New York show, her first in
more than ten years. For some three decades she has been quietly
painting portraits that are contemporary both in form and psychology, proving that the portrait as an art form is still vital. . . .
Her capacity for portraying people—the whole conglomerate of
inner selves that one can contain simultaneously and the resulting tension, without artifice, with the unavoidable and stunning
honest, is astonishing. The presences that people her canvases
are extraordinarily alive: she paints the shells they have chosen,
and penetrating their shell, probes and exposes their inner being, their thoughts, their panics. . . . Hubert Crehan becomes a
granite-faced pugnacious Madonna holding a wide-eyed baby
on his knee; Julian Beck, a John the Baptist lost in financial
meditations. . . . The newest paintings are achieved with least—a
black line tells everything about a chin, two grey splashes can
define a suit jacket; bare canvas works with thin paint for an open
unfinished look. Miss Neel's work falls somewhere in the realm
where the sensibility is so acute that it defies definition; her portraits are not only people; they are art.

Even the *New York Post* weighed in, "The art scene came alive this
week with a number of one-man shows, among them Alice Neel at the
Graham."

Neel's work was kept on the second floor of the three-story gallery, then
at 1014 Madison. Recalls Robin Graham, "The significant thing about the
gallery as it relates to Alice, is that taking her on was very much my father's stepping out into the contemporary art world, which he had a great
passion for. He loved mingling and socializing with artists. He and Joan
were very much on that scene and Alice was very much part of that scene.
She seemed to be able to connect to some fairly important people—
Geldzahler, Warhol—even if they didn't buy the pictures. The people she
painted were a rather impressive group."

In December 1963, Richard married Nancy Greene, and the couple
moved in with Neel for the next two years. Richard graduated from Columbia Law School the following spring.

Starting in 1964, Neel began receiving an annual stipend of six thousand dollars, which would continue for the rest of her life. The gift was from
Dr. Muriel Gardiner, an extraordinary philanthropist, whom Neel had

met through John Rothschild. (Gardiner knew Rothschild's first wife, the painter Erica Feist, who lived near her in Pennsylvania.)

Typically, Neel managed to conceal Gardiner's extraordinary gift from Rothschild, so she could continue to benefit from his generosity. John was furious when he later learned of it.

Dr. Muriel Gardiner was a psychoanalyst who, as a student in Vienna in 1932, had helped hundreds of people escape from Austria. As previously mentioned, her story was the basis of Julia in Lillian Hellman's *Pentimento: A Book of Portraits*. Vanessa Redgrave played the eponymous character in the 1977 film version. Dr. Gardiner later wrote her own memoir, *Code Name Mary*, which was published in 1983. She went on to help establish the Sigmund Freud Museum in Hampstead, England.

Says Constance Harvey, Dr. Gardiner's daughter, "My mother helped a lot of people. They didn't have to be artists. I think she [Neel] did a portrait of my mother. I didn't like it much; it was rather unflattering, to say the least. And my former daughter-in-law ended up with a picture of two Puerto Rican boys."

Neel appeared in several group shows between 1964 and 1965. In May 1964, her painting of Bobby Schiller (priced at one thousand dollars) was included in a large figurative show at the Wadsworth Atheneum in Hartford, Connecticut, along with paintings by Willem de Kooning, Elaine de Kooning, Fairfield Porter, Philip Pearlstein, Paul Resika, Andy Warhol, and Robert De Niro. In January 1965, she had a solo show of fifteen recent paintings at the Hopkins Center at Dartmouth College (where Hartley was doing a masters' program in chemistry). The work on display included her portraits of James Farmer, Randal Bailey, Edward Avedisian, Mary Shoemaker, and Kristan and Stewart Mott, and was priced from $1,200 to $2,500.

Sometime in the mid-1960s, Alice affected a rapprochement with her long-lost lover from the Village days, Kenneth Doolittle, who was now working as an elevator operator at Mt. Sinai Hospital. She had run into him at Symphony Space, where Gus Hall was putting in an appearance. He was with his friend Stanley Maron.

Recalls Maron, "Gus Hall just made an international world trip. He was at Symphony Space around 1964. Kenneth hadn't seen her in a long time. We saw this husky [little] woman with a big head of blond hair. We wound up going to her house. We started walking up Broadway and stopped at a deli to get some corned beef. She showed us her paintings." The two lost no time reminiscing about the old days. "She and Kenneth were talking about this person, that person," says Maron.

That summer, Neel traveled to Europe for the first time, with Hartley and Nancy Selvage. They made stops in Paris, Rome, Florence, and Madrid. "She wanted to go to every museum," said Selvage.

Neel's sixties revival reached its peak in early 1966, when she finally went from *Mainstream* to the mainstream. Neel had her second solo show at the Graham Gallery, "Alice Neel; Recent Paintings and Paintings from the Thirties," from January 5 to 29. *Newsweek* art critic Jack Kroll relegated his entire January 31 column to it, annointing Neel, for the first time in a general-interest publication, as a major American artist. Memorably dubbing her a "Curator of Souls," he declared:

> . . . Alice Neel is like an old pagan priestess somehow overlooked in the triumph of a new religion. Indeed with her shrewdly cherubic face, her witty and wizard eyes, she has the mischievous look of a maternal witch whose only harm lies in her compulsion to tell the truth. Now in her late 50's [*sic*], Neel's painted truths have made her magnificently unfashionable in the art marts, and the most powerfully original portrait painter of her time.

If Crehan's piece four years earlier had "introduced" Neel to the current art world, Kroll's piece put the definitive public spin on Neel for the rest of her life:

> Neel's new show at New York's Graham Gallery makes an extraordinary impression. The walls are alive with people—not "real people," but "art people," humans caught in the torrid, temperate and frigid zones of their passage through the human span. . . .
>
> Alice Neel's portraits strike all the senses with the superbly scary impact of mortality. She is uncanny at bodying forth the history of compromise, surrender and curdled victory that is written in the flesh of human beings. Her "Human Comedy," as she calls it, is thus a symphony of vitimizations—except for children, whom she paints masterfully in their wary sweetness. Here are bitter kids from Spanish Harlem, slightly hysterical, cozily shrill ladies, millionaire art collectors wearing luck like cologne. . . . Neel is the heir of the European Expressionist

painters who saw modern man distorted by unable demons. But
the weather in her world is not depressing, it shows deep affection
for the hard work the ego must do to find reasons for comfort and
self-love. . . . Alice Neel is like a curator of human souls in a brave
or something new world.

The exhibit showed the scope of Neel's tireless effort, ranging from
strong early works such as the Fearing portrait and her painting of Isabetta
to more recent works, including the picture of former CORE head James
Farmer, looking, according to Kroll, "tight, controlled, efficient," and the
mathematician and poet Jerry Sokol, caught twice, once in 1964 and once
in 65.

As the poet Ted Berrigan pointed out in his article "The Portrait and Its
Double," published just before Neel's show, in the January 1966 issue of
ARTnews, Neel sometimes did several telling portraits of the same subject: Miles Kreuger (1959), Frank O'Hara (1960), Randall Bailey (1961),
Maynard Stone (1965), Lida Moser (1962). (And, of course, Ellie Poindexter, not mentioned in the piece.) She also sometimes made, unbeknownst to
the buyers of her work, exact duplicates of paintings, and she had no compunction, if it suited her, about altering their dates. For instance, there is
a portrait of David Brody, painted from life in 1968, that is nearly identical
to the portrait which sold at auction at Christies in 2010 for $782,500. (The
Brody family has consigned their painting to Sotheby's.)

The show also got strong reviews in the *New York Post* and *Arts* magazine. *Arts* magazine said of Neel, "She may well be the only painter today
making an original and vital statement in portrait form."

Wrote Charlotte Willard in the *Post,* "Alice Neel puts them all down
sharply: the intelligent glance, the talon hands, the hostile stare, defensive
gesture, the suspicious eyes, and the wasted body, the brave mouth, the
debonair gesture." (Neel returned the favor: Her elegant 1967 portrait of
Willard is unusually sympathetic. Willard's face appears both kindly and
intelligent, although Alice later said she was thinking of her as a rat when
she posed, and actually told her, "Your paw isn't in the right position.")

Millen Brand met Alice at the Graham show on January 8, writing it up
in his journal:

> *She wanted to be with me while I saw it. . . . The devil painting
> of Sam was there, glowering, and the portraits of Kenneth Fear-
> ing and Sam Putnam. The naked young girl with her hands on*

her hips and the wonderful flaring hair. Joe Gould's head. Men-
tal hospital scenes and maternity wards. And magnificent new
work including a Sergeant-like [sic] full-length portrait of a
woman in evening dress. "I haven't seen that," I said. "I know I
just did it." And a new portrait of Hartley with his shirt in a
blaze of light. "I did that last Sunday." She said, "In two years I
can have another show and that one will be Recent Paintings
and Paintings from the Forties. You know, if I can't have a retro-
spective, I'll have it in pieces. I'll put you in the next one." "You
ought to sell from this one." "I ought to, don't you think so?"

She's getting reviews and articles in the Herald Tribune
Magazine Section, the NY Post, a big article with color repro-
ductions in ART NEWS [sic], and a notice in Newsweek.

Neel told Brand she wanted to paint Charlotte Willard, who was planning to review the show the following week.

According to Brand, Neel's explanation for her recent success was
simple: "This is the most coverage I ever had. All this has come since I
broke with Sam, got free of him. All I could think of then was him. Oh, he
was so destructive. A genius, but he destroyed everything."

The poet Robert Lowell was so impressed with Neel's painting of Kenneth Fearing that he asked Neel to paint him in exchange for one of his
own manuscripts. Ultimately, the trade never happened; Lowell had a nervous breakdown and was hospitalized. His wife, the writer and critic Elizabeth Hardwick, wanted to buy Neel's painting of Sam Putnam but couldn't
afford it. She actually rented the portrait for fifty dollars a month for three
months. But Hardwick returned it after only a month and a half, complaining, "We don't think any man who was such a great translator could look
like that."

On May 15, 1967, Mike Gold, Neel's close friend and mentor (and occasional lover), died. Neel created a moving tribute within the context of a
Mexican funerary motif; she painted a framed image of her original 1952
portrait of him, placed ceremonially on a dresser; a table with a skull and
lilacs in the foreground, with the legend "Mike Gold, In Memoriam, born
April 12, 1893, died May 15, 1967."

Neel's next show was on the West Coast, in June 1967 at the Maxwell
Gallery in San Francisco. She stayed with Hartley's friends Julie Hall and
Algis Alkaitis. She painted even when she was on the road. Struck by the
light in the afternoons, she painted Julie, beautiful, pensive, and pregnant,

with her half-hidden husband behind her on a mattress on the floor. This would be among the earliest of Neel's signature pregnant nudes. (The first one, done in 1964, was *Pregnant Maria*.)

The show had been arranged by Peter Homitsky, whose wife, Betty, painted in 1968, became another in the series. Neel was in part drawn to the subject of pregnancy by being in close proximity to her pregnant daughter-in-law, Nancy, who had given birth to her first child, Olivia, on February 11, 1967.

Neel's pregnant nudes speak volumes about both her style and subject matter. They are a culmination of themes Neel had explored in her earliest work, *The Family*, *Well Baby Clinic*, and *Futility of Effort*. Neel herself became a grandmother in the midst of the sixties revolution—a major upheaval of twentieth-century values, including family values. The pregnant nude provided her with a unique and powerful expression—literally a physical embodiment—of women's basic conflicts.

Even at a time that celebrated sexual freedom, portraying a pregnant nude remained taboo. There are very few such paintings in the canon of art history. Gustav Klimt's *Hope 1*, 1903 is one example. The German artist Paula Modersohn-Becker did several pregnant nudes, most famously the sensitive 1906 self-portrait, done on her sixth wedding anniversary, in which she was probably not yet even pregnant; she died of an embolism after giving birth to her first child in 1907. And, in 1910, Egon Schiele, whose work Neel had been familiar with since her student days, painted several pregnant nudes, including one entitled *Red Nude, Pregnant*.

Neel may have been unconsciously inspired by this painting. Its composition, including the delicate outline around the body—a trope Neel shares with Schiele—strongly resembles *Margaret Evans Pregnant*, 1978. (Unlike Schiele, however, who has stripped things down to an elegant essence, Neel psychologically fleshes her image out with a lovely, expressive background and an evocative mirror reflection.) That same year, Schiele also painted a newborn baby with visible genitalia, a motif Neel would also employ as she continued to deconstruct the conventional notions of motherhood (*Andrew*, 1978).

The Soyer brothers also tried their hand at the subject, preceeding Neel by a decade or so when they painted their regular models as they became pregnant. But their staid academic style had little or nothing to do with Neel's typically honest treatment of naked women on the verge of giving birth.

Neel established her mature style in the mid to late 1960s, creating a series of canvases that are among her best-known. Who can forget her ironic vision of *Thanksgiving*, 1965, a naked capon in a kitchen sink (Neel jokingly referred to it as her "answer to Pop art"). Or her incongruously grinning concentration-camp survivor, the indomitable *Fuller Brush Man*, painted the same year.

The model for this portrait was Dewald Strauss, who had been rounded up on Kristallnacht, in November 1938, and interred in Dachau, then released and sent to an immigration camp in England. Thanks to his brother and sister, who had already left Germany, he was able to get an affidavit permitting him to emigrate to the United States. He subsequently returned to Germany as an American soldier, earning a Purple Heart after being wounded by shrapnel.

According to his son, Jerry, Strauss's territory ran from 100 to 110th street, from Central Park West to Riverside Drive. He sold everything from personal grooming aids to household goods. Alice was a customer. Recalls Jerry, "If we delivered to Riverside or West End Avenue or Central Park West, it was great, it was safe, we got tips, but if we delivered to, like, Manhattan Avenue, Columbus Avenue, we were worried about being mugged—in fact, he was mugged on the job around that time—because the neighborhood then was pretty crappy. His stockroom was about a block and a half away at Broadway and 106th Street. He knew everybody in the neighborhood. I think she captured the essence of my father with that positive, can-do, survivor kind of attitude."

Then there is her moody *Hartley*, whose akimbo arms and legs anchor the frame, from the same year. And in 1967, her painted payback to Henry Geldzahler, with whom she had a double-edged relationship. Geldzahler, who had recently been named the curator of 20th century art at the Metropolitan Museum, was putting together a seminal show, "New York Painting and Sculpture: 1940–1970." When Neel asked him to include her, he responded, "Oh, so you want to be a *professional?*" (It was Geldzahler who did the last published interview with Neel for *Interview* magazine, which appeared posthumously in 1985.) Skewered to his chair; he frowns straight at Neel, his pinkie finger disdainfully (or painfully) cocked.

Her 1967 portrait of her daughter-in-law, Nancy (Richard's then wife), anxiously clutching her first child, Olivia, continues Neel's original and unsentimental take, established back in the 1920s, on the trials and tribulations of motherhood. The bold *Ginny in a Striped Shirt*, 1969, a splaylegged portrait of Hartley's soon-to-be wife, Ginny, who had actually met and become friendly with Neel before meeting Hartley, is a quintessential

Neel painting of the late sixties and early seventies: The subject, full of attitude, is juxtaposed against a minimal background. A similar-looking
image was done in 1976, for a poster for the Montreal Olympics.

Neel had her third show at the Graham Gallery from January 6 to February 3, 1968. In addition to her bitchy rendition of Geldzahler, there was
her telling portrait of Red Grooms and Mimi Gross, whose marriage would
break up less than a decade later ("Don't they look like a vaudeville team?"
Neel later remarked. "They show it's not enough to be an artist today, you
also have to be a performer, because they look as though in a few minutes
they're going to get up and dance.") and her picture of Walter Gutman,
who was "the bulls and bears market."

Writing in *The New York Times*, Hilton Kramer, never a fan of Neel's,
doled out a left-handed compliment:

> Mrs. Neel has become somewhat of a legend on the New York art
> scene for her portraits. They are stress pictures, nervous and
> coarse in their drawing, often brutal in observation and com-
> pletely devoid of delicacy of nuance . . . the coarseness of the ex-
> ecution supports a penetrating psychological vision. Often the
> pictures engage one's interest at a level beyond—or beneath—the
> esthetic, and are sometimes unforgettable in a way that much
> finer pictures are not.

In *Arts* magazine, Cindy Nemser called her, "Probably one of the greatest portraitists of our day . . . All the vulnerability, anxiety, and hostility
that is inherent in contemporary living is expressed in the wary faces of
Neel's subjects."

Charlotte Willard included her as one of three "New Faces" in her January 27, 1968, column:

> The Alice Neel exhibition is perhaps the most original and
> interesting. . . . Her likenesses hover on the edge of caricature that
> is at once sharp, penetrating and visually powerful. In color and
> stance she pins her subjects to the wall like so many specimens for
> study and analysis. One would not be surprised if the latter day
> psychoanalysts will be able to diagnose the traumas and charac-
> teristic neuroses of her subjects from these observations of her
> keen brush.

Neel remained a hard sell, despite the critical success—or at least attention—she was receiving, says Robin Graham. "Most of that time, her shows hardly sold at all. We weren't making any money, and she wasn't making any money to speak of. My father stuck with her for years and years. It was a struggle on both sides. At that time, her work was considered much more difficult than it looks to people today—people look ugly and grotesque in the way they are portrayed. A lot of people didn't want to have portraits done in that manner. The work was considered pretty tough. I am surprised myself when I look at it now and it appears so mild. I found it difficult at the time. But Alice always stuck to her guns, she was who she was, and painted the way she painted."

Says Joan Washburn, who worked on the third (avant-garde) floor of the gallery at the time, where Neel frequently popped up to chat, "Alice was Alice and that's the nature of her work. I never thought of her as fitting in. She enjoyed the role of the nonconformist completely." (Washburn recalls the gold space shoes that were Neel's signature footwear at the peak of her Graham period.)

And she continued to parade her beliefs. In the fall of 1968, Neel participated in a protest against the Whitney's exhibit "The 1930s: Painting and Sculpture in America" because it omitted women and African-American artists.

Hartley left for Pakistan that August, and Sam was in town, visiting. Millen Brand paid Neel a visit, only to run into Sam. As he noted in his journal:

> No evidence of the former feuding, when he called me a monster. . . . He looked good, even if his hair is white, the element of intelligence and humor still evident, but God help Alice if she gets involved with him again. . . .
>
> Alice has painted Jonny and Monika, separate portraits. The one of Jonny she did hurriedly and it isn't good, but the one of Monika she spent more time on than almost any other recent portrait—"Five sittings and I worked on it when she wasn't here too: she has a subtle thing I wanted to get"—and it's magnificent. Utterly gets her. You have to look at it for a minute until you realize it, then it's hard not to keep looking at it, it's so true and attractive. A triangular faint blue background and an unusual outlining of the jaw in the same faint color. A shadow in

*the middle of the forehead (secret sadness, hint of approaching
age?) and a minor jaggedness of the lips. She sit partly sideways, the skirt sliding back and revealing much of the upper leg
as girls do now. But all beautifully and strongly done.*

Neel chided herself for not doing more landscapes: "I can usually sell
them. Dumb of me not to do more? I don't look out for myself." But she
looked out for herself enough to part with one of her few paintings of Isabetta, which she sold during this visit to Millen's son, Jonathan.

*The second painting Jonny was buying was an early one of Isa-
betta, Alice's daughter by the Cuban—a curious one, multiply
slashed by Doolittle, that looked like a primitive. The great one
of Isabetta in the nude, Alice still has. I was surprised at her selling Isabetta to Jonny. But he paid $1000 for it, slashes and all.
Neither of Jonny's pictures had Alice's signature so she put them
in the easel in the living room . . . and signed them.*

  *. . . To sign them, Alice filled one of two small cups on her pal-
ette with turpentine (the palette is a large conventionally shaped
one—"I only use a few colors") and dipped the brush in brown
and briefly in black. She was signing Isabetta, the tone of which
was a muted brown. The signature came out too light and she increased the black, but still keeping it relatively light . . . she said
"If somebody examined the painting with infra-red, they'll find it
was signed later and may think it's a fake." She wrote Isabetta's
full name on the frame, and "1930."*

In September 1968, Joe Lasker, who had known Neel for several decades, and whose portrait Neel painted that year, wrote a letter to Jack
Bauer, the director of the Whitney, on her behalf:

The painter, Alice Neel, has never shown at the Whitney, yet for
years, her work has been highly thought of by serious figurative
painters. A number of prominent abstract painters turned
figurative and had one eye on Neel when they "discovered" the
figure. . . . Miss Neel has been painting in New York City since
the 30's. Her recent canvases are the boldest and most colorful.
Lloyd Goodrich, Thomas Hess and Mr. Agee have been to her
last one-man show at the Graham. What does an American

painter have to do to be shown at the Whitney? Would it be
possible for you to view her work for possible inclusion in a
forthcoming show?

Baur answered him a month later:

> We have no exhibition this season for which Alice Neel might
> qualify since our Annual this year is devoted to sculpture. We
> will be glad to consider her for possible inclusion in our Painting
> Annual next fall, though I am sure you will understand I cannot
> make a definite commitment this far in advance.

Neel wrote a note to Lasker, expressing her gratitude, and adding,
"Everything has results although I wish they'd hurry as I think I've really
waited too long. . . ."

As she told Jonathan Brand the following year, "I would like to have a
retrospective before I die, but I don't know that that would add anything
for me because lots of times I show the slides and people like the modern
ones the best. I would love to have a retrospective, but I never knew how
to go about getting it."

In January, 1969, Neel's work appeared in the Graham Gallery's two-
hundred year survey, "Mom, Apple Pie and the American Flag," which
included everyone from Mary Cassatt and N. C. Wyeth to Neel. Reviewing
the show in *New York* magazine, John Gruen, who called it "splendid," commented, "There are endless apples—raw and cooked in the show—and an
array of the dearest mothers imaginable—all that is except the two painted
by Alice Neel who look refreshingly out of their minds."

While *Time* magazine opined, "[Neel] paints neurasthenic portraits of
tired-looking hippies, scrunched-up museum curators and tense Park Avenue housewives. Her deliberately crude technique makes each picture a
devastating microcosm of all that is both magnificent and maddening
about the megalopolis of Manhattan. Yet perhaps, her cosseted, uneasy
little children are the most unforgettable." The piece was accompanied by
a reproduction of Neel's portrait of Mrs. Paul Gardner and her son Christopher Samuel (Sam), the grand-nephew of Ernest Hemingway.

Neel called Millen Brand to boast about the mention—and to try to sell
him the portrait of his daughter-in-law, Monika, according to his January
6, 1969, journal entry: "Isn't it great? It's the best notice I've had, really
understands me."

As for the painting of Monika, "I'd take a hundred dollars off the gallery price and make it fourteen hundred. You know I have to get something. My prices are going up. Oh, you know I was at the gallery and they had a Thomas Benton there—smaller than my paintings. I asked how much it was. They said, $25,000. It made me sick. I almost passed out. That crap. He's nothing, you know. . . . So you better buy Monika. . . ."

A photograph of Brand had appeared in *Time* the month before, along with a review of his most recent novel *Savage Sleep* (published in June 1968). He was shown in his apartment, with a Neel nude of Nancy Selvage on the wall. Sam Brody, out on the West Coast, saw the portrait and called Neel. ("Sam called up from the coast and knew it was my work, even though he never saw the portrait," Neel said.)

The mid to late sixties was, in many ways, like one big long protest, and Neel, as always, did her share of marching. Ever the activist, Neel made antiwar posters and contributed her work to anti–Vietnam War shows. She described one such work to Hills: "I did a poster for an anti-war exhibition. It was a brand-new canvas 40 by 30 inches, using collage. . . . I also did a drawing of Che Guevara. . . . The Green Berets murdered him."

As noted earlier, she even wrote a letter to Fidel Castro. And of course, Neel picketed, often against the very institutions she hoped would show her work, but which somehow continued to give minorities (read: women and African Americans) short shrift. The late painter Benny Andrews recalled Neel marching in the "Harlem on My Mind" protest in early 1969. The two had first met in the early 1960s, when they had a show together in Spanish Harlem. They became close friends in 1966, when they had a second show together, this time at what is now the Schomburg Center.

Said Andrews, "Once we got to know each other, it was just like a love affair. I would get involved in other things and Alice always wanted to be involved in things. She always reminded me of someone like a carpetbagger in a positive way—that she would just gather up her things and join in. One thing I always remember her for is that during the protest of the "Harlem on My Mind" exhibition at the Metropolitan [Museum of Art, January 1969] Alice came and she was out there and it was cold, and we had a very small group there at the beginning. There were only four or five white people: Raphael Soyer, Mel Ramos, and John Dobbs, and Alice was out there. And of course Alice was having trouble with her legs and everything, but that protest just brought her spirits up."

That February, she was included in a show at the National Institute of Arts and Letters. "I'm allowed eighteen linear feet," she told Brand on

February 28, when she invited him to that evening's opening. "It's quite a problem because my paintings are big—you know. I guess I'll be bumper to bumper." She added that she hoped she wouldn't be "behind a door—I always seem to be somewhere where you can't see me."

On May 21, Neel received an award, at the Institute's annual ceremony, presented by William Maxwell. The event drew an illustrious crowd, including Stephen Spender, Virgil Thomson, Leopold Stokowski, John Hersey (whose piece on Hiroshima Neel had read to her sons), Tennessee Williams, Marcel Breuer, Malcolm Cowley, Robert Penn Warren, Allen Ginsberg, Arthur Schlesinger, Jr., S. J. Perelman, John Ashbery, Jacques Lipchitz, and Saul Steinberg; in all ninety-eight luminaries of arts and letters.

Neel was seated in the next-to-the-last row, next to Chaim Gross. Wrote Millen Brand in his journal, "Alice looked sweet in a plain pastel dress, beaming and clapping everybody, and the applause for her award was louder and more enthusiastic than any other." She herself would be formally inducted as a member in 1976.

Neel spent part of 1969 traveling, something she had rarely done up to this point. In April, she went to the Soviet Union with John Rothschild on one of the trips organized by his Open Road agency. That summer, she saw José Santiago Negron, who had become an Episcopal priest, when she, Richard, and Nancy went to San Miguel, Mexico. She also saw her old friend from Havana, Marcelo Pogolotti, and met the Mexican muralist David Alfaro Siqueiros. She continued on from Mexico to San Francisco to visit Hartley and Ginny. Neel stayed in San Francisco for nearly two months, and completed some ten paintings, including the portrait of *Ginny in a Blue Shirt*. (Hartley filmed Ginny sitting for Alice.) She was also introduced to Linus Pauling, who lived near Big Sur, where she painted him.

For Neel, the trip was apparently a bit of a busman's holiday. Wrote Brand in his journal on September 28, 1969:

> *I just got Alice Neel on the phone after a number of intermittent tries and she said, "Oh, I've been in San Francisco and in Mexico. Hartley is in San Francisco now. He has this cute little apartment looking out over the bay and I was staying there. I painted Linus Pauling." She also painted Felix Greene, and she was in Mexico City with Richard and Sally [sic] and at first they were in a hotel, but she was patining portraits in a family (loaded evidently) who had her live there and paint. During a*

visit to Mexico City, she stayed with a family. [Doctora Enelda
Fox and her daughter, Enelda Fox Luttman. Doctora Fox and
her late husband Charles were friends of John's.] They had
their walls filled with Siqueiros and put me up there with him.
You know what I felt like. You know how Velasquez painted the
portrait of the king—well, that was me going into the home and
painting. I never did it before, but I did some great paintings.
But I worked like mad, it wasn't a vacation, I didn't get to Cuer-
navaca or anywhere—just worked.

Alice, Nancy, and Richard visited Sequeiros at his studio in Mexico
City, and later that evening had dinner with Sequeiros and his wife at the
Luttmans, where Alice gave the famous muralist a slide show.

The eventful decade ended with Neel on the road again, this time traveling to Denmark, and Spain with Richard, Nancy, and their first child,
Olivia. In Copenhagen, Neel visited Jonathan and Monika Brand, Millen's
son and daughter-in-law, and stayed with them for several weeks. She then
continued alone to Norway, before joining John Rothschild in Spain.

Neel had finally found her rightful place in the sixties, but it was the
next decade that would truly revolutionize her career.

CHAPTER TWENTY-FOUR

Their Balls Are Just Higher Up

Neel's entry into the 1970s, like her entry into the 1960s (*Pull My Daisy*), began with an iconic cultural image. In August 1970, *Time* magazine asked Neel to do a portrait of the radical feminist Kate Millett, whose ground-breaking book, *Sexual Politics,* had just been published. When Millet refused to pose because she didn't want to be portrayed as a leader, Neel painted her from a photograph. Widely reproduced, it is not one of her best pieces. But it nonetheless branded Neel—and her work—as inextricable from the second wave of the feminist movement, and the beginning of an extraordinary era of "feminist art."

As she herself put it, Neel was, in effect, a feminist before there was feminism. Although she did not identify herself as a feminist per se—"The women's lib movement is giving the women the right to openly practice what I had to do in an underground way" she said during her Moore doctoral address in 1971—Neel and her career benefited enormously from being adopted by the movement as an emblem of artistic integrity and freedom. Feminists took a page from the challenging—and unorthodox—choices she had made in both her life and her work. Unlike the other well-known female artists of her generation, Neel had done it her way, and alone, without attaching herself to a powerful male.

Nineteen seventy marked the advent of the second wave of feminism and the blossoming of feminist art. If the civil rights movement dominated the 1960s, feminism dominated the 1970s. The first wave, unleashed by Betty Friedan's 1963 book, *The Feminine Mystique,* fought fiercely to create sociological and economic change and established major women's organizations to fight for women's rights, including the National Organization of Women (NOW), founded in 1966. (Neel criticized Friedan's book with characteristic bluntness: "I couldn't read Betty Friedan because . . . I was

such a snob. I couldn't identify with the housewife in Queens. I didn't have
her aids—her washing machine and her security.")

A decade later, Western cultural history itself came under the feminist
knife. First, Kate Millett's *Sexual Politics* incisively deconstructed the
sexism of the patriarchal literary canon. Then came art historian Linda
Nochlin's 1971 groundbreaking essay in *ARTnews*, "Why Have There
Been No Great Women Artists?" The piece, which soon became feminist
gospel, proclaimed that "The fault lies not in our stars, our hormones, our
menstrual cycles, or in our empty internal spaces, but in our institutions
and our education . . ." As Nochlin pointed out, historically women artists
were not even allowed to paint from the nude until the early twentieth century. In other words, the key issue was the ongoing patriarchal attitude of
the white Western academies, not any trait inherent in the "weaker" sex itself.

Nochlin's essay instantly created a ripple effect throughout the already
burgeoning women's art coalitions. These included WAR (Women Artists
in Revolution); LACWA (Los Angeles Council of Women Artists); Ad Hoc
Women's Artists' Group, which focused on the sexist programs of museums; Women in the Arts (WIA), which emerged out of a series of informal
meetings with female artists, including Ce Roser, Fay Lanser, Alice Neel,
Elaine de Kooning, and Pat Passlof; West-East Bag (WEB), a registry
that assigned delegates and representatives across the country to keep track
of events on both coasts; and the Women's Caucus for Art (WCA). (Alice
Neel would be one of five artists to receive the WCA's first Honor Awards
for lifetime achievement in 1979.)

This formidable grass-roots political movement coalesced into an impressive generation of feminist artists, including Judy Chicago, Miriam
Schapiro, May Stevens, Faith Ringgold, June Blum, Nancy Spero, and
Sylvia Sleigh, as well as a powerful cadre of feminist critics and historians
(many of whom were also artists). Besides Nochlin, there were Lucy Lippard, Grace Glueck, Cindy Nemser, Mary Garrard, Norma Broude, Ann
Sutherland Harris, and Elizabeth Hess, among others, who all made
themselves volubly heard. An explosion of feminist journals and publications emerged, including *Feminist Art Journal* (founded by Nemser,
Patricia Mainardi, and Irene Moss; Nemser's husband, Chuck, was an
editor), *Woman and Art, Heresies, Metamorphosis, Womanart,* and
Chrysalis. The first official issue of *Ms. Magazine* was published in July
1972. A.I.R., the first female cooperative art gallery, was founded in SoHo
later that year.

"The early 1970s was entirely exhilirating," says Chicago. "We were discovering our history and reinvigorating our work by moving into areas openly and freely that had been taboo. It was thrilling and terrifying and we were breaking new ground." Chicago was an early pioneer: One of the seminal works of the new movement was the avant-garde art project Womanhouse, which she codirected with Miriam Schapiro in 1972. A seventeen-room abandoned house in Hollywood was used to stunning and much-publicized effect to stage installations and performances that satirized and subverted conventional female rites and roles—from menstruation to marriage to pregnancy. Two years later, Chicago began work on her iconic piece, *The Dinner Party.* One of the best-known (and controversial) feminist artworks ever created, it consists of dinner-place settings representing 1,038 female innovators, 39 of whom have their own "vulval" plates.

"The personal is the political" became a popular mantra. It was the era of consciousness-raising groups and (thanks, in part, to the 1973 publication of *Our Bodies, Ourselves*) vaginal self-examinations. That same year, Erica Jong nailed the Zeitgeist with her best-seller *Fear of Flying*, in which she coined the infamous phrase "zipless fuck." (Just four years later, Diane Keaton would discover the dark side of such sexual freedom in *Looking for Mr. Goodbar.*)

"What made those early moments of feminism so electric was that the whole movement was like letting a million powerhouses out of a box," says painter and critic Mira Schor. (A student at the time, she contributed several pieces to Womanhouse.) "All this intelligence and ambition and energy suddenly focused on the world, saying whatever we wanted and confronting the galleries and museums. And the sort of humor that came out of a kind of imprisonment that had gone on for centuries. I guess I understood that I was at the moment where these stories were beginning to be told, and wanted to be told, and I wanted to tell them. That was the excitement."

Mary Garrard, coeditor of the seminal *The Power of Feminist Art*, summed the 1970s up as "that magical moment in time when astounding new things seemed possible for women." To her, the phrase "women's liberation" said it all—women were finally attempting to liberate themselves from the ongoing sexual and social tyranny of the previous generations. "It's hard for younger people to understand what the word liberation meant to our generation. Liberation from all the social role expectations and social constraints. You can't imagine what it was like to grow up in the fifties."

As women fought to gain equality in academic and cultural institutions,

and, most importantly, in the cultural canon itself, there was a virtual eruption of protests, shows, panels, and publications. And while Neel herself
had little interest in feminist rhetoric, she readily participated in the growing number of feminist activities multiplying across the country. Both because of her natural antipathy toward bureaucracy (she wasn't a good Party
member, either) and, perhaps, her fear of once again being marginalized
with a special-interest group, this time as a feminist artist, rather than a
Social Realist, she refused to label herself as a feminist.

Neel's attitude toward feminism was conflicted and complex. "I believe
in Feminism. I was born believing in it. My mother used to say, 'I don't
know what you expect to do in the world. You're only a girl.' But if anything,
that made me more ambitious," she had told Barbaralee Diamonstein.
At the same time, she seemed to have inculcated her mother's conditioned
Victorian misogyny. "I much preferred men to women. Women terrified
me. I thought they were stupid because all they did was keep children and
dogs in order. Even though they were 'the conscience of the world,' I didn't
think they had all the brains they should have, nor all the answers. I
thought the most they ever did was back some man they thought was important." Or, as she told students at one lecture, "I felt women represented a
dreary way of life, always helping a man and never performing themselves,
whereas I wanted to be an artist myself! I could certainly have accomplished much more with a good wife. This is quite male chauvinist, but this
was the world with which I was confronted."

Neel readily acknowledged that she had been discriminated against as a
female artist, "I was a woman. That was partly it," she said to Joan Kuflin,
about receiving recognition so late in her career. "Women are second-class
citizens and they still are." But she insisted gender itself was never an issue
for her. "When I was in a room working, I wasn't aware of being a woman
artist. I don't think there's basically a difference between women's art and
men's art. I don't agree with any of that poppycock. It's either good art or
bad art, and that's it," she told Judith Higgins in 1984 *ARTnews*. (Neel
wasn't alone in distancing herself from feminism. It was a position that a
number of female artists of the prefeminist generation seemed to take. Lee
Krasner and Georgia O'Keeffe vocally disclaimed feminism, as did Grace
Hartigan, who exhibited under the name George Hartigan until the mid-
1950s (supposedly an homage to George Sand and George Eliot), and alienated the sixties feminists with pointed remarks.

Still, Neel was more than happy to grab the pedestal offered to her by
the feminist art movement. That meant media, being considered a mentor,

and being memorialized. Neel even became a cause célèbre when Women in the Arts circulated a petition drafted by Cindy Nemser, demanding that Neel be included in the Whitney's Annual: "To us the Whitney's neglect of an artist like Alice Neel is a symbolic action. It is a gesture which embodies completely the unjust and biased treatment that women artists have received from the big establishment museums all over the world."

The first issue of *Women's Art Journal* in 1972 printed a similar petition, along with Neel's 1971 doctoral address at Moore College of Art and Design. Ultimately, the Whitney, which had been picketed for several years by various women's organizations, did include Neel. Says Chicago, "Neel was one of the women artists, like O'Keeffe and Kahlo, that the feminist art movement brought into visibility."

One of the movement's milestone events was the first national Conference on Women in the Visual Arts, which took place from April 20 to 22, 1972, at the Corcoran School of Art in Washington, D.C. Neel didn't just attend the event; she literally left her mark. Years later, people remembered how she had to be physically "dragged from the stage," according to Mary Garrard, after showing nearly forty years' worth of slides.

Then, apparently unwilling to wait in line for the ladies' room, she brazenly peed in the Corcoran's corridor. "With this aggressive, outrageous behavior, Alice Neel showed us what it might mean to be *really* free of feminine constraints," wrote Garrard in *Women's Art Journal* in 2006, comparing Neel's action to Jackson Pollock's celebrated antics—including peeing into fireplaces. (Actually, as much simple necessity as feminist performance, the aging Neel didn't hesitate to pee in public places, says her son Hartley. "But she also got some satisfaction in just doing that. I think it was both. Alice was saying something.")

For Garrard, "Her own idiosyncratic feminism, her outrageous gestures, helped expand the definition of feminism in the seventies. There is, and was, such a huge range of kinds of ways that one could be a feminist, and she was a large figure in creating one kind of type, a role model. . . . she was Rabelaisian, like Gulley Jimson in *The Horse's Mouth*, a kind of over-the-top figure usually associated with being a male artist."

Still, Neel was scarcely a team player. Says May Stevens, "She wasn't a feminist—she was an *Alice Neelist*. . . . She was totally antifeminist and antiwomen, and as far as politically, she knew everybody on the Left. . . . I was one of the leaders. I didn't want anything to do with Alice. She showed up at our parades and demonstrations. She wanted to be seen and whatever glory, but she was not . . . a kindred spirit. We supported her not as a

friend or supporter. She took advantage of the situation and we were proud
to have a good artist on our side. Alice concentrated on Alice. Everyone
knew she wasn't really a feminist."

Sylvia Sleigh, who participated in several feminist shows with Neel, including the "Sister Chapel," for which Neel painted Bella Abzug (her little
round breasts are depicted more or less as "balls higher up"), describes
Neel as "opportunistic, narcissistic. I think she was a person who didn't
think the rest of the world really existed. . . . I know from the Sister Chapel. She said her painting was the best. She was the only one that didn't
fulfill the requirements—her piece should have been nine feet high and it
wasn't. I did manage to bully her once, when May Stevens and I had a show
with her, and we were asked afterward to talk about our work. We were going to show slides. She had thirty-six slides, and I know what she's like.
What she tried to do was to talk so long we would not have a chance to say
anything, so I said, 'I think you better go last.' She said, 'Oh no, I'll be
quick. I'll be quick.' She had a certain fear of me, I think."

In the end, though, Neel's ambivalent and sometimes troublesome attitude didn't matter to the feminists, who embraced her wholeheartedly as
an icon and ready-made role model. Says Chicago, "She exemplified the
struggles a major woman artist of her generation faced in order to participate, to be taken seriously, to be able to have her work acknowledged. She
led the life few women had the courage to live. She didn't have a strong
male mentor to ease it. She faced life with all of its obstacles, with all of its
difficulties, with all of its pain and rejections, and eventually she overcame
it—at huge cost to herself. She faced it alone. Isn't that the paradigm for
heroism? That's why she became a feminist heroine."

And then there was the work, which in its style and subject matter an-
ticipated the feminist art movement, from Neel's choice of portraiture as a
genre to her many ruthlessly honest depictions of motherhood—including
pregnancy. As Chicago said back in the 1970s, "The agenda for women artists was to transform our circumstances into our subject matter . . . to use
them to reveal the whole nature of the human condition." Neel, of course,
had been doing just that from the start.

In her essay "Some Women Realists," Linda Nochlin argues that portraiture, by its very nature, lends itself to such female characteristics (innate or conditioned) as empathy, and the desire—or need—for emotional
interaction. "In the field of portraiture, women have been active among the
subverters of the natural laws of modernism," she noted. "This hardly
seems accidental: women have, after all, been encouraged, if not coerced,

into making responsiveness to the moods, attentiveness to the character traits (and not always the most attractive ones) of others into a lifetime's occupation. . . . For the portrait is implicated, to some degree at least— whether artist, sitter, or critic wish to admit it or not—in 'that terrible need for contact' [referred to by Katherine Mansfield]. Unlike any other genre, the portrait demands the meeting of two subjectivities: if the artist watches, judges the sitter, the sitter is privileged, by the portrait relation, to watch and judge back."

As for Neel's subject matter and its treatment, "much of Alice's work prefigured the feminist movement in terms of its content," Chicago says, singling out Neel's watercolor *The Family* as an early example. "It only became comprehensible in retrospect. Now looking backward, we can see all of these impulses that had not been identified or discussed before the feminist art movement—to be able to express oneself as a woman prior to a time when there was an actual sort of formulated visual language. As a feminist, you look at her paintings of Linda Nochlin, of her pregnant daughter-in-law. Those are not women as objects. Those are women with power and agency and individuality, who walk off the canvas into the world. They are not splayed out there for the male gaze. There is no male viewer in mind. And one of the things about Alice Neel's portraits of men is they are not aggrandized, they are not heroic, they are human and vulnerable. Joe Gould—he's an object of amusement, empathy, scorn, pity, and compassion all at once. That's very unusual historically. Andy Warhol, instead of being presented as an iconic art hero, is presented as wounded, bandaged, and vulnerable. I remember Anaïs Nin said something that always stayed with me. She talked about Virginia Woolf's *To the Lighthouse*, and she talked about what was a singular aspect of female intelligence—which was the ability, like a lighthouse beam, to penetrate to the deepest layers of the psyche. And I think you can really see that in Alice Neel's paintings."

And then there are Neel's pregnant nudes. Simply by creating them, and thereby correcting their glaring absence in art history, Neel was, consciously or not, performing a feminist act, according to Garrard. "Neel herself observed that the whole picture of women without pregnancy is trivial, saying that that was treating them as sex objects. If you think about how many pregnant women are actually visible in the world at any given moment, the absence of that image in art is really unusual. It's a taboo that she's breaking. So her pregnant nudes are inherently feminist as a refutation of the absence of women's real lived experience in art." As Neel told Hills, "It's a very important part of life and it was neglected. I feel as a subject it's perfectly legitimate, and people out of false modesty, or being sissies, never showed it. . . ."

Just as she had painted the Communist and civil rights leaders of earlier decades, Neel documented a number of influential women during the 1970s and 80s, most of whom were outspoken feminists. In addition to Linda Nochlin and Cindy Nemser, these included Faith Ringgold, Ann Sutherland Harris, Mary Garrard, Ellen Johnson, Mimi Gross (shown with her then husband, Red Grooms), Isabel Bishop, Sari Dienes, June Blum, Irene Peslikis, Marisol, Susan Rossen, Dianne Vanderlip, Catherine Jordan, and Bella Abzug.

Finally, there is what is unquestionably Neel's masterwork from a feminist perspective: her late nude self-portrait. Says Garrard of this tour de force, "She's the subject gazing back at the viewer and she's deploying the gaze both as subject and as artist, and I think she's very aware of all the complications of self-portraiture and the gender conventions and all those things—plus age. It's not hard to break it down into all those component elements. But what's beautiful about it is that it says it in one gestalt. It's not like 'Here are itemized points I am making'; it's that the image contains, as a kind of potent object, all those ideas. I can't think of any counterpart. It would be as if the Venus de Willendorf came to life and started painting. It really is quite extraordinary. It's something that is both unique and deeply in dialogue with all of art history."

*   *   *

The seventies marked a pinnacle for Neel. At a point in life when many people begin to slow down, Neel, if anything, seemed to speed up. Suddenly, Neel was everywhere, painting everyone. The 1970s was the most rewarding decade of the artist's hard-won career. She seemed to be ubiquitous—at feminist-related events, on college campuses, and, more than anything else, in art shows.

Neel's work itself grew even stronger in terms of expression and technique. She seemed more confident, often boldly leaving portions of the canvas incomplete or blank, thus emphasizing the subject. During this decade, she produced some of her best pieces, including some gender-bending classics. She was particularly adept at navigating the subtle sexual nuances in the body language of transgender and gay couples: Warhol superstar and drag queen Jackie Curtis with her friend Ritta Redd (1970) and their prurient feet; the critics David Bourdon and Gregory Battcock (1970), one stripped down to his underwear, the other fully suited and shod; Geoffrey

Hendricks and Brian (1978), a louche Geoffrey in an unbuttoned shirt, between them a suggestive bowl of fruit.

Her personal life also shifted during this period: Hartley Neel married Ginny Taylor on August 15, 1970, and the couple moved to Cambridge, Massachussetts, where Hartley was a resident at Massachussetts General Hospital. Ginny, who met Neel through her college friend Nancy Selvage, then going out with Hartley, had bonded with Alice even before she and Hartley got romantically involved. She saw Neel as a role model, and they maintained a close relationship.

That same month, John Rothschild moved in. He would live with Neel until his death, five years later. Neel ridiculed his fastidious ways. "He just wanted to bring in little tables and bourgeois it," Neel told Hills. "His habit for organization is a goddamn nuisance in my house," she said in an interview with Jonathan Brand.

Free from the daily responsibilities of motherhood and the constraints—or tumult—of a romantic relationship (if she and John still had sex, it was certainly not frequent), Neel was able to devote herself completely to her work. Although Richard and Nancy still lived in New York and Nancy had soon become Neel's hands-on amanuensis and constant companion, she clearly missed the proximity of her sons, as evidenced by her wistful painting *Loneliness*—an empty chair by a window—done not long after Hartley got married.

In 1970, Neel had her fourth solo show at the Graham, which ran from October 13 through through November 7. The works included a number of contemporary cultural figures, from poet and Warhol acolyte Gerard Malanga to Dorothy Pearlstein to Raphael Soyer and scientist Linus Pauling. As was often the case, Neel's work elicited a mixed response. Lawrence Campbell wrote in his review in *ARTnews*: "All together they make an astonishing, somewhat dismaying survey of our period. . . . Miss Neel seems to detect a hidden weakness in her sitters, which she drags out, yelping, into the clear light of day."

Art International, however, trashed the show. Wrote Gerrit Henry, ". . . Miss Neel paints her sitters in a kind of dumb Expressionist style whose ancestry can be traced directly back to the pages of Mad Magazine. She leaves parts of her paintings unfinished to prove, I suppose, that they are modern art . . ."

And, of course, Hilton Kramer predictably criticized both the painter and the paintings:

Mrs. Neel exhibits her familiar strength and weaknesses. The
strengths are all in the faces of her subjects, which Mrs. Neel renders with an uncommon intensity. The weaknesses are all in the
realization of the painting as a formal entity. Mrs. Neel is one of
those artists who are forever hostage to their most immediate
feelings, and in her case it is character she responds to: the making of a pictorial structure is of much less interest to her . . .

Still, the opening was a memorable event; Andy Warhol showed up and
Alice was photographed with his portrait for *The Village Voice*. The invitation reproduced Neel's striking portrait of the Gruen family—art critic
John Gruen, his wife, the painter Jane Wilson, who also showed at Graham,
and their daughter, Julia, who now heads the Keith Haring Foundation—
notable for their shiny patent-leather shoes (Neel jokingly referred to the
painting as "Six Patent Leather Shoes"). "Jane Wilson is the painter. John
Gruen is a critic, and the little girl was studying ballet," Neel remarked.

Neel, true to form, captured her subjects at their most recognizable and
then froze them there; portraiture as taxidermy. (Except, of course, that
the painting looks startlingly alive: Gruen and Wilson are dark, smolder-
ing, and intense, while Julia's blasé expression is worldly beyond her years.)
Neel commented that "John Gruen reminded me of a gypsy father and
Jane Wilson looked so much like a fashion model that I was amazed later to
find out that she had been a fashion model before she was an artist."

Gruen had been one of the first art writers to single Neel out as exceptional, shortly after her 1966 Graham show. As he recalls, "I said to Jane,
'Guess what? Alice Neel wants to paint our portrait.' And Jane said, 'Oh, how
wonderful!' and Julia said, 'Oooh,' and I said, 'Yes, you, too, my darling, and
she is a very great artist and you are going to come along anytime she wants
us, because this is going to be history.'"

When the Gruens arrived, they found Alice prepared with her easel and
a very large canvas; she had never before tackled a portrait of three people.
Like everyone else, the Gruens were impressed by the number of paintings
in the apartment. "Every room was stacked with paintings. And she would
just ramble. I remember her rambling," recalls John. "Rambling in the
sense of 'Well and then I went to Cuba and you know Cubans, they have a
funny way of being . . .' but she would go off into tangents. She didn't keep
to one subject. She digressed, and she digressed interestingly. She was
never boring."

Adds Jane Wilson, "She never lost her concentration with the painting.

That was straight as an arrow. I thought it was really very interesting to start with blue. Usually my understanding of it is that the color of the outline, for some artists, is one that feeds the interior color, the color areas, so I wondered how that worked in her head. But it seemed to be something that helped her build the form, define the form, not just with the outline but the color."

Neel immediately fixated on their shoes. "She said, 'Oh, how wonderful, you're all wearing patent-leather shoes.' And that was so intriguing to her, and I believe that when she started putting color, she started with the shoes. They are very prominent," recalls John.

Despite Neel's chattering, "we were very conscious of being the subject matter. We had not ever posed except in photography. We were photographed a lot—Jane and Julia and I, and we have beautiful, gorgeous portraits. It was an amazing experience, and we looked forward to going back and being with Alice, and every time, of course, there was more of us on the canvas, and that was wonderful to see. Even Julia was intrigued. I had always loved Alice's work, because it was a mixture of the sublime and the grotesque. The sublime and the grotesque to me were part of her aesthetic, were part of what she was conveying to the world, that people are beautiful and grotesque, that people are poignant and tragic, that they had big interior lives. She gave them big interior lives. She saw the lives in them that even they did not recognize. What emerged was a kind of desperate beauty, that made itself felt. It was like sound."

The Gruens were thrilled with the final painting, which they considered "a masterpiece." Says John, "I thought that the painting had great strength and we had also, of course, been used to our seeing ourselves in photographs as being, you know, beautiful." Adds Jane, "Or glamorous. Whereas Alice's portrait did not make us look beautiful. I think it's very beautiful, but you know what I'm saying. It's not Avedon. It's you, not a model."

Neel seemed to assume the Gruens would purchase the portrait, which she offered to them for twelve hundred dollars. "I said, 'Alice, I don't know what to say. We don't have the money,'" John recalls. "And she said, 'Maybe you could pay it off in big chunks. I don't have any money, either.' This came as a shock that she wanted to sell it, because, of course, it placed into my evil mind that she asked us to pose so she could sell us the painting. I mean, that never occurred to me, ever. I thought she just wanted to paint us, and I was a little taken aback. The only bad blood was that we really couldn't afford to have it, and certainly if we did buy it, we wouldn't have known where to put it. So that was it and it was never brought up again."

The high point of the show was her unforgettable portrait of Andy Warhol, generally considered one of her best works, and one of Neel's personal
favorites. The painting, which took four or five sittings, was completed just
before the show opened, with Brigid Berlin taking Polaroid shots of one
portrait master documenting another.

It's an astonishing portrait on every level. Warhol, a maverick at coining
the throwaway phrase, had pronounced in *The Philosophy of Andy Warhol* that "nudity is a threat to my existence." Nonetheless, the artist, who
never even appeared without his trademark wig (and, usually, sunglasses),
offered to strip to the waist for Neel, revealing the scars from the assassina-
tion attempt by Valerie Solanas in 1968, as well as the surgical corset he
was now forced to wear.

Neel exaggerated these disturbing details to indelible affect. She also
painted one of the most voyeuristic—and perceptive—artists of the twentieth century with his eyes tightly closed. She gives the androgynous Warhol an almost feminine form, with small drooping breasts and wide hips.
And, perhaps alluding to Warhol's own beginnings as a commercial illustrator who did shoe advertisements for I. Miller, she renders his shoes in
beautiful, shiny detail. The portrait is memorable for Neel's nervy perspi-
cacity in depicting Warhol's vulnerability, as a perpetual outsider (like
herself) and as a literal victim of his own celebrity. But Warhol's input is
also key: His courageous self-exposure is in itself an artistic act. Of all
Neel's paintings, this portrait comes the closest to a collaboration.

The two had originally met in 1963. "We were both hanging in the penthouse at the Museum of Modern Art, Neel explained. And he said, 'Oh,
you're that woman that paints those wonderful portraits. I want a portrait. . . . I'll put you in a movie.' But I was even more overweight then. I
thought I'd look frightful, so I never called him. But then in '70, I saw him
again . . . and then I painted him. . . . The reason he wears that corset,
when they took the bullets out they had to cut all of his stomach muscles."

Neel recalled that she ran into Warhol at the Gotham Book Mart, and he
suggested, " 'Why don't you paint me with my scars?' I admired him for
just taking off his shirt like that." And that it was actually Warhol's idea to
shut his eyes, "because all my pictures look at you. I really thought he
shut them because as an adolescent he was ashamed of his state. . . . We
were both so sophisticated," said Neel. "We never mentioned the fact that
he's an androgyne."

According to Neel, Andy later said, when asked, that she and Louise
Nevelson were the best women artists. "Not that I should be flattered by

that, but I was, Well, it's advertising. Andy was the biggest advertiser ever."

The following year began with Neel's triumphant return to her alma mater, the Philadelphia School of Design for Women, now called Moore College, for a retrospective exhibit that ran from January 15 through February 19. Thumbing her nose (as always) at Main Line society, Neel was escorted to the show's opening by none other than Jackie Curtis and Ritta Redd, the infamous transgender couple of her mesmerizing 1970 portrait, proudly on display at Moore. As Richard recalls, "Alice, Nancy, Ginny, and I drove out to Moore in a van with Ritta Redd and Jackie Curtis, who was primping himself the whole way."

Among the fifty paintings in the show were *Joe Gould*, *Andy Warhol*, *Raphael Soyer*, *Linus Pauling*, *Walter Gutman*, *Frank O'Hara*, *Jerry Malanga*, *David Bourdon and Gregory Battcock*, *Mimi Gross and Red Grooms*, and the triple portrait of the Gruens. Wrote Hubert Crehan of Neel in the *San Franciso Sunday Examiner and Chronicle* on March 7:

> Today she is the most original portrait painter I know: sophisticated in craft, passionate in expression and wizardly in wresting potent psychological insights from her subjects. . . . Alice Neel never left figure painting and now in her mature years she is working at the height of her powers. She had been scorned as a woman artist but her long career is coming into its own, and she becomes a force in women's liberation. Her work is one of the most artistic efforts of the protest against some of the inequities of our time. And by itself, her painting is an achievement of a high order.

Victoria Donohoe, the critic for the *Philadelphia Inquirer*, an old acquaintance of Neel, wrote two pieces, one in the Friday and one in the Sunday edition of the paper: "Portrait painting is alive and well in the hands of Alice Neel, America's most probing and stunningly original portrait painter. . . ." Donohoe wrote on Friday, while Sunday's paper proclaimed, "Not the least of Alice Neel's claim to contemporary fame is the fact that this sensitive and resourceful ex-Philadelphia artist has single-handedly put the once-creative art of portrait painting back on the map in America."

Neel would receive an honorary doctoral degree from her alma mater six months later, on June 1, 1971:

Alice Neel, your people are real: they have presence on the street and in the galleries where your works hang. One is transfixed by you penetration of character. Yours are portraits which express inadequacy, hostility, virility, energy—each with a unique face and feature. Only after the impact of the personality does one re- member to look at shadows, facets of light, the lines that contain the portrait—to be astonished at the formal excellence of each work. You have done in art what writers do in the characteriza- tion in a novel. You have called yourself a collector of souls; you have said that you would like to make the world happy. Every saviour must see as you have seen; the sorrow, the pain, the madness—the human need—before any set of salvation is possi- ble. We confer this honor upon you because you have seen, have pitied, have loved, and have kept a record. To you, Alice Neel, we award the Doctor of Fine Arts Degree.

Neel's doctoral address was printed later that year in the feminist jour- nal *Women and Art.* She spoke about the current times and her response to them, quoted (and refuted) a comment by Simone de Beauvoir, and in- voked her familiar self-mythologizing Balzac leitmotif. It stands as her most complete artistic statement:

This is a great era of change and it is very exciting to be an artist— even with the terrible things that are going on, such as the war in Vietnam and the fact that society is almost in a state of chaos. . . . Things move so fast today that before a movement dies the next movement is already felt. . . .

Destruction and bitter criticism are a reflection of the overall picture. However, great attention is being paid to art and the art- ist is being lifted out of his idiosyncratic alienation (witness me) and all society is taking an interest in him. . . .

The women's lib movement is giving women the right to practice openly what I had to do in an underground way. I have always believed that women should resent and refuse to accept all the gratuitous insults that men impose upon them. The woman artist is especially vulnerable and could be robbed of her confidence. . . .

I have only become really known in the sixties because before I could not defend myself. I read a quote from Simone de Beauvoir

1. Alice Neel at age five

2. Alice's parents, George Washington
Neel and Alice Hartley Neel

3. Alice Neel as a young woman

4. Carlos in Philadelphia, 1924

5. Carlos and Alice on their bench at
Chester Springs, 1924

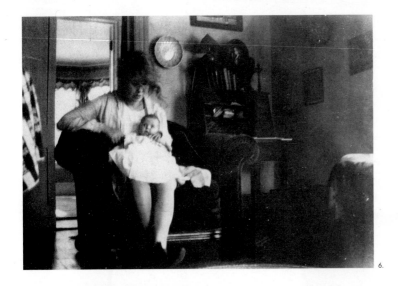

6. Alice and Isabetta, New York, 1929

7. Alice with Carlos and Marcelo Pogolotti
in Havana, 1926

8. Alice and Santillana, Sedgwick Avenue,
the Bronx, 1927

9. Alice with Isabetta, age 11 months,
New York, 1929

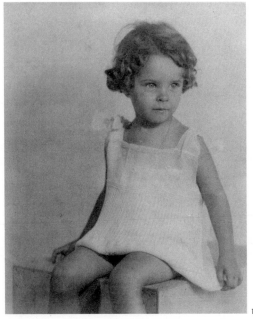

10. Isabetta

11. Kenneth Doolittle and Alice, circa 1932-33

12. Nude Alice, 1931

13.

14.

15.

13. Alice and Nadya Olyanova

14. Alice and Fanya Fox on Cornelia Street, 1933

15. Alice and Kenneth with the first version of the Isabetta portrait, 1934

16. Isabetta, age 6

16.

17. José with his sister Jenny

18. John Rothschild, 1940

19. Alice and Sam Brody, 1940

20. Sam Brody

21.

24.

22.

25.

23.

21. Hartley and Richard on the rocking horse, c. 1944

22. Alice with Richard and Hartley, 1946

23. Richard and Hartley at Spring Lake, 1954

24. Alice on the set of *Pull My Daisy* with Allen Ginsberg, 1960

25. Alice with her painting of Bella Abzug

To Alice — My friend : Next time without fy leaf Ed Koch 26.

27.

28.

29.

30.

31.

26. Alice with Mayor Ed Koch and his portrait, 1982

27. Alice picketing the Whitney, 1971

28 Alice with Ritta Redd and Jackie Curtis and their portrait,
at the Moore College show, 1971

29. Alice celebrating her Whitney retrospective, 1974

30. Alice on *The Tonight Show* with Johnny Carson, 1984

31. Alice with her nude self-portrait, 1980

32.

32. Alice by Sam Brody

saying that no woman had ever had a world view because she had always lived in a man's world. For me this was not true. I do not think the world up to now should be given to men only. No matter what the rules are, when one is painting, one creates one's own world. Injustice has no sex and one of the primary motives of my work was to reveal the inequalities and pressures as shown in the psychology of the people I painted. It is not for nothing that Samuel Beckett won the Nobel Prize. His world view, encapsulated capitalism, carries the theory of dog eat dog to its ultimate outpost.

When El Greco and Raphael painted, religion was powerful and the great art was done in relation to faith and the church. A Campbell's soup can has supplanted Christ on the cross. Money is king and advertising and technology religion for the arts, and now complete destruction and anti-art.

My choices perhaps were not always conscious, but I have felt that people's images reflect the era in a way that nothing else could. When portraits are good art, they reflect the culture, the time and many other things. . . .

Never has prejudice of all sorts come under attack as it has to-day. There is a new freedom for women to be themselves, to find out what they really are. Freud's "What to do they want?" is easy to answer. They know what they do not want, but just as the slave who can only dream of what he will have after freedom knows what he wants, women must first be free and live and discover what they want. . . .

. . . The human image for many years was not considered im-portant. In 1962 when the Museum of Modern Art had its Recent Painting USA: The Figure show, I went to a symposium (all men by the way and none of the speakers really connected with the kernel of the subject). "Man is the mirror of all things: says the Bible, and this is true. . . ."

Neel then quoted her *Hasty Papers* statement, which began, "As for myself, being born I looked around and the world and its people terrified and fascinated me. I was attracted by the morbid and excessive and every-thing connected with death had a dark power over me. . . ." She continued:

. . . Now Things have changed and there are hopeful signs that a new humanism is taking place. Everything is being questioned,

all relationships, education, western man, and the very ethos of
the west. Allen Ginsberg chants Buddhist chants.

It is a great time to be . . . an artist; who knows where these
new investigations will lead. Also everything has been and is being tried in art and this will enrich . . . consciousness. Art is
hard work but it is a great way of life. . . . Of course one cannot
omit the fact that one must be a good artist and since esthetics are
in a complete state of confusion, this is not easy.

In late January of 1971, Neel joined nineteen women, including Pat
Mainardi, Lois Dodd, Ann Tabachnick, and Marcia Marcus, at the Alliance of Figurative Artists, to protest the dominance of male speakers. The
feminist group took over the January 29 weekly meeting and demanded
their own session, which, according to the March issue of *Arts* magazine,
was used to discuss "painting the figure, naked and clothed, the male tradition of painting woman as erotic object, and the differences in sexual attitude. During the after-discussion, the hostility from the men was almost
unanimous." It was one of several protests Neel would participate in over a
period of just a few months.

Neel, who had attended the Club in the 50s and 60s, became a regular
part of the Figurative Artists Alliance in the early 70s, and still had an active member's card in 1982. Founded in February 1969, the vociferous
group met every Friday at the Educational Alliance at 197 East Broadway.

"She was a major player in the Alliance," says Marjorie Kramer, who
became friendly with Neel at that time, and helped champion one of the
petitions to the Whitney, insisting that the museum include Neel in its Annual. "The petition that was passed around at the Alliance got more than
three hundred names," she says. (Kramer was also involved with organizing the first open show of feminist art at a space called Museum, on Broadway, where Neel showed, among other paintings, her image of Joe Gould.)

Over the course of the next half a dozen years, she would be in some six
panels at the Alliance, and was a vocal audience member. Says Kramer's husband, Sam Thurston, "It could be a scrappy place. I remember her bringing
up Sequeiros the week after he died. She always brought in some of her work
on 'work night.' Neel also made some invaluable friends and connections.

Recalls Philip Pearlstein, "The first few meetings were at Alfred Leslie's place, but so many people showed up that he investigated the neighborhood and found the Educational Alliance and got space there. Between
two and three hundred people showed up at these meetings. I started going

down there regularly, because it was terrific, it was very exciting. All they wanted to do was have panels and guest speakers, and just talk about the problems of figurative art representation, and the battles became terrific. It was mostly split between the intellectuals and the expressionists; the 'heads and the guts.'"

Pearlstein would regularly give Alice, who lived nearby, a ride. "I had a Volkswagen bus, so I would pick her up and drive her down. . . . And of course that's where she discovered how to speak publically. She had an evening presenting her ideas and work, and was greeted with great enthusiasm. She spoke a number of times, either from the audience or as a speaker. That's where she learned that she had this ability to communicate verbally. . . . She had great popularity and began getting invited places. . . .

"One night I picked up Alice and also Katherine Kuh who had been the director of the Chicago Art Institute . . . and she heard about it and wanted to write about it [for *The Saturday Evening Post*]. She and Alice got involved in a wild discussion afterward about their respective love affairs. . . . It was quite loud between these two older ladies, outdoing each other with their lovers."

As Pearlstein remembers it, the evenings at the Alliance could get quite rowdy. "I had invited Chuck Close—this is when he was a young strapping man—and Robert Rosenblum, the art historian, and the audience ended up throwing beer cans at him, and not empty cans. . . . They attacked him, there were all kinds of crazy accusations, and since I was instrumental in getting him to talk there, I was so embarrassed I never went back. That was after about five years of going regularly. Alice must have gone to at least a third of them, I picked her up a lot."

The painter Paul Resika, who fondly called Neel, "Alice Neel the Squeaking Wheel," because she "called anytime with any bit of publicity about her," remembers Neel latching on to Isabel Bishop as she hailed a cab. "At that time Isabel Bishop was a real art-world madam, and had great power and Alice envied her terrifically and wanted her approval. So one snowy night, Isabel was getting into a cab and Alice worked so hard and elbowed everyone in her path to get into the taxi with her to go uptown. I remember her delight and her passion when she got into that cab." (Neel would paint Bishop in 1974.)

Says Don Perlis, who became close to Neel in 1970 when they were both showing at the Graham Gallery (Neel painted Perlis with his son Jonathan), "Was the Alliance important to her? All those young people talking about figurative art? It was incredibly important to her. After the panels, there would be audience discussions, and she would sit in the front row talking like a sailor. Alice was vocal, she was very outspoken. I remember sitting in the audience and being astounded by her. To hear a grandmotherly woman with a mouth like that, and who was very opinionated."

In late February, Neel's painting of Red Grooms and Mimi Gross won the Benjamin Altman Figure Prize of $2,500 when it was shown in the National Academy of Design's 146th annual exhibition. As Neel later explained, "I was new blood. The National Academy of Design in New York would never hang my pictures because they thought they were a little outlandish. And then all of the sudden they took in me, they took in Pearlstein. They took in about fifteen people. It's new blood."

On April 17, Neel published a piece in the *Daily World*, giving a nod to feminism, in anticipation of the doctoral award she would soon be receiving:

> It's a great thing to see women demanding the right to be human beings and to have their product taken just as seriously as that of men. For me, art was really an uphill fight, for not only was I a woman, but I also painted people and until recently this technological society's art critics thought that was a very unimportant thing to paint. . . . It is true that women's real liberation cannot occur without some change in the social organization, which, of course, would include a change in thinking. Property relations which reduced everything to the status of "things" and objects have also reduced women to the status of sexual objects and have bound them and crushed them in many ways. This has been and still is largely a male world. In an office, a man is boss—a woman is secretary. In the museums it is the same thing. All the insults and discrimination are just part of the terrible rat race to which the human race has been reduced, and men, finding themselves with an advantage, take it. . . .
>
> Art was a struggle also because 29 or 30 years ago it was not regarded as "real work." I went my own way as much as I could. I have always painted seriously and often at great sacrifice. I lived in Spanish Harlem for 25 years and painted the life there. It was too hard to fight the establishment, so much of my work went on shelves. To produce was the thing! Still, one lives in the real world, and in the last two years especially, I have become known, perhaps because, even though so many terrible things are going

on, there are great changes taking place: the Black Panthers struggle for first class citizenship, the revolt of the youth against a moribund educational system, and also women's liberation opening new horizons and hopes for half the human race.

In May, Neel, along with her friend Benny Andrews, picketed the Whitney Museum of American Art's exhibition "Contemporary Black Artists in America." Recalled Robin Graham, "Alice had this wonderful little grandmotherly look and little impish smile and the vocabulary of a drunken sailor. There was a protest that had to do with a Whitney show and Alice was one of the people picketing. . . . Alice was carrying a sign that said, 'Doty [the curator] is a four-letter word.' That's sort of emblematic of the two sides of her." (Like many, Doty was beguiled by Neel's in-your-face attitude. He sent out Christmas cards bearing the image of the artist with her "four-letter" placard, adding the inscription, "So is love.")

In September, Neel joined the protest against MoMA organized by the Black Emergency Cultural Coalition (headed by Andrews) and Artists and Writers Protest the War in Vietnam, against Governor Nelson Rockefeller's handling of the Attica prison riot. There is a photograph of Neel with her oldest grandchild, Olivia, then four. Neel is holding a placard that says ATTICA: ROCKEFELLER CALLS THE SHOTS. She also contributed to the Attica art book created by the two organizations, along with Andrews, Sylvia Sleigh, Antonio Frasconi, and John Dobbs, which MoMA refused to sell. (The ever-vigilant FBI added it to Neel's file.) Said Andrews, "Since I was involved in these protest things, the Attica book and things like that, that added another dimension to our relationship, and then it kept going because we both kept doing things."

For Andrews, Neel's political engagement and social activism were as central to her personality as her need to paint: "It was as important as her having her breakfast. She was that before she became an artist. That's who Alice Neel was and art became a vehicle for her to be that."

Andrews spoke passionately about Neel's ongoing political commitment. "She was always reaching out to try to do something about what she saw as the inhumanity of man. And she was available for that and I think she literally led with her chin that way. To a certain point her agenda was much more nebulous—it was harder to put your fingers on, but you knew that she was trying to stand for something that was better than what was. You know she felt that there was so much injustice in a broad way. It's almost saying she couldn't achieve what she wanted; there was almost no way to do that, because it was so big. And I just think that we are so lucky that she was able to get it out in paint."

Neel never stopped being the rebel artist, but as she entered her seventies, she became more image-conscious, packaging herself as a kind of grandmotherly muckraker, as politically aware as she was outrageously outspoken. Invited everywhere, she took her show on the road, becoming a cult figure on the college lecture scene, famed for her idiosyncratic off-color remarks and quick wit. When a man heckled her during a panel discussion by shouting, "The reason women don't succeed is they don't have balls," Neel instantly replied, "Women have balls. They're just higher up."

In an interview with author Barbaralee Diamonstein, she didn't mince words about gender politics and the art world. "What amazed me was that all of the women critics respect you if you paint your own pussy as a woman's libber, but they didn't have any respect for being able to see politically and appraise the third world. So nobody mentioned that I managed to even see beyond my pussy politically, but I thought that was really a good thing. If they had a little more brains, they should have given me credit for being able to see not the feminine world, but my own world."

*   *   *

For Neel as for feminism, 1972 was a big year. Her notorious appearance at the Corcoran inspired her to embark on a series of college lectures. (Between 1972 and her death, Neel gave more than forty lectures.) She was an artist in residence at Pennsylvania's Bloomsburg State College, where her nephew, Georgie Neel, taught foreign languages, and had a show from March 7 to March 28 at the university's Haas Gallery. As she told students in her lecture, "I think I have painted to try not to lose life—it seemed terrible to have things happen and disappear. I have tried to keep a record." In April, she gave a lecture at a gallery in Nairobi. She also spent a week that summer at Skowhegan, Maine, as a visiting artist.

In late 1972, John Perreault made Neel an offer she couldn't refuse when he invited her to contribute to a "male nude" show at the School of Visual Arts. He specifically had her Joe Gould portrait in mind, which had first been shown publically at Moore College in 1971, but Neel insisted on creating a brand-new work for the show.

"It was the first show I ever curated," Perreault recalls. Neel wanted to know who else would be included. "She quizzed me with her fierce blue eyes," he says. When Perreault told her that Pearlstein would be represented by a recently completed painting, Neel retorted, "And you want me to be represented by a painting I made in 1933? I have to have a new painting in there." "She was kind of competitive. And she said, 'And you know, I think you would be great; why don't you take off your clothes and lie on the sofa,' and then she chalked me." (Neel told Hills that Perreault had volunteered to pose nude when she said she wanted to do a new painting.)

Sylvia Sleigh firmly believes that Neel originally got the idea for a Perreault nude portrait from her. "John Perreault was very brave," she says. "He made an exhibition of male nudes, I was very proud of him for that. And he chose my *Turkish Bath* painting, which wasn't even finished. So she [Alice] saw my painting of the Turkish bath and immediately took him home to her house and painted the nude for the show."

Whoever's idea it initially was, Neel lost no time starting the new canvas. She drew an outline in chalk around Perreault so she would remember his position when he returned for the next sitting. "I don't know if she knew it was going to take that long—it ultimately took seventeen sittings—but it did, and it would have been hard to get at the same pose. When I came back, she worked on it diligently, talking all the time."

But Neel wasn't happy with the first sitting. "And the second time when I came back she said, 'Oh, it didn't work out right.' She actually replaced my body the way it is now. It was kind of cut off and she wasn't pleased with her initial drawing with paint the way she did on a white canvas. Actually, it was more like what Phil Pearlstein would have done where he truncates things, so she said, 'Oh, we have to start all over again,' so she got it centered that time."

Neel gave Perreault the Matisse treatment, placing him odalisque-style on a couch, his explicitly rendered genitalia, dead center, anchoring the canvas. The painting also evokes Manet's *Olympia*, Goya's *The Naked Maja*, and Thomas Eakins's photograph of a nude male model, *Bill Duckett in the Rooms of the Philadelphia Art Students League*. "She captured my inner faun," Perreault later said. "I see myself in it and I think it's a great collaboration. We were both being wicked." The painting was exhibited at "The Male Nude" show, which opened the day after Valentine's Day, 1973. *Joe Gould* was also shown.

The previous month, Neel was included in the "Women Choose Women" show at the New York Cultural Center, which ran from January 12 to February 18, 1973. Initiated by Women in the Arts, the original plan, proposed during a huge demonstration on the doorstep of the Museum of Modern Art the previous April, was to mount a show of some five hundred of WIA's members throughout six different museums. Ultimately, the work of 109 female artists, chosen by a jury including Linda Nochlin, Pat Passlof, and Sylvia

Sleigh, was shown at a single venue. "It was important. It was the first big show of women's art," says Sleigh.

The catalog essay, by Lucy Lippard, summed up the still-dismal state of the art for female artists in the early 1970s:

> A large-scale exhibition of women's art in New York is necessary at this time for a variety of reasons: because so few women have up until now been taken seriously enough to be considered for, still less included in, general group shows; because there are so few women in the major commercial galleries; because young women artists are lucky if they can find ten successful older women artists to whom to look as role models; because although 75 per cent of the undergraduate art student body is female, only 2 per cent of their teachers are female. And, above all, because the New York museums have been particularly discriminatory, usually under the guise of being discriminating.

Among the better-known artists in the exhibit were Nell Blaine, Betty Parsons, Yvonne Jacquette, Joyce Kozloff, Faith Ringgold, Pat Passlof, Mary Frank, Joan Mitchell, and Alice Neel, represented by her painting *Pregnant Woman* (1971), a portrait of her daughter-in-law Nancy, reclining, with an image of Richard's head looming in the background. According to Harry F. Gaugh (who recalled it six years later in in *Arts* magazine), Neel's "grisly prenatal odalisque" of Nancy was one of the "sensations" of the show.

Newsweek captured the spirit of the event, which was, in the end, more meaningful than the art, in its January 29 issue:

> Opening night at the Cultural Center, jam-packed with more than a thousand guests, had much more of the aura of radical politics than of radical art. "It was just like the demonstrations last spring," said WIA activist Anne King. "There was a lot of warmth, excitement and a terrific sense of adventure."

Meanwhile, Neel, never one to follow the pack, wrote a revealing piece that was published in the winter 1971, quarterly issue of *Women in Art*, expressing her keen skepticism regarding the existence of a "feminine sensibility" (and of the goals of feminism in general).

Since God was made a man and all the symbols of strength and power have been made by men, naturally women are male chauvinist enough to wish to identify utterly with these magnificent beings, so there can be no feminine sensibility because per se it would be inferior. I have always wanted to paint as a woman but not as the oppressive and power mad world thought a woman should paint.

In a draft of the piece, the two following sentences, which shed some light on her prescient sensitivity towards gays, were crossed out: "Perhaps women care more deeply and feel more. Every homosexual and transvestite is a compliment to women." She then continued:

Actually there is so much variation that a scientific study would have to be carried out to discover if there is such a thing as feminine sensibility, and this on a being not corrupted by the whole network of cultural pressures. For practical purposes the aim of women should be to break the insulting and limiting life to which they are subjected. The enemy perhaps is not men but the very system itself which also encourages women to oppress each other. Women should be proud to be women and paint as that. Only negative remarks about "feminine sensibility" have raised this question. P.S. Freud said "When two go to bed four go to bed."

Still, in the next two years, Neel, whom Faith Ringgold accurately described as someone "who could work both sides of the street," would participate in some eight exhibits devoted solely to the work of women.

In June of 1972, Neel traveled with Hartley and John Rothschild to Greece and Africa, where Neel had a show at the Paa Ya Paa Art Gallery and Studio in Nairobi, gave a slide lecture, and appeared on television. Recalls Hartley, "We had a good time in Nairobi. We went to Ngorongoro Crater and we went to Murchison Falls, the source of the Nile. I was in this boat with Alice paddling around. It was the most incredible scene. Alice was always up to something amusing. Once we were out in the bush in the middle of nowhere, and all of sudden there were some elephants. I jumped out of car with my camera and Alice started yelling at me. One night we roasted a whole pig. We ate zebra meat in Tanzania. It was most amazing to see Alice in the back hinterlands of Africa. I remember once John threw some little wrapper out the window of the car and Alice went after him for polluting the countryside and not showing respect."

In the summer of 1973, Neel received a $7,500 grant from the National Endowment for the Arts. That fall, Neel had her fifth solo show at the Graham Gallery, "Recent Paintings," which ran from September 18 through October 13. She received an impressive amount of press. Pegged to the show, Diane Cochrane wrote a cover story on Neel for the September issue of *American Artist* (Neel's portrait of the Soyer brothers was the cover art), and Cindy Nemser wrote a major piece for the October issue of *Ms. Magazine*. Neel painted a portrait of Cochrane that year.

Both posited Neel as a living legend, with Cochrane comparing Neel to Miss Jean Brodie in her prime: "Only this woman, I suspect, has always been in her prime, both as a young woman and now that her hair has faded and extra pounds blur her Liv Ullmann–type beauty. This woman is renowned as the most powerfully original portraitist of her time." Nemser, recapping four decades of Neel's life and work, took the opportunity to chastise the Whitney once again for waiting so long to recognize the artist's formidable talent.

The reviews of the show were more or less glowing. Neel snagged a brief write-up in *The New York Times*, which said,

> Alice Neel's portraits . . . strike somewhere between benevolent caricature and expressionism as a vehicle for personal release. But you don't have to know exactly what Alice Neel's target is to know that she is right on.

ARTnews, with a few humorous disclaimers, highly praised the work:

> Neel's style is very much her own—falling somewhere between van Gogh and *Mad* magazine. Her colors, gangrenous greens and blues, have the lurid, off-key quality of early color television. Offensive to the sensibilities as Neel's painting can be, they have an ungainly, engaging counter-charm. They can be understood as a major contribution to the high caricature tradition of Daumier that relatively few fine artists have explored.

In the *Christian Science Monitor*, Diana Loercher wrote,

> It is no accident that Alice Neel is finally coming into her own at this point in time, when it is fashionable to 'discover' neglected

women artists . . . Moreover, realism is becoming respectable again in its new guises as superrealism, new realism, photorealism, etc., and Miss Neel's portraits look, at first glance, as if they might fit into one of those categories.

But they don't. Her paintings . . . are much too personal, too rich and psychological in nuance and perception, to accord with these dispassionate approaches . . . In an entirely contemporary manner she gives universal significance to the individual and realizes the portraitist's traditional ideal of the portrait as a mirror of the mind.

*   *   *

Nineteen seventy-four marked the apotheosis of Neel's career: After several years of active campaigning by both feminists and family members, she was finally given a retrospective at the Whitney Museum of American Art.

"I don't think there is any question the women's movement helped," says Hartley, who had arranged a meeting with Jack Baur after Baur had broached the topic. "But I called up and got an appointment to see him and went over there to the Whitney and sat for around half an hour. We discussed things about Alice and he said he thought she was a great artist, and they were interested in sometime perhaps giving her a show. I finally said, 'If the Whitney's going to do this, they should do it as soon as possible.' She had problems with arthritis, some cardiac stuff, and mature-onset diabetes. He told me he would look into it and we found out after the fact that it was Jack Baur who did it, in terms of getting that show for her. He was sympathetic. He really did love Alice's work." (Hartley had had a similar meeting on his mother's behalf with Richard Oldenburg at the Museum of Modern Art, who "basically expressed no interest whatsoever in Alice Neel.")

Joseph Solman recalled Alice telling him she had buttonholed Baur when they were on a flight returning from a juried show. "She was invited to be on the jury of a show of American paintings, and so was Baur, who was the head of the Whitney. When they flew home together she said, 'You've got to come up and see my work.' And he came up, and he was so impressed with the variety of stuff, and the great amount of paintings that she did, that he gave her a show, and good for her."

According to Richard, initially Alice was only supposed to have been given a small room on the ground floor but, typically, "once she got her foot in the door," she personally persuaded Baur to expand the show to the Whitney's whole second floor.

However it ultimately came about, Neel was utterly thrilled. "I was delighted to have the Whitney show. It covered five decades of figure work. Jack Baur wanted to give me the credit for having preserved the figure when the whole world was against it," Neel told Hills. Although she still took exception to the word "portrait" because of "the horrible connotations that cling to it," Neel said that Baur assured her, "You're going to change all that."

Now nearly three-quarters of a century old, Neel at last felt vindicated. "The show finally convinced me that I had a perfect right to paint," she told NPR's Terry Gross. "I had always felt in a sense that I didn't have a right to paint because I had two sons and I had so many things I should be doing and here I was painting. After the show I didn't feel that way anymore."

Fifty-eight portraits, produced over the previous forty years, were crammed onto the second floor. The show was curated by Elke Solomon, curator of Prints and Drawings, rather than the late Marcia Tucker, then curator of Paintings and Sculpture, and was accompanied by an eight-page brochure, with an essay by Solomon that oddly focused on Neel's portraits of John Rothschild. The brochure began with Neel's personal statement published in *The Hasty Papers* the previous decade. It ended with an update, in which Neel declared:

> I feel both justified and vindicated that my fifty-year quest to depict the soul and psychology of 20th-century man is being seen in this retrospective at the Whitney Museum of American Art. The label "American" is especially appropriate since although I have always thought of my work as universal, it yet remains, because of physical and unavoidable reality, an odyssey particularly American. I have always considered the human being the first premise—I feel his condition is a barometer of his era . . . we must trot back to the human size and human feelings. At the present moment there is a permissive air of "let all flowers bloom" which is perhaps a good thing.

Many of Neel's supporters felt that it was a less than gracious exhibition—and that the museum, after ignoring Neel for so long, owed her at least another floor. Others saw it as a somewhat grudging capitulation to the various petitions that had been circulated on Neel's behalf.

As Pat Mainardi put it in *Art in America*, "Alice Neel may be the only artist whose way into the Whitney was paved by petitions from the art community," adding, "She has become to many a symbol of both the discrimination and neglect women artists have had to endure, and artistic integrity and courage in the face of official hostility." But for Neel herself, who had for so long been famously obscure, it was an unalloyed personal triumph.

"Alice was overjoyed to get into the Whitney," recalls Hartley. "She was aware that it was only one floor, and this and that and so forth, but she was not about to complain about it, given what it meant to her career. It was fabulously exciting for her. She was in heaven with the whole thing."

The retrospective gathered paintings from 1933 through 1973, including some of Neel's strongest work: the double nude of Nadya and Nona; the portrait of José Santiago; *T. B. Harlem; Dead Father; Last Sickness; Pregnant Julie and Algis; My Mother; Andy Warhol; David Bourdon and Gregory Battcock; Jackie Curtis and Ritta Redd; The Family; John Perreault; The Soyer Brothers.*

But where were her incisive images of Frank O'Hara? (The absence of these two remarkable portraits was strange, especially since Neel's show ran concurrently with another Whitney show on the floor below, "Frank O'Hara, Poet Among Painters.") And what about Neel's portraits of Robert Smithson, Joe Gould, Kenneth Fearing, Ellen Poindexter, and Linda Nochlin? With a few exceptions—Warhol and his acolytes, John Perreault, and *Randall in Extremis*—these were some of Neel's more palatable paintings.

And, by eliminating much of her work from the WPA period, the strong social and political content of Neel's art was muffled, if not entirely muted. John Rothschild, Neel's intimate personal friend, is represented by no fewer than three portraits, but Sam Brody, her longtime partner and Hartley's father, of whom Neel painted many more pictures, didn't appear at all. Although it was certainly prestigious, and key to Neel's burgeoning career in the last two decades of her life, the retrospective was, ultimately, a narrow and one-dimensional representation of Neel's powerful oeuvre.

The curator, Elke Solomon, whose area was actually prints (particularly WPA-period prints), later acknowledged that she didn't think that Alice was an important painter. Moreover, in organizing the show, she had taken a personal dislike to her. "She was a nasty piece of work," Solomon said. Still, Neel deserved a retrospective because "she was a woman painter who represented a kind of paradigm of someone who persisted in making paintings that represented a certain ideological position." As to the limited size of the show, Solomon said, "That's a ridiculous criticism. One floor is enough for anybody."

The numerous reviews covered the gamut. Here was Hilton Kramer, in
The New York Times, once again carping on how Neel's sensationalist
tendencies overwhelmed her artistic craft (he went so far as to question
her "basic competence"). Calling Neel, "a collector of faces rather than of
souls," he wrote:

> Most of them are in Mrs. Neel's "late style," a very personal ver-
> sion of expressionist caricature that turns everyone—the famous
> and the obscure, the young and the old, the beautiful and the
> ugly—into a compelling grotesque. To see a few of these por-
> traits, especially the paintings of the cultural celebrities, is an
> arresting experience. To see the entire floor of a museum devoted
> to them is something else. . . . Mrs. Neel is simply not the kind of
> artist whose work can withstand such scrutiny.

Weighing in two weeks later in *The New York Times*, James R. Mellow,
was not much kinder:

> Alice Neel is a portrait painter with a vengeance. The large retro-
> spective of her portraits . . . is more like a savage chronicle of the
> cultural celebrities of the American art scene and the Bohemian
> lifestyles of the past decade or more, when Mrs. Neel began to ac-
> quire a serious reputation among New York artists and critics. It
> is a very personal record, in which the artist seems to have fixed
> upon the angst, anguish, wretchedness, vanity or arrogance of her
> subjects—as if life were, always, some form of interminable disease.

He goes on to call much of her later work "cruel." The review engendered at least one angry letter, accusing Mellow of "sexism" and making
the point that de Kooning had never been panned for "grotesqueries."
    The Times may have been reacting, in part, to the subtext of the show
itself: Politics played a large part in getting Neel through the Whitney's
reluctant door, and the Whitney's halfheartedness remained apparent in
how the show was both curated and mounted. Lawrence Alloway, in *The
Nation* dealt with these issues head-on:

> Before discussing Neel's admirable paintings in some detail, I
> want to consider the show in the kind of political terms that forced
> the museum's hand. She is represented by nearly sixty paintings

on the second floor, in a show organized by Elke Solomon, the associate curator for Prints and Drawings. Neel is showing only
paintings. The question arises, why did she not receive the attention of a senior curator accustomed to dealing with paintings?
Neither James Monte nor Marcia Tucker . . . took the assignment. To judge from Solomon's other shows, she is not particularly attuned to realism. If she had given us a marvelous show,
one would have taken pleasure in a wrong righted, and in, so to
say, the understudy going on so successfully, but we are denied
that reaction. It is not the fault of Neel's work, but the show looks
terrible, badly hung and incoherently selected.

Alloway also took issue with the skimpy catalog, which he described
as "entirely inadequate: 8 printed pages and printing on the cover: one
illustration in color and six small black and whites. A 2-page text by Solomon gets nowhere and indicates no grasp of the actual course of Neel's
development. . . ."

He then suggested that this might be, on the part of the museum, both
ageist and sexist, comparing it to a similarly flimsy catalog done by the
Whitechapel Art Gallery ("hardly a prosperous institution") for a retrospective of Neel's contemporary—another artist as old as the century—
Betty Parsons.

Neel, it seems, even when apparently embraced by the establishment,
never really lost her outsider status, as evidenced by this mixed review in
Newsweek:

> Neel is a figure of some controversy. From the start, her main
> passion has been the portrait, hardly a fashionable genre. More-
> over, she is interested less in the form the painting takes than in
> the psychology of her subject—again, not the latest fad. . . . The
> result is an art that hovers between caricature and in-depth analy-
> sis, often falling to the wrong side. But when she is right, Alice
> Neel crafts portraits that are both savage and incisive. . . .

It had always been Neel's nature to go against the grain, a position she
clearly reveled in. Even in her latter days as somewhat of a media darling,
Neel made sure that her unconventional behavior placed her outside the
mainstream. Her outrageous Johnny Carson appearances in the last months
of her life would be a case in point.

Still, *Artforum, Art in America,* and *New York* magazine all gave Neel
her due, although Thomas B. Hess in *New York,* who called Neel "a born
draftsman," had a few minor reservations, including the "jittery sense of
malaise" that resulted from "reducing humans to types." (Which he called a
"crime against humanity.") *Artforum* wrote, "The strength of Neel's work
lies in her ability to essentialize the foibles of her subjects without resorting
to cruel caricature. Her people stare out directly at the viewer as if to de-
mand an empathetic response to their raw humanity." And Kenneth Evett,
in *The New Republic,* gave Neel a bona fide rave:

> Neel has undertaken the serious risks of the painting game. She
> has contemplated the variegated visual and psychic aspects of life
> and has objectified her vision by accountable definitions of forms
> in space, thereby placing herself in competition with the big-
> league painters of the Western tradition. . . . Neel is one of the
> few original and significant American painters of the past 30
> years.

Neel herself told an interviewer, "It was an advance for the Whitney to
have me there in place of a haystack or a piece of painted gray board. Don't
you think the fact that they gave me a show at the Whitney indicates a return
to humanism?" Later that year, Neel painted the Whitney's director, Jack
Baur. Alice had warned him that he wouldn't like the result and she was
right. "He was terrified for weeks and months because he didn't know how
she was going to paint him, and he didn't want to be painted naked and he
just didn't know how to refuse and he was mortified. And then he got painted
in a blue suit," says the Whitney's Anita Duquette. Despite nine sittings,
Baur, of whom Neel was fond, ended up looking like a corporate cipher—
and not buying the portrait.

The retrospective ran from February 7 to March 17. Tom Armstrong,
then associate director at the Whitney, became fast friends with Neel
around this time, and arranged for a major show of her work at the Summit
Art Center in Summit, New Jersey, from May 26 to June 16. "She used to
meet me downstairs from her apartment in her negligee and we'd go upstairs and there'd be scotch on the kitchen table, and we'd drink and she'd
constantly ask me if I wouldn't let her paint me in the nude. She wanted to
paint my wife as a religious fanatic. We got along very well. The show had
been accomplished. She didn't have an ax to grind. We could just be two
people, not an artist and a museum director. She asked me to arrange some

cocktail parties, and just invite men. In exchange, she lent me her painting of June Blum."

Armstrong remembers Neel's salty tongue shocking some of the New Jersey locals. "The dinners after the lectures were pretty upsetting. The president of the museum would take us to dinner and she would find ways to say 'penis' about every fifth word. I told her after one of those meals that either she stopped or I was leaving. It became sort of a joke, the way she tried to shock the rubes of the countryside. I think she thought it was colorful to be an artist and to talk that way was amusing." Today, the Whitney owns ten Neel paintings, including *Andy Warhol* and *John Perreault*.

Vindication

Neel turned seventy-five on January 28, 1975. Jack Baur (who had just retired from the Whitney) celebrated her birthday with a poem:

TO ALICE AT 75

Ah what innocent blue eyes,
Soft as violets, sharp as knives,
Dissecting all our private lives.
And when moans betray we suffer
Alice only gets the rougher.
But ratified at last by fame,
They're gorgeous paintings just the same.

Neel had reached real fame quite late in her life, and she intended to make the most of every moment. Says Hartley, "She felt it was something she deserved. She basked in it. She really enjoyed it. When we were young, she struggled, waiting around for some critic to review her work, up or down. All of the sudden they were saying good things about her. Her paintings were on the walls, and people were buying her work. It was all different. She wasn't bitter. She had a very upbeat attitude toward the whole thing."

Recalled Joseph Solman, "I remember coming out of some exhibition at the Whitney musuem uptown, and she shouted, 'I made it Joe, I made it!' She was so delighted that she'd become well known. I was delighted for her, too."

Not that Neel sat on her laurels. She continued to paint every day. And she had some ripe, recent subject matter: her five grandchildren. Nancy and Richard's daughter Olivia, now eight, had been born in 1967 (Neel had painted her at five months, squirming on Nancy's lap); their twins, Alexandria and Antonia, were born in 1971 (*Nancy and the Twins*, 1971); and their daughter Victoria was born in 1974. In January 1975, Hartley and Ginny had had their first child, Elizabeth (*Ginny and the Baby*, 1975). A grandson, Andrew, would be born in 1978. Neel took full advantage of this new generation of in-house models, painting them at every stage of their young lives.

On Sunday, April 27, 1975, John Rothschild, who had lived with Neel for five years, died of a heart attack at age seventy-eight. He had been in Midtown Hospital for nearly a week, after complaining of chest pains, around the same time that Richard had been hospitalized for an eye problem. Neel casually remarked at the time, "John is just competing with Richard." Rothschild had requested that there be no service, and his wishes were respected. Instead, his son Joel arranged a gathering of family and friends on May 21 at the Community Church on Madison Avenue. Alice attended the memorial.

Just the year before, John had written to Hartley complaining of Neel's behavior toward him. "Alice's reactions to me are autocratic compulsive and not governed by reason," he wrote on March 24, 1974. "In order to build up her self-esteem, her psychiatrist had to discredit me." But he also wrote in July of that year, saying he was concerned about Neel's medical care.

He made similar complaints to Richard, over the course of several lunches at the Harvard Club. Alice, he said, had been much nicer before she had gone into therapy. (John would never learn that Sterrett, whom he knew only as his son's podiatrist, was, in fact, Neel's therapist.) And John reported yet another major insult: He had found Alice's will, which did not include him. The basic dynamic of their relationship, it seemed, had remained the same until the very end.

Not long after John died, Neel actually gave some of his clothing— including a suit and a Panama hat—to Kenneth Doolittle. (She had stayed in touch with him ever since they had run into each other at Symphony Space in the mid-sixties.) As Neel told Munro, "Only this year did he ever say he was sorry. Guess what I did. He came to see me. He's an old man now. He worked as an elevator operator at Mount Sinai. John had died, and I had all John's clothes, and it just so happened they fit him. Of course he was just wretched, he never had any decent clothes. So I gave him a Panama hat worth about eighty dollars from Brooks Brothers."

Although Neel was still regularly in touch with Sam Brody, who lived in Connecticut with his current wife, Sondra, and often served as Neel's confidant, John Rothschild was the last of Neel's live-in companions. She had told Jonathan Brand that John was a good traveling companion, that he "wasn't stupid," and that their relationship was "just old habit." As Hartley aptly described it, "I don't count John as a player, because he was like scenery."

Neel had once insisted to Phillip Bonosky that her dubious choices in men had been driven by her sex drive: "I had to reach my sexual aim!" But she had also told Hills that by the time John was living with her, "he was always at my bedroom door and I just couldn't stand it." According to Neel, John gave her "a beautiful accordion nightgown. I didn't want to be ravaged. . . . Do you know when men give you up? When you get to be about 70. They don't try to flirt with you anymore. You're pursued your whole life until you're say 65—especially when you are pregnant."

Whatever her feelings about sex and love were at this point in her life, Neel did not experience any late-in-life romances, unlike many of her male contemporaries, such as the famously priapic Picasso, who married his last wife, Jacqueline, when he was seventy-nine (and she was thirty-four), or even Willem de Kooning, who at the age of sixty-six fell deeply in love with the thirtyish Emilie ("Mimi") Kilgore. Nor, like Georgia O'Keefe—who took on the young Juan Hamilton to serve as her domestic helpmeet and companion from 1984 until her death in 1998, and lived with him for the last decade of her life—did Neel have anything like a spouse equivalent.

Still, she remained a femme fatale of sorts, fascinating everyone from Michel Auder to Johnny Carson. When she was sixty-nine, she did sleep at least once with Vladimir Bogachev, a correspondent for TASS whom she had met in the late 1950s.

Nonetheless, between her burgeoning career and her two sons and six grandchildren, Neel's life was quite full. At the apartment in New York, Nancy was almost always by her side. By now, they had developed a sort of symbiotic routine, with Neel wheedling and commanding, and Nancy serving as her willing aide. For her part, despite her often domineering treatment of her, Neel was genuinely grateful for Nancy's assistance, and made sure to credit her, at least publically. "If it wasn't for her, I don't believe I'd be able to paint, because she helps me so much," Neel told several interviewers. She also praised Nancy's innate sense of art. "I just have the good luck to have a daughter-in-law that *sees* art and very few people see art . . . many people with Ph.D.s don't see it," Neel told Richard Polsky. "I'd rather have her opinion than any art historian," Neel said in the film, *Three Women Artists.*

Recalls John Cheim, who was then the director of the Robert Miller Gallery, "Nancy Neel was always there, her constant companion, throughout the whole time I knew her. Nancy brought her to the gallery; Nancy at-

tended to her at 107th Street. She treated Nancy the way you might expect
a bossy husband to treat a wife that you've had for a long time. She just
kind of barked out at her. Nancy waited on Alice and did whatever Alice
wanted. I think Nancy loved and adored Alice, and knew she was a great
artist and treated her as such."

When Neel wasn't in New York, she was out in Spring Lake or, increasingly, up in Stowe. (By 1976, Alice had requested and paid for the conver-
sion of a small two-story log building on Hartley and Ginny's property into
a cozy studio. It still contains some of her work.) Wherever she was, she
found ample opportunities to paint her growing brood.

Neel spent many weekends and most of the summer out in Spring Lake,
usually surrounded by family, which could include not just her sons and
their wives and children but sometimes various members of the Brody
family: David, of whom Alice was fond, and even Sam and Sondra. One of
Neel's portraits of David was painted in the dining room.

The modest but comfortable house, which Neel bought in 1959 and the
Neel family still maintains (although it has deteriorated), is larger than her
original place at 506 Monmouth Avenue. Surrounded by a pleasant lawn
and trees, it has an eat-in kitchen, a dining room, a long, narrow parlor with
a piano, a screened-in porch, what Alice called the "animal room" (it has a
turkey head on the wall), and, up the bright blue staircase, are three bedrooms on the second floor.

One bedroom is rhubarb pink, the other blue, and the master bedroom,
which belonged to Alice, is painted mauve except for its front wall, which
is covered in a wild sixties-inflected floral wallpaper, nearly psychedelic in
its orange, purple, and magenta hues. The green-flowered muumuu Neel
wore for painting is still stashed in the bottom drawer of the oak dresser;
displayed on the top are various knickknacks: a bamboo fan, a bottle of
4711 perfume, and an Eskimo figure given to her by Sam. There's a white
rocker near the small double bed.

It's easy to imagine Neel holding court there—and painting many
paintings (such as *Nancy and the Twins*, 1971), whether out on the lawn or
in the parlor, where the Olympics poster she did using Ginny as a model
still hangs. Neel had her favorite haunts: she liked to walk by the beach,
feed the ducks, eat grilled cheese sandwiches at Dale's, and forage for sweets
(which she sometimes helped herself to without paying) at the local candy
store, Jean Louise Homemade Candy. And she still bought her fruit and
vegetables from a stand that used to deliver them by buggy back in the
1930s. Since she didn't really drive (although she had a license, and at

some point she had bought Hartley a red Porsche and later a green one), Nancy would drive would her back and forth to Manhattan.

*   *   *

The mid-seventies were good to Neel. Her career, newly revved up by the women's movement, continued to accelerate. It was as if, in the penulti-mate decade of her life, she had just been discovered as a potent and prodi-gious talent. And her talent continued to evolve. Her canvases of the mid to late 1970s are confident, colorful, and full of a painterly authority, from the beautifully realized portrait *Nancy and the Rubber Plant*, 1975, to the austere but expressive *Windows*, 1977.

Nineteen seventy-five, which was the United Nations designated Inter-national Women's Year, was another major year for Neel. She seemed to be in a show or two nearly every month, and gave her slide lectures just as of-ten. She also regularly participated on panels, from "Women in the Media" at her alma mater, where she spoke along with Lucy Lippard, Tana Hoban, and Carolee Schneeman, to "Women Artists, Seventy Plus" at the Brooklyn Museum, where she held forth along with Isabel Bishop, Lilly Brody, Sari Dienes, and Lil Picard. As Moore's alumnae journal gushed, "Alice is a woman of such strength, independence and beautiful honesty that she held the audience enthralled."

That year, Neel had what was arguably the most exhaustive retrospective of her career at the Georgia Museum of Art, in Athens. She also had six other solo exhibitions, from a show of thirty portraits at the Portland Center for the Visual Arts in Oregon to a show at the American Can Collective in San Francisco, to a show at the Smith College Museum of Art, in Northampton, Massachusetts, all accompanied by one of her celebrated lectures.

"Everyone who meets her remarks on her engaging personality," wrote Leonard Kimbrall in *ArtWeek* of the Portland show, which ran from Janu-ary 8 to February 9. "Elke Solomon has remarked, 'Critics writing about Alice Neel seem more interested in her personality than her paintings.' If this is so, it would certainly be, despite the power of that personality, that they failed to look at her work, for the paintings carry with them, each one in this show, at least, a power that is at times an embarrassment." Alfred Frankenstein, in the *San Francisco Chronicle* called the American Can Show, which ran from February 23 to March 28, "an encounter with human personality such as we have not seen in American portraiture since the days of Thomas Eakins."

Neel was also included in a dozen group shows, including "Sons and Oth-ers: Women Artists See Men" at the Queens Museum; "Works on Paper:

Women Artists," at the Brooklyn Museum; a traveling show, "Three Centuries of the American Nude," which originated at the New York Cultural Center; a show at the Women's Interart Center in New York, "Color, Light and Image," "Figure as Form: American Painting 1930–1975" at the Museum of Fine Arts in Saint Petersburg, Florida; and "From Pedestal to Pavement: the Image of Women in American Art, 1875–1975" at the Mount Holyoke College Art Museum. A portfolio of her work was printed in the summer edition of the feminist journal *Painted Bride Quarterly*, which featured her double portrait of Cindy and Chuck Nemser on the cover.

The University of Georgia's Museum of Art show, which ran from September 7 to October 19, was a full-scale celebration of the artist's career. It gave Neel her due in a way the Whitney retrospective had not. On display were eighty-three works, done from 1926 through 1975, Neel's earliest paintings in Havana through her heyday in the 1970s. It included such great, up until then little-seen, works as *Well Baby Clinic, Futility of Effort*, and *Symbols*, as well as *Andy Warhol, Virgil Thompson*, and *Duane Hanson* (her quirky 1972 painting of the sculptor in a fur-collared coat and matching sideburns).

The show explored the entire spectrum of her talent: her still lifes, landscapes, and streetscapes, in addition to her multitudinous paintings of people, from the anonymous to the famous. It was Neel revealed in her totality: One plate in the catalog was a fetching nude photograph of the artist herself taken in 1931. The text included an essay by Cindy Nemser and statements by Dorothy Pearlstein and Raphael Soyer, in addition to Neel's doctoral address (which, as her most complete artistic statement, was frequently quoted and reprinted). The only downside was that the reproductions of the paintings (all eighty-three were printed in the catalog), right up to the most recent, the portrait *Nancy and the Rubber Plant* (with Audrey McMahon peering darkly through the leaves), were in black and white.

Painter and art professor Neill Slaughter recalls wheeling Neel, who, although she could walk, usually preferred a wheelchair at large events, around the University of Georgia art museum, accompanied by an entourage of students. "I remember her having a real wit, and this beguiling smile. She seemed sort of flirtatious, and said she wanted to paint me. She left an impression upon one, and it reminded me of her paintings. A little quirky, bent, a little off. Not what you would ordinarily expect of an older woman. Like her paintings—the proportion or perspective a little off, the colors a little off. She had that incisive way of delving into the character, and she had that same way about her. She was very beguiling and she had this kind of wink and nod."

Neel was interviewed on *Forum*, a show on the university's television channel, WGTV. As usual, she shocked and charmed the audience, even managing to slip the word "penis" into a discussion about Claes Oldenburg's famous *Lipstick* sculpture, and holding forth on her foibles and philosophies.

"Is there any art that you don't like?"

"Well I'm sort of prejudiced in favor of the thing I do. I like people and for so many years they wouldn't show anything that was people. But my art, although it's people is not just simple. I know how to divide up canvases. I'm aware of abstraction. . . . Actually one of the greatest pleasures I have is the freedom to just divide up the canvas. And that of course is not just painting people, that smacks of abstraction, mathematics, all sorts of things. But I think there is a terrific amount of junk on the market today. But then I think in general, junk is riding high. Don't you?"

Neel finished off the year with several more solo shows. She had a solo exhibition of thirty recent paintings at the Fairlawn, New Jersey, Public Library, from November 23, 1975 through January 2, 1976, with a catalog with commentary by Cindy Nemser, whose book *Art Talk: Conversations with 12 Women Artists*, which included Neel, had recently been published. Both were accompanied by slide shows.

Finally, that December, she lectured at the St. Louis Art Museum. True to form, she "held her listeners in uncontrolled giggles as she showed slides of her work, according to the *St. Louis Post-Dispatch*, which described her as "a roly-poly little old lady in a long black dress with gleaming green eyes and such a blithe, chirpy manner that she soon has everyone she meets eating out of her hand." As she told her audience, with a "whoop," "When I picked men, I picked them the way rich businessmen pick ladies. I picked ones who are beautiful. One reason I liked far out people is that boring childhood in that small town. You know people think I'm a Bohemian, just jumping from one thing to another, but I went through Hell each time. I have so much history, if I didn't unload it, I wouldn't have any present."

What the *St. Louis Post-Dispatch* didn't include was Neel's brash insistence that the slide show continue much longer than planned. "I can now control an audience," she boasted to Munro. "Out in St. Louis, I was giving a slide lecture, and they said we have to turn the lights on. I said, 'Why, it will take at least an hour and a half more; I haven't shown Andy Warhol yet. Don't you dare turn the lights on.' And they left the lights off for two hours more."

"As she visited art classes and artists' organizations here during her four-day stay, students clustered about her as though hungering for half the gladness that her brain must know," the paper went on to note. Neel also revealed her "sentimental" side, actually shedding a tear or two in recalling the headmistress of High Mowing, who had given both her sons scholarships. "Oh isn't this awful," she told her interviewer. "It's the goodness of people that does it, you know. It's always so embarrassing."

The momentum didn't let up the following year, with Neel engaged in an avalanche of activities, from shows to award ceremonies. Neel received several major honors in 1976. On January 25, she was inducted into the National Institute of Arts and Letters (now the American Academy and Institute of Arts and Letters). The actual ceremony was held later, on May 19, along with a small exhibit of Neel's work.

Her hair in a prim gray twist, wearing the same dress she had worn to her Whitney opening—a high-necked navy blue gown with rhinestone trim at the throat and wrists, Neel radiated sheer delight at hearing her name and citation read. It was loudly interrupted by applause and Alice's "thank you"—despite the secretary of the institute's admonition to wait until the citation was over. "Alice Neel, painter. A unique figure in contemporary American art, Alice Neel is in this age of photography a portrait painter. She probes courageously, almost violently into the human psyche. Hers is a difficult art to bear—without ingratiation, without pretty nuances of color and drawing, but with great validity. Like most serious accomplishment in the arts, it supplies the viewer with energy for its own delight."

Like the Whitney retrospective, her induction into the Institute was a validation of Neel's long professional struggle. She was understandably proud, telling Hills that "it is the greatest honor this country can give an artist." Still, that didn't stop her from chiding the institute on another occasion for only inducting old people. "Blame yourself, not me. I was always in New York. Why didn't you take me instead of having a cellar full of Speicher paintings. That bad painter! It just took you that long to know I was good, so don't blame me."

Neel had her sixth solo show, "Recent Paintings," at the Graham Gallery, from January 31 to February 28, 1976. Her portrait *Linda Nochlin and Daisy* was reproduced on the cover of the brochure. Thomas Hess wrote a somewhat backhanded review in *New York* magazine, commenting on how "comparatively mild" Neel's work had become: While "Alice Neel's portraits—which are among the art world's most beloved open scandals . . . can take an ordinary face . . . (like Frank O'Hara or Virgil Thompson) dig into it, and mine enough brimstone to fire all of Scarsdale and Gomorrah," her current works—which included her portraits of Jack Baur, Sari Dienes, Isabel Bishop, and several grandchildren—were, he observed, "milder, almost rosy," and have an "Indian summer glow."

Hess seemed bemused by Neel's "growing *succès d'estime*" which, he suggested, had dulled the "spur of neglect and misunderstanding" that gave her work its edge. "Young artists and poets admire her as a free spirit, a feminist guerilla, a survivor of the 1930s art projects, a dedicated (*pace* Tom Wolfe) Boho." Nonetheless, he commended Neel's current confidence in handling paint, concluding, "She became the master of her own eclectic idiom. . . . if some of Neel's former throbbing, visionary quality got lost in the process, her art became richer for it."

John Russell in *The New York Times* singled out Neel's 1974 portrait of Bishop (who had told Neel she thought the portrait made her look like a "mosquito"), and her townscapes. "The two metropolitan views at the Graham are one of the treats of the season: observant, well-composed and painted with a succulence that elsewhere seems to curdle at human contact." (Neel, ever competitive, was probably less than happy that her two-paragraph review was in a roundup headlined HEROIC INVENTIVE NUDES OF PHILIP PEARLSTEIN.)

On February 26, Neel received the International Women's Year Award, "in recognition of outstanding cultural contributions and dedication to women and art." That same month, she and Sylvia Sleigh were in a two-woman show at the A.I.R. Gallery in SoHo.

The following month, Neel appeared along with Studs Terkel in a documentary on the WPA, which was broadcast on PBS. She also reunited with her former Moore schoolmate and friend, Rhoda Medary, who ran the art-supply store at Beaver College, where Neel had a solo show from March 31 to April 16. (Neel had last seen her, for the first time in forty years, in 1973, when she, Medary, and Ethel Ashton met at an alumnae art show at Moore College; at the time, Ethel was humiliated by the prominent placement of the heavy nude Neel had done of her in 1930.)

That spring, Victoria Donohoe, an art critic for the *Philadelphia Inquirer* and a longtime acquaintance of Neel, got her a once-in-a-lifetime commission—to paint the portrait of Archbishop Jean Jadot, an apostolic delegate for the Liturgical Arts show which accompanied the 41st International Eucharistic Congress. Donohoe was the director of a selections committee made up of five volunteers (including herself) associated with the arts.

As Donohoe, who initially contacted eight hundred artists, explained, "There were twenty-five commissioned works being set for the exhibit, and we wanted to involve painters. We were doing this with Alice as a way of continuing the tradition of the Thomas Eakins clergy portraits. In fact, Alice was intending to go to the National Gallery to look at Eakins's 1905 portrait of Monsignor Diomede Falconio. I had been thinking of various people and had admired her work a long time. We also asked Philip Pearlstein to paint Cardinal Krol, after Fairfield Porter, who was originally commissioned to do the cardinal's portrait, suddenly died. Alice was to have gotten the biggest commission: eight thousand dollars, paid for by the Philadelphia philanthropist Samuel P. Mandell, while the other painters, including Pearlstein, were to get five thousand. Pearlstein was supposed to do just the head and neck of the cardinal, but instead he painted a huge portrait, to have been paid for by Edward Piszek, the head of Mrs. Paul's Kitchens. When Piszek saw the painting, he hated it, and refused to pay for it. We were beside ourselves."

Ultimately, the cardinal himself paid for it—$25,000. "Alice was rather jealous," says Donohoe. (The incident was yet another episode in Neel's long-standing rivalry with Pearlstein.)

The Exhibition of Liturgical Arts ran from July 29 to August 7. Pearlstein vividly described Neel's typically unorthodox behavior during the opening. "I painted Cardinal Krol. So the time came for this big event. At the opening festivities you could see my painting and Alice's, which were near each other in the exhibition hall. Cardinal Krol hated the painting and he made no secret of it. He was very funny about it. He spoke like W. C. Fields. So he came up to me. Cardinal Krol was a very large man and said hello, and just at that moment, Alice appeared and greeted me, and she asked the cardinal how he liked my painting. And the cardinal said, 'I told Philip at the beginning it would be perceived that I was doing this as a penance,' and a few other remarks like that. And I told him I was going to give his painting to an institution for the blind. So she punched me and said, 'Oh, you are a terrible man.' And then Alice asked, 'How do you like my painting?' And before Cardinal Krol could answer, she said, 'When I

was young nobody thought women could do anything serious like this.'
And the cardinal said, 'Well, I don't think anything has changed.'"

This might have been enough for most people, but according to Pearlstein, Alice had just begun her jousting match. "So Alice said to the cardinal, 'Oh, can I kiss your ring? I've always wanted to do that.' She was still
young enough to be able to kneel. She knelt down on one knee and kissed
the ring, and she looked up and said, 'Oh, how sensual!' And the cardinal
raised his hand, and she yelled out, 'Oh, he's going to hit me!' And the
cardinal said 'No, I won't hit you.' And they continued this wild exchange."

Later, there was a dinner at the Barclay Hotel, where, Neel told Hills,
she was the "guest of honor." After her performance at the opening, one
can only imagine Neel at a gathering made up primarily, as she described
it, of "bishops and collectors." (She was seated next to a cleric.)

Pearlstein's painting hung for a year at the Philadelphia Museum of Art.
Alice's was displayed at the Saint Charles Borromeo Seminary of the Arch-
diocese of Philadelphia, where today they hang side by side. Says Donohoe, "I think Alice Neel's Jean Jadot portrait represents her at the strongest
level of her mature accomplishment. As in all her best work, Alice never
lets the intensity of this portrayal reduce the human element to a minimum." Vivien Raynor called it "one of her most restrained and successful
efforts, in pleasantly warm colors."

The painter and her subject were a good match: Jadot was known for his
progressive thinking. As Neel told Hills, "He was completely for the working class. He worked fourteen years in Africa. He loved the oppressed."
Neel spent a week working on the painting, standing at a "frightful" easel,
and frequently dropping her brush, which the archbishop kindly fetched
for her. According to Neel, he told her she was "the bravest person he had
ever met."

Typically, Neel managed to inject much of the archbishop's character
into his twisted hands, particularly the one bearing the ring; when he "objected a little," Neel told him, "Oh well, you have to give me some artistic
license."

During her trek to Washington, where the portrait was painted, Neel recalled attending a party for "détente with Russia." As she told Yetta Groshans, "The President of the Academy of Sciences, Philip Handler, took me
to a party in the biggest department store in Washington, where they showed
Russian still lifes and landscape painters and where Dobrynin was there.
The Russians put on a snack, and what a snack. Wonderful champagne and
caviar and a whole big sturgeon. Oh it was gorgeous, and Russian bread.

There is no bread like Russian bread." Neel was impressed by the dress code of the Russian women, and mentioned it to Jadot, who remarked, "The rich care nothing for the poor."

In September, Neel participated in the show "Paintings by Three American Realists: Alice Neel, Sylvia Sleigh, and May Stevens," at the Everson Museum of Art in Syracuse, New York, which ran from September 17 through October 31 and included twenty-five paintings. In October, she had a show at the Fendrick Gallery in Georgetown. Writer Paul Richard accompanied her to the gallery, and described her in *The Washington Post* as someone who "looks sweet, but isn't really. . . . She is 76 and wears her grey hair in a bun. It would take an Alice Neel to portray Alice Neel. One should not be misled by the twinkle in her eyes, the sweetness of her smile, or her grandmotherly demeanor. She is as tough as they come. Part grand dame, part Bohemian, part cunning politician, she tells her oft-told stories as if trying to implant the right image in your mind. . . ." Alice, always one step ahead of the game, told her interviewer, "If I were young and beautiful, I'd have a great future."

In late October, the Wildenstein Gallery held an exhibit organized by then Columbia University art history professor Kirk Varnedoe, "Modern Portraits: The Self and Others," of the work of some one hundred artists, which included drawings, paintings, and photographs. *The New York Times* asked four artists, Lucas Samaras, Philip Pearlstein, Chuck Close, and Neel to write pieces explaining their process. Neel's piece, entitled "I Paint Tragedy and Joy," ran on October 31, 1976. After explaining that she tried to capture the person and the Zeitgeist, and enumerating the sacrifices she had made "for freedom to paint," Neel gave a condensed version of her modus operandi:

I am never arbitrary. Before painting I talk to my sitters and they unconsciously assume their most typical pose—which, in a way, involved all their character and social standing; what the world has done to them and their retaliation. What I feel, what I think, and my involvement with the sitter all comes out in the painting. I like it to look spontaneous, not labored.

Part of the interpretation lies in the structure, and I enjoy dividing that white unsullied canvas according to the composition that best interprets the person. Usually I place everything when I start by drawing on the canvas in thin blue or black paint directly from the model. For me, drawing is the great discipline of art, but

I've been painting so long I do not think consciously of technique and I do not believe one should concentrate on technique. I feel the art in my work is the way I do it, an ongoing thing that happens while I work. . . .

As one works, a profounder conception often develops, so sometimes I have painted two canvases of the same person. For instance, I once painted a very romantic, falconlike profile of the late poet Frank O'Hara. Beside him was a table with lilacs. He came to sit four or five times but the last time he looked much more beat than the romantic image I'd painted.

I asked him if I could do another canvas. I put the circle of his mouth on the canvas first, with teeth like tombstones. Then I made a rather savage painting of him, with the lilacs now dead. When he saw it, he said, "My God! Those freckles. But the Fauves went that far." I think the second painting is as valid as the first.

As for people who want flattering paintings of themselves, even if I wanted to do them, I wouldn't know what flattery is. To me, as Keats said, beauty is truth, truth beauty. Altered noses always look much worse. I paint to try to reveal the struggle, tragedy and joy of life.

In December, Neel had a major painting in one of the milestone shows of the decade. Her haunting portrait of José's ailing brother, *T. B. Harlem*, was included in the seminal show "Women Artists: 1550 to 1950," which was curated by Linda Nochlin and Ann Sutherland Harris, and originated at the Los Angeles County Museum of Art before traveling to several other institutions, including the Brooklyn Museum.

Although Neel was once painted by her contemporary John Koch (*John Koch Painting Alice Neel*, 1969), it would not be until 1980, when she posed for herself, that a memorable portrait in paint would be created. However, Michel Auder, the avant-garde video artist, who met Neel at a SoHo party in 1976 and was instantly drawn to her, expertly captured the artist and her mise-en-scène during the mid-seventies—videotaping her at regular intervals over the next six years.

"I came to the party with Larry Rivers and I think Alice liked my nose," Auder recalls of his first encounter with Neel. "She was sitting there talking and I thought she would make amazing material for a video, just looking at her. I didn't know who she was and I didn't know her work. I love people who tell stories without being actors, so it was perfect for me to make a portrait of a woman who spoke about all kinds of things—about sex, about men, about how people love, about a painful life and a beautiful life. She spoke very well about sex. I brought Taylor Mead with me because Taylor knew her, and I didn't know if she was going to talk to me a lot, so I figured he could be like a semi-interviewer. My videotape opens with her showing her work to me and to Taylor Mead. And we had some food, and that day, we sealed our friendship, and then for many years I went to see her all the time—at least once or twice a week." In Neel, Auder found a kindred spirit, and vice versa, as is evident from her openness with him on tape.

Auder, then age thirty-one, was, possibly unbeknownst to Neel, a heroin addict. (He smoked, rather than injected, the drug.) For him, Neel was a wise (but not old) soul with whom he could talk intimately and honestly. "Basically she was vital to me, because it was a difficult time for me," he says. "I was fighting a heroin habit that I had, and for me, being there took me away from my other life. So it was great. And also she understood video. She looked at a lot of my video work and liked it, and I was kind of being frustrated by not really being able to make money out of my work, and she also had the kind of life similar to mine at that time, when I was struggling and nobody paid attention to my work. Plus, I loved her paintings. I thought they were amazing. So I got also very seduced by her work, and she was a great woman and we became friends. It gave me a lot of energy to keep going on and do what I do. And she was very important for my survival, my mental state, to have this person talking to me as a friend, and we communicated really well together. Basically she was my best friend for many, many years. Not like my grandmother, my friend, on equal terms."

Auder showed her his current work. "I would play it on the machine, and she would ask for more; she was one of my fans. It was kind of amazing to have this person that understood what I was doing. She also gave me a lot of energy because I respected her and I could feel that she seriously understood what I was getting at in my work."

In addition to videotaping her regularly, he used her in several other films, including *Chasing the Dragon*, where she riffs on life, death, money, and art with Eric Bogosian, and *A Coupla White Faggots Sitting Around Talking*, in which there is an hilarious exchange with Cookie Mueller regarding both Kate Millett and the poet Adrienne Rich, whom Neel had recently drawn. Neel, looking somewhat glamorous in sunglasses, starts by reading a line or two from Auder's script, but the rest is totally ad-libbed.

NEEL: But the funny thing was when she [Kate Millett] was admiring and worshipping Sita, her conversation was just like that of a man admiring a woman. You know she admired her elegance, her charm. She even admired her for being a little bit of a liar at times. You know she made allowances for her. I think Kate Millett, I think she is before the sexual differentiation. I think she's everything, you know. That's what it is. Would you like to be that way?

MUELLER: I am.

NEEL: You are? Oh you are a two-way street. Oh how wonderful. I never knew that. [She laughs.] You like the girls as well?

MUELLER: Umhm

NEEL: You do?

MUELLER: Umhm

NEEL: Better?

MUELLER: No not better.

NEEL: Just the same you are—you're addictive. Do you get nice girls? I mean writers and people like that?

MUELLER: No.

NEEL: I drove Adrienne Rich, crazy. . . . I did a drawing of her for *Parnassus*, that poetry magazine. So I said—I don't know why I said this just to be perverse—I said, "I never did want to be a muff diver," I said, and you know that's a very vulgar phrase for lesbianism and I could feel her freeze in front of me. You see, she is a muff diver.

MUELLER: I don't see why she had to get upset about it, even if you used that kind of phrase.

For her part, Rich, when asked about sitting for Neel, refused to comment. She did say she didn't like the drawing.

*　　　*　　　*

Neel's bustling schedule did not slow down much during the next three years. In 1977, she had another five solo shows, from a large exhibition at Lehigh University's Alumni Memorial Gallery in March to her seventh Graham Gallery show in October. She also appeared in an array of group shows, including several that focused on WPA art, garnering Neel her first praise from *The New York Times'* Hilton Kramer, who otherwise panned both the show in November at New York University's Grey Gallery and a second, simultaneous show at the Parsons School of Design.

Kramer singled out Neel's work at the Grey Gallery show: "Here and there of course, there are pictures that remain authentic and touching. Alice Neel, for example, comes off remarkably well with her pictures of the 1930's. . . ." And in his scathing review of the Parsons show, which he called a "debacle," he again had kind words for Neel: "Here again Alice Neel's work suggested that she was as good then (or perhaps better?) than she is today."

The Graham show, which ran from October 4 through October 29, included twenty-six drawings and paintings. Many of the pictures were portraits of her immediate and extended family, from grandchildren to David Brody—Sam's son and Hartley's half brother. The prices of the work ranged from $7,500 for *Still Life with Fruit and Bottles* to $15,000 for a painting of Stephen Schaffer. The film *Alice Neel: Collector of Souls,* by Nancy Baer, which had been produced for the PBS film series *The Originals,* was screened at the opening. Norman Turner, writing in the December issue of *Arts Magazine,* used the occasion for a full-page meditation on Neel's work.

While he rather unfairly suggested that Neel's paintings are "pretty much just knocked off," as opposed to extensively worked on, he nonetheless arrived at the conclusion that Neel was an important artist. Referring to *T. B. Harlem,* which he had seen in the "Women Artists: 1550–1950" show, he wrote:

> The bluntness and moral authenticity of this picture alone should have secured for Neel the most respectful consideration, and it was painted over thirty-five years ago. In recent years, her work has taken on a more cool, distanced and sardonic turn while her

palette, reflecting this shift of mood, has become lighter and more buoyant while its visual taste has become distinctly acid. The range of her expression has been considerable.

Commenting on Neel's "categorical decisions" about the "proper concerns of art," he wrote that Neel was one of those painters who

have acted on their convictions with dictatorial intent. These solitary artists, following their bent regardless of the price, often in painful isolation, have forceably reminded us that art encompasses any human occasion, and that its limitations are defined only by the limitations of the race. Neel is one of those artists.

Reviewing the show in *ARTnews*, Gerrit Henry called Neel "a force of nature. Her paintings, portraits of friends and relatives and still lifes are filled with the same marvelous freshness and vitality and sunlight that she exudes personally."

He went on to describe some of the paintings in the show in stylistic terms more often associated with Bonnard than with Neel.

As her brushes whirl across the canvas, they are filled with glowing color—deep blues, soft pinks, burgundies . . . clear, positive, happy, life-enhancing colors. . . . Her granddaughter Olivia sits in a bower of hovering leaves that seems to hug her intense and delicate little frame. Lilly Brody perches on the edge of her chair, both feet squarely planted, her tendril-like fingers spread articulately as she is captured in mid-breath. Susan Rosen [sic] a symphony of pinks and burgundies, her face veiled by the drooping brim of a velvet hat, clenches her hands. Dr. Stephen Herbert relaxes quietly, at peace with the world and himself, his long, thin, bony body outlined in a luminous blue aura.

In the late 1970s, Neel, freed from domestic responsibilities and romantic entanglements, allowed her spirited aesthetic sensibility to soar. It was as if she had been liberated by her "vindication" by the establishment and could now allow herself the pure, absolute joy of paint, without any constraint. This is reflected equally in her juicy still lifes, her luminous window scenes, and, of course, her portraits, which, in their psychological surgery, became noticeably more forgiving.

While many reviewers criticized Neel's tendency, especially in her later work, to skimp on the background, or leave it out altogether, Neel's use of the canvas was never arbitrary; but in fact, quite canny. As she told her Harvard audience, in describing her portrait of Stewart Mott (1961), "The reason this is so unfinished is because I had reached a point in art where I didn't want to finish the whole thing." (Although she quipped that the Mott portrait looked unfinished because *he* was unfinished.)

Neel chose to render the background fully in some paintings—such as *Nancy and the Rubber Plant* and *Ginny and the Baby*, both done in 1975, or sparely but tellingly in *Margaret Evans Pregnant*, 1978, in which the model's partial reflection in a background mirror serves as a memento mori. Or she dispenses with it entirely, as in the formidable *Ellen Johnson*, 1976, whose authoritative pose in an elegant chair is set up against nothing more than a pale blue wash, which becomes just slightly denser around her head. In *Olivia*, 1976, Neel not only jettisoned the background but left as mere outlines the legs of her granddaughter and the chair she is perched in. In the eighties, Neel often went even further in eliminating extraneous details.

As Neel told a radio interviewer (WBAI) about her work, "I want it to spring right out of the canvas. I want it to live. They can't forgive me for that. I just make it as living—with a terrific immediacy—because that's an important part of art. But they want you to work every little inch. I just don't work that way."

Some artists, as they approach their own demise, seem to become transcendant, superlight. The very airiness of Neel's late work emulates, to a certain degree, the paper cutouts of Matisse and the incandescent late interiors of Bonnard.

Auder documented Neel's painting of her extraordinary portrait *Margaret Evans Pregnant* in a thirty-minute video. Neel is quite precise in posing her model, whom she has at first on a love seat, before putting her in an armchair, before finally positioning her, hands tentatively clutching its sides, on a funny pincushion-like ochre chair.

Tilting back and forth in her own creaky chair, Neel starts with an outline of Evans's right leg. Her application of brush to canvas is sure and unerring. She might as well be using a pencil or stick of charcoal as she draws, rather than paints, a delicate outline of her model, moving to the left leg, the arms, the breasts, the nipples, the oval head, with its cleft chin and dark, tendrilled hair.

She is able to get a remarkable amount onto the canvas in just one session; Evans would come back two more times to pose. "I remember when she first picked up her brush to start, she said 'This is always the hardest part.'" Evans recalled. The video is shot in black and white, so it is impossible to see that Neel has outlined Evans in black, or to determine what shades are on the brushes she sometimes clutches a bunch at a time. But at one point, Margaret gets up to stretch and remarks, "The colors are wonderful."

Neel has infused Evans, who was pregnant with twins, with a golden glow, the shading of the floor matching her large sepia nipples, her flesh mottled here and there with deeper pink. This is a glimpse of Neel at her apex, where the mastery of her art has become second nature, as intimate and comfortable as her paint-smeared smock.

Neel celebrated the birth of her only grandson, Andrew (May 18, 1978), with a small, charming nude that does full justice to his infant genitalia. Remarked Neel soon after completing the painting, "Don't you just love it? I love to look at his little penis—looks like an acorn attached to a plum." Splayed on a towel and blankets that are gently twisted to mirror his jointless wriggling, Andrew already sports a handsome, fine-featured face.

This affirmation of life is in contrast to her paintings of both Hartley and Richard the following year. In *Hartley*, 1979, Neel showed her younger son in a white chair circa the 1950s, his legs crossed, his chin resting on his hand. He looks pensive and somewhat careworn.

But it is in her portrait of Richard that Neel felt she had captured the "zeitgeist." Seated in the same chair and pallidly reflected in a mirror, Richard, Neel said, "just looks used up, you know. He'd go to work early in the morning. By the time he got home at night he wouldn't have any energy left for anything." She called the picture *Richard in the Era of the Corporation*, explaining to Terry Gross on NPR's *Fresh Air*, "I did one of him when he was working for Pan Am and that was in the seventies, and the truth is I didn't know what the seventies was about until I painted him. And then I realized that it was the time when the corporation enslaved all these bright young men. Because he looks just about ready to die of being enslaved by Pan Am."

At the end of the year, the Skowhegan School of Painting and Sculpture honored Neel, along with fifty other artists, at the Metropolitan Club. Among the 275 other guests there on December 9, were Louise Nevelson, Robert Indiana, and James Brooks. Even at seventy-seven, Neel was something of a party animal. Wearing the pale mink toque she favored at the time, her eyes "twinkling with delight," she told *New York Times* writer Enid Nemy, "If you keep your nose to the grindstone for fifty years, you get to stand on this beautiful carpet at this elegantly stacked party."

* * *

Auder's video portrait of Neel, entitled *Alice Neel 1976–1982*, actually begins with footage shot in 1978. This may be the time when he brought Taylor Mead up to Neel's apartment; in any case, the three have a great deal of fun during a marathon conversation with Neel, as the artist, with the assistance of Nancy, ferrets through her vast archive of paintings to show them gem after gem. Calling herself her own long-term "curator," she breezily acknowledges her failure to sell most of her work. "But then I get to have it all here," she tells Auder.

Neel at seventy-eight has wispy white hair swept into a bun, glasses perched on her nose, through which eyes more green than blue dart, and smooth, round cheeks. She says Georgie Arce, the Puerto Rican teen and seductive con artist she befriended and frequently painted until he was jailed for murder in 1974, told her she should say she is fifty-three. Neel scarcely looks that young, but she certainly doesn't look—or act—her age. Nothing has dampened her keen curiosity, razor-sharp wit, or roving mind, and her sense of humor is mercilessly intact.

She's capable of starting a sentence discussing world politics and ending it quoting a poem by Byron. She'll mimick Ginsberg chanting on *Dick Cavett*, or dismiss Joseph Mitchell's *New Yorker* profile of Joe Gould as erroneous: "He said he kept copying the same thing, but Harvard just bought 11 of his essays." She recalls Audrey McMahon's nickname: "Arsenic and Old Face." When asked if she is jealous of another artist, she gleefully tells an anecdote about the ultracompetitive Robert Frost: On receiving a book from a friend, he first opened it, then stamped on it, then burned it, then tore it up. "That shows what competition really is." The video reveals the quintessential Neel—a charismatic, quirky, well-read intellect with a quick tongue and raucous laugh.

Nineteen seventy-eight began with a small show, organized by June Blum, at Valencia Community College, in Orlando, Florida, from January 24 through February 24: "Three Realist Painters: Alice Neel, Audrey Flack, and June Blum" (which had originated, with a slightly different title, at the Miami-Dade Community College in December, 1977). Neel's work included four "Studies of the New Woman."

As she wrote in the catalog, the images reflected different stages of women affected by feminism: "The woman who resembles Louis XIV is June Blum, one of the first feminist woman curators of a museum and a participant in this show . . . Another one, *Olivia*, is a child born in the middle of the great struggle of Women's Liberation, and shows the fearlessness and aggression of the new woman. The fourth painting, *Kitty Pearson*, has force, and the lack of sentimental wiles coming from liberation. *Mrs. Paul Gardner and Sam* shows a woman of the same era, affected, but not actively participating."

Neel had a larger solo show at the Fort Lauderdale Museum of Art, which ran from February 8 to February 26. It featured a selection of thirty-three of Neel's better-known paintings from the 1960s and 1970s, including *Robert Smithson, Andy Warhol, Dorothy Pearlstein, The Soyer Brothers, The Family, Red Grooms and Mimi Gross, Virgil Thompson, Linda Nochlin and Daisy,* and *Jackie Curtis and Ritta Redd.*

The extensive catalog essay by Henry R. Hope includes his own notes of sitting with his wife for a commissioned portrait by Neel, *Henry and Sally Hope,* also included in the show. Sally was not at first pleased with the "gray, slightly wrinkled, tired looking and depressed" visage Neel gave her. Hope observed "Her first remark was 'It looks like my father!'"

"When Neel looks at her subject (some would say victim) she sees something else. Not necessarily ugliness nor hypocrisy, but her scrutiny gets beyond the image that most of us believe we see in the looking glass. Sometimes it reveals hidden secrets, idiosyncracies, vulnerabilities," Hope wrote in his introduction, which was later reprinted in full with some revised text in the summer 1979 issue of *Art Journal,* where he was the editor.

But the Fort Lauderdale show was remarkable for a unique reason that had nothing to do with art. It was at the lecture and reception for this show that Neel missed her last opportunity to connect with her long-lost daughter, Isabetta.

"Alice Neel hurt my mother terribly," Cristina Lancella, Isabetta's daughter, says simply. "My mother denied her existence to us. I never knew I had a grandmother until after my mother's death." Still, family lore includes a poignant anecdote about Isabetta's futile attempt to meet Alice—for what would have been only the second or third time in her adult life—at the Fort Lauderdale show.

"Do you know what my mother did one time? This is so freaky weird. Alice Neel was lecturing, giving a seminar in Fort Lauderdale, which is the next town up from Miami, where my mother lived. And my mother paid the entrance to get into the seminar, and sat in the very first row, and

Alice Neel did not recognize her! And she looked just like Alice," says Cristina. "And she came home and she went directly to the psychiatrist for three or four sessions because she was so freaked out. But can you imagine to expose yourself to that kind of thing?"

Isabetta, who was fifty years old at the time of this incident, told her aunts (Carlos's sisters, now living in the United States) about it. According to Marisa Diaz, a close friend, the aunts said that after Alice hadn't recognized her, Isabetta was very frustrated and left the lecture. And, both Diaz and Isabetta's cousin, Adoris Mendoza, said that she found her mother's failure to recognize her deeply depressing. Apparently, she had been too distraught at the time to stay and introduce herself at the reception, even though she walked right by Alice.

Would this episode have played out differently if Neel had shown slides of earlier work—her portraits of Carlos, say, or even the stunning painting of the young Isabetta, nude, triggering memories in both that might have somehow coalesced? As it was, Isabetta, upset and disappointed, left the museum, not having found what she sought.

Given that Neel hadn't seen Isabetta since about 1948, when she was twenty years old, and then only once or, at most twice, briefly, it is not so surprising that in the midst of a lecture and the flurry of the subsequent cocktail party, she might have overlooked her own daughter, now middle-aged. Neel also had cataracts and did not have the best vision. (Moreover, according to an interview she did with Eleanor Munro, she was under the misimpression that Isabetta lived in Venezuela and was married to a football star.)

Still, it must have compounded what for Isabetta was a lifelong sense of rejection and abandonment by her mother. Says Pablo Lancella, Isabetta's husband, "She was really bitter about her mother. She couldn't understand why her mother would have left her at that time way back there. It wasn't Alice Neel, the painter. It was just another mother, but she needed her." Isabetta, like Alice, had at one point had a nervous breakdown and had already attempted suicide several times. She would succeed on her last attempt, four and a half years later.

As Marilyn Schmitt wrote in a review in *Arts Magazine* of Neel's dual appearance in Florida (she had a retrospective of works on paper that opened a few days later at the Virginia Miller Galleries in Coconut Grove, Miami): "There is nothing domesticated about Alice Neel. From the beginning of her career in the 1920s she has stood outside—and sometimes outrageously beyond—convention and pursued her freedom with a relentless

determination, in her art, in her politics, most of all in her life. No intellectual, she: Neel's life and art tell us that the vitality of freedom dwells
elsewhere than in the cerebrum, and that its price is high." Just how high,
not only to Neel but to her partners and family, Schmitt could not possibly
have known.

Describing her as an "apple-cheeked lady, all sweetness and shock,"
Schmitt went on to say, "At 78, Alice Neel, like the Soyers, is a survivor. In
the decades when they, Reginald Marsh, Ben Shahn and a host of lesser
lights were making their way into art history books, she was a phantom,
stealing past unseen. . . . She is a major artist of the 20th century. We can
judge for ourselves an art world that celebrated far weaker stuff while ignoring her. Against that backdrop, Alice Neel is a giant."

Among Neel's paintings in the Virginia Miller show were such early
works as *Kenneth Doolittle*, *Judge Medina*, and *Christopher Lazar*. Also
included was a very recent portrait of the gallery owner, Virginia Miller,
who had first met Neel a year earlier, when both were on panels at the New
School—Miller on a panel with Louise Nevelson and Jacques Truman and
Alice on one with Ivan Karp and Henry Geldzahler, with whom Neel got
into a bit of a "row" over the fact that he had (once) excluded her from a
show (perhaps his famous 1970 show, "New York Painting and Sculpture").
Geldzahler retorted that it was because she was not "modern" enough.
Soon afterward, Miller convinced Alice to allow her and her husband to
scavenge for some of her more obscure works "under her bed and in the
depths of her closet."

"When I first met Alice, she said she liked what I was wearing and
asked if I would sit for her. She said, 'You have to wear that same outfit.'" It
was during the big blizzard of 1977, and Miller was wearing cowboy boots.
"I sat for her for four or five days," Miller recalls, "and on the last day she
became agitated when she remembered Geldzahler's comment to her on
the panel. And she screamed, 'I'll show him who's modern,' and began
making slashing movements across the canvas. I was horrified at what she
seemed to be doing to my portrait. She continued to slash, slash, slash and
rail against the injustice of it all, and then when I walked around and saw
the canvas, and saw those green slashes across the background, I didn't
mind. They seemed to work. Mine is the only portrait with an Abstract
Expressionist background, or even a green background. Some years later,
Betty Parsons told me I was very brave, and said she never had the nerve to
sit for Alice."

Miller also recalled screening Nancy Baer's film on Neel, *Collector of Souls* at her gallery during the opening. "We showed the film three times; people were still there at midnight. We had hundreds and hundreds of people. I never realized what a cult figure she was. Women were coming, and saying how much they loved her work, and what an influence she had been, and asking for her autograph."

One person who approached her was Miller's brother, a tall man with a big red beard. "Alice immediately said to him, 'I'd love to have your head on a silver platter,'" Miller recalls. During the dinner afterward, at a local place called Charades, Neel apparently shocked some of the bigwigs seated with her, including the top brass from the Fort Lauderdale Museum, with her colorful language. "One word she used was *muff diver*," Miller remembers. "It was incredible. People didn't know what to say."

Neel was a frequent guest on panels; in mid-April, she participated in a two-day weekend workshop at the Maryland Institute, College of Art, "offering practical information on how to function in the art world," a rather ironic topic given the wildly uneven trajectory of Neel's own career.

A month later, on May 15, Neel had an unusual show: a preview of new works in clay at the Clayworks Studio Workshop on Great Jones Street in New York. As at the Virginia Miller Galleries, the film, *Alice Neel: Collector of Souls* was shown. Neel didn't do many works in clay; one of her best is a cat.

On May 18, Neel's grandson, Andrew, was born; on a warm spring day twenty-nine years later, his critically acclaimed documentary on his grandmother would premiere at Cinema Village in Greenwich Village.

Neel had a smattering of shows that October. An exhibit at the Artemisia Gallery in Chicago ran from October 3 to November 5. Franz Schulze, of the *Chicago Sun-Times*, called her "the fabled Alice Neel of New York, darling of the national feminist art lobby and a good painter as well, and nothing if not in a class by herself." Schulze rather naïvely marveled over the "shocking contrast between apparent lack of technical skill on the one hand (anatomical gracelessness, sloppy paint, drawing that is often a model of the maladroit) and, on the other, awesomely precise perceptions and a craft that is unfailingly articulate in its own weird way, that the viewer is obliged to conclude he has never seen anything quite like it."

But Neel was not on hand to elucidate her work for the writer. She had been invited to participate in the fifth anniversary convention of Wisconsin Women in the Arts, which included a show at Alverno College in

Milwaukee, and ran from October 15 to November 3. As usual, she gave a
two-hour slide lecture. She also spent a day "holding court" at the gallery,
as described by James Auer in the *Milwaukee Journal*:

> White-haired and grandmotherly, but with a waspish wit that
> held her immediate circle in awed (and frequently amused) si-
> lence, she expounded on everything from her lifelong struggle
> for liberation to the role of children in a woman's personal and
> artistic growth. . . .
>
> "This is still a male chauvinist world," she told her admirers,
> "but women are struggling and there is much more opportunity.
> My advice to young people is, Find your own road and then work.
> There's a terrific rat race, but you can't even get in the rat race
> unless you have a road of your own."

From November 1 to December 2, Neel had twenty-three drawings in a
two-man exhibit with her old acquaintance John Dobbs, at the Summit
Gallery on fifty-seventh Street. That same month, the Graham Gallery
mounted the first retrospective of the artist's works on paper. Neel called it
a "swan song." The exhibit, which ran from November 1 to November 25,
included fifty-seven rarely shown watercolors and drawings. Neel's statement for the catalog, which included an essay by Ann Sutherland Harris,
testified to her ever-acerbic point of view:

> If I had died 20 years ago, think how many of these things
> wouldn't be here. What if my mother had strangled me when I
> was a baby. Should she have? Think of it, none of this would have
> existed. Here I am, standing on the edge of the grave. What will
> they think of me, afterwards? You know, I had to do this. I
> couldn't have lived, otherwise.

While some of the works—the watercolors of Kenneth Doolittle, or
Alienation and *Joie de Vivre*, which wryly captured her early relationship
with John Rothschild—were well known, others, like *Suicidal Ward, Men
from Bleecker Street, City Hospital,* and *Che Guevara,* were, not surprisingly, quite obscure.

The exhibit revealed that throughout her prolific life, especially in the
early years, when she couldn't afford more ambitious materials, Neel continued to create numerous works on paper, including drawings, sketches,

watercolors, and gouaches. These smaller, more intimate works, which were often also highly autobiographical, sometimes served, as Harris pointed out in her essay, as "a sort of diary."

They also focus attention on the fact that even in her paintings, drawing remained, for Neel, the starting point, the compass through which she navigated her craft. One has only to look at the video snippets of Neel, wielding a brush like a pencil, as she tackles an empty canvas.

As Harris pointed out in her essay: "We realize again that her paintings are full of visible drawing, sketched passages, emphatic contour lines. . . . Throughout this exhibition we are reminded that Neel was trained to draw by the most academic and traditional of methods and that she knows her craft. But her formidable gifts have never been used to describe the surface of life. Her drawings, as much as her paintings, probe for the truth and contribute to her incisive, idiosyncratic but compassionate record of life in America in this century as she had seen it and as she continues to see it."

Neel had a solo show of two dozen paintings from the 1960s and 1970s at the New Art Center at Skidmore College from November 16 to December 12, and gave a gallery talk on December 5. Harry F. Gaugh, who wrote the introduction to the brochure for her Skidmore show, summed up the artist and her work in a piece in the March 1979 issue of *Arts Magazine* that covers her Graham show, her Summit show, and her Skidmore show:

> Neel's work during the last 15 years has been a relentless confrontation with portraiture. Her subjects, usually life-sized, are as physically there as van Gogh's *Postman Roulin*. (It used to be everyone could spot a van Gogh miles away. Now it's a Neel.). . . .
> In a way de Kooning was more considerate, more gentlemanly—in wrestling with *Woman 1*. By broadening her formally, he amplified her identity. In contrast Neel's insistence on retaining, simultaneously, a subject's singular identity while zooming in on tell-tale features intensifies specificity to a painful threshold. Only Avedon, in photography, is more excruciating in an overkill of likeness. . . . An ability to expose psyche through pose and drawing remains one of the most emphatic aspects of her art. . . . Neel is an American monument along with such other epochal women as O'Keefe, Nevelson, Graham and Hepburn.

The "American monument" was featured in the November *ARTnews* in an excerpt from Suzanne Slesin's "New York Artist in Residence."

Regally esconced in a corner of her sprawling apartment, in front of the windows through which she painted the world, Neel, the icon, sits in one of the chairs on which she sometimes skewered her models.

Undoubtedly to her own delight, Neel ended the year with a small but juicy scandal: *The New York Times* printed a story about a contretemps between Neel and the Standard Oil heiress Pat Ladew: "Two of the city's saltier-tongued women are back in touch, if not very devotedly, since Pat Ladew found in her morning mail a 1948 nude painting of herself," the item began, going on to say that Ladew had immediately threatened to sue. (She didn't.)

Thirty years earlier, John Rothschild had wrangled a commission for Neel to paint Ladew, then nineteen years old. The artist, of course, had painted her nude. Ladew had originally accepted the painting, for which she paid either three hundred dollars (according to Ladew) or five hundred dollars (according to Neel). Ladew had returned the painting, asking to have her pubic hair covered with little red panties. "It embarrassed her," Neel told *The Times*. "She has the same attitude towards a nude as some hard-hat." Neel uncharacteristically obliged, but Ladew was still not satisfied. Apparently, her crowd now found the painting too tame, so Ladew returned the painting for good. Neel lost no time happily restoring the pubic hair.

Recalls Joel Rothschild, "Living through the whole process, I saw the original one, I saw and lamented the fact that she put pants on it, and I saw Alice's glee when it was returned, and John's distress that a commission had been lost. He was amused also, but he was well aware of the fact that one way or another Alice's commissions didn't work out, and another commission was gone. If you x-rayed it, you would see three paintings."

Ladew was not amused when the painting was printed on the cover of a catalog for a benefit auction on December 8 for the Artists Mobilization for Survival. Still, she said she was grateful that the reproduction hadn't run in "*Town and Country* and my grandmother would have seen it in Palm Beach." The item also made Page Six of the *New York Post*, which reported that Ladew's lawyer had convinced the auction house to take her name off the cover.

The Ladew saga continued: In the meantime, according to a letter from Brian Buczac to Neel, Ray Johnson had apparently turned the Plaza auction house cover reproduction of Neel's portrait into a piece of his chain-mail art—writing "Rhode Island" on Ladew's belly, and "what year, what year" near Neel's signature. And Neel herself wrote a letter to Plaza Auction house about the incident, declaring definitively, "In closing, I want you to know that I consider this painting a work of art."

The snafu resurfaced in *People* magazine's March 19, 1979, issue, which used it as an opportunity to print a two-page spread on Neel, noting that the painting had gone for $7,750 at the auction. (The piece also mentioned that Neel had a poster of Lenin on her kitchen wall.)

Said Ladew this time around, "I respect Alice, but her stuff is too intimate to live with. . . . Alice won't tell me who bought it. It could end up as a poster at a gynecologist's convention."

*   *   *

Neel started 1979, the last year of the last full decade of her life, on a high note: She received the first National Women's Caucus for Art Lifetime Achievement Award, along with Isabel Bishop, Selma Burke, Louise Nevelson, and Georgia O'Keeffe. The recently established award, for lifetime achievement in art by senior women artists, was presented by President Jimmy Carter at a ceremony in the Oval Office:

> We honor Alice Neel, who has been painting for more than fifty years, for creating an incomparable visual record of the life of one of America's great cities, New York. Her pictures have captured the souls of the very old and the very young, of the rich and the poor, of laborers and intellectuals, artists and businessmen, of poets and salesmen, eccentrics and squares. Her portraits are profoundly democratic for she has understood and recorded the psyche of a range of personalities unprecedented in the art of portraiture. The vitality, truth and humanity of her work make her one of America's great artists.

Neel told an interviewer how pleased she was with the honor, and that the fact that it came from the government made it even more special. But, ever the cynic, she later told an audience during a slide lecture that she knew the medal would be presented in the Oval Office because "I, with my Machiavellian mind, after he fired Bella Abzug I knew he would give it in the Oval Room [*sic*]. Before that it was doubtful, but 44 women resigned with her because he let his personal feelings overcome his intellect. . . ."

Neel had seven solo shows during 1979, including a two-part retrospective that originated at the University of Bridgeport, before it traveled to the Silvermine Guild of Artists in New Canaan, Connecticut, to the Madison Art Center in Wisconsin, and finally to the Diane Gilson Gallery in Seattle. The show encompassed much of her career, from the 1930s to the present. Neel gave slide lectures at each venue. The show ran in Bridgeport

from February 25 to April 11, in Silvermine from March 18 to April 8, and
ended in Seattle, where it opened on October 18.

Wrote Martha B. Scott in the catalog essay:

> Alice Neel is seventy-nine years old. Yet she is closer to the youth
> of today than most artists half her age. . . . She is the darling of
> college campuses. She is the heroine of feminist magazines (even
> though she feels there is no such thing as feminine or masculine
> painting). While she has bluntly rejected tradition in her art and
> bourgeois conventions in her living, she has longed for official
> recognition. Now she has her official acknowledgement. The peak
> of her popularity has been crowned recently by an award dear to
> her heart—a presentation in the Oval Room [sic] from President
> Carter.
>
> . . . Alice Neel steered her own clear-headed course, alone,
> throughout the storms of the Abstract Expressionist, Pop, mini-
> mal and conceptual movements. She formed her own vocabulary
> in which she could make a positive statement, one without flat-
> tery or sentiment. Her language is her own, both in painting and
> speaking, and whether wielded by a brush or with the tongue,
> it can be brutal, aggressive, lively, intelligent, witty and always
> straightforward.

Included was a broad swath of her work, from 1930s watercolors to a
1978 lithograph of Benny Andrews. The paintings ranged in price from
$5,000 for a watercolor of Kenneth Doolittle, to $25,000 each for the portraits of Linda Nochlin and Daisy, Henry Geldzahler, and Red Grooms and
Mimi Gross.

Neel's next solo show, "Paintings by Alice Neel," ran from March 7 to
March 28 at the Williams College Museum of Art. On display was a selec-
tion of about two dozen paintings, including *Dead Father, Isabetta, Sam,
Bessie Boris,* and *The De Vegh Twins.* Neel also gave a slide lecture.

Although Neel had by now been giving lectures regularly for over a decade (she gave over a dozen in 1975 alone), she was extraordinarily proud
of the lecture she gave at Harvard on March 21, 1979, boasting that Harvard's president, Derek Bok, had given her a gold star for "giving the best
lecture on art."

Neel's slide lectures were an extension of the spontaneous, voluble presentations she did whenever she had a visitor in her studio—the sort of personal performance that had thrilled everyone from Joel Rothschild to Jack Baur. The slide box was a portable version of the stacks of paintings that filled every nook and cranny of her home.

Says Hartley, "She had her whole world of her art with her in those slides. It's like taking hundreds of people and walking them through a private show. It was almost like a concert—it was like a performance; it had a life of its own in many ways. You see she could get her stuff out there by talking about it. It was certainly the second-best thing to having it on a wall in an important museum. She was presenting basically her whole life, and the people in it, and around her—the people she was interested in: It was *her*."

Neel had worked in isolation for years, hauling out her life's work whenever a new guest crossed her threshold. Many found it revelatory. Mimi Gross recalls the first time she and Red Grooms went to Neel's home to pose in 1967: "This only happened about three times in my life, where crossing a threshold changed one's life forever. Alice was incredibly disheveled. She made me feel neat and clean. She had a bathrobe on, that was sideways off the shoulder, apparently without underwear underneath, and just completely comfortable. It wasn't that she was in any way showing off, or not showing off, or being a different person from what she probably always was. She was essentially just being herself in that way that was so welcoming. Anyway, she had a really high voice. And she was tall and big, so you can imagine it against the backlight of her standing in the doorway. When we came in, that left a really big impression. And then right from the start, there were her paintings. And they filled the entire apartment. She had not sold anything at that time. So every painting that has since become iconic, like the shot of Andy Warhol, or her daughter-in-law pregnant, paintings like that, that really since then have become trademarks of Alice Neel, were lying around. She had to show us *everything*."

Now Neel was the toast of the town and invited to do essentially the same thing at college campuses all over America. Neel knew better than to make her lectures cerebral. She kept them entertaining and down-to-earth—and, more than anything else, highly humorous. Neel was determined to milk the drama of her life to get her message out there with her art. It was almost as if she had been given the chance to make all those tragic mistakes worth something in retrospect. She played her life, and the characters in it, for laughs. Neel's audiences didn't scratch their heads every time Neel made a comment about one of her works; they literally guffawed their heads off.

Her Harvard lecture was a quintessential Neel performance: witty, worldly, whimsical, and of course jam-packed with juicy autobiographical tidbits; at once self-deprecating and self-aggrandizing.

Referring to her painting of Ethel Ashton, she remarked, "Think of all that furniture she is carrying, you know. And also, it's very good for women's lib, because she looks terrified. . . . I put her in a show at my alma mater . . . and the family were going to sue. . . . I never, until about ten years ago, could have a slide because there was a law in this country that you couldn't have a slide of anything with pubic hair. And you see she has quite a bit of pubic hair."

Commenting on her shocking 1934 nude portrait of Isabetta, Neel said, "Now this is a little girl I painted in 1934. I couldn't show this either. Why they said, it's indecent. Think of it. And by the time it got to be the 60's they said it was Lolita. It wasn't Lolita at all, it was just very frank, you know. I mean that's the way we come." [Audience laughter.] Of two portraits of Sam, she remarked, "This is a man I met on the art project, a genius, really, but insane, you know: mad. He looks here as though he's dropping poison in someone's wine, maybe. [Laughter.] Oh and here's when I knew him better." [Both Alice Neel and the audience laughed even louder.]

While these antics made Neel an extremely popular performer, and, as Hartley points out, got her work out to a wide audience, it didn't necessarily enhance the art historical approach to her work. She was presenting herself as something of a novelty act.

As Mira Schor has observed: "There are two types of myth in art: the wild man's stories, which coexist with and enhance his myth as a great artist; and the wild woman's story, likely to create a lot of appeal without necessarily enhancing the perceived aesthetic value of the work. . . . In what might have been a deliberate effort to confront this double standard head-on, Neel was a primary source of the biographical and anecdotal approach to her work, one that has continued to dominate the critical and historical perception of her work. . . . Neel deserved the attention and at that point in her life was entitled to have an audience in the palm of her hands. . . . But what might it have meant . . . if Neel had also revealed something of her more serious aesthetic views . . . If the intellectual were allowed space along with the personal, it would build another idea of what a woman artist could be."

But regardless of how Neel may have tried to, in effect, dumb her lectures down by making fun of her subjects and soft-pedaling the pain of her relationships with Carlos, Kenneth, Sam, or even Isabetta, the paintings themselves unflinchingly express the truth. Neel's lectures packed such a wallop not just because they were a practiced form of performance art but because the sheer power of the paintings created a lasting resonance. In the end, Neel wasn't so much an intellectual painter as a *visceral* one, and her highly animated slide lectures brought every bit of that into play.

Ultimately it was people—and their stories—that fueled Neel's paintings. She had always prided herself on being a self-described "humanist" and "collector of souls," and while she clearly understood the value of making her lectures good theater, Neel was, in part, simply transmitting her own burning fascination with the human condition.

"Don't leave, don't leave," Neel shouted at the audience during the brief interval when her slide tray was being changed at Harvard. "I see somebody leaving. Look Andy Warhol is coming!" In her lectures, as in her life, Neel never wanted to leave the stage.

"Celebrity for me is acceptance," Neel told *New York* magazine in July. "I don't enjoy it for itself. What I enjoy is being able to communicate. I'm not as famous as I'd really like to be, because they [the public] don't really know me yet. I'd like to have my work seen for what it is, and most people don't know how truly profound and serious it is. They're carried away by the surface gloss, and my personality reinforces that. You see, I'm not just a simple figure painter. The abstract elements and the geometric layout of the canvas are very important to me. When I paint, I throw everything out of my brain and simply react to the image I'm going to do."

*   *   *

In April, a selection of musings was published in the journal *Night*, including an "interview" with Neel:

—How would you describe yourself?
—*I am a morbid person.*

—Do you ever participate in unrequited love?
—*No, I ruined more men's illusions than anyone living.*

—Have you ever been fascinated with death?
—*All my life I have wanted to commit suicide and I never look out a window without wanting to jump.*

—What were you thinking moments before you attempted suicide in 1930?
—*I heard voices. I thought I heard my parents talking. I was at the point of a nervous breakdown. I thought I had gone mad.*

—What is the most reckless thing you do?
—*My paintings.*

Neel had two small solo shows that month. One at the Tomasulo Gallery at Union College in Cranford, New Jersey, from April 6 to April 27, which coincided with a show at Montclair State College.

That fall, Neel had a solo show at the Fort Wayne Museum of Art, in Indiana, which ran from September 14 to November 1. The director of the gallery, James Bell, wrote to thank her for attending the opening reception and giving a lecture. "Fort Wayne cannot stop talking about you! Since the opening the galleries are filled with groups of all ages studying your work."

A notice from November 15 trumpets a "Slide Lecture by Alice Neel, One of the Major American Artists of the 20th Century" at the Strauss Lounge, Union College, in Cranford, New Jersey, for $3.00 ($1.00 for students), including refreshments. "With a fresh and insightful vision, Alice Neel has been a figurative painter of people for 60 years. She has bluntly rejected tradition and records all people in her art: The Poor and Wretched; The Rich and Pampered; The Famous and Infamous," it read.

Neel participated in the group show "Woman" at the Harold Reed Gallery later that month. On exhibit was her piece, "Kristen Walker."

In 1979, Neel painted John Cheim, then director of the Robert Miller Gallery, who would be pivotal both in the shows which took place in the last few years of Neel's life and in her posthumous career. Cheim, who had just recently graduated from the Rhode Island School of Design, where he was studying painting, usually preferred abstract work. But, he says, "I remember being very attracted to Alice Neel, much in the way that I am attracted to van Gogh. There are a lot of abstract qualities about Alice's painting, and I think there's just an intensity, whether they are literal or abstract, in the same manner as van Gogh. I remember chasing after her, and wanting to show her work. I remember her showing at the Graham Gallery and thinking it was just not the best spot for her at that point in time. I thought it wasn't being presented properly." Cheim, who also worked with Joan Mitchell and Louise Bourgeois, would eventually succeed in bringing Neel into the Robert Miller Gallery, where his curatorial style would bring a whole new appreciation to her work.

Bowing Out

"Come celebrate Alice Neel's 80th Birthday," read the announcement. Then a mordant Neel touch: The otherwise-innocent invitation was illustrated with a "self-portrait by Alice Neel," her ghoulish 1958 ink drawing of her own skull, one eye socket darkly oozing, the death head's grin missing a few teeth.

It was an odd choice, given that the "self-portrait" had been done at a pivotally low point in Neel's life—just when her relationship with Sam Brody was ending and she was entering therapy with Dr. Anthony Sterrett. The eighty-year-old Alice Neel was, in many ways, a far more fulfilled woman than the she had been at fifty-eight, when she was painting in almost total obscurity and bringing up two young sons.

In the last two decades of her life, her straggling career had fully blossomed. Her painting had become richer and freer, much more expansive. She was widely considered an important, if not major, twentieth-century American artist, with the awards and accolades to prove it. And she was now not only a mother but the grandmother of six thriving grandchildren.

The eightieth-birthday event was an exhibit preview to benefit the Women in the Arts Foundation. It was held on January 8 at the Sarah Institute on East Sixty-fifth Street. The ten paintings on view through January 24 ranged in price from $12,000 for the skull self-portrait to $35,000 for her inimitable image of Henry Geldzahler.

The next night, along with some 2,500 other A-list guests, Neel attended the Whitney Museum of American Art's big fiftieth-birthday bash. *The New York Times* ran a piece on the star-studded party, which included such other notable artists as Jasper Johns, Lee Krasner, Cristo, Isamu Noguchi, Raphael Soyer, Alex Katz, Tom Wesselmann, and Philip Pearlstein. There, topping the column of photos, was a beaming Neel, mink toque on head and drink in hand. As the artist "gleefully" boasted to the photographer, "I'm 80 years old and I'm still here!"

Alice's actual birthday party was thrown by Stewart Mott (whom she had memorably painted in a Scottish kilt in 1961) in his elegant Fifth Avenue penthouse. More than a hundred guests were invited, including some of Alice's peers from the Academy and Institute of Arts and Letters.

Wrote Millen Brand on January 29, 1980, in his journal:

> *Alice Neel had her eightieth birthday party last night at Stewart Mott's penthouse at 1133 Fifth Avenue (94th Street). Penthouse being remodeled, two floors, enormous space and two great single-paned picture windows looking out at the south end of Central Park. . . .*
>
> *Alice was sitting in state in a large alcove on the second floor and Nancy was standing near her. I said Hello to Nancy and wished Alice a happy birthday and kissed her. Others were coming up and I slipped away into the massed crowd. I ran into Raphael Soyer and his wife Rebecca standing alone and they were delighted to see me. . . . I had debated coming at all and I now at once made my way downstairs and left. I had done my duty.*

Richard toasted his mother, commenting on how she was just starting her career at an age when most people were already retired. But before he could even finish his remark, Alice interrupted him, shouting, "I didn't have sex with you!"

Richard was mortified, but Mott used the remark as a takeoff point. Raising a glass to Alice, he said that he "felt like a son, but unlike her sons, had never slept in the same bed with her." Neel, who even in her eighties was still something of a flirt, no doubt relished the remark.

Although Mott and Neel never had an intimate relationship, back in the 1960s he frequently "schlepped" her around the city and to Spring Lake in his station wagon. He had originally met her through John Rothschild. "I was at a brunch at John's and I must have worn my kilt. I remember Alice looking at me from across the table, using a forefinger and thumb to frame me," he recalled. "I was immediately charmed by her sense of humor and politics. She was a larger-than-life person to me, as a young twenty-two-year-old student finding my way. She was such a commanding presence. Adjectives that come to mind are: raucous, intense, and funny, imaginative, provocative, voluptuous. There was no sexual interaction between us, but I must say, her talking about her sexual escapades and her paintings, like the one of Joe Gould, all prompted discussion of sex."

Portfolio magazine also celebrated Neel's eightieth birthday and her work. Ann Sutherland Harris, then the head of Academic Affairs at the Metropolitan Museum, wrote a feature story, with the headline ENGAGING AND OUTRAGEOUS AT EIGHTY, ALICE NEEL STILL CREATES PSYCHOLOGICAL PORTRAITS OF EXTRAORDINARY STRENGTH.

Wrote Harris:

> Portraits that seek to record a truthful and complete image of an individual psyche instead of a partial but flattering account are difficult for most people to accept. For this reason, Neel's work is admired rather than loved. . . . It is Neel's portraits of the sixties and seventies that have made her famous. Many critics regard them as her best work, some as her only works worth serious consideration. Even when discussing her last masterpieces, some critics overlook the artist's extraordinary empathy with a range of sitters who represent a cross-section of society unparalleled in the work of any other portraitist. . . . Neel can find the extraordinary and the unique where no one else would dream of looking.

Sutherland herself was the subject of a compelling Neel portrait in 1978, when the art historian was the young mother of a strapping blond infant son. "She was the first sweater girl as a mother that I ever painted," Neel coyly said during her Harvard lecture, recounting how Harris had observed that her connection with her child was not as strong as it would have been in a Mary Cassatt painting. "So I told her that that was middle-class France in the late 1800's and early 1900's. But actually Mary and Jesus have no connection like that. He's always completely separate, you know holding a little world or something. . . . But she is very much a career woman, although I didn't *mean* to separate them. It's just that I didn't have that, you know, Mary Cassatt's, they look as though they're all kissing each other."

Nobody could accuse Neel of taking that tack: Her entire career, from her specific choice of art schools on, had been dictated by her relentless direction as something of an anti-Cassatt—a ruthlessly unsentimental chronicler of humanity. Even her harshest critics would have to agree that at the very least, Neel had triumphed in her own self-created genre, a genre that had arisen as much out of her own subconscious as her social conscience. "I think every good artist paints largely with his subconscious. . . . But the world is like the subconscious also," she told her Harvard audience.

As a painter, Neel brings her survivor's sensibility to the canvas. By the time she was barely thirty, she had experienced the death of a child, the loss of her husband and another child, and would soon survive several botched suicide attempts. "I love to see what the pressure of life does to the human psyche," Neel told Sutherland, echoing her oft-repeated quote about people and the rat race. Neel didn't see her subjects just as victims; she also saw them as survivors, however scarred. As such, almost all Neel's subjects mirror her own identity.

Although she had fewer shows and gave fewer lectures than she had the previous year, 1980 included several significant milestones in Neel's life. She completed and showed her first bona fide self-portrait, and she had a pacemaker installed, both in their way bearing testimony to her formidable tenacity.

Neel's work was included in the Graham Gallery's group show of women artists, "Originals" (inspired by Eleanor Munro's eponymous 1979 book of interviews with important women artists, which included an in-depth interview with Neel), from January 15 to February 20. The work ranged from paintings by Mary Cassatt to Helen Frankenthaler to Neel, whose 1978 portrait of her framer, Dennis Florio, in an elegant red velvet suit and a Proustian pose, got a bad mention in *Arts Magazine,* suggesting that it "revealed the weakness of much contemporary art" in that the artist "remained glued to her material" and it was "formal rather than expressive." Actually, it's a rather wistful, empathetic portrait of Neel's close friend, whom she called simply "Florio." He would later introduce her to performance artist Annie Sprinkle.

Neel had a solo show at the Lancaster Community Gallery in Pennsylvania, from March 2 to April 27. And her work was included in a show of painting, from the Whitney's collection; entitled, "American Painting of the Sixties and Seventies: The Real, The Ideal, The Fantastic," at the Montgomery Museum of Fine Arts in Alabama, which ran from April 3 to May 25, along with Andy Warhol, Roy Lichtenstein, Philip Pearlstein, and Fairfield Porter (whom Neel referred to as a "mild dish"), among others. The catalog actually compared her to de Kooning, and acknowledged her awareness of Abstract Expressionism: "Neel's acerbic portraits of art world personalities seem painted in a frenzy of activity, influenced by Abstract Expressionism, and Willem de Kooning in particular."

Neel had another major solo show, "Alice Neel: Paintings of Two

Decades," at Boston University from October 9 through November 2. Curated by Patricia Hills, who wrote the catalog essay, it included fifty-five of
some of Neel's better-known works from the 1960s and 1970s: *Frank
O'Hara, David Bourdon and Gregory Battcock, Duane Hanson, Cindy
Nemser and Chuck,* and *Nancy and the Rubber Plant.* Also exhibited
were some rarely shown works, including a portrait of Joseph Papp (not
one of her best) and the black playwright Hugh Hurd.

In late 1979, Hills conducted a series of lengthy interviews with Neel for
a book to be published by Harry N. Abrams. She completed another eight
hours of interviews as she prepared for the Boston show. These edited interviews, embellished with some written material by Neel, including comments
on her own paintings, became her book *Alice Neel,* which was published in
1983, and remains the best introduction to the artist and her work. (Hills
continues to be one of the most articulate art historians to champion Neel,
with a perceptive understanding of Neel's unique contribution and its place
in art history.)

Neel had another solo show, at Drury College in Springfield, Missouri,
later that October. In addition to a dozen paintings, the show included fourteen prints and fifteen drawings, providing a well-rounded view of Neel's
talent. The show ran from October 22 through November 25 and included
a slide lecture.

In early November, Neel had what would be her last solo show at the
Graham Gallery. This exhibit of "recent paintings" included twenty-five
pieces done between 1978 and 1980. At this point, Neel's work was selling
for up to thirty thousand dollars. The show included a number of pictures
of family members and friends, including *The Family,* a painting of Nancy
with three of her four daughters, done in 1980; Neel's 1979 painting of cellist David Soyer, and her just-completed painting of Michel Auder. Wrote
ARTnews, "Neel is one of the most exciting portraitists active today. She
neither sacrifices likeness to style nor style to likeness. Each work has the
ring of truth." The reviewer particularly raved about the Auder portrait:

> With its drippy washes and rough broad strokes of color, bright
> yellow-green sandal straps on unpainted outlined feet, an orangy-
> yellow floor next to a burnt sienna table and chest that suddenly
> acquired color behind the snaky globs of blue, burnt umber and
> gray that form the sitter's curly hair—this is one of Neel's most
> brilliant performances to date.

But the pièce de résistance of the entire year was the unveiling of Neel's iconic *Self-Portrait*, which debuted at a benefit dinner for the Third Street Music School Settlement on October 14 at the Harold Reed Gallery, where it was included in the show "Selected 20th Century American Self-Portraits." Neel was the only artist who chose to portray herself nude. To say that it caused a stir would be an understatement. Neel had outdone even herself. The painting is the audacious and unexpected grand gesture of an artist at the top of her form.

Lucian Freud, the master of outrageous nudes, whose often hard-to-view work bears a direct connection to Neel's, seems to flirt with a similar notion in a nude self-portrait at age sixty-three (*Reflection*, 1985), but the image stops, with uncharacteristic modesty, just below his collarbone. And, like Neel, he dared to paint a frank image of himself at age eighty— except he's fully clothed. Neel knowingly crashed right through the boundaries of self-portraiture with her late, great masterpiece, gouging a new niche in the canon. She's arguably the only artist in history to have painted her first self-portrait so late in life, and to have compounded the breakthrough by stripping herself bare.

But it's not its shock value that gives Neel's self-portrait such potency. Neel has basically turned the notion of the "gaze," whether artist's or viewer's, male or female, inside out. She's the artist depicting herself as subject, no holds barred. She's defied gender stereotypes by deliberately casting the female body as the furthest possibility from a sex object. And she's challenged art history itself, which is studded with famous self-portraits—from Rembrandt's celebrated images of himself as an old man to van Gogh's harrowing self-depictions—by painting one that is sui generis.

At her most essential, distilled down to her core, Neel presents herself as an artist not only undiminished by age but at the very peak of her powers, her flesh-toned paintbrush growing out of her hand like an organic extension of her body. ("I live for this little thing in my hand," she once said.) Enthroned in the familiar blue-striped chair, Neel is clearly the mistress/master of all she portrays. This is a picture of sheer, triumphant will.

And yet, ironically, Neel didn't initially set out to make such a sweeping statement. In fact, she did anything but. For most of her career, she neatly avoided the self-portrait. True, she had done a pencil drawing of herself at age thirty-two, and she showed herself with others in several works: with Santillana in *The Family*; in the erotic watercolors she made of herself and John Rothschild; the watercolor of herself in bed with José; the disturbing picture where she is clutching a terrified Richard; and a few others including the tiny image of herself in a mirror in the painting *Hartley on the Rocking Horse*, and the *Mother and Child* painting set in a cemetery. But she had never attempted a full-blown oil painting of herself, never deliberately committed herself to canvas as the sole subject.

When a student at Harvard earlier that year had asked her why, Neel gave a rather superficial answer. "Well, my type doesn't interest me, you know. No, I hate this type. I don't know why I look like this. I never did anything about it. Now Louise wears those big eyelashes and she's already exotic because she was born in Russia, you know, long ago. . . . I always thought it was artsy-craftsy people that tried to look like an artist. I thought you didn't have to look like it, you just had to *be* it. . . . I don't like my type. I think I look like, you know what, somebody at one of my shows invited me to a great concert of the DAR [Daughters of the American Revolution] and I went there and if I didn't look like all those women—it was just frightful, you know. . . . Picasso had a great face, with those commanding eyes. But I never had—I didn't bother with that. I was *anonymous*." Or, as she told another interviewer, "I have always been reluctant to do a self-portrait. I thought if I was going to be a great painter I had to have a big nose and no chin. I had such a plain little face."

Frederick Ted Castle got a slightly more thoughtful response when he asked the same question. "I hate the way I looked! I don't look like I am! I look very sissy—I was a very pretty girl and I liked to use that with the boys, but I wasn't like me. My spirit looked nothing like my body. By the time I got old, I could reveal. . . . nobody could think of being sorry for that wretch . . . but I never had any arches in my feet. My feet hurt me all my life and I never had any comfort until at 58 I got these molded shoes in and they saved my feet. In my self-portrait I showed that I have a prehensile toe—I was just an ape a while ago, hanging onto a tree—and I liked to put the flesh dropping off my bones, and the reason my cheeks got so pink was that it was so hard for me to paint that, I almost killed myself painting it." (Neel used a mirror to paint herself, which is why, although she was left-handed, the portrait shows her holding her brush in her right hand.)

In fact, the genesis of the startling self-portrait was surprisingly banal. Neel told Terry Gross in a 1980 *Fresh Air* interview that the idea initially came from William Paul, the director of the Georgia Museum of Art, where Neel had her 1975 survey. He had promised Neel that if she did a self-portrait, he would reproduce it in color in the otherwise-black-and white catalog.

As Neel went on to explain: "So I thought I'll try to do one. So I don't know if I was making fun of myself, or what I was doing. I couldn't tell you. But I did a self-portrait. I began it. Then I had nothing on, it was hot summer weather . . . at first I'd put a bathrobe on after I'd paint, but then I didn't bother, it was so hot. But I looked out the window, and even though I'm not in Spanish Harlem, there are still a lot of Spanish where I live, 107th and Broadway, and I saw a middle-aged Spanish man looking up and grinning. So I thought 'My God, he can see in the window,' you know. So then I didn't work on it anymore. It never got into that show."

Neel added that although she had already drawn in the entire figure, she had gotten tired of the image and put it away. "But then several years later, a chap named Hal Reed gave a show at this gallery and it was self-portraits. So I got it out. I was always going to scrape it, but my sons both thought it was a great composition. So I got it out and I worked on it for a whole week. And it came to be what it is now. And I sent it to that show there. Well, the night that show opened, it came out the next day in *Newsweek*, even *The New York Times*. Everybody was amazed at this portrait, you know."

Reed himself recalls his surprise when he first saw the painting, which he had commissioned for his show. "When I was putting together the exhibit, I called Alice, whom I had known since the late sixties, and asked her if she had a self-portrait. She said she had one that wasn't that great and she would do another one for the show. Two or three weeks passed, and I told Alice I was sending my assistant, David Ebony, over. He brought it back to me wrapped in a sheet, all excited, and said, 'Wait until you see this!' So we unwrapped it, and there was Alice Neel, nude!"

As ingenuous as she sounds in the interview, Neel was clearly aware of the significance of the work, started when she was seventy-five and completed when she was eighty. "There is almost a taboo in this society about showing people naked," she told Gross. "I broke all the rules, yes, sure. Well, I did and since it was myself, I could do as I pleased, you know. . . . I got so much notoriety with that portrait, but I didn't do it for that."

Two days after the self-portrait was revealed at the Reed Gallery's benefit dinner, *The New York Times* made it and Neel the lead item of its October 16 "Notes on People" column:

To help drum up support for the 86th anniversary fund-raising luncheon for the Third Street Music School Settlement, Harold Reed gave a preview Tuesday night of his new exhibition, "Selected 20th Century American Self-Portraits. . . . But what caught the immediate attention of the 200 or so arriving guests was a quite large nude self-portrait of the prolific, 81-year-old [sic] artist Alice Neel. In the portrait, painted from life especially for the exhibition and completed only a couple of weeks ago, Miss Neel is seated in an armchair wearing only her eyeglasses. Sitting exactly opposite the nude self portrait was Miss Neel herself, wearing the same glasses but bundled up in a beige coat, which she kept on for the more than two hours she was at the Reed gallery.

As Neel quipped to *Newsweek*, which featured her in its October 27 "Newsmakers" column, old age "is a deliverance. All my life I wanted to do a nude self-portrait, but I put it off till now—when people would accuse me of insanity rather than vanity."

The Harold Reed dinner generated not only publicity but a new commission—to paint New York's then mayor, Edward Koch. "Mayor Koch came to the opening," says Reed, "and Alice, who was very assertive, got into a conversation with him. I think that's how she got to paint his portrait." Adds Reed, "Alice was always sort of wild and interesting and seductive. She had a certain gleam in her eye." As Koch later told *Interview* magazine, Neel took him upstairs to see the portrait and "I fell in love."

The painting would also be featured two years later in a show of self-portraits at the Allan Frumkin Gallery. "From the Mirror," the first of a two-part invitational exhibit that ran from November 27, 1982 through January 27, 1983, included pieces by Jack Beal, Paul Georges, Red Grooms, Alfred Leslie, Marisol, and Philip Pearlstein.

Once again, Neel's was the only nude self-portrait. Reviewing the show in *The New York Times*, John Russell wrote, "Alice Neel's well-known nude self-portrait at a very advanced age is as touching and surprising as it ever was." While *The Christian Science Monitor* said, "Alice Neel, in particular, insists we see her precisely as she sees herself in the cold light of day—with the result that her self-portrait is as frank and heartbreakingly revealing as any painted in recent years."

"I remember distinctly Alice coming in to see the show and critiquing the entire thing as she went around, because I went around with her," says George Adams, now director of the George Adams Gallery. "She particularly disapproved of Paul Georges's self-portrait, where he's taking a leak. She said she thought it was 'adolescent.' She clearly thought her painting was gutsier than everybody else's."

Adams also recalls that a collector, Marvin Kantor, requested that Neel's painting be put on hold, but ultimately decided against buying it. The reason, Kantor told Adams, was "There is just not enough paint on it for fifty thousand dollars" (its price at the time). Neel's nude self-portrait has become one of her most famous works. It was purchased by the National Portrait Gallery after her death and is now in its permanent collection.

Neel spent that Thanksgiving with Stewart Mott at his house in Bermuda. Mott had invited a small group of people to join him and his then wife, Kappy, including Michel Auder, Tana Hoban (my aunt, a photographer), and Neel's granddaughter Olivia. Auder captured Neel on videotape: Sitting on the veranda, her long white hair billowing softly around her face, she talks openly about her innate jealousy of other artists.

In late 1980, Neel, who had been suffering from blackouts for several months, had a pacemaker installed. Although Neel's health appeared to be basically good, she had diabetes and had been complaining for years of various neurological symptoms. She also had cataracts, which she lived with, opting not to have an operation. She was already on a variety of medications, and would take her assorted army of pills each day. The brain scans arranged by Hartley at the hospital in St. Johnsbury, Vermont, proved negative. (In fact, Neel's brain appeared to be remarkably youthful.) Hartley booked her into Massachussetts General Hospital for a complete work-up. When Neel had a blackout during "grand rounds" at the hospital, they immediately did an EKG and discovered that her blood pressure was dangerously low and Neel received a pacemaker.

Whatever her health issues, her humor remained intact. As Neel later told an interviewer, "You know I had a pacemaker put in and for several days you can't turn over because they put it in your heart and if you turn over the wire falls out of your heart. And so for three days and three nights you can't turn. So the first night I could turn over I dreamed that I was Ann Sutherland Harris. She's an art historian. And this filled me with such horror that I began screaming in my sleep, and they came and woke me up and I said, 'Oh I dreamed I was an art historian!'"

*   *   *

At eighty-one, Neel was still a major presence. Just a week after her eighty-first birthday, she had a retrospective at the C. Grimaldis Gallery in Baltimore, Maryland. *The Evening Sun* described her holding court to a rapt group of art students:

> Alice Neel has the look of some ageless natural wonder. . . . She's dressed all in warm earth tones; dark solid shoes, sand-colored dress, camel cape, brown fur cap. Wisps of white hair flutter around her face like the tag ends of memory. And her face is pink and glowing and as American as a huckleberry. A cane stout as a scepter supports her left hand. She holds her glasses and a yellow tissue in her right. . . . And if her bearing is regal, as befits one of the great survivors in contemporary art, her conversation is blunt, honest, witty, straightforward, hard-edged and often downright salty. Just about like the nude self-portrait she did of herself in her 80th year.

Neel's talks were often like theater, but this one had an added dimension of drama. The paper went on to note the "slightly late" arrival of Grace Hartigan at the gallery, causing Neel to interrupt her comments and exclaim, "Are you Grace Hartigan? I had no idea you looked like that! Take off your hat a minute. You are for me the 'Grand Street Brides,' and 'Tess of the D'Urbervilles,' which I read when I was a child. . . ." (Neel was referring to Hartigan's renowned *Grand Street Brides* (1954), a painting of mannequins in a bridal store, based on Goya's *Royal Family*. Hartigan, who moved to Baltimore in the 1960s, was first the director, then a teacher at the Hoffberger School of Painting, a graduate school created for her at the Maryland Institute College of Art.)

It was a unique art historical moment: two generations of feisty but very different New York artists, meeting for the first time. Hartigan was a disciple of Pollock and de Kooning and gained fame as a second-generation Abstract Expressionist in the 1950s. (In 1958, *Life* magazine referred to her as "the most celebrated of the young American women painters.") Eventually, she began to use figurative imagery, in part because of the influence of Frank O'Hara's poetry.

Neel, seated in front of her double portrait of O'Hara, continued her talk, peppered with typically caustic remarks. At one point, Hartigan commented on a remark Neel made about death. "Death is always in your hand," Hartigan said. Neel didn't skip a beat before one-upping her. "Suicide? Oh, but it's not easy, have you ever tried? When I was 30 I put my head in the oven." Of Warhol, Neel stated, "It may not be an important contribution to art, but it shows great powers of adjustment," adding, "I'm not being especially vicious, only mildly vicious."

The retrospective—"From 1926 to 1981"—included thirty-two pieces and ran from February 5 to March 1. Neel gave a slide lecture on February 6. Among the works, which ranged from her 1926 *Beggars, Havana, Cuba* to a 1980 silk screen of Olivia, was her 1979 portrait of Tom Freudenheim, the former director of the Baltimore Museum of Art, looking, as the *News-American* put it, "like José Ferrer's impersonation of Toulouse-Lautrec."

Freudenheim recalled how the painting came about: "I was giving a lecture at the New School in 1977, and at the end of it there was a note sent up to me and it said 'I must paint you before I go to the happy hunting grounds,' signed by Alice Neel. So I went over and said, 'Do you really mean this?' and she said very crustily, 'I wouldn't have sent the note if I didn't.' Eventually I called and said, 'What am I supposed to wear?' She said, 'I don't care. Why are you asking me?' and I said, 'Because you always paint people in states of undress.' I went back I don't remember how many times, and sat in the usual striped chair. We had all these conversations about literature. I was reading Edmund Wilson's *Memoirs of Hecate County*, and she remembered everything about it, even though she had only read it once, when it came out in 1946."

Freudenheim wanted to buy the painting, which Neel was selling for thirteen thousand dollars. Freudenheim offered to barter diamonds from his father, who was in the jewelry business. Neel adamamantly refused, saying she had "gotten screwed all her life." (Neel also said she wanted to do a crucifixion painting of Freudenheim as Jesus, because he "looked so Talmudic," but they were never able to arrange it.)

Overlapping with the Grimaldis retrospective, Neel had a solo show closer to home, at the Fine Arts Center, State University of New York at Stony Brook, from January 26 to March 20. The director had requested portraits done from 1967 to the present. These included *Red Grooms and Mimi Gross, Benny and Mary Ellen Andrews, Linda Nochlin and Daisy*, and Neel's self-portrait, the most recent of the batch—and the most expensive at $35,000—the same price being charged for *David Bourdon and Gregory Battcock, The Family*, and *Linda Nochlin and Daisy*.

That July, Neel achieved another milestone: She became the first living American artist to have a retrospective in the Soviet Union. Neel had traveled there for pleasure with John Rothschild in 1969, and she and her old friend Phillip Bonosky had attempted to organize a show in the 1960s. But it wasn't until 1981, when Bonosky was finishing up his stint as the Moscow correspondent for the *Daily World* that the complicated arrangements fell into place. Neel said she had done the show in "the cause of détente." Or, as she told Hills, "My idea was that anything that stimulates détente makes the danger of nuclear war less. That's why I wanted to go."

The show, at the Moscow Artists' Union, was Neel's largest since her retrospective at the University of Georgia in Athens in 1975. On display were some eighty-five paintings and drawings. Bonosky, to his amazement, received a telegram asking that the work be insured for $1.5 million, which caused some tension between him and Neel. "I was in this correspondence back and forth with her in the Teletype and one day I got a Teletype from the people who were handling her show from the American side and they told me that the paintings in Moscow were insured for over a million and a half," he recalled. "And the way it was voiced, it sounded as though I was responsible for it. That if anything went wrong, I stood to lose a million and a half dollars. And I thought, Oh my God, how did I get into this? The last time I had anything to do financially with Alice, I paid her two hundred dollars for a painting, and I paid in four installments, and it was hard to make it. That was the level at which I dealt with her financially—and now to be at a million and a half. I thought, Oh my God, she's pricing me out of her life. And in effect she did, although she insisted on giving me this painting [that's behind you] in return for making the show for her."

Whatever the awkwardness over the financial arrangements, the show was viewed by some eight hundred people a day. Says Bonosky, "It was a very successful show. I had arranged it all. They were the guests of the Artists' Union, the whole family was, and it was one of the best galleries in Moscow. It was on Gorky Street. My time as a correspondent ended about a month before her show. It was a great show; she loved every moment of it. She was interviewed right and left." (Although Moscow television wouldn't show the nude portraits of Isabetta and Elizabeth.)

Neel told Frederick Ted Castle in 1983: "I had a friend who was a correspondent for the Daily World in Russia, and he always thought my images told more about life in New York than anything else could tell. So he fixed it that I had a show on Gorky Street at the Artists' Union. I took my whole family with me [Richard, Nancy, Olivia, Hartley, Ginny, Elizabeth, and Andrew]. I had some money in the bank from prints and I spent every nickel. We all just

1. *Loneliness*, 1970, oil on canvas 80 x 38 inches:
Neel painted this not long after the year Hartley
married Ginny and moved to Massachusetts, and
she has referred to it as a self-portrait.

2 & 3. *Hartley*, 1965, oil on canvas, 50 x 36 inches:
An exhausted Hartley during his medical school
days; *Richard in the Era of the Corporation*, 1979,
oil on canvas, 60 x 45 inches: Richard was a lawyer
for Pan Am. Neel said it was only after she painted
this that she realized the impact of corporate
America on its youth.

4.

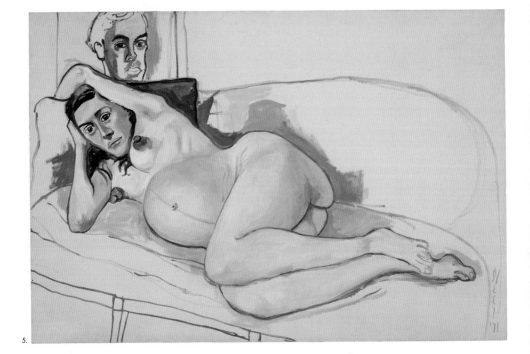

5.

6.

4. *Ginny in a Striped Shirt*, 1969, oil on canvas, 60 x 40 inches: Ginny, who in this painting is not yet married to Neel's younger son, Hartley, was part of a new wave of feminist women who saw Neel as a role model; she bonded with Neel before she became involved with her son.

5. *Pregnant Woman*, 1971, oil on canvas, 40 x 60 inches: Neel painted Nancy, pregnant with her first child, Olivia, with an image of Richard looming in the background. The painting captures an anxious edge of pregnancy rarely, if ever, depicted.

6. *Margaret Evans, Pregnant*, 1978, oil on canvas, 57 ¼ x 38 inches: This painting epitomizes Neel's bold approach to the taboo subject of pregnant nudes; it closely resembles Egon Schiele's earlier version.

7. Egon Schiele: *Red Nude, Pregnant*, 1919.

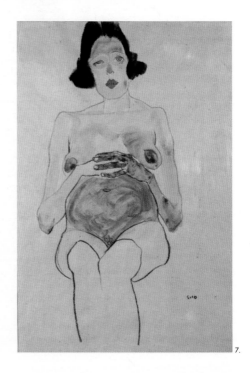

7.

8.

9.

10.

8. *Frank O'Hara*, 1960, oil on canvas, 34 x 16 inches: This portrait of the famous poet and critic was one of the first of Neel's series of art world figures. She twinned this with a second portrait, as ravaged as this is idyllic.

9. *Henry Geldzahler*, 1967, oil on canvas, 50 x 33 ½ inches: Neel's painted payback to curator Henry Geldzahler, with whom she had a pointed relationship.

10. *Red Grooms and Mimi Gross*, 1967, oil on canvas, 60 x 50 inches: Neel was adept at catching the angst between couples, sometimes even before they were aware of it themselves. Great art collaborators, this pair look totally estranged.

11. *Jackie Curtis and Ritta Redd*, 1970, oil on canvas, 60 x 42 inches: Neel was particularly adept at navigating the subtle sexual nuances in the body language of gay couples: take the prurient feet of Jackie Curtis with his boyfriend, Ritta Redd.

11.

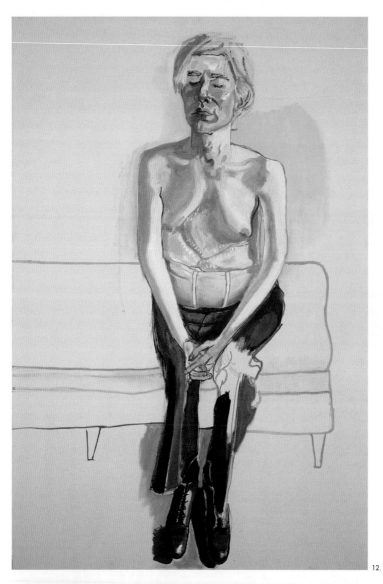

12.

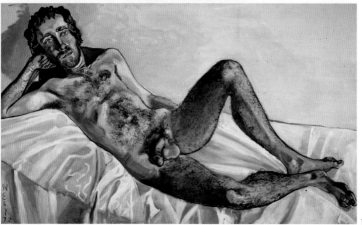

13.

14.

15.

12. *Andy Warhol*, 1970, oil on canvas, 60 x 40 inches: This is one of the most memorable images ever made of the cultural icon; it portrays Warhol as the vulnerable victim of his own celebrity, a voyeur with closed eyes. But Warhol's input is also key; his courageous self-exposure is in itself an artistic act.

13. *John Perreault*, 1972, oil on canvas, 38 x 63 ½ inches: Neel turned Perreault, an art critic and curator, into a Fauvist odalisque in this naughty nude, as titillating now as it was when she first painted it.

14. *The Family*, 1970, oil on canvas, 58 x 60 inches: A crafty portrait of the dauntingly glamorous Gruen family, frequently photographed in *Vogue*, Neel has great fun with this intense threesome and their six patent leather shoes.

15. *The Soyer Brothers*, 1973, oil on canvas 60 x 46 inches: Neel knew the Soyer brothers from her Village days, and they, like she, remained loyal to figurativism during its darkest days.

16. *Linda Nochlin and Daisy*, 1973, oil on canvas, 55 ½ x 44 inches: Neel was sometimes called the court painter to the feminists. Here she's caught feminist scholar Linda Nochlin with her vibrant red-headed daughter, both exuding taut intelligence.

16.

17.

17. *Self-portrait*, 1980, oil on canvas, 54 x 40 inches:
Done when she was eighty, this is one of Neel's
masterworks, breaking through genre barriers,
inverting the gaze of subject and artist, and radically
subverting the female form.

went to Russia for ten days. I sent them seventy paintings. I must say that
they do not have as much interest in individual psychology as I have, and of
course, I couldn't get along with the party here. . . . The people in Russia are
wonderful. They don't want war and they're very poor. We had a translator
who was one of the most ruined creatures I ever met in my life. All she
wanted was money. She tried to shake everybody down. Don't put this in the
paper, though, because I would never criticize the Communist Party, although I don't think there's any haven of the soul today."

Neel had told Jonathan Brand that she planned to send work that was
"not just class-conscious . . . I'll send my regular paintings." In fact, the
paintings on exhibit ranged from her portraits of CPUSA leaders and
members (*Gus Hall, Art Shields, Bill McKie, The Death of Mother
Bloor*) to paintings of art-world personalities (*Frank O'Hara, Duane Hanson, Red Grooms and Mimi Gross*) to paintings of family members, with a
few Depression-era works thrown in (*Synthesis of New York: The Great
Depression* and *Ninth Avenue El*). Interestingly, the paintings came with
a capitalist price list: *Gus Hall* and *The Death of Mother Bloor,* for instance, were marked at $25,000 each. (Gus Hall had objected vociferously
to having his portraits shown, because he felt it was "immodest and im-
proper," unless you were head of state. Neel was furious when it had to be
taken out of the show.)

Bonosky himself wrote the catalog essay, insistently evoking Neel's left-
ist, pro-Soviet politics and, of course, her long-term ties to the Communist
Party, and, whenever possible, framing her work as a painted critique of
American culture:

> . . . she depicts every subject in a style that no "society" artist
> would ever dare use. . . . if people's faces can express an epoch,
> then Alice Neel's portraits in that sense have a rare eloquence. In
> them appears an America which no other painter (either male or
> female) has seen with such an intent prophetic look of almost piti-
> less objectivity. . . .
>
> Her paintings are personal impressions of men and women in
> the America of yesterday and today. Her art reveals to us in the
> individual what usually is not seen. And although that sometimes
> maybe be shocking, it certainly does not stray from the truth of
> life. . . .
>
> The 1930's depression aroused her (and all of her generation)

to life, struggle, and art. At that time she became a member of the Communist party. In the period when the American economy collapsed, and millions of workers found themselves without work, the situation for the artist was truly critical. . . . American capitalism plainly and directly announced to them: You're useless. . . . 'Go left' Mike Gold exhorted the artists in the pages of the *New Masses*. And they were going left in the thousands.

Bonosky went on to describe Neel's WPA years, and subsequent obscurity in the wake of the dissolution of the WPA and the rise of McCarthyism:

Her paintings of this period portray scenes of protest, mass demonstrations, against Hitlerism and starvation and in support of Spain. . . . Alice Neel had a difficult time of it after the war, before she received recognition. Around that time the main positions in art had been taken over rather aggressively by abstract and other non-figurative forms. And to the degree that their emergence in time coincided with the politics of McCarthyism in the 50's, they were also politically sanctioned. Almost all the so-called figurative painters of that time in America had come from the left. They were realists—they tried to portray the world as it is.

Only the left listened to her. As for the attitude of the bourgeoisie, which now makes such a fuss about her name, well at that time Alice Neel simply had ceased to exist. It would be hard to imagine greater neglect and scorn . . . Frankly speaking, Alice Neel was saved from this death in life by the unexpected flowering of the counter culture in the 60's . . .

She was discovered by the new left, hippies and participants in the movement for women's liberation and by the official press, which as it accepted Alice Neel, distorted the meaning of the creative work of this protesting artist of the 30s and 40s who was concerned about the fate of the world. . . . Her constant support of Socialism, her friendship with the Soviet Union, her inseparability from the activites of the Communists in the USA, can all that really have been simply in order to provoke someone's indignation? What about her participation in the struggle for peace. . . .

All her life she has dreamed of showing her works in the Soviet
Union. Of one thing she is certain. Here she can speak openly,
forthrightly. Alice Neel knows that here she is among friends.

Nonetheless, Ginny recalls that when the Neel caravan left to return to the
United States, they found that film in Hartley's camera had been "jammed,"
and that some things were missing from their luggage. Says Hartley, "More
than once my camera disappeared and came back mysteriously filmless. We
were watched every minute. Our interpreter never took her eyes off us."
The Neels were also trailed on the train to Leningrad by someone they
thought was a KGB agent.

But for Neel, in her early eighties, the show seemed to represent a once-
in-a-lifetime opportunity to exhibit her work in the place she believed was
most closely aligned with her long-held politics. Organizing and attending
the show at all was an audacious move on her part, given that official détente with the United States had completely ended with the Soviet invasion
of Afghanistan in December 1979. Moreover, the Reagan years were characterized by a hard anti-Soviet line and a range of American policies against
the Soviet Union, from an embargo against grain shipments (this was lifted
in April, 1981, just a few months before Neel arrived), to the United States
withdrawing from the 1980 Summer Olympics, the eventual abandonment of the SALT treaty, boycotting the sale of technology, and the elimi-
nation any cultural exchange. But while it may have been historical, the
moment for Neel's show had passed. The reality of the Soviet Union in
1981, under the rule of Brezhnev, was neither the enemy-empire depicted
in the press and by the U.S. government during the first Reagan administration, nor anything like a successful socialist society. And the 1980s Soviet audience must have been somewhat mystified by Neel's subject matter
and style.

Neel was clearly dismayed by the level of suffering, poverty, and corrup-
tion she witnessed in this pre-perestroika state. According to Ginny, she
and the whole family were surprised to see that "it was a Third World
country in many ways." But if Neel was disappointed in finally seeing the
Soviet bureaucracy at work, she didn't say so for the record. Instead, she
stated to a reporter for the *Daily World*, "The Soviet Union wants peace
and friendship and Brezhnev has offered any number of times to talk to this
country. . . . This country is now warlike and a threat to the world. Reagan
says the government doesn't owe anybody anything. In the Soviet Union

you get free medical care—everything is free. There the government owes you everything."

As for the Soviet Union's response to Neel, despite the fact that the show was a crowd pleaser—after all, Neel was the *first* living American artist to have been given a show of this stature—it is not at all clear who the real audience for Neel's work, at this point in Soviet history, might have been. As Pamela Allara observed, during this "period of late Communism," neither old-fashioned American Social Realism nor its party-line Soviet analogue, official "socialist realism," was exactly au courant.

In the post–Cold War world, both, in fact, were more or less completely obsolete. The Soviet public had been exposed since the 1970s, for instance, to the sophisticated SOTS artists, who made postmodern use of Soviet propaganda, appropriating heretofore sacrosanct images of Stalin, Lenin, and Brezhnev in order to deconstruct and parody them. Just the year after Neel's show, the famous SOTS artists Komar & Melamid would overtly criticize Stalin with a cynical image entitled *Stalin in Front of a Mirror*. Neel's sincere posterlike images of Pat Whalen and Bill McKie must have seemed irrelevant, if not downright anachronistic.

As for her day-to-day experience there, Neel, unfortunately, didn't get much of a chance to interact with the Soviet artists, most of whom were away because it was summer. And Ginny recalls that the family ran into red tape almost immediately, because Neel had gotten off the plane and was put onto a stretcher, rather than a wheelchair as had been requested. The interpreter who had been hired to assist the family was not on the scene to explain the situation, and a tangle ensued over whether she was going to the hotel or a hospital. Then Andrew got chicken pox, and the Russians at first feared it might be smallpox.

The Neels stayed at the Metropol Hotel in Moscow for seven days. Then they spent three days in Leningrad, where they stayed in the Astoria Hotel. The high point there was a private in-house tour of the Hermitage. Ginny recalls some of the family visiting Red Square and seeing Lenin. (Neel had done that back in 1969 with John, and was too busy with the show to do it again.) Says Ginny, "To have a show in a place she had admired for so many years was an important thing for her. But I think she was disappointed to see that not everything was rosy and that a 'utopian' society is not necessarily more liberal." "She was glad to be there," says Hartley, "but she came away disillusioned."

Neel disguised her disappointment in the current-day Soviet Union by focusing on Russia's illustrious cultural tradition. "Russia has a great past," Richard recalls Alice saying. Still, when she was asked by Soviet television if she could be called a member of Communist Party, she said yes.

On October 29, Neel returned to the Harold Reed Gallery for the official unveiling of the portrait she had painted of Mayor Koch. "You should give me a public kiss," Neel commanded Koch, kissing him smack on the lips as flashbulbs popped. "Two beauties!" she exclaimed.

Although Koch said Neel had suggested that he pose nude, the mayor sat for her in his shirtsleeves. According to *The New York Times*:

> Last spring, Mayor Koch was going around telling people he had "fallen in love" with a self-portrait of Alice Neel, the 82-year-old [*sic*] painter who got around to acting as her own model only last October. . . . Commenting on the painting, Mr. Koch said, "I wanted an informal portrait, but I'm not as beautiful as dear Alice. In some parts of town, removing my jacket is considered controversial. Alice has tastefully captured my shirtsleeves. This is where I've worn my heart since the first day I saw her self-portrait."

Reed later priced the portrait at fifty thousand dollars. Neel told *ARTnews* that "the quizzical expression shows a kinder side that many people don't see. But his eyes always twinkle. I think it's because he just loves being mayor." Says Koch of the portrait, "It was her style. And certainly not a style that any post office has. So it's not one of those paintings that you look at and you say, 'Gee, doesn't he look handsome.' It was an honor to be painted by her."

The National Academy of Sciences mounted Neel's first solo show in Washington, D.C., in early November. Twenty-two paintings were on view, a mixed assortment of work that included *Loneliness, Linus Pauling, Hydrangeas, Red Grooms and Mimi Gross,* and *Duane Hanson. The Washington Post* said, strangely, "To stand in a gallery filled with portraits by Alice Neel is an unsettling, if rewarding, experience. The effect is somewhat akin to the queasiness a person might feel during a ghostly appearance at his own funeral." The show ran through January 28, 1982. Perhaps the reviewer was projecting: None of the pieces, except perhaps the poignant *Loneliness,* showed any indication of Neel's sometimes morbid sensibility.

On Februrary 1, 1982, Neel's portrait of Franklin Delano Roosevelt, celebrating the centennial of his birth, appeared on the cover of *Time* magazine, with the headline THE NEW DEAL: FDR'S DISPUTED LEGACY. (Inside the issue, Neel, who is quoted in "A Letter From the Publisher," praised both the president, "A compassionate man," and the project, which she called "A great creative venture. The WPA kept me and a lot of other artists from starving.") It was her second, and last, *Time* magazine cover.

*   *   *

Neel's eighty-second birthday party, held on March 29, was a bona fide event. For one thing, it took place at Gracie Mansion, where a group of Neel's portraits, including the recently completed portrait of Mayor Edward Koch and her own nude self-portrait, were formally on display.

A letter from Koch had gone out in February:

> *On January 27 [sic], Alice Neel celebrated her 82nd birthday. On January 30th [sic] her portrait of FDR appeared on the cover of Time magazine, and throughout February her WPA murals are on exhibit at the Hirshorn Musuem and Sculpture Garden in Washington. On February 15, she will be honored at the Phila-delphia Academy of Fine Arts.*
>
> *With so many accolades around the country, there is barely time for the City of New York to pay her a just tribute. Our city and its citizens, many of whom have borne their bodies and souls upon her canvases, will celebrate her birthday on March 1st [sic]. It would be wonderful if you would join me that eve-ning at 7:30 pm at a dinner in her honor at Gracie Mansion. As no time spent with Alice would be complete without her portraits present, there will be a display of some of her favorite works at the mansion that night.*

The Neel entourage arrived early. Neel, resplendent in a sequined gold-toned jacket, greeted guests as they appeared, including Andy Warhol. Bending to give Neel a kiss, he said, "Can I take your picture?" (Warhol, omnivorous collector of ephemera, actually saved the menu from the dinner. [The entrée was fillet of sole Florentine, with carrots and potatoes.] Signed by Neel, Koch, and Duane Hanson, it is now in the collection of the Andy Warhol Museum in Pittsburgh.)

The guest list included many of Neel's famous subjects, among them: Raphael Soyer, and his wife, Rebecca, David Soyer, and his wife, Janet, Henry Geldzahler, Virgil Thomson, Ann Sutherland Harris, Stewart Mott and his wife, Kappy, John Perreault, Michel Auder (of course taping), Red Grooms, and Warhol, camera at the ready. As always, the juxtaposition of people with their portraits emphasized Neel's uncanny ability for identifying their most defining gesture. Besides members of Neel's immediate family, there were paintings of Geldzahler, Thomson, Mott, Soyer, Florio, Freudenheim, and Grooms, propped around the mansion on easels.

Recalled David Soyer, the cellist with the Guanari String Quartet, which played a musical interlude, "Ed Koch was fond of her. All the people she had painted were there at Gracie Mansion. It was very nice."

The hundred or so guests were seated at nine tables. Alice sat at the table of honor with the Honorable Edward I. Koch, Richard and Nancy Neel, and the Freudenheims. Ginny and Hartley were seated at the next table, along with the Whitney Museum's then director, Thomas Armstrong, and his wife, Bunty. There was only one guest, however, whose presence attracted almost as much attention as that of Neel herself.

Porn star and performance artist Annie Sprinkle, whose portrait Neel had just finished—in fact, it was still up on her easel in her apartment on 107th Street—had come as Dennis Florio's date. According to Ginny, when Alice sent Koch's office her guest list, the question of whether Annie Sprinkle would be an appropriate guest at Gracie Mansion came up. At the time, Koch was concentrating on cleaning up Times Square. Neel protested, saying, "If I invite someone to a party, don't tell me whom they can bring. Florio asked Annie Sprinkle—and I am not going to change that."

Recalls Tom Freudenheim, "I was invited to that famous dinner at Gracie Mansion, and Annie Sprinkle was there. There were police surrounding the place to prevent anyone photographing a stripper going into Gracie Mansion."

(However, Mary Tierney, who worked at City Hall at that time and had helped arrange the party, says that the mayor's office never objected to Sprinkle's presence, and that Gracie Mansion is always guarded by police.)

In any case, Sprinkle showed up fully clothed, wearing a leather miniskirt and tasteful white blouse, rather than the topless bottomless leather corset (which clearly revealed her pierced labia), garters, stockings, and high heels she sported in Neel's portrait. Even Andrew Neel, then about four years old, expressed relief. "I'm glad she didn't wear her other outfit," he told his mother.

Sprinkle later described sitting for her portrait to *New York* magazine: "I found the experience very erotic. I thought she was a very sexy, powerful woman. She was passionate about every little thing. She would almost have an orgasm over my high heels. I brought lots of costumes. I had just gotten my labia pierced, and she really liked that."

Sprinkle had met Neel through Dennis Florio, who used to share pornographic material he got from Sprinkle with Neel, who got a kick out of it. After a few months, Alice asked if she could paint Sprinkle, who brought over an entire selection of outfits. Neel picked the "fetish" look. "We talked about sex the whole time. Her painting me was like doing me with her brushes," Sprinkle told former Philadelphia Museum curator Ann Temkin, who interviewed her in the 1990s for a show the museum mounted in 2000.

Tierney, who became friends with Neel during the period when Koch's portrait was being painted (she used to accompany the mayor when he posed at Neel's apartment) recalls, "Alice was extremely energetic. She had such spirit. She would call me up sometimes, and say, 'Oh Mary, guess what? I'm alive!' One time, I was visiting her, and she said, 'I think I must be losing it. I don't even have any sexual desires whatsoever left.'"

*   *   *

That May, Neel made a major career move. John Cheim, the director of the Robert Miller Gallery, had been actively pursuing her for several years. In fact, he had made the arrangements for a show of her nonfigurative work to be exhibited at the Miller Gallery while she was still officially at Graham. He had also commissioned three portraits: of himself, Betsy Miller, and Bob Miller, all completed in 1979.

Meanwhile Michel Auder had personally introduced Neel to Bob and Betsy Miller, who, thanks in part to Cheim's interest, wanted to meet her. A luncheon was arranged at the Algonquin Hotel. Finally, Cheim's persistence and Auder's attentions paid off: Neel signed up with the gallery in May 1982. Neel would be represented by the Robert Miller Gallery for about two and a half years during her lifetime. Over the next sixteen years, the gallery would mount a number of important shows. It also financed the 1983 Patricia Hills book, for which John Cheim acted as design consultant. For most of that time, Robert Miller, the gallery's founder and owner, promoted and sold the work (his wife Betsy took over in later years), while John Cheim, its director, conceived of and curated all the shows.

Recalls Cheim, "The first show we had was Alice's nonfigurative works. I was trying to come up with something to show people about Alice Neel that was unexpected, and of course everyone thought Alice Neel was a figure painter. But in going through all her work, I realized that she'd done a lot of beautiful still lifes, landscapes, interiors and urbans scapes, going back to the thirties and forties, like *Ninth Avenue El*, so I put together a show about that subject, and it got quite a bit of attention because it was a surprise. I think it opened up people's eyes to a different aspect of her work. So this was the sort of show I did to prove we were capable of reframing her work for a newer audience, a younger audience. The Graham Gallery showed nineteenth-century American Realism. Some of the works were *Loneliness*, *Philodendron*, and a seascape from the forties, very kind of Munch-y [*Cutglass Sea*, 1947]."

Cheim's inventive gambit was an immediate success. Neel's debut show at the Robert Miller Gallery—and her only solo show that year—garnered mostly rave reviews from everyone, from John Russell in *The New York Times* to Roberta Smith in *The Village Voice*.

Russell's review appeared in a roundup in which Neel was the lead (Jasper Johns came next). Wrote Russell:

> Alice Neel, now in her 80's is best known for portraits that go far beyond the traditional exchange of courtesies between artist and sitter. To be painted by Miss Neel is not simply the equivalent of a body search. It is the equivalent of a body-and-soul search. . . . "What have you done with yourself and with your life?" is the question Miss Neel asks of her sitters, and rare is the man or woman who comes up with a triumphant answer. . . .
>
> So it is an unfamiliar Miss Neel that we see in this show. . . . In particular, we realize that she has kept a sharp eye on 20th century tradition, whether in this country or elsewhere. . . . We see her tackling the open-window theme that preoccupied Matisse throughout the greater part of his long career . . . quite apart from that, we see the metropolitan scene as it was manipulated by Edward Hopper, the glare of sunlight on a distant wall, the windows turned to melodrama by deep shadow, the sense of loss and loneliness for which just one empty chair can speak out loud and clear.

Calling her land- and seascapes, "visionary" and "transcendental," Russell went on to say, "It is given to few artists to dart so freely from one preoccupation to another and to give every one of them so strong a personality. Above all, Miss Neel brings to her many different subjects a vigor and clarity of expression that should be a model to her juniors. . . ."

In *ARTnews*, Deborah C. Phillips wrote:

This recent survey of Neel's non-portrait work from the past 30-odd years shows to great advantage her capacity for bringing real, expressive power to any subject she chooses. The anxious energy that makes her better-known portraits so memorable infects every one of these landscapes, interiors and still lifes. . . . Throughout these canvases, the restless contours, encroaching shadows, jarring colors and foreshortened perspectives instill even the most benign domestic objects with a sense of foreboding. Neel perceives an incipient danger in all of the daily matter of our lives. It is this quality of hypersensitivity and emotional projection that makes the artist's non-portrait works every bit as complex and psychologically compelling as her portraits.

Arts Magazine devoted an entire page to the show. "The world these paintings depict is the creation of a gifted and powerful expressionist," wrote Jon R. Friedman, going on to contrast Neel's version of the genre with the usual understanding of the term "expressionist" "obsessively subjective" work "in which everything is portrayed as seen through dark and distorted lenses":

. . . There is another mode of expressionism in which subjectivity functions in an altogether different way. Rather than a fist that strikes, the artist is the open palm, more exposed and hypersensitive to experience than are the rest of us . . . the effect when successful is one of heightened verisimilitude. We feel that some aspect of the experience has been revealed with shocking clarity, and more often than not we perceive this to have been accomplished with a noteworthy spareness and focus. Van Gogh manages such revelations as does Kokoschka in his early portraits, Munch in many of his pre-1900 works, and Neel in many of the paintings on view here. Her paintings are the real thing.

The exhibit, which ran from May 4 through June 5, showcased Neel's ability to condense a complex narrative into a single potent image. A painting like *Loneliness*, of an empty chair by a window (reminiscent of van Gogh's *Gauguin's Chair*) or *Thanksgiving*, of a raw, scrawny fowl in a kitchen sink, have all the poetic subtext of a short story by Henry James or Paul Bowles, both, in very different ways, masters of subtle foreboding.

Neel would have one more solo show at the Miller Gallery: "Alice Neel,"

which ran from January 31 to February 25, 1984, before her death later
that year. John Cheim's exacting eye and original take on Neel's work
would pay off in a number of well-received posthumous shows, first at the
Miller Gallery and later at the Cheim & Read gallery, founded with Howard Read in 1997. The Miller Gallery would continue to mount shows of
Neel's work through 2008, after which the Neel estate left the gallery. In
2009, the David Zwirner Gallery began representing the Neel estate.

Neel had eight group exhibits in 1982, mostly shows dealing with the figure, which, in these early days of Neo-Expressionism, was in the forefront
again, as was painting itself. Julian Schnabel, David Salle, and Jean-Michel
Basquiat were among the stars of a new generation of painters who had much
more in common with Neel's Realist-Expressionism than with the Minimal-
ism of the previous decade. (Neel was quite aware of the new movement:
"What do you think of Julian Schnabel?" Neel asked Frederick Ted Castle
when he interviewed her in 1983. "I think he's better than Kossoff.")

Neel had three paintings at the Tibor de Nagy Gallery—which special-
ized in the New York School—in a show called, appropriately enough, "The
Figure," from December 5, 1981, through January 7, 1982. She was in "Realism and Realities, the Other Side of American Painting, 1940–1960," at
Rutgers, from January 17 to March 26, 1982, which traveled to two other
venues.

The Whitney Museum of Art's Fairfield County branch in Stamford,
Connecticut, included Neel in its show "Five Artists and the Figure," from
April 9 through June 9. As the catalog text observed: "1982 seems to be
the year of the figure. After a long period during which figurative art was
disparagingly referred to as a holding tactic until something better came
along, the pendulum is now swinging in the opposite direction. This year
the 'new figuration' is an explosive gallery phenomenon and major institutions throughout the country are devoting exhibitions to the subject." Neel
was grouped with Alex Katz, Duane Hanson, Philip Pearlstein, and George
Segal, all "artists who kept the figurative tradition alive during the period
when it was out of favor."

Neel's self-portrait was in a show called "Homo Sapiens" at the Aldrich
Museum, in Ridgefield, Connecticut, from May 9 to September 5. "Did
you see my self-portrait in the Aldrich catalogue?" she asked Castle.
"Frightful, isn't it? I love it. At least it shows a certain revolt against everything decent."

Neel was also in two shows devoted to Roosevelt's centennial and the
Depression era: "Five Distinguished Alumni: The WPA Federal Art

Project," earlier in the year, at the Hirshhorn Museum and Sculpture Garden, in Washington, D.C., from January 21 to February 22, where she gave
a slide lecture, and a show at The Sierra Nevada Museum of Art in Reno,
"1931 America: the Artists' View," from September 10 to November 7. Finally, she was in "New Portraits, Behind Faces," from October 19, 1982
through February 6, 1983 at the Dayton Art Institute's Contemporary Art
Center in Ohio.

*   *   *

One of the more significant events of the year, from a biographical point
of view, even though Neel herself didn't learn about it until later, was a
tragedy that had been decades in the making. On August 20, 1982, Neel's
daughter Isabetta, whom she hadn't seen in over thirty years, killed herself. Her fourth attempt at suicide had finally succeeded. She was just short
of fifty-four years old at the time of her death.

Oddly, the Neel family learned of Isabetta's suicide from a New York
dentist who had a connection with the Lancellas in Miami. During a routine visit, the dentist, Dr. Victor Caronia, bluntly asked Richard if he had
a sister, and then informed him of her death. It was Richard who told Alice. Her only comment upon hearing the news was "I had a dream about
Isabetta last night."

Did Neel dream of Isabetta as a girl or as a woman? She had only seen
her once—or at most twice—as an adult, when she was about twenty, and
came to New York after her marriage. The fiercely naked little girl grew up
into a glamorous woman of the world. And although she never realized a
relationship with her mother, that nonrelationship would significantly shape
her life, just as an artwork's negative space is sometimes its defining mark.
Neel's portrait of her beautiful young daughter may have captured her striking features. But it didn't capture her vulnerability, something she apparently never outgrew.

Isabetta was only about one and a half years old when Carlos took her to
Havana, where he deposited her with his two sisters, Julia and Sylvia. Julia
and Sylvia were the youngest of six children born to Carlos Enríquez Costa
and Isabel Gómez Diez. They were a year apart in age, born in 1904 and
1905, respectively, although Sylvia would outlive Julia by fifteen years. An
older sister, Aldofina, was the mother of an only child, Adoris, Isabetta's
cousin, who grew up with her in Havana and would remain quite close to
her until her death. There was also a beloved brother, Antonio, who died
young of tetanus after stepping on a nail.

Julia, apparently a warm, maternal type, was known as "Mami," while

Sylvia, who was called "Tita," also had another nickname—"la Vibora" ("the Viper.") These two women would bring up not only Isabetta but, later, in the United States, help care for Isabetta's own two children, Pablo Jr., and Cristina. "We were raised like sisters," says her cousin Adoris Mendoza. "Isabetta looked like a little doll, with blond hair and blue eyes." Until Antonio's death, he also lived with them, and Isabetta called him "Pappy."

The aunts' idea of the proper upbringing of a little girl, consistent with the mores of Cuba in the mid-1900s, was much different from Alice's. "She was raised like a little bourgeois," says her childhood friend Marisa Diaz.

Isabetta was initially brought up in the beautiful house in the Vedado that Alice had lived in with Carlos during their early days in Havana. Her grandmother, Isabel Gómez Diez, with whom Isabetta was quite close, died in 1933. Four years later, her grandfather, Carlos Enríquez Costa, died. The two sisters and Antonio, who would die a year and a half later, moved with Isabetta to another house in the Vedado, which Carlos decorated with paintings and murals.

Recalls Adoris, "It was in the Vedado, on top of a little hill. When you came in, on the right-hand side, there was a painting Carlos did in the living room. On the left, in the dining room, there was another mural. Upstairs there were three bedrooms and a terrace. I remember it was not a pretentious house. It was a nice home. I remember the paintings, because they were in every room—everything was painted by Carlos. In the dining room, they had a mural he painted of the whole family on a picnic."

As previously noted, Carlos was away for most of the early part of Isabetta's childhood. Staunchly opposed to the dictatorship of Machado, he left Havana in August 1930, traveling to Italy, France, and Spain, encouraged by his friends, including Marcelo Pogolotti.

Enríquez returned to Cuba in January 1934, when Isabetta was five years old, but he never lived with his daughter. The show that opened shortly after he came home, was closed down due to its erotic content, reopening at the law offices of Emilio Roia de Leuchsenring. Throughout his career, much of Carlos's work would be noted for its explicit use of the female nude. Although their styles were quite different, both he and Neel continued to share a passionate mutual interest in the brazenly political and/or erotic. And both also loved to scandalize, and had racy nude paintings ousted from shows. His life and his work were often controversial—if not downright salacious—and no doubt the aunts were just as happy to bring Isabetta up on their own.

Isabetta, Mami, and Tita would visit Carlos on weekends, at El Hurón

Azul, the charming cottage and studio he had built in 1939 on the rural
outskirts of Havana with money inherited after his father died. Carlos invited his friends to join him there every Sunday, and throughout the mid-
1940s El Hurón Azul was a famous cultural salon. There was a lot of
drinking, and people would stay until the wee hours. Despite her bourgeois
upbringing, Isabetta was certainly exposed to the *vie bohème* through Carlos. "Hurón Azul was famous for its wild parties," says Marisa.

Although she admired her father, Isabetta grew up essentially without
parents. Carlos, who was, if anything, even more antibourgeois than Alice,
was leading a life parallel to Neel's in the United States. They both had
multiple partners (although Carlos had no more children). And when they
were each in their late thirties, they both geographically removed themselves from the center of their respective art worlds.

Says Adoris Mendoza, "Isabetta was not very close to Carlos because he
had all these women, so she didn't live with him. She would go out to his
cottage and stay for a day. Recalls America Villiers, an old family friend,
"Carlos had this energy. His eyes were like hot coals, embers. All the
women were in love with him. He was half angel, half devil."

Isabetta spent two summers on the New Jersey shore visiting Alice, as
previously mentioned, at her summer cottage when she was six, and then
again when she was eleven, never to return. However, she did go back to
her aunt's house in Teaneck when she was seventeen, spending the entire
third year of high school there. Her only other sightings of Alice were the
brief meeting in a New York hotel sometime around 1950, when she was
pregnant with her first child, Pablo; possibly the dinner in Teaneck that,
according to George Neel, Alice had ambushed, and ultimately her unfor-
tunate attempt to connect with Alice during her show and lecture in Fort
Lauderdale.

According to Villiers, "Isabetta said she wouldn't use the word *mother*.
She said, 'She didn't recognize me,' when she told me about Fort Lauderdale,
not 'My mother didn't recognize me.'" She never saw her mother again.
When Isabetta's own children were born, she never told them about Alice.

Says Marisa, "She never talked about her mother. Most of her problems
in life were due to her upbringing. Neither her mother nor her father was
responsible." According to both Adoris and Marisa, the primal sense of
being rejected by her parents was central to Isabetta's personality. "Every
time she was rejected by a man, she would break down. She couldn't take
rejection," says Marisa.

Isabetta treated Mami like her mother. But she was acutely aware of

Alice's absence. "She was probably not a very happy child," says Adoris. "Everybody had a mother and father, and she had no mother or father, even though they were alive. And she never talked about it." According to Adoris, "Isabetta never asked about her mother. She never asked because Alice never asked for her again after Carlos told her he was taking Isabetta. Even when she was visiting her Aunt Lily in Teaneck, she didn't see Alice." Says Isabetta's close friend Eileen Goudie, "Isabetta always asked herself that question. Why didn't her mother put her foot down when Carlos took her away? Because she loved Mami and she loved Tita, but it wasn't her mom."

It is unclear how much correspondence there was between Isabetta, or her aunts, and Alice. But at least early on, Isabetta and Alice were in touch by letter, as evidenced by two notes that the little girl sent her mother.

The first, dated February 2, 1940 (when Isabetta was about eleven years old) is written in a neat penmanship:

> *I am sorry you did not receive the other letter. I sended [sic] you. As I told you in my last letter, I think the cape is beautiful. And I love the color too. I am going to school and have very much to study that is why I am not writing very much and besides I cannot fill my pen because I can't find the ink. You can see in the writing that it needs a good feeling [sic].*
>
> *With much love, Isabetta.*
> *P.S. excuse my writing. Turn the page please.* [Isabetta has drawn what looks like a little squirrel on a tree branch near the P.S.]

On the other side, the letter reads:

> *Please send me all the stamps you can find from any country. I do not care from where. I am collecting stamps.*

It is signed "me," accompanied by a number of doodles—one quite advanced—of a girl in profile, with a thought balloon: *"By-By, Ain't she got hair—whistle do it. By By. I am going to open my ear when I am a little more brave. He ho. My tooth doesn't ache. Thanks Grandpa. Love to all, says Isabetta? Who is she? Anyway? Ah fun for me. Do not forget my stamps."*

Then there is this simple but sad Christmas card, dated December 21, 1941:

> *Dear Mother, why don't you ever write. I've written and written and never get an answer. I'm waiting to hear from you.*
>
> *With love, Isabetta*

Isabetta's daughter Cristina believes that it is possible that Alice wrote to Isabetta and that Tita hid the letters. Certainly Tita was in touch with Alice's sister, Lily, about Isabetta. And she seemed to write to Alice when she saw fit. Olivia Neel (Alice's oldest grandchild) says she saw other "mommy" letters from Isabetta stashed in Alice's apartment.

When she was seventeen, Isabetta was engaged to be married to Ulises Carbo Yaniz, the son of a wealthy family. His father was a newspaperman, his mother a socialite. Everything had been finalized, including the wedding dress. Then, just two weeks before the wedding, after the invitations had already been sent out, his mother apparently had second thoughts about Isabetta's pedigree (after all, both her parents were notorious Bohemians) and suddenly broke off her son's engagement. Ulises, "a mama's boy," according to Marisa, left the country. Isabetta, then eighteen, had to deal with this abandonment on her own. It was a devastating disappointment, from which Isabetta never quite recovered. "It left a very strong mark on her life," says Marisa.

Cristina says that she believes that Isabetta's first suicide attempt occurred shortly after she was jilted. Marisa says Adoris told her the same thing, but she never heard it firsthand.

A year later, still on the rebound, Isabetta married a somewhat older admirer, Pablo Lancella, in June 1948. (A wedding announcement was sent to Mrs. George W. Neel in Darby, Pennsylvania: "Carlos Enríquez, Pablo Lancella and Alicia Cruz de Lancella invite you to the wedding of Isabett y Pablo in Havana.")

Lancella, an upper-middle-class, well-bred man with degrees in both agricultural and chemical engineering, was working at the time for Hershey, the largest sugar company in Cuba. His father had worked for the Ford Motor Company before becoming a successful importer. Lancella's office was in the same building as the National City Bank, where, he says, Isabetta worked as bilingual secretary.

"I used to see her on the street, and I was attracted to her," Lancella recalls. He finally met her when he joined friends at a summer resort called Varadero. Unbeknownst to him, his friends had arranged a meeting with Isabetta. "So we hit it off. She was very young. I was twenty-seven, about seven years older than she was," says Lancella. He courted her at the house where she lived with Tita and Julia.

"They were very nice," recalls Lancella. "Tita was married for a very short spell. I don't even know that story. And Julia had a boyfriend on a cruise ship, or something like that, but she never married, and I never saw her dating anybody. And of course Carlos. Carlos was a character. He had that place on the outskirts of Havana. After we married, Carlos would come and visit with us, but not too often."

The young couple lived in Havana, eventually saving enough money to design and build their own house in "a very nice residential section. I was doing well," says Lancella says. "I was always doing well." They had two children, Pablo Jr., born in 1951, and Cristina, born in 1954.

Like so many others, the family left Cuba when Castro took over, moving to the United States in 1960. Lancella got a job with Procter & Gamble in Cincinnati. Recalls Cristina, "We lived in a small apartment in Cincinnati. Sylvia and Julia lived with us, and my brother and I and Sylvia and Julia were in the one room. And my mom and dad lived in another. It was very crowded." According to Cristina, "Julia raised me. She and Sylvia took care of the house, cleaned and cooked."

Pablo and Isabetta were married for ten years before separating. Isabetta, it seemed, had been having an affair with a lover who lived in Havana. When Pablo found out about the affair, which had been going on for some time, he left, relocating to New Orleans. They didn't get legally divorced. Pablo and Cristina remained with their mother.

Says Lancella, "We separated in 1961. She came to live in Miami and I went to New Orleans. She had a job in Cincinnati, but they had moved the offices here [Miami], so she moved with them. We were on friendly terms. I always sent her money, and every time she was ill or something like that, because she was ill a couple of times seriously, I'd come over. I always took a full month's vacation in August and I would come and stay with them. I would stay in the guest room, but I was with them in the house. And on Christmas it was the same thing. It was a very friendly separation."

Isabetta began working, first as an executive secretary to "an international investor, Frank (Franco) Torresi," according to Cristina. After that, she briefly worked as a secretary for Maurice Ferre, Miami's mayor in the early 1970s, and finally became a real estate broker for a company called Lago Realty, that she started with a friend and colleague, Eileen Goudie, whom she had met at Arco Realty. The company name, LAGO, was an acronym of their two last names, Lancella and Goudie. Recalls Goudie, "I thought she was a beautiful lady and very witty."

"My mother was a party person. She liked to spend money on good clothes, good food, good travel, expensive hotels. She went first class," says Cristina. Isabetta was also a heavy drinker. Still, she was a good mother—when she was at home. Her job required extensive traveling, which she enjoyed. "She was away a lot," says Marisa. "She wanted to live a bourgeois life, but at the same time she had a wild streak that was something unbelievable."

Stylish and sophisticated, Isabetta never lacked for male companions, and for many years was involved with a lawyer named Frank Cosio, whose nickname was "Cuco," and who became quite close to her family. "My mom went out with Cuco for twelve years," says Cristina. "He wanted to get married, but he was never good enough for her. She was a very beautiful, very bright woman, and she wanted somebody who was rich and powerful."

After she and Cosio broke up, she had ongoing relationships with several married men, with whom she remained on a friendly basis even after the romance was over. Later, she had a serious relationship with another married man, one that she believed might lead to marriage, but he died suddenly of a heart attack. "At the time of her death, she was seeing a married man from Ecuador. She was in love with love. She needed that attention," says Goudie. "She used to say in her past life she must have been a courtesan."

Beneath Isabetta's seductive exterior lurked a dark undertow. Her first suicide attempt after marrying Pablo, which occurred when the family was still living in Cuba, was when she was only about twenty-eight years old. Says Pablo Lancella, "When I was working at Hershey, they called me and told me she was in the hospital—she had taken sleeping pills."

"She had a split personality," says Marisa. "One part of her, she was an excellent housewife and mother and wife, and the other part of her, she wanted to live life to its maximum. Her life was like a soap opera; she was always traveling, always having affairs and things like that. She wanted to have security, but she also wanted to have excitement. She was so beauti-

ful, very few men didn't fall for her charms, and she used that a lot to get
whatever she wanted in life. She knew that part of her life was going to end
because of age, and I think it made her very uncomfortable to know she
was going to lose that power."

In her forties, Isabetta had also had some very serious medical problems, including complications from a severe case of chicken pox, which
caused her to become paralyzed. "She fought like a tiger," says Goudie.
She was just about to be put on a respirator when the paralysis stopped. Afterward, she was incontinent, and during her long recuperation was forced
to carry a portable bag, which, according to Goudie, didn't interfere with
her nights on the town. But Pablo says the incontinence, even when she
stopped using the bag, depressed her. She was very vain, and the idea of aging deeply distressed her. Before she was fifty, she had already had plastic
surgery, Pablo says. "I even hate the number forty-eight," she told her friend
Marisa when she turned forty-eight.

During the 1970s, Isabetta suffered a nervous breakdown after a visit to
Cuba. She had gone there to retrieve some of Carlos's paintings and to help
a political prisoner being released through the Colombian embassy. (The
second part of her mission failed.) She was completely traumatized by seeing her radically changed homeland, and the vandalism that had destroyed
her home. Isabetta left Cuba early and returned to the United States.

"She told me when she came back from Cuba it was the first time in her
life she understood what it meant to be mentally ill and what the mind
could do to you. She said when she saw the house, when she saw the streets
she was so familiar with, she almost couldn't breathe, because of the pain
of seeing all that," says Marisa.

Isabetta's next suicide attempt occurred in Miami, during the time she
was seeing Cuco. When she didn't answer the phone, he broke into her
house and found her unconscious. "Cuco found her one time," says Cristina. "And he broke the window to get in. He was calling and calling, and
he knew that she was home and she wasn't answering. He broke the window
through the back and he found her all passed out." She was found before
the fatal dose of sleeping pills had done their work, and recovered after a
short stay in the hospital.

When it came to her last suicide attempt, Isabetta had learned from her
past mistakes. This time, she made certain she would not be found in time.
The beautiful fifty-three-year-old woman took sleeping pills, then walked
down to the bay and lay quietly down on the seawall. The tide took her out

and she drowned. Her body was found a day later. Her son and Cuco had to
identify her. Isabetta would have appreciated that, based on her appearance, the newspapers had reported her age as thirty-five.

In the days before her death, Isabetta had told Marisa that her current
relationship wasn't going well. " 'This is my last chance, because I am getting old,' she said. She dreaded to get old; she hated to get old. She didn't
want to be old at all. She'd always been so attractive, so charismatic, so
beautiful, and part of what she had achieved in life was because of how she
looked. And I think she realized the man she was seeing wasn't going to
leave his wife. Everything accumulated," says Marisa.

The night of her death, Isabetta, true to form, had been out celebrating
with her Ecuadorian married friend at the Four Ambassadors Hotel. She
made multiple calls—to Cristina, Adoris, and Eileen, asking each of them
to join her. She was clearly quite tipsy. Nobody was available, and they all
declined.

Recalls Goudie, "It was a Friday night and she had a very important
closing with Daniel, a former lover and business associate, and this Ecuadorian client of hers she was having a relationship with. She called me at
around ten-thirty to ask me to go to the Four Ambassadors to celebrate. I
told her I didn't have a baby-sitter. I felt so guilty afterward, because I wish
I had gone."

Goudie says that later "the Ecuadorian told me she had gotten drunk
and he had driven her to her car and left her there. Then all night long he
kept calling the house and leaving messages. But I know he was at Isabetta's house, because he had a private line there. I don't know if they had a
fight, but I think he went home with her." Goudie doesn't believe that Isabetta
killed herself, but thinks she could have been the victim of an accident or
foul play. "I find everything about it very fishy," she says.

Although Isabetta did have a fight that night with her companion, according to Adoris (who also mentioned it to Marisa), there seems to be no
doubt that her death was a suicide. Besides the fact that she had taken sleeping pills, there was the tear-stained note she left for her family, telling them
that she loved them, how she wanted her property disposed of, that she
wanted to be cremated, and where her ashes should be scattered. (Goudie
believes the note could have been written long before, in case something
happened to her.) "I believe it was destiny and it was her day. But I never
saw the note."

But Marisa, says, "I read the note. It was very clear that she was going to
terminate her life."

Isabetta's fate was influenced by a number of powerful forces, from her fear of aging, to her failure to find a permanent life partner, to the early void created by the absence of her parents. It is also possible that, like Alice, she was born "hypersensitive." Perhaps she had genetically inherited Neel's early tendency toward self-destruction. Both mother and daughter suffered at least one nervous breakdown and attempted suicide several times. (In fact, Alice's major breakdown was caused by losing her family—first Santillana, then Carlos and Isabetta.) But Alice's will to survive was paramount, and she channeled her demons, including the terrible loss of Isabetta, directly into her work. Isabetta had less to fall back on.

"Whenever she had a love rejection, it would trigger something in her that could result in a suicide attempt," says Marisa. "Because she was very sick for quite some time, and she didn't try anything. And she had problems with her children, and she didn't try anything. Whenever she tried to commit suicide or something like that, it was because she had some sort of love rejection. If you think it over, it starts with the rejection of her father and mother."

According to her wishes, Isabetta's ashes were scattered in Biscayne Bay, with Frank Sinatra playing in the background. Says Cristina, "She used to say, 'When I die, I want everybody to have this big party. I want there to be French champagne, I want Frank Sinatra on the stereo, and I want everybody to have a good time. And Luis Felipe [a friend], you are going to distribute my ashes over Biscayne Bay.'" (She had reiterated this in her note.)

After their mother's death, Pablo Jr. and Cristina were told for the first time about Alice's existence—Cristina by their father, and Pablo by Tita. After seeing Alice on television, Tita had written to her in June 1983, saying that during Isabetta's lifetime, she had respected her wishes, but now she was finally telling them about their maternal grandmother. In September, Tita sent Alice a picture of Isabetta, Pablo, and both children taken at Pablo Jr.'s wedding. In return, Neel sent her a copy of the Patricia Hills book *Alice Neel*.

That October, Pablo Jr. went to New York with his wife, Roxy, to visit Alice. They spent the weekend with her, Richard, and Nancy in Spring Lake. Alice called him "her vest-pocket Cuban," said she wanted to paint him, and, when they were at the beach, observed that he had powerful thighs.

Cristina never met Alice. "I told my father I didn't want to go to New York, because if she had not bothered to ever look for me, why should I bother. I said, 'Daddy, I've never kissed her on the cheek. Why would she care about me?' So the pain carried over from one generation to the other."

*   *   *

In the last two decades of her life, Neel went from being virtually ostracized to being ardently sought after. Her popularity—as a painter and a personality—would transcend her death. Posthumously, Neel would continue to achieve the level of success she had earned so late in life.

In early 1983, Neel received another honor. She participated in the National Academy of Design's 158th annual exhibition and was awarded the Benjamin Altman Figure Prize of three thousand dollars for her portrait *Benny and Mary Ellen Andrews*. The prize was presented at the Academy's exhibition preview on March 17.

In March, Neel was featured in a show at Bucknell University which ran until April 17, "Faces Since the 50s: A Generation of American Portraiture." The brochure singled out her dedication to the genre: "Of the many artists brought together in this exhibition, Alice Neel is perhaps the only one who has devoted the larger portion of her career to making portraits, the sole purpose of which is to reveal the sitter's character."

That spring, Neel had her very first show in Los Angeles, at Loyola Marymount University. A striking selection of thirty-five paintings, it focussed on work of the past two decades, right up to *Georgie and Annemarie*, 1982, Neel's quirky but affectionate rendering of her nephew and his much older wife. Of her early works, only *Snow on Cornelia Street*, 1933, was shown, and just two paintings from the 1950s, *Last Sickness* and *David Rosenberg*. Ann Sutherland Harris wrote the lucid catalog essay. The show opened on March 29 and ran through May 7.

The eighty-three-year-old Neel wowed Los Angeles, getting the kind of treatment that Tinseltown usually reserved for starlets du jour—or at least the latest young art-world superstars. According to the July/August issue of *Images & Issues*, her mobbed show and sold-out lecture drew as much "attention as Julian Schnabel the year before." She got a standing ovation from the crowd, who "hung on every word" of her March 30 lecture, and then went on to do a "marathon of other public appearances." She also met Johnny Carson's "alter ego," Shirley Wood, who called Neel a "pistol" and would later help get her booked onto the show. Said Neel in response, "I'm not a pistol, I'm a cannon."

The L.A. press gave both the artist and her art star placement, with profiles and reviews in all the major papers. In the *Los Angeles Times* "Sunday Calendar," William Wilson said the show was:

. . . as much a coup in its way as the recent Edvard Munch exhibition. The connoisseur of pure vision is constantly startled at
the juice and variety Neel wrests from what are basically traditional portrait poses. Her painterly powers validate the product,
but they are not essentially aesthetic delights. Their structural
honesty is only a side effect of the search for emotive accuracy
and makes us realize how bloody sick we are of art that is all style.
Neel makes us suspect that the downfall of Modernism was its
progressive involvement in products that were all form and no
substance.

"I got up out of the grave to come here," Neel told journalist Sandy Nelson, who described her as "Ms. Dynamite," writing that in addition to her
X-ray vision, "she possessed the tact of a pack of six-year-olds. . . . I've
known her for all of thirty seconds and already we are intimate. I sense
that the next few days will be something like an extended trip to the gynecologist." (Indeed, within half an hour, Neel was asking the writer to send
her pictures of her husband, nude, so Neel could make a sculpture of him.)
Nelson goes on, more seriously, to say:

> Seeing the torrent of expressionism and figuration that floods
> galleries today and noting that these portraits stretch back to
> 1953, we cannot help but be impressed with Neel's tenacity and
> idiosyncratic brilliance. No, like Philip Guston's images, which
> also predate current individualism, Neel's natural expressionism
> is being seen for what it is; singularly hers, prophetic and brave.
> Approached from any point of view—psychological, emotional,
> intellectual, aesethetic—her pictures convey a solidity of purpose
> and meaning superior to much new expressionism that seeks emo-
> tional and pictorial power, but does not possess it. . . . One can
> compare her works directly to an opposite pole. David Salle's paint-
> ings, for example: Salle's pictures say nothing about their sub-
> jects, while Neel's say everything.

In a review entitled "Triumphant Images Highlight Exhibit," Christopher Knight of the *Los Angeles Herald Examiner* wrote:

> In her most compelling works, the world which Neel depicts is off
> balance and about to be upset: there is no such thing as terra firma.

And the people that populate her discordant, heaving world are squarely at its center, seemingly the focus of its torque.

There is such a confidence to the complex orchestration of these paintings, however, such straightforward, wide-open mastery at the heart of her convulsive worlds, that one cannot help but feel that this is what these paintings really are about—an eyeball-to-eyeball confrontation with whatever situation presents itself on the horizon. Neel's are paintings of intense moral honesty.

Neel's work, seen in the context of the early infatuation with Neo-Expressionism, had an unmistakable gravitas. Compared to the brash new breed of figurative painters, whose work ranged from the clever, cartoony canvases of Keith Haring and Kenny Scharf to the sheer excess of Schnabel, famous at the time for his broken-dish paintings, or the poetic polemics of Basquiat, Neel came across like an old master. Certainly her portraits revealed a level of technique and vision not found in David Salle's postmodern appropriations. Eric Fischl's beautifully rendered bedroom (and other) scenes—psychosexual dramas fraught with ambiguous tension—come closest to the spirit, if not the style, of Neel's work. Perhaps that was why, as Nelson wrote, "Many artists, I have noticed, are taking note of Neel's work with great respect and awe."

In the spring of 1983, Neel received $25,000 from the National Endowment for the Arts. Shortly afterward, Patricia Hills's book *Alice Neel* was published by Harry N. Abrams. The coffee table–size book is filled with Neel's commentary on her life and work, as well as more than one hundred full-color images of her paintings.

An exhibit of the first four decades of Neel's work was mounted at Bard College, Annandale-on-Hudson, New York, in July and ran through August 28. Neel gave a gallery talk at the opening on July 17. Sixty paintings were culled from Neel's crowded shelves. In her essay, the curator, Linda Weintraub, evokes Neel in her "narrow-strapped black nightgown and unlaced space shoes," ferreting out the works, with Nancy's help and Neel's lively nonstop commentary.

Neel gave another gallery talk September 1, in Provincetown, Massachusetts, where she had a show at the Provincetown Art Association and Museum. Mira Schor and Raphael Soyer (who would outlive Neel by three years) were among those who attended. Wrote Schor some twenty years later about the lecture, "It was a kick to hear her tell the stories I already knew. . . .

Nevertheless, her self-presentation made me slightly uneasy. I feared it encouraged a view of her that was consolidated by her very well-received February 21, 1984, appearance on the *Tonight Show with Johnny Carson* as a slightly scandalous but endearingly cute little old lady, a performance that obscured her skills as an artist and her depth as an intellectual. . . ."

But Neel wasn't trying to impress her audiences with her intellectual weight. Neel never felt she had to prove herself to anyone. If the popular—and populist—slide shows burnished her reputation and stoked her celebrity, all the better. A born storyteller—in her painting as well as in her lectures—Neel clearly loved both giving the performance and the audience adulation. "I give a slide lecture of fifty years of art. I enjoy it for this reason: it gets your art before the public. Now it's not in a practical way, it's true. But so what! I'll never learn to do that . . . I don't worry whether it's legitimate or not. I make it legitimate. I gave a lecture at the Metropolitan even. I don't think anyone else ever gave a slide lecture there."

At the end of that month, Neel had a second solo show at the C. Grimaldis Gallery in Baltimore, this time a retrospective of the first five decades of her work, from such obscure paintings as the 1932 *Martin Jay* and the 1944 *Dorothy Koppelman* to the notorious 1933 *Joe Gould*, and Neel's somber 1955 *Death of Mother Bloor*. A stark head shot of Neel, her face behind an old-fashioned net veil, was on the cover of the brochure. Neel, of course, gave a slide lecture. If Grace Hartigan showed up this time, there is no record of it.

In her eighties, Neel gave no sign of going gentle into that good night. After all those years of Sturm and Drang, of economic and emotional instability, she had settled into what seemed like a comfortable niche. She may have lost her sex drive, but she certainly hadn't lost the drive to paint, which she would continue to do nearly to her dying day—her last painting is that of her attending physician: Dr. James Dineen.

Unlike many artists, most famously de Kooning, for instance, Neel's late work shows no diminution of her talent. Her 1983 painting of Hartley, with Andrew on his knee, has a commanding presence, and captures both her son and grandson with economical precision. The sunny wash just behind the duo is the only effort at a background, and yet the painting looks absolutely complete. Neel's second portrait of Meyer Schapiro, also done in 1983, thirty-six years after the first, which portrayed Schapiro as a passionate young art historian, shows the elderly intellectual against empty windowpanes, his face, although wizened, lively, with clear, still-seeking eyes. Although it has none of the morbidness of Neel's double portrait of the elderly Soyer brothers, done a full decade earlier, it is nonetheless reminiscent, with its clear intimations of mortality, of Neel's great portrait of her mother, *Last Sickness*.

CHAPTER TWENTY-SEVEN

Last Look

Q: Do you think about the end of life?
A: Oh yes, Death and I live here together. I wonder how I'll die. . . .

Q: What are you interested in now?
*A: I always used to tell them I'm an old-fashioned painter, still
lifes, country scenes and people. People have been my overriding
interest. I did a great one of Broadway with the shadow on the
building. That was Death, of course, creeping over here. Art takes
an awful lot of discipline. But I'm not supposed to work more than
two hours at a time with my cataracts and my heart. If you have
sufficient will you can do anything. . . . I often say that I'm serving
a sentence here.*

Q: What do you mean?
A: Well, life.
    —FREDERICK TED CASTLE INTERVIEW WITH ALICE NEEL,
    ARTFORUM, OCTOBER 1983.

Neel's eighty-fourth year began with her second solo show at the Robert
Miller Gallery. It included forty portraits and ran from January 31 through
February 25. Writing in *The New York Times*, Michael Brenson called the
paintings, which ranged from her 1935 portrait of Max White through the
80s, including her nude self-portrait, "expressive, tough, sympathetic and
funny."

Earlier that January, she was awarded the Gold Medal in Visual Arts at
the National Arts Club, where a dinner was held in her honor. Recalls the
club's president, Aldon James, "She admitted to not feeling well, but she
said it was a night she would always remember fondly. She said it was like a

vitamin shot. She was very happy that she was here in an institution that admitted women in 1898. And she loved getting the medal, in that it put her in the context of history."

On February 21, Neel had the ultimate celebrity experience: She made what would be the first of two smash appearances on *The Tonight Show with Johnny Carson.* All Neel's life, she had been anything but a crowd pleaser. Now, in her final year, she proved herself a master entertainer on network television. Dressed to the nines in a full-length gown and brandishing a silver-handled cane, Neel bantered flirtatiously with Carson. "You have a wonderful sense of humor," Carson told her. Repeating her green-room remark to Carson, that he "looked like a decadent Prince of Wales, quite amused"—she added, "And then he offered to marry me." The banter continued: "You were kidding me about my marriages," Carson said, "You've had a pretty good run yourself, haven't you?" "Well, yes I did, but I learned all I needed to know in one," Neel replied.

In her second appearance, on June 19, she asked Carson, "Oh, I wonder if you wouldn't like to pose nude." If not, she said, she would paint him in his red jacket, "You know why? because the audience wants to see more of you." She had the audience in her palm (and in stitches) with her deadpan descriptions of her work, from *Loneliness* to two of her lovers shown in quick succession: Kenneth Doolittle, "one of my boyfriends," who "slashed up about sixty paintings and burned about thirty . . . actually because this gentleman"—here a picture of John Rothschild was shown—"was sending me flowers," she said, greeted by loud audience laughter. She even managed to sneak the word "shat" past the censors.

If Neel had any inkling she was mortally ill, she didn't let it show. In early March, she went to Massachusetts General Hospital, where she was scheduled for a routine appointment to have her pacemaker checked. There she learned that she had advanced colon cancer, which had already spread to her liver. Hartley, who happened to walk into a lecture room just after his mother was examined, but before he had spoken to her doctors, saw Neel's slides up on the screen. Her prognosis wasn't good. She immediately underwent surgery, then stayed in Stowe for several months to recuperate.

She didn't return home to New York until late April. She would spend the last six months of her life dividing her time between Stowe, Spring Lake, and New York. But despite her ill health, Neel kept working, completing as many as eight new paintings. She had a solo show: A "small, rather uneven sampling of work," at the Makler gallery, in Philadelphia, through June 9, reviewed by her old friend Victoria Donohoe in the May

26 *Philadelphia Inquirer*, who called her "one of the great portraitists of our time. . . ."

In the early summer, she returned to Vermont, where she was interviewed by Judith Higgins for a cover story celebrating her life and work for the October issue of *ARTNews*. The interview was completed in New York and Spring Lake, where the photographs, including the cover picture, were taken. Neel gave one of her last slide lectures at Berkshire Community College in Pittsfield, Massachussetts, on June 15, where she also had a show, which ran from May 21 through June 17, during the "Focus on Women '84 Conference."

Just four days later, she flew out to Los Angeles for her second appearance with Johnny Carson. She seemed sharp as a whip, making Carson squirm when, in addition to trying to get him to pose in the nude, she asked him for the address of his New York City apartment. Like the audience, Carson was totally charmed by Neel, telling her she had an open invitation to return to the show.

Her last lecture was given in July, Ginny says at the Vermont Studio School, in Johnson, Vermont. Shortly afterward, she began chemotherapy, which greatly weakened her. It was clear that she was not going to recover. Neel spent the remainder of the summer in Spring Lake, surrounded by her family and attended by Dr. James Dineen, whom Hartley had brought in as her personal physician.

But even in what she knew to be her dying days, Neel couldn't part with her paintbrush: her very last portrait, completed just days before her death, was of her doctor. As she once said, "The thing that made me happiest in the world was to paint a good picture."

In mid-September, Neel returned to 107th Street, where she would remain, housebound, until her death. In early October, Robert Mapplethorpe, who was also represented by the Robert Miller Gallery, went up to her apartment to photograph her, at Neel's request. The tables had been turned: Neel was now another artist's subject. He captured her in a stark, regal black-and-white photograph, perched on a chair like one of her own models, wearing the simple black slip she favored at the time.

"She had the reputation for being hard as nails, but right before she died she somehow went to heaven, she was just this angelic creature. She closed her eyes through half the shooting. She knew she was giving me her death mask," Mapplethorpe later recalled. She told a writer it was "so I can see what I will look like when I'm dead."

"She was very, very sick then," says Hartley. "You can see from the photograph, she could hardly keep her eyes open. But one of the things Alice said about being sick was, 'I'm not scared of death. I just don't want to miss anything.' That was her attitude. Alice hated to miss anything. Nobody loved life more than Alice." She died several days later.

For the weeks leading up to Neel's death, the New York branch of the family kept vigil, and Hartley frequently flew down to the city. Richard, Nancy, and the children would have dinner with Neel, and Richard would spend the night there. On the morning of October 13, Richard went in to see his mother and found her dead. Alice had apparently died during the night.

The family gathered in her bedroom. Richard took some pictures of Alice on her deathbed. "I think that's what she would have wanted. She was always interested, after all she painted her father in his coffin," he says. In a sense it was at Neel's own request: she had said she wanted Duane Hanson (whose portrait she painted in 1972) to make a sculpture of her in her coffin, and she had voiced curiosity about how she would look in death.

When Dr. Dineen came later that day to make out the death certificate, he took his portrait with him.

Earlier that summer, when Neel was up in Vermont, she and Hartley had walked the property by the house in Stowe, and picked the place that is now registered as the family plot, with a bird's-eye view of her log studio. Although her parents, her brother Albert, and her infant daughter Santillana are all buried at Arlington Cemetery in Darby, Pennsylvania, Neel didn't want to be buried there. "She felt connected to us," says Ginny. "She wanted to be where all of us would be."

Neel's body was taken to Frank E. Campbell's funeral home before being flown up to Stowe, where the coffin remained in the studio for several days, as family members arrived to say good-bye. At one point, Neel's granddaughter, Elizabeth, asked if she could see her grandmother, and the coffin was briefly opened.

On an unusually warm day in October, the Neels held a simple ceremony. Dalton Putvain, who had worked on the Stowe farm for years, and his three brothers, served as pallbearers, carrying the coffin to the grave. At the last minute, Neel's granddaughter, Elizabeth, asked if she could walk her pony, Lisa, over to the grave site. The white pony stood like a ghostly sentinel as the family recited the Twenty-third Psalm, which begins, "The Lord is my shepherd; I shall not want."

Richard read "Paul's Letter to the Corinthians." Olivia read the Dylan Thomas poem, "And Death Shall Have No Dominion," which ends, "Though they be mad and dead as nails, Heads of the characters hammer through daisies; Break in the sun till the sun breaks down, And Death shall have no dominion." Then Richard and the girls sang William Byrd's lovely, "Non nobis Domine." Each of the ten Neel family members placed a single shovelful of dirt on the coffin.

There were no flowers, but that Thanksgiving, as always, Hartley, Ginny, Richard, Nancy, and Alice's six grandchildren celebrated the holiday in Stowe. It was their very first Thanksgiving without Alice, and the grandchildren commemorated her by planting daffodil bulbs on her grave, which now bloom every spring.

A few years after Neel's death, the family marked the grave, which has no tombstone, with a sculpture made by a local artist, Judith Brown. The piece, a graceful rearing horse called "St. Mawr," after D. H. Lawrence's 1925 novella, now serves as Neel's monument. By coincidence, the singular protagonists in *St. Mawr* and Alice Neel share several core qualities: The story is about a young girl, who visits from Havana en route to San Antonio, Texas, and her spirited stallion, St. Mawr, a wild and indomitably willful horse that stubbornly refuses to be tamed.

The pomp and circumstance of a major ceremony were reserved for Neel's official memorial, which took place at the Whitney Museum on February 7, 1985. Tom Armstrong, then the Whitney's director, introduced the speakers, who included Jack Baur, Edward Koch, Patricia Hills, and Raphael Soyer, who called Alice "Shakespearean." Allen Ginsberg read his poem "White Shroud," dedicated to his mother:

> *A shopping-bag lady lived in the side alley on a mattress, her*
> *wooden bed above the pavement, many blankets and sheets,*
> *Pots, pans, and plates beside her, fan, electric stove by the wall.*
> *She looked desolate, white-haired, but strong enough to cook*
> *and stare. . . .*
> *she'd weathered many snows stubborn alone in her motheaten*
> *rabbit-fur hat.*
> *. . . I'm a great woman, I came here by myself, I wanted to*
> *live . . .*

And David Soyer, along with members of the Guarnari String Quartet, played a piece by Beethoven.

Said Baur, "It seems to me extraordinary that Alice Neel is dead. She was such a vital being, even in old age, that she seemed to wear a cloak of immortality which shielded her against the normal process of aging. Some important threads in that cloak were her personal courage and her indomitable sense of humor. But of course, the real secret of Alice's immortality lay in her art."

*   *   *

Neel received obituaries in all the major newspapers and magazines, including several pages in *The Philadelphia Inquirer*. She would have loved the fact that almost all the notices, including the one in *Time* magazine, used the same key word to describe her life and art: *unconventional*.

"ALICE NEEL, UNCONVENTIONAL ARTIST, DIES AT 84," ran the October 15 headline for the *The Times* obituary, written by William G. Blair, who recalled the apt description of Neel as "the quintessential Bohemian," and wrote that her "unconventional and intense representational portraits . . . were neglected, even resented in official art world circles. . . ." *The Philadelphia Inquirer* said of her life and work: "Steadfast in the pursuit of her own vision and amused by her ability to shock both the art world and the arbiters of American taste, Miss Neel lived a singular life devoted utterly to painting and to the laughing, suffering world around her." In *ARTnews*, Judith Higgins, who had interviewed her just several months before her death, wrote, "She was unique, and she paid for her uniqueness with her sometimes tragic but finally triumphant life. 'I have always been what you could call a loner,' she once said. 'If I could have met myself, it would have been wonderful, but I never met such a person.'"

But typically, it is Neel herself who best articulates her own achievement: "I do not know if the truth that I have told will benefit the world in any way. I managed to do it at great cost to myself and perhaps to others. It is hard to go against the tide of one's time, milieu and position. But at least I tried to reflect innocently the twentieth century and my feelings and perceptions as a girl and a woman. . . .

"A good portrait of mine has even more than just the accurate features. It has some other thing. If I have any talent in relation to people, apart from planning the whole canvas, it is my identification with them. I get so identified when I paint them, when they go home I feel frightful. I have no self—I have gone into this other person. And by doing that, there's a kind of something I get that other artists don't get. . . . It is my way of overcoming the alienation. It is my ticket to reality."

Coda

In October 2009, there was a tiny but historical show at the reopening of El Museo del Barrio, located in Harlem, not far from where Neel had lived in the 1940s. It was the very first time the work of Neel and Enríquez had ever been shown together in America.

There was Alice's romantic rendition of Carlos, portrayed as the passionate Latin lover in Havana—the exciting entrée to the new life that had awakened so much in this extraordinary young woman from provincial Pennsylvania. And then there was Alice, depicted as a lovely pink nude perched on a bed. Next came the jagged splinters of their saga: a picture of the two of them with their first child, Santillana, before she died as an infant, and a picture of Julia, Carlos's sister, who raised their second daughter, Isabetta, in Cuba after she was basically abandoned by both parents; then two portraits of Isabetta herself—a wide-eyed, romantic image by Carlos of Isabetta at six, and the wild-eyed toddler clutching a stuffed animal, frightened, and frightening, done by Neel from memory four years earlier, just after Isabetta had been taken from her.

It might as well be a self-portrait: Those are Neel's crazed blue eyes staring out of Isabetta's childish face. The painful pentimento of this painting cuts straight to the heart. That systematic, grid-like slashing, mended during Alice's time, but still violently visible, of Kenneth Doolittle's angry knife rending the canvas, and several lives, asunder.

On the night the show opened, a flesh and blood image almost as powerful stood in front of Carlos's and Alice's dual portraits of Isabetta, as if willed into life by the vital energy of the paint itself. Cristina, Isabetta's only daughter, was meeting Hartley Neel, her uncle, for the very first time. The encounter was unplanned; both had lent work to the exhibition.

Hartley gave Cristina a kiss before Cristina clasped him in a hug. Blood relatives but total strangers, they chatted politely. The two-year-old Isabetta looked on, through the tragic blue eyes of the traumatized thirty-year-old woman who had just registered the unbearable loss of two great loves of her life. For a moment, Neel's painting tangibly bridged the gap between art and life.

Enduring Images: Neel's Artistic Legacy

When the gavel came down on the second lot at Sotheby's Contemporary Art Evening Sale on November 11, 2009, it marked a record sale for a Neel painting. The energetic bidding culminated in *Jackie Curtis and Ritta Redd*, an iconic work from 1970, being bought by the Cleveland Museum of Art for $165,500,000, three times its high estimate.

Said the auctioneer, Tobias Meyer, Sotheby's worldwide head of contemporary art, "It's an important piece and she's an important painter. She's a great artist who has been overlooked for years and is finally being recognized." Anthony Grant, international senior specialist of contemporary art, said simply: "The painting spoke for itself."

A quarter of a century after her death, Neel remains a larger-than-life figure. As a painter and a personality, she still generates a palpable buzz. Mention Alice Neel and ears instantly perk up. In art-world circles she is considered a grande, if often rude, dame, her work as sharp as her tongue. Although during her lifetime, Neel was a fashion victim—boldly out of sync with contemporary art movements, particularly Abstract Expressionism, Neel's work has always stubbornly transcended style.

"I tried to capture life as it went by—art records so much, the feeling, the beliefs, the changes," she wrote. "Art in many ways is similar to a religious experience. Something of which you are not completely aware speaks through you. 'Not my will but thine.' But one has to work all the time for this to happen. I have painted life itself right off the vine—not a copy of an old master with new figures inserted—because now is *now*."

In devoting her life's work to capturing what she called the "Zeitgeist," Neel made several lasting contributions to art history. She radicalized portraiture, virtually turning it inside out. She documented an age, the American twentieth century. She transformed the nude—both male and female—with her genre-bending depictions of both genders, whether male odalisques or pregnant females. And, long before the adjective even existed, Neel established herself as a multicultural painter. From her earliest work on, Neel's social conscience and political views merged seamlessly with her aesthetic vision.

At the time that Neel began painting portraits, the genre was so dead that Neel herself banned the term from her own vocabulary, preferring to call her work "pictures of people." Although Neel was fascinated by people's exterior appearance, it was their interior life that she sought to reflect. She did this by focusing on individual psychology as it manifested itself in body language and physiognomy.

"That is the microcosm. Everything can be there—the person, his position in life, how he feels, how he thinks, what life does to him, how he retaliates, the spirit of the times, everything," she stated. The exercise in exploring someone else's reality was also an escape from her own. As Neel remarked more than once, "Actually, it was a matter of identification. I would leave myself behind and enter the painting and the sitter, and afterward feel like an empty house with no self."

Like the WPA photographers, including Walker Evans, Neel was democratic in her portrayal of people—the rich, the poor, the underdogs, whites, blacks, Hispanics. She also produced some of the last century's—or any other's—most memorable portraits of children. Like the late photographer Helen Levitt, Neel found children a valid and fascinating subject in their own right. They were, she said, "not contaminated yet." Whether she depicted them alone or with one or both their parents, she never sentimentalized them. Her portraits of children epitomize her ruthless honesty.

Georgie Arce, her seductive and cunning young neighbor (who would later be convicted of manslaughter) is a case in point. Georgie, of whom Neel did several portraits, is never depicted as a one-dimensional character. Across his lively features play a wide range of emotions, from wily worldliness to sheer youthful energy. And there are hordes of other examples, from the hyperalert Daisy to the precocious Julia Gruen to the often edgy pictures of her own children and grandchildren. Who can ever forget her fierce nude portrait of her lost daughter, Isabetta? In *Two Girls, Spanish Harlem*, a picture of young black sisters, Neel artfully emphasizes the girls' eyes and mouths to capture two unique personalities—one passive, the other inquisitive.

Neel's empathetic depiction of gay and transgender couples arguably stands alone in art history. Rather than exploiting the potentially prurient aspect, Neel validates the emotional bond between two people. At the same time, she doesn't avoid the obvious sexual innuendos. Take her dual portrait *David Bourdon and Gregory Battcock*, with its provocative subtext (done in 1970, just a year after the Stonewall Riots), or *Geoffrey Hendricks and Brian* and their ripe bowl of fruit. Her painting of cross-dressing Jackie Curtis and Ritta Redd raises this self-invented genre to a new level.

Neel has been called the court painter to the feminists and to the art world, because she painted the power brokers of both. She could just have well have been called the court painter to the Communist Party and the Barrio. In fact, Neel was the court painter to nobody but herself, and her court was the world at large.

In its subject matter, diversity, and style, Neel's often precedent-setting work can be examined from a variety of perspectives. While she suffered from a lack of attention for most of her lifetime, posthumously she has rarely been out of the public eye. For the last twenty-five years, Alice Neel's legacy has not only survived her but continued to grow exponentially. Her reputation, if anything, is greater than it was during the last two decades of her life.

Since 1984, there has not been a single year when Neel's work hasn't been exhibited in both solo and group shows. Between 2000 and 2010 alone, there were three major museum retrospectives. Neel is now not only considered a major American twentieth-century artist, but a major twentieth-century artist. Neel was represented by the Robert Miller Gallery from 1982 to 2008. In early 2009, the Neel Estate began to be represented by the David Zwirner Gallery, widely considered one of the most powerful in the world. Says überdealer Zwirner, "You could make a strong case that the most important female artists of the twentieth century are Georgia O'Keeffe and Alice Neel," a statement he also made to *The Wall Street Journal* in April 2009. (He later amended that to "in America.")

The list of Neel's posthumous exhibits is too extensive to describe in detail. But a dozen or so major shows in the last two decades have securely anchored Neel's place in art history. The following is a brief overview.

*   *   *

Originally planned as a celebration of Neel's eighty-fifth birthday, "Alice Neel, Paintings Since 1970," curated by John Cheim, ran from January 26 to March 17, 1985, at the Pennsylvania Academy of the Fine Arts. The catalog included Neel's typically quirky and outspoken interview with Frederick Ted Castle, done for *Artforum* the year before her death. The forty-one paintings were a richly representative sampling of Neel's late style, including such well-known works as *John Perreault, The Family, Margaret Evans, Pregnant, The Soyer Brothers, Loneliness, David Bourdon and Gregory Battcock*, and Neel's own nude self-portrait.

Although the review itself was mixed, the headline of Theodore F. Wolff's piece in *The Christian Science Monitor*, WILL SHE BE KNOWN AS THE AMERI-CAN VAN GOGH? granted Neel and her work a newly influential perspective. Like most of the reviews of the show, it emphasized Neel's quintessential honesty.

> As an artist, Alice Neel always spoke the truth, without embel-lishments or evasions, and with little concern for the social ame-nities. Confronted by reality, she preferred to depict it as it was rather than as it should be and to present it starkly, regardless of whose feelings were hurt or whose ideals were offended. . . .
>
> . . . Unfortunately, we still don't how how large a purely ar-tistic victory she achieved. Two things are certain however: Her art is much too true to be dismissed, and any and all arguments as to her importance must take her technical idiosyncracies into account. The latter is inevitable, because her expressive and some-what simplistic manner of drawing and painting often calls at-tention to itself in ways that undermine her images' credibility as major art. . . .
>
> For her fans, of course, such aberrations are of no consequence in the light of her uncompromising honesty. If we can overlook van Gogh's technical weaknesses, they ask, why can't we ignore Alice Neel's?
>
> . . . If art continues to expand as it has this past century . . . then Alice Neel may well be counted among the most valuable American artists of the post–World War II period.
>
> Writing in *The Philadelphia Inquirer*, Edward J. Sozanski wrote, "A considerable portion of Neel's appeal derives from the way she lived and the views she held. She represents virtues we hold dear: intellectual honesty, perserverance, determination, re-spect for common humanity, love of the underdog."

It wasn't a major show, but at the end of 1985, Neel was included in the American Academy and Institute of Arts and Letters Memorial Exhibition, from November 18 through December 15, which honored Academy mem-bers who had recently died. Neel, who was justifiably proud of her mem-bership in the Academy, was represented by twelve paintings.

Neel's first posthumous exhibit at the Robert Miller Gallery, "Drawings and Watercolors," which ran from December 2, 1986, through January 3,

1987, was important in that it introduced a new generation to both Neel's early work from the 1920s and 1930s, and her drawings, including her only other real self-portait: a delicate, lovely rendering of Alice at thirty-two years old. As Roberta Smith wrote in *The New York Times*:

> [The show] simultaneously reveals the foundation of Neel's achievement and expands her stature considerably, for it gives her a serious historical position prior to the onset of Abstract Express-sionism . . . it seems possible to consider that, in the gap between the generation of John Marin and Marsden Hartley . . . and that of Jackson Pollock and Willem de Kooning, Neel may qualify as one of this country's most important and singular artists. Given the time and her gender, she proceeded along her chosen path much as Georgia O'Keeffe proceeded along hers: with almost unbelievable self assurance.

John Cheim, then director of the Robert Miller Gallery, next curated the show "Alice Neel and Diane Arbus: Children," which ran from April 25 through May 20, 1989. Like the "Drawings and Watercolors" show, it got a full page in *The New York Times*. Wrote Smith:

> This exhibition, which brings together nearly 40 portraits of children by the photographer Diane Arbus and the painter Alice Neel, is a great and simple thing. . . . The pairing of the two artists, with all they share and don't share, is so obvious it's brilliant. . . . Whether or not it was a sex-related trait, both Arbus and Neel had a special skill for depicting children. Their first rule of thumb was to grant their subjects the autonomy and psychological complexity of adults. . . .
>
> In all cases, Neel's sitters brim with a potential and self-awareness that is underscored by the artist's own eccentric realism, a combination of hearty light-filled colors and improvisational paint handling, anchored in the achievements of van Gogh and Matisse. Neel gave every part of her pictures—furniture, wallpaper, clothing—its own vividness without overwhelming the painting's raison d'etre. This is especially visible in the Nochlin double portrait, in which the lush treatment of a sea-green love seat, gently dotted with pink and white, is held in check by the child's open curiosity and the mother's scrutinizing gaze.

Elizabeth Hess, in *The Village Voice*, focused on the frequently disturbing quality of Neel's portraits of children:

> This is a theme show on children that is more about adults. . . .
> Neel made mincemeat out of mirror reflections, cutting through
> layers of skin-deep surface in search of a person's less recogniz-
> able, more unknown, qualities . . . Her canvases are a psychoana-
> lytic battle between artist and subject (or patient and therapist)
> demonstrating that Neel not only knew many of her subjects, but
> was emotionally entangled with them. . . .
>
> Neel's wizened children, ensconced in lavish chairs and
> comfortable living rooms, presage a terrifying psychological adult-
> hood. Her family portraits turn pathology into a chilling, but
> rudimentary household product. Neel also celebrated children,
> straightforwardly, but her real power is in messing up their faces
> and bodies, leaving only a trail of recognizable characteristics on
> the canvas. Neel made her subjects more than themselves by de-
> constructing, or simply removing, their security blankets—even
> their clothes. Arbus went right to a nudist colony to find people
> who didn't wear any to begin with. In either case, nudity is not
> the issue: nakedness is.

Neel's often neglected cityscapes, landscapes, and still lifes were the focus of "Exterior/Interior," the inaugural show of Tufts University's Tisch Gallery, which ran from October 1 through December 20, 1991, with a catalog by Pamela Allara. Even Neel's non-figurative work was autobiographical—specifically, as in *After the Death of the Child*, 1927, and *Symbols*, 1932, or more obliquely, as in *Snow on Cornelia Street*, 1933, painted to celebrate her inclusion in the PWAP, and *Loneliness*, 1970, a picture of an empty chair, which she did after Hartley got married and moved away.

Neel's unique documentation of her Spanish Harlem neighborhood was explored in several shows in the early 1990s. The first, "Alice Neel in Spanish Harlem," was shown at the Dia Center for the Arts in Bridgehampton, New York, from June 29 through July 28, 1991, before traveling to the Linda Cathcart Gallery in Santa Monica in 1992. The catalog was by Henry Geldzahler.

Wrote Phyllis Braff in *The New York Times* about the show:

> Ms. Neel's move from Greenwich Village to Spanish Harlem in
> 1938 was more than a search for an affordable rent. She devel-

oped a keen social conscience in the 30's and identified with those she perceived to be victims of exploitation. . . . Ms. Neel's portraits come across as social statements, and the breadth of interpretation possible adds significantly to their appeal. Faces show frustration, and sometimes anger and oppression. Dignity is consistent, but is often combined with a tenseness achieved through posture, color, gaze or the set of a mouth. . . . *Rag in the Window* [which Neel referred to as *The 20th Century*] may well be the most remarkable work here. . . . It also combines a flat two-dimensional objectlike quality with a surface of runs, drips and scumbles that suggest Abstract Expressionism's use of paint. . . . Ms. Neel was clearly one of those artists who believed that having a philosophy of life and making art were inseperately intertwined.

Roberta Smith also wrote about the show in *The New York Times:* "This is a great little show. It gives a glimpse of one of the strongest phases of Neel's career, emphasizing once more that she ranks as one of this century's best portrait painters."

A larger show, "Alice Neel: The Years in Spanish Harlem 1938–1961," ran at the Robert Miller Gallery from February 15 through March 19, 1994. Elizabeth Hess, in *The Village Voice,* called the work, "some of the painter's darkest and most affecting canvases. . . . The real shock of this show is how contemporary it feels. . . . Neel's portraits beg comparison with artists ranging from Picasso to contemporary sculptor John Ahearn."

Writing in *Artforum*, Thomas McEvilley said:

The works in this show . . . demonstrate an uncanny sense of sympathy and directness . . . Four portraits of the Latino boy Georgie Arce seem to show an incredible amount of affection and openness between the eccentric white woman and her young friend met in the street. . . . These works are moving in the humanity they bring to the practice of easel painting . . . the hints of the primitive that Neel allowed to remain in her work—an occasional asymmetry in the eyes, a perspectival incommensurability in the rendering of furniture—do not clash with her mastery of the fretful surface and its wide-ranging set of associations, from Edouard Manet to Egon Schiele and beyond.

More pointedly, Carol Diehl in *ARTnews* wrote:

> It's time we stopped thinking of Alice Neel as a quaint little old
> lady who painted "primitive" portraits. Her strength was espe-
> cially evident in the haunting paintings and drawings on view in
> her recent show, "The Years in Spanish Harlem (1938–61)." It
> opened on the heels of the Lucian Freud blowout at the Metro-
> politan Museum, underscoring the similarity in style between the
> two artists, and one wonders what fame Neel might have achieved
> had she been male and endowed with a famous psychoanalyst's
> last name.

Neel's prolific work lends itself to curatorial themes, and Neel's pregnant
nudes are a subcategory unto themselves. A show of eight of these remarkable paintings opened at Robert Miller in 1996, "The Pregnant Nudes of
Alice Neel," which ran from January 9 to February 3.

Ken Johnson, in *Art in America*, compared the physicality of Neel's
portraiture favorably to that of Philip Pearlstein and Lucian Freud:

> Neel's affectionate anti-idealizing portraits insisted on the hum-
> bling entrapment of spirit in flesh that consitutes our inescapable
> human condition. . . . Although Neel was attentive to intimate
> details of anatomical tyopography (veins, freckles, skin tone, nip-
> ples, etc.), the pregnant nudes are not just gross bodyscapes à la
> Pearlstein or Freud. They read, rather, as penetrating psychologi-
> cal essays on a complicated, often scary experience.

In March 1997, a stunning show, "Alice Neel: Paintings from the Thirties," curated by Cheim, opened at Robert Miller. It was accompanied by a
catalog with a meditation on Neel's work by Wayne Koestenbaum, and text
consisting of comments on the paintings (and life) from Neel herself, who
was shown in a 1931 nude photograph on the first page.

The thirty-seven paintings created a vivid impression of Neel's singular
early style, her idiosyncratic blend of Expressionism and Social Realism.
Painted in the dark, noirish palette she favored then, they also document
her days in the Village and on the WPA during the Depression. The works
ranged from such politically pointed pieces as *Investigation of Poverty at
the Russell Sage Foundation* and *Nazis Murder Jews* to some reliable
show-stoppers like *Joe Gould*, Neel's erotic watercolors of herself and John

Rothschild, *Alienation*, and *Untitled* (Alice Neel and John Rothschild in Bathroom). There were also portraits of three of Neel's lovers at the time: Doolittle, Rothschild, and José. The show demonstrated that, even in her early years, Neel was already a consummate painter—not just of portraits but also of cityscapes.

As *The New Yorker* put it:

> "Paintings from the Thirties," is an extraordinary show of early works from a period when the artist was still experimenting with various styles. Her characteristically precise yet sympathetic observation is abundantly evident in several of the portraits. At the same time, she borrows freely, and often successfully, from Social Realism, Expressionism and Surrealism.

Grace Glueck, in a full-page piece in *The New York Times* wrote:

> In these paintings, made early in her career, Neel already demonstrates her superb skills with portraiture, the best part of her work. A self-styled "collector of souls," she homed in on the faces and body language of her subjects with penetrating insight and shrewd judgement. . . . Shunning the steady run of trends ushered in by Abstract Expressionism in the 1940s, Neel remained true to her figurative style. . . . But while catching the souls of others, she rarely again revealed her own as she did in these deeply engaged works from the gritty 30s.

In *Art in America*, Eleanor Heartney wrote:

> In the best of the portraits in this exhibition, Neel's penchant for social commentary, her passion for justice and her fury at human villainy are distilled in individual faces. . . . This exhibition demonstrated that despite her occasional excursions into a more public rhetorical mode, Neel's politics were ultimately ground in the personal. She sought truth in the individual human soul and laid bare whatever mixture of compassion, greed, vanity and despair she found locked within.

By 1998, Cheim had left Robert Miller to found his own gallery with Howard Read—Cheim & Read. One of the first shows he organized was a clever take on the Neel oeuvre. Entitled "Men in Suits," it paired Neel's paintings of—what else?—men wearing suits with the photographs of August Sander (whom Neel admired). Thanks to its ingenious conceit, this relatively small show (thirteen Neel paintings and twenty-seven Sander photographs) got an inordinate amount of press. Among the Neels were, *Richard in the Era of the Corporation, Timothy Collins, Jack Baur,* and *Fuller Brush Man.*

Wrote Ken Johnson in *The New York Times:*

> No artist extended the life of post–World War II portraiture with such painterly verve, humor and psychological acuity as did Alice Neel. . . . There's autobiography and social history in these paintings. Neel was a lifelong Bohemian leftist, which might explain why her subjects seem a little ridiculous in their standardized business attire.

Peter Schjeldahl, writing in *The Village Voice*, said:

> An authentic 20th century heroine, Neel contended in her gypsyish life with more than a few aggressive and bolting men, all infected with unconscious condescension by the old male privilege. . . . What would the men around her have said if told back then that, eclipsing them all, she would emerge as the premier artist of their world and time?
>
> . . . Neel's style, which used to trigger the epithet "eccentric," looks even more classic now, a joltingly efficient application of Expressionism—with important lessons from Edvard Munch and Chaim Soutine—to hard human faces. There is absolutely nothing mannered about it. It conveys sheer truth, though of an inextricably tangled kind: truth about the subject, truth of the artist. Every picture tells what it's like to be Alice Neel while making room in that existential condition for another, explosively living soul. The result is poor etiquette and great art.

In 2000, Neel finally got the major Whitney retrospective she deserved (due at least in part to prodding by Richard and his wife, Constance Hoguet, an old schoolmate of the late Philadelphia Museum director, Anne D'harnoncourt). Ann Temkin, who organized the show that originated at the Philadelphia Museum of Art where she was then curator of modern and contemporary art, said that the museum wanted to celebrate the centennial of this native Philadelphian. The exhibit, which included seventy-six works, forcefully brought Neel's work into the twenty-first century. It was accompanied by a comprehensive, 198-page catalog.

Roberta Smith, in *The New York Times*, credited Neel with "making some of the 20th century's best paintings, especially portraits." But she felt that the "illuminating but insufficient" show didn't do the artist justice, that it skimped on her early work, and was too small and cramped. "Neel should not be a one-floor artist," she wrote.

Art in America devoted a seven-page illustrated spread to the show, entitled "Eros in Spanish Harlem," detailing the various periods of Neel's career. Still, writer Raphael Rubinstein, like Smith, felt that not enough space was devoted to Neel's pre-1960 work. "It is regrettable that the earlier work wasn't more fully represented. Despite the considerable charm, visual intelligence and historical value of her later portraits, to my eye the emotional depth and sense of distinctive purpose visible in Neel's pre-1960 work represented the greater achievement."

In *The New Yorker*, Hilton Als called Neel "New York's painter laureate," who recorded "a new vanished way of life in Spanish Harlem, in the fuck-it attitude the most compelling of her subjects shared, who ranged from the street prophet Joe Gould to the great transvestite performer Jackie Curtis. Neel embraced the marginal, and the word defined more than half her life as an artist."

(That certainly was no longer the case. By the time of the Whitney show, Neel had become emphatically what she wasn't for most of her life: a critics' darling, and among the outpourings of press on the retrospective was a full-length feature in *Vanity Fair*.)

Says Temkin, now chief curator of painting and sculpture at the Museum of Modern Art, "I would say the independence with which Neel worked from the beginning to the end is an inspiration, because not only did she make portraits, but she made portraits of people who ordinarily would not be the subjects of portraits, and that perserverence in regard to an individual vision is striking. Her curiosity about her fellow human beings is clear and so is her empathy, and like any painter of a portrait, what comes out on the canvas is a collaboration between sitter and painter. I think in her case the nature of that collaboration is part of her gift."

In late 2005, the National Museum of Women in the Arts mounted an extensive, theme-oriented retrospective: "Alice Neel's Women," which ran from October 28, 2005, through January 15, 2006. It was co-curated by

Susan Sterling and Carolyn Carr, and included some eighty paintings and drawings. The show came about when Ginny, who has worked to promote Neel's reputation over the last decade, approached Carr to do a book on Alice Neel's portraits of women. (Published by Rizzoli in 2002, the book also served as the show's catalog.) The exhibit presented an extraordinary array of portraits from every period of Neel's life, including many little-seen works.

By focusing exclusively on Neel's handling of this single rich subject (Neel painted a great many women over the course of her career), the show definitively mapped the phases of Neel's artistic evolution. It also emphasized the degree to which she reflected the Zeitgeist, at the same time as celebrating women who were leaders in their fields. Included were portraits of Linda Nochlin, Faith Ringgold, Adrienne Rich, Bella Abzug, Isabel Bishop, Mary Garrard, Dore Ashton, Audrey McMahon, Cindy Nemser, Ann Sutherland Harris, June Blum, and of course, Neel herself.

Blake Gopnik, in *The Washington Post*, called the show "important" and said:

> The show's focus on women isn't just a nod to this museum's mandate. It gets at what makes Neel's art important and at why it's her later art that matters most . . . In the second half of her career Neel gives up on going head-to-head against the ego-baring styles of male artists, each of whose chest-thumping innovations showed that he was better than the guy who came before. Instead, she decides that what matters more, by far, than her own style, are the female subjects of her portrait art.

In 2004, former Tate curator and director of collections Jeremy Lewison, who became the Neel Estate's advisor several years earlier, organized the first of several shows at the Victoria Miro Gallery in London, which represents Neel, bringing her work to an international audience. Says Miro, "It's like mining an undiscovered trove. It's very exciting." "A Chronicle of New York 1950–1976," which ran from June 1, 2004, through July 31, 2004, was a show of twenty-four paintings and drawings: five paintings were concurrently displayed in a dedicated room at the Tate. A second show at Miro, "Alice Neel: The Cycle of Life," ran from May 23 through July 21, 2007, concurrent with a screening of *Alice Neel*, Andrew Neel's 2007 documentary about his grandmother. The show included ten paintings, mostly from the 1960s and 1970s. The catalog, by Yale University's Dean of Art, Robert Storr, featured an interview with Andrew Neel. A third show at Miro, "Alice Neel: Works on Paper," ran from April 18 through May 14, 2009.

The David Zwirner Gallery got maximum mileage out of two shows co-curated by Lewison that ran concurrently in May 2009. "Nudes of the 1930s," a small but powerful show at Zwirner's uptown gallery (Zwirner & Wirth), from May 6 through June 20, displayed a dozen early Neel nudes, including two erotic watercolors of herself with Rothschild and a somewhat tropical one of Neel with a full-frontal José, reminiscent of Gauguin. Among the better-known nudes were the powerful *Nadya and Nona,* and *Rhoda Myers in a Blue Hat.* There were also a few lesser-known pictures, including a buxom blond nude, *Winifred Mesmer* (who, according to Neel, had slept with both Sam Brody and José) and two delicate nude images (one in an open fur-trimmed coat) of Katherine Hogle, the friend who introduced Neel to Linus Pauling.

The second show, "Selected Works," at the Zwirner Gallery in Chelsea from May 14 through June 20, consisted of sixteen somewhat randomly selected portraits from 1945 through 1982. Among the earliest were several of Sam Brody (with a terrified looking young boy—this time, Hartley) and one of Brody in profile entitled *Sam, Snow (How Like the Winter),* reading a wartime newspaper (suspended in the background are striking Surrealist doodles). The latest was Neel's in-your-face burlesque of Annie Sprinkle (1982). Three of the best paintings in the show were of children: The anxious-looking *Cindy,* 1960, a pensive *Georgie Arce,* 1959, and the brightly-hued but serious *Hartley,* 1952.

Roberta Smith once again anointed Neel "One of the outstanding portraitists of the 20th century":

> As these two exhibitions confirm, Neel excelled at heightening the triangulated tensions inherent in portraiture: painter-sitter-viewer; figure-space-surface; line-brushwork-stain; biography-autobiography-history. Her portraits and self-portraits define her as a feminist before the fact, a left-leaning Bohemian drawn to other nonconformists and a sybarite at ease with her body.

In *The New Yorker,* Peter Schjeldahl wrote two pages on Neel's extraordinary life and work, singling out her Georgie Arce portrait, "a terrific painterly cadenza," in the downtown show (which he generally found "bit disappointing in its undoubtedly market conscious emphasis on formally

accomplished pictures") and the erotic watercolors of Neel and John Rothschild in the uptown show.

> It includes a watercolor from 1935 that is the funniest and funki-
> est visualization of intimacy I know. Cute, blowsy Alice urinates
> on a toilet while her solemn boyfriend John Rothschild does the
> same in the sink . . . Another watercolor from that year has Alice
> voluptuously supine on a bed, while Rothschild stands over her,
> wearing only slippers, in a tense, withdrawn posture . . . Both
> pictures are beautifully drawn. Rougher, and ruthlessly honest,
> are paintings and drawings of women Neel knew . . . The nudes
> aren't erotic, but they exude carnal wisdom. They are modern in
> their frontality, nudging subjects off the wall and into the room,
> while utterly free of stylistic affectation . . . Lots of celebrated
> twentieth-century art has seemed dated and tame lately. Not Neel's,
> which, beyond being something to look at, is something that hap-
> pens to you.

T. J. Carlin gave both shows five out of six stars in *Time Out*:

> The nudes provide good examples of Neel's multifaceted ap-
> proach to line and her correspondingly deep understanding of
> the psychology of her subjects . . . Her compassion for her sub-
> jects and her commitment to reflect the world around her, even
> when it cost her deeply, were acts of true courage and a boon for
> the rest of us.

The third retrospective of the decade, "Alice Neel: Painted Truths," was
organized by the Houston Museum of Fine Arts, and co-curated by Jeremy
Lewison and Barry Walker. The show examined Neel's oeuvre thematically,
rather than chronologically, dividing the sixty-seven paintings up into seven
categories: "Maternity," "The Allegorical Portrait," "The Psychological
Portrait," "Nudes," "Cityscapes," "Old Age," and the "Detached Gaze." The
Houston show traveled to the newly renovated Whitechapel in London from
July 8 to September 17 and then on to the Moderno Museet in Malmo, Sweden, from October 9, 2010, to January 21, 2011. More like a large gallery
show than a standard retrospective, the Houston show emphasized the thoroughly modern essence of Neel's work.

Indeed, Neel's artistic influence, even when not immediately obvious, is apparent in the work of many contemporary figure painters. Take the atmosphere of innuendo in Eric Fischl's suggestive, sexually-fraught narratives. Like Neel, he is a master of depicting the palpable but unspoken. Fischl first became known in the early 1980s for his provocative bedroom scenes and louche nudes, which often look like painterly freeze-frames. Says Fischl, "The thing that I love about Neel's work, and feel close to, is that she is one of those artists where you remember every painting of hers that you see: it burns in the back of your brain. That's something I try to do in my work; give people a sort of monumentalized moment. But there's something about Neel. I wish I could do her even more than I do. She really is an expressionist. I'm more repressed than that."

Then there is Neel's often-stated goal of "capturing the Zeitgeist," which is shared in different ways by both Elizabeth Peyton, who chronicles contemporary culture in her deadpan portraits, and Marlene Dumas, whose imagery frequently refers to hot-button political and social issues, and who is, as Neel said of herself, "attracted to the morbid and excessive."

Dumas's striking portrait of her daughter with paint-stained hands, *The Painter*, has, in common with Neel's haunting *Andy Warhol* a pale, ethereal palette and an extreme spareness. Both are tinted in hues more typical of dead than living bodies. In an appreciation of Neel that Dumas wrote for the Houston show's catalog, she called her piece, "an homage to her portrait, *Andy Warhol*, which is one of the most beautiful paintings of the 20th century.

"I really like in that painting that there are such a lot of things together. He looks a bit like a woman, male and female in one," Dumas says. "You have vulnerability, artificiality, a lot of qualities together. Warhol was also enigmatic. There is a total fake, artificial aspect, then there is the lonely aspect of an alienated character. And there is that simplicity, that economy of means. There is almost nothing redundant in this painting. It's very difficult and complicated to do a complicated subject in a simple image. She captured it beautifully. It's very much Alice Neel, but also very much Andy Warhol.

"That also links it to *The Painter*. You could call the painting of Warhol, and also the portrait of my daughter, the portrait of the artist. She was an alter-ego for me. Instead of making a self-portrait with a brush, there was this child. I use the body and Neel uses the body to get to the spirit, because the spirit has some form. One has got a figure, but it's not about flesh or about materiality, it's about trying to capture the spirit."

Elizabeth Peyton, like Neel, records her era in portraits of the cultural elite (Kurt Cobain), people in her immediate milieu, and those who are both. She even did a nude image of Neel. As Peyton puts it, "I was most interested in people, and that seemed like the most important thing— humans; humanity. I can't say if I make pictures of people for the same reason as Alice Neel, but I feel pictures of people contain their time in an important way that communicates to other times. Alice Neel seems more interested in humans in general than I am, and seemed to be able to connect with all kinds of people, and you can really see it in the magic of how she made the faces. In a way, you could say she took on the whole thing [of people] and all that encompasses in a fearless way. I love that she doesn't try to 'get it right,' that the gesture or feeling is always more important in her work than an exact description of the sitter. Sometimes this can seem mannered in the bodies, but never feels like that in the faces—they are really their own universe created by her."

Philip Pearlstein believes that Neel's reach has never been greater. "In a crazy way, like Andy Warhol, she is much more significant now than when she was alive. Her kind of drawing and painting are not quite the opposite of academic, but more in line with what's now called 'outsider art.' She probably established a taste for outsider art, for the non-correct. I think she helped break down, or made the acceptance of alternative ways of drawing, acceptable. She broke the ground for Eric Fischl and for John Currin as far as that goes. In a sense she paved the way."

Chuck Close tells a funny story about running into Neel on the street with a mutual friend, who introduced the two artists. Said Neel to Close, "Chuck Close? I hate your work!" Close responded, "That's interesting, because I'm a fan of yours." Neel gave it a moment's thought before replying, "In that case, I'll have to take another look."

Says Close, "Neel is an artist's artist, never hot but always respected. That's a very nice status to have, actually. You don't make a lot of money and you are not constantly on the cover of magazines, but it's also a reputation that is sustainable over many decades. That's what can be said about her."

John Cheim says of Neel, "The best of her paintings wipe out anything else that's on the wall in a lot of exhibitions that have to do with figurative painting, or even abstraction. You could put an Alice Neel next to a Basquiat. You could put an Alice Neel next to a Twombly, a de Kooning, a Joan

Mitchell. And you know the paint quality and intensity holds up in their company. And I think you can even relate her to Philip Guston. Philip Guston went back to Goya, went back to storytelling."

In May 2007, *Alice Neel*, a documentary made by then twenty-eight-year-old Andrew Neel, Neel's youngest grandchild, opened. As idiosyncratic as Neel herself, the film pieced together footage from a number of Neel interviews, as well as intimate interviews with Andrew's father, Hartley, and his uncle, Richard, and Isabetta's children and husband. Combined with high-definition shots of Neel's paintings, the film provided a prismatic, compelling view of the artist.

Speaking about his film, Andrew Neel says, "The thing about great people with sensational lives, is that what's most important about them and what they've done is what they've left. I mean, Alice Neel without any paintings was like many, many other people. There's a lot of eccentrics in the world. What's amazing is that she left these paintings, and maybe some of those details in her life can inform that legacy. People are very complicated. They can make horrible mistakes at one point, and then they can be saintly at other times. I think a lot of especially interesting people are enigmatic, and I think Alice was enigmatic."

Despite the obvious "messiness," Neel's life and art were—and remain—inspirational. "She teaches you to follow your bliss," says Hartley Neel in the film, eyes moistening.

Alice Neel herself always eschewed the sentimental. "I try to paint the scene. A human comedy like Balzac—the past, present, and future interlaced with the levels of society, like Proust. It's terrible to think that life happens and just goes, disappears. I paint my time using the people as evidence," Neel wrote. "I believe in art as history. The swirl of the era is what you're in and what you paint. I love, pity, hate, and fear all at once, and try to keep a record."

Chapter Notes

CHAPTER ONE: *Studio Still Life*

p. 1   Her paintbrushes and glasses: visit to Neel apartment at 107th and Broadway, 2001.

p. 2   "I'm cursed to be": comment by Benny Andrews in Ann Temkin, ed., "Undergoing Scrutiny: Sitting for Alice Neel," *Alice Neel*, Philadelphia: Philadelphia Museum of Art, 2000, 73 (published on the occasion of the Alice Neel retrospective).

p. 2   When *Time* magazine: Neel did an oil portrait of Kate Millett for the cover of *Time* magazine, August 31, 1970.

p. 3   "the Human Comedy": Neel frequently compared her oeuvre to Honoré de Balzac's *The Human Comedy*, a parallel she originally made in a personal statement she wrote in 1960 for the *The Hasty Papers: A One-Shot Review*, Alfred Leslie, ed.; reissued as a hardcover Millennium edition, Host Publications, Austin, Texas, 2000, 91. She reiterated this remark in her doctoral address, delivered at Moore College of Art in June 1971.

p. 3   "I paint my time": Alice Neel, "Artists on Their Art," *Art International*, Vol. 12, No. 5, May 15, 1958, 4; quoted in Susan Rothenberg, "People as Evidence," Philadelphia Museum of Art catalog, 47.

p. 4   Curator John Perreault: Edie Newhall, "Neel Life Stories," *New York* magazine, June 19, 2000, 38–43.

p. 4   Another model, artist Benny Andrews: "Undergoing Scrutiny: Sitting For Alice Neel," comment by Benny Andrews in Ann Temkin, ed., *Alice Neel*, "Undergoing Scrutiny: Sitting for Alice Neel," 76.

p. 5   "dropping off the bone": Frederick Ted Castle, "Alice Neel," *Artforum*, Vol. 22, No. 2, October 1983, 36–41; reprinted in *Alice Neel, Paintings Since 1970*, Pennsylvania Academy of the Fine Arts, 9.

p. 5   "The road that I pursued": Barbaralee Diamonstein, *Inside New York's Art World*, New York: Rizzoli, 1979, 256.

CHAPTER TWO: *Childhood's Canvas*

p. 6   Her "Rosebud" moment: "Rosebud" refers to the name of the emblematic child-hood sled of Charles Foster Kane, the William Randolph Hearst-like protagonist of the 1941 Orson Welles film classic, *Citizen Kane*. The iconic sled appears at the beginning, middle, and end of the film; "Rosebud" is Kane's last dying word.

p. 6   "Whenever I think of writing": first page of unedited transcript of an interview with Eleanor Munro for *Originals: American Women Artists*, New York: Simon and Schuster, 1979; 120–130 (outgrowth of series *The Originals/Women in Art* produced by WNET Channel 13).

p. 6   "I tried to capture life": *The Christian Science Monitor*, "Artists and their Inspiration," Alice Neel, October 31, 1977.

p. 6   "One of the reasons": Lucille Rhodes and Margaret Murphy, *Three Women Artists: Anna Sokolow, Alice Neel, Muriel Rukhauser*, The Museum of Modern Art, 1978; Kultur Video, 1998, 2001.

p. 7   "My mother . . . saw Alice": author's phone interview with Mary-Lou Usher, May 2008.

p. 7   "If I could have met myself": Terry Gross interview, *Fresh Air*, March 3, 1983. A similar quote appears in *ARTnews*, Vasari Diary, Judith Higgins, "Alice Neel: An American Artist, 1900–1984."

p. 7   "If I ever write": Alice Neel, interview with Yetta Groshans and Werner Groshans, March 20, 1979, "Yetta and Werner Groshans Papers," Smithsonian Archives of American Art. Similar quote in Richard Polsky, Interview 1, April 8, 1981, Columbia University Oral History Collection, 7; Harvard lecture transcript, March 21, 1979, 3 18; Colwyn had a population of about 1,200: Old Chester, PA, Delaware County Population and Census; 1789–1980, Delaware County Planning Department.

p. 7   Neel's family history: Patricia Hills, *Alice Neel*, New York: Harry N. Abrams, Inc., 1983 (reprint 1995), 12.

p. 8   who died when he was between: ibid.; 18. Richard Polsky, Interview 1, April 8, 1981, 5, Columbia University Oral History Collection.

p. 8   "I forget which opera": transcript of Alice Neel interview for *Three Women Artists*.

p. 8   The most definitive link: Stockton family background from interview and correspondence with Russell Stockton, Richard Stockton descendant, who has researched the family tree; author's phone interview with Russell Stockton, Richard Stockton descendant, December, 2009; Stockton family tree Web site: thehomemarket.info/Stockton/STOCKTONfamilytree, 41–50, Thomas Coates Stockton, *The Stockton Family Tree*, Carnahan Press, 1911.

p. 8   Hartley fought in the Civil War: Neel identifies her grandfather as a Civil War veteran in Joan Kufrin, *Uncommon Women*, Piscataway. N.J.: New Century Publishers Inc., 1981, 138.

p. 8   "Rhoda Stockton was a sister": Polsky, Interview 2, April 29, 1981, 82.

p. 8   "courier in the cavalry in the Civil War": transcript of Eleanor Munro interview for *Originals*, 22. Neel says her *maternal* grandfather, William Hartley, was a courier in the calvary; Alice Neel, undated written reminiscence.

p. 8   Apparently, there was also a wealthy side: Alice Neel interview with Jonathan Brand, 1969, Philadelphia Museum of Art, transcript, 3.

p. 9   he was vehemently "anti-Bohemian": Barbaralee Diamonstein, *Inside New York's Art World*, 255; Polsky, Interview 1, 5.

p. 9   Alice had a picture: Polsky, Interview 2, April 29, 1981, 82.

p. 9   his mother died: George Neel, interview with Gerald and Margaret Belcher, July 17, 1987.

p. 9   "little gray man": Hills, *Alice Neel*, 19 (caption for *The Family*).

p. 9   "the most disciplined Victorian": George Neel, taped interview with Gerald L. and Margaret L. Belcher, July 18, 1987 (authors of *Collecting Souls, Gathering Dust*, New York: Paragon House, 1991).

p. 9   a younger sister Florence, had died of diphtheria: Richard Polsky, Interview 2, 76.

p. 10   "My mother was the real head-of-the-house type": Frederick Ted Castle interview, 3.

p. 10   "My grandfather was": George Neel, interview with Gerald and Margaret Belcher.

p. 10   "Alice did everything": ibid.

p. 10   the family had moved twice: Philadelphia Museum catalog.

p. 10   cream-colored, with forest green trim: George Neel, interview with Gerald and Margaret Belcher.

p. 10   All three houses still stand: author's visit to Colwyn, August 1, 2004.

p. 11   Description of interior and furnishings: George Neel, interview with Gerald and Margaret Belcher.

p. 11   As Neel recalled it: Alice Neel, written reminiscence, February 23, Neel Archives 1963.

p. 11   George Neel painted a telling picture: George Neel, interview with Gerald and Margaret Belcher.

p. 12   "You're only a girl": Patti Goldstein, "Soul on Canvas," *New York* magazine, July 9–16, 1979, 78; Joan Kufrin, *Uncommon Women*, New Jersey: New Century Publishers Inc., 1981, 138; Polsky, Interview 1, 10; Diamonstein, *Inside New York's Art World*, 261.

p. 12   "Everything in her life": Hills, *Alice Neel*, 35.

p. 12   "None of us will": Munro, *Originals*, 122.

p. 12   "there was already a wall": ibid., 122.

p. 12   duly noted by the family doctor: Henry R. Hope, "Alice Neel: Portraits of an Era," *Art Journal*, Vol. 38, No. 4, Summer 1979, 273.

p. 12   "I was hypersensitive": Munro, *Originals*, 122.

p. 12   "If a fly lit on me": ibid., 121.

p. 12   "The tale of Christ": John Gruen, "Collector of Souls," *The Herald Tribune*, June 9, 1966.

p. 12   "going into a fever": Munro, *Originals*, 122.

p. 13   "jumpy as a cricket": Fanya Foss, undated reminiscence, newsletter, L.A. Gallery.

p. 13   "Other people loomed too large": Munro, *Originals*, 121.

p. 13   "I was an unknown quantity": Kufrin, *Uncommon Women*, 138.

p. 13   "Even as a child," Munro, *Originals*, 122.

p. 13   "I always wanted to be an artist": Hills, *Alice Neel*, 12.

p. 13   "When I was very small": Karl Fortess Collection, Smithsonian Archives of American Art, audio interview, September 12, 1975.

p. 13   "the bug, the virus": Jonathan Brand interview, December 4, 5, 1969.

p. 13   "When I first began to paint": ibid.

p. 13   "swamp things": George Neel, interview with Gerald and Margaret Belcher.

p. 13   "the only real farm": Alice Neel, written reminiscence, February 23, 1963, Neel Archives.

p. 14   "I was just a child then": Munro, *Originals*, 122.

p. 14   "I was a romantic," ibid.

p. 14   "I read how Picasso": Fortess, audio interview.

p. 14   "At night I'd turn on my side": Munro, *Originals*, 122, 123.

p. 14   "extremely attached": ibid., 121.

p. 14   "She had a strong . . . run the roost": ibid., 121, 122.

p. 14   "My grandmother, who was": George Neel, interview with Gerald and Margaret Belcher.

p. 15   "She was so superior": Munro, unedited transcript of interview for *Originals*, 15.

p. 15   her therapist hypothesized: Judith Higgins, "Alice Neel and the Human Comedy," *ARTnews*, October, 1984, 72.

p. 15   "needed sunshine because": Alice Neel, written reminiscence, February 23, 1963, Neel Archives.

p. 15   "Do you remember": ibid.

p. 16   "Small and dark": Nancy Neel interview, July 22, 2003.

p. 16   "My sister made the most magnificent clothes": Munro, unedited transcript for *Originals*, 30.

p. 16   "When Alice was born": Nancy Neel interview.

p. 16   one of the architects of the Holland Tunnel: George Neel interview with Gerald and Margaret Belcher.

p. 16   son named Jimmy: Polsky, Interview 1, 9.

p. 16   "Later on she became a bone in my throat": Polsky, Interview 1, 33.

p. 16   "She was wonderful": Jonathan Brand interview, December, 1969.

p. 16   had died of diphtheria: Polsky, Interview 2, 76.

p. 16   *Obie's Corner*: Nancy Neel interview.

p. 16   dance a jig: Richard Neel interview, April 10, 2010.

p. 16   leaving the infant: Gerald and Margaret Belcher, *Collecting Souls, Gathering Dust*, New York: Paragon House, 1991, 138.

p. 16   became the dean of Monmouth . . . burned to death: Hartley Neel interview, June 11, 2008.

p. 16   "None of them had any grace": George Neel interview.

p. 16   Although Hartley says: June 11, 2008.

p. 17   "She'd tell the other kids": Richard Neel interview, April 7, 2010.

p. 17   she excelled in math: Munro, *Originals*, 123.

p. 17   very edges of the page: Hills, *Alice Neel*, 12.

p. 17   covers of *The Saturday Evening Post*: Henry Geldzahler, *Making It New*, New York: Turtle Point Press, 1994, 234.

p. 17   "benighted": Higgins, *ARTnews*, 72.

p. 17   "Although in the spring": Hills, *Alice Neel*, 12.

p. 17   Neel recalled seeing *Faust*: ibid., 12.

p. 17   "so I wouldn't get pregnant": ibid., 12.

p. 17   "I felt like their parent": Polsky, Interview 1, 11.

p. 18   "a dim silence fell": ibid., 11.

p. 18   "This was the stupidest thing": Fortess interview.

p. 18   "I had a small nervous breakdown": Munro, *Originals*, 123; Patricia Hills, taped
          interview with Alice Neel, July 17, 20, 1982.

p. 18   "Well you see": excerpt of undated personal writing, entitled, "Money," tran-
          scribed by the Philadelphia Museum of Art, Neel Archives.

p. 18   "I did love New York": *Three Women Artists*, interview transcript, November 8,
          1975; (also mentioned in Munro, *Originals*, transcript).

p. 18   Darby High School yearbook: *Utelum, The Classbook of Darby High School,
          1919*, published by the graduation class under direction of the faculty. Will: "My
          client, the Class of 1919, has expressed a desire to have all friends and relatives
          gather around her bedside during the few remaining hours of her life. She hopes
          they will act in an orderly manner when they gather, as she does not like a scene
          such as was enacted last year as a result of a similar request by the Class of 1918."

p. 19   job with the Army Air Corps: Hills, *Alice Neel*, 13.

p. 19   "meeting lots of Air Force officers": Fortess interview.

p. 19   "Well, that isn't the way . . . before you conquer art": Hills, *Alice Neel*, 13; anec-
          dote also told in Fortess interview; Polsky, Interview 1, 29.

p. 19   "You know what it takes to be an artist?": Goldstein, "Soul on Canvas," 78.

p. 19   "Hypersensitivity, because in order to be an artist": Munro, *Originals*, 121.

          CHAPTER THREE: *Designing Women*

p. 20   She had just returned: Richard Polsky, Interview 1, 31.

p. 20   earning thirty-five: Hills, *Alice Neel*, 13.

p. 20   "Art was in the back of my mind": ibid.

p. 20   "For me art was a necessity": Nancy Baer, "Alice Neel: Collector of Souls,"
          (1976 or 1978) broadcast on PBS in 1978 as part of *The Originals: Women in
          Art*, now in video library of The Museum of Modern Art.

p. 20   "I was very beautiful then": Munro, *Originals*, 124.

p. 20   "I didn't want to be taught Impressionism": Hills, *Alice Neel*, 13.

p. 20   "I didn't want to be taught a formal form": Fortess interview.

p. 21   The school's registration pages indicate: Moore College of Art, registration pages, 1921, 264: "Alice H. Neel, Colwyn Pa, recommended by James A. Bunham, Darby, Pa., Fine Arts, Nov. 1st, 1921."

p. 21   switched to illustration about a year later: ibid., 320, "Alice H. Neel, 408, Colwyn Ave, Colwyn, Pa., Illustration, admitted October 3, 1922."

p. 21   "because I still had the idea": Karl Fortess interview.

p. 21   "The truth is I deceived them": Cindy Nemser, *Art Talk: Conversations with 12 Women Artists*, New York: Charles Scribner's Sons, 1975; Hills, *Alice Neel*, 99.

p. 21   Neel paid the one-hundred-dollar: Hills, *Alice Neel*, 14.

p. 21   As the school's 1922 pamphlet: Theodore C. Knauff, *An Experiment in Training for the Useful and the Beautiful: A History*, published by the Philadelphia School of Design for Women, 1922, 5.

p. 22   Founded in 1848: Nina de Angeli Walls, "Art and Industry in Philadelphia: Origins of the Philadelphia School of Design for Women," *The Pennsylvania Magazine of History and Biography*: July 1993, 177–199. Although for decades, including during the 1920s, earlier histories referred to the founding date as 1844—both in the Knauff book (ibid., 8,) and in the yearbooks for the years Neel attended the school, according to contemporary scholarship, including the article by de Angeli Walls, the founding date was probably 1848. This material later appeared in de Angeli Walls' book, *Art, Industry and Women's Education in Philadelphia*, Westport, CT: Bergin & Garvey, 2001.

p. 22   Initially established in a single room: ibid.

p. 22   it started out with one drawing teacher: ibid., 12.

p. 22   The idea was that women could be taught: ibid., 13.

p. 22   Eventually, the endeavor outgrew: ibid.

p. 22   By 1851, the school was doing so well: ibid., 15.

p. 22   of which they kept three-quarters: *Design for Women, A History of the Moore College of Art*, Wynewood, PA: Livingston Publishing Co., 1968, 23.

p. 22   In 1853, when Mrs. Peter moved: Knauff, *An Experiment in Training . . .* , 19.

p. 22   At that time, the school had just three departments: ibid., 23, 24.

p. 22   In 1880, the school moved: *Design for Women, A History . . .* , 36, 37.

p. 23   The Forrest mansion is now: National Historic Landmarks Program; National Register Number 93001608.

p. 23   "The school had great towering rooms": Fortess interview.

p. 23   "They had a magnificent": ibid.

p. 23   The Fine Arts Course: The Philadelphia School of Design for Women, 77th Year, 1921–1922, 18. (The Neel painting is on page 22 of catalog.)

p. 23   "It is so arranged": ibid., 18.

p. 23   "For me, drawing is the great discipline of art": Alice Neel, "I Paint Tragedy and Joy," *The New York Times*, October 31, 1976; similar statement in Kufrin, *Uncommon Women*, 141.

p. 23   "the Philadelphia School for Designing Women": Belcher and Belcher, *Collecting Souls, Gathering Dust*, 8.

p. 24   Robert Henri, *The Art Spirit*, New York: J. B. Lipincott Co., 1923; Boulder Colorado: Westview Press, 1984.

p. 24   gave it, as a token of friendship: Hills, *Alice Neel*, 21.

p. 24   "Paint what you feel": The Minnesota Museum of American Art, Resource Library Magazine, October 26–December 31, 2002, 3.

p. 24   Robert Henri history and background: As one of the instigators of the Philadelphia Four . . . Ashcan School: The Minnesota Museum of American Art, *Resource Library Magazine*, October 26–December 31, 2002, 3.

p. 24   "work with great speed": Robert Henri, *The Art Spirit*, Margery Ryerson ed., Philadelphia: J.B. Lippincott Co., 1951, 10.

p. 24   "I am not interested in making copies of pretty children": *Robert Henri: His Life and Letters*, 99.

p. 25   She was a member of an eminent: *Design for Women, A History* . . . , 53, 54.

p. 25   It was Emily who instituted a life class: ibid., 40.

p. 25   Fortess interview.

p. 25   "even though the male model": interview with Terry Gross, *Fresh Air*, March 3, 1983.

p. 25   "very conventional lady": Hills, *Alice Neel*, 14.

p. 25   "beauty in the largest sense": *Design for Women, A History* . . . , 54.

p. 25   "Tradition is our springboard": ibid.

p. 25   which Neel represented as "romantic": Karl Fortress interview.

p. 25   "the daughter of the Weber:" ibid.

p. 25   best painting in life class: Commencement Program, Kern Dodge Prize: $25.00
           Progress in Painting from Life, Alice Neel.

p. 25   girls required to wear hats and gloves: Belcher and Belcher, *Collecting Souls,
           Gathering Dust*, 9.

p. 25   "There was one very good teacher": Fortess interview; similar statement in Hills,
           Alice Neel, 15.

p. 26   Neel had nothing but "contempt": Fortess interview.

p. 26   "Uncle Harry": Belcher and Belcher, *Collecting Souls, Gathering Dust*, 51, 56.

p. 26   "Once I took him": Fortess interview; similar statement in Hills, *Alice Neel*, 15.

p. 26   hard time doing the lettering: Hills, *Alice Neel*, 15.

p. 26   "Now, if you could add your clever drawing": ibid.

p. 26   "Of course that to me was heaven": Fortess interview.

p. 26   Until the end of the nineteenth century: Linda Nochlin, "Why Have There Been
           No Great Women Artists," *Women, Art and Power and Other Essays*, New
           York: Harper & Row Publishers, 1988, 159: "While individual artists and pri-
           vate academies employed the female model extensively, the female nude was for-
           bidden in almost all public art schools as late as 1850, and after. . . . Far more
           believable, unfortunately, was the complete unavailability to the aspiring woman
           artist of any nude models at all, male or female. As late as 1893, 'lady' students
           were not admitted to life drawing classes at the Royal Academy in London, and
           even when they were, after that date, the model had to be partially draped."

p. 26   "We had another teacher": Fortess interview.

p. 27   "too rough for the Philadelphia School": Hills, *Alice Neel*, 16.

p. 27   she didn't receive: ibid., 17.

p. 27   "they liked pictures of girls in fluffy dresses": ibid., 16.

p. 27   To escape the staid confines: Belcher and Belcher, *Collecting Souls, Gathering
           Dust*, 18, 19.

p. 27   "old, poor and city people, an Asian and a young black child": ibid.

p. 27   "There were all these rich girls": Munro, *Originals*, p. 124.

p. 27   Every day, Neel would travel: Polsky, Interview 1, 41.

p. 27   "I'd go wait at Penn Station": ibid., 45.

p. 27   Alice also occasionally painted: Belcher and Belcher, *Collecting Souls, Gather-
           ing Dust*, 58.

p. 28   "from going to the theater": Munro, *Originals*, 124.

p. 28   "I didn't like him physically": Fortess interview.

p. 28   "Well, then there was Jim": Alice Neel, "Money," Neel Archives.

p. 28   She paid her tuition: ibid.

p. 28   "If I liked a boy physically": Munro, *Originals*, 124.

CHAPTER FOUR: *En Plein Air*

p. 30   Established in 1916: History of Chester Springs taken from www.yellowsprings
.org; Historic Yellow Springs Archives; school circular, 1917; also in 1923 Pennsylvania Academy of the Fine Arts Summer School Catalog, Historic Yellow
Springs Archives, and author's interview with Sandy S. Momyer, archivist, Historic Yellow Springs, Inc.

p. 30   Situated on one hundred rolling acres: description of property and buildings
from www.yellowsprings.org; Historic Yellow Springs Archives (the Oriental
Bog may have been landscaped after 1924, when Neel was there); author's interview with Sandy S. Momyer.

p. 30   "The chief object": "Art and Artists in the Making of the PAFA Summer School
at Chester Springs," August 30, 1925, unsourced newspaper article, Historic
Yellow Springs Archives.

p. 31   he was from one of the wealthiest families: Juan Sanchez, *Vida de Carlos Enriquez*, La Habana, Cuba: Instituto Cubano Del Libro, 1996, 9.

p. 31   after he had proven: ibid., 16, 19, 19; Candler College (where he met Marcelo
Pogolotti) and Newton Academy, before studying with the Episcopalians.

p. 31   "gorgeous": Hills, *Alice Neel*, 17.

p. 31   nicknamed "the Mosquito": Marcelo Pogolotti, *Del Barro y las Voces* (unknown
publisher), Havana, Cuba, 1982, 54–55; reprinted in 2004 by Editorial Letras
Cubanas, Havana, Cuba; Sanchez, *Vida De Carlos Enriquez*, 16.

p. 31   "That was the first time": Munro, *Originals*, 124.

p. 31   As a boy: Sanchez, *Vida de Carlos Enriquez*, 17. Carlos also enjoyed Cervantes
and Byron.

p. 31   Dumas and Scott: Pogolotti, *Del Barro y las Voces*, 54, 54.

p. 31   his school magazine: The name of the school magazine was *Heredida*. Sanchez,
Vida de Carlos Enriquez, 17.

p. 31   "Well, doctor, your son,": Sanchez, *Vida de Carlos Enriquez*, 10.

p. 32   "whiz at mathematics": Munro, *Originals*, 123.

p. 32   "But he really loved art": Nemser, *Art Talk; Alice Neel*, 99.

p. 32   According to the school's records: copies of records provided by The Pennsylvania Academy of the Fine Arts.

p. 32   "the most repressed creature": Hills, *Alice Neel*, 17.

p. 32   "the forced gaiety": Munro, *Originals*, 124.

p. 32   "nothing much more than taking walks": Hills, *Alice Neel*, 17.

p. 32   "After failing in various prep schools": Sanchez, *Vida de Carlos Enríquez*, 20.

p. 32   "When the student" ibid., 20.

p. 32   he fought with the head: Munro, unedited transcript of interview for *Originals*, 21.

p. 32   Carlos and Alice had already: Belcher and Belcher, *Collecting Souls, Gathering Dust*, 61.

p. 32   Not that the colony was so staid: author's interview with Sandy Momyer, Chester Springs archivist, April 2008.

p. 33   "Now by then I'd had": Munro, unedited interview transcript for *Originals*, 21.

· p. 33   surviving letter to Alice: copy of letter, Neel Archives; Juan A. Martínez, Enríquez scholar; also quoted in the Philadelphia Museum of Art catalog, 160.

CHAPTER FIVE: *Limbo*

p. 35   "Well then one summer": Alice Neel, "Money," Neel Archives.

p. 35   "After I met Carlos": Munro, *Originals*, 124; unedited transcript of interview for *Originals*, 21.

p. 36   She began to spend more time: Belcher and Belcher, *Collecting Souls, Gathering Dust*, 62.

p. 36   She became much more vocal: ibid., 63.

p. 36   A photograph of Neel: Philadelphia School of Design for Women, 1925–26 yearbook, Moore College Archives.

p. 36   naked on a vase: copy of image of Neel as Lady Godiva provided by Moore College archives.

p. 36   portrait of a girl "en plein air": Sanchez, *Vida de Carlos Enríquez*, 22.

p. 36   "Carlos exhibited a portrait": Pogolotti, *Del Barro y las Voces*, 141.

p. 36   The meeting rekindled: Sanchez, *La Vida de Carlos Enríquez*, 22, 23.

p. 36   "For me, there was not": Sanchez, *Vida de Carlos Enríquez*, 22; Pogolotti, *Del Barrio y las Voces*, 191.

p. 36   Enríquez and Pogolotti: Pogolotti, *Del Barro y las Voces*, 142.

p. 36   huge house in Reina: Pogolotti, *Del Barro y las Voces*, 140–143.

p. 37   Nuevo Mundo restaurant: Sanchez, *Vida de Carlos Enríquez*, 23.

p. 37   "Our points of view": Pogolotti, *Del Barro y las Voces*, ibid.

p. 37   "After some intense work": Pogolotti, *Del Barro y las Voces*, 141, 142.

p. 37   "a huge influence on Carlos": Sanchez, *Vida de Carlos Enríquez*, 24.

p. 37   He would translate: Fortess interview.

p. 37   her mother had still not forgiven: Belcher and Belcher, *Collecting Souls, Gathering Dust*, 62.

p. 37   "Then I did a dirty trick": Alice Neel, "Money," Neel Archives.

p. 37   "Could you come as far as Colwyn": unsent letter: Philadelphia Museum of Art catalog, 160; Neel Archives.

p. 38   Alice's mother "absolutely adored": George Neel, interview with Gerald and Margaret Belcher.

p. 38   "He is very interesting": Polsky, Interview 1, 51.

p. 38   In the days after Carlos returned: Belcher and Belcher, *Collecting Souls, Gathering Dust*, 64.

p. 38   The marriage certificate: certified copy of marriage certificate, obtained from Orphans' Court, Division of Delaware County, PA.

p. 38   The ceremony took place . . . "the manse": Register of Marriages, Darby Presbyterian Church.

p. 38   "Well, I couldn't help it": Alice Neel, "Money," Neel Archives.

p. 38   The commencement took place: program of "Commencement Excercises, Wednesday, June Third, Nineteen Twenty-Five at Three O'Clock," Moore College Archives.

p. 38   When the awards: ibid.

p. 38   Still, Neel's talent was: ibid.

p. 38   Her sister, Lily: Belcher and Belcher, *Collecting Souls, Gathering Dust*, 71.

p. 39   Alice fled the house: ibid., 73.

p. 39   the "awful dichotomy": Hills, *Alice Neel*, 29.

p. 39   "He sent me money": Munro, *Originals*, 125.

p. 39   "So he came back in February": ibid.

CHAPTER SIX: *Tropical Soul*

p. 40   Neel recalled having a private compartment: Polsky, Interview 2, 62.

p. 40   The Peninsular and Occidental Steamship Company: period brochures and schedules of the Peninsular and Occidental (P&O) Steamship Company; Wendy Gimbel, *Havana Dreams*, New York: Random House, 1998, 92–93.

p. 40   According to an unidentified newspaper account: Philadelphia Museum of Art catalog, 160, from unidentified article supplied by Juan Martínez.

p. 41   The ships arrived: author's visit to Havana, Cuba, June 2007.

p. 41   "Spain touched everywhere": Joseph Hergesheimer, *San Cristobal de la Habana*, New York: Alfred A. Knopf, 1927, 15.

p. 41   "You see tortuous cobbled streets": Consuelo Hermer and Marjorie May, *Havana Manana: A Guide to Cuba and the Cubans*, New York: Random House, 1941, 47.

p. 41   "crystal light" and "printed shadows": Joseph Hergesheimer, *San Cristobal de la Habana*, 42.

p. 41   gracious rooms, wide hallways: author's visit to presumed house in Havana, June 2007.

p. 41   Alice referred to it as a "palace": Hills, *Alice Neel*, 20.

p. 41   There was even a charming balcony: Hills, *Alice Neel*, ibid.

p. 42   At six each day: Belcher and Belcher, *Collecting Souls, Gathering Dust*, 76.

p. 42   "You can't imagine how they lived": Hills, *Alice Neel*, ibid.; in Goldstein, "*Soul on Canvas*," *New York Magazine*, 78, Neel says there were seven servants and a Rolls Royce.

p. 42   Alice was certainly not expected to conform: Wendy Gimbel, *Havana Dreams*, 61.

p. 42   "What struck me at once": Joseph Hergesheimer, *San Cristobal de la Habana*, 22.

p. 42   According to the historian Louis Pérez: author's phone interview with Louis Pérez, May 20, 2008.

p. 43   Louis A. Pérez, Chapel Hill: *On Becoming Cuban*, The University of North Carolina Press, 1999, 319.

p. 43   "Siempre en la calle": Nemser, *Art Talk: Conversations with 12 Women Artists*, 100.

p. 43   "I wasn't made": Polsky, Interview 2, 67.

p. 43   "I should have had some birth control": Hills, *Alice Neel*, 21.

p. 43   And by July 1926: Belcher and Belcher, *Collecting Souls, Gathering Dust*, 78.

p. 43   "like van Gogh": Hills, *Alice Neel*, 20.

p. 43   "All we did was paint day and night": Karl Fortess interview.

p. 43   "too happy": William Luvaas, "Making It: An Interview," *Art Times*, December, 1986, 11 (reprint of interview done with Neel in 1979); Neel also complained about "heat and sun," in Hills, *Alice Neel*, 20.

p. 43   "tropical light": Hills, *Alice Neel*, 29.

p. 43   "There the Afro-Cubans": ibid., 20.

p. 44   "They have more self": Hills, *Alice Neel*, ibid.

p. 44   "There were people": Diamonstein, *Inside New York's Art World*, 256.

p. 44   "The rich used to cut": Rhodes and Murphy, interview transcript for *Three Women Artists*, January 3, 1976, 4.

p. 44   "We completely lived the vie Bohemienne": Nemser, *Art Talk: Conversations with 12 Women Artists*, 99.

p. 44   "It was more civilized": Luvaas, "Artists on Their Art," *Art International*, Vol. 12, No. 5; May 15, 1958, 11 [quoted in Susan Rothenberg, "People as Evidence," Philadelphia Museum of Art catalog (2000), 47].

p. 44   "My life in Cuba": Hills, *Alice Neel*, 21.

p. 44   "Latin mentality": ibid., 33.

p. 45   In January 1899: Dick Cluster and Rafael Hernandez, *The History of Havana*, New York: Palgrave (Macmillan), 2006.

p. 45   José Martí's dream of a "Cuba Libre": Cluster and Hernandez, *The History of Havana*, 106.

p. 45   "the coming of age": author's interview with Louis Pérez, May, 2008.

p. 45   "Second dance of the Millions": Donald J. Mabray, The Historical Text Archive, Mississippi State University; author's e-mail correspondence with Donald J. Mabray.

p. 45   the price of sugar: Louis A. Pérez, Jr., *Cuba and the United States; Ties of Singular Intimacy*, Athens, GA: The University of Georgia Press, 2003, 180.

p. 45   In May 1925: Cluster and Hernandez, *The History of Havana*, 162, 163.

p. 45   In 1926, however: ibid., 138.

p. 45   Havana Biltmore Yacht and Country Club: Pérez, *Cuba and the United States* 139; Pérez, *On Becoming Cuban*, 175, 179.

p. 45   "the Monte Carlo of the Western Hemisphere": Pérez, *Cuba and the United States*, 141, 142.

p. 46   "Havana is becoming a second home": ibid., 141.

p. 46   "It is hot, it is wet": ibid., 142.

p. 46   Pérez describes it vividly: author's interview with Louis Pérez.

p. 46   "The moment to go to Havana": Hergesheimer, *San Cristobal de la Habana*, 198.

p. 46   "Foot It and Go": Cluster and Hernandez, *The History of Havana*, 136.

p. 46   the Junta for National Renovation: Juan A. Martinez, *Cuban Art and National Identity*, Miami: University Press of Florida, 1994, 37.

p. 46   1925 alone saw the formation: Pérez, *Cuba and the United States*, 173, 174.

p. 46   the Grupo Minorista published its manifesto: Martinez, *Cuban Art and National Identity*, 39.

p. 47   "We fully condemn and negate": ibid., 11.

p. 47   "embryonic" period of modern Cuban painting: ibid., 5.

p. 47   the Cuban academic style: ibid., 2.

p. 47   "lo Cubano": ibid., 5.

p. 47   possibly at a small gallery: Belcher and Belcher, *Collecting Souls, Gathering Dust*, 80.

p. 47   Pogolotti dramatically described: Pogolotti, *Del Barro y las Voces*, 167, 168.

p. 48   "You can't mix people": Rhodes and Murphy, transcript of interview for *Three Women Artists*.

p. 48   named Santillana del Mar, after a small town: author's interview with Pablo Lancella, May 27, 2003; Sanchez, p. 31.

p. 48   Neel never forgot: Hills, *Alice Neel*, 21.

p. 48   "They're more animal": Munro, *Originals*, 125.

p. 48   La Vibora: Hills, *Alice Neel*, 20; Richard Polsky, Interview 1, 51.

p. 48   "two steps from the bus stop": Pogolotti, *Del Barro y las Voces*, 165.

p. 48   "Every Saturday we would meet": Pogolotti, *Del Barro y las Voces*, 165.

p. 49   "Anglo-Saxon" gullibility: ibid.

p. 49   looking at it upside down: author's interview with America Villiers, January 6, 2004.

p. 49   "Carlos was fond": Pogolotti, *Del Barro y las Voces*, 165.

p. 49   showed their work at the XII Salón de Bellas Artes: pamphlet for the XII Salon de Bellas Artes, Marzo–Abril, 1927.

p. 49   According to the pamphlet: ibid.

p. 49   In a glowing review: Marti Casanovas, undated Paqueta Gaceta article; translated and excerpted in Philadelphia Museum of Art catalog, 161.

p. 49   Images of their work were reproduced in two issues: *Revista de Avance*, La Habana, Abril 15 de 1927, Ano 1, Num. 3; *La Habana*, Abril 30 de 1927, Año 1, Num. 4.

p. 49   "the extraordinary marriage": Philadelphia Museum translation; Neel Archives.

p. 49   "wide and juicy brushstroke," its "spontaneity and great richness of temperament": ibid.

p. 50   "militant," "new," and "avantgarde": Juan Martinez, *Cuban Art and National Identity*, 6, 10.

p. 50   "mild versions of European modern styles": ibid., 6.

p. 50   Neel showed portraits: list of artists' works in show from *Special Edition of Revista de Avance for the Exposicion de Art Nuevo*: "Orginizada por 1927 revista de avance, Primera Exposcion de Art Nuevo, Mayo de 1927," Asociacion de Pintores Y Escultores, La Habana.

p. 50   column by Martí Casanovas: *El Mundo*, Havana, 1927.

p. 51   she and her in-laws: Belcher and Belcher, *Collecting Souls, Gathering Dust*, 83; Polsky, Interview 1, 51, 52. Neel told Polsky that Carlos had lost his job with the coal company, "so rather than go and live with his family again—that's what I should have done, but you know they had very definite ideas about what women should do, you know." She also said she came back to the States, "to visit my mother."

p. 51   "Since Carlos' wife left": Pogolotti, *Del Barro y las Voces*, 170. (In one later adventure, Carlos, acting like a school boy, stole an enormous rosary from a public place and hung it in his room, like a trophy; ibid., 211.)

CHAPTER SEVEN: *(You Can Go) Home Again*

p. 52   At thirty-nine, Albert was finally: Belcher and Belcher, *Collecting Souls, Gathering Dust*, 85.

p. 52   "quiet desperation": Hills, *Alice Neel*, 21.

p. 53   "My brother is upstairs": ibid., 19.

p. 53   Carlos resurfaced in Colwyn that fall: Philadelphia Museum catalog, 161; Juan Sanchez, "La Vida de Carlos Enríquez," 30.

p. 53   an apartment on West Eighty-first Street: Philadelphia Museum of Art catalog, 161.

p. 53   "great number of watercolors": Hills, *Alice Neel*, 21.

p. 53   "street scenes of New York": Nemser, *Art Talk*, 100.

p. 54   Fanya Foss's Art Deco store: author's interviews with Toni and Michael Lawrence (daughter and son of Fanya).

p. 54   at National City Bank: Philadelphia Museum catalog, 162; Hills, *Alice Neel*, 21.

p. 54   "a modern scene in action": Ann Douglas, *Terrible Honesty: Mongrel Manhattan*, New York: The Monday Press, Farrar, Straus and Giroux, 1995, 59.

p. 54   As Fitzgerald wrote: ibid., 22.

p. 54   New York City's population: ibid., 15.

p. 54   the Bohemian A-list: ibid.

p. 54   literature, film, theater: ibid., 13–16.

p. 54   "was a magnet": ibid., 25.

p. 55   De Kooning had just recently moved: Mark Stevens and Analyn Swan, *De Kooning*, New York: Knopf, 2004, 69.

p. 55   Arshile Gorky settled in: Hayden Herrera, *Arshile Gorky*, New York: Farrar, Straus and Giroux, 2003, 127.

p. 55   One of Edward Hopper's: Gail Levin, *Edward Hopper*, Berkeley: University of California Press, 1995, 201.

p. 55   Jackson Pollock would arrive: Steven Naifeh and Gregory White Smith, *Jackson Pollock: An American Saga*, New York: Clarkson N. Potter, 1989, 151. "Jackson began classes at the Art Students' League on September 19, 1950."

p. 55   Mark Rothko had studied: James E. B. Breslin, *Mark Rothko*, Chicago: University of Chicago Press, 1993, 55, 56.

p. 55   Armory statement: Made by John Quinn, the president of the Association of
            American Painters and Sculptors; Milton R. Brown, *The Story of The Armory
            Show*, New York: Abbeville Press, 1988, 43.

p. 56   "The Armory Show was a complete disaster": Mark Stevens and Analyn Swan,
            De Kooning, 78.

p. 57   "When we were together": Munro, unedited interview transcript for *Originals*, 20.

p. 57   "stupid" drawings for American newspapers: Hills, *Alice Neel*, 29.

p. 57   Gordon Kingman: Philadelphia Museum catalog, 36.

p. 57   Background on Fanya Foss: author's phone interviews with Michael Lawrence
            and Toni Lawrence.

p. 56   Ibid.

p. 57   kindred spirit in Neel: author's interview with Michael Lawrence.

p. 57   "shared an early feminist independence": Letters to the Editor, *Art in America*,
            May, 2001.

p. 58   surrounded herself with artists: author's interview with Toni Lawrence.

p. 58   The street scenes owned by Fanya Foss were *Snow Scene*, 1938, and *Spanish
            Harlem House*, circa 1930s: author's interview with Amy Wolf, Amy Wolf Fine
            Art, New York.

p. 58   "I bought Alice's early periods": Fanya Foss, undated reminiscence for a gallery
            in Los Angeles.

p. 58   "She was a friend of mine": Hills, *Alice Neel*, 26.

p. 58   In Foss, Neel found an equal: author's phone interviews with Michael Lawrence
            and Toni Lawrence.

p. 58   "I met Alice": Foss, undated reminiscence for a gallery in Los Angeles.

p. 59   Foss not only witnessed: author's interview with Michael Lawrence.

p. 59   apartment on Sedgwick Avenue: Philadelphia Museum catalog, 162. In Nemser,
            Art Talk, 101, Neel says they moved right after Santillana died.

p. 59   "My grandmother said": George Neel, interview with Gerald and Margaret Belcher.

p. 59   "Malice Neel": author's interview with Barbara Hollister, November 8, 2007;
            author's interview with Victorio Korjhan; November 16, 2007.

p. 60   "a very beautiful, healthy child": Hills, *Alice Neel*, 21.

p. 60   "burning a spiritus lamp": Belcher and Belcher, *Collecting Souls, Gathering
            Dust*, 89.

p. 60   Santillana had also been malnourished: author's interview with Graziella Pogolotti, Havana, June 14, 2007.

p. 60   "Do you know how much an oil stove costs?": Alice Neel, "Money," Neel Archives.

p. 60   "She must have died there": George Neel, interview with Gerald and Margaret Belcher.

p. 61   "It was so horrible": author's interview with Hartley and Ginny Neel, June 11, 2008.

p. 61   There are no tombstones: author's visit to Arlington Cemetery in Drexel Hill, PA; interview with Arlington Family Services representative Dennis Hancock; Arlington Cemetery records for December 8, 9, 1927 *re:* burial of Santillana Enríquez.

p. 61   "In the beginning, I didn't want children": Hills, *Alice Neel*, 21.

p. 62   "Even Picasso only used gray": Nemser, *Art Talk*, 101.

p. 62   "I had had that child": Munro, *Originals*, 125.

CHAPTER EIGHT: *Futility of Effort*

p. 63   "After Santillana's death": Hills, *Alice Neel*, 21.

p. 63   "The two little lamps": Neel, undated personal writings, Neel Archives.

p. 64   "When I was pregnant": Munro, unedited interview transcript for *Originals*, 20.

p. 64   "All this you do": Alice Neel, undated personal writings, Neel Archives; typed on The National City Company letterhead.

p. 64   "You enter a splendid building": ibid.; Philadelphia Museum catalog, Rothenberg, "People as Evidence," 40.

p. 65   "A terrible rivalry": Hills, *Alice Neel*, 29.

p. 65   Enríquez also sent illustrations of New York scenes: Juan A. Martínez, *Carlos Enríquez: The Painter of Cuban Ballads*, Coral Gables, Fl., Cernude Art, 2010, 42.

p. 65   "we really almost starved": Polsky, Interview 2, 75.

p. 65   "consumed by an actual fire": Alice Neel, personal papers, November 8, 1928, Neel Archives.

p. 65   "I lay in bed": ibid., November 12, 1928.

p. 66   "I feel sorry for them all": ibid.

p. 66   According to Isabetta's husband: interview with Pablo Lancella, May 27, 2003.

p. 66   Her birth certificate states: copy of Isabetta's birth certificate.

p. 66   *"Well Baby Clinic* makes my attitude": Hills, *Alice Neel*, 23.

p. 66   "When people would mewl": ibid., 21.

p. 66   "that nice-looking one": ibid., 23.

p. 67   "sloppy humanity there": ibid., 23; Nemser, *Art Talks*, 102.

p. 67   Neel suffered from phlebitis: Hills, *Alice Neel*, 24.

p. 67   "The Dark Picture of the Kallikaks": Hills, *Alice Neel*, 24, 25.

p. 68   in several poems: ibid., 29.

p. 68   According to George Neel: George interview with Gerald and Margaret Belcher.

p. 69   Photographs of Neel with Isabetta: courtesy of the Neel Archives, Pablo Lancella, Jr.

p. 69   In another poem written: Alice Neel, poem written in the winter, 1929, Smithsonian Archives of American Art, Alice Neel Papers, Reel 4964.

p. 69   Neel was forced to ask her sister: George Neel, interview with Gerald and Margaret Belcher.

p. 69   "People starved": Rhodes and Murphy, *Three Women Artists*, interview transcript, November 8, 1975.

p. 69   Carlos drew a Christmas card: Philadelphia Museum catalog, 162.

CHAPTER NINE: *The Bell Jar*

p. 70   "Oh I was full of theories": Hills, *Alice Neel*, 41.

p. 70   "He abandoned New York": translation done by Philadelphia Museum of telegram "directed to" Marcelo Pogolotti.

p. 70   His friends had been criticizing: Hills, *Alice Neel*, 32.

p. 71   "I realized that was just the end": ibid.

p. 71   "Carlos went away": Alice Neel, personal papers, Neel archives; Philadelphia Museum catalog, 162.

p. 71   Martínez doubts: author's interview with Juan Martínez, January 6, 2004.

p. 72   According to Marisa Diaz: author's phone interview with Marisa Diaz, June 3, 2003.

p. 72   But Martínez heard: author's interview with Juan Martínez, January 6, 2004.

p. 72   From the Cubans' point of view: Philadelphia Museum catalog, 15. "Resentful of Neel's maternal ineptitude, Enríquez took their second child Isabella home with him to Cuba when he left Neel in 1930."

p. 72   "I had always had this awful dichotomy": Hills, *Alice Neel*, 29.

p. 72   "At first all I did was paint": ibid.

p. 73   "I asked my mother": ibid., 32.

p. 73   According to Diaz: author's phone interview with Marisa Diaz, June 3, 2003.

p. 73   "the Cuban inlaws": Hills, *Alice Neel*, 53.

p. 73   "His family would have brought": Goldstein, "Soul on Canvas," 78.

p. 73   "it would be too bourgeois": Philadelphia Museum transcript of interview with Jonathan Brand, 1969.

p. 73   "Isabetta was bitter": author's interview with Pablo Landella, May 27, 2003.

p. 73   she lost nearly twenty-five pounds: Hills, *Alice Neel*, 32.

p. 74   "I had a terrible life": ibid.

p. 74   "Your senses are never more acute": Munro, *Originals*, 125.

p. 74   "One of the reasons": Hills, *Alice Neel*, 32.

p. 74   "dying spells . . . dreading falling apart": ibid., 32, 33.

p. 74   "It's a complete breakdown": ibid., 33.

p. 74   the "pathogenic mechanism": Sigmund Freud, *Five Lectures, on Psychoanalysis*, translated and edited by James Strachey, New York: W.W. Norton & Company, 1977, 24.

p. 75   "If I'd only had five hundred dollars": Munro, *Originals*, 125.

p. 75   "Instead of being able": Rhodes and Murphy, transcript of interview for *Three Women Artists*.

p. 75   "great masterpieces": Hills, *Alice Neel*, 33.

p. 75   "a little girl chained": ibid.

p. 75   "A suicidal depression is a kind of": A. Alvarez, *The Savage God; A Study of Suicide*, New York: W.W. Norton & Company, 1990, 103.

p. 76   Lily had summoned from Paris: Hills, *Alice Neel*, 33.

p. 76   "Carlos wanted to return to Paris," ibid., 35.

p. 76   taxi ride: Hills, *Alice Neel*, ibid.

p. 76   It was a threat: Hills, *Alice Neel*, ibid.

p. 76   "During one of my periodic visits": Fanya Foss, reminiscence for Los Angeles gallery show.

p. 76   tried to swallow the shards: Hills, *Alice Neel*, 35.

p. 76   "my grandmother refused to go": George Neel, interview with Gerald and Margaret Belcher.

p. 76   "He was a frivolous character": Hills, *Alice Neel*, 36.

p. 76   "to see if I had a venereal disease": *Alice Neel*, 36.

p. 76   She was surrounded by others: ibid., 36.

p. 77   "oblivion . . . between the cries and groans": ibid., 40.

p. 77   She soon became incontinent: Munro, *Originals*, 126.

p. 77   "I couldn't pull long enough": Hills, *Alice Neel*, 36.

p. 77   "Well I'm a famous artist": ibid., 38.

p. 77   "You're the enemy": ibid.

p. 77   "It was the drawing": *Originals*, 126.

CHAPTER TEN: *Resurrection*

p. 78   "I was a neurotic": Rhodes and Murphy, interview transcript for *Three Women Artists*.

p. 78   according to data: Natalie Angier, "An Old Idea about Artistic Genius Wins New Scientific Support," *The New York Times*, October 12, 1993.

p. 78   Bourgeois has stated: Joan Acocella, "The Spider's Web, Louise Bourgeois and Her Art," *The New Yorker*, February 4, 2002.

p. 78   Arshile Gorky hanged himself: Hayden Herrera, *Arshile Gorky*, Farrar, Straus and Giroux, New York, 2003, pp. 595, 612, 620.

p. 79   "no psychosis" Hills, *Alice Neel*, 32.

p. 79   "Freud's classic hysteria": ibid.

p. 79   "If I don't paint": Hills, *Alice Neel*, 192.

p. 79   "But guess what?": Goldstein, "Soul on Canvas," 80.

p. 79   "I'm a trained neurotic": Kufrin, *Uncommon Women*, 145.

p. 79   who had first come across . . . in 1910, bought the property in 1912: Joseph S. Kennedy, *The Philadelphia Inquirer*, September 19, 2004; Rebecca V. Quinn, "The Gladwyne Colony," Lower Merion High School Psychology Course, June 5, 1977, 3, information corroborated with Sandy Ronan, granddaughter of Seymour Ludlum.

p. 80   Biographical background on Dr. Seymour DeWitt Ludlum: Charles Rupp, M.D., Secretary of the American Neurological Association, written appreciation of Seymour DeWitt Ludlum, December 1956; provided by Sandy Ronan, Rebecca V. Quinn, "The Gladwyne Colony," 8, corroborated by Sandy Ronan.

p. 80   published more than fifty-five papers: Rebecca V. Quinn, "The Gladwyne Colony," 4, corroborated by Sandy Ronan.

p. 80   some of his mentally disturbed patients: ibid.

p. 80   At its peak: Joseph S. Kennedy; Rebecca V. Quinn, 11, corroborated with Sandy Ronan.

p. 80   locked rooms . . . simply old people: ibid., 7; author's interview with Helen Dixon, daughter of Ellen Porter, nurse who worked at Gladwyne during Alice Neel's time, June 30, 2008.

p. 80   Number of staff, patients: Joseph S. Kennedy; Kathi Kaufman, *The Philadelphia Inquirer*, September 8, 1991; Lower Merion Historical Society Oral History Project, Ann Bagley interviewing DeWitt Ludlum, November 21, 1997.

p. 80   therapeutic methods: Rebecca V. Quinn "The Gladwyne Colony," 5.

p. 80   "When able, patients": Lower Merion Historical Society, *The First 300*, 96.

p. 80   "If you were to drive": *Mainline Chronicle*, March 28, 1957.

p. 81   "There were people in straitjackets": author's interview with Sandy Ronan, June 9, 2008.

p. 81   Physically, Gladwyne Colony: author's visit to grounds of former Gladwyne Colony.

p. 81   Description of grounds and buildings: author's interview with Helen Dixon.

p. 81   It is likely that after being evaluated: ibid.

p. 81   Dr. Ludlum's home, Fernside . . . impeccably renovated: author's visit to grounds of former Gladwyne Colony.

p. 81   "a wonderful experimental psychologist": Hills, *Alice Neel*, 38, 39.

p. 82   Recalled Millen Brand's son: Jonathan Brand, Gallery Programs/Exhibitions, University Art Museum, Berkeley, April 85; author's interview with Jonathan Brand.

p. 82   "suicidal ward": Hills, *Alice Neel*, 38.

p. 82   But Helen Dixon, the daughter of Ellen Porter: author's interview with Helen Dixon.

p. 82   Neel's first memory: Munro, *Originals*, 127; Hills, *Alice Neel*, 38.

p. 82   "You wouldn't have to be here": ibid.

p. 82   although Dixon states: author's interview with Helen Dixon.

p. 82   A tall, distinguished-looking man: author's interview with Helen Dixon.

p. 82   "a connoisseur of good food": Charles Rupp, written appreciation.

p. 82   According to Dixon: author's interview with Helen Dixon.

p. 83   Neel's quirky anecdotes: Hills, *Alice Neel*, 38.

p. 83   "Dr. Ludlum used to hug me": ibid., 39; Neel made a similar statement, "for one thing I was very beautiful and people used to love to hug me," in Munro, unedited transcript for *Originals*, 31.

p. 83   Neel's self-prescribed therapy: ibid.; Munro, *Originals*, 126.

p. 83   "Body that had lain": Millen Brand, *The Outward Room*, Simon and Schuster, New York, 1937, 5.

p. 83   "I worked at getting well": Munro, *Originals*, 126; unedited interview transcript Munro, for *Originals*, 31.

p. 83   She tried to follow the advice: ibid., 30; Munro, *Originals*, 127.

p. 83   "I began to try to explain it to myself": Munro, *Originals*, 127.

p. 83   "I learned to realize": Hills, *Alice Neel*, 40.

p. 83   Eventually, she became continent: Hills, *Alice Neel*, 39.

p. 83   "Dr. Ludlum had a wonderful house": ibid.

p. 83   "I never saw him hugging": author's interview with Helen Dixon.

p. 84   Dixon recalls: ibid.

p. 84   But according to Neel's account: Hills, *Alice Neel*, 39.

p. 84   Dixon says that on: author's interview with Helen Dixon.

p. 84   "Ever since he had known her": Millen Brand, *The Outward Room*, 15, 16.

p. 84   "Is there any other reason": ibid., 23, 24.

p. 85   "I think you know": ibid., 24.

p. 85   "I have always had a perfect horror": Hills, *Alice Neel*, 39.

CHAPTER ELEVEN: *Next Stop, Greenwich Village*

p. 86   Her inclusion in the WPA easel program: Hills, *Alice Neel*, 57.

p. 86   she had joined the Public Works Art Project: ibid., 53.

p. 86   in 1935 she joined the Communist Party: ibid., 60.

p. 86   The Washington Square studio: Belcher and Belcher, *Collecting Souls, Gathering Dust*, 155.

p. 86   "great renunciation": Hills, *Alice Neel*, p. 41; personal papers, Neel Archives.

p. 87   Nadya was now living with her husband: Hills, ibid.; Munro, unedited transcript of interview *Originals*, 30.

p. 87   According to her great-nephew: author's interview with Victorio Korjahn, November 16, 2007.

p. 87   "her preoccupation with people": Nadya Olyanova, *Handwriting Tells*, North Hollywood, California: Melvin Powers Wilshire Book Company, 1969, 194.

p. 87   Born in Kiev: *The New York Times*, obituary, Nadya Olyanova, May 26, 1991.

p. 87   "She represented Decadence": Hills, *Alice Neel*, 41.

p. 88   "return to real life": ibid.

p. 88   compelling anecdotes: Belcher and Belcher, *Collecting Souls, Gathering Dust*, 155.

p. 88   "He was very clever": Hills, *Alice Neel*, 44.

p. 88   "an interesting fellow": Munro, *Originals*, 127.

p. 88   "Why don't you go stay" Hills, *Alice Neel*, 44.

p. 88   33½ Cornelia Street: ibid.; Philadelphia Museum catalog, 163.

p. 88   The four-story rear building: author's visit to property at 33 ½ Cornelia Street.

p. 88   "I lived with a sailor": Nemser, *Art Talks*, p. 104.

p. 89   Biographical background on Kenneth Doolittle: author's interviews with Kenneth Doolittle's children, Karla Doolittle Buch, Sarah Eisner, December 10, 2008; Thomas Doolittle, December 19, 2009; author's interview with Kenneth Doolittle's friend, Stanley Maron, October 24, 2008.

p. 90   military papers: Doolittle family archives.

p. 92   Originally called Green Village: Ross Wetzsteon, *Republic of Dreams, Greenwich*

Village: The American Bohemia, 1910–1960, New York: Simon and Schuster, 2002, 4, 5.

p. 92   Greenwich Village was unofficially: ibid., 1–3.

p. 93   By the time Neel arrived: ibid., 250.

p. 93   Mabel Dodge: ibid., 15.

p. 93   Max Eastman: ibid., 49.

p. 93   Jig Cook and Eugene O'Neill: ibid., 92–108.

p. 93   In his book, *Exile's Return*: Dore Ashton, *The New York School*, New York: The Viking Press and Compass Books, 1973, 16.

p. 93   As Ross Wetzsteon puts it: ibid., Preface, ix.

p. 93   Wetzsteon's list: ibid., Preface, xiii, xiv.

p. 93   the Belmar, etc.: Joseph Mitchell, *Up in the Old Hotel*, Vintage Books, New York, 1993, 635, 63.

p. 94   Stewart's Cafeteria: ibid., 652.

p. 94   Although according to Gould: ibid., 650.

p. 94   Aunt Clemmy's and Minetta Tavern: ibid., 651, 652.

p. 94   "one free meal": Hills, *Alice Neel*, 53; Philadelphia Museum catalog, p. 164; Joe Gould, "My Life," 1933, 11, "This is all that I will say about my life as I write these lines at ten minutes past three in the afternoon of Sunday, December 31, 1933, in the Fair at 103 W. Third St. New York City, where I am at the free dinner . . ."
         I discovered the essay, "My Life," among the Millen Brand Papers, Columbia Rare Manuscript Library, along with several other essays and a cache of letters.

p. 94   As Gould himself wrote: Gould, "My Life," 1933, 10.

p. 94   "an underground masterpiece" Mitchell, *Up in the Old Hotel*, 628, 629.

p. 94   Neel said this was an advertisement: phone interview with Virginia Neel.

p. 94   "Variations on an Old Theme": Alice Neel, Harvard lecture, March 21, 1979.

p. 94   "The trouble with you": Hills, *Alice Neel*, 48.

p. 95   "Joe Gould Fund": Mitchell, *Up in the Old Hotel*, Philip Bonosky journals, May 31, 1960, entry.

p. 95   "spinach and vinegar": ibid.

p. 95   Ibid.; Philip Bonosky reprints a "transcript" of Neel's writing "Requiem for Joe Gould," in his May 31, 1960, entry.

p. 95   Joseph Mitchell, *Up In the Old Hotel*: "Professor Seagull," 52–70; "Joe Gould's Secret," 623–716; list of publications essays were included in 647, 648.

p. 96   He left about half a dozen: these essays are included in the Millen Brand Papers, Rare Book and Manuscript Library, Columbia University.

p. 96   Wrote Mitchell of the portrait: Joseph Mitchell, *Up in the Old Hotel*, "Joe Gould's Secret," 630.

p. 96   Neel later criticized Mitchell: Polsky, Interview 3, 114; Michel Auder video; Alice Neel, 1976–1984.

p. 96   Kenneth Fearing, Christopher Lazar, Max White, Sam Putnam: Hills, *Alice Neel*, 47, 49, 54, 63.

p. 97   "dipsomaniac and broken ruin": Alice Neel, Harvard Lecture, March 21, 1979.

p. 97   "the Beat of those days": Leslie, *The Hasty Papers*, 91.

p. 97   "Those were the days": Phillip Bonosky journal, May 31, 1960 entry.

p. 97   "I never palled around with them": Polsky, Interview 1, 47.

p. 97   Harold Rosenberg: ibid., 94; Munro, interview transcript for *The Originals*, 37.

p. 97   "queen of homosexuals": Hills, *Alice Neel*, 47.

p. 97   Millen Brand, *Some Love, Some Hunger*, New York: Crown Publishers, 1955.

p. 97   Millen Brand journals, October 2, 1934 entry, Millen Brand Papers, Rare Book and Manuscript Library, Columbia University.

p. 98   Fanya Foss's depiction, "plump, with thick legs": Fanya Foss, manuscript of untitled, unpublished novel, 39.

p. 98   "I must paint his picture": ibid., 38.

p. 98   "Sometimes I have the illusion": ibid., 42.

p. 98   "In the beginning, when I loved him": Alice Neel, personal papers, undated poem, Neel Archives.

p. 99   As *The New York Times* described it: Philadelphia Museum catalog, 163, 164; "Open Air Art Shows Gaining Favor," *The New York Times Magazine*, June 5, 1932.

p. 99   "All of this is humanity": Hills, *Alice Neel*, 45.

p. 99   Joseph Solman: *The Ten; Birth of the American Avant-Garde*, Boston: Mercury Gallery, 1998; "The Ten," introduction by Isabelle Dervaux, 5.

p. 100   Recalled Solman: author's interview with Joseph Solman, March 3, 2003.

p. 100   Recalled Herman Rose: author's interview with Herman Rose, March 20, 2003.

p. 101   Description of John Rothschild: Hills, *Alice Neel*, 47.

p. 101   Dr. Lehvy: Fanya Foss, untitled novel, 57.

p. 101   November 20 tea and discussion at the Jumble Shop: Philadelphia Museum catalog, 162.

p. 101   small show at a bookstore: ibid.; Belcher and Belcher, *Collecting Souls, Gathering Dust*, 160.

p. 101   she received her first American review: J. B. Neumann, *The Philadelphia Inquirer*, March 19, 1933; Philadelphia Museum catalog, 164.

p. 101   She was also mentioned: "Painting from Six Countries on View at Mellon Galleries," *The Philadelphia Ledger*, March 19, 1933.

p. 101   On December 26, 1933, Neel enrolled: Hills, *Alice Neel*, 53.

CHAPTER TWELVE: *The Easel Project*

p. 103   "I came to Greenwich Village": Judith Zilczer, interview with Alice Neel, October 27, 1981, for the catalog, "Five Distinguished Alumni: The WPA Federal Art Project," Hirschorn Museum and Sculpture Garden, January 21–February 22, 1982; "WPA," Herter Art Gallery, University of Massachusetts, Amherst; 1977, Preface. Author's interview with Bernarda Bryson, October 3, 2003.

p. 103   25 percent—some fifteen million: Hills, "Social Concern and Urban Realism, American Painting of the 1930s," Boston University Art Gallery, 1983; "The Socially Concerned Painters of the 1930s: An Introduction," 10.

p. 103   Bernarda Bryson, Ben Shahn's widow: author's interview with Bernarda Bryson, October 3, 2003.

p. 103   When Neel attended: Hills, *Alice Neel*, 57.

p. 103   "When I first came to New York": author's interview with Will Barnet, July 8, 2003; although Barnet was on the WPA at the same time as Neel, he didn't know her at that time.

p. 104   By early 1933: Janet Feldman, "WPA," Amherst: Herter Art Gallery, University of Massachussetts, 1.

p. 104   "arsenic and old face": Neel used this sobriquet in the Michel Auder video when talking about her painting of McMahon.

p. 104   3,749 artists: Janet Feldman, "WPA," Herter Art Gallery, 2.

p. 104   Neel was so happy: Hills, *Alice Neel*, 53.

p. 104   15,633 works of art: Janet Feldman, "WPA," 3.

p. 104   According to her employment records: transcript of Employment for Alice Neel, General Services Administration, National Personnel Records Center, Civilian Personnel Records, St. Louis, Missouri, courtesy of Francis V. O'Connor.

p. 105   The Art Project alone had eight divisions: Hills, "The Socially Concerned Artists of the 1930s," 11; Janet Feldman, "WPA," Herter Art Gallery, 3.

p. 105   According to Hills: Hills, "The Socially Concerned Artists of the 1930s," 13; Janet Feldman, "WPA," Herter Art Gallery, 3. More specific numbers: 2,566 murals, 17,744 sculptures, 108,900 paintings, and 200,000 prints, 2 million posters; catalog preface for "New York WPA Artists Then and Now," November 8–Dec 10, 1977, Parsons School of Design, 1.

p. 105   There was, however, a prohibition against nudes: Hills, "The Socially Concerned Artists of the 1930s," 12.

p. 105   According to Neel: Alice Neel, transcript of question and answer session at Harvard University Lecture, March 3, 1979, 13.

p. 105   As Raphael Soyer recalled: Hills, "Social Concern and Urban Realism," 30; "An Art of Protest and Despair," *Art in America*, December, 1983, 98.

p. 106   Says Barnet: author's interview with Will Barnet.

p. 106   Neel was on the easel project: Francis V. O'Connor, ed. *The New Deal Art Projects: An Anthology of Memoirs*, Washington, DC: Smithsonian Institution Press, 1972: Joseph Solman essay, "The Easel Divisions of the WPA Federal Art Project," 117.

p. 106   As Neel recalled in 1981: Alice Neel, October 27, 1981, interview with Judith Zilczer.

p. 106   In a statement made: "New York WPA Artists Then 1934–1943 and Now 1960–1977," November 8 to December 10, 1977, 66.

p. 107   As Barnet puts it: author's interview with Will Barnet.

p. 107   By September 1935: transcript of Employment for Alice Neel, General Services Administration.

p. 107   *The Great Depression*, which she never turned in: Hills, *Alice Neel*, 58; (the painting is still in the Estate of Alice Neel).

p. 107   "Not everyone likes blood": Patricia Marlene Park, "New Deal for Art: the Government Art Projects of the 1930's, with Examples from New York City and State," Hamilton, N.Y.: Gallery Association of New York State Inc., 1977, 80.

p. 107   when Neel discovered: *Life* magazine, April 17, 1944.

p. 107   John Reed Club: Hills, "The Socially Concerned Artists of the 1930s," 15, 16.

p. 108   Neel attended the John Reed Club: Hills, *Alice Neel*, 59.

p. 108   In September 1933: Hills, "Socially Concerned Artists of the 1930's," 12; Andrew Hemingway, "Artists on the Left," New Haven: Yale University Press, 2002, 84–86.

p. 108   just such an intervention: author's interview with Joseph Solman; also mentioned in Joseph Solman, "The Easel Divisions of the WPA Federal Art Project," 119.

p. 108   McMahon recalls one revealing: O'Connor, ed. *The New Deal Art Projects: An Anthology* of *Memoirs*, 67.

p. 109   Solman recollected an incident: Solman, "The Easel Divisions of the WPA Federal Art Project," 120.

p. 109   219 sitdown strike: Hills, "Socially Concerned Artists of the 1930's," 21.

p. 109   strike against May's department store: Hills, *Alice Neel*, 60.

p. 109   *Art Front*: Hills, "Socially Concerned Artists of the 1930's," 16.

p. 109   Solman became its editor: author's interview with Joseph Solman.

p. 109   In 1935, another important artists' organization: Hills, "Socially Concerned Artists of the 1930's," 16.

p. 110   Recalls Barnet: author's interview with Will Barnet.

p. 110   The papers from the conference: American Artist's Congress discussed in Hills, "Socially Concerned Artists of the 1930's," 16; Serge Guilbaut, *How New York Stole the Idea of Modern Art*, Chicago: The University of Chicago Press, 19–21; Dore Ashton, *The New York School: A Cultural Reckoning*, New York: Penguin, 1973, 63, 64; Andrew Hemingway, *Artists on the Left*, 123, 124; David Schapiro, *Social Realism: Art as a Weapon*, New York: Frederick Ungar Publishing Co.: 1973, 22, 23.

p. 110   the legendary ACA Gallery: founded in August, 1932 by Ellie and Herman Baron. Hemingway, *Artists on the Left*, 47–48; A Concise History of the ACA Galleries, acagalleries.com.

p. 110   Stewart's Cafeteria: Stevens and Swan, *De Kooning*, 148.

p. 110   Bernarda Bryson met her future husband: author's interview with Bernarda Bryson.

p. 110   When Rockfeller asked Rivera: Hills, "Socially Concerned Artists of the 1930's," 14.

p. 110   Wrote Rivera in his 1932 essay, "The Revolutionary Spirit in Modern Art": David Schapiro, *Social Realism; Art as a Weapon*; 55.

p. 111   Jackson Pollock studied: Hills, "Socially Concerned Artists of the 1930's," 14.

p. 111 Willem de Kooning worked for the mural division: Stevens and Swan, *De Kooning*, New York: Knopf, 2004, 125.

p. 111 Stuart Davis's abstract mural for radio station: O'Connor, ed., *The New Deal Art Projects*; Rosalind Bengelsdorf Browne, "The American Abstract Artists and the WPA Federal Art Project," 232.

p. 111 Gorky's stunning *Modern Aviation*: O'Connor, *Federal Art Patronage*, 33–35.

p. 111 In 1937, twenty-eight abstract artists: *The New Deal Art Projects*, Rosalind Bengelsdorf Browne, "The American Abstract Artists and the WPA Federal Art Project," 228; Stevens and Swann, *De Kooning*, 130.

p. 111 a specter was haunting: Karl Marx and Friedrich Engels, *The Communist Manifesto*. First line: "A spectre is haunting Europe, the spectre of Communism . . ."

p. 111 In his 2002 book: Andrew Hemingway, *Authors on the Left*, New Haven: Yale University Press, 2002, p. 1.

p. 112 The Communist Party "were the only ones": author's interview with Annette Rubinstein, June 10, 2004. Brief biographical information on Rubinstein can be found in: *Monthly Review*, June 2007, "Remembering Annette Rubinstein":

> In the 1940s she founded and led the Robert Louis Stevenson school, an innovative primary and secondary school in New York, and during the Second World War served on Mayor LaGuardia's commission on the status of children in wartime. She was an unsuccessful candidate for congress on the American Labor Party (ALP) ticket in a district on the Upper West Side of Manhattan, and also served as state vice chair of the ALP. In 1958 she ran for Lieutenant Governor of New York State as an Independent Socialist candidate. Annette took the 5th amendment when asked by Senator Joseph R. McCarthy if she were a member of the Communist party. McCarthy replied that she was the most charming communist who had sat before his committee, to which she responded, "Aren't you jumping to conclusions, Senator?" She was also a key advisor to the radical New York congressman Vito Marcantonio.

p. 112 Benjamin's seminal essay: Walter Benjamin, "The Work of Art in the Age of Mechanical Reproduction," Preface. Benjamin ends his essay:

> Mankind, which in Homer's time was an object of contemplation for the Olympian gods, now is one for itself. Its self-alienation has reached such a degree that it can experience its own destruction as an aesthetic pleasure of the first order. This is the situation of politics which Fascism is rendering aesthetic. Communism responds by politicizing art.

p. 112 The Congress itself: Hills, "Socially Concerned Artists of the 1930's," 17.

p. 112 "The Popular Front was a haven": Serge Guilbaut, *How New York Stole the Idea of Modern Art*, 18.

p. 112 Guilbaut quotes Daniel Aaron: Guilbaut, ibid.

p. 112 "It was very heady": author's interview with Charles Keller, December 3, 2002.

p. 113   Joseph Solman recalled: author's interview with Joseph Solman.

p. 113   In *Art and Politics*: Susan Noyes Platt, *Art and Politics in the 1930's, Modern-
            ism, Marxism and Americanism*, New York: Midmarch Arts Press, 1999, Intro-
            duction, xiii, xiv.

p. 113   As Solman wrote: Joseph Solman, The Easel Divisions of the WPA Federal Art
            Project, 119.

p. 114   "Participation of the Communist Party": O'Connor, ed. "The New Deal Art
            Projects," Lincoln Rothschild, "Artists Organization of the Depression Decade,"
            218.

p. 114   Bryson . . . recalled: author's interview with Bernarda Bryson.

p. 114   Said Charles Keller: author's interview with Charles Keller.

p. 115   "If the Communist system": Pamela Allara, *Pictures of People*, Hanover, NH:
            Brandeis University Press, 1998, 65–66.

p. 115   Explains Guilbaut: Guilbaut, *How New York Stole the Idea of Modern Art*, 29.

p. 116   Neel joined the Party in 1935: Hills, *Alice Neel*, 60.

p. 116   writing a letter to him: author's interview with Virgina Neel.

p. 116   poster of Lenin: author's visit to to 107th Street.

p. 116   Says her friend: author's interview with Philip Bonosky.

p. 116   "One of the key things": author's interview with Andrew Hemingway.

p. 116   taking classes with V. J. Jerome and Andrew Selsam: Patricia Hills's interview
            with Alice Neel, July 17, 20, 1982.

p. 116   She also accompanied: author's interview with Annette Rubinstein; Andrew
            Hemingway, *Artists on the Left*, 247.

p. 116   "V. J. Jerome was a very good friend": Patricia Hills's interview with Alice Neel,
            July 17, 20, 1982.

p. 116   Neel even made a special visit: Hills, *Alice Neel*, 87.

p. 117   According to Hemingway: author's interview with Andrew Hemingway.

p. 117   although she said she quit twice: Neel told both Hills and Nancy Baer, the film-
            maker of *Alice Neel: Collector of Souls*, that she had joined and quit the Party
            more than once.

p. 117   Rubinstein, for instance: author's interview with Annette Rubinstein; author's
            interview with Gerald Meyer.

p. 117   "She remained absolutely": author's interview with Andrew Hemingway.

p. 117   What Allara refers to as: Pamela Allara, *Pictures of People*, 65.

p. 118   Gus Hall: letter from Gus Hall, February 5, 1982.

p. 118   Wrote Gold in his essay "Towards Proletarian Art": Pamela Allara, *Pictures of People*, 67.

p. 118   As Gerald Meyer observed: Gerald Meyers, "Alice Neel: The Painter and Her Politics," *Columbia Journal of American Studies*, p. 169.

p. 118   Neel's FBI file: copy courtesy of and obtained by Pamela Allara through Freedom of Information Act:
          Federal Bureau of Investigation report on Alice Neel; First page of the report is dated July 9, 1951. According to the reports filed, she appears to have been surveilled through 1959, as a "subject retained on Communist Index." In early January 1961, "this Reserve Index case is being re-opened," On Febraury 20, 1961, it was recommended that "the subject be deleted from the Reserve Index as her last CP membership was in 1948 and there is no evidence of current front group participation" and her file was closed.

p. 118   "I joined the Party several times . . . *anarchic humanist*": Nancy Baer, *Alice Neel: Collector of Souls*; Hills, *Alice Neel*, 60; Patricia Hills interview with Alice Neel:
          "Well the first time I joined it was in the 30's, I guess around when I did Patty Whalen (1935). Yes, but I was never a good communist. You know why? I hate bureaucracy . . . even the meetings used to drive me crazy."

p. 118   "She never showed any particular discipline": author's interview with Charles Keller.

CHAPTER THIRTEEN: *A Man's a Man for All That*

p. 119   "You know I picked husbands": Munro, unedited interview transcript for *Originals*, 36.

p. 119   "When I lived with him": Goldstein, *Soul on Canvas*, 79.

p. 119   "I really didn't care too much": Diamonstein, *Inside New York's Art World*, 257.

p. 119   Carlos even sent his sisters as would-be emissaries: Jonathan Brand interview with Alice Neel, 1969.

p. 120   "Now that year, in 1934": Hills, *Alice Neel*, 53.

p. 120   "His mother had died": Sanchez, *Carlos Enríquez*, chronology.

p. 120   Foss offered a hint: Fanya Foss, untitled novel, 40.

p. 120   "The hell with them. I've learned to do as they do": ibid.

p. 120   "one of the phases of New York City life": Philadelphia Museum catalog, 165.

p. 120   "the night before": ibid.

p. 120   rented a small cottage: Hills, *Alice Neel*, 50.

p. 121   there's even a picture: Philadelphia Museum catalog, 165.

p. 122   "My second child came back": Munro, unedited interview transcript for *Originals*, 39.

p. 122   As Neel told Brand: transcript of Jonathan Brand interview with Alice Neel, January 1981, 13. Millen Brand mentions in his journals (August 25, 1968) that Neel sold Jonathan the slashed painting for $1,000. Jonathan eventually also bought the naked Isabetta portrait.

p. 122   "He was very jealous": Diamonstein, *Inside New York's Art World*, 257.

p. 122   "Doolittle was a real male chauvinist": Henry R. Hope, "Alice Neel: Portraits of an Era," *Art Journal*, Vol. 38, No. 4, Summer, 1979.

p. 122   "You know what the problem was?": Goldstein, *Soul on Canvas*, 79.

p. 122   at least as fictionalized: Fanya Foss, untitled novel, 288.

p. 122   Allara describes the relationship: Allara, *Pictures of People*, 227.

p. 123   As she described it to Munro: unedited interview transcript for *Originals*, 38; Munro, *Originals*, 127, 128.

p. 123   She embellished the story: Nemser, *Art Talks*, 107.

p. 123   She gave a slightly different account: Hills, *Alice Neel*, 56.

p. 123   Doolittle told his friend: author's interview with Stanley Maron.

p. 124   Author's interview with Doolittle's daughters, Sarah Eisenberg and Karla Buch, and his granddaughter, Ilana, December 10, 2008.

p. 124   Tom has a totally different: author's interview with Tom Doolittle, December 12, 2009, and several subsequent phone interviews in December, 2009, and January and February, 2010.

p. 124   Doolittle's children: interview with Sarah Eisenberg and Karla Buch.

p. 125   "It was ironical that she": Fanya Foss, untitled novel, 273.

p. 125   "When I left Cornelia Street": Jonathan Brand interview with Alice Neel, December 4, 5, 1969.

CHAPTER FOURTEEN: *Moving On*

p. 126   "I cry and my tears": Alice Neel, excerpt from undated poem, personal papers, Neel Archives.

p. 126   "holocaust": Munro, *Originals*, p. 128; Jonathan Brand interview, December, 4, 5 1969, Alice's Spanish Harlem neighbor, whom she painted in 1938, Mr. Green, called John her benefactor.

p. 126   according to the Neel family: interview with Virginia Neel; interview with Richard Neel.

p. 126   "He used to love me and then a big white stomach": Alice Neel, excerpt from undated poem.

p. 126   "Alice told me": interview with Richard Neel.

p. 126   "that swank hotel": Munro, unedited interview transcript for *Originals*, 36.

p. 127   "super-aesthete": Judith Higgins, "Alice Neel and the Human Comedy," *ARTnews*, October, 1984, 74.

p. 127   "Benefactor": Jonathan Brand interview, December, 4, 5 1969; Alice's Village friend, Mr. Green, called John her benefactor.

p. 127   "A Harvard man par excellence": Rhodes, transcript for *Three Women Artists*.

p. 127   biographical background on John Rothschild: author's interview with Joel Rothschild, August 18, 2005; author's interview with Marc Bernstein, archivist, Society for Ethical Culture.

p. 127   explains Marc Bernstein: author's interview with Marc Bernstein, archivist, Society for Ethical Culture.

p. 127   At Harvard, he had become friendly: author's interview with Joel Rothschild.

p. 128   According to Joel: ibid.

p. 129   in a little house: author's interview with Virginia Neel.

p. 129   The red-shingle, one-story cottage: author's interview with Richard Neel.

p. 129   "I painted him in a hat": Patricia Hills interview with Alice Neel, July 17, 20, 1982.

p. 130   "It had nothing to do with sex": Hills, *Alice Neel*, 55.

p. 130   While Allara describes: Allara, *Pictures of People*, 230.

p. 130   In September 1935: Hills, *Alice Neel*, 57; transcript of Employment for Alice Neel, General Services Administration.

p. 130   she went out and found an apartment: Alexander Russo, *Profiles on Women Artists*, Maryland: University Publications of America, 1985, 202.

p. 130   Neel actually spent the weekend: Patricia Hills interview with Alice Neel, July 17, 20, 1982.

p. 130   As to why: ibid.

p. 131   The apartment on West Seventeenth: Hills, *Alice Neel*, 57.

p. 131   "loved to take care of the laundry": ibid.

p. 131   "an elegant apartment": ibid.

p. 131   "He had a Filipino cook": ibid., 59.

p. 131   "I enjoyed the luxuries of the rich": Belcher and Belcher, *Collecting Souls, Gathering Dust*, 162.

p. 131   "I always loved the most wretched": Hills, *Alice Neel*, 64.

p. 131   "One of the fascinations": Diamonstein, *Inside New York's Art World*, 257.

p. 131   "He was a great companion . . . The only compatible life": Hills, *Alice Neel*, 64.

p. 131   "He pursued me all his life": Diamonstein, *Inside New York's Art World*, 257.

p. 131   "He was absolutely convinced": author's interview with Joel Rothschild.

p. 132   "take that Fauntleroy": Hills, *Alice Neel*, 62; Nancy Baer, *Alice Neel: Collector of Souls*.

p. 132   "When I painted Patty Whalen": Hills, *Alice Neel*, 64.

CHAPTER FIFTEEN: *José and Spanish Harlem*

p. 133   "I spent evening after evening": author's interview with Joel Rothschild.

p. 133   "It was as though": ibid.

p. 134   "You know what he was?": Nemser, *Art Talks*, 108.

p. 134   "I went to the nightclub with John": Patricia Hills, interview with Alice Neel, July 17, 20, 1982; Hills, *Alice Neel*, 65.

p. 134   "Maybe it was Vermont": Patricia Hills interview with Alice Neel.

p. 134   "I wish I had a record": ibid.; Hills, *Alice Neel*, 66.

p. 134   "who took most of their dances from houses of prostitution": Patricia Hills interview with Alice Neel.

p. 134   "I remember my mother noticing some wrinkles": ibid.

p. 134   "José had a spiritual streak": Hills, *Alice Neel*, 66.

p. 135   biographical background on José Santiago Negron: author's interview with Jenny Santiago, March 11, 2006.

p. 135   according to Sheila de Tuya: author's interview with Sheila De Tuya, December 15, 2008.

p. 135   Not long after Alice met José: Philadelphia Museum catalog, 165.

p. 135   "I guess he captured Alice's heart": author's interview with Ralph Marrero, January 21, 2009.

p. 135   "During the Depression": Rhodes and Murphy, interview transcript for *Three Women Artists*, January 3, 1976.

p. 135   "I think it was a very revolutionary painting": Nemser, *Art Talks*, 101; Munro transcript.

p. 136   Wrote Emily Grenauer: Emily Grenauer, *New York World Telegram*, September 12, 1936, "New Fall Art Exhibits Feature by Tyros' Promising Efforts"; also quoted in Philadelphia Museum catalog, 165, 166; Hills, *Alice Neel*, 60.

p. 136   "For how I have loved you": Alice Neel, excerpt from undated, untitled poem, Neel Archives.

p. 136   "I don't live with a pregnant woman": ibid.

p. 136   in July 1937: Philadelphia Museum catalog, 166.

p. 137   Excerpt from letter from Neel's mother, July 12, 1937, ibid.; full transcription of letter in Neel Archives.

p. 137   Excerpt of letter from Nadya Olyanova, July 16, 1937, ibid.

p. 137   129 MacDougal Street: Hills, *Alice Neel*, 66; undated letter to Millen Brand from MacDougal Street, Millen Brand Papers, Rare Book and Manuscript Library, Columbia University.

p. 137   "I'm horribly broke": undated letter to Millen Brand from MacDougal Street, Millen Brand Papers, Rare Book and Manuscript Library, Columbia University.

p. 137   the Village had become too honky-tonk: transcript for *Three Women Artists*, 4.

p. 138   She and José moved: Philadelphia Museum catalog has address as 8 West 107th Street, but Neel told Hills it was 10 West 107th Street.

p. 138   Recalls Ralph Marrera: author's interview with Ralph Marrera.

p. 138   "Now when I was on the WPA": Lynn F. Miller and Sally Swenson, *Lives and Works: Talks with Women Artists*, New Jersey: The Scarecrow Press, Inc., 1981, 125.

p. 138   As Solman put it: Belcher and Belcher, *Collecting Souls, Gathering Dust*, 175.

p. 138   Neel had her very first solo show: Philadelphia Museum catalog, 166.

p. 138   "At Contemporary Arts": *ARTnews*, "New Exhibitions of the Week," Vol. 36, No. 33, May 14, 1938.

p. 139   *The New York Times* also reviewed: Henry Devere, "A Reviewer's Notebook: Brief Comment on Some of the Recently Opened Exhibitions in the Galleries," *The New York Times*, May 8, 1938, 7; quoted in Philadelphia Museum catalog, 166.

p. 139   "You know what I thought I would find": Nemser, *Art Talks*, 108.

p. 140   "I love you Harlem": Alice Neel, Neel Archives; Smithsonian Archives of American Art; Neel Papers.

p. 140   Within the next three years: brochures/price lists for Contemporary Arts Shows for "20 Artists Look North from Radio City," from May 23 to July 16, 1938, Neel showed one painting: *Other Points of View*; an untitled show that ran from September 19 to October 1, 1938, Neel showed *Shades of Night*, priced at $75; a show called Paintings for the Five to Fifty Christmas Budget, December 5 to 25, 1938, Neel showed *Puerto Rican Baby* priced at $50; and a show called Painters Paint Painters, June, 1939; Mid-season Retrospective, February 26 to March 16, 1940; Allara, *Pictures of People*, chapter notes, 283.

p. 141   "Drawings and paintings can fight too": Gerald Meyer, *Alice Neel: The Artist and Her Politics*, 164.

p. 141   "The New York Group": Philadelphia Museum catalog, 166.

p. 141   Neel had two paintings in the exhibition: Allara, *Pictures of People*, 88.

p. 141   mentioned all the artists but Neel: Belcher and Belcher, *Collecting Souls Gathering Dust*, 175.

p. 142   "I was out in nightclubs": Jonathan Brand interview with Alice Neel, December 4, 5, 1969.

CHAPTER SIXTEEN: *More Truth*

p. 143   Wrote Kenneth Fearing: flyer for New York Group Exhibition, February 5–18, 1939.

p. 143   Wrote Philip Rahv: Guilbaut, *How New York Stole the Idea of Modern Art*, 28.

p. 143   disintegration of the American Artists Congress: Breslin, *Rothko*, 147, 154.

p. 144   "The Congress no longer deserves": Guilbaut, *How New York Stole the Idea of Modern Art*, 40.

p. 144   "poor art, for poor people": Irving Sandler, *The Triumph of American Painting: A History of Abstract Expressionism*, New York: Prager Publishers, Inc., 1970, 10.

p. 144   "the soap box speaking instead of the man": ibid., 12.

p. 144   the Federation of Modern Painters: Breslin, *Rothko*, 155.

p. 144   Harold Rosenberg memorialized: Harold Rosenberg, *Tradition of the New*, Cambridge, MA: Da Capo Press, 1994; "The Fall of Paris," 210, 211, 220.

p. 145   In July 1939, Neel's WPA payments: Philadelphia Museum catalog, 167.

p. 145   in August: ibid., 167.

p. 145   Neel was staying along with her parents: author's interview with Virginia Neel.

p. 145   Marisa Diaz, a childhood friend: author's interview with Marisa Diaz, June 3, 2003.

p. 145   According to a family friend, America Villiers: author's interview with America Villiers, January 6, 2004.

p. 145   Nancy Neel, Alice's daughter-in-law: author's interview with Nancy Neel, July 22, 2003.

p. 146   "She came to see me when she was ten": Munro, undated interview transcript for *Originals*, 39.

p. 146   A photograph at the time: group shot of Neel's parents, José, and Sheila, Neel Archives.

p. 146   On September 14, 1939: Philadelphia Museum catalog, 167.

p. 147   "I was in the hospital": Hills, *Alice Neel*, 66; Allara, *Pictures of People*, 91.

p. 147   Although she was terminated: Philadelphia Museum catalog, 167.

p. 147   Marrero remembers visiting: author's interview with Ralph Marrero.

p. 147   "Well, you know how Spanish men are?": Nemser, *Art Talks*, 109.

p. 147   "I was tired of getting horns": author's interview with Jenny Santiago, March 11, 2006.

p. 148   "Of course José should never have done": Philadelphia Museum transcript of Jonathan Brand interview with Alice Neel, 1969.

p. 148   "I kept on living in Spanish Harlem": Nemser, *Art Talks*,

p. 148   she described José's abandonment: Hills, *Alice Neel*, 66.

p. 148   "My mother was sixteen years old": author's interview with Paul Negron, January 21, 2009.

p. 148   Family lore: author's interview with Joseph Negron, January 21, 2009.

p. 148   For a time: author's interview with John Negron, January 21, 2009.

p. 148   Says Jenny Santiago: author's interview with Jenny Santiago.

p. 149   "I don't think he was curious": author's interview with Ralph Marrero.

p. 149   Recalls Richard: author's interview with Richard Neel.

p. 149   According to José's medical records: Author's interview with Joseph Negron, January 21, 2009, follow-up on October 6, 2009. When José's family first tried to place him in a nursing home, they were told that the home could not accept him since his records indicated that he had syphilis, and that proof would have to be given that the disease was no longer active. After that proof was obtained, the nursing home accepted José. He died there several years later.

p. 149   Although it is unclear what caused: author's interview with Richard Neel.

p. 149   Neel told several friends: author's interview with Barbara Hollister.

p. 150   Author's off-the-record interview with a close friend of Alice Neel's.

p. 150   Richard himself acknowledges: author's interview with Richard Neel.

p. 150   Richard's eyes were apparently fine at birth: author's interviews with Richard Neel and Nancy Neel.

p. 150   According to Richard, it was Sam: author's interview with Richard Neel.

p. 150   Background on Dr. Max Goldschmidt: "Boy 11, Stranded in Reich, Returns," *The New York Times*, March 5, 1940:
          "The physician, ironically, is a refugee from Germany who for eighteen years before the advent of Hitler was a professor at the University of Leipzig. He is Dr. Max Goldschmidt."
          Obituary for Dr. Max Goldschmidt, *The New York Times*, November, 11, 1964.

p. 151   Richard says that, according to Alice: author's interview with Richard Neel.

p. 151   as per the following note: copy of doctor's note provided by Richard Neel.

p. 151   Dr. Goldchmidt was Richard's ophthalmologist: author's interview with Richard Neel.

p. 152   According to Dr. Gerald W. Zaidman: author's interviews with Dr. Gerald W. Zaidman, December, 2009, April and May, 2010.

p. 152   Dr. Frederick Wang, a clinical professor: author's interview with Dr. Frederick Wang, December 2009, April and May, 2010.

p. 152   Alice told members of her family: author's interviews with family members.

p. 152   Both Dr. Wang and Dr. Zaidman: author's interviews with both doctors in April and May, 2010.

p. 153 Neel told a confidante: off-the-record interview with close friend of Alice Neel's.

p. 154 Says one person close to Alice: interview with Hartley Neel, April, 2009.

p. 154 Alice often told Hartley: ibid.

p. 154 Richard was sent: author's interview with Richard Neel.

p. 154 Says Hartley, "Whatever happened": author's interview with Hartley Neel.

p. 155 Isak Dinesen, whose father: Judith Thurman, *Isak Dinesen*, New York: Picador, 1982, 258.

p. 155 In the early 1940s: author's interview with Paul Negron.

p. 155 By that time, he and Ruth had two sons: author's interviews with Paul, Joseph, and John Negron.

p. 155 "He had a roaming eye": author's interview with Paul Negron.

p. 155 "He chased everything in a skirt": author's interview with Joseph Negron.

p. 155 Richard visited Palm Beach: author's interviews with Richard Neel, Joseph Negron, David Freeman.

p. 156 Helen Mabbott: author's interview with Paul Negron.

p. 156 Neel didn't see José: author's interviews with Richard Neel and Nancy Neel.

p. 156 he developed Parkinson's disease: author's interview with Joseph Negron.

p. 156 his obituary: "A Tribute," *The Ledger*, Lakeland, Fla. February 26, 1992; information about church affiliations also mentioned in unidentified newspaper clipping about a church trip to Louisiana

p. 156 In later years: Jonathan Brand interview with Alice Neel, December 4, 5, 1969.

CHAPTER SEVENTEEN: *Enter Sam*

p. 157 Neel met Sam Brody: author's interviews with David Brody, April 29, 2004; May 22, 2004.

p. 157 "some obscene loyalty oath": Tony Safford, "Samuel Brody Interview, The Camera as a Weapon in Class Struggle," *Jump Cut: A Review of Contemporary Media*, No. 14, 1977; 2004, 28–30, 30.

p. 157 introduced . . . by a sculptor named Blanche Angel: Jonathan Brand interview with Alice Neel, 1969.

p. 157 "He was such a show off": Jonathan Brand interview with Alice Neel, 1969.

p. 157 Says his widow: author's interview with Sondra Brody, June 4, 2004.

p. 158   "[Sam] came a couple of times for dinner": Jonathan Brand interview with Alice Neel, 1969.

p. 158   Biographical information on Sam: author's interview with David Brody, May 22, 2004; March, 2009; author's interviews with Sondra Brody, June 4, 2004, March 18, 2009.

p. 158   "poor intellectual fare": Jonathan Brand interview with Alice Neel, 1969.

p. 158   Brody was born: copy of Sam Brody birth certificate provided by David Brody.

p. 158   "He was an extraordinary person": author's interview with David Brody.

p. 159   "My old man was a journeyman": Safford, "Samuel Brody Interview," *Jump cut*, 28.

p. 159   "My formal education": ibid.

p. 159   According to his *New York Times* obituary: *The New York Times*, obituary, "Sam Brody, Maker of Films on Labor and Social Justice," September 22, 1987.

p. 159   "doing a little editing, Jack of all trades": Tom Brandon interview with Sam Brody, Venice, California, March 19, 1974, 1.

p. 159   "The earliest film I can remember": Sam Brody interview with David Platt, filmed by Judy Pomer, Old Saybrook, CT; 1987.

p. 159   Brody saved up: Brandon interview, 3.

p. 160   He went to France briefly: Safford, "Samuel Brody Interview," *Jump Cut*, 30.

p. 160   "It is nine o'clock": *Close Up*, Vol. VI, No. 4, April, 1930; reprinted in *Jump Cut*, No. 14, 1977, 30.

p. 160   "several people suggested": Sam Brody interview with David Platt, filmed by Judy Pomer.

p. 160   "Little by little": ibid.

p. 160   Whether that was the birth: Safford, "Samuel Brody Interview," *Jump Cut*, 28.

p. 160   "The camera as a weapon in the class struggle": ibid.

p. 160   he wrote in the *Daily Worker*: Russell Campbell, "Film and Photo League: Radical Cinema in the 1930's," *Jump Cut*, No. 14, 23.

p. 161   To accomplish this: Safford, "Samuel Brody Interview," *Jump Cut*, 28.

p. 161   "I was a member": Campbell, "Film and Photo League," *Jump Cut*, 24; also mentioned in Safford, "Samuel Brody Interview," *Jump Cut*, 28.

p. 161   "The Workers Film and Photo League carried on": Safford, ibid., 29.

p. 161   "the Soviet films and the writings": Safford, "Samuel Brody Interview," *Jump Cut*, 29.

p. 162   Brody later wrote film criticism: references to column for the *Daily Worker*, and work for Experimental Cinema, Tony Safford, "Interview with Samuel Brody," 29; *Daily Worker* columns quoted in Campbell, "Film and Photo League," *Jump Cut*, 22; references to "From Up in the Gallery," by Lens, *Film Front*, issues from February and March, 1935; Samuel Brody on *Thunder over Mexico*, *The New Masses*, Screenscan, September 1933; Samuel Brody on *Holiday*, *The New Masses*, Screenscan, December, 1950; Samuel Brody, "How to Strike Effective Blow at Hollywood Anti-Labor Films," the *Daily Worker*, July 15, 1935.

p. 162   "revolutionary content": Safford, "Samuel Brody Interview," *Jump Cut*, 29.

p. 162   "helped push the intellectuals": ibid.

p. 162   "He was very clever": Hills, *Alice Neel*, 68.

p. 162   "He was so smart": ibid.

p. 162   "Sam in a tirade": author's interview with Philip and Faith Bonosky, May 21, 2004.

p. 162   "Out of the chaos": Hartley Neel, speaking in the Andrew Neel documentary *Alice Neel*, SeeThink Productions, 2007, (Andrew, Alice's grandson, is the son of Hartley and Ginny).

p. 162   "Alice was sure": author's interview with Philip and Faith Bonosky.

p. 163   "They would have screaming matches": author's interview with Mady McCoy, *neé* Brody, November 11, 2006.

p. 163   "cowering at the bottom of the stairs": author's interview with Hartley Neel, April 5, 2009.

p. 163   Joe Lasker, a fellow artist: author's interview with Joseph Lasker, July 24, 2003; Neel also told Joseph Solman that Sam "sometimes beat her up," author's interview with Joseph Solman.

p. 163   "Sam knocked him out": author's interview with Sondra Brody, June 4, 2004.

p. 163   "as time went on": Patricia Hills interview with Alice Neel, July 17, 20, 1982.

p. 163   "He used to kick me under the table": Richard Neel, in *Alice Neel* documentary.

p. 164   When Brody later discovered: Hills, *Alice Neel*, 68.

p. 164   Still, in January, 1941: Philadelphia Museum catalog, p. 167.

p. 164   Winifred Wheeler Day Nursery: ibid.

p. 164   Says Sondra: author's interviews with Sondra Brody, June 4, 2004; March 18, 2009.

p. 164   "Sam's attitude toward Hartley": Hills, *Alice Neel*, 68; Patricia Hills interview with Alice Neel, July 17, 20, 1982.

p. 165   "I am holding Richard": Hills, *Alice Neel*, 75.

p. 165   1943 portrait of herself with Richard: This picture is reproduced in "Alice Neel; Drawings and Watercolors," Robert Miller Gallery, New York, 1986.

p. 165   "Part of me is very inert": Jonathan Brand interview with Alice Neel, 1969.

p. 165   "My mother heard about it": author's interview with Jenny Santiago.

p. 165   Alice told several people: Philip Bonoksy journal, May 21, 1949; author's interview with Nancy Neel.

p. 165   "I was too young": author's interview with Richard Neel. Hartley Neel, April 1, 2010.

p. 166   "It was just a very lousy situation": interview with Richard Neel, April 7, 2010; according to Hartley, he never thought of Sam as a father or felt any emotional connection to him.

p. 166   Hartley frequently came to Richard's rescue: author's interview with Hartley Neel, April 5, 2009.

p. 166   "The fact is that she tolerated": Richard Neel in *Alice Neel* documentary, 2007.

p. 166   Fiona True, codirector: author's interview and e-mail correspondence with Fiona True, codirector of the Center for Children and Relational Trauma, The Ackerman Institute for the Family.

p. 167   "If she had been satisfied": Hartley Neel, in *Alice Neel* documentary, 2007.

p. 167   Richard even goes so far as to say: Richard Neel, ibid.

p. 167   In November 1942: Philadelphia Museum catalog, 168.

p. 167   among the last artists to come off the payroll of the WPA: Neel's employment records: Hills, *Alice Neel*, 72.

p. 167   "They made people on the Art Project": Hills, *Alice Neel*, 77.

p. 167   "I never corrected one": Patricia Hills interview with Alice Neel, July 17, 20, 1982.

CHAPTER EIGHTEEN: *Painting in Oblivion*

p. 169   A 1944 photograph: photograph taken by Samuel Brody; brochure for the Pinacotheca Show, opening Sunday, March 5 from 4:30 to 7 pm; according to the brochure, the show ran from March 6 through March 22.

p. 169   decidedly mixed review in *ARTnews*: *ARTnews*, Vol. XlIII, No.3, March 15–31, 1944, 20.

p. 169   Howard Devere, in *The New York Times*: Howard Devere, "A Reviewer's Notes," *The New York Times*, March 12, 1944.

p. 170   But, as Neel put it: transcript of Harvard Lecture, 1979, 12.

p. 170   "I never followed any school": Munro, unedited interview transcript for *Originals*, 35.

p. 170   Sale of WPA canvases: *Life* magazine, April 17, 1944, "End of WPA Art," 85.

p. 170   later inspired a scene: Kenneth Fearing, *The Big Clock*, New York: *The New York Review of Books*, 1974 (with introduction by Nicholas Christopher, 2006):

> On page 47 of *The Big Clock*, Louise Patterson, modeled on Neel, is described as a "big, monolithic brunette, sloppily dressed and with a face like an arrested cyclone," who "unchained a whoop of laughter . . ."
>
> Vermin infested loft: "I've been poking around a studio-loft she lives in— God what a paradise for rats and vermin—looking at acres and acres of paintings . . ." 122
>
> Four love children: ". . . four children, where the two younger ones, Pete's and Mike's, were helping the older pair, Ralph's," 151–154. Even Doolittle's destruction of Neel's work: "His large grey eyes bugged out just the way Ralph's had when he showed me the pile of scraps and ashes and charred fragments, all that was left of five years work . . ." 154.

p. 170   "Selling the WPA paintings": Hills, *Alice Neel*, 79.

p. 170   "In response to World War II": Sandler, *The Triumph of American Painting*, 1.

p. 171   In the fall of 1936: Ashton, *The New York School*, 76; Sandler, *The Triumph of American Painting*, 15.

p. 171   The Museum of Modern Art mounted: Sandler, *The Triumph of American Painting*, 13.

p. 171   Neel was familiar: Salvador Dalí exhibition announcement, Neel Archives.

p. 171   Bonwit Teller: Naifeh and Smith, *Jackson Pollock*, 377.

p. 171   A major Picasso exhibit: Sandler, *The Triumph of American Painting*, 13.

p. 171   the Museum of Non-Objective Painting: Anton Gill, *Art Lover: A Biography of Peggy Guggenheim*, HarperCollins, New York; 2002, 277, 278.

p. 171   *Partisan Review*: Guilbaut, *How New York Stole the Idea of Modern Art*, 31.

p. 171   published Clement Greenberg's: ibid., 33.

p. 172   "Capitalism in decline": Clement Greenberg, *The Collected Essays and Criticism*, Chicago: The University of Chicago Press, 1986, "Avant-Garde and Kitsch," 22, 8; originally published in *The Partisan Review*, 1939, 34–39.

p. 172   "Some day it will have to be told": Guilbaut, *How New York Stole the Idea of Modern Art*, 38.

p. 172   Greenberg . . . art critic of *The Partisan Review* . . . *The Nation*: Norman L. Kleeblatt, ed. *Action Abstraction*, CT: Yale University Press, 2008, 14, 15 (catalog for the *Action Abstraction* show at the Jewish Museum, May 4–September 21, 2008).

p. 173   cleverly mounted . . . resembled sawed-off baseball bats: Gill, *Art Lover*, 305; Stevens and Swan, *de Kooning*, 171.

p. 173   early work of Jackson Pollock: Steven Naifeh and Gregory White Smith, *Jackson Pollock: An American Saga*, New York: Clarkson N. Potter, Inc., 1990, 408, 409. Pollock was included in the Spring Salon thanks to the endorsement of Mondrian.

p. 173   *Life* magazine had somewhat sardonically: *Life* magazine, August 8, 1949, "Is he the greatest living painter in the United States?"; Naifeh and Smith, *Jackson Pollock*, 549.

p. 173   Remarkably, she also mounted: Cornelia Butler and Lisa Gabrielle Mark, *WACK! Art and the Feminist Revolution*, Cambridge, MA: MIT Press, 2007, 474; *re*: Dorothea Tanning later marrying Max Ernst; Gill, *The Art Lover*, 287.

p. 173   Neel had, however, thanks to her WPA connection: Hills, *Alice Neel*, 79; also listed in Neel's group shows on David Zwirner Gallery Web site; Cheim and Read gallery Web site.

p. 173   description of Sam Kootz's Macy's show: "179 paintings by 72 artists . . . and nearly every other Modernist Painter in New York": Sandler, *The Triumph of American Painting*, 32, 33; also mentioned in: Ashton, *The New York School*, 146; Breslin, *Mark Rothko*, 160.

p. 173   Just the year before: Sandler, *The Triumph of American Painting*, 32.

p. 173   Kootz letter: Sandler, ibid.; Guilbaut, *How New York Stole the Idea of Modern Art*, 65, 66.

p. 174   Edward Alden Jewell, described . . . "truly shattering bombshell": ibid.; chapter notes, 219; Jewell's article appeared in *The New York Times*, August, 10, 1941, section 9, page 7.

p. 174   Sparked by Jewell's suggestion: Sandler, *The Trimph of American Art*, 32; Guilbaut, *How New York Stole the Idea of Modern Art*, 67.

p. 174   "Bombshell Group": Guilbaut, *How New York Stole the Idea of Modern Art*, 66; Sandler, *The Triumph of American Painting*, 32.

p. 174   One of the last organized stands of the Social Realist movement: ibid, 69

p. 174   Artists for Victory show and American Modern Artists show: Guilbaut, *How New York Stole the Idea of Modern Art*, ibid., 68, 69.

p. 174   Wrote Barnett Newman: ibid.

p. 175   "You will have to make of Marcus Rothko's": Breslin, *Mark Rothko*, 187; Guil-
          baut, *How New York Stole the Idea of Modern Art*, 73

p. 175   "We do not intend to defend": Breslin, *Mark Rothko*, 192, 193; Guilbaut, *How
          New York Stole the Idea of Modern Art*, 75.

p. 175   influenced by . . . Freud and Jung: Sandler, *The Triumph of American Paint-
          ing*, 62.

p. 175   As Arshile Gorky put it: Kleeblatt, ed. *Action Abstraction*, 15.

p. 175   Rosenberg borrowing paintings: Munro, unedited interview transcript for *Origi-
          nals*, 37.

p. 175   John Graham . . . used to visit: Hills, *Alice Neel*, 66.

p. 176   "I just went my own way": Neel, Harvard lecture, 11.

p. 176   "All during the forties and fifties": Diamonstein, *Inside New York's Art World*,
          258.

p. 176   In her innovative essay: Mira Schor, "Some Notes on Women and Abstraction and a
          Curious Case History: Alice Neel as a Great Abstract Painter," *Differences, A Jour-
          nal of Feminist Cultural Studies*, Brown University, Washington, DC; 2003, 13.

p. 177   Schor on Neel's technique in Dore Ashton portrait: Schor, "Alice Neel as an Ab-
          stract Painter," *Women's Art Journal*, Fall/Winter, 2006, 15.

p. 177   Schor *re:* Neel's Robert Smithson portrait: Schor, "Some Notes . . . ," 22, 23.

p. 177   "The way I would describe it": author's interview with Mira Schor.

p. 178   a member of United American Artists: Allara, *Pictures of People*, 91.

p. 178   "Abstract Expressionism was becoming": Hills, *Alice Neel*, 80.

p. 178   "I am a humanist": Munro, unedited interview transcript for *Originals*, 40.

p. 178   Neel summed up her professional fate: Baer, *Alice Neel, Collector of Souls*.

CHAPTER NINETEEN: *Domestic Dramas*

p. 179   "He was a good and kind man": Hills, *Alice Neel*, 81.

p. 179   she told Henry Geldzahler: Henry Geldzahler, *Making It New*, New York: Turtle
          Point Press, 1994, 235.

p. 180   "I realized later that the willow tree": Hills, *Alice Neel*, 83.

p. 180   "The paintings were always there": author's interview with Richard Neel.

p. 180   Recalls Hartley: author's interview with Hartley Neel, June 11, 2008.

p. 180   a classic six-and-a-half: author's interviews with Hartley Neel, April 5, 2009; June 11, 2008.

p. 181   "Our room was the transition": Hartley Neel, in *Alice Neel* documentary, 2007.

p. 181   "Alice had a lot of interesting friends": author's interview with Hartley Neel, June 11, 2008.

p. 181   And then there were the intermittent: author's interview with Richard Neel, April 7, 2010.

p. 181   government investigator: author's interview with Hartley Neel, April 5, 2009; June 11, 2008.

p. 181   "We knew pretty early": author's interview with Richard Neel, April 7, 2010.

p. 182   "Alice was a resourceful mother": ibid.

p. 182   Despite living close to the bone: author's interviews with Hartley Neel, April 5, 2009; June 11, 2008.

p. 182   Author's interviews with Hartley Neel, April 5, 2009; June 11, 2008.

p. 182   "We didn't feel deprived": author's interview with Hartley Neel, June 11, 2008.

p. 183   including one young woman . . . tried to kill herself: Phillip Bonosky journal, February 23, 1948; April 1, 1948; *re:* suicide, furniture.

p. 183   "a promiscuous girl who had posed for me nude": Jonathan Brand interview with Alice Neel, December 1969, 11.

p. 183   Janice Loeb: ibid., 7.

p. 183   "Hartley said to me": ibid., 9.

p. 183   Around the same time: ibid., 21.

p. 183   Brody actually even got married: ibid., 10.

p. 183   "Hartley as a boy": ibid., 12.

p. 183   "Don't publish me as a female Don Juan": ibid., 18.

p. 184   "The great thing about John": Jonathan Brand interview with Alice Neel, December 4, 5 1969.

p. 184   "John never gave me up": Hills, *Alice Neel*, 83.

p. 184   John adroitly managed: author's interview with Joel Rothschild, August 18, 2005.

p. 184   Despite the difficult of dealing with Sam: ibid.

p. 184   During this time, Phillip Bonosky: interview with Phillip Bonosky; Phillip Bonosky journals.

p. 184   Hartley Neel in *Alice Neel* documentary, 2007; author's interview with Hartley Neel, April, 2009.

p. 184   asked Richard to do the same: interview with Richard Neel, April, 2010.

p. 184   "I don't like Bohemian culture": Richard Neel in *Alice Neel* documentary, 2007.

p. 185   Back in Havana: author's interviews with Marisa Diaz and Adoris Mendoza.

p. 185   wedding announcement: Neel Archives.

p. 185   According to Isabetta's cousin: author's interview with Marisa Diaz, June 3, 2003; phone follow-up with Marisa Diaz, August 3, 2009.

p. 185   But according to her friend, Eileen Goudie: author's interview with Eileen Goudie, January 5, 2004.

p. 185   Nancy Neel says: author's interview with Nancy Neel, July 22, 2003.

p. 185   Pablo Lancella actually saw: author's interview with Pablo Lancella, phone follow-up to May 27, 2003.

p. 185   Alice had also apparently invited: author's interviews with Richard Neel, April 2010.

p. 185   And there is also another story: George Neel interview with Gerald and Margaret Belcher.

CHAPTER TWENTY: *Monsters and Victims*

p. 187   Bonosky was born: author's interview with Phillip and Faith Bonosky, May 21, 2004.

p. 188   All journal excerpts and personal details in this chapter are taken directly from a typescript of Phillip Bonosky's journal provided to me by Phillip Bonosky and his daughter, Nora Bonosky, and published with permission.

p. 201   illustrations of Bonosky's: Phillip Bonosky journal, April 21, 1949; *re:* Judge Medina and Angela Calomaris, Hills, *Alice Neel*, 87; Pamela Allara, *Pictures of People*, 99, 100.

p. 202   Copies of handwritten letters from Alice Neel to Phillip Bonosky provided by Nora Bonosky.

p. 202   Hartley recalls the terrible visit: author's interview with Hartley Neel, April 5, 2009.

p. 202   "The worst I saw was to have him walk": author's interview with Joel Rothschild, August 18, 2005.

p. 203   Rothschild, who recalls Neel's place as: ibid.

p. 205   "You know Sam was always crazy about these children": Jonathan Brand inter-
          view, December, 1969, 9.

p. 205   Bonosky recounts Neel saying: June 10, 1958 journal entry.

p. 205   According to Bonosky: October 19, 1958 journal entry.

p. 205   But, as she would say to Bonosky: November 21, 1959 journal entry.

p. 205   Sam liked to spit at people when he was angry: author's interview with Sondra
          Brody, June 4, 2004.

p. 205   "He was abusive to Alice": author's interview with Richard Neel, April 7, 2010.

p. 206   "[He was] not a hitter": author's interview with Sondra Brody, June 4, 2004.

p. 206   "Alice claimed my father abused Richard": author's interviews with David
          Brody, April 29, 2004; May 22, 2004.

p. 207   "Homicidal meets suicidal": Jonathan Brand interview with Alice Neel, Decem-
          ber 4, 5, 1969.

p. 207   Some sixty years later, Hartley: author's interview with Hartley Neel, April 5,
          2009.

p. 208   "You know, Phil was good": author's interview with Richard Neel, April 7, 2010.

p. 208   when Sam went on a tirade: author's interview with Hartley Neel, April 5, 2009.

p. 208   "I mean if things were going too smoothly": author's interview with Richard
          Neel, April 7, 2010.

p. 208   Olivia, Neel's oldest granddaughter, also remembers: author's interview with
          Olivia Neel, April 20, 2010.

p. 208   "Alice really liked the Sturm and Drang": author's interview with Hartley Neel,
          April 5, 2009.

CHAPTER TWENTY-ONE: *In the Middle of the Road*

p. 211   drawing called *Relief Cut* was published: Philadelphia Museum catalog, 168;
          prices *ARTnews*, January, 1951.

p. 211   The day after Christmas: ibid.

p. 211   In a 1986 letter: Belcher and Belcher, *Collecting Souls, Gathering Dust*, 204;
          chapter notes; 282.

p. 211   Recalls Herman Rose's wife, Elia: author's interview with Herman and Elia
          Rose, March 20, 2003.

p. 212   Solman wrote an exacting introduction: Philadelphia Museum catalog, 168.

p. 212   Seventeen paintings were included: ibid.; prices *ARTnews*, Vol. 49, No. 9, January, 1951.

p. 212   "Emotional values predominate": *The New York Times*, December 31, 1950.

p. 212   "Alice Neel, whose paintings": Mike Gold, "Alice Neel Paints Scenes and Portraits from Life In Harlem," *The Daily Worker*, December 27, 1950.

p. 213   "I am against abstract and non-objective art": ibid.

p. 213   "Alice Neel has vigor": "Alice Neel," *Arts Digest*, January 1, 1951, Vol. 25, No. 7, 17.

p. 213   Wrote Stanton Catlin: *ARTnews*, Vol. 49, No. 9, January 1951.

p. 214   in late 1949, when Charles Egan: Phillip Bonosky, December 2, 1949:
           We went out for coffee and talk, and she told me that Eagen [*sic*] was up to see her work, but didn't seem to be too impressed and she doubts that she'll get a show from him.

p. 214   Although she didn't know it: March 10, 1951.

p. 214   Millen Brand: Dec 27, 1954; telegram to appear for McCarthy Hearings, March 26, 1953; appearance scheduled for March 27 at 9:45 a.m., Millen Brand Papers.

p. 214   "The subject appears to suffer": FBI file on Alice Neel; November 20, 1953, p. 2 of 5-page memorandum, also refers to statements made about Alice in 1948.

p. 214   Flyer from New Playwrights Theater with list of works and Mike Gold introduction: Gold introduction quoted in Hills, *Alice Neel*, 89; Philadelphia Museum catalog, 169.

p. 214   duly attracting the attention of the FBI: FBI file on Alice Neel; two-page write-up March 10, 1951; Neel's show: May 4, 1951; May 14, 1951.

p. 214   It included two dozen works: flyer for show.

p. 214   The opening of the show featured a panel discussion: ibid.

p. 214   "Pioneer of Social Realism": ibid.; also mentioned in Philadelphia Museum catalog, 169.

p. 215   The FBI may have also been the only agency: Neel FBI File, June 8, 1951 *re:* the Brevort Hotel show.

p. 215   The Ninth Street Show: Calvin Tomkins, *Off The Wall*, New York: Penguin Books, 1981, 61; *The Irascibles* was first published in *Life* magazine, January 18, 1951; also cited in Norman L. Kleeblatt, ed., *Action Abstraction*, 23.

p. 216   "to be with other artists": Hills, *Alice Neel*, 97.

p. 216   It was at the club: ibid., 104.

p. 216   Harold Rosenberg, *The Tradition of the New*, Chicago: University of Chicago Press, 1960, "The American Action Painters," 25, 26, 30; I have deliberately moved the quotes into a different sequence.

p. 217   Wrote Bonosky: Phillip Bonosky journal, April 27, 1953.

p. 217   "She was very bitter": author's interview with Phillip Bonosky.

p. 217   "We were mugged": author's interview with Jack Levine, March 7, 2003.

p. 217   "Abstract Expressionism was the new broom": author's interview with Joe Lasker.

p. 217   As Joel Rothschild recalled: author's interview with Joel Rothschild, August 18, 2005.

p. 218   It was Bonosky who realized: author's interview with Phillip and Faith Bonosky, May 21, 2004.

p. 218   "On the last of the Friday evenings, March 27": Alice Neel FBI file; copy of *Daily Worker* article, April 2, 1953; also mentioned in Philadelphia Museum catalog, 169.

p. 218   Philip Pearlstein remembers: author's interview with Philip Pearlstein, December 18, 2003.

p. 218   Benny Andrews remembers: author's interview with Benny Andrews, August 15, 2005.

p. 218   That same March: author's interview with Richard Neel, April 7, 2010.

p. 218   "I'm tired of death": Phillip Bonosky journal, May 5, 1955.

p. 219   "Alice Neel, Class in Painting and Drawing": FBI file on Alice Neel, May 25, 1953.

p. 219   "I used to give classes": Kufrin, *Uncommon Women*, 140.

p. 219   "Look what happened to the poor Rosenbergs": Hills interview with Alice Neel, July 17, 20, 1982.

p. 219   "A reliable informant": FBI file on Alice Neel, November 30, 1953.

p. 219   Richard Neel entered High Mowing: Philadelphia Museum catalog, 169.

p. 219   Copies of letters from Alice Neel to Phillip Bonosky provided by Nora Bonosky.

p. 221   Philadelphia Museum catalog, 169, incorrectly states that her mother died from cancer.

p. 221   As Bonosky wrote: Phillip Bonosky journal, June 14, 1955.

p. 222   "muddled, romantic, Bohemian type Communist": FBI file on Alice Neel, March 4, 1954, p. 3 of 3-page memo emanating from Miami office, this description was contained in a March 4, 1954 letter from a male informant.

p. 222   In the summer of 1954: flyer from ACA Gallery, "Two One-Man Exhibitions," August 30–September 11, 1954.

p. 222   thanks to the efforts of . . . Joseph Solman: Belcher and Belcher, *Collecting Souls, Gathering Dust*, 208.

p. 222   The show received a mention *ARTnews*: "Capt. Hugh Mulzac and Alice Neel," *ARTnews*, Vol 53, No. 6, October, 1954, 58–89.

p. 222   There was also a dismissive review: *Arts Digest*, "Mulzac and Neel," Vol. 28, September 15, 1954, 26.

p. 222   In mid-April: Phillip Bonosky journal, April 17, 1955.

p. 222   That same spring, Neel made a fictional appearance: Millen Brand, *Some Love, Some Hunger*, New York: Crown Publishers Inc., 1955, 33–37.

p. 224   "Foxy and Catty": Phillip Bonosky journal, May 15, 1955.

p. 225   Throughout most of the fifties: Alice Neel FBI File; October 11, 17, 1955.

p. 225   Hartley recalls the incident: author's interview with Hartley Neel, June 11, 2008.

p. 225   Description of visits: Alice Neel FBI File, October 31, 1955.

p. 225   Neel was quite upset by the intrusion: Phillip Bonosky journal, October 20, 1955.

p. 226   A review of instant file: FBI File on Alice Neel, October 25, 1958; February 27, 1959.

p. 226   three years later . . . and in 1959 Neel's status: ibid.

p. 226   In a late entry: FBI File on Alice Neel, undated entry.

p. 226   Neel's case was finally closed in 1961: ibid.

p. 226   Phillip Bonosky journal, April 11, April 15, 1957.

p. 226   In May 1957, Neel received: ibid., May 23, 1957.

p. 227   According to Bonsky's journal: ibid., May 29, 1957.

p. 228   A few weeks later: ibid., June 5, 1957.

CHAPTER TWENTY-TWO: *Romancero Guajiro*

p. 229   In the twenty-seven years: Juan A. Martínez: *Carlos Enríquez: The Painter of Cuban Ballads*, Coral Gables, FL., Cernude Art, 2010.

p. 229   publication of books: ibid., At a Glance Chronology, 282.

p. 229   "He is one of the most important artists": author's interview with Graziella Pogolotti, June 14, 2007.

p. 229 Carlos had his first show: Juan A. Martínez, *Carlos Enríquez*, At a Glance Chronology, 281, 282; Juan Sanchez, *Carlos Enríquez*, Chronology; *Carlos Enríquez*, Serie Cuban Painters, 3, biblio, 45.

p. 229 Recalls Graziella Pogolotti: author's interview with Graziella Pogolotti.

p. 230 In his work: Juan Martínez, *Cuban Art and National Identity*, 119.

p. 230 As Enríquez himself explained: ibid., 119–122.

p. 231 Quotation from *Tilín García*: Rocio Aranda-Alvarado, thesis, 168.

p. 231 Says Pogolotti: author's interview with Graziella Pogolotti.

p. 231 "Enríquez was out to scandalize": author's interview with Juan Martínez.

p. 232 "When Tilín met her": Arnada-Alvarado, thesis, 156.

p. 232 Ibid., 179.

p. 232 "The technique is soft": Juan Martínez, *Cuban Art and National Identity*, 122; letter to Alfred Barr dated February 8, 1943.

p. 232 Comparison of Enríquez and Neel paintings: notes from author's visit to Museo Nacional de Bellas Artes, Havana, June, 2007.

p. 233 In early 1936: Juan Martínez, *Enríquez*, At a Glance Chronology, 282; *Carlos Enríquez*, Serie Cuban Painters, 3, 45.

p. 233 In 1938, Enríquez's work was shown in Mexico City: Juan Martínez, ibid.

p. 233 1939 was an important year: Juan Martínez, ibid.; according to Serie 3, Enríquez's second novel, *La Feria De Guancanama*, was first published in 1940.

p. 233 As Graziella Pogolotti: author's interview with Graziella Pogolotti.

p. 233 But, as her father recalled: Marcelo Pogolotti, *Of Clay and Voices*, 267; translated for the author by Robert Gibbons.

p. 234 Enríquez painted a gauzy nude: author's visit to El Hurón Azul, June 2007.

p. 234 The sparkling rum bottles: author's visit, June 10, 2007.

p. 234 El Hurón Azul: ibid.; author's interviews with Juan Martínez, Graziella Pogolotti, Esperanza Maynulet; June 2007; Juan Martínez, August 14, 2007.

p. 234 "It was the splendid era": author's interview with Graziella Pogolotti.

p. 234 From 1940 to 1943: Juan Martínez, *Carlos Enríquez*, Chronology At A Glance, 283.

p. 235 Enríquez and Frejaville: ibid.

p. 235 1944 was another banner year: ibid.

p. 235   Enríquez participated in a second show: ibid.

p. 235   In 1945, Enríquez went to Haiti: ibid.

p. 235   In 1946, he was given an award: ibid., 284.

p. 235   In 1947, Enríquez had another solo show: ibid., 284.

p. 235   He collaborated on: ibid.

p. 235   In 1949, Enríquez participated: ibid.

p. 235   In 1950, Geramine left him: ibid.

p. 236   But Enríquez's habitual drinking: author's interview with Graziella Pogolotti.

p. 236   His painting, *Dos Ríos*: Martínez, *Enríquez*, Chronology at a Glance, 285.

p. 236   Two years later: Martínez, *Enríquez*, Chronology at a Glance, ibid.

p. 236   The year before his death: ibid.

p. 236   "The last years of Carlos": author's interview with Graziella Pogolotti.

p. 236   it was the day that his sixth solo show: author's interview with Juan Martínez, August 14, 2007.

p. 236   The show opened a few weeks later: ibid.

p. 237   El Hurón Azul became a museum; further description of El Hurón Azul: author's visit to El Hurón Azul, June 2007.

p. 237   Richard graduated from High Mowing: Philadelpia Museum catalog, 169.

p. 237   serious relationship with a woman named Sondra: author's interviews with Sondra Brody.

p. 237   "I met him": ibid.

p. 237   according to Sondra: ibid.

p. 237   although Alice was somewhat in the dark: This assumption is based on follow-up interviews with Sondra Brody in May, 2009, and various Bonosky journal entries from 1956 and 1957, indicating that Alice was unaware of the extent of the relationship.

p. 238   "She complains and grieves": Phillip Bonosky journal, June 10, 1958.

p. 238   Sondra and Sam's son: author's interviews with Sondra Brody.

p. 238   Richard recalls a 1958 episode: author's interview with Richard Neel, April 1, 2010.

p. 238   a youngish man in his mid-thirties: author's interview with Joel Rothschild.

p. 239   "I was analyzed in 1958": Hills, *Alice Neel*, 101.

p. 239   "Still, in March, 1958, she complained": Bonosky journal entry, March 5, 1958.

p. 239   According to Neel: Hills, *Alice Neel*, 103.

p. 239   Neel told Jonathan Brand: Jonathan Brand interview, December 1969.

p. 239   Sam would die in 1987: author's interviews with Sondra and David Brody.

CHAPTER TWENTY-THREE:

Pull My Daisy (from Flower to Power)

p. 240   "Poverty isn't enough for me anymore": Phillip Bonosky journal, May 31, 1960.

p. 240   Background on *Pull My Daisy*: Blaine Allan, *The Making and Unmaking of Pull My Daisy*, Taylor and Francis, 1988, 185.

p. 240   Notes from author's viewing of the film.

p. 240   The movie was produced: Walter Gutman Notes from Film Anthology Archives Retrospective, April 15 to 26, 1981; Gutman obituary, *Variety*, May 14, 1986.

p. 240   Neel painted him in 1965: Hills, *Alice Neel*, 113; Neel describes his pose.

p. 240   With its free-form: notes from author's viewing of *Pull My Daisy*.

p. 240   the third act of his play: author's interview with Alfred Leslie, November 2004.

p. 240   "I never understood": Larry Rivers, *What Did I Do? The Unauthorized Biography of Larry Rivers*, with Arnold Weinstein, New York: HarperCollins, 1992, 173.

p. 241   As Bonosky remarks in his journal: Phillip Bonosky journal, April 12, 1960.

p. 241   Says Leslie: author's interview with Alfred Leslie, November, 2004.

p. 241   Recalls Amram: author's interview with David Amram, November 2004.

p. 241   According to Neel: Hills, *Alice Neel*, 104.

p. 241   *The Hasty Papers*: Alfred Leslie, ed., *The Hasty Papers: A One-Shot Review*, 91.

p. 242   Geza de Vegh's Old Mill Gallery: Belcher and Belcher, *Collecting Souls, Gathering Dust*, 216.

p. 242   her 1935 Kenneth Fearing portrait appeared: Philadelphia Museum catalog, 170.

p. 242   Critic Lawrence Campbell singled out her work: Lawrence Campbell, "Reviews and Previews; Alice Neel, Jonah Kingstein, Anthony Toney, Giacomo Porzano," *ARTnews*, December 1960, Vol. 59, No. 8, 13, 14.

p. 243   Wrote Stuart Preston: Stuart Preston, Art: "Stoneware Works from Sweden," *The New York Times*, October 8, 1960, 46.

p. 243   Just as importantly: author's interview with Richard Neel.

p. 243   including the art critic Hubert Crehan: Hills, *Alice Neel*, 104.

p. 243   Nemser, *Art Talks*, 112.

p. 244   Neel called him "wolf boy": Hills, *Alice Neel*, 114.

p. 244   "Why Robert, you wouldn't let me": ibid., 112.

p. 244   breakthrough year: Belcher and Belcher, *Collecting Souls, Gathering Dust*, 239.

p. 244   This was also the year: Philadelphia Museum catalog, 170.

p. 244   Ibid.

p. 245   Neel was in excellent company: flyer for Kornblee Gallery.

p. 245   The show, along with several others, engendered: Valerie Peterson, "U.S. Figure Painting; Continuity and Cliché," *ARTnews*, Vol. 61, No. 4, Summer 1962.

p. 245   "Alice Neel's portrait of Edward Avidisian": ibid., 38.

p. 245   placed her in context with several dozen celebrated artists: flyer for Zabriskie Gallery; Philadelphia Museum catalog, 170.

p. 245   At her invitation: author's interview with Richard Neel.

p. 245   "She stole my technique": Jonathan Brand interview with Alice Neel, December 4, 5, 1969.

p. 246   Irving Sandler recalls: author's interview with Irving Sandler.

p. 246   In September, Neel made the move: Philadelphia Museum catalog, 170.

p. 246   two-man show at the Camino Gallery: *ARTnews*, October, 1962, Vol. 61, No. 6, 14.

p. 246   triumphant *ARTnews* piece: Hubert Crehan, "*Introducing the Portraits of Alice Neel*," *ARTnews*, October, 1962, Vol. 61, No. 6, 44–47.

p. 247   Background history of the Graham Gallery: Betsy Fahlman, James Graham & Sons, 1857–2007, 150th year anniversary book; history of the gallery, 9; list of Neel's seven shows, 96: Neel actually had nine shows at the Graham.

p. 248   In September 1963, Neel saw her old friend: Millen Brand journals, September 14, 1963.

p. 248   It garnered the lead review: Kim Levin, "Reviews and Previews," *ARTnews*, Vol. 67, No. 6, October, 1963, 11.

p. 249   Even the *New York Post* weighed in: In the Art Galleries, *The New York Post*, October 6, 1963, 14.

p. 249   Recalls Robin Graham: author's interview with Robin Graham, May 2009.

p. 249   In December 1963, Richard married: Philadelphia Museum catalog, 171.

p. 249   Richard graduated from Columbia: ibid.

p. 249   Starting in 1964: ibid.

p. 249   Neel had met through John Rothschild: author's interview with Joel Rothschild.

p. 250   Biographical background on Dr. Muriel Gardiner: *The New York Times*, obituary, Muriel Gardiner, February 7, 1985.

p. 250   Says Constance Harvey: author's interview with Constance Harvey, January 17, 2007.

p. 250   Neel appeared in several group shows: Wadsworth Atheneum, Hartford, *News*, (this is a newsletter) May 1964; "Some Contemporary Figure Painters," with price list.

p. 250   Dartmouth Show; New from the Hopkins Center: Dartmouth College, January 12, 1965; Hartley, then doing his masters program at Dartmouth, helped arrange this show.

p. 250   Sometime in the mid-1960s: author's interview with Stanley Maron, October 24, 2008.

p. 250   Recalls Maron: ibid.

p. 251   That summer, Neel traveled to Europe: Philadelphia Museum catalog, 171.

p. 251   *Newsweek* art critic Jack Kroll relegated: Jack Kroll, "Curator of Souls," *Newsweek*, January 31, 1966, 82.

p. 252   As the poet Ted Berrigan pointed out: Ted Berrigan, "The Portrait and Its Double," *ARTnews*, January, 1966, 30–32, 63.

p. 252   For instance: auction price from Christie's Web site, corroborated with Christie's. Includes buyer's premium. Existence of second portrait; interview with Sondra Brody, author's visit to Brody home in 2004.

p. 252   John Gruen said simply: John Gruen, "Collector of Souls," *The Herald Tribune*, January 9, 1966.

p. 252   *Arts* magazine said of Neel: Vol. 40, No. 5, March, 1966, 55.

p. 252   Wrote Charlotte Willard: Charlotte Willard, "In the Art Galleries," *The New York Post*, January 16, 1966.

p. 252   Millen Brand met Alice: Millen Brand journal, January 8, 1966.

p. 253   The poet Robert Lowell: Hills, *Alice Neel*, 112, 113.

p. 253 On May 15, 1967: Mike Gold obituary, May 15, 1967; Neel repainted her original portrait of Mike Gold as a shrine, *Mike Gold, In Memoriam*, 1967, Pamela Allara, *Pictures of People*, 114, 115.

p. 253 Neel's next show was on the West Coast: Maxwell Gallery Flyer, "Alice Neel, A one man Exhibition of Oil Paintings," June 9–30, 1967; mentioned in Philadelphia Museum catalog, 171.

p. 254 Gustav Klimt, *Hope 1*, 1903.

p. 254 Paula Modersohn-Becker, self-portrait, 1906.

p. 254 Egon Schiele . . . *Red Nude*: Jeanette Zwingenberger, *Egon Schiele*, New York: Parkstone Press, 2000, 64, 65, Figures 30, 31; *Red Nude*, pregnant, 1910, watercolor and charcoal; *Newborn Baby*, watercolor and charcoal, 1910; the Neue Gallery showed three more pregnant nudes, cat. no. D30, D31, and D32, all done in 1910, in the Egon Schiele show which ran from October 20, 2005–February 21, 2006; reproduced in the catalog "Egon Schiele," The Ronald S. Lauder and Serge Sabarsky Collections, New York: Prestel, 212, 214, 215.

p. 254 The Soyer brothers also tried their hand: Pamela Allara, "Matter of Fact: Alice Neel's Pregnant Nudes," *American Art*, Spring, 1994, 16.

p. 255 "answer to Pop art": Jonathan Brand interview with Alice Neel, January, 1981.

p. 255 According to his son, Jerry: author's interview with Jerry Strauss, October 19, 2007.

p. 255 "Oh, so you want to be a *professional?*": Allara, *Pictures of Paintings*, 178, 179; David C. Berliner, *Cosmopolitan*, "Women Artists Today, How Are They Doing vis a vis the Men?" October 1973, 219; Munro, *Originals*, interview transcript, 41; Henry Geldzahler, *Making it New*, Turtle Point Press, 1994.

p. 256 Neel had her third show: Graham Gallery catalog, January 6–February 3, 1968, opening 1–4 p.m.; Neel's 1967, *Mother and Child*, of Nancy and Olivia on the cover.

p. 256 "They show it's not enough to be an artist": transcript of Harvard lecture, 1979, 14.

p. 256 "bulls and bears market": Hills, *Alice Neel*, 112.

p. 256 Writing in *The New York Times*: Hilton Kramer, "Marsden Hartley, American Yet Cosmopolitan," *The New York Times*, January 20, 1968.

p. 256 "Probably one of the greatest portraitists": Cindy Nemser, "Alice Neel," *Arts Magazine*, Vol. 42, No. 4, February, 1968, 60.

p. 256 Charlotte Willard included her: Charlotte Willard, "In the Art Galleries: New Faces," *New York Post*, January 27, 1969.

p. 257 Neel remained a hard sell: author's interview with Robin Graham.

p. 257   Says Joan Washburn: author's interview with Joan Washburn.

p. 257   Millen Brand paid Neel a visit: Millen Brand journal, August 25, 1968.

p. 258   In September 1968, Joseph Lasker: letters given to me by Joe Lasker; September 27 letter from Joe Lasker to John Bauer; October 1, 1968, letter from John Bauer to Joe Lasker; October 19, 1968, note from Alice Neel to Joe Lasker.

p. 259   As she told Jonathan Brand the following year: Jonathan Brand interview with Alice Neel, December 4, 5, 1969.

p. 259   "Mom, Apple Pie and the American Flag": John Gruen, "Monster and Mom," *New York* magazine, January 27, 1969.

p. 259   While *Time* magazine opined: *Time* magazine, January 3, 1969, 49.

p. 259   Neel called Millen Brand to boast: Millen Brand journal, January 6, 1969.

p. 260   "I did a poster": Hills, *Alice Neel*, 124.

p. 260   The late painter Benny Andrews: author's interview with Benny Andrews, August 15, 2005.

p. 260   "I'm allowed eighteen linear feet": Millen Brand journal, February 28, 1969.

p. 261   On May 21, Neel received an award: Philadelphia Museum catalog, 172.

p. 261   Neel was seated in the next-to-last row: May 21, 1969 Program for Annual Ceremonial, National Institute of Arts and Letters; seating chart.

p. 261   Wrote Millen Brand in his journal: Millen Brand journal, May 21, 1969.

p. 261   Neel spent part of 1969 traveling: Philadelphia Museum catalog, 172.

p. 261   Neel stayed in San Francisco for nearly two months: interview with Virginia Neel.

p. 261   a busman's holiday: Millen Brand journal, September 28, 1969.

p. 261   Ibid.

p. 262   Alice, Nancy, and Richard: author's interview with Richard Neel, author's interview with Nancy Neel.

CHAPTER TWENTY-FOUR:
Their Balls Are Just Higher Up

p. 263   *Time* magazine . . . portrait of . . . Kate Millett: "The Politics of Sex," *Time* magazine, August 31, 1970.

p. 263   When Millett refused to pose: Allara, *Pictures of People*, 193.

p. 263 "The women's lib movement is giving the women": Doctoral Address, Moore College of Art, June 3, 1971.

p. 263 Betty Friedan's 1963 book: *The Feminine Mystique*, New York: W.W. Norton, 1963; Norton paperback 2001; mentioned in Norma Broude and Mary D. Garrard, ed., *The Power of Feminist Art*, New York: Harry N. Abrams, 1996 paperback edition, 90.

p. 263 "I couldn't read Betty Friedan": Nemser, *Art Talk*, 118.

p. 264 Kate Millett, *Sexual Politics*, New York: Doubleday, 1970.

p. 264 "The fault lies not in our stars": Linda Nochlin, *Women, Art, and Power and Other Essays*, New York: Harper & Row, Icon Edition, 1988, 150; quoted in Norma Broude and Mary D. Garrard, ed., *The Power of Feminist Art*, New York: Harry N. Abrams, 1996 paperback edition, 122.

p. 264 already burgeoning women's art coalitions: ibid., Broude and Garrard, *The Power of Feminist Art*, 122.

p. 264 An explosion of feminist journals: ibid.; *re*: Chuck Nemser: Allara, *Pictures of People*, 201.

p. 265 "The early 1970s was entirely exhilarating": author's interview with Judy Chicago, May 17, 2009.

p. 265 Womanhouse: Broude and Garrard, ed., *The Power of Feminist Art*, 48–66.

p. 265 *The Dinner Party*: Phoebe Hoban, *ARTnews*, "We're Finally Infiltrating," Feminist Issue, February, 2007, 111; Broude and Garrard, *The Power of Feminist Art*, 227, 228; author's interview with Judy Chicago, December, 2007.

p. 265 vaginal self-examinations: *Our Bodies, Ourselves*, Boston: Boston's Women's Health Book Collective, 1973.

p. 265 Erica Jong nailed the Zeitgeist: Erica Jong, *Fear of Flying*, New York: Holt, Rhinehart & Winston, 1973.

p. 265 Richard Brooks, screenwriter, director, *Looking for Mr. Goodbar*, movie released by Paramount Pictures on October 19, 1977; based on the novel by Judith Rossner, New York: Washington Square Press, 1975.

p. 265 "All this intelligence and ambition": author's interview with Mira Schor.

p. 265 "that magical moment": Mary D. Garrard, "Alice Neel and Me," *Women's Arts Journal*, Fall/Winter, 2006, 3.

p. 265 "It's hard for younger people": author's interview with Mary Garrard.

p. 266 "I believe in Feminism": Diamonstein, *Inside New York's Art World*, 261.

p. 266 "I much preferred men to women": Hills, *Alice Neel*, 13, 14.

p. 266   "I felt women represented a dreary": Alice Neel, Bloomsburg State College (now University) lecture, March 21, 1972.

p. 266   "I was a woman": Kufrin, *Uncommon Women*, 237.

p. 266   "When I was in a room working": Judith Higgins, "Alice Neel and the Human Comedy," *ARTnews*, October, 1984, 79.

p. 267   Neel even became a cause célèbre: Allara, *Pictures of People*, 195.

p. 267   The first issue of *Women's Art Journal*: ibid. Neel was included in the Whitney's annual show in 1972.

p. 267   "Neel was one of the women artists": author's interview with Judy Chicago.

p. 267   "With this aggressive, outrageous behavior": Garrard, "Alice and Me," 5; Broude and Garrard, ed., *The Power of Feminist Art*, 93; "No one present has forgotten the virtually unknown septuagenarian Alice Neel who seized the stage uninvited and presented a marathon slide show of her own work . . ."

p. 267   "But she also got some satisfaction": author's interview with Hartley Neel, June 11, 2008.

p. 267   "Her own idiosyncratic feminism": author's interview with Mary D. Garrard.

p. 267   "She wasn't a feminist": author's interview with May Stevens, October 8, 2006.

p. 268   Sylvia Sleigh, who participated: author's interview with Sylvia Sleigh, June 2009.

p. 268   "She exemplified the struggles": author's interview with Judy Chicago.

p. 268   "The agenda for women artists": Broude and Garrard, ed., *The Power of Feminist Art*, 22.

p. 268   In her essay: Linda Nochlin, *Women, Art, and Power and Other Essays*, "Some Women Realists," 99.

p. 269   "It only became comprehensible in retrospect": author's interview with Judy Chicago.

p. 269   "Neel herself observed": author's interview with Mary Garrard.

p. 269   "It's a very important part of life": Hills, *Alice Neel*, 162.

p. 270   "She is a subject gazing": author's interview with Mary Garrard.

p. 271   Hartley Neel married Ginny Taylor: Philadelphia Museum catalog, 172.

p. 271   That same month, John Rothschild moved in: ibid.

p. 271   "He just wanted to bring in": Hills, *Alice Neel*, 82.

p. 271 "His habit for organization": Jonathan Brand interview with Alice Neel, December 4, 5, 1969.

p. 271 In 1970, Neel had her fourth solo show: brochure for Graham show.

p. 271 "All together they make": Lawrence Campbell, "Reviews and Previews," *ARTnews*, November 1970, Vol. 69, No. 7, 24.

p. 271 Wrote Gerrit Henry: Gerrit Henry, *Art International*, December 1970, Vol. 14, No. 10, 77–78.

p. 271 And, of course, Hilton Kramer: Hilton Kramer, *The New York Times*, October 24, 1970.

p. 272 Andy Warhol showed up: *The Village Voice*, "The Other Real Andy Warhol" (photo with Alice Neel at her Graham Gallery exhibit, October 22, 1970).

p. 272 "Six Patent Leather Shoes": Alice Neel, Harvard slide lecture, March 21, 1979, transcript of tape 2, 10, "The Title is *The Gruen Family or Six Patent Leather Shoes*"; Phoebe Hoban, "A Desperate Beauty," *ARTnews*, March 2010.

p. 272 Neel commented that: Hills, *Alice Neel*, 129.

p. 272 "I said to Jane": all descriptions and comments on following pages from author's interview with John Gruen and Jane Wilson, October 25, 2007; I did a follow-up interview on November 6, 2007.

p. 274 Warhol . . . one of Neel's personal favorites: Nessa Forman, *The Sunday Bulletin*, Philadelphia, January 24, 1971.

p. 274 "nudity is a threat to my existence": Andy Warhol, *The Philosophy of Andy Warhol, From A to B and Back Again*, New York: Harcourt Brace Jovanovich, 11; mentioned in Philadelphia Museum catalog, 49.

p. 274 offered to strip: Alice Neel, lecture at Whitney Museum of American Art, December 2, 1982; tape/transcript in the collection of the Whitney Museum of American Art archives.

p. 274 "We were both hanging in": Alice Neel, Harvard slide lecture, 23.

p. 274 she ran into Warhol at the Gotham Book Mart: Alice Neel, lecture at Whitney Museum of American Art.

p. 274 "Why don't you paint me with my scars": ibid.

p. 274 "because all my pictures look at you": ibid.

p. 274 "We were both so sophisticated": William Luvass, "Making It: An Interview," *Art Times*, December 1986, 10.

p. 274 she and Louise Nevelson were the best women artists: ibid.

p. 275 The following year began with Neel's triumphant return: Philadelphia Museum catalog, 172.

p. 275 Jackie Curtis and Ritta Redd: ibid.
Neel amused her Harvard and Whitney audiences with her hilarious anecdote about taking Jackie and Ritta to the women's section of the Harvard Club, the night before they posed, where they were thrown out because "gentlemen in the Harvard Club must wear jackets. I can't imagine how he knew she was a gentleman, you know . . . the skin on her neck and arms, any woman would envy." Two years later, the Club referred to the two as "her sons."

p. 275 "Today she is the most . . .": Hubert Crehan, "A Different Breed of Portraitist," *San Francisco Chronicle*, March 7, 1971, 32.

p. 275 "Portrait painting is alive and well": Victoria Donohoe, "Alice Neel Comes Home After 30 Years of Portraiture Triumphs," *The Philadelphia Inquirer*, January 15, 1971, 14.

p. 275 While Sunday's paper proclaimed: Victoria Donohoe, "Homecoming Collector of Souls Displays Portraits at Moore," *The Philadelphia Inquirer*, Sunday, January 24, 1971, 8.

p. 275 Moore College of Art PHD Citation, reprinted in *Women and Art*, Winter, 1971, 12, 13; Belcher and Belcher, *Collecting Souls, Gathering Dust*, 247.

p. 276 Neel's doctoral address: copy of doctoral address, Moore College of Art, June, 1971; reprinted in *Woman and Art*, Winter, 1971, 12, 13.

p. 278 In late January of 1971, Neel joined: "The Political Scene," write-up of Figurative Alliance Protest, *Arts Magazine*, Vol. 45, No. 3, March 1971; mentioned in Philadelphia Museum catalog, 172.

p. 278 "She was a major player in the Alliance": author's interview with Marjorie Kramer, June 5, 2010.

p. 278 "It could be a scrappy place": author's interview with Sam Thurston, June 5, 2010.

p. 278 Recalls Philip Pearlstein: author's interview with Philip Pearlstein, December 18, 2003.

p. 279 Pearlstein would regularly: author's interview with Philip Pearlstein, December 18, 2003.

p. 279 The painter Paul Resika: author's interview with Paul Resika, March 2010.

p. 279 Says Don Perlis: author's interview with Don Perlis, March 2010.

p. 280 Benjamin Altman Figure Prize: Philadelphia Museum catalog, 172.

p. 280 "I was new blood": Neel made this comment during an interview conducted in October, 1975 for University of Georgia Television Station, WGTV, the *Forum* program, in conjunction with her retrospective at the University of Georgia Museum of Art in September 1975.

p. 280   Alice Neel, *Daily World*, April 17, 1971.

p. 281   Recalled Robin Graham: author's interview with Robin Graham.

p. 281   Like many, Doty was beguiled: Piri Halasz, "I Have this Obsession with Life,"
          ARTnews, January, 1974, 47.

p. 281   "Since I was involved in these protest things": author's interview with Benny
          Andrews.

p. 282   "Women have balls": David C. Berliner, "Women Artists Today: How Are They
          Doing Vis a Vis the Men," *Cosmopolitan*, October 1973, 174, 5.

p. 282   "What amazed me was that all of these women critics": Diamonstein, *Inside
          New York's Art World*, 258.

p. 282   "I think I have painted": Alice Neel, Bloomsburg State College (now University)
          lecture, March 21, 1972.

p. 282   She also spent a week that summer at Skowhegan, Maine: Philadelphia Museum
          catalog, 173.

p. 282   In late 1972, John Perreault: author's interview with John Perreault.

p. 282   "It was the first show I ever curated": ibid.

p. 283   Neel told Hills: Hills, *Alice Neel*, 152.

p. 283   Sleigh firmly believes: author's interview with Sylvia Sleigh.

p. 283   "I don't know if she knew": author's interview with John Perreault.

p. 283   "inner faun": author's interview with John Perreault; Perreault refers to Neel
          seeing him as a faun in Edie Newhall, "Neel Life Stories," *New York*, June 19,
          2000, 40.

p. 283   "I see myself in it and I think it's a great collaboration": author's interview with
          John Perreault.

p. 283   The previous month, Neel was included in: catalog for the Women Choose
          Women show.

p. 284   "It was important": author's interview with Sylvia Sleigh.

p. 284   The catalog essay . . . summed up: Lucy R. Lippard, catalog for Women
          Choose Women show, "A Note on the Politics and Aesthetics of a Women's
          Show," 6.

p. 284   "grisly prenatal odalisque": Harry F. Gaugh: *Arts* magazine, March 1979.

p. 284   *Newsweek* captured the spirit: Douglas Davis, "Women, Women, Women," *News-
          week*, January 29, 1973, 77.

p. 285   "Since God was made": Alice Neel, *Women in Art*, winter 1971, draft of piece in Neel Archives.

p. 285   "who could work both sides": author's interview of Faith Ringgold, November 13, 2008.

p. 285   Neel also traveled: author's interview with Hartley Neel, June 23, 2009.

p. 286   Neel received a $7,500 grant: Philadelphia Museum catalog, 173.

p. 286   Pegged to the show, Diane Cochrane: Diane Cochrane, "Alice Neel, Collector of Souls," *American Artist*, September 1973, Vol. 37, Issue 374, 32.

p. 286   Cindy Nemser wrote a major piece: Cindy Nemser, "Alice Neel: Portraits of Four Decades," *Ms. Magazine*, Vol. 2, No. 4, October 1973. On page 53, she wrote:
  "Never has she received the recognition due her superb body of work. It was only a few years ago that the Whitney Museum in New York finally purchased its first Alice Neel. Now in her seventy-third year, she will have her first exhibition (October, 1974) at that prestigious museum."

p. 286   "Only this woman, I suspect": Cochrane, "Alice Neel, Collector of Souls," *American Artist*, 32.

p. 286   Neel snagged a brief write-up in *The New York Times*: *The New York Times*, October 6, 1973.

p. 286   *ARTnews*, with a few humorous: *ARTnews*, "Reviews and Previews," Vol. 73, No. 6, November 1973.

p. 286   In *The Christian Science Monitor*: Diana Loercher, "Will Barnet, Alice Neel and Others on Display," *The Christian Science Monitor*, October 11, 1973.

p. 287   "I don't think there is any question": author's interview with Hartley Neel, June 23, 2009.

p. 287   Joseph Solman recalled: author's interview with Joseph Solman.

p. 287   According to Richard: author's interview with Richard Neel, April 2010.

p. 288   "I was delighted to have the Whitney show": Hills, *Alice Neel*, 136.

p. 288   Although she still took exception to the word "portrait": Diane Leorcher, "Alice Neel, American Portraitist," *The Christian Science Monitor*, Vol. 66, No. 6, March 1974.

p. 288   "The show finally convinced me": Terry Gross interview with Alice Neel on *Fresh Air*, WNYC, March 3, 1983.

p. 288   Fifty-eight portraits: Whitney Retrospective catalog, Alice Neel.

p. 288   The brochure began: ibid.

p. 288   "Alice Neel may be the only artist": Pat Mainardi, *Art in America*, "Alice Neel at the Whitney Museum," Vol. 62, No. 3, May/June, 1974.

p. 289   "Alice was overjoyed": author's interview with Hartley Neel, June 23, 2009.

p. 289   The retrospective gathered: Whitney Museum catalog, list of works in the exhibition.

p. 289   The curator, Elke Solomon . . . later acknowledged: author's interview with Elke Solomon.

p. 290   "a collector of faces, rather than souls": Hilton Kramer, "Art: Alice Neel Retrospective," *The New York Times*, February 9, 1974.

p. 290   Weighing in two weeks later: James R. Mellow, "When Does a Portrait Become a Memento Mori," *The New York Times*, February 24, 1974.

p. 290   The review engendered: "Sexism," Susan Rappaport, Staten Island, letter to the editor, *The New York Times*, March 31, 1974.

p. 290   Lawrence Alloway, in *The Nation*: Lawrence Alloway, "Art," *The Nation*, March 9, 1974, Vol. 218, No. 10, 318.

p. 291   Neel, it seems, even when: "Country Art and City Art," *Newsweek*, March 11, 1974, Vol. 83, No. 10, 90.

p. 292   Although Thomas B. Hess: Thomas B. Hess, "Behind the Taboo Curtain," *New York* magazine, 1974, 68.

p. 292   *Artforum* wrote: Alice Neel, The Whitney Museum, Vol. 12, No. 9, May 1974, 74–75.

p. 292   And Kenneth Evett, in *The New Republic*: Kenneth Evett, "From Top to Bottom at the Whitney," *The New Republic*, May 4, 1974, 30.

p. 292   Neel herself told an interviewer: Diana Loercher, "Alice Neel, American Portraitist," *The Christian Science Monitor*.

p. 292   Neel painted the Whitney's director: Belcher and Belcher, *Collecting Souls, Gathering Dust*, 245; author's interview with Anita Duquette.

p. 292   Tom Armstrong . . . became fast friends: author's interview with Tom Armstrong.

p. 293   Today the Whitney owns: list provided by the Whitney Museum of American Art.

CHAPTER TWENTY-FIVE: *Vindication*

p. 294   Jack Baur . . . celebrated her birthday with a poem: Jack Baur "To Alice at 75"; Smithsonian Archives of American Art; also printed in Robert Miller catalog.

p. 294   "She felt it was something": author's interview with Hartley Neel.

p. 294   Recalled Joseph Solman: author's interview with Joseph Solman.

p. 295   On Sunday, April 25, 1975, John Rothschild: author's interview with Joel Roth-
          schild; author's interview with Ginny and Hartley Neel, April 5, 2009.

p. 295   Just the year before: copy of John's letter, on his letterhead, from Neel Ar-
          chives.

p. 295   He made similar complaints to Richard: author's interviews with Richard Neel,
          April 1 and April 7, 2010.

p. 295   Not long after John died: author's interview with Stanley Maron.

p. 295   "Only this year did he ever say he was sorry": Munro, unedited interview tran-
          script for *Originals*, 38.

p. 295   She had told Jonathan Brand: Jonathan Brand interview with Alice Neel, De-
          cember 4, 5, 1969.

p. 296   "I don't count John as a player": author's interview with Hartley Neel, April 5,
          2009.

p. 296   "I had to reach my sexual aim!": Phillip Bonosky journal, January 16, 1949.

p. 296   "he was always at my bedroom door": Patricia Hills, Alice Neel interview, July
          17, 20, 1982.

p. 296   "a beautiful accordion nightgown": Michel Auder video.

p. 296   "I didn't want to be ravaged": Munro, unedited interview transcript for *Origi-
          nals*, 42.

p. 296   When she was sixty-nine: Jonathan Brand interview with Alice Neel, December
          4, 5, 1969.

p. 296   "I just have the good luck": Richard Polsky, Interview 2, 139.

p. 296   "I'd rather have her opinion": Rhodes, *Three Women Artists*.

p. 296   Recalls John Cheim: author's interview with John Cheim, March 30, 2009.

p. 297   By 1976, Alice had requested: correspondence with Ginny Neel; Philadelphia
          Museum catalog, 174; Neel had been regularly spending time up in Stowe ever
          since Hartley and Ginny moved there in 1973; The catalog says the log studio
          was renovated in 1975.

p. 297   The modest but comfortable house: author's visit to Spring Lake, September 20,
          2006; author's interview with Nancy Neel during visit.

p. 297   Neel had her favorite haunts: ibid.

p. 298   She also regularly participated on panels: Susan Swinland, "Women in the Me-
          dia," *MCA Alumnae Journal*, Moore College of Art, May 7, 2005.

p. 298   "Women Artists, Seventy Plus": June Blum, "Women and Success at the Brooklyn Museum," *The Feminist Art Journal*, Vol. 4, No. 3, Fall 1975; "Works on Paper—Women Artists," September 24 to November 9, 1975; "Women Artists Seventy-Plus" panel on November 2, 1975.

p. 298   a show at the Smith College Museum of Art: May 18, 1999, Smith College Memo to Philadelphia Museum curators, *re:* "Alice Neel Paintings," April 8–May 11, 1975 at Smith College Museum of Art.

p. 298   "Everyone who meets her": Leonard Kimbrell, "Alice Neel's Portraits," *Art-Week*, February 1, 1975, Vol. 6, No. 5; review of Alice Neel's show at the Portland Center for Visual Arts.

p. 298   Alfred Frankenstein: Alfred Frankenstein, "Neel Exhibition Is a Human Encounter," *San Francisco Chronicle*, March 9, 1975.

p. 298   Brochure for "Sons and Others: Women Artists See Men," The Queens Museum, Flushing, N.Y. March 15–April 27, 1975; David L. Shirey, "Men as Viewed by Women Artists," *The New York Times*, March 30, 1975, wrote a review of this show: "Alice Neel, who possessed a piquantly subtle sense of humor, emphasizes man's social mask and his vulnerability in a double portrait of Gregory Battcock and David Bourdon. One is casually facing the world in a protective suit and the other, sitting in his underwear and socks, looks as helpless as a bird in a cage."

p. 299   "Three Centuries of the American Nude": brochure for "Three Centuries of the American Nude," May 9 through July 13, 1975 (traveled to Minneapolis Institute of Art and the University of Houston Fine Art Center).

p. 299   "Color, Light, and Image": flyer for "Color, Light, and Image, Words and Statements, November 13 to January 30, In Celebration of the United Nations Designated International Women's Year 1975."

p. 299   "Figure as Form": The "Figure as Form" show ran from November 25, 1975, through January 4, 1976 at the Museum of Fine Arts; mentioned in Philadelphia Museum catalog, 191.

p. 299   "From Pedestal to Pavement": "From Pedestal to Pavement" ran from December 5, 1975 through January 30, 1976 at the Mount Holyoke College Art Museum, ibid.

p. 299   A portfolio of her work: *Painted Bride Quarterly*, Vol. 2, No. 3, Summer 1975; portfolio included, *Anne Deagon, Frank O'Hara, Kenneth Fearing, John Perreault, Jackie Curtis and Ritta Red, Andy Warhol, Linda Nochlin and Daisy, Randall in Extremis.*

p. 299   a full-scale celebration of the artist's career: The University of Georgia Museum of Art Show catalog, "The Woman and Her Work," September 7–October 19, 1975; Cindy Nemser, "Alice Neel—Teller of Truth," essay; "To Alice at 75," Jack Baur poem; statements by Dorothy Pearlstein, Raphael Soyer, and Alice Neel.

p. 299   Painter and art professor Neill Slaughter: author's interview with Neill Slaughter.

p. 300   Neel was interviewed on *Forum*: interview conducted in October 1975 for University of Georgia Television Station WGTV, the *Forum* program, Georgia Museum of Art, with Bill Paul, director of the Georgia Museum of Art.

p. 300   She had a solo exhibit of thirty recent paintings: brochure for "Alice Neel, Collector of Souls," Fairlawn New Jersey Public Library, November 23, 1975–January 2, 1976.

p. 300   Finally, that December, she lectured at the St. Louis Art Museum: E. F. Foster, Jr., "Blithe Spirit, Collector of Souls," *St. Louis Dispatch*.

p. 300   "I can now control an audience": Munro, unedited interview transcript for *Originals*, 41.

p. 301   Her hair in a prim gray twist: author's viewing and transcript of video footage of Neel's induction, from Nancy Baer's, *Collector of Souls* video; included in Andrew Neel's documentary *Alice Neel*, 2007.

p. 301   "it is the greatest honor": Hills, *Alice Neel*, 177.

p. 301   Neel had her sixth solo show: Graham Gallery brochure for show.

p. 301   Thomas Hess wrote a somewhat backhanded review: Thomas Hess, "Sitting Prettier," *New York* magazine, February 23, 1976, 62.

p. 302   John Russell in *The New York Times*: John Russell, "Heroic Inventive Nudes of Philip Pearlstein," *The New York Times*, February 7, 1976.

p. 302   portrait of Bishop . . . made her look like a "mosquito": Isabel Bishop transcript, Smithsonian Archives of American Art; Neel mentions "mosquito" remark in Harvard lecture, 32.

p. 302   On February 26, Neel received the International Women's Year Award: Philadelphia Museum catalog, 174.

p. 302   That same month: Allara, *Pictures of People*, 207.

p. 302   She also reunited: Belcher and Belcher, *Collecting Souls*, *Gathering Dust*, 256.

p. 302   That spring, Victoria Donohoe: author's interview with Victoria Donohoe, July 16, 2009; Donohoe discussed her role in the exhibit in an article, "Religious art thrives, and here's a sample," in the *Philadelphia Inquirer*, December 5, 1979.

p. 303   Pearlstein vividly described: author's interview with Philip Pearlstein.

p. 304   Later, there was a dinner: Hills, *Alice Neel*, 177.

p. 304   Says Donohoe: author's interview with Victoria Donohoe.

p. 304   Vivien Raynor called it: Vivien Raynor, "The Church as Art Patron; Why It Doesn't Work," *The New York Times*, August 1, 1976.

p. 304   As Neel told Hills: Hills, *Alice Neel*, 173, 177.

p. 304   As she told Yetta Groshans: Yetta and Werner Groshans interview; Yetta and Werner Groshans Papers, 1926–1997, Smithsonian Archives of American Art.

p. 305   In September, Neel participated in the show: brochure for "Three American Realists," Everson Museum of Art, Syracuse, NY, September 17–October 31.

p. 305   Writer Paul Richard accompanied her: Paul Richard, "Alice Neel, Portraits and the Artist," *The Washington Post*, October 8, 1976.

p. 305   *The New York Times* asked four artists: "The Art of Portraiture," *The New York Times*, October 31, 1976:
          With the revival of interest in realist painting has come an appreciation of portraiture. The age-old genre is now celebrated by a lively new show, "The Self and Others," at the Wildenstein Gallery. . . . To mark the occasion, *The Times* asked four artists represented in the show to explain how they go about making a portrait, The artists were: Lucas Samaras, Philip Pearlstein, Alice Neel, and Chuck Close.

p. 305   Neel gave a condensed version of her modus operandi: "I Paint Tragedy and Joy," *The New York Times*, October 31, 1976.

p. 306   In December, Neel had a major painting: Philadelphia Museum catalog, 174.

p. 306   "I came to the party with Larry Rivers": author's interview with Michel Auder, June 24, 2009.

p. 307   videotaping her regularly: Michel Auder, documentary *Alice Neel, 1976–1982*, New York: Michel Auder Videos, 2000.

p. 307   Neel . . . starts by reading a line or two from Auder's script: author's transcript of audio of clip from *A Couple of White Faggots Sitting Around Talking*, Michel Auder.

p. 309   Rich, when asked about sitting for Neel: author's brief conversation with Adrienne Rich at the Michael Rosenfeld Gallery, September 2009.

p. 309   large exhibition at Lehigh University's Alumni Memorial Gallery: brochure for Lehigh University Alumni Memorial Gallery show, Bethlehem, PA, March 4–April 1, 1977.

p. 309   Kramer singled out Neel's work: Hilton Kramer, reviews of "New Deal For Art," Grey Art Gallery and "New York W.P.A." at the Exhibition Center of Parsons School of Design, *The New York Times*, November 18, 1977.

p. 309   The Graham show: Graham Gallery catalog for 1977 "Drawings and Paintings" show with Ginny and Elizabeth on cover; includes price list.

p. 309   Norman Turner, writing in the December issue: Norman Turner, "Alice Neel," *Arts Magazine*, December 1977, 14.

p. 310   Reviewing the show in *ARTnews*, Gerrit Henry: Gerrit Henry, "Alice Neel,"
          ARTnews, Vol. 76, No. 10, December 1977.

p. 311   As she told her Harvard audience: Alice Neel, Harvard lecture, 14.

p. 311   As Neel told a radio interviewer: "Talking About Portraits," transcript of
          WBAI-FM Pacifica radio interview with Pat Mainardi, Marcia Marcus, and Alice
          Neel by Judith Vivell, printed in *Feminist Art Journal*, Summer 1974; broad-
          cast on April 7, 1974.

p. 311   Auder documented Neel's painting ... *Margaret Evans, Pregnant*: author's
          viewing of Michel Auder video clip.

p. 312   "I remember when she first picked up her brush": author's interview with Marga-
          ret Evans.

p. 312   "Don't you just love it?": Goldstein, *Soul on Canvas*, 76.

p. 312   "I did one of him when he was working": Terry Gross, *Fresh Air* interview.

p. 312   At the end of the year: Enid Nemy, "On a Night for Artists, Glitter Bows to Tal-
          ent," *The New York Times*, December 9, 1977.

p. 313   Auder's video portrait of Neel: author's viewing of Michel Auder, *Portrait of Al-
          ice Neel, 1976–1982*.

p. 313   As she wrote in the catalog: artist's statement in brochure for "Three Contm-
          porary Women Artists," Miami-Dade Community College, December 5–6,
          1977.

p. 314   Neel had a larger solo show: Fort Lauderdale Museum of Art catalog, catalog es-
          say by Henry R. Hope, introduction; 1–6.

p. 314   "gray, slightly wrinkled . . . Her first remark": Henry R. Hope, personal notes
          on posing at end of Fort Lauderdale Museum of Art catalog.

p. 314   "When Neel looks at her subject": ibid., introduction.

p. 314   "Alice Neel hurt my mother terribly": author's interview with Cristina Lancella,
          May 2003.

p. 315   According to Marisa Diaz: author's interview with Marisa Diaz, June 3, 2003;
          phone follow-up, August 3, 2009.

p. 315   And another friend: ibid., author's interview, Adoris Mendoza, June 3, 2003.

p. 315   according to the Neels: author's interview with Ginny Neel.

p. 315   Moreover, according to an interview: Munro, unedited transcript for *Origi-
          nals*.

p. 315   Says Pablo Lancella: author's interview with Pablo Lancella, May 27, 2003.

p. 315   As Marilyn Schmitt wrote: Marilyn Schmitt, "Alice Neel," *Arts* magazine, Vol. 52, No. 9, May 1978, 9.

p. 316   Virginia Miller, who had first met Neel: author's interview with Virginia Miller.

p. 317   Neel was a frequent guest on panels: flyer for The Artist and Survival, The Maryland Institute College of Art, April 15–16, 1978.

p. 317   A month later . . . Neel had an unusual show: flyer for the Clayworks Studio Workshop, New York, Monday, May 15, 1978.

p. 317   On May 18: Philadelphia Museum catalog, 174.

p. 317   Franz Schulze, of the *Chicago Sun-Times*, called her: Franz Schulze, "3 Artists Defy Trend" *Chicago Sunday Sun-Times*, October 15, 1978.

p. 318   as described by James Auer: James Auer, "Alice Neel Reflects on Art, Life," *The Milwaukee Journal*, October 16, 1978, 6.

p. 318   Neel had twenty-three drawings: flyer for opening reception at the Summit Gallery, West 57th Street, October 31, 1978, 4–7 p.m.

p. 318   Neel called it a "swan song": Alice Neel, Harvard lecture.

p. 318   Neel's statement for the catalog: catalog for Graham Gallery, "Alice Neel, A Retrospective Exhibition of Drawings and Watercolors," November 5 to 8, 1978, with list of works in exhibition.

p. 319   as Harris pointed out in her essay: ibid., Ann Sutherland Harris essay, 4.

p. 319   Neel had a solo show of two dozen paintings: flyer for "Alice Neel, Paintings," Skidmore College, New Art Center, Saratoga Springs, NY, November 16–December 12, 1978; gallery talk with Alice Neel, December 5.

p. 319   "Neel's work during the last 15 years": Harry F. Gaugh, "Alice Neel," *Arts*, March, 1979.

p. 319   The "American monument" was featured: Suzanne Slesin, "The New York Artist in Residence; Alice Neel," *ARTnews*, November 1978.

p. 320   "Two of the city's saltier-tongued women": "All the Nude Not Fit to Be Shown, Artist Says," *The New York Times*, December 14, 1978.

p. 320   "It embarrassed her": ibid.

p. 320   Recalls Joel Rothschild: author's interview with Joel Rothschild.

p. 320   Still, she said she was grateful: "All the Nude Not Fit to Be Shown, Artist Says," *The New York Times*.

p. 320   The item also made Page Six: "Heiress Miffed by Nude Portrait," *The New York Post*, December, 12, 1978.

p. 320 December 14, 1978, letter from Brian Buczak to Alice Neel: "This was Ray Johnson's response to your portrait of Pat Ladew.

December 12, 1978 Letter from Alice Neel to Mr. James C. Couri, Chairman of the Board, Plaza Art Galleries, Inc.:

In 1948, Pat Ladew asked me to do a nude of her and I painted what I considered a work of art. However, she was embarrassed by it and asked me to paint red panties on. A month laster, she came back to me with the painting and said that her friends thought she must be a masochist to hang such a picture of herself. I exchanged this painting for a still life which I gave to Pat Ladew.

Pat Ladew's painting was shelved until 78, when to help save the world, I donated it to the Artists' mobilization for survival. When I donated the painting I told the Artists' mobilization that the paintings was entitled, "Pat Ladew." Last Friday, December 8 I cam home from lunch and received a telephone call from a man later identified to me as Ellaiot Hoffman who insulted me as I have never been insulted in my life. He said I was malicious and told me I had better not say a word to the New York Post or the mass media or I would be languishing in Jail. In closing, I want you to know that I consider this painting a work of art. Sincerely, Alice Neel.

Author's interview with Geoffrey Hendricks, August 25, 2010 Author's interview with Frances Beatty, Richard L. Feigen & Co. August 25, 2010.

p. 321 The snafu resurfaced: Patricia Burstein, "Painter Alice Neel Strips her Subjects to the Bone—And some then Rage in their Nakedness," *People* magazine, March 19, 1979, 63, 64.

p. 321 Women's Caucus for Art Lifetime Achiviement Award: Philadelphia Museum catalog, 174.

p. 321 "We honor Alice Neel": copy of Award Statement, "Women's Caucus for Art Honors Bishop, Burke, Neel, Nevelson, O'Keefe, January 30–March 3, 1979."

p. 321 Neel told an interviewer: Anita Velez Mitchell, "A Visit with Alice Neel."

p. 321 she later told an audience: Harvard Slide Lecture, March 21, 1979 question and answer session, 9.

p. 322 Wrote Martha B. Scott: catalog for University of Bridgeport exhibit.

p. 322 Neel's next solo show: catalog for "Paintings by Alice Neel," Williams College Museum of Art, March 7–28, 1979.

p. 322 Derek Bok had given her a gold star: Hills, *Alice Neel*, 136.

p. 323 "She had her whole world of her art": author's interview with Hartley Neel, May 15, 2009.

p. 323 Mimi Gross recalls the first time: author's interview with Mimi Gross.

p. 324 Excerpts are from the Harvard Slide Lecture, March 21, 1979: comments regarding Ethel Ashton, 1; Isabetta, 6; Sam, 8.

p. 324 As Mira Schor has observed: Mira Schor, "Some Notes on Woman and Abstraction," *re:* myth, 16; *re:* Neel's entertaining approach to her lectures, 13; *re:* Raphael Soyer remark, 12.

p. 325   "Don't leave, don't leave": Harvard Slide Lecture.

p. 325   "Celebrity for me is acceptance": Goldstein, "Soul on Canvas," *New York* magazine, 80.

p. 325   In April . . . an "interview": Alice Neel, "Interview," published in *Night*, Vol. 2, No. 3, April, 1979; Alice Neel Papers, Smithsonian Archives of American Art, Reel 4964.

p. 326   That fall, Neel had a solo show: Fort Wayne Museum of Art, September 24, 1979, letter from James Bell, with a check for a $500 honorarium and $30 cab fare.

p. 326   A notice from November 15: flyer for "Slide Lecture by 'One of the Major American Artists of the 20th Century,' Alice Neel."

p. 326   "I remember being very attracted to Alice Neel": author's interview with John Cheim, March 30, 2009.

CHAPTER TWENTY-SIX : *Bowing Out*

p. 328   "Come celebrate Alice Neel's 80th Birthday": invitation/flyer from the Sarah Institute, 42 East 65th Street.

p. 328   The next night, along with some 2,500: Judy Kelmesrud, "A Tale of Two Parties; Whitney Has Its 50th and Mary Hartman," *The New York Times*, January 11, 1980.

p. 329   Wrote Millen Brand: Millen Brand journals, January 29, 1980; journal page provided by Jonathan Brand.

p. 329   Richard toasted his mother: author's interview with Richard Neel.

p. 329   "felt like a son": author's interview with Hartley Neel.

p. 329   "schlepped" . . . "I was at a brunch": author's interview with Stewart Mott.

p. 330   *Portfolio* magazine also celebrated: Ann Sutherland Harris, "The Human Creature," *Portfolio* magazine, December/January 1980, 71, 73.

p. 330   "She was the first sweater girl as a mother": Harvard slide lecture, 34.

p. 331   "I think every good artist paints": Harvard lecture, question and answer session transcript, 16.

p. 331   "I love to see what the pressure of life does to the human psyche": Sutherland, "The Human Creature," *Portfolio*, 71.

p. 331   "revealed the weakness": "Originals," *Arts* magazine, Vol. 54, No. 9, May 1980, 34, Graham Gallery review.

p. 331   whom Neel referred to as a "mild dish": Frederick Ted Castle, interview with Alice Neel, reprinted from *Artforum*, October, 1983, used as catalog essay for Pennsylvania Academy of Fine Arts, "Alice Neel: Paintings Since 1970," January 26–March 17, 1985, 4.

p. 331   The catalog actually compared her to de Kooning: catalog for "American Painting of the Sixties and Seventies/the Real/the Ideal/the Fantastic."

p. 331   Neel had another major solo show: Patricia Hills, "Alice Neel: Paintings of Two Decades," Boston University Gallery, October 9–November 21, 1980. "Alice Neel: Art as a Form of History," essay by Patricia Hills.

p. 332   In late 1979, Hills conducted a series: author's interview with Patricia Hills.

p. 332   Neel had another solo show: catalog for "Alice Neel '80," Drury College, Springfield, MO, introduction by John H. Simmons, chairman, Department of Fine Arts.

p. 332   Neel had what would be her last solo show: Graham Gallery catalog, "Recent Paintings," November 8–December 13, 1980; price list.

p. 332   Wrote *ARTnews*: Ann Bass, "New York Reviews," *ARTnews*, Vol. 80, No. 1, January 1981, 67, 68.

p. 333   *Self-Portrait*, which debuted at a benefit dinner: "A Revealing Glimpse of an Artist's Twilight Years," *The New York Times*, October 10, 1980.

p. 333   Neel was the only artist: author's interview with Harold Reed.

p. 333   "I live for this little thing": Patricia Burstein, "Painter Alice Neel Strips Her Subjects to the Bone," *People* magazine.

p. 334   "Well, my type doesn't interest me": Harvard lecture, March 21, 1979.

p. 334   "I have always been reluctant": Rita Mercedes, "Alice Neel Talks to Rita Mercedes," *Connoisseur*, Vol. 208, No. 835, September 1981, 2, 3.

p. 334   "I hate the way I looked!": Castle, "Alice Neel," *Artforum*.

p. 335   "So I thought I'll try to do one": Terry Gross interview with Alice Neel, *Fresh Air*.

p. 335   Reed himself recalls his surprise: author's interview with Harold Reed.

p. 335   *The New York Times* made it and Neel the lead item: "A Revealing Glimpse," *The New York Times*.

p. 336   As Neel quipped to *Newsweek*: Barbara Graustark, "Newsmakers," *Newsweek*, October 27, 1980, 81.

p. 336   "Mayor Koch came to the opening": author's interview with Harold Reed.

p. 336   The painting would also be featured: "Self-Portraits" catalog, Alan Frumkin Gallery; "From the Mirror," Part 1.

p. 336 Once again, Neel's was the only nude: John Russell, "Contemporary Self-Portraits," *The New York Times*, December 10, 1982.

p. 336 While *The Christian Science Monitor* said: Theodore F. Wolff, "Ancient and Modern Self-portraits; Some Vain, Some Candid," *The Christian Science Monitor*, January 4, 1983.

p. 336 "I remember distinctly Alice coming": author's interview with George Adams.

p. 337 Neel spent that Thanksgiving with Stewart Mott: Michel Auder video; Tana Hoban, my aunt, was on that trip and took pictures of Neel and her granddaughter Olivia.

p. 337 In late 1980, Neel who had been suffering: author's interview with Hartley Neel.

p. 337 "You know I had a pacemaker put in": Paul Tschinkel, "Alice Neel, 1900–1984," ART/New York, Inner-Tube video, No. 32; Carl Schoetler, "Alice Neel Decided you Might as Well Live," *The Evening Sun*, February 26, 1981.

p. 338 Just a week after her eighty-first birthday: Grimaldis Gallery catalog for "A Retrospective, 1926–1981," which ran from February 5 through March 1; price list.

p. 338 *The Evening Sun* described her holding court: Carl Schoettler, "The Artist as Survivor; Alice Neel decided you might as well live," *The Evening Sun*, February 26, 1981.

p. 339 "like José Ferrer's impersonation of Toulouse-Lautrec": R. P. Harris, "Super-realist LaRose blossoming into a stylist," Lively Arts, the *News-American*, February 22, 1981.

p. 339 Freudenheim recalled how the painting: author's interview with Tom Freudenheim.

p. 339 The director had requested portraits: December 31, 1980 letter from the director, Fine Arts Center, State University of New York at Stony Brook.

p. 340 she and her old friend Phillip Bonosky: author's interview with Phillip Bonosky.

p. 340 "cause of détente": Jenny Burman, A press release from Bennington College, undated.

p. 340 "My idea was that anything that stimulates détente": Hills, *Alice Neel*, 177.

p. 340 Bonosky, to his amazement: author's interview with Philip Bonosky.

p. 340 the show was viewed by some eight hundred people a day: *Bennington College Newsletter, re:* number of people, "It was viewed by more than eight hundred people daily."

p. 340 "It was a very successful show": author's interview with Phillip Bonosky.

p. 340 Although Moscow television wouldn't show: author's interview with Ginny Neel.

p. 340 Neel told . . . Castle: Castle, "Alice Neel," *Artforum*.

p. 341   Neel had told Jonathan Brand: Jonathan Brand interview with Alice Neel, December 1969.

p. 341   Gus Hall had objected vociferously: author's interview with Phillip Bonosky; letter from Gus Hall, February 5, 1982.

p. 341   Bonosky himself wrote the catalog essay: Philip Bonosky, "Meet Alice Neel," Soviet Union Show Catalog.

p. 343   Nonetheless, Ginny recalls: author's interview with Ginny and Hartley Neel, August 2009.

p. 343   "it was a Third World country": author's interview with Ginny Neel.

p. 343   Instead, she stated to a reporter for the *Daily World*: Susan Ortega, "Art for Détente," the *Daily World*, December, 1981; quoted in Allara, *Pictures of People*, chapter notes, 290.

p. 344   As Pamela Allara observed: Allara, *Pictures of People*, 125, 226.

p. 344   As for her day-to-day experience: author's interview with Ginny and Hartley Neel.

p. 344   Neel disguised her disappointment: author's interview with Richard Neel, April 2010.

p. 345   "You should give me a public kiss": Michel Auder, *Alice Neel, 1976–1982*, author's transcript of video clip.

p. 345   According to *The New York Times*: Robin Krebs and Robert McB Thomas, Notes on People, "Image of Koch in Shirtsleeves Preserved on Canvas," *The New York Times*, October 30, 1981.

p. 345   Reed later priced the painting: ibid.

p. 345   Neel told *ARTnews* that "the quizzical expression": *ARTnews*, "The Vasari Diary," January 1982.

p. 345   Says Koch of the portrait: author's interview with Mayor Koch, September 28, 2004.

p. 345   The National Academy of Sciences mounted: brochure for The National Academy of Sciences for Alice Neel show, November 12, 1981–January 28, 1982, with list of works.

p. 345   "To stand in a gallery filled with portraits": Benjamin Forgey, "Alice Neel's Unsettling Portraits," *The Washington Post*, November 30, 1981.

p. 345   Copy of *Time* magazine cover, February 1, 1982, with Neel's distinctive signature on lower lefthand side; copy of "A Letter from the Publisher."

p. 346   A letter from Koch had gone out in February: Letter from The City of New York, Office of the Mayor, February 5, 1982, to Dennis Florio; Dennis Florio Collection, Smithsonian Archives of American Art.

p. 346   "Can I take your picture?" Michel Auder, *Alice Neel, 1976–1982*, video footage of the event.

p. 346   The entrée was fillet of sole Florentine: Philadelphia Museum catalog, 175.

p. 346   The guest list: copy of birthday-party guest list and table seatings and list of paintings to be shown at Gracie Mansion.

p. 347   Recalls David Soyer: author's interview with David Soyer.

p. 347   The hundred or so guests were seated: copy of table seating list.

p. 347   According to Ginny: author's interview with Ginny Neel.

p. 347   Recalls Tom Freudenheim: author's interview with Tom Freudenheim.

p. 347   Mary Tierney, who worked at City Hall: author's interview with Mary Tierney.

p. 347   Even Andrew Neel: author's interview with Ginny Neel.

p. 347   "I found the experience very erotic": Edie Newhall, "Neel Life Stories," *New York* magazine.

p. 348   Neel picked the "fetish" look: transcript of Ann Temkin interview with Annie Sprinkle for Philadelphia Museum catalog.

p. 348   Tierney, who became friends with Neel: author's interview with Mary Tierney.

p. 348   John Cheim . . . had been actively pursuing her: author's interview with John Cheim, March 30, 2009.

p. 348   Meanwhile, Michel Auder had personally introduced: author's interview with Michel Auder, June 24, 2009.

p. 348   Recalls Cheim: author's interview with John Cheim.

p. 349   Russell's review appeared in a roundup: John Russell, "Art: Offbeat Alice Neel, Not a Portrait Around," *The New York Times*, May 28, 1982.

p. 349   In *ARTnews*, Deborah C. Phillips wrote: Deborah C. Phillips, "Alice Neel," *New York Reviews*, Vol. 81, No. 8, 150.

p. 350   *Arts* magazine devoted an entire page: John R. Friedman, "Alice Neel," *Arts Magazine*, September, 1982.

p. 351   Neel had eight group exhibits in 1982: Philadelphia Museum catalog, Exhibition History, 192.

p. 351   "What do you think of Julian Schnabel?": Castle, "Alice Neel," *Artforum*.

p. 351   Neel had three paintings at the Tibor de Nagy: flyer for Tibor De Nagy, "The Figure," December 5–January 7, 1982.

p. 351   She was in "Realism and Realities": Philadelphia Museum catalog, 192.

p. 351   The Whitney Musem of Art's Fairfield County branch: flyer for "Five Artists and The Figure," Whitney Museum of American Art Fairfield County, April 9–June 9, 1982.

p. 351   Neel's self-portrait was in a show: copy of Loan Agreement for Aldrich Museum, *Self Portrait*.

p. 351   Neel was also in two shows devoted to Roosevelt's: flyer for "Five Distinguished Alumni: The WPA Federal Art Projects, January 2–February 22, 1982."

p. 352   During a routine visit, the dentist: author's interviews with Richard Neel, Hartley Neel

p. 352   Enríquez family history: family tree provided by Pablo Lancella.

p. 353   "We were raised like sisters": author's interview with Adoris Mendoza.

p. 353   "She was raised like a little bourgeois": author's interview with Marisa Diaz.

p. 353   Recalls Adoris: ibid.

p. 354   Carlos invited his friends: author's interview with Graziella Pogolotti.

p. 354   "Isabetta was not very close to Carlos": author's interview with Adoris Mendoza.

p. 354   "Carlos had this energy": author's interview with America Villiers.

p. 354   However, she did go back to her aunt's house in Teaneck: author's interview with Marisa Diaz and Adoris Mendoza.

p. 354   "Isabetta said she wouldn't use the word *mother*": author's interview with America Villiers.

p. 354   Says Marisa: author's interview with Marisa Diaz.

p. 355   "She was probably not a very happy child": author's interview with Adoris Mendoza.

p. 355   Says . . . Eileen Goudie: author's interview with Eileen Goudie.

p. 355   It is unclear how much correspondence: copies of letter; postcard from Neel Archives.

p. 356   Cristina believes that it is possible: author's interview with Cristina Lancella.

p. 356   Olivia Neel . . . says: author's interview with Olivia Neel.

p. 356   When she was seventeen: author's interviews with Adoris Mendoza and Marisa Diaz.

p. 356   first suicide attempt: author's interviews with Cristina Lancella, Adoris Mendoza, June 2010.

p. 356   "Carlos Enríquez, Pablo Lancella and Alicia Cruz de Lancella": copy of wedding announcement from Neel Archives.

p. 357   "I used to see her on the street": author's interview with Pablo Lancella.

p. 357   The young couple lived in Havana: ibid.

p. 357   "We lived in a small apartment": author's interview with Cristina Lancella.

p. 357   When Pablo found out about the affair: author's interview with Pablo Lancella.

p. 357   "We separated in 1961": ibid.

p. 357   Isabetta began working: author's interview with Cristina Lancella.

p. 358   After that, she briefly worked: author's interviews with Eileen Goudie, Cristina Lancella, Marisa Diaz.

p. 358   Recalls Goudie: author's interview with Eileen Goudie.

p. 358   "My mother was a party person": author's interview with Cristina Lancella.

p. 358   "At the time of her death, she was seeing": author's interview with Eileen Goudie.

p. 358   "When I was working at Hershey": author's interview with Pablo Lancella.

p. 358   "She had a split personality": author's interview with Marisa Diaz.

p. 359   "She fought like a tiger": author's interview with Eileen Goudie.

p. 359   Before she was fifty: author's interview with Pablo Lancella; Cristina says this was simply an eye lift.

p. 359   "I even hate the number forty-eight": author's interview with Marisa Diaz.

p. 359   "She told me when she came back from Cuba": ibid.

p. 359   Isabetta's next suicide attempt: author's interview with Cristina Lancella.

p. 359   When it came to her last suicide attempt: ibid.; author's interview with Pablo Lancella.

p. 360   "This is my last chance": author's interview with Marisa Diaz.

p. 360   The night of her death: author's interviews with Cristina Lancella, Adoris Mendoza, Eileen Goudie.

p. 360   "It was a Friday night": author's interview with Eileen Goudie.

p. 360   "I find . . . it very fishy": ibid.

p. 360   Although Isabetta did have a fight that night: author's interview with Adoris Mendoza.

p. 360   Goudie believes the note could have been written: author's interview with Eileen Goudie.

p. 360   But Marisa says: author's interview with Marisa Diaz.

p. 361   "Whenever she had a love rejection": author's interview with Marisa Diaz.

p. 361   Isabetta's ashes were scattered: author's interview with Cristina Lancella.

p. 361   After seeing Alice on television: copy of letter from Sylvia, Neel Archives; this was Neel's appearance on *The Tonight Show Starring Johnny Carson*.

p. 361   Alice called him her "vest-pocket Cuban": author's interview with Pablo Lancella Jr.

p. 361   Cristina never met Alice: author's interview with Cristina Lancella.

p. 362   In early 1983, Neel received another honor: letter from John Dobkin, Director of the National Academy of Design, February 8, 1983.

p. 362   In March, Neel was featured in a show at Bucknell: flyer for "Faces Since the 50's: A Generation of American Portraiture," Center Gallery, Bucknell University, March 11–April 17, 1983.

p. 362   A striking selection of thirty-five paintings: catalog for "Alice Neel, Paintings 1933–1982," Loyola Marymount University, Los Angeles, California March 30–May 7, 1983, with an essay by Ann Sutherland Harris.

p. 362   According to the July/August issue: Sandy Nelson, "Looking at Alice Looking at Us, Alice Neel in Los Angeles," *Images and Issues*, July/August, 1983.

p. 362   She got a standing ovation . . . "marathon of other public appearances": Suzanne Muchnic, "Beneath the Skin with Alice Neel," April 10, 1983.

p. 362   She also met Johnny Carson's "alter ego": ibid.

p. 362   William Wilson said the show was: William Wilson, "Finding a Neel in a Haystack," *Los Angeles Sunday Times Calendar*, April 10, 1983.

p. 363   "I got up out of the grave": Nelson, "Looking At Alice Looking at Us."

p. 363   "Seeing the torrent of expressionism": ibid.

p. 363   In a review entitled: Christopher Knight, "Triumphant Images Highlight Exhibit," *Los Angeles Herald Examiner*, April 5, 1983; the review was paired with a profile by Eileen Warren, "Alice Neel, 83, Loves Painting City 'Freaks'," both under the headline "Her Work Bares the Souls of Her Victims."

p. 364 $25,000 from the National Endowment for the Arts: Philadelphia Museum catalog, 175.

p. 364   *Alice Neel*: *Alice Neel* by Patricia Hills, published by Harry N. Abrams; Philadelphia Museum catalog, 175; the book was reviewed, among other publications, by Lawrence Alloway, *Art Journal*, Vol. 44, No. 2, Summer, 1984.

p. 364   "narrow-strapped black nightgown and unlaced space shoes": Linda Weintraub, brochure essay, Edith C. Blum Institute, Bard College.

p. 364   Neel gave another gallery talk: Mary Abell, "Lecturing and Showing Slides, Alice Neel At Art Association," *The Advocate*, September 1, 1983.

p. 364   "It was a kick to hear her tell the stories": Mira Schor, "Some Notes."

p. 365   "I give a slide lecture of fifty years of art": William Luvaas, "Making It," *Art Times*.

p. 365   a retrospective of the first five decades: C. Grimaldis Gallery catalog, "Five Decades of Painting," September 29–October 30, 1983.

p. 365   her face behind an old-fashioned net veil: ibid.; the photograph was taken by Samuel Brody.

p. 365   her last painting: author's interview with Hartley Neel.

CHAPTER TWENTY-SEVEN: *Last Look*

p. 367   "Do you think about the end of life?": Frederick Ted Castle interview with Alice Neel, *Artforum*, October, 1983.

p. 367   her second solo show at the Robert Miller Gallery: Philadelphia Museum catalog, 176.

p. 367   Writing in *The New York Times*: Michael Brenson, "Charles Burchfield, A Timely Retrospective,"

p. 367   Earlier that January, she was awarded the Gold Medal: author's interview with Aldon James, President of the National Arts Club; the award is mentioned in Stephen Salisbury, "Oil and Vinegar; As a Person and a Painter, She's An Original," *The Philadelphia Inquirer*, March 4, 1984.

p. 368   On February 21, Neel had the ultimate celebrity experience: Philadelphia Museum catalog, 176.

p. 368   "You have a wonderful sense of humor": transcript of video of Carson shows.

p. 368   In her second appearance: ibid.

p. 368   In early March: author's interview with Hartley Neel.

p. 368   Neel kept working, completing as many as eight new paintings: correspondence with Ginny Neel.

p. 368   Victoria Donohoe review.

p. 369   interviewed by Judith Higgins for a cover story: Judith Higgins, "Alice Neel and the Human Comedy," *ARTnews*, October, 1984, 72–79.

p. 369   Neel gave one of her last slide lectures: Berkshire Community College flyer for

"Important Paintings by Alice Neel: May 21–June 17, 1984; slide lecture on June 15 in conjunction with the "Focus on Women '84 Conference."

p. 369   she asked him for the address: transcript of Johnny Carson show, June 21, 1984.

p. 369   Her last lecture was . . . at the Vermont Studio School: interview with Ginny Neel, August, 7, 2009.

p. 369   "The thing that made me happiest in the world": Hills, *Alice Neel*, 179.

p. 369   In mid-September, Neel returned: Philadelphia Museum catalog, 176.

p. 369   In early October, Robert Mapplethorpe: profile of Robert Mapplethorpe, *Art in America*, November 1986, 146.

p. 369   "She had a reputation for being hard as nails": Robert Mapplethorpe: Stephen Koch, "Guild, Grace, and Robert Mapplethorpe," *Art in America*, November, 1986, 146.

p. 370   For the weeks leading up to Neel's death: author's interviews with Ginny Neel, Nancy Neel.

p. 370   Richard took some pictures of Alice on her deathbed: interviews with Nancy Neel, Richard Neel.

p. 370   When Dr. Dineen came later: ibid.

p. 370   Earlier that summer: author's interview with Ginny Neel, August 7, 2009.

p. 370   Neel's body was taken to Frank E. Campbell's funeral home: ibid.

p. 370   On an unusually warm day in October: ibid.

p. 370   Richard read "Paul's Letter to the Corinthians": correspondence from Richard and Nancy Neel.

p. 371   There were no flowers: author's interview with Ginny Neel, August 7, 2009.

p. 371   A few years after Neel's death: ibid.

p. 371   after D. H. Lawrence's 1925 novella: D. H. Lawrence, *The Woman Who Rode Away / St. Mawr / The Princess*; Penguin Classics, London: 2006, 148, 149.

p. 371   The pomp and circumstance of a major ceremony: copy of memorial program and speakers remarks.

p. 371   Allen Ginsberg read his poem "White Shroud": Allen Ginsberg, "White Shroud," Harper & Row Publishers, New York; 1986, 48, 49.

p. 371   "It seems to me extraordinary that Alice Neel": copy of address by Jack Baur at Memorial Service for Alice Neel, Whitney Museum of American Art, February 7, 1985.

p. 372   Neel received obituaries in all the major: including *The New York Times*, William

G. Blair, "Alice Neel Dead; Portrait Artist," October 14, 1984; Paul Richard, "Appreciation; Alice Neel, Painting's Piercing Soul," *The Washington Post*, October 16, 1984; "Milestones," *Time*, October 29, 1984; Roberta Smith, "Alice Neel, 1900–1984," *The Village Voice*, October 30, 1984; Stephen Salisbury, "Alice Neel, 84, whose fame as a painter came late in life," *The Philadelphia Inquirer*, October 16, 1984.

p. 372 "Alice Neel, Unconventional Artist Dies at 84": William G. Blair, "Alice Neel, Unconventional Artist, Dies at 84," *The New York Times*, October 15, 1984; the previous day's version of Blair's obituary was headlined: "Alice Neel Dead; Portrait Artist."

p. 372 "She was unique, and she paid for her uniqueness": Judith Higgins, "Alice Neel, 1900–1984," Vasari Diary, *ARTnews*, Vol. 13, No. 18, December 1984.

p. 372 "I do not know if the truth": Hills, *Alice Neel*, 183.

p. 372 "A good portrait of mine has even more": Ingrid Sischy, "Artist Interrupted," *Vanity Fair*, July 2000, 177.

CODA

p. 373 In October 2009: I attended the opening for Nexus New York, Latin American Artists in the Modern Metropolis, El Museo Del Barrio, New York, October 17, 2009 through February 28, 2010.

p. 373 a flesh and blood image: author's interview with Cristina Lancella on the night of the opening.

EPILOGUE:
Enduring Images: Alice Neel's Artistic Legacy

p. 375 When the gavel came down: I was present at the Sotheby's Contemporary Art Evening Sale, November 11, 2009.

p. 375 $1,650,500; final price corroborated with Sotheby's. Includes buyer's premium. Estimate was $400,000 to $500,000.

p. 375 Author's interviews that evening with Tobias Meyer; Anthony Grant.

p. 375 "I tried to capture life as it went by": Alice Neel for "Artists and their Inspiration," *The Christian Science Monitor*, October 31, 1977; artist's statement.

p. 376 "That is the microcosm": ibid.

p. 376 "not contaminated yet": Richard Polsky, Interview 3, June 5, 1981, 162.

p. 376 who would later be convicted: Hills, *Alice Neel*, 149; Arce was sentenced to serve a term in Attica Prison; Thomas McEvilley mentions his manslaughter conviction in *Artforum*, May 1994.

p. 377   Between 2000 and 2010: I attended all three retrospectives: The Whitney, The National Museum of Women in the Arts, and "Painted Truths," the show at the Houston Museum of Fine Arts.

p. 377   from 1982 to 2008: author's interview with John Cheim.

p. 377   In early 2009: notice from David Zwirner Gallery, announcing that they were to represent The Estate of Alice Neel; author's interview with Ginny Neel.

p. 377   "You could make a strong case": David Zwirner interview with Kelly Crow, More Q&A with NYC Gallerist David Zwirner, *The Wall Street Journal Online*, April 30, 2009; "in America": author's interview with David Zwirner, September 22, 2009.

p. 377   Originally planned as a celebration: Sally Friedman, "Alice Neel's Human Comedy," Welcomat, *After Dark*, February 13, 1985.

p. 378   "As an artist, Alice Neel always spoke the truth": Theodore F. Wolff, "Will She Be Known as the American Van Gogh?", *The Christian Science Monitor*, July 11, 1985.

p. 378   It wasn't a major show: brochure for Memorial Exhibition, "Ivan Albright, Jimmy Ernst, Armin Landeck, Alice Neel," American Academy and Institute of Arts and Letters, November 18–December 15, 1985.

p. 378   Neel's first posthumous exibit: catalog for "Drawings and Watercolors."

p. 379   As Roberta Smith wrote: Roberta Smith, "Art: Alice Neel Show," *The New York Times*, December 16, 1986.

p. 379   John Cheim, then director: author's interview with John Cheim, March 30, 2009.

p. 379   Wrote Smith: Roberta Smith, "Diane Arbus and Alice Neel, With Attention to the Child," *The New York Times*, May 19, 1989.

p. 380   Elizabeth Hess, in *The Village Voice*: Elizabeth Hess, "The Company of Strangers," *The Village Voice*, May 21, 1989.

p. 380   Neel's often neglected cityscapes: catalog for "Exterior/Interior" inaugural show at the Tisch Family Gallery at Tufts University, Shirley and Alex Aidekman Arts Center.

p. 380   Neel's unique documentation: Phyllis Braff, "How Neel Saw Spanish Harlem," *The New York Times*, July 21, 1994.

p. 379   Christine Temin, "Revelations Abound at Alice Neel Show," *The Boston Globe*, October 18, 1991.

p. 381   Roberta Smith also wrote about the show: Roberta Smith, "On Long Island, Photos, Portraits, Pollock and Stereotypes," *The New York Times*, July 21, 1991.

p. 381   "some of the painter's darkest and most affecting": Elizabeth Hess, "Artist and Models," *The Village Voice*, March 22, 1994.

p. 381   Writing in *Artforum*: Thomas McEvilly, "Alice Neel," The Robert Miller Gallery, *Artforum*, Vol. 32, No. 9, May 1994, 98, 99.

p. 382   More pointedly: Carol Diehl, Alice Neel, Robert Miller, *ARTnews*, September 1994.

p. 382   compared the physicality: Ken Johnson, Alice Neel at Robert Miller, *Art in America*, 119; Pamela Allara, "The Pregnant Nudes of Alice Neel," *Artforum*, Vol. 34, January, 1996.

p. 382   In March 1997, a stunning show: catalog for "Alice Neel: Paintings from the Thirties," the Robert Miller Gallery.

p. 383   As *The New Yorker* put it: *The New Yorker*, "Alice's Wonderland," April 7, 1997.

p. 383   "In these paintings": Grace Glueck, "Alice Neel, Self-Styled Collector of Souls, Unfurls Her Own, in Glee and Heartbreak," *The New York Times*, March 21, 1997.

p. 383   "In the best of the portraits": Eleanor Heartney, "Portrait of a Decade," *Art in America*, Vol. 85, No. 10, October 1991, 104.

p. 384   "Men in Suits": Cheim and Read catalog for "Alice Neel: Men in Suits," March 4–April 25, 1998.

p. 384   "No artist extended the life": Ken Johnson, "Alice Neel and August Sander," *The New York Times*, April 10, 1998.

p. 384   "An authentic 20th century heroine": Peter Schjeldahl, "A Guy Thing," *The Village Voice*, March 31, 1998.

p. 384   In 2000, Neel finally got the major: "Alice Neel," Philadelphia Museum catalog, Edited by Ann Temkin; Philadelphia Museum of Art, 2000.

p. 385   "making some of the 20th century's best paintings": Roberta Smith, "How Alice Neel Used Talk in Service to Her Painting," *The New York Times*, June 30, 2000.

p. 385   *Art in America* devoted: Raphael Rubinstein, "Eros in Spanish Harlem," *Art in America*, December 2000.

p. 385   "New York's painter laureate": Hilton Als, "Alice Neel's Eye," July 3, 2000.

p. 385   full-length feature in *Vanity Fair*: Ingrid Sischy, "Artist, Interrupted," *Vanity Fair*, July, 2000, 150–156.

p. 385   Says Temkin, now: author's interview with Ann Temkin, June 10, 2010.

p. 385   In late 2005: *Alice Neel: Women*, Rizzoli; I attended the National Museum of Women in the Arts retrospective.

p. 386   The show came about when Ginny . . . approached Carolyn Carr: author's interview with Hartley Neel, August 23, 2010; author's interview with Carolyn Carr, August 23, 2010.

p. 386   "The show's focus on women": Blake Gopnik, "Alice Neel and Portraiture's Alternative Face," *The Washington Post*, November 13, 2005.

p. 386   In 2004, former Tate curator and director of collections: author's interview with Hartley Neel, Ginny Neel, August 23, 2010.

p. 386   the Victoria Miro Gallery: author's interview with Victoria Miro; Victoria Miro catalog for "Alice Neel: The Cycle of Life."

p. 387   The David Zwirner Gallery got maximum mileage: David Zwirner brochure for "Nudes in the 1930's."

p. 387   Roberta Smith once again anointed Neel: Roberta Smith, "Alice Neel," *The New York Times*, May 29, 2009.

p. 387   In *The New Yorker*: Peter Schjeldahl, "Wild Life," *The New Yorker*, May 25, 2009.

p. 388   five out of six stars: T. J. Carlin, "Alice Neel," *Time Out New York*, June 11–17, 2009.

p. 388   The third retrospective of the decade: "Painted Truths" catalog, New Haven: Yale University Press, 2010; I attended "Painted Truths" in Houston, Texas, March 19, 2010.

p. 389   Indeed, Neel's artistic influence: author's interviews with Eric Fischl, Elizabeth Peyton, and Marlene Dumas; Phoebe Hoban, "Portraits: Alice Neel's Legacy of Realism," *The New York Times*, Arts and Leisure, April 25, 2010, 20.

p. 390   Phillip Pearlstein believes that Neel's reach: author's interview with Philip Pearlstein.

p. 390   Chuck Close tells a funny story: author's interview with Chuck Close.

p. 390   John Cheim says of Neel: author's interview with John Cheim.

p. 391   *Alice Neel*, a documentary: author's interview with Andrew Neel.

p. 391   Alice Neel herself always eschewed the sentimental: "I try to paint the scene . . ." *Arts International*, Vol. 12, No. May 18, 1968, 48.

Acknowledgments

An enormous number of people helped me, in one way or another, during the long odyssey of this book. First, I would like to thank my numerous sources, listed in alphabetical order. Special thanks go to those who were interviewed multiple times.

George Adams, Pamela Allara, David Amram, Tom Armstrong, Michel Auder, Benny Andrews, Will Barnet, Margaret Belcher, Jonathan Brand, David Brody, Sondra Brody, Bernarda Bryson, Philip, Faith and Nora Bonosky, Karla Buch, John Cheim, Chuck Close, Marisa Diaz, Helen Dixon, John Dobbs, Victoria Donohoe, Tom Doolittle, Marlene Dumas, Sarah Eisenberg, Margaret Evans, Eric Fischl, Antonio Frasconi, Tom Freudenheim, Mary Garrard, Wendy Gimbel, Ted Goldsborough, Eileen Goudie, Mimi Gross, John Gruen, Ann Sutherland Harris, Constance Harvey, Andrew Hemingway, Patricia Hills, Barbara Hollister, Aldon James, Charles Keller, Dorothy Koppelman, Cristina Lancella, Pablo Lancella, Sr., Pablo Lancella, Jr., Michael Lawrence, Toni Lawrence, Alfred Leslie, Joe Lasker, Jack Levine, Ralph Marrero, Luz Marino, Adoris Mendoza, Mady McCoy, Malachi McCormick, Sandy Momyer, Stanley Maron, Esperanza Maynulet, Gerry Meyer, Virginia Miller, Victoria Miro, Stewart Mott, Hartley Neel, Richard Neel, Ginny Neel, Nancy Neel, Andrew Neel, Olivia Neel, Paul Negron, Joseph Negron, John Negron, Linda Nochlin, Philip and Faith Pearlstein, Don Perlis, John Perreault, Graziella Pogolotti, Richard Polsky, Elizabeth Peyton, Paul Resika, Sandy Ronan, Herman Rose, Elia Rose, Annette Rubinstein, Jenny Santiago, Joseph Solman, Neill Slaughter, Elke Solomon, David Soyer, Janet Soyer, David and Mary Soyer, May Stevens, Jerry Strauss, Ann Temkin, Mary Tierney, Jane Wilson, Sheila de Tuya, Marilou Usher, Ramon Vasquez, America Villers, David Zwirner.

I would also like to thank the various institutions and libraries that provided invaluable resources: The Smithsonian Archives of American Art, The Columbia Rare Book and Manuscript Library, The Whitney Museum of American Art Library, The Moore College Library, The Darby Free Library, The Gladwyne Free Library, The Lower Merion Historical Society, The University of Miami Library, The National Museum of Women in the Arts, and The Museum of Modern Art. Special thanks to The Philadelphia Museum of Art for allowing me to use their extraordinary Neel archives.

Enormous thanks are also due to Patricia Hills, whose book was one of my main reference sources, and who also provided valuable input and support, including the loan of interview tapes; and Eleanor Munro, whose wonderful interview with Neel, from her book *Orginals*, as well as the transcript on which it was based, provided many insights.

Thanks also to Joy Weiner and Judy Throm at the Smithsonian, Jennifer Lee at Columbia, Caroline Rusk at the Whitney, Betty Schell at the Darby Free Library and Carolyn Conti at the Gladwyne Free Library. I am also grateful to the David Zwirner Gallery, the Victoria Miro Gallery, and the Cheim & Read Gallery.

My Havana research would not have been possible without the extraordinary assistance of Carole and Alex Rosenberg, and the Ludwig Foundation of Cuba, including Helmo Hernández and Wilfredo Benítez, who helped with everything from protocol to itinerary to setting up interviews with key sources.

Juan Martínez was an invaluable resource for my chapter on Carlos Enríquez, as well as my Cuba chapter; I am also grateful for the assistance of Wendy Gimbel and Louis Pérez. For my foray to Colwyn and the surrounding area, thanks to my cousin Miela Ford, and Jan and John Haigis, local historians. My Gladwyne trip came about thanks to Ted Goldsborough, Dennis Milstein, and Richard Lebert.

Special thanks to Phillip Bonosky and his daughter Nora for permitting me to use extensive material from his extraordinary journals. Also to Toni and Michael Lawrence for allowing me to use excerpts from their mother's unpublished manuscript, and to Jonathan Brand, for his 1969 interviews with Alice Neel and assistance with material by his father, Millen Brand. Thanks to Pamela Allara for background material including the loan of a copy of Neel's FBI files.

Thanks to Pablo Lancella, Jr. and Cristina Lancella, Karen Buch and Sarah Eisenberg, Sondra Brody, Sheil de Tuya, and Ralph Marrero for the loan of family photographs, and to David Brody for background background material on Sam Brody. Thanks also to Andrew Neel and See Think Productions for help with photographs, and to Ginny Neel for handling all the images.

The sincerest of thanks to my wonderful editor, Michael Flamini, whose great sensitivity, enthusiasm, and patience helped me at all times, but especially through the daunting rough patches. And to his associate editor, the plucky Vicki Lame, always at the ready.

Enormous thanks also to the members of the Neel family, including Hartley Neel, Ginny Neel, Richard Neel, and Nancy Neel, as well as their children, whose love and memories of Alice Neel helped keep her alive in my mind—and on these pages—and who so generously allowed me to reproduce her brilliant and inspiring work.

Finally, this book would not have been possible without the staunch support of my family and friends.

I would like to thank my father, Russell Hoban, who inspired me to become a writer, and who stood by me throughout the writing of this book. The memory of my mother, Lillian Hoban, was never far from me during this long, arduous process. Thanks also to my brother and sisters, Brom, Esme, and Julia, and their families.

I would also like to thank my friends, whose intelligence, support, and companionship enabled me to complete this book: Mark Alan Stamaty, Gwenda Blair, Lorraine Monchak, Mark Moore, Patti Cohen, Edward Sutton, Kathleen McCauliffe, Josh Cohn, Cheryl Kaplan, Steven Levy, Teresa Carpenter, Mark Tansey, Josephine Schmidt, Karen Cattan, Barry Rutizer, Dani Shapiro, Linda Eckstein, Edward Bekkerman, Mark Wiener, Linda DiGusta, Liana Perez, Catherine Texier, and Kim Uchiyama. Thanks also to Phyllis Schimel.

I am indebted to the following friends who were also early readers: Gwenda Blair, Cheryl Kaplan, Mark Moore, Kim Uchiyama, Josephine Schmidt, Kathleen McAuliffe, Jon Gould, and Catherine Texier.

As a long-time member of the National Arts Club, I consider it to be my artistic family. Special thanks to its president, Aldon James, always a loyal supporter.

I have also benefited from residencies at several writers' colonies. My first draft was begun at The MacDowell Colony in August of 2003, a writer's haven, thanks to its wonderful history, the camaraderie of fellow residents, and the loyalty and dedication of its staff. Much background was done at The Bau Institute's residency in Otranto, Italy, where I spent three weeks in June, 2007. Thanks especially to Marthe Keller and Paola Iucci. I was honored to be the first writer granted a fellowship at The Watermill Center, founded by Robert Wilson, in May, 2009, where I completed the first draft of my chapter on feminism. Special thanks to its director, Sherry Dobbin.

More images of Alice Neel's work can be found at www.aliceneel.com.

Index